AMERICAN FOREIGN POLICY

AMERICAN FOREIGN POLICY

History, Politics, and Policy

Daniel S. Papp
University System of Georgia

Loch K. Johnson
The University of Georgia

John E. Endicott
Georgia Institute of Technology

PEARSON
Longman

New York   San Francisco   Boston
London   Toronto   Sydney   Tokyo   Singapore   Madrid
Mexico City   Munich   Paris   Cape Town   Hong Kong   Montreal

Executive Editor: Eric Stano
Senior Marketing Manager: Elizabeth Fogarty
Supplements Editor: Kristi Olson
Managing Editor: Bob Ginsberg
Production Manager: Joseph Vella
Project Coordination, Text Design, and Electronic Page Makeup: Electronic Publishing Services Inc., NYC
Senior Cover Design Manager: Nancy Danahy
Cover Design Manager: John Callahan
Cover Designer: Kay Petronio
Cover Illustrations: Courtesy of Corbis, Inc. and Getty Images, Inc.
Photo Research: Photosearch, Inc.
Manufacturing Manager: Mary Fischer
Manufacturing Buyer: Alfred C. Dorsey
Printer and Binder: Hamilton Printing Company
Cover Printer: Coral Graphics Services

Library of Congress Cataloging-in-Publication Data
Papp, Daniel S., 1947–
American foreign policy : history, politics, and policy / by Daniel S. Papp, Loch K. Johnson, and John E. Endicott.
    p. cm.
    Includes bibliographical references and index.
    ISBN 0-321-07902-7 (pbk.)
    1. United States—Foreign relations.   I. Johnson, Loch K., 1942–   II. Endicott, John E.   III. Title.
    E183.7.P18 2005
    327.73'009—dc22
                2004016760

Please visit our website at http://www.ablongman.com.

ISBN: 0-321-07902-7

1 2 3 4 5 6 7 8 9 10—HT—07 06 05 04

Contents

Preface

American foreign policy is not easy to understand. It has a long and sometimes confusing history. It is often perceived and interpreted in amazingly different ways by different Americans, and often even more so by citizens of other countries. Many American players are involved in its formulation and implementation, and many international actors—individuals, states, international governmental organizations, nongovernmental organizations, multinational corporations, and so on—are affected by what the United States does in its foreign policy. Many of these domestic players and international actors have different values and perceptions from those that underlie American foreign policy, and many have objectives that differ from, and sometimes run counter to, those of the United States. American foreign policy also encompasses many issues, ranging from but not limited to homeland security and economic well-being, to human rights, to the use of military force overseas, all of which are examined in this text.

We wrote *American Foreign Policy: History, Politics, and Policy* to help students see that, even though American foreign policy is a challenge to understand, that challenge can be met. We undertake this effort in three ways.

First, in Chapters 1 and 2, we provide the analytical frameworks of levels of analysis, unifying concepts, and competing themes to help our analysis and improve our understanding of American foreign policy. These frameworks are carried throughout the book.

Second, from our perspective, students must understand, at a minimum, how the United States got to where it is in foreign policy, the way that American foreign policy is made, and the issues that confront the United States in its foreign policy, if they are to gain an in-depth understanding of American foreign policy. Put differently, students must understand the history, politics, and policy content of American foreign policy. Yet few introductory American foreign policy texts address all three of these critical components that, in our eyes, are required to develop such an understanding.

Thus, we wrote *American Foreign Policy: History, Politics, and Policy* to provide a rarely presented approach to the study of American foreign policy. Unlike other American foreign policy texts, this book has three primary foci: (1) the background and history of U.S. foreign policy; (2) the politics and processes of U.S. foreign policy formulation; and (3) analyses of critical current U.S. foreign policy issues. Almost all other American foreign policy texts concentrate on one or at most two of these areas, leaving students with an inadequate understanding of either the history of American foreign policy, the processes of and players behind American foreign policy, or the foreign policy issues that confront the United States today.

Third, *American Foreign Policy: History, Politics, and Policy* provides detail and depth sufficient for understanding, but avoids the detail and depth that may lead to boredom. Many American foreign policy texts are superbly detailed books that in some cases may even be used for research. They provide large quantities of data and information that undergraduate students—and sometimes professors—find superfluous. Such detail may be good for graduate students, but for students in introductory American foreign policy courses, it is overkill. By avoiding excessive detail, *American Foreign Policy: History, Politics, and Policy* is able to cover all three primary focuses of American foreign policy without being too long.

Our writing approach is therefore straightforward, with students in mind. We seek to provide information, understanding, and knowledge for students. The writing is clear and concise, with complex ideas and concepts explained in comprehensible ways with easily understood words. Details are provided, but not too many. Footnotes are included, but not excessively. We hope to keep students interested in what they are reading, not to impress readers with our knowledge.

Each chapter begins with a list of bulleted questions that are examined in the chapter. Each chapter concludes with a list of key terms and concepts. Each term or concept is highlighted in bold text the first time it is discussed in the text. Each chapter also has a significant number of headings, subheadings, and even sub-subheadings to help focus the readers' attention.

At the end of the book, we also provide a few concluding thoughts, urging students—Americans and citizens of other countries as well—to think about where they want their homeland to go in its future foreign policy, and how they wish it to get there. It is only with an informed and educated populace that the United States—and other countries as well—will realize fully the potential that they have.

We owe debts of gratitude to many people. These include but are not limited to Sylvia Smith, executive assistant at the Board of Regents of the University System of Georgia; Georgia Tech students Bernard Gourley, Sarah Tourtellott, and Nate Edwards, who provided invaluable research assistance; Eric Stano, our editor, who gave us continual encouragement and much-needed occasional prodding; Kara Wylie and Lake Lloyd, who shepherded us through the publication process; and our reviewers: Kelechi A. Kalu, University of Northern Colorado; Peter O. Hefron, Troy State University; Linda L. Petrou, High Point University; Andrew Bennett, Georgetown University; Phil Kelly, Emporia State University; Richard A. Nolan, University of Florida; Patrick J. Haney, Miami University; David A. Reilly, Niagara University; Adam Resnick, Western Washington University; Jeffrey S. Morton, Florida Atlantic University; Timothy J. White, Xavier University; Trevor Morris, Methodist College; Domenic Maffei, Caldwell College; Brian C. Schmidt, SUNY New Paltz; Karl K. Schonberg, St. Lawrence University; Joseph E. Thompson, Villanova University; Melissa Butler, Wabash College; Roy Licklider, Rutgers University; David Houghton, University of Central Florida; Samuel B. Hoff, Delaware State University; Robert Schelin, St. Thomas Aquinas College; Michael J. Siler, California State University, Los Angeles; Walton Brown Foster, Central Connecticut State University; Tomasz Inglot, Minnesota State University; David H. Bearce, University of Pittsburgh.

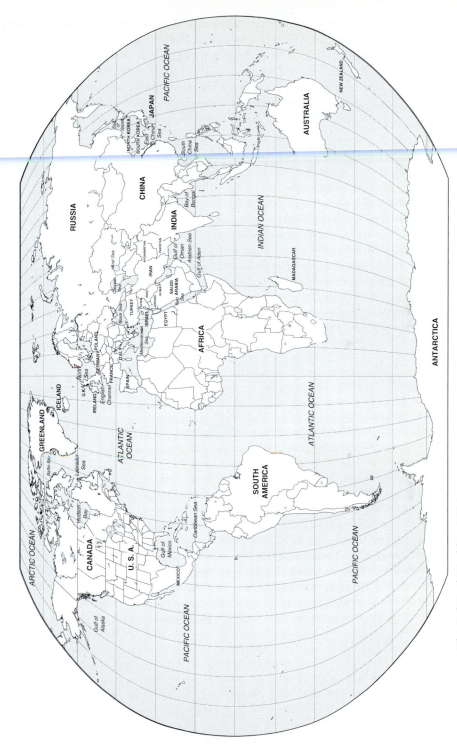

The Political World in 2004

We also wish to dedicate this book to Susan Papp, Billy, Alex, Michael, and Ben, as well as granddaughter Elena; to Kristin Johnson and the next generation of foreign policy leaders, as well as Leena Johnson, Loch's indispensable partner in all things; and to Mitsuyo Endicott, who has been at John's side for 45 years.

We hope that this book in a small way enables all of its readers to fashion a safer, saner, and more humane world for themselves, their families, and future generations.

DANIEL S. PAPP
LOCH K. JOHNSON
JOHN E. ENDICOTT

Introduction

WHY STUDY AMERICAN FOREIGN POLICY?

At the beginning of the twenty-first century, no country rivaled the United States in military power, economic strength, political clout, and cultural influence. Having enjoyed during the 1990s the longest period of uninterrupted economic expansion in its history, the U.S. economy was almost twice as large as that of Japan, the state with the second largest economy. After the Soviet Union and its military collapsed in 1991, the United States' armed forces were unparalleled, projecting American power to every corner of the globe. Washington's position on every important international political issue was a matter of utmost concern to all involved with any issue, and the U.S. political system was the model for many states. American culture—music, food, fashion, movies, television, and so on—for better or worse, penetrated many non-U.S. cultures and extended American influence throughout the world.

Pleased with themselves and their country, many Americans lost interest in foreign policy and world affairs. Indeed, Bill Clinton ran for the White House in 1992 on a platform that largely ignored foreign affairs. A general disregard for foreign affairs continued throughout most of the 1990s except when occasional crises unfolded, such as the Kosovo War. In the 2000 presidential election, foreign policy was again a little remarked issue.

As 2001 unfolded, Americans focused their attention on how well President George W. Bush could govern after assuming office following one of the most confused and contentious presidential elections in American history. Americans were worried about the slowing economy and whether a tax cut could revive it. They were concerned about who would win the 2001 Emmy awards, whether Barry Bonds would break Mark McGuire's home run record, and about the extent to which the dot-com crash would slow the economy. Few people believed that foreign policy and world affairs affected them. Even fewer knew about a fanatical Saudi Arabian former businessman named Osama bin Laden who had turned to terrorism and who was harbored by the Taliban, a repressive religious regime that ruled the primitive country of Afghanistan half a world away.

All that changed on September 11, 2001, when 19 members of bin Laden's terrorist network, al Qaeda, hijacked four U.S. airliners, flying two into the twin towers of the World Trade Center, destroying both buildings and killing nearly 3,000 people, and crashing one into the Pentagon. The fourth plane plummeted into a field in western Pennsylvania after the passengers rushed the cockpit of the hijacked aircraft and attacked the hijackers.

Americans were stunned and terrified. Suddenly, foreign policy and world affairs were critically important. The horror of September 11 focused American attention on foreign policy and world affairs like no event since the December 7, 1941, attack on Pearl Harbor. Bin Laden, al Qaeda, Afghanistan, and the Taliban became household terms much the way that the Bataan Death March, Midway, and Tojo had become topics of everyday discussion 60 years earlier. Even though the United States did not declare war following the September 11 attacks, most Americans accepted that their country was at war, even as it had been after Pearl Harbor.

"Why did this happen?" Americans asked. "Why do these people hate us so much?" "What can we do to prevent this from happening again?" "How can we get even?" Most realized that the answers to these questions could only be obtained if they, their leaders, and their country paid increased attention to foreign policy and world affairs.

The questions Americans asked about foreign policy and world affairs following September 11, 2001, were important, but they were not the only questions about U.S. foreign policy that needed to be asked and answered. Even before the hijackings, analysts and scholars had other concerns about American foreign policy and the role of the United States in the world:

- Was the United States as preeminent as it appeared?

- How secure was American preeminence?

- How did the United States acquire such wealth, power, and influence?

- Was American preeminence the result of a conscious effort, or did a constellation of situations and events simply come together to allow the United States to become so powerful?

- What challenges did the United States face in foreign policy and its relations with the external world?

- How did the United States make foreign policy, and what objectives did it seek?

- Who played what role in making U.S. foreign policy, and how did they acquire these roles?

- Did the United States—either its government or its people—really know what it wanted to achieve in world affairs?

We explore these issues later in this book, but in this introduction, we examine a more basic question: "Why study U.S. foreign policy?"

Reason 1. Foreign threats can endanger U.S. security and affect the day-to-day lives of Americans. Following the 1991 collapse of the Soviet Union and the end of the Cold War, the United States enjoyed a decade of relative freedom from perceived foreign threats. However, the events of September 11 reaffirmed that foreign threats to American security were real. Fears that terrorists or other U.S. enemies might acquire biological, chemical, or nuclear weapons—"weapons of mass destruction"—increased even more after prominent politicians and media outlets in later 2001 received anthrax-laced letters that killed five people. The fear that Iraqi president Saddam Hussein would provide weapons of mass destruction to terrorist groups or order his country's military

to use them against others was a prominent reason that [   ]
with Iraq in 2003.

American responses to the terrorist threat also affec[   ]
United States. Airport security was heightened, barricades were put in place around public buildings, and mail was screened for anthrax. Immigration checks were tightened, identity cards were checked more frequently, and police and military presence became increasingly visible. President George W. Bush even created a cabinet-level department, Homeland Security, whose responsibility was to develop policies to protect the American homeland.

As novel and intrusive as these responses were for many Americans, it was not the first time that foreign threats affected daily American life. The American experience during the Cold War provides an excellent example from an earlier era. For almost half a century, from shortly after World War II until 1991, Americans were fixated on the USSR, communism, and the fear of nuclear war because of the global confrontation between the United States and the Soviet Union. A generation of American children grew up during the 1950s and 1960s practicing air raid drills at school. Many of their parents built bomb shelters at home. Indeed, the entire U.S. interstate highway system was rationalized as a key element of U.S. national security policy designed to help counter the Soviet threat.

By the 1970s and 1980s, air raid drills had ended, bomb shelters had been converted to basements or wine cellars, and no one thought of the interstate system as a key element of national security. Nevertheless, the United States spent billions of dollars on defense and millions of American served in the armed forces. As late as 1985, 2.2 million Americans served in the armed forces, and U.S. defense spending totaled $368 billion, consuming 6.5 percent of the U.S. gross domestic product (GDP).

Clearly, the Soviet threat had an immense impact on American life. But when the Soviet Union dissolved in 1991, the Cold War faded into history and the threat of intentional nuclear war ended. This too had an impact on the United States. Thus, by 1997, U.S. defense spending had declined to $273 billion, only 3.4 percent of the U.S. GDP. Only 1.4 million people were in the military.[1] Just as the Soviet threat had had a major impact on how Americans lived their lives and on how the United States spent its money, the end of the threat likewise changed how many Americans lived as foreign threats receded into the background.

Reason 2. The United States is deeply involved in the international economic system. Like it or not, the United States is deeply involved in the global economy. In 2003, the United States imported over $1.5 trillion of goods and services and exported another $1 trillion. And this involvement is growing. The 2003 statistics represented a doubling of the U.S. trade turnover since 1990.

American involvement in the global economy is extremely diverse. Each day, the United States imports millions of barrels of oil from the Middle East and thousands of cars made in Germany and Japan. Even a U.S. car company like General Motors manufactures or assembles its cars and automobile parts in over 30 countries. That means that almost every GM car sold in the United States has components made outside the country. Thousands of tons of minerals mined in Africa, Australia, and Canada enter the

United States each day. Each day, Americans eat thousands of tons of fruits and vegetables grown in Mexico, Brazil, and elsewhere in Latin America. Many flowers sold in local florist shops are also grown there.

Supporters of extensive U.S. involvement in world trade argue that it improves living standards by increasing employment, lowering prices, and, as a result of global competition, improving product quality. On the other hand, critics of U.S. involvement in world trade argue that U.S. jobs are exported, U.S. national security is compromised, and U.S. economic strength is squandered as a result of the large U.S. foreign trade deficit.

Obviously, considerable disagreement exists over whether or not the United States benefits from world trade. However, on one point consensus exists: U.S. involvement in world trade has an immense impact on what is happening economically in the United States.

Reason 3. What occurs around the world, near and far, sometimes spills into the United States. The United States is an immense country. It has thousands of miles of seacoast, and it shares thousands of miles of borders with Canada and Mexico. This presents the United States with a simple reality: its borders can never be completely or perfectly secured or sealed.

More often than not, when Americans think of this reality, they think first of illegal immigration and next of drug smuggling. Both are significant issues that have a major impact on life within the United States, in the case of illegal immigration primarily in the American Southwest and South and in urban areas, and in the case of drugs, in all regions of the country and socioeconomic sectors of society. Low standards of living, and in some cases political repression, in the Caribbean islands, Central American states, and Mexico contribute substantially to the flow of illegal immigrants to the United States, and many Latin Americans see no alternative to the drug trade as an assured source of income. Standards of living outside the United States thus combine with permeable American borders to have an immediate and direct impact on American society.

But these are not the only issues with which the United States must cope as a result of the permeability of American borders. For example, American borders cannot protect the United States from worldwide environmental problems such as global warming or the deterioration of the ozone layer, and American borders are equally valueless in protecting the southwestern United States from lax environmental standards for industry in Mexico, just as Canada's border with the United States cannot protect Canadian lakes and forests from American-produced acid rain.

Nor can borders prevent the entry of sickness and disease. In 2003 alone, the SARS virus and a new strain of flu entered the United States, sickening thousands of Americans and killing over 100 people. Another disease that traced its roots to locations outside the United States, AIDS, killed thousands of Americans in the 1980s and 1990s and continues to take its toll today.

Clearly, then, some of what occurs in America's neighbors both near and far can spill over American borders into the United States. The impossibility of perfectly securing American borders warrants that Americans stay abreast of foreign affairs and American foreign policy.

Reason 4. American lifestyles and culture are deeply influenced by foreign lifestyles and cultures. In many American cities—Boston, Miami, New York, San Francisco, and others—people who have come from outside the United States congregate in a "Little Italy," "Little Havana," "Chinatown," or other area where the people seek to keep the lifestyles and cultures of their homelands. Inevitably, their lifestyles and cultures spread beyond their neighborhoods and influence mainstream American life. During the 1980s and 1990s, rhythms imported from the Caribbean and Latin America had an immense impact on U.S. music. Only a few decades ago, it was hard to find blini, calamari, crepes, falafel, knockwurst, rigatoni, sushi, tamales, and wonton soup outside their countries of origin. Today, most large U.S. cities have restaurants serving Russian, Greek, French, Moroccan, German, Italian, Japanese, Mexican, or Chinese food and drink.

A few years ago, few people in the United States played "the world's game," soccer, known outside the United States as football. Today, youth soccer rivals American football in popularity in the United States, and soccer moms are everywhere. The U.S. Women's National Soccer team has become so good that much of the world of women's soccer emulates its training methods and style of play, and after the excellent performance of the U.S. men's team in the 2002 World Cup, many sports writers predicted an upsurge in interest in men's soccer.

The examples are many from the realms of lifestyle and culture of how the world impacts American life. It is not much of an overstatement to say that Americans cannot understand their own lifestyle and culture if they do not understand the lifestyles and cultures of other countries.

Reason 5. The United States has an immense impact on the world. Another reason to study American foreign policy is the immense role that the United States plays in the world. While some countries may have a *concern* about international political, economic, military, and cultural issues and others may have a *presence* that involves them directly on a given issue, only the United States, with its political clout, economic strength, military reach, and cultural pervasiveness, has the potential to *influence* (but not *control*) most international political, economic, military, and cultural issues of note.[2]

Politically, the United States often plays a major role in key international issues. National leaders and others involved with issues as diverse as disputes between Argentina and Chile over the Beagle Channel, famine in Sudan and Somalia, Palestinian statehood, piracy in Indonesia, the drug trade in Latin America, and language content on the Internet all want to know what the U.S. position is, often because the United States has the potential to influence the outcome.

Economically, American tourists keep Caribbean economies prosperous, American oil imports help build bank accounts in many Middle Eastern states, and American car purchases help keep Japanese auto workers employed. Currencies of many countries are pegged to the U.S. dollar, and despite the increased importance of other stock markets and the growth of global electronic trading in the stock market, the New York Stock Exchange remains the most important barometer of international financial health.

At the same time, the United States exports large quantities of grain and other food and has led the world in grain exports for decades. The United States also dominates the world's entertainment markets, giving rise to charges in some countries that the United States, because of rock music, movies, and television, engages in cultural imperialism.

In high-tech areas, the United States has over 50 percent of the world export market for airliners, while U.S. companies, networks, and service providers are positioned to dominate e-commerce, at least for a short time. In addition, American culture—music, food, fashion, movies, television—for better or worse has penetrated many non-U.S. cultures and is expanding its influence in many countries. MTV can be seen in Moscow, blue jeans are found in Bombay, Madonna sells out in Tokyo, hamburgers can be ordered in Paris, a U.S. football league is in Europe, baseball is the national sport of Japan and Cuba, and Coca-Cola is everywhere.

None of this means that the United States attempts to influence or control every issue with which it is concerned. Note American inaction in the Sudanese and Rwandan civil wars in the early and middle 1990s. Had the United States become involved in these conflicts, the course of events in both countries would have been changed. Paradoxically, American inaction in Sudan and Rwanda influenced events in both countries. As it became clear that the United States would not intervene, those involved in the conflicts engaged in increasingly awful assaults on human rights and life. Tragically, American inaction encouraged escalation of violence.

The key point here is that the United States plays an immense role in world affairs. It is therefore critically important that Americans—and non-Americans as well—understand what the United States is attempting to accomplish in its foreign policy.

Reason 6. American citizens—and citizens of other democracies—can influence what their country does in foreign policy. If you are a citizen of the United States, or of any of the world's almost 90 democracies, you have a responsibility to be an informed citizen. Through the electoral process and your ability to comment on issues in a number of ways, you can influence your country's foreign policy. In the absence of extensive public opposition to the Vietnam War, would Lyndon Johnson have begun to withdraw U.S. forces from Vietnam, or would Richard Nixon have ended U.S. involvement there? Without public support, would George H. W. Bush have deployed troops to Saudi Arabia and launched Operation Desert Storm to expel Iraqi forces from Kuwait? In the absence of public support, would Bill Clinton have been able to initiate air attacks against Serbian forces who were driving Kosovars from their homes, or would George W. Bush have been able to order the invasion of Iraq?

In each of these examples, the probable answer is "No." Demonstrably, Americans—and citizens of other democracies—influence their homeland's foreign policy. Studying and understanding U.S. foreign policy is therefore a critical responsibility for U.S. citizens.

Reason 7. In the eyes of many, the United States has a moral obligation to care about, and in some cases respond to, human suffering and abuses of human rights. It was an unfortunate truth of the late twentieth century that the world was rife with human suffering and abuses of human rights, and it remains an ugly reality of international affairs in the early twenty-first century that suffering and abuses of human rights continue. In the Balkans, governments used rape and murder as a tool of policy. Genocide ran rampant in Rwanda. Hundreds of thousands starved in Somalia, Sudan, and North Korea. Saddam Hussein killed thousands who opposed his rule in Iraq. The list goes on.

Sometimes the United States responds to suffering and abuse, and other times it does not. For numerous reasons the United States chose in some instances to respond to suffering and abuse and in other cases opted not to respond—but this is not the place to explore these reasons. Almost always, however, Americans as individuals were touched by the suffering and condemned the abuses, and many Americans believe their country has a moral obligation to alleviate, if not eliminate, suffering and to oppose, if not end, abuses of human rights.

There are multiple reasons, then, for Americans and others to be concerned about world affairs, and about how the United States, the world's most powerful single actor, is engaged in world affairs through its foreign policy. This text offers students a *tour de horizon* through which they may gain an understanding of American foreign policy from the perspectives of history, politics and process, and current issues.

NOTES

1. International Institute for Strategic Studies, *The Military Balance 1998/99* (Oxford: Oxford University Press, 1998), p. 295.

2. We must differentiate between four levels of foreign policy involvement: *concern, presence, influence,* and *control*—all of which will be key terms used throughout this text.

   Concern means that the United States, or another country or international actor, displays interest in an issue, a country, or a region. It does not mean that the United States or another actor necessarily seeks to affect the course of events.

   Presence means that the United States or another international actor has actual human or material assets in a country or region. Presence does not mean that the United States or other actor necessarily has influence, although influence may result from presence or, in some cases, even concern.

   Influence indicates that the United States or another actor has the ability to induce a different actor to undertake an action, adopt a policy, or otherwise behave as the United States or other actor would prefer. Influence is not absolute; different degrees exist. The degree of influence that the United States or other international actor has often changes from issue to issue and on the same issue over time. For example, the United States may be influential in one capital on some issues but not on others, or it may find that its ability to influence outlooks or actions on an issue in another capital may change on a day-to-day basis. Neither concern nor presence guarantees influence, but either may provide influence.

   Control is extreme influence, but in foreign policy it rarely exists. For example, despite its military strength, the United States could not control events in Vietnam during the 1960s nor in Kosovo in 1999. Similarly, despite its economic strength, the United States cannot dictate the outcome of trade disputes with Latin American states or the European Union, nor can it control the price of oil.

The Study of American Foreign Policy

Introduction to Part One

If it is important to study American foreign policy for all of the reasons put forward in the introduction to this book, the question that comes quickly to mind is, "How should it be studied?"

In this text, American foreign policy will be approached from three directions: (1) the background and history of U.S. foreign policy, (2) the politics and processes of U.S. foreign policy formulation, and (3) analyses of current critical U.S. foreign policy issues. These directions are discussed in detail in Chapter 1. Before we begin our detailed study of the history, politics and processes, and issues of American foreign policy, it is first necessary to provide conceptual frameworks through which to view American foreign policy. The two chapters in Part I of this text undertake that task.

Chapter 1 offers a conceptual framework for the study of foreign policy on three levels of analysis: the international, national, and individual levels. This framework helps students understand that regardless of whether one is examining American foreign policy from the perspective of history, politics and processes, or current issues, there are multiple angles from which to look at foreign policy. Levels of analysis as a conceptual framework are useful for examining not just American foreign policy but all types of policies of every nation and state.

Chapter 2 provides several unifying concepts and competing themes that flow throughout past and present American foreign policy and that doubtlessly will play significant roles in future American foreign policy. From the time of the Founding Fathers through the current war on terrorism, American foreign policy has been imbued with a sense of mission, has pursued a set of national interests, and has claimed to be based on a set of principles. Chapter 2 examines American missions, interests, and principles and traces their evolution over time. Chapter 2 also identifies and discusses three sets of competing themes that have prominent roles in American foreign policy: the competition between realism and idealism, isolationism and involvement, and unilateralism and multilateralism. To a great extent, these three sets of competing themes flow from the missions, interests, and principles that underlie American foreign policy.

Throughout this text, we will return to levels of analysis, unifying thoughts, and competing themes to help improve our understanding of American foreign policy. They are not the only tools through which American foreign policy may be analyzed and understood, but they are among the most useful.

CHAPTER 1

Key Dimensions of Foreign Policy Analysis

The 2003 war in Iraq and its aftermath illustrated the importance of levels of analysis. The war was an international event (Level One), with different parts of the U.S. government having different views about what would and should happen during and after the war (Level Two). Individual policymakers also had different motivations and views about the conflict and its aftermath (Level Three). Here, U.S. troops in Iraq guard a roadblock in front of a picture of radical cleric Moqtada al-Sadr and his father.

- How should American foreign policy be analyzed?
- What is the international context in which American foreign policy takes place?
- How is American foreign policy affected by the nation's domestic issues and constitutional principles?
- What role does the individual decision maker play in the crafting of foreign policy?
- Can the United States have both a democratic and an effective foreign policy?

Colonel Paul W. Tibbets pushed the throttles full forward on the B-29 bomber under his command, a part of the 509th Composite of the 20th Air Force. Named *Enola Gay* in honor of his mother, the airplane lumbered down the runway on Tinian Island in the Pacific, lifted, and headed toward Japan. In the darkness of the plane's belly lay a special cargo: an experimental bomb ten feet long, two feet wide, 9,000 pounds in weight, and packed with enough high explosives to trigger a uranium-235 chain reaction. In ironic misnomer, the crew called the weapon "Little Boy."

As dawn began to break, weather planes and two B-29 escorts joined the *Enola Gay* over Iwo Jima. The weather reports were good for each authorized Japanese target: Nagasaki, Kokura, and, the top priority on the list, Hiroshima. In his mind's eye, the bombardier, Major Thomas W. Ferebee, could see the briefing maps of Hiroshima, with the Aioi Bridge at the center of this city famous for its graceful willow trees.

The sky turned bright and clear as the bomber approached Hiroshima. Local time: 8:15 a.m., the sixth day of August, 1945. The speed of the *Enola Gay:* 200 miles per hour. Altitude: 31,060 feet. The Aioi Bridge moved swiftly into the cross hairs of the bombsight. Ferebee opened the belly of the plane and pressed the cargo-release button.

As quickly as Colonel Tibbets could maneuver the controls of the sluggish airplane, the *Enola Gay* pulled upward, back, away. Little Boy fell until its altimeter registered the correct height of 1,890 feet above the unsuspecting city.

Burst.

A blinding flash of light.

Tumbling helixes of white-hot mass rising in a glassy column.

The sun come to earth.

A world changed forever.

In an instant, an energy force equivalent to the detonation of 12,000 tons of TNT struck Hiroshima. Ground zero became an oven set at 50 million degrees centigrade. Above the maelstrom of death and destruction, a stately mushroom cloud rose 20,000 feet into the sky, its stem darkened by urban debris, at its top a white plume trailing off toward the horizon. Of Hiroshima's 255,000 population, 78,150 perished in the witchfire of the nuclear explosion; another 100,000 suffered serious burns; 13,425 were never found.

Three days following the destruction of Hiroshima, another B-29 (named *Boxcar*) dropped a second atomic bomb on Japan, this time using a plutonium nuclear reaction. The target: Nagasaki. The result: 35,000 killed or missing, 40,000 injured. At long last, with a stunning use of physical power that left the world in awe, the United States had brought to an end the agony of the island-to-island warfare in the Pacific.

HIROSHIMA, TRUMAN, AND THE LEVELS OF ANALYSIS

President Harry Truman's decision to use atomic weapons against Japan in 1945 was momentous. The world had never seen a single bomb that could destroy an entire city. The president knew that Hiroshima and Nagasaki were of no military value and that thousands of innocent civilians would die in the attacks. "I am going to have to make a decision which no man in history has ever had to make," he said to aides immediately after being briefed about the terrible weapon, adding: "I'll make the decision, but it is terrifying to think about what I will have to decide."[1]

What led Truman to approve the bombing? One useful way to examine this and other foreign policy decisions is through a conceptual framework based on three **levels of analysis:** the international, the national (or domestic), and the individual.[2] According to this conceptual framework, foreign policy decisions can best be understood by analyzing which factors—international, national, or individual—influence decision makers' choices.

Kenneth N. Waltz offers a discussion of this framework in his book *Man, the State, and War,* observing that, at the international level, relationships among nations can be thought of as the product of global anarchy. By anarchy, Waltz means that no government exists above the nations of the world to regulate their behavior. Waltz also posits a second view of relations among nations, that nations' behavior toward one another is a result mainly of each nation's internal structure: politics at the domestic level. Waltz adds a third view as well, the possibility that the most important consideration in international relations is the behavior of the human beings who make decisions on behalf of a nation: the individual level of analysis. He refers to these three levels—international, internal (domestic), and individual—as distinct "images" of how the world works.[3]

Waltz is persuaded that the international—or "systemic"—level of analysis best explains how nations behave. On this international level, policymakers face strong-willed and often well-armed nations (usually called "states" or "units" by theorists), each with goals of its own. In Waltz's characterization, "Each state arrives at policies and decides on actions according to its own internal processes, but its *decisions are shaped by the very presence of other states as well as by interactions with them*" (emphasis added).[4] He stresses, too, that the number of powerful states in the world can affect their relations with one another. Sometimes, he notes, the world is dominated by one state (a unipolar international setting), by two states (bipolar), or by several states (multipolar). Hollis and Smith, two international relations theorists, summarize Waltz's view of the world in these words: "The international system acts to determine the behavior of its units by virtue of its anarchical structure and its polar structure."[5]

Certainly the Second World War reflected a condition of anarchy in the international system. With respect to the devastating atomic blows dealt Japan in 1945, nothing concerned President Truman so much as U.S. intelligence reports indicating that an American invasion of the Japanese homeland would meet stiff resistance. Military experts estimated that an invasion would last at least 18 months and cost the lives of anywhere from 40,000 to 500,000 American fighters. Eager to end the war without further loss of American life, Truman turned to the new weapon invented by a team of government scientists working secretly at a camp in New Mexico (the Manhattan Project). "You break your head and your heart to save one life," recalled Truman after the war. "No man could fail to use the bomb and look his countrymen in the face."[6]

Another event on the international level may have contributed to Truman's decision to use a nuclear weapon against Japan. The Truman Administration understood the Soviet Union would soon join the war in the east, raising the prospect that the Red Army might outrace the Americans to Tokyo and control that part of the world. Perhaps, some analysts argue, Truman resorted to the A-bomb chiefly to prevent communism from dominating Japan and all of its industrial might.

Theorists critical of Waltz's emphasis on the international level of analysis maintain that it is important to look not just at the system of nations but also "the properties of its units,"[7] that is, the internal structure of each state's government. On this national level of analysis, policymakers must deal with the vagaries of domestic politics and institutional conflicts within their own governing institutions. As Foyle states simply: "domestic political calculations influence foreign policy choices."[8]

Truman's atomic bomb decision faced fewer domestic pressures than is normally the case, since the Manhattan Project was a secret tightly kept. Not a single member of Congress knew about the atomic bomb until it was used against Japan. Nevertheless, inside the confines of the Oval Office, the president heard arguments from some scientists against dropping the bomb on the enemy without first displaying its horrific power to Japanese authorities by demolishing a nearby uninhabited island in the Pacific. Conversely, other scientists and the military director of the Manhattan Project argued that only this direct application of force would convince this stubborn enemy to surrender. Besides, they argued, a demonstration on a deserted island would waste one of the few nuclear weapons in the American arsenal. And what if the demonstration bomb proved to be a dud? In these internal debates among a small circle of bureaucrats, scientists, and White House advisers, President Truman decided to side with the director of the Manhattan Project.

Least visible of all to the scholar is the level of the individual government official, where decision making is subject to peer group and other psychological pressures. The supposition is that individual leaders perceive, assess, and act upon information in different ways, depending on their personalities, life experiences, and political calculations.[9]

This level is a murky domain for scholars to probe, because no one is a mind reader and the inner workings of a person's thought processes can be difficult, if not impossible, to fathom. Yet, as Harold Lasswell once observed, "Political science without biography is a form of taxidermy." So is the study of foreign policy. The personalities and attitudes of individual government officials can matter, as Woodrow Wilson's emotional support for a League of Nations and Ronald Reagan's ideological crusade against international communism illustrate. The influence of individuals should not be, but often is, ignored in efforts to understand foreign policy.

With respect to the nuclear bombing of Japan, we know little about the psychological dimensions of Truman's thinking, but we do know that he witnessed firsthand the carnage of the battlefield during the First World War as an infantry officer. Based on this experience, he could appreciate the profound suffering on both sides that an invasion of Japan would entail. These memories may have exercised some influence, however subliminal, on the president's approval of the *Enola Gay*'s fateful mission. Truman may have concluded that, as horrific as nuclear weapons are, the harvest of death, destruction, and suffering that would result from the bombing of Hiroshima and Nagasaki would still be less than the carnage of a full-scale ground invasion.

Which of the three levels of analysis is most important for understanding the bombing of Japan in 1945 and other foreign policy decisions? The three levels of analysis intersect in intricate, often baffling ways to shape the course of foreign policy; often there is no definitive answer as to which level has been most significant. Each level warrants closer examination.

LEVEL ONE: THE INTERNATIONAL SETTING

Almost every scholar of foreign policy agrees with Waltz's conception regarding the anarchical nature of the world. As Ferguson and Mansbach write, "No central government exists with a range of authority compared to that found in contemporary states."[10] Or as another scholar observes, we live in "a world of egoists without central authority."[11] This setting makes the goal of international cooperation often difficult and sometimes impossible.

For the foreseeable future, states remain the basic entities in international affairs, as fundamental to an understanding of foreign policy as the atom is to an understanding of physics. A **state** may be defined as a gathering together of individuals under a single government that controls a well-defined territory, while a **nation** is a group of people who view themselves as being linked to one another in some manner.[12] A nation is as much a psychological fixation as anything else. A **nation-state** combines both territorial and psychological dimensions, with citizens living in a single state but sharing a cultural identity, including a common language and allegiance to a distinctive flag and national anthem.

For example, the United States may be considered a nation-state, even though Americans come from all ethnic groups, cultural backgrounds, political and religious beliefs, economic levels, and historical experiences. This is because Americans consider themselves one people and one nation under a single government. Conversely, the former Soviet Union was a state but never a nation-state, since Soviet citizens lived in a single state for over 70 years without ever considering themselves a nation. The existence today of 15 separate states in place of a now-defunct Soviet Union is evidence of this. While it is useful to appreciate these distinctions between "state" (or "unit"), "nation" (or "country"), and "nation-state," in common usage analysts tend to use these expressions interchangeably.

If the formation of a new state is widely recognized by other established states, the new state is considered sovereign. **Sovereignty** may be defined as "the legal capacity of an independent state to regulate its affairs as it pleases, without having to obtain permission from any outside source."[13] In the aftermath of the 1991 Persian Gulf War, a United Nations coalition led by the United States stripped Iraq of some aspects of its sovereignty as a punishment for renegade ("rogue") behavior—most notably, its invasion of Kuwait in 1990. Against Iraqi protests, UN weapons inspectors (backed by America's military and intelligence presence in the Persian Gulf region) entered the nation and conducted searches for hidden weapons laboratories. The UN established "no-fly zones" in the north and south of Iraq in 1992, policed mainly by U.S. fighter planes—a further erosion of Iraqi sovereignty.

In March 2003, the United States with the support of 34 other nations in a "coalition of the willing" (as President George W. Bush referred to the ad hoc alliance) decided to attack Iraq again. The president had grown impatient with Iraq's leader, Saddam Hussein, fearing that he had a continuing interest in developing weapons of mass destruction (WMDs) and angered by his uneven cooperation with a new team of UN weapons inspectors. The attack was controversial; several of America's leading allies, including France and Germany, opposed the immediate use of military force and sought to extend the period of UN inspections and diplomatic negotiations over the future of Iraq. Nevertheless, the American-led attack on Iraq proceeded and Iraq's sovereignty lay in tatters.

Despite their importance in the international system, states are not the only international actors. Indeed, the international setting is crowded with many other entities in addition to sovereign nations, such as various international governmental organizations (IGOs), which are formal organizations with specific objectives and are composed of state members, and nongovernmental organizations (NGOs), which are formal organizations with specific objectives and are composed of individuals, professional groups, or other gatherings of people with shared interests and objectives. The World Health Organization (WHO) is an example of an IGO, and the human rights organization Amnesty International is an example of an NGO. With their cross-national ties, some of these organizations help damp down the tensions endemic in a system of competing and distrustful nations.

With these features of the international setting in mind, **American foreign policy** may be defined as those decisions and actions taken by the United States with respect to other international actors in pursuit of the well-being of its citizens and the advancement of their interests and ideals. As only one of nearly 200 nations, the United States often finds its interests and objectives in conflict with those of other sovereign nations. The world is a rich tapestry of disparate states, trading blocs, military alliances, ethnic and religious groups, tribes, terrorist cells, parties, and factions. Each state has its own goals and ambitions, its own territory and culture, and its own population and ideals to defend, along with its own means of defense—from punji stakes dipped in primitive poisons (used against U.S. soldiers during the war in Vietnam) to the modern intercontinental ballistic missiles (ICBMs) armed with multi-megaton warheads that are a part of the military arsenals in the United States, Russia, China, and several other nations. As the United States tragically learned on September 11, 2001, even commercial airliners can be used as weapons by terrorists hijacking the fuel-laden planes and flying them into skyscrapers and government buildings.

Scholarly attempts to explain why states behave as they do toward one another vary widely and are often contradictory. No single theory of American foreign policy stands preeminent. Some explanations, though, have wider currency than others. On the international level of analysis, the most influential perspectives focus on the balance of power between nations, the concepts of "realism" versus "idealism," a range of geographical opportunities and constraints (geopolitics), and, most recently, the idea of "globalization."

The Balance of Power

In the foreign policy model based on the **balance of power** concept, the central notion is that if one state becomes dominant, it will attempt to manipulate—even conquer—other states. Therefore, argues this model, leaders of other states will try to form coalitions to prevent any single country from achieving superiority over the rest.[14] In Rosecrance's formulation, balance of power is "a theory based on the assumption that nations will rally around a potential victim state, providing arms, military guarantees, and general support, thereby helping it to fend off a potential aggressor."[15]

In the Western world, states have been unwilling to allow any individual country to dominate the European continent. When Adolf Hitler sent Panzer tanks rumbling into Poland in 1939, Great Britain honored a treaty with the Polish government and immediately declared war on Germany, since the British believed that an expanded Third Reich would make Hitler a grave threat to the security of the United Kingdom. When Hitler then threatened Great Britain, President Franklin D. Roosevelt similarly concluded that the United States had to resist his attempt to disrupt the balance of power in Europe, since

America could well be the next target of the Nazi war machine, backed by the industrial might of Europe in Germany's hands.

Yet the balance of power approach offers no panacea to curb global conflict. In Rosecrance's words, "nations can by no means rely on the automatic creation of a reliable balance against aggression."[16] Especially in recent years, he notes, the balance of power concept may still apply to large, strong nations, but less so with respect to those nations in the post–Cold War world that are smaller and weaker.

Realism versus Idealism

The balance of power concept is central to the philosophy of **realism**. This school of thought—sometimes referred to as "realpolitik"—argues that a nation's external relations should rest on a foundation of military and economic strength, since international politics is a struggle for power in a setting "unmediated by any referee."[17] As Tony Smith observes, "Faced with the law of the jungle, nice distinctions of legal or ethical theory are not compelling discourses."[18] According to realists, national security—and especially territorial security—is the first order of business for any state; therefore, a state's military and economic power matter most.

The roots of the realist tradition are long, extending back to the writings of Niccoló Machiavelli (1469–1527) and even Thucydides (circa 460–400 B.C.). Classical realism displays a fundamental pessimism about human nature, as reflected in Thomas Hobbes's famous aphorism that the life of man is "solitary, poor, nasty, brutish, and short." The plight of human beings, according to Hobbes, boils down to "a condition of war of everyone against everyone."[19] In this tradition, Machiavelli proposed during the sixteenth century that princes fashion their state policies based on the hard realities of political life, not Christian ethics—on life as it is, not as it should be. This outlook has provided the conceptual underpinnings for modern statecraft.

Hans Morgenthau became the leading proponent of realism in the United States after the Second World War.[20] In *Politics among Nations*, he emphasized that the world is driven by considerations of national interests.[21] For Morgenthau, the international system and its anarchical structure demanded, to avoid the outbreak of war, the use of skillful diplomacy to maintain a balance of power in the world. Since nations are self-interested maximizers of power, they have to be checked by countervailing power.

A subsequent generation of scholars, led by Kenneth Waltz, expanded upon Morgenthau's writings to develop the philosophy of **neo-realism**.[22] The neo-realists approached the study of world politics armed with more advanced, scientific tools of analysis. Further, they placed a stronger emphasis on the international level of analysis, while downplaying the importance of morality and elevating issues of economic relations among nations. Their philosophy remained true, though, to the pessimism about human nature found in the roots of classical realism. Given Waltz's interest in the theoretical significance of how many strong nations existed in the world at any given time (that is, the degree of global polarity), some analysts have labeled this approach "structural realism."[23] Other variations of neo-realism have also arisen, such as Mearsheimer's concept of "offensive realism," which highlights the balance of power concept and the tenet that strong states seek to maximize their share of world power as a means for ensuring their own survival in a competitive and anarchical world.[24]

Other scholars and policymakers are drawn more to the concept of moral principle or **idealism** in foreign affairs. Idealists advocate the settlement of international disputes according to international law, as well as through the promotion of collective security arrangements and organizations such as the UN to preserve and promote world peace. They also underscore human rights norms that outlaw genocide and other violations of basic freedoms and dignity. "Idealists downplay the role of the international system," note Hollis and Smith. "Conflict was avoidable, and its causes could be found in the domestic settings of states."[25] **Neo-liberalism,** a related approach to the study of international relations, displays a strong dose of idealism. Its proponents advocate the worldwide development of democracy, open markets, and free trade. They place a premium as well on international law and institutions, ethics, human rights, and multilateral diplomacy—all of which, they argue, can mitigate the negative effects of power competition among states.[26] Yet another related school, **constructivism,** focuses on the question of how social norms and ideas—the social construction—of international politics influence relations among states.[27] Like the neo-liberals, constructivists concentrate on issues like human rights, multilateralism, and the value of international institutions for enhancing world peace.

Government officials often evoke the idea of idealism in foreign policy by referring to morality as a guiding principle of America's foreign relations. For example, a chairman of the Senate Foreign Relations Committee, reflecting on how the United States may have diminished its standing in the world by using the Central Intelligence Agency (CIA) to carry out assassination plots against foreign leaders, concluded: "I suggest we have lost—or grievously impaired—the good name and reputation of the United States from which we once drew a unique capacity to exercise matchless moral leadership."[28] In another expression of idealism, a prominent member of the House Foreign Affairs Committee (now called the International Relations Committee) stressed that in the conduct of U.S. foreign policy, "the best way to promote our interests is to promote our ideals."[29]

In sum, realists and neo-realists exhibit a skeptical outlook on international law and ethical considerations in international affairs. They believe that a nation's external relations should rest more prudently on a foundation of military and economic strength. Realism, writes Stanley Hoffmann, "looks at the international system as a milieu in which states compete, seek to increase their power, try to prevent the rise of rivals or hegemons through unilateral moves as well as through balances of power, and depend for their survival and success above all on military might and the economic underpinning of it."[30] In contrast, idealists, neo-liberals, and constructivists embrace the goals of optimism, community, and non-elitism in international affairs, along with the promotion of worldwide egalitarianism and economic prosperity.[31]

The conflict between realism and idealism has long been a part of American foreign policy, even though the terms themselves were not widely used until the twentieth century. Indeed, as we will see in Chapter 2 and Part II of this book, the conflict is one of the three competing themes of American foreign policy that can be traced through the eighteenth and nineteenth centuries. The competition between idealism and realism was especially evident in the twentieth century, during and after Woodrow Wilson's presidency. Wilson held idealistic hopes after World War I that the League of Nations, open diplomacy, and collective security would usher in an era of international peace for the United States and the world. Wilson's idealism was frustrated, however, when the League failed to keep the peace, in part because the U.S. Senate blocked America's participation in the League, and when the nations of the world proved unwilling to pursue open diplomacy and collective security.[32]

The failure of Wilson's idealism, combined with British Prime Minister Neville Chamberlain's feckless attempts to satiate Hitler's imperial appetites with a policy of appeasement, added to the ranks of those who came to be called realists. Thus, during and after World War II, idealism became "an epithet for naivete."[33] As Nye has written: "The horrors of Hitler's war made a post-war generation of scholars worry about idealism in foreign policy, and the conventional wisdom in the professional study of international relations since 1945 has awarded the 'realists' a clear victory over the 'idealists.'"[34]

Still, idealism continues to exercise a strong attraction for many Americans. Even President George H. W. Bush, who, like his son, President George W. Bush, is normally viewed as a proponent of the realist perspective, encouraged U.S. intervention in Somalia

Idealism and realism sometimes clash in U.S. foreign policy, as when U.S. citizens, shown here in Niger helping vaccinate people against polio, undertake actions that the U.S. government opts not to pursue.

in his last weeks in office in 1992, on the grounds that the United States should provide humanitarian assistance to the poor and starving citizens of that African nation. In one of his final speeches, the first President Bush emphasized that "our country's tradition of idealism" has made us "unique among nations." Commonly, the foreign policy views of public officials (like private citizens) in the United States are a mixture of idealism and realism. The clash between idealism and realism hence remains one of the key competing themes in American foreign policy.

Geopolitics

In addition to agreeing about the importance of balance-of-power considerations, students of foreign policy usually acknowledge the centrality of another proposition regarding the affairs of nations, namely, that geography can play a major role. Nicholas J. Spykman (1893–1943), a famous geopolitical thinker, overstated the case when he argued that geography was "the most fundamentally conditioning factor" in the shaping of foreign affairs. Nonetheless, **geopolitics**—that aspect of foreign policy influenced by the number, size, strength, location, and topography of states—is a prominent feature in the writings of scholars and the decisions of government leaders. As will be discussed in more detail in Chapter 2, perhaps no one has stated this perspective more poignantly than Mexican President Porfirio Diaz in a *fin de siècle* lament that his country was "so far from God and so close to the United States."

But the United States is not the only country that has a strong influence on its neighbors. Most large countries with powerful armies acquire a "sphere of influence" beyond their borders, an area into which other nations tread only at the peril of triggering a military response. Since the proclamation of the Monroe Doctrine in 1823, the United States has officially claimed the Western Hemisphere as its sphere of influence. During the Cold War, the USSR viewed weak countries on its perimeter as within Moscow's sphere of influence. Finland, the Baltic states, Eastern Europe, and Afghanistan all found themselves in the shadow—and at times under the foot—of the Soviet military behemoth.

Strategic Resources

Some geopolitical analysts point to the significance of **strategic resources** in the foreign policy calculations of states. For instance, vital to the United States is access to nickel and zinc in Canada; tin in Bolivia; bauxite in Jamaica and Guinea; platinum, industrial diamonds, and chromite in South Africa; manganese ore in Brazil; and oil in the Middle East. Analysts of this persuasion argue that the essential reason the United States fought the Persian Gulf War in 1991 was to repel the Iraqi takeover of oil fields in Kuwait and block a possible Iraqi invasion of Saudi Arabia. Some attribute similar oil-related motives to the war against Iraq in 2003, although the official reason from the second Bush Administration was to prevent the regime of Saddam Hussein from developing weapons of mass destruction—even though no sign of WMDs were discovered by the U.S.-led invasion force.

Falling Dominoes

During the Cold War, American geostrategists warned of another danger related to the balance-of-power concept: the spread of communism from one regime to another, like a row of falling dominoes. As President Dwight D. Eisenhower stated in 1954, this **domino theory** meant that if Southeast Asia, then Japan and Formosa, the Philippines, Australia, and New Zealand fell into communist hands, "you could have a beginning of a disintegration that would have the most profound influences."[35] The domino theory played a major role in convincing U.S. officials to intervene in Vietnam in 1964, resulting in over 58,000 battlefield deaths for the United States and the nation's first military defeat overseas.

Sometimes the fear of falling dominoes can reach exaggerated proportions. Advocating covert military assistance to pro-West factions in Angola, the U.S. ambassador to the UN, Daniel P. Moynihan, opined in 1975: "The Communists will take over Angola and will thereby considerably control the oil shipping lanes from the Persian Gulf to Europe. They will be next to Brazil. They will have a large chunk of Africa and the world will be different in the aftermath."[36] A majority of lawmakers in Congress were unimpressed by this logic and rejected the argument. During the Reagan Administration (1981–1989), officials again used the domino theory to rally support for U.S. intervention in Central America. Again, many in Congress disagreed, including a skeptical Representative (now Senator) Barbara Mikulski (D-Maryland): "When they get ready to send helicopters to El Salvador, they talk about saving the country from Communism. I want them to start talking about saving the country from birth defects. I'm talking about children in my district who are more likely to die of birth defects than from some communist who's going to come up the Chesapeake Bay."[37]

The chief weakness of the domino theory lies in its assumption that if one country is dominated by a hostile ideology, its neighbors will inevitably be infected by that ideology. History suggests that, on the contrary, there is nothing inexorable about anything, and states are often protected against outside threats by their strong economies, robust military defenses, or vibrant nationalism. Thus, when Cuba attempted to establish, with Soviet assistance, a communist regime in Angola, the relatively weak African nations bordering Angola successfully fought against communist expansion into their territories. They no more wished to be under the thumb of Havana or Moscow than under the thumb of European colonial powers in an earlier era.

Dramatic changes in modern transportation and communications, the stunning destructive power of modern weapons, and the swiftness of intercontinental missiles and modern aircraft have diminished the importance of geography in world affairs. Even so, the notion of falling dominoes—most recently, Islamic nations falling away from modernity to embrace anti-American fundamentalism of the kind that inspired the terrorist attacks against the United States in 2001—remains a part of the debate about U.S. foreign policy.

Globalization

The central role that geopolitical analyses once held in international affairs is being replaced to some extent by an even more comprehensive concept, **globalization,** defined by Nye as "the growth of worldwide networks of interdependence."[38] Proponents of globalization argue not only that geography is less important in international affairs than it once was, but, more importantly, that states are in decline as the key actors in world affairs. They point to the growing role of multinational corporations; a sense of common identity among groups that reaches across state boundaries; the dependence of nations on one another's economic decisions; increased trade across state borders with fewer and fewer impediments; rapid communications and transportation—indeed, the entire intricate interplay of world events that washes across national boundaries and weakens the influence of the state.

Today, components of a single consumer end product, say an automobile, are manufactured in many different countries and assembled somewhere else; American and Russian physicians issue joint statements against the use of nuclear weapons; youth around the globe share the latest fads in rock music, film, and fashion; and terrorists groups forge secret linkages across national borders. "A new pattern of international politics is emerging," forecast political scientist Zbigniew Brzezinski over two decades ago (he served as President Jimmy Carter's national security adviser). According to Brzezinski, "The world is ceasing to be an arena in which relatively self-sustained, 'sovereign,' and homogeneous nations interact, collaborate, clash, or make war. . . . Transnational ties are gaining in importance, while the claims of nationalism, though still intense, are nevertheless becoming diluted."[39]

Linkages brought about by technology are a central part of globalization. Television transmitted the battlefields of Vietnam, the Persian Gulf, Somalia, Bosnia, Kosovo, Afghanistan, and Iraq into the homes of millions of Americans. It also brought pictures of worldwide public demonstrations against some of these wars, as well as protests from Seattle to Genoa against international economic conferences that promoted globalization (which dissenters claim has a pernicious effect on the working classes and developing countries). Few modern influences on the shaping of American foreign policy have been as profound as television, especially the worldwide, around the clock coverage of breaking events provided by CNN.

"If there had been live [television] coverage of the Civil War," political scientist Austin Ranney once speculated, "it would have ended in 1862 with the establishment of the Confederacy, because it was a terribly bloody war and the North was losing most of the early part of it."[40] While of course there is no way to determine if this particular counterfactual view might be true, it is clear that television images are ever present in the minds of those who must make decisions about how the United States should react to world events and conditions. Television coverage of American soldiers killed in battle can quickly turn public opinion in the United States against involvement overseas in particularly dangerous places, as happened in Somalia in 1993. Similarly, in 2004, as a mounting number of body bags returned to the United States from the war zone, the second Bush Administration feared that the American public would lose faith in the U.S. occupation and reconstruction of Iraq.

The emergence of the Internet in the late twentieth century is another vital force behind globalization. Like television, the Internet allows millions of people to communicate across national boundaries, sharing opinions, ideas, information, outlooks, pictures, and films. Already the Internet has had an immense influence on global commerce, as trillions of dollars are transferred every day across national boundaries electronically—for the most part beyond the control of individual state governments.

Television and the Internet have the potential to draw people closer together into a "global village," in Marshall McLuhan's vivid phrase. Some say that as television and the Internet are more widely used, they will nurture global peace as people share the same soap operas, athletic events, and rock concerts, creating transnational ties that will eventually overcome the anarchy of today's international system. Others are more skeptical, believing that the state and its interests will withstand the challenges of globalization and technology, because so many powerful groups have invested in the status quo and fear the uncertainty that would accompany an abandonment of the current state system.

LEVEL TWO: THE NATIONAL SETTING

Below the international level, policymakers must also deal with domestic politics and institutional conflicts within their own state as they formulate and implement foreign policy. Domestic debates about foreign policy are influenced by many considerations, and each state has its own specific issues and circumstances. Of special importance for an understanding of American foreign policy are the unique historical experiences of the United States, as well as its constitutional framework, contemporary institutional arrangements, and pluralist politics.

Historical Experiences

"History is the memory of states," wrote Henry Kissinger, who served as national security adviser during the Nixon Administration and as secretary of state during the Ford Administration.[41] He properly emphasized the importance of **historical experiences** in the evolution of a nation's relations with the rest of the world. American foreign policy can be thought of as an ongoing experiment, marked by a deep-seated ambivalence about the appropriate degree of U.S. involvement abroad.

Throughout its history, as we will discuss in detail in Chapter 2 and in Part II, the United States has oscillated between two contradictory impulses: an isolationist detachment from the affairs of other nations, and involvement with and interventions into the affairs of other nations (sometimes openly, sometimes secretly). Though often unsure which impulse would better serve the nation, Americans on balance have preferred some degree of detachment. Yet the United States has been happy to accept friendly assistance from overseas in times of military need, as when Great Britain and other nations rallied to America's side against terrorism after the September 11 attacks, and when it gained the endorsement of some nations for the U.S.-led attack against Iraq in 2003.

In light of their experiences with the Second World War, the rise of the Soviet empire during the Cold War, and the homeland terrorist attacks of 2001, most Americans have concluded that isolationism is ill advised. Public opinion surveys continue to indicate, though, a longing to be "free from the wrangling world," in Thomas Paine's quaint phrase of 1776. Thus, even during one of the hottest periods of the Cold War, a majority of Americans polled in 1986 expressed opposition to direct U.S. military intervention in such trouble spots as Angola, Indochina, and Central America.[42] Even so, the United States has intervened overseas many times, chiefly in the developing world, to curb the rise of Marxist-Leninist regimes, as in Korea from 1950 to 1953, Vietnam from 1964 to 1975, and Nicaragua from 1983 to 1987. More recently, the United States has intervened overseas to oppose aggressive dictators or terrorists in Panama in 1989, Iraq and Kuwait in 1991, Somalia in 1993, Bosnia and Kosovo between 1993 and 1999, Afghanistan in 2001 through today, and again in Iraq from 2003 through today.

Constitutional Framework

The **constitutional framework** for governance drafted by the American founders, led in this task by James Madison, is significant to an understanding of American foreign policy. The Constitution was guided by the founders' deep distrust of centralized power. King George III had taught them a searing lesson about its corrosive effects. "Power, lodged as it must be in human hands, is ever liable to abuse," warned Madison. The founders had a remedy against this danger: the dispersal of power. As historian Joseph Ellis writes, the Constitution was a "victory of diffusion over consolidation."[43] Power, for both domestic and foreign affairs, would be divided among three branches of government. "Ambition must be made to counteract ambition," Madison declared in a celebrated phrase from *Federalist Paper No. 51*. Checks and balances would be the order of the day, as the founders attempted (in Thomas Jefferson's prescription) to restrain government with "the chains of the Constitution."

The **separation of powers doctrine** that the founders wrote into the Constitution provides the legal framework for American governance to this day. Richard E. Neustadt accurately described the reality of day-to-day policymaking, noting that America's government is required by constitutional design to *share* power across the institutions of government: the legislature, the executive, and the judiciary.[44] The power to approve treaties, for example, requires participation by both the legislative and the executive branches, with occasional arbitration by the judicial branch.

Yet power sharing creates tensions and ambiguities within the government. Who will ultimately assume the responsibility to commit the nation to war or to enter into binding agreements with other countries? By spreading the authority for such decisions across the branches of government, the American Constitution pitted one institution against another—precisely what Madison had in mind as a check against any one branch becoming too strong.

The sharing of authority has the virtue of keeping it under better control, but this method carries with it the makings of a recipe for conflict and inefficiency. As constitutional expert Edward S. Corwin famously observed, "The Constitution . . . is an invitation to struggle for the privilege of directing American foreign policy."[45] The founders understood that governance involved a balancing act between liberty and efficiency, and they tilted toward liberty. In 1926, Justice Louis Brandeis of the Supreme Court commented on the wisdom of this choice: "The doctrine of separation of powers was adopted by the Convention of 1787, not to promote efficiency but to preclude the exercise of arbitrary power. The purpose was, not to avoid friction, but, by means of the inevitable friction incident to the distribution of governmental powers among three departments, to save the people from autocracy."[46]

During the Reagan presidency, executive branch frustration over having to share foreign policy powers with Congress led officials in the administration to bypass lawmakers and set up a secret scheme to sell weapons to Iran. The officials hoped to persuade the Iranian government during 1985–1986 to intervene with terrorist groups in Lebanon and bring about the release of U.S. hostages held there. The U.S. officials then used the profits from this weapons sale to support, again secretly, anti-Marxist *contra* rebels in Nicaragua. They also acquired additional funding for the *contras* from wealthy private American citizens, as well as from foreign rulers such as the king of Saudi Arabia and the sultan of Brunei. Thus, the administration skirted laws requiring reports to Congress on the use of secret operations, including the Hughes-Ryan Act of 1974, which mandated reports on all important covert actions; the Arms Export Control Act of 1976, which prohibited the sales of arms to nations like Iran that supported terrorists; and, most directly, the Boland Amendments, named after Representative Edward P. Boland (D-Massachusetts), chairman of the House Intelligence Committee at the time, which specifically prohibited covert actions in Nicaragua.

According to Article I, Section 8, of the Constitution, the power to spend is placed in the hands of Congress. Going beyond the defiance of the various statutes mentioned above, the secret operations in Iran and Nicaragua also dismissed this core constitutional provision. The ensuing domestic crisis brought about by these infringements, known as the Iran-*contra* scandal, caused President Ronald Reagan's popularity to plunge 21 points in public opinion polls.

Later investigations into the Iran-*contra* affair disclosed that administration officials had sought an "off-the-shelf, self-sustaining, stand-alone" capability to conduct secret foreign policy, free from the "interference" of Congress.[47] Had this scheme succeeded, the appropriations process—a key element in the American system of checks and balances—would have become irrelevant. These clandestine machinations inflicted a dangerous blow against limited, constitutional government, carried out by misguided presidential aides who decided they knew more about what was good for the United States than the elected representatives of the American people in Congress. Senator Warren Rudman (R-New Hampshire), a leading lawmaker who helped investigate the abuses, concluded that these officials had "wrapped themselves in the flag and [went] around spitting on the Constitution."[48]

Institutional Fragmentation

Just as the U.S. Constitution's insistence on shared power leads to friction among the branches over the conduct of foreign policy, so, too, does its requirement for a government of separate institutions. On one side of the coin, some observers believe that the structural arrangements of America's government have led to excessive **institutional fragmentation.** Critics complain of 535 would-be secretaries of state on Capitol Hill (100 senators and 435 representatives), along with too many committee hearings that sap the time and energy of the real secretary of state, as well as too many laws that require the executive branch to report to Congress on foreign policy too often.

On the other side of the coin are those who, in the spirit of the founders, are suspicious of power that resides exclusively within the executive branch. They complain of undue secrecy by administration officials who seek to conceal from lawmakers faulty premises underlying their foreign policy initiatives. They lament as well the slippery dealings that pass authority from the White House to the CIA, the Department of Defense, and other agencies in a shell game within the executive branch that prevents

Congress from following the formulation of foreign policy. Moreover, they object to attempts by the executive to take detours around the Congress by using groups outside the government as a means for achieving foreign policy goals blocked by law, as occurred with the privatization of American foreign policy during the Iran-*contra* affair.

Even within (as opposed to between) the executive and legislative branches of government, the friction that results from having too many parts in the policymaking machinery has become a sore point for critics. On Capitol Hill, numerous subcommittees jostle over legislative jurisdiction and compete for the same witnesses from the executive branch for public hearings. Junior members of Congress travel abroad to barter with heads of states over policy or attempt, as did Representative George Hansen (R-Idaho) during the Cold War, to gain the release of U.S. hostages in the Middle East while professional diplomats in the Department of State look on in dismay.

Inside the executive branch, multiple actors—including the State, Defense, Treasury, and Commerce Departments, the 15 intelligence agencies, the National Security Council, and the United States Trade Representative—vie for influence and often pursue their own separate agendas. At times, officials appear to be conducting their own personal notions of proper foreign policy, not just beyond the purview of lawmakers but outside the supervision of the president and the Cabinet as well. Without presidential—let alone congressional—authority, the CIA entered into secret contracts with the Mafia as part of a plan to assassinate Cuban leader Fidel Castro during the 1960s; mid-level White House officials established Swiss bank accounts for the private funding of covert operations in Nicaragua during the Reagan years; and CIA officials prepared a manual on how to "neutralize" (a euphemism for "assassinate") political opponents in Nicaragua in 1984, despite a 1976 executive order signed by President Gerald R. Ford that banned murder as an instrument of American foreign policy. In consideration of these and other operations, one can appreciate the conclusion reached by historian Arthur M. Schlesinger Jr. that "students of public administration have never taken sufficient account of the capacity of lower levels of government to sabotage or defy even a masterful President."[49]

The complexity of foreign policy is reflected in the models of decision making advanced by political scientists Graham Allison and Philip Zelikow.[50] As Allison put it in his initial formulation of this approach, the **rational actor model** (Model I) attempts "to understand happenings as the more or less purposive acts of unified national governments." The objective of this first model, he wrote, is "to show how the nation or government could have chosen the action in question, given the strategic problem that it faced."[51] From this model's vantage point, decisions are calculated responses to a strategic problem, that is, a reasonable choice in light of the circumstances faced by a state. Using the missile crisis of 1962 as an illustration, Allison and Zelikow show how the Soviet installation of missiles in Cuba was a reasonable act from the perspective of the Soviet Union, given (among other reasons) the Kremlin's interest in shoring up its eroding strategic posture. The Soviets had only 20 ICBMs in 1962, compared to 180 for the United States—a 1:9 imbalance.

In contrast to the idea of rational behavior carried out by a unified political leadership, Allison and Zelikow raise other possibilities that underscore the role of organizational constraints and bureaucratic dynamics. An **organizational process model** (Model II) attempts to identify the relevant governmental organizations involved in a crisis, then determine both the interests and the standard operating procedures (SOPs) that influenced the behavior of the organizations. Regarding the Cuban missile crisis, Allison and Zelikow point to military SOPs as central to understanding the Pentagon's response during the crisis, such as the U.S. Navy's specific rules for carrying out a blockade at sea to halt the Soviet missile-carrying ships headed for Cuba.

Finally, a **bureaucratic politics model** (Model III) looks at "the internal politics of a government. Happenings in foreign affairs are understood . . . neither as choices nor as outputs," Alison emphasizes. "Instead, what happens is categorized as *outcomes* of various overlapping bargaining games among players arranged hierarchically in the national government. In confronting the problem posed by Soviet missiles in Cuba, a Model III analyst displays the perceptions, motivations, positions, power, and maneuvers of principal players from which the outcome emerged."[52]

In sum, leaders act to maximize national strategic objectives; organizations behave according to SOPs; bureaucracies engage in compromise, bargaining, coalition building, and competition. Here are the lenses through which Allison and Zelikow invite us to examine the intricacies of foreign policy, noting that no single model will serve by itself. As they emphasize, "*multiple, overlapping competing conceptual models are the best that the current understanding of foreign policy provides.*"[53]

Taking into consideration the unified leadership model—Model I in the Allison-Zelikow framework—and their two organizational models (II and III), some scholars have suggested that it is useful to think of Level Two analysis (the national level) in terms of two different tiers: a cohesive state-centric core of rational leaders surrounded by bargaining bureaucracies with specialized SOPs. From this vantage point, one can think of foreign policymaking in terms of four levels of analysis, not just the three we have emphasized in this chapter. We prefer the simpler approach for this text, although we acknowledge that Level Two contains within it both a rational actor dimension and an organizational dimension.

Whichever models the analyst finds most useful, one feature of American foreign policy is certain: it is a dispersed enterprise. The end result is that presidents and lawmakers face a difficult challenge, since they must try to piece together the fragments into some semblance of coherence and purpose. Sometimes they succeed, most notably when the United States faces an emergency, such as an economic depression or a surprise attack as occurred at Pearl Harbor in 1941 and against the World Trade Center 60 years later. But often the whole unwieldy machinery threatens to break down in what James MacGregor Burns referred to as a "deadlock of democracy."[54]

Pluralism

As if the institutional fragmentation inside the government were an insufficient complication, American society is also characterized by the participation of many groups in the shaping of foreign policy decisions. The term **pluralism** is often used to describe these multiple centers of influence within the United States—not just a plethora of government institutions but a wide array of organizations, groups, and movements that have an interest in shaping America's relations with the rest of the world. Some groups have strong foreign policy agendas that they press with varying degrees of success upon officials.

Among the most prominent are political parties, notably the Democrats and the Republicans; interest or "pressure" groups, like the American-Israeli Public Affairs Committee (AIPAC); and occasional mass movements, such as the protests against the war in Vietnam in the 1960s or the anti-nuclear demonstrations of the 1980s.

Critics worry that the influence of these outside power centers has become too great, especially when officeholders bend toward those groups that have the most campaign funds to offer them in exchange for foreign policy favors. Moreover, as the number of power centers grows, the end result could be a clogging of the arteries of decision making, with so many officials and lobbyists involved in shaping a decision that everything shuts down from overload. Historian Paul Kennedy fears that the dispersal of power encouraged by the nation's founders "may be less serviceable now that the United States is a global superpower often called upon to make swift decisions vis-à-vis countries that enjoy far fewer constraints," and that the "cumulative effect [of power dispersal] is to make it difficult to carry out policy changes that seem to hurt special interests and occur in an election year."[55]

LEVEL THREE: THE INDIVIDUAL DECISION MAKER

According to some scholars and analysts, the third level of analysis—the individual decision maker—has been substantially ignored by scholars because of the analytic difficulties it presents; as a consequence, our understanding of foreign policy decision making has been distorted. The American diplomat and scholar George F. Kennan maintains that academics and other analysts have underestimated "psychological and political reactions—of such things as fear, ambition, insecurity, jealousy, and perhaps even boredom—as prime movers of events."[56] The tendency has been (as in Allison's Model I) to assume that decision makers are rational people who work together in harness, engaged in clear-headed analysis and with access to perfect information. Yet the emotions, personal idiosyncrasies, and other psychological traits of human beings in high office also play a part in the making of foreign (as well as domestic) policy and should not be dismissed. Scholars of social psychology and cognitive psychology have long been aware of how an individual's personal traits can shape decision making. "Perceptions of the world and of other actors diverge from reality," writes political scientist Robert Jervis, who maintains that an understanding of foreign policy can benefit from studying the patterns of divergence among those in high office.[57]

Consider the importance of human perceptions in the following description of relations between high-ranking foreign policy officials in the Reagan Administration. "Think of someone you really hate," noted a close observer during those years. "Multiply that by twenty and raise the answer to the fourth power, then you will have an idea of how [Secretary of State George P.] Shultz and [Secretary of Defense Caspar W.] Weinberger feel toward one another."[58] According to a senior official in the Reagan Administration, the assistant secretary of state for Latin American affairs and a key staff aide on the National Security Council (NSC) "fought like cats and dogs and would not speak to each other."[59] And a reporter wrote at the time that Secretary Shultz "had come to loathe" CIA Director William J. Casey."[60] Inevitably, such conflicts of personality at the highest levels of government have an effect on the course of foreign policy. How well decision makers relate to one another is important. "The real organization of government at higher echelons is not what you find in textbooks or organization charts," Secretary of State Dean Rusk once remarked. "It is how confidence flows down from the President."[61]

From among the many avenues of inquiry one might follow in assessing the influence of individuals in the shaping of foreign policy, three are especially revealing: the role-playing that policymakers engage in, the degree to which perceptual screens block out factual information, and the fundamental personality traits of decision makers.

Role-Playing

The concept of **role-playing** affects policy when the office a policymaker holds causes him or her to advocate and implement views traditional to that office. A former State Department official has referred to this phenomenon as the "curator mentality," lamenting that—regardless of their personal views—country desk officers in the department are expected to maintain policies that are already in place and to make sure that U.S. relations abroad are carefully preserved "under glass, untampered with, and dusted," as if the officials were simply museum curators.[62] Hence the nature of the office itself, coupled with peer expectations about how the job ought to be conducted, becomes critical influences on foreign policy decisions—as suggested by the phrase attributed to the civil servant Arnold Miles: "Where you stand depends on where you sit."[63]

Role-playing, however, is hardly an infallible predictor of how officials will behave. State Department policy does in fact change from time to time, and sometimes individuals and departments advocate unexpected positions. For example, during the Reagan Administration, the Department of State often advocated military intervention to achieve U.S. foreign policy goals, while the Department of Defense—still reeling from the frustrations of the Vietnam War—was inclined to encourage a diplomatic approach to foreign affairs. The reader will notice that individual role-playing at Level III is analogous to the aggregated institutional role-playing of Models II and III in the Allison-Zelikow conceptual framework: both individuals and organizations (that is, aggregates of individuals) can, and often do, reflect traditions that are part and parcel of the job descriptions and government buildings they inhabit.

Distorted Perceptions

As psychologists have long understood, how one perceives reality can be more important than reality itself. From time to time, foreign policy officials have erred because of a failure to accurately comprehend the world around them. **Self-delusion** is one important cause of misunderstanding, as officials brush aside—or bend—facts that fail to conform to their worldview. Of Kaiser Wilhelm I (1797–1888), the king of Prussia and the first emperor of modern Germany, Tuchman has written: "[He] was interested in gold-plated news only and disliked above all else those tiresome visits from ministers with their reports of inconvenient facts that did not fit in with his schemes."[64] Similarly, one of Hitler's close associates remembers how the Nazi leader "gladly sought advice from persons who saw the situation even more optimistically and delusively than he himself."[65]

Self-delusion is hardly limited to former German leaders. It can occur anywhere. Looking back at the early years of the Vietnam War, a senior U.S. intelligence official regretted "that the policymakers did not better exercise their own power to listen," since the evidence against a quick American victory in Indochina was available, compelling— and ignored.[66] Another intelligence official recalled that in 1966 U.S. policymakers began to "lose interest in an objective description of the outside world and were beginning to scramble for evidence that they were going to win the war in Vietnam." Increasingly from 1969 to 1974, "there was almost total dissent from the real world around us."[67] In 2003, intelligence officials in the United States and England complained in anonymous newspaper leaks that policy officers had exaggerated, selectively used ("cherry picked"), or simply dismissed out of hand various intelligence reports as they sought information to support their preconceived plans to attack Iraq. Policy officials in both countries claimed that Iraq was on the verge of producing, or already had, weapons of mass destruction. These officials lost considerable credibility with the public when the U.S.-led coalition that invaded Iraq in 2003 failed to find WMDs as they scoured the countryside. Even Pat Roberts (R-Kansas), the chairman of the Senate Intelligence Committee and normally a strong supporter of the CIA, called the agency's discredited allegation that Iraq had mobile weapons labs "embarrassing."[68]

Leadership isolation is another way in which policymakers are sometimes cut off from an accurate perception of reality. Before the 1961 Bay of Pigs invasion of Cuba by CIA-supported forces, experts inside the agency expressed skepticism that Cuban leader Fidel Castro could be so easily overthrown. The Cuban premier was "likely to grow stronger rather than weaker as time goes by," summed up a top-secret CIA report, since declassified. The study warned that Castro "now has established a formidable structure of control over the daily lives of the Cuban people."[69]

Unfortunately, President John F. Kennedy neither saw this study nor spoke with a single CIA analyst regarding the Bay of Pigs scheme. Ambitious, persuasive, a member of Kennedy's Georgetown social milieu, Richard M. Bissell Jr., the CIA officer in charge of the invasion plans (and sitting in a section of the CIA building far removed from the expert Cuban analysts), assured President Kennedy that Castro could be removed by a swift covert action. This was happy news to President Kennedy for the moment, but it soon proved disastrously wrong. The Cuban military quickly defeated the CIA invaders as they landed at the Bay of Pigs. An analyst from the CIA or from the Department of State, whose Cuban experts were also excluded from White House planning sessions, could have warned the president of the odds against success. At a minimum they could have pointed out that the contingency escape route to the Escambray Mountains was unrealistic, because of the intervening and impenetrable marshlands of the Zapata Swamp.

Perceptions of reality can be distorted as well by a phenomenon of interaction within small groups of individuals that psychologist Irving L. Janis labeled **groupthink,** the tendency of individuals in groups to cast aside realistic views of alternative courses of action in favor of cohesiveness among group members. According to the groupthink hypothesis, it becomes more important for members to conform to group expectations than to be correct. Regarding the Bay of Pigs fiasco, Janis wrote: "The failure of Kennedy's inner circle to detect any of the false assumptions behind the Bay of Pigs invasion plan can be at least partially accounted for by the group's tendency to seek concurrence at the expense of seeking information, critical appraisal, and debate."[70]

A policymaker's basic **personality traits**, evolved from childhood, can also have a significant influence on foreign policy decisions. One study correlates the willingness of some decision makers to use military force as a policy option to their "high-dominance personalities." Such individuals have a tendency to "run the show" while in office, imposing their will forcefully on subordinates, berating them, often ignoring them altogether as they set policy directions by themselves—say, a strong-willed national security adviser like Henry Kissinger compared to the more passive Secretary of State William P. Rogers during the Nixon Administration.[71]

A ROAD MAP FOR FOREIGN POLICY ANALYSIS

The influences on foreign policymaking that converge from the three levels of analysis—the international milieu, the domestic setting, and the individual decision maker—are depicted in Figure 1.1[72] The figure stresses the importance in American foreign policy of historical and constitutional antecedents (panel I in the figure), the competitive and bargaining nature of policymaking institutions (panel II), and the human influences (panel III) that stand between the decision maker and a range of foreign policy choices (panel IV).

Officials in Washington, D.C., face a wide range of **foreign policy choices,** as displayed in Figure 1.1. They may decide to order the gathering of more information about a world situation (intelligence); use the CIA to secretly manipulate events abroad (covert action); pursue negotiated resolutions to international disputes (diplomacy); take up arms

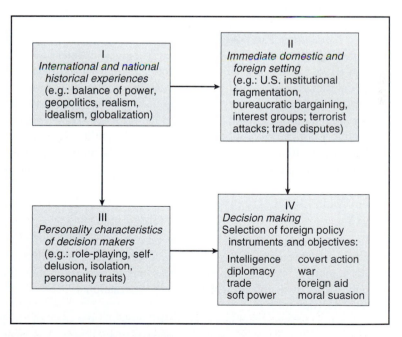

FIGURE 1.1
A Framework for Foreign Policy Analysis

against an adversary (war); use the blandishment of commerce as an inducement, or economic sanctions as a threat (trade); provide development assistance (foreign aid); win support overseas through the appeal of American culture (soft power);[73] or seek influence in the world through the embrace of high principle, from a strong human rights agenda overseas to the protection of civil liberties at home (moral suasion). The arrows in the figure indicate that foreign policy decisions are the result of a complex interplay between historical and institutional circumstances on the one hand, and the psychological orientations and personal attributes of the decision makers on the other hand.

Behind this abstract and simplified outline lies an intricate reality. The complexity can be underscored by a contrast with the game of chess. In chess, there are only six distinct pieces, a handful of rules, and a board that is just eight-by-eight units square. Yet even in chess, the number of possible sequences of moves is incredibly large: some 10^{120} or, essentially, infinity. But chess is simple compared to the sequence of possible moves that policymakers face in real-life situations. Take, for example, the interaction between two naval forces at war. Far more than six distinct "pieces" are involved in a naval operation. The standard operating procedures (the "rules") for moving just one destroyer are more intricate than for a chess piece, and the topographical "board" of the world's oceans is vast and far more difficult to assess than the confined parameters of a chessboard.[74]

Clearly, the conduct of American foreign policy is deeply challenging and endlessly fascinating, but how should one study it? Three views predominate. The first holds that an understanding of U.S. and world history is essential; a second focuses on the people and institutions that sometimes cooperate and sometimes clash as they make foreign policy; a third concentrates on the specific policies and activities currently being carried out abroad by the United States. This book uses all three approaches—history, politics, and policy implementation—in search of a 360° perspective on foreign policy.

We continue Part I of this book with an examination in the next chapter of the missions, interests, principles, and competing themes in American foreign policy. Then, in Part II, we explore how this nation's foreign policy has unfolded since the earliest days of the Republic—the vital historical backdrop for understanding America's contemporary relations with the rest of the world. Part III takes up an analysis of how foreign policy is made in the United States. Part IV discusses the most important global issues facing America. Finally, some Concluding Thoughts challenge students to use their knowledge and understanding to help the United States choose appropriate and constructive foreign policies.

SUMMARY

Foreign policy may be analyzed in several ways. One of the most useful ways is through a conceptual framework based on three levels of analysis: the international, the national (or domestic), and the individual. Under this framework, policy decisions can best be understood by analyzing which factors—international, national, or individual—influence decision makers.

At the international level, analysis focuses on the state and its interests, and what decision makers do to promote the interests of their state. However, states are not the only international actors. Various international governmental organizations (IGOs) and nongovernmental organizations (NGOs) are also active in international affairs. Thus, as decision makers formulate and implement foreign policies, they often must take these other actors into account.

Scholarly attempts to explain why states and state decision makers behave as they do vary widely. No single theory stands preeminent. Some explanations, though, have wider currency than others. On the international level, the most influential perspectives focus on the balance of power, realism versus idealism, geopolitics, and the idea of globalization.

The second level of analysis recognizes that decision makers must also deal with domestic politics and institutional conflicts in their own state as they formulate and implement foreign policy. Domestic debates about foreign policy are influenced by many considerations, with each state having its own issues and circumstances. Thus, at this level, American historical experiences, the U.S. constitutional framework, contemporary institutional arrangements, and pluralist politics must all be considered.

The third level of analysis, the individual decision maker, maintains that personal perceptions, emotions, idiosyncrasies, and other psychological traits of people in high office play a part in the making of policy. Three of the many avenues of inquiry one might follow in analyzing the influence of individuals in shaping of foreign policy are especially revealing: the role-playing that policymakers engage in, the degree to which perceptual screens block factual information, and the personality traits of decision makers.

The influences on foreign policymaking that emerge from the three levels of analysis—the international milieu, the domestic setting, and the individual decision maker—mean that foreign policy decisions are the culmination of a complex interplay between historical situations, institutional circumstances, and psychological orientations and personal attributes of decision makers.

KEY TERMS AND CONCEPTS

levels of analysis	historical experiences
state (nation, nation-state)	constitutional framework
sovereignty	separation of powers doctrine
American foreign policy	institutional fragmentation
balance of power	rational policy model
realism	organizational process model
neo-realism	bureaucratic politics model
idealism	pluralism
neo-liberalism	role-playing
constructivism	self-delusion
geopolitics	leadership isolation
strategic resources	groupthink
domino theory	personality traits
globalization	foreign policy choices

THINKING CRITICALLY

1. Identify and explain the three levels of analysis discussed in this chapter.

2. Explain how the three levels of analysis may be used to understand President Harry Truman's decision to drop atomic bombs on Hiroshima and Nagasaki.

3. Use the three levels of analysis to provide a critique of the U.S. decision to go to war in Iraq in 2003.

4. In international affairs, how does the balance of power work?

5. Explain what realism and idealism are in foreign policy, and why there is often tension between the two concepts.

6. In international affairs, what is globalization?

7. How does the structure of the U.S. government—specifically the constitutional framework, separation of powers, and institutional fragmentation—affect the formulation and implementation of U.S. foreign policy?

8. Explain the rational actor model, the organizational process model, and the bureaucratic politics model of foreign policy decision making.

9. Explain role-playing, self-delusion, leadership isolation, and groupthink in the context of foreign policy analysis, and how each may affect foreign policy decision making.

NOTES

1. Clark Clifford with Richard Holbrooke, *Counsel to the President: A Memoir* (New York: Random House, 1991), p. 58.

2. J. David Singer, "The Level-of-Analysis Problem in International Relations," in *The International System: Theoretical Essays,* ed. Klaus Knorr and Sidney Verba (Princeton: Princeton University Press, 1961), pp. 72–92.

3. Kenneth N. Waltz, *Man, the State and War: A Theoretical Analysis* (New York: Columbia University Press, 1959), and *Theory of International Politics* (Reading, Mass.: Addison-Wesley, 1979).

4. Waltz, *Theory of International Politics,* p. 65.

5. Martin Hollis and Steve Smith, *Explaining and Understanding International Relations* (Oxford: Clarendon Press, 1990), p. 110.

6. President Harry S. Truman, interviewed in *Truman and the Atomic Bomb,* a Learning Corporation film, 1969.

7. Hollis and Smith, p. 111.

8. Douglas Foyle, "Foreign Policy Analysis and Globalization: Public Opinion, World Opinion, and the Individual," *International Studies Review* 5 (June 2003): 168. See also David Auerswald, *Disarmed Democracies: Domestic Institutions and the Use of Force* (Ann Arbor: University of Michigan Press, 2000), and Bruce Bueno de Mesquita, "Domestic Politics and International Relations," *International Studies Quarterly* 46 (March 2002): 1–9.

9. Daniel L. Byman and Kenneth M. Pollack, "Let Us Now Praise Great Men: Bringing the Statesman Back In," *International Security* 25 (March 2001): 107–146; Margaret G. Hermann and Joe D. Hagan, "International Decision Making: Leadership Matters," *Foreign Policy* 110 (Spring 1998): 124–137; and Loch K. Johnson, "Operational Codes and the Prediction of Leadership Behavior," in *A Psychological Examination of Political Leaders,* ed. Margaret G. Hermann with Thomas W. Milburn (New York: Free Press, 1977), pp. 82–119.

10. Yale H. Ferguson and Richard W. Mansbach, *The Elusive Quest: Theory and International Politics* (Columbia: University of South Carolina Press, 1988), p. 187.

11. Edward A. Kolodziej, "Renaissance in Security Studies? Caveat Lector!" *International Studies Quarterly* 36 (December 1992): 424.

12. See David W. Ziegler, *War, Peace, and International Politics*, 2nd ed. (Boston: Little, Brown, 1981), p. 97.

13. Hollis W. Barber, *Foreign Policies of the United States* (New York: Dryden, 1953), p. 9.

14. See Morton Kaplan, *System and Process in International Politics* (New York: Wiley, 1957), and Robert Jervis, *System Effects* (Princeton: Princeton University Press, 1997).

15. Richard N. Rosecrance, "Balance of Power," in *Encyclopedia of U.S. Foreign Relations*, I, ed. Bruce W. Jentleson and Thomas G. Paterson (New York: Oxford University Press, 1997), p. 130.

16. Rosecrance, "Balance of Power," p. 131. See also Richard N. Rosecrance, "A New Concert of Powers," *Foreign Affairs* 71 (Spring 1992): 64–82.

17. J. Martin Rochester, *Between Two Epochs: What's Ahead for America, the World and Global Politics in the Twenty-First Century* (Upper Saddle River, N.J.: Prentice Hall, 2002), p. 61.

18. Tony Smith, *America's Mission: The United States and the Worldwide Struggle for Democracy in the Twentieth Century* (Princeton: Princeton University Press, 1994), p. 352.

19. Thomas Hobbes, *Leviathan*, ed. Richard Tuck (New York: Cambridge University Press), part 1, chs. 4, 13.

20. For the perspective before the war, see the influential realist book of E. H. Carr, *The Twenty Year Crisis, 1919–1939* (London: Macmillan, 1939). Along with Morgenthau's writings, see also Robert G. Gilpin Jr., *War and Change in World Politics* (Princeton: Princeton University Press, 1981); George Kennan, *American Diplomacy, 1900–1950* (New York: New American Library, 1951); Reinhold Niebuhr, *Moral Man and Immoral Society* (New York: Scribner's, 1947); and Kenneth W. Thompson, *Political Realism and the Crisis of World Politics* (Princeton: Princeton University Press, 1960).

21. Hans Morgenthau, *Politics among Nations: The Struggle for Power and Peace* (New York: Knopf, 1948).

22. Waltz's key formulation is in his *Theory of International Politics*. See also Hedley Bull, *The Anarchical Society* (New York: Columbia University Press, 1977), and Robert Keohane, ed., *Neo-Realism and Its Critics* (New York: Columbia University Press, 1986).

23. See, for example, Robert O. Keohane, "Theory of World Politics: Structural Realism and Beyond," in *Political Science: The State of the Discipline*, ed. Ada W. Finifter (Washington, D.C.: American Political Science Association, 1983), pp. 503–540.

24. John J. Mearsheimer, *The Tragedy of Great Power Politics* (New York: Norton, 2001).

25. Hollis and Smith, p. 96.

26. See, for example, Howard J. Wiarda, *Political Development in Emerging Nations* (Belmont, Calif.: Thomson, 2004).

27. J. Samuel Barkin, "Realist Constructivism," *International Studies Review* 5 (September 2003): 325–342, and Alexander Wendt, *Social Theory of International Politics* (Cambridge: Cambridge University Press, 1999); John Gerard Ruggie, "What Makes the World Hang Together? Neo-Utilitarianism and the Social Constructivist Challenge," *International Organization* 52 (Autumn 1998): 855–885.

28. Senator Frank Church (D-Idaho), "Covert Action: Swampland of American Foreign Policy," *Bulletin of the Atomic Scientists* 32 (February 1976): 11.

29. Representative Stephen J. Solarz (D-New York), C-Span Television (May 22, 1988).

30. Stanley Hoffmann, "Reconsiderations: A New World and Its Troubles," in *Sea-Changes*, ed. Nicholas X. Rizopoulos (New York: Council on Foreign Relations Press, 1990), p. 277.

31. See Yale H. Ferguson and Richard W. Mansbach, *The Elusive Quest Continues: Theory and Global Politics* (Upper Saddle River, N.J.: Prentice Hall, 2003), p. 63.

32. August Heckscher, *Woodrow Wilson: A Biography* (Newtown, Conn.: Scribner and the American Political Biography Press, 2000).

33. Wendt, p. 33.

34. Joseph S. Nye Jr., "Ethics and Foreign Policy," *Occasional Paper* (Aspen Institute, 1985), p. vii.

35. News conference (April 7, 1954), *Public Papers of the Presidents,* 1954 (Washington, D.C.: Office of the Federal Register, National Archives, 1960), p. 382.

36. Quoted by Graham Hovey, "Fog and Worse on Angola," *New York Times* (December 30, 1975): 25.

37. Quoted by Judy Mann, "Hunger," *Washington Post* (March 5, 1982): 21.

38. Joseph S. Nye Jr., *The Paradox of American Power* (New York: Oxford University Press, 2002), p. 78.

39. Zbigniew Brzezinski, *Between Two Ages* (New York: Viking, 1983), p. 275.

40. Quoted in *U.S. News & World Report* (July 15, 1985): 24. Noted Civil War historian James M. McPherson disagrees, believing that—unlike during the Vietnam War—Americans on both sides of the Civil War held such strong views that they would have supported continuation of the conflict, despite the televised gore. Public remarks January 24, 2002, University of Georgia, Athens, Georgia.

41. Henry Kissinger, *A World Restored* (Boston: Houghton Mifflin, 1957), p. 331.

42. John E. Rielly, "America's State of Mind," *Foreign Policy* 66 (Spring 1987): 48.

43. Joseph J. Ellis, *Founding Brothers* (New York: Knopf, 2001), p. 79.

44. Richard E. Neustadt, *Presidential Power and the Modern Presidents*, 5th ed. (New York: Free Press, 1990).

45. Edward S. Corwin, *The President: Office and Powers, 1787–1957*, 4th rev. ed. (New York: New York University Press, 1957), p. 171.

46. *Myers v. United States*, 272 U.S. 52, 293.

47. Congressional Committees Investigating the Iran-Contra Affair, *Hearings*, S. Rept. No.100-16 and H. Rept. No. 100-433 (Washington, D.C.: U.S. Government Printing Office, November 1987), testimony respectively of Lt. Col. Oliver L. North (July 13, 1987) and Vice Admiral John M. Poindexter (July 15,1987), the president's national security adviser.

48. Press conference, Washington, D.C., May 7, 1989, quoted by William S. Cohen and George J. Mitchell, *Men of Zeal* (New York: Viking, 1988), p. 76.

49. Arthur M. Schlesinger Jr., *The Age of Roosevelt* (Boston: Houghton Mifflin, 1958), p. 536.

50. Graham Allison and Philip Zelikow, *Essence of Decision: Explaining the Cuban Missile Crisis*, 2nd ed. (New York: Longman, 1999).

51. Graham Allison, "Conceptual Models and the Cuban Missile Crisis," *American Political Science Review* 63 (March 1969): 689–718.

52. Allison, "Conceptual Models" (original emphasis).

53. Allison and Zelikow, p. 401 (original emphasis).

54. James MacGregor Burns, *Deadlock of Democracy* (Englewood Cliffs, N.J.: Prentice-Hall, 1963).

55. "The (Relative) Decline of America," *Atlantic Monthly* (August 1987): 38.

56. George F. Kennan, *American Diplomacy, 1900–1950* (Chicago: University of Chicago Press, 1951), p. 11.

57. Robert Jervis, *Perception and Misperception in International Politics* (Princeton: Princeton University Press, 1976), p. 3. See also Yuen Foong Khong, *Analogies at War: Korea, Munich, Dien Bien Phu, and the Vietnam Decisions of 1965* (Princeton: Princeton University Press, 1999), and Deborah Welch Larson, *Origins of Containment: A Psychological Explanation* (Princeton: Princeton University Press, 1985).

58. Professor Michael Nacht, remark, Harvard-MIT Program on Nuclear Weapons, Cambridge, Massachusetts, June 20, 1985.

59. Quoted by John Felton, "Testimony Sheds New Light on North's Role," *Congressional Quarterly Weekly Report* 45 (August 29, 1987): 66.

60. Bob Woodward, "The Man Who Wasn't There," *Newsweek* (October 5, 1987): 66.

61. Quoted in *Life,* January 17, 1969, as cited by I. M. Destler, "National Security Advice to U.S. Presidents: Some Lessons from Thirty Years," *World Politics* 29 (January 1977): 143–176.

62. James C. Thomson, "Vietnam: An Autopsy," *Atlantic Monthly* (April 1968): 47.

63. Cited in Richard E. Neustadt and Ernest R. May, *Thinking in Times: The Uses of History for Decision Makers* (New York: Free Press, 1986), p. 157.

64. Barbara Tuchman, *The Zimmerman Telegram* (New York: Viking, 1958), p. 26.

65. Albert Speer, *Inside the Third Reich* (New York: Macmillan, 1970), p. 243.

66. Thomas L. Hughes, "The Power to Speak and the Power to Listen: Reflections in Bureaucratic Politics and a Recommendation on Information Flows," in *Secrecy and Foreign Policy*, ed. Thomas M. Franck and Edward Weisband (New York: Oxford University Press, 1974), p. 28.

67. Ray Cline, quoted in Roy Godson, ed., *Intelligence Requirements for the 1980s: Analysis and Estimates* (Washington, D.C.: National Strategy Information Center, 1980), p. 79.

68. Bob Drogin, "Key Senator Criticizes Prewar Data," *Los Angeles Times* (April 5, 2004): A1.

69. Cited in Peter Wyden, *Bay of Pigs* (New York: Simon & Schuster, 1979), p. 99.

70. Irving L. Janis, *Groupthink,* 2nd ed. (Boston: Houghton Mifflin, 1982), p. 47.

71. Graham H. Shepard, "Personality Effects on American Foreign Policy, 1969–84: A Second Test of Interpersonal Generalization Theory," *International Studies Quarterly* 32 (March 1988): 91–123.

72. This framework, although considerably modified, draws on M. Brewster Smith's heuristic "scanning devise," in "A Map for the Analysis of Personality and Politics," *Journal of Social Issues* 24 (July 1968): 15–28.

73. Nye, *The Paradox of American Power*, p. 9.

74. Jonathan Bendor and Thomas H. Hammond, "Rethinking Allison's Models," *American Political Science Review* 86 (June 1992): 301–322.

The American Declaration of Independence and later documents such as the Constitution gave many U.S. citizens a sense that their country was exceptional, that is, better than other countries. Here, the Declaration of Independence is signed in 1776.

CHAPTER 2

Unifying Concepts and Competing Themes

- What foreign policy missions does the U.S. believe it has?
- What are America's national interests?
- Upon what principles does the United States base its foreign policy?
- How have the competing themes of realism and idealism, isolationism and involvement, and unilateralism and multilateralism affected American foreign policy?
- How may other countries view the United States?

Americans have many views about and positions on U.S. foreign policy. Often, they disagree about issues such as the Vietnam War, free trade, immigration policy, foreign aid, the United Nations, and military intervention in places like Somalia, Kosovo, Afghanistan, and Iraq. Most Americans accept such debate as a good and inevitable result of the democratic American political process.

Despite their differences on foreign policy issues, most Americans share an underlying consensus about the missions, national interests, and principles of U.S. foreign policy. This set of unifying concepts is rooted in over two centuries of American experience, tradition, practice, and political culture. Such unifying concepts are not unique to the United States and its citizens. Indeed, the views that any country and its citizens hold not only of their own missions, interests, and principles, but also of their own and others' roles in the international arena, are products of their own experience, tradition, practice, and political culture.

At the same time, popular views of missions, national interests, and principles do not always conform to documented facts. For example, even though most Americans think that the principle of isolationism drove foreign policy for most of American history before World War II, it is difficult to make that case. Similarly, although many British citizens believe that the centuries of British colonial rule brought enlightenment and education to most British colonies, this occurred rather infrequently.

The concepts of missions, interests, and principles are deeply intertwined. We will separate them by defining **missions** as fundamental long-term objectives that a country claims to pursue in its foreign policy. In the American context, "spreading democracy" and "defending human rights" may aptly be categorized as missions. Often a country's missions are outwardly focused, future oriented, and phrased in abstract and even grandiose terms.

By comparison, **interests** are more concrete objectives of foreign policy such as national security, economic well-being, and providing a homeland for an identifiable group of people, often an ethnic group. One must be careful to differentiate between interests and ways to achieve or defend interests. For example, few Americans oppose the proposition that it is in the United States' interest to be economically strong. However, extensive disagreement exists about whether the best way to protect and enhance American economic strength is through an open economy and free trade or by protecting American jobs and production with quotas, tariffs, and laws that curtail imports.

Principles are the beliefs and premises that a country claims underlie its foreign policy. In the American context, the beliefs that each human being has the rights of life, liberty, and the pursuit of happiness and that individuals should have freedom of religion, speech, press, and assembly are often regarded as principles. The same principles are often claimed to underlie both a country's domestic and foreign policies.

In an ideal world, a country's missions, interests, and principles might convince its leaders and its citizens to have a single well-focused, internally consistent, and noncontradictory set of foreign and domestic policies. But given the complexity of both foreign and domestic affairs and the multitude of viewpoints that Americans—and the leaders and citizens of other countries—hold on foreign and domestic issues, such an ideal world does not exist.

Not surprisingly, then, American foreign policy has not always been well focused, internally consistent, and noncontradictory. Indeed, throughout American history, three pairs of **competing themes** have dominated U.S. foreign policy: the competition between realism and idealism, isolationism and involvement, and unilateralism and multilateralism. It is perhaps a paradox that these three pairs of competing themes flow from the missions, interests, and principles that underlie American foreign policy. These competing themes will be detailed later in this chapter and explored throughout this text.

AMERICAN MISSIONS

Throughout their country's history, most Americans have believed that the United States was different from other nations. Immodestly describing their country as the world's "first new nation," American politicians, statesmen, writers, poets—indeed, men and women from every walk of life—have viewed the United States as a country with a special destiny, a sense of mission.

The view that the United States was somehow different from other countries, sometimes described as American **exceptionalism,** dates back to the nation's founders.[1] No less a person than Thomas Jefferson called the United States "the last best hope of mankind" and a "barrier against the return of ignorance and barbarism." Alexander Hamilton, who agreed with Jefferson on little else, predicted that the American Revolution would force Europe to make "inquiries which may shake it to its deepest foundations." As early as 1782, Benjamin Franklin declared that the creation of the United States and the political liberties found within it would not only "make that people happy," but would also "have some effect in diminishing the misery of those who in other parts of the world groan under despotism, by rendering it more circumspect, and inducing it to govern with a lighter hand." Three years later, John Adams, who became the United States' second president, predicted an even more outstanding future for the United States, declaring that it was "destined beyond a doubt to be the greatest power on earth."

American writers and poets waxed as eloquent as politicians and statesmen in praising the self-proclaimed "first new nation." Ralph Waldo Emerson viewed the formation of the United States as "a last effort of the Divine Providence in behalf of the human race." Herman Melville considered his countrymen a "peculiar, chosen people, the Israel of our times; we bear the ark of the liberties of the world." Walt Whitman was even so bold to describe how he believed the rest of the world viewed the United States:

> Thou, too, sail on, O Ship of State!
> Sail on, O Union, strong and great!
> Humanity with all its fears,
> With all the hopes of future years
> Is hanging breathless on thy fate!

American exceptionalism carried with it a sense of mission. Although the nature of the mission changed over time, the sense of mission endured. Thus, it is instructive to compare Thomas Jefferson's eighteenth-century view of the American mission with twentieth- and twenty-first-century views. Writing in the late eighteenth century, Jefferson opined that the American mission was "to consecrate a sanctuary for those whom the misrule of Europe may compel to seek happiness in other climes. This refuge once known will produce reaction on the happiness even of those who remain there." Jefferson clearly believed that the United States' mission was to provide a safe haven for those who sought a better life and, in so doing, to offer hope for those who could not relocate to the United States.[2]

A century and a half later, the world had changed significantly. So, too, had the United States. Two world wars had been fought, and the United States had become a global power. Not surprisingly, the American mission as defined by the president, this time Harry Truman, had also changed, though in a subtle way. Rather than serving primarily as an example, Truman asserted in his 1947 Truman Doctrine speech, the United States had to adopt an activist stance in foreign policy. "The free peoples of the world look to us for support in maintaining their freedoms," Truman observed, and "great responsibilities have been placed upon us by the swift movement of events."[3] The United States had no choice, he believed, but to support and aid foreign nations and individuals who desired political freedom as defined by the United States. This was a far cry from serving primarily as an example, but it was still a mission closely connected to that of Jefferson's time.

Subsequent twentieth-century American presidents—both Republican and Democratic—and their foreign policies followed in Truman's mission-oriented footsteps. For example, in 1960, the Eisenhower Administration's *Presidential Commission on National Goals* postulated that U.S. foreign policy objectives should be "to extend the areas of freedom throughout the world" and to "help build a world in which every human being shall be free to develop his capacities to the fullest."[4] Similarly, over 30 years later, the Clinton Administration, following the collapse of the Soviet Union, adopted a foreign policy that included as one of its primary tenets "enlargement," that is, a policy of promoting democracy, open markets, and other U.S. and Western political, economic, and social values around the world.[5]

A sense of mission has continued into the twenty-first century. Thus, in 2001, following the terrorist attacks on the World Trade Center and the Pentagon, President George W. Bush declared: "We did not ask for this mission, but we will fulfill it.... We defend not only our precious freedoms, but also the freedom of people everywhere to live and raise their children free from fear."[6] Bush also appealed to the American sense of mission to help legitimize the 2003 war against Iraq. The war was initiated, the president declared, not only to rid the world of the threat of Iraqi weapons of mass destruction but also to free Iraq's people from Saddam Hussein's tyranny and bring freedom to Iraq. Two centuries had passed between Jefferson and Bush, with Truman, Eisenhower, Clinton, and many other presidents in between. Clearly, however, the American sense of mission, of exceptionalism, remains strong.

The American mission, however, has also changed. During Jefferson's time and throughout the first century and a half of its existence, the United States saw its mission primarily to serve as an example for those who sought and fought for political freedoms. Then, as circumstances changed following World War II, the United States adopted a more activist way to pursue its mission as it supported and aided foreign nations and individuals who desired political freedom as defined by the United States. Thus, the United States in 2003 had both the capability and the will to overthrow Saddam Hussein in Iraq and bring freedom to the Iraqi people.

A sense of mission, then, has been a central precept of American foreign policy. At the same time, the nature of the mission has changed over time, leaving some Americans—and others as well—to question whether it was best for the United States to serve as a model for others who desired democracy and a freer way of life, or to act militarily, economically, and politically to provide others such opportunities.[7]

AMERICAN NATIONAL INTERESTS

Like all states, the United States on most issues recognizes and accepts no international authority higher than itself.[8] As we saw in Chapter 1, this concept of sovereignty means that the United States defines its own national interests and determines how it will attempt to achieve them. Even so, this does not mean that every American defines American interests in the same way. Indeed, in analytical and academic communities, whether the concept of "national interest" can be effectively defined and meaningfully used has been widely debated.[9] Nevertheless, it is widely used in public discussions and widely embraced in policy communities in the United States and throughout the world. Thus, we will use it here.

Defining Interests

Defining U.S. national interests is a difficult task. Who within the United States actually defines U.S. interests? Is it the president, the president's administration, or other groups such as businesses, special interest groups, or the general public? If it is the president and his administration, do American interests change when one president and his administration leave office and another with a different foreign policy viewpoint assumes the presidency? Or does the United States have long-term interests that extend from one administration to another that are determined by geography, resource base, population, cultural ties, and other factors that transcend narrowly based issues of the day?

These questions are more than academic inquiries relevant only to the classroom. Throughout U.S. history, different individuals and groups have claimed that the policies that they preferred were the true interests of the United States. Even so, the president and his administration usually define American interests. For example, even though many Americans disagreed with him, President Bill Clinton in 1999 concluded that American interests were served by launching air attacks against Serbian-controlled Yugoslavia in retaliation for Serbian brutality against ethnic Albanians living in the Yugoslavian province of Kosovo. Clinton was president and had concluded that the attacks were in the American interest. Hence the attacks proceeded.

More recently, President George W. Bush in 2003 asserted that war against Iraq was in the American interest to eliminate the danger of Iraq developing weapons of mass destruction, to end Iraq's support of terrorism, and to provide Iraq's people the opportunity to escape from Saddam Hussein's tyranny and live under a democratic government. Other Americans argued differently, maintaining that proof did not exist that Iraq had programs to develop weapons of mass destruction, that the real threat from terrorism came from elsewhere, and that as bad as Saddam was, removing him and instituting a democratic government in Iraq was not a core American interest.[10] Despite this disagreement, Bush chose to go to war.

Not surprisingly, presidents sometimes define U.S. interests differently after they assume office than they did when they were candidates for the presidency. For example, before he became president in 1801, Thomas Jefferson had a reputation as being pro-French. Before he assumed the presidency, he also opposed a strong central government. However, after he became president, he heard that Napoleon intended to occupy New Orleans as part of a secret agreement with Spain. Jefferson therefore informed the French emperor that the United States considered whoever possessed New Orleans to be "our natural and habitual enemy." Jefferson then expanded the power of the U.S. government by buying not only New Orleans but also the entire Louisiana Territory. To Jefferson, this action was in the U.S. interest even though others disagreed with it and it was counter to positions that he previously had held.[11]

What, then, is the American national interest, and who should define it? Do interests change over time? What factors should be considered when an attempt is made to define interest? Perhaps the most significant question is what should "count" when interest is being defined. In the American context, there are several answers.

Identifying National Interests

Policymakers, scholars, and analysts have identified at least six different primary American national interests. Not surprisingly, there is no consensus about which is the most important. Indeed, not all policymakers, scholars, and analysts even agree about whether all six may be legitimately described as interests.

Acquiring and augmenting **power** is the most controversial. Hans Morgenthau, a leading scholar of international relations, defined power as anything that allows one state to establish and maintain control over another.[12] According to Morgenthau, any policy that enhances a state's power is in its interest. To Morgenthau, power permits a state to survive, and therefore it is in the interest of all states to acquire power.

Power, of course, can be acquired and augmented in a variety of ways, for example by enhancing military capabilities, improving economic strength, developing a technological breakthrough, or by using ideological persuasion. Proponents of the view that acquiring and augmenting power is an American national interest argue that any policy that enhances American power is in the U.S. interest and should be pursued, and any policy that does not enhance U.S. power is not in the U.S. interest and should be avoided.

Critics of this approach to defining interest counter by asserting that power is too general a concept to be of any utility in defining interests. They also criticize Morgenthau's emphasis on control as opposed to influence.[13]

There is almost no debate over the relevance or importance of a second interest, **military security and/or advantage.** With force playing such a prominent role in global affairs, the United States and other countries only naturally look to military security as a minimum determinant of national interest. Proponents of military security argue that a chief responsibility of any state is to provide safety for its inhabitants; proponents of military advantage argue that the best way to achieve safety is through military advantage. Both views are widely espoused in the United States, with the second receiving increased emphasis especially since the September 11, 2001, terrorist attacks.

While most Americans agree that the U.S. government should provide military security and/or advantage, the question of how the government should provide military security and/or advantage is more difficult to answer. Should nuclear weapons be a central element of U.S. defense, or should they be deemphasized? What about other weapons of mass destruction such as biological and chemical weapons? Should the United States develop capabilities in these areas? The debate during George W. Bush's presidency over whether the United States should renounce the 1972 Anti-Ballistic Missile Treaty (ABM

Treaty) with Russia and develop a defense against ballistic missiles provides a good case in point. According to the Bush Administration, the ABM Treaty had to be renounced because technology and the changing world situation rendered it obsolete. Conversely, according to other defense analysts not involved with the Bush Administration, the ABM Treaty added significantly to American security even though it was 30 years old. The Bush Administration eventually renounced the treaty, but who was right?

Economic strength is another frequently identified and widely accepted American interest. Thus, any policy that enhances the American economic position could be argued to be in the United States' interest. Improving the United States' balance of trade, strengthening its technological base, or expanding its access to reliable sources of energy and nonfuel mineral resources could all be considered in the American interest.

Sometimes economic criteria may conflict with other criteria. For example, should the United States trade with a country if the country uses the material that it buys or the money it receives to subjugate other countries? That was the dilemma that the United States found itself in immediately before World War II in its relations with Germany and Japan, and again in 1990 in its relations with Iraq after Iraq invaded Kuwait. Similarly, should the United States buy minerals from a country if that country has an internal social system that is repugnant to most American citizens? That was the dilemma that the United States found itself in with its relations with South Africa before South Africa abandoned apartheid.

Ideological criteria are also sometimes used to define the United States' interest. For example, President Woodrow Wilson argued that the United States should enter World War I on the side of the Allied powers to help "make the world safe for democracy," and throughout the Cold War the United States legitimized its foreign policy as a crusade against communism. This was particularly apparent during the 1940s and 1950s under Presidents Truman, Eisenhower, and Kennedy and again during the 1980s under President Reagan.

Even after the collapse of the Soviet Union, ideology remained an important although less visible element of American foreign policy as Bill Clinton emphasized "enlargement," that is, the policy of increasing the number of states that were ruled by democratic governments and that used capitalist economic systems. Although George W. Bush did not formally accept enlargement as part of his foreign policy, his administration nevertheless followed many of the precepts adopted by Clinton in his effort to expand the domain of democracy and capitalism.

Morality and the rule of law are also sometimes considered American interests. As we will see later, morality is central to the American self-image in foreign policy and may even be regarded as an American foreign policy principle. Nevertheless, despite the United States' and most Americans' claims that morality is a national interest, close examination of U.S. policies often clouds what at first blush may have been a clear moral or ethical position.

The United States also often argues that the rule of law both domestically and internationally is in its national interest. It is a long-standing tenet of the United States' political philosophy that all people are subject to the rule of law, and so, too, is the government. On occasion, however, the United States has been less than willing to become party to international legal conventions. For example, despite its claims that it desired an international rule of law, the United States for over two years refused to accept the 1998 statutes that created the International Criminal Court, fearing that the court would pursue politically motivated prosecutions against U.S. military personnel stationed overseas. Eventually, in late 2000, President Clinton signed the treaty even though many Americans still had reservations about it. This, however, was not the end of the saga, since George W. Bush renounced the treaty after he became president.

Finally, **cultural identity** is sometimes considered an American interest. Hence, American interests are seen to coincide with the interests of other states or peoples whose traditions, language, and/or ethnicity are the same as or similar to those found in the United States. Thus, many Americans have had a special affinity for Great Britain. Similarly, during the 1970s and 1980s, many Americans argued that it was in the United States' interest to support the struggle of South Africa's blacks to overthrow apartheid.

For the United States, defining interests in terms of cultural identity is exceedingly difficult. The United States views and defines itself as a country in which peoples of many cultures, traditions, languages, and ethnic backgrounds can be at home. It may be argued that American affinity for Great Britain as a nation and South African blacks as an ethnic group are special cases arising from unique circumstances. However, any country that maintains that it is a melting pot must define its interests carefully in terms of cultural identity.

The American national interest, then, is a difficult concept to define specifically. Different Americans and different groups of Americans define the American national interest differently, even at the same time. Unfortunately, "the American national interest" has no universally accepted meaning. Even with this shortcoming, however, national interest is a useful concept, providing a tool with which we can understand, in general terms, the interests that the United States has and seeks in foreign policy.

AMERICAN PRINCIPLES

Throughout American history, most U.S. citizens would probably have agreed that four fundamental principles underlie American foreign policy. First, they probably would agree that until World War II, isolationism was a central principle of U.S. foreign policy. Second, they probably would accept that, with occasional lapses and exceptions, American foreign policy was moralistic. Third, they probably would concede, perhaps even proudly, that U.S. foreign policy was pragmatic and that pragmatism on occasion overshadowed isolationism and moralism. Finally, they would agree that, until World War II, the United States stressed unilateralism in its foreign policy, that is, acting alone, usually without consulting others, when action became desirable. Each principle requires separate discussion.

Isolationism

Before World War II, the United States rarely sought close alignment with other states and infrequently intervened in the political affairs of states outside the Western Hemisphere. The causes of this predilection for isolation were geographical, emotional, and psychological. At the same time, in economic affairs—and, as we shall see, often in political affairs as well—American isolationism was more self-proclaimed fantasy than objective fact. Even so, isolationism has been part of the American foreign policy self-image.

Geographically, there were reasons for this. The United States was separated from Europe by a vast ocean that took weeks or even months to cross, and there was little threat of invasion from Canada or Mexico. Also, the western frontier gave the United States the opportunity not only to absorb immigrants disaffected with their old lives in Europe but also to enhance its own size and strength without challenging the interests of most European states. Politically and diplomatically, the United States and many of its people believed that the United States did not need Europe. Fortuitously for the United States, as we will see in Chapter 3, most European states also were not concerned about the upstart United States.

Geographic isolation went hand-in-hand with emotional and psychological isolation. As the self-proclaimed "last best hope of mankind," the United States consciously sought to develop a society devoid of the feudalistic baggage of Europe.[14] With a population of immigrants who had fled the religious, social, and economic bigotry of Europe, the United States developed a new style of government in which, ideally, power was shared among three branches, church was separated from state, individual human beings were equally valued, and a social contract of justice existed between governed and the government. Even if these ideals were sometimes overlooked and ignored in practice,

A perceived strength of the United States is that it is a country that people of many cultures, traditions, languages, and ethnic backgrounds can call home. Many immigrants from many countries came to America through New York, where one of their first views of the United States was the Statue of Liberty.

they were ideals significantly different from those espoused in most of the states of the Old World during the eighteenth, nineteenth, and even early twentieth centuries.

Indeed, George Washington in his 1796 Farewell Address set the course claimed to be central to most of American pre-World War II foreign policy:

> Europe has a set of primary interests, which to us have none, or a very remote relation. Hence she must be engaged in frequent controversies, the causes of which are essentially foreign to our concerns.... Our detached and distant situation invites and enables us to pursue a different course.... Why forego the advantages of so peculiar a situation? Why quit our own to stand upon a foreign ground? Why, by intertwining our destiny with that of Europe, entangle our peace and prosperity in the toils of European Ambition, Rivalship, Interest, Humour, and Caprice?[15]

Isolationism was also the product of a growing American superiority complex. Although the new republic was not a military or economic match for any established European power, it considered its ideals and its government superior to any in Europe. American leaders intended for the United States to lead by example and to develop economically to an extent unparalleled elsewhere in the world. A foreign policy of isolationism allowed the United States to concentrate on its own growth and permitted Americans to savor and develop a sense of uniqueness.

But how real was American isolationism? For decades, even centuries, foreign policy scholars, analysts, and experts within the United States, and many others in other countries as well, have questioned the degree to which the United States was truly an isolationist state at any time in its history. Indeed, one can make a persuasive case that as much as most Americans believe that isolationism was a prevailing principle of American foreign policy before World War II, tension between international isolationism and international involvement has been a prevailing theme in American foreign policy throughout U.S. history. We will return to the tension between isolationism and involvement later in this chapter.

Moralism

Most Americans believe that moralism is one of the key principles of American foreign policy. As implied in our earlier discussion of the American mission and American interests, many Americans see moralism as the foundation upon which U.S. foreign policy missions are based and consider morality to be one of the interests that the United States has among its foreign policy objectives.

Over the years, moralism has played out in U.S. foreign policy in different ways. During the United States' formative years, the nation's founders and philosophers, as already noted, asserted that the American form of government, and therefore American foreign policy, was superior to that of other states. As the United States expanded during the nineteenth century from a country on the Atlantic coast to a country of continental dimensions, the concept of **manifest destiny**—that is, the belief that it was a divinely mandated U.S. obligation to expand across North America from the Atlantic to the Pacific and acquire all territory in between—was used to rationalize American expansion. Although manifest destiny was in reality fueled by a complex mix of economics, politics, ideology, strategy, and racism, many Americans truly believed that it was divinely mandated. And if manifest destiny was divinely mandated, how could it not be moral?[16]

Americans also used moralism at the end of the nineteenth century and the beginning of the twentieth century to explain the United States' increasingly interventionist policies in Latin America and elsewhere. As the United States during this era searched for markets, sites for naval bases to protect trading lanes, and, in the eyes of some, empire, many Americans argued that the country's interventions were undertaken in the name of liberty and justice. Instead of spreading its ideals and values by example, the United States would spread them by intervention.

Indeed, morality became a watchword for intervention, as evidenced by the 1898 Spanish-American War, a watershed in U.S. foreign policy, since for the first time the United States used the moral imperative to rationalize territorial acquisition outside continental North America. The war and the territory that the United States acquired during the war, especially Cuba and the Philippines, were explained in moralistic terms, with President William McKinley positing that the United States had "accepted war for humanity. We can accept no terms of peace which shall not be in the interests of humanity."[17] In subsequent years throughout McKinley's administration and on into the presidencies of Theodore Roosevelt, William Taft, and Woodrow Wilson, the United States often legitimized interventions in the Philippines, China, Central America, Mexico, and the Caribbean on the basis of morality and humanity. Roosevelt clearly stated this in 1904 when, fearing European intervention in Latin America and the Caribbean, he put forward the **Roosevelt Corollary** to the Monroe Doctrine, which linked morality, finance, and American interests:

> If a nation shows that it knows how to act with decency in industrial and political matters, if it keeps order and pays its obligations, then it need fear no interference from the United States. Brutal wrong-doing, or an impotence which results in a general loosening of the ties of civilized society, may finally require intervention by some civilized nation, and in the Western Hemisphere the United States might act as a policeman, at least in the Caribbean region.[18]

Woodrow Wilson couched America's 1917 entry into World War I in similarly moralistic terms, declaring that the United States was fighting to "make the world safe for democracy" in "a war to end all wars." Near the end of the war, Wilson unveiled his "Fourteen Points," in which he appealed for open diplomacy, self-determination, freedom of the seas, arms reduction, and the League of Nations, a new international organization that he claimed would guarantee peace through collective security.[19] Never before had American moralism so occupied the center stage in world affairs.

American moralism in foreign policy continued throughout the twentieth and on into the twenty-first century. President Ronald Reagan reflected the prevailing American attitude toward the Soviet Union when in 1983 he declared it "an evil empire." Eight years later, President George H. W. Bush denounced Saddam Hussein's invasion of Kuwait and treatment of his own people as "evil." In 2001, following the terrorist attacks on the World Trade Center and the Pentagon, President George W. Bush proclaimed that the United States would rid the world of "the evil of Osama bin Laden and his terrorist network." Bush also argued that morality legitimized the 2003 war against Iraq.

Moralism, then, has been a central principle of American foreign policy, used both to justify the American sense of mission and to legitimize American interventions. Whereas a British patriot might say, "My country right or wrong," an American patriot would say, "My country because it is right." While many Americans acknowledge occasional U.S. moral lapses, most see morality as a central American foreign policy principle.[20]

Pragmatism

Although many Americans couch U.S. foreign policy in moralistic terms, they also on occasion admit to an underlying **pragmatism**. The history of American foreign policy reveals numerous examples of pragmatism. For example, during the last decade of the eighteenth century and the first decade of the nineteenth, American business people and traders found lucrative profit by selling to all sides in the Napoleonic Wars that raged across Europe. Only when Great Britain and France began interfering with trade did the United States argue that moral issues were involved. American pragmatism was well illustrated by the American response to British and French interference.

At first, Thomas Jefferson, arguing that U.S. commerce was so valuable to Europeans that "they will be glad to purchase it when the only price we ask is to do us justice," took an idealistic approach to the interference, implementing the Embargo of 1807, which barred American ships from entering foreign ports. Unfortunately for Jefferson, the embargo was a disaster for American trade. Cotton exports fell by 75 percent, and farm prices by 34 percent. Especially in New England, Americans pragmatically ignored the embargo, concluding that the economic impact of the embargo was worse than either impressment of American sailors or seizures of ships by the British and French navies.

The embargo was removed in 1809 and replaced by the Non-Intercourse Act that banned exports to and imports from Great Britain and France. Impressment and ship seizures remained problems that led to public agitation for and congressional support of war against Great Britain. Once again, Americans living in what was then the western United States (western Pennsylvania, Ohio, and elsewhere) pragmatically seized on these issues to further their own cause: territorial expansion. Despite their limited interest in maritime issues, they realized that impressment and ship seizures could be converted into issues that would legitimize territorial acquisitions from Great Britain in Canada. The War of 1812, then, was not fought over the morality of impressment and ship seizures alone. It was also a war fought for the pragmatic cause of territorial expansion.

The nineteenth century has other examples of American pragmatism. Most Americans remember the Barbary War as a series of naval and marine encounters that, in a moral sense, were undertaken because "Americans do not pay bribes." They overlook that after the Barbary War the United States continued to make payments, though at a reduced rate, to the Barbary states to guarantee safe passage of American ships through North African waters. Similarly, they remember that the United States fought the 1846 Mexican War not just to gain Texas but to acquire additional Mexican territory. Even the American Civil War, fought in American lore for the moral issue of ending slavery, had as its primary objective maintaining the Union. And we have already examined the moral dimension of the Spanish-American War and seen that American pragmatism was integrally involved there as well.

The late twentieth and early twenty-first centuries also have many examples of American pragmatism, several of which will be discussed later in this chapter in the context of the competing themes of idealism versus realism. With American moralism underlying American idealism, and American pragmatism underlying realism, it is inevitable that tension exists between these competing themes. Even so, throughout their history, Americans have been proud of their pragmatism, and they remain so today.

Unilateralism

Throughout most of its history, the United States has stressed **unilateralism**—acting alone and independently, usually without consulting others—as a foreign policy principle. Even though the 13 colonies benefited immensely from their cooperation with France during the Revolutionary War, and in the eyes of many may not have won their independence in the absence of French support, unilateralism was evident in American foreign policy from the earliest days of the American republic. George Washington's statement in his Farewell Address that the United States' "true policy" was to "steer clear of permanent alliances with any portion of the foreign world" is often used to argue that the United States' first president supported isolationism, but it can just as easily be used to argue that he advocated a unilateralist approach to foreign policy.

Indeed, in the United States' first three major confrontations with foreign states—the late 1790s undeclared naval war with France, the Barbary War against the North African Barbary states in the early nineteenth century, and the Anglo-American War of 1812—the United States acted alone against foreign powers. Of course, unilateralism in these three cases was as much a matter of necessity as choice. No foreign state was in the least interested in joining the upstart North American state in any of these conflicts.

The American preference for unilateralism continued throughout the nineteenth and into the early twentieth century as the United States pursued policies that promoted trade, commerce, and continental expansion, and that expanded overseas influence and territorial acquisition. However, as the twentieth century proceeded, the United States, especially after World War I and then again after World War II, moved away from unilateralism as a principle and began to favor **multilateralism:** the belief that foreign policy decisions should be made and actions undertaken in conjunction with other states. Following World War I, Woodrow Wilson, as we have seen, made multilateralism a central tenet of his plan for peace in the form of the League of Nations and collective security. Similarly, after World War II, Franklin Roosevelt and many of his successors emphasized the United Nations, multilateral military alliances, and a collective approach to international financial and monetary issues as central tenets of American foreign policy.

Even so, the debate between unilateralists and multilateralists continues today, as we will see later in this chapter. Indeed, the conflict between unilateralism and multilateralism has joined the conflicts between isolationism and involvement and between idealism and realism as one of the competing themes that dominate American foreign policy debates. We turn now to these three pairs of competing themes.

COMPETING THEMES

Unfortunately for policymakers and students, American foreign policy missions, interests, and principles sometimes conflict with one another. This has given rise over the more than two and a quarter centuries of U.S. foreign policy to several conflicting themes in foreign policy. Three are most important: (1) the conflict between idealism and realism that in one form or another has troubled American foreign policymakers since the Republic was founded; (2) the contradiction between isolationism and involvement, which also dates back to America's founding; and (3) more recently, the tension between unilateralism and multilateralism. Each of these three sets of competing themes is critically important to contemporary American foreign policy.

Idealism versus Realism

As we saw in Chapter 1, idealism is a school of thought in international affairs that says that international relations and foreign policy should ideally be based on international law and norms of peaceful behavior among states. Peaceful resolution of disputes through negotiations, diplomacy, and discussion; the role of international organizations and international law; and emphasis on human rights, arms control, and disarmament are usually central elements in the foreign policy preferences that idealists put forward.

As explained in Chapter 1, idealism is often juxtaposed to realism, a school of thought that argues that a country's external relations should be based on military and economic strength. Realists emphasize elements of foreign policy such as the perceived need for a balance of power, military preparedness and deterrence, war and the use of force, and economic capabilities. In Chapter 1 we briefly explored the debate that exists between idealists and realists. Here and in later chapters, we will examine how these two competing themes have played out in U.S. foreign policy.

At the outset, it must be stressed that few if any American presidents and their administrations held viewpoints or implemented policies that could be labeled exclusively "idealistic" or exclusively "realistic." Thus, for purposes of analysis and understanding, it is most useful to think of idealism and realism as polar extremes on a spectrum, as shown in Figure 2.1. The debate between realists and idealists over foreign policy, then, is usually better framed as a debate over where on a realist-to-idealist spectrum an administration's foreign policy should be, as opposed to which polar extreme an administration should adopt.

As specific terms, *idealism* and *realism* are products of the twentieth century. But the underlying conflict between idealism and realism in American foreign policy can be traced

FIGURE 2.1
The Foreign Policy Spectrum: From Realism to Idealism

back to the earliest days of the American republic as the United States' founders struggled to craft the new country's foreign policy. Should they base the new foreign policy on ideals, that is, on the way they wanted the world to be? Or should they base it on economic strength and military power? And what should they strive for as they formulated and conducted foreign policy: ideals and morality, or economic strength and military power?

One early example of the clash between idealism and realism was the disagreement between John Adams, the United States' second president, and Thomas Jefferson, who succeeded Adams as president, over policy toward Great Britain. Convinced that Great Britain was the world's most powerful country with the world's strongest military and economy, Adams charted a policy course that recognized this reality and that avoided conflict with Great Britain. Conversely, Thomas Jefferson, committed to friendship with France and the ideals that France espoused after the French Revolution, and despite the excesses committed in France under the names of democracy and equality, opposed Great Britain and Adams's policies toward it. Arguably, at this point in their careers, Adams could be labeled an early American realist and Jefferson an early American idealist.[21]

Idealism and realism continued to compete throughout nineteenth-century American foreign policy, with Americans disagreeing, for example, over the proper policy toward Texas and Mexico during the 1840s. No one called it realism, but many Americans wanted to attach Texas to the United States and go to war with Mexico so the United States could expand, gain economic strength, and increase its military might. No one called it idealism, but other Americans opposed war with Mexico because it ran counter to what they saw as American ideals. The same debates occurred in the late nineteenth century and the twentieth century, with many Americans supporting the expansion of American power and influence in the Caribbean, Latin America, and the Pacific, and many others decrying this expansion as alien to the United States' democratic ideals.

Woodrow Wilson was the first American president specifically identified with the term *idealism*. Wilson and his fellow idealists, sometimes called "liberal idealists," based their worldview and their policy preferences on several optimistic premises about human beings and human nature, including:

- Human nature is basically good and human beings prefer to help each other rather than live in conflict.
- Bad behavior such as war is usually the product of flawed institutions rather than flawed human nature.
- War and conflict are not inevitable and can often be avoided if the correct international institutions are in place.
- Collective multilateral efforts are more effective in preventing war and conflict than unilateral national efforts.
- Ethics, morality, and humanitarianism are important in both domestic and international affairs.
- The likelihood of international peace can be increased by the presence of self-determination and democracy within states and the creation of international institutions that stress collective action and the creation of a global community.

By the 1920s, Wilsonian idealism had become a watchword in foreign policy analysis identified with international organizations, especially the League of Nations; improving the international system and the conduct of foreign policy via national self-determination, open diplomacy, arms control, and the end of power politics; and because of Wilson's inability to bring the United States into the League and because of the League's eventual failure, naivete.[22] Not surprisingly, then, as the United States during the 1920s returned to isolationism, and the world's nations during the 1930s began the slippery slide into World War II, opposition developed to Wilsonian idealism. Although opponents of idealism were not yet called realists, their foreign policy beliefs were the forerunners of realism. The high-minded moralism of idealism sounded good, skeptics granted, but when it came to foreign policy, economic strength and military capabilities were what really mattered.[23]

Realism and realists came into their own after World War II, often blaming the horror of the war on the claimed inadequacies of idealism. Postwar realists such as George Kennan, Hans J. Morgenthau, Reinhold Niebuhr, and Kenneth W. Thompson had a decidedly different view of human beings and human nature than the idealists.[24] The post–World War II realists argued, among other things, that:

- Human nature is basically flawed, with human beings preferring to dominate and control each other rather than help each other.

- The drive for the power to control others is difficult if not impossible to control or eliminate, and behavior such as war and conflict is therefore inevitable.

- International affairs is a struggle for power, and states have to acquire power to promote and defend their national interest.

- Military power is the most important component of power, but economic strength is important too, primarily because of its ability to enhance military power.

- Alliances can be used to add to national power, but the loyalty of allies should never be assumed.

- States should never rely on international organizations or international law alone to defend national interests and national security.

- If all states seek to maximize their power, the chances of international peace will increase because a balance of power will be created, especially if flexible alliances are in place.

But realism did not explain everything that happened in world affairs in the 1940s and 1950s. Thus, as American policymakers and leaders of other states pondered how to restructure and reform the international system after World War II, they often concluded that international cooperation and intentionally limiting power provided the best opportunities to construct a path toward lasting peace. As a result, a "new and improved" international organization was created, the United Nations, and a cooperative international economic system, the Bretton Woods system, was put into place by at least some of the international community.

Nor did realists always agree among themselves about the proper course of foreign policy action. Realists soon disagreed about the wisdom of the United States joining a new peacetime alliance, the North Atlantic Treaty Organization, the first alliance that the United States had ever belonged to during peacetime. Realists also disagreed over the wisdom of fighting the Korean War in the 1950s and the Vietnam War in the 1960s.

Thus, the debate between realists and idealists raged on. Could a new and better world be based on ideals such as international law, international organizations, arms control, and human rights, or did security and prosperity depend on military might and economic strength, the very elements that many people believed had led directly to World Wars I and II? Could international organizations reduce the chances that war would occur, or did states continue to have to rely on themselves for security? Could economic security best be obtained by self-reliance, or was international economic cooperation a better way to achieve economic security? Were military and economic power the only critical components of power, or did other things also contribute to power?

The debate was heated, and it goes on today, although in more sophisticated terms. In the analytical and academic communities, as we saw in Chapter 1, "structural realism" (also called neo-realism)[25] and "offensive realism"[26] have joined realism, and "neo-liberalism"[27] has joined idealism, as explanations for the way the international system works and as the intellectual foundations upon which policies are proposed and implemented. Since Chapter 1 explored the differences between these more sophisticated analytical perspectives, we will not repeat the distinctions between them here. Suffice it to repeat here that each at its core remains true to its origins in either realism or idealism.

And how have realism and idealism affected post–World War II American foreign policy? Since World War II, every American president has blended idealism and realism in his foreign policy. Most emphasized realism, some strongly. Only Jimmy Carter, early in his administration before the twin 1979 shocks of the Iranian takeover of the U.S. embassy in Teheran and the Soviet invasion of Afghanistan, and Bill Clinton, on issues such as the environment and human rights, could arguably be labeled idealists. Even so, both Carter and Clinton had strong realist elements in their foreign policies, as evidenced by Carter's 1979 declaration, called "the Carter Doctrine," that the United States would counter any Soviet move toward the Persian Gulf with military force, and as evidenced by Clinton's delayed but nonetheless forceful deployment of U.S. forces to Bosnia and Kosovo.

Conversely, realist presidents often included elements of idealism in their foreign policy. Ronald Reagan, who called the Soviet Union "the evil empire" and initiated the largest peacetime military build-up in American history, also negotiated sizeable arms reduction agreements with the Soviets and held more summit meetings with Soviet leaders than any previous U.S. president. Similarly, George W. Bush initiated the war on terrorism and the 2003 war in Iraq while simultaneously proclaiming his hope to build a better world in which the rule of law was respected and human rights were protected.

Realism and idealism, then, have been competing themes in American foreign policy since World War II, with precursor versions of the competition evident as early as the founding of the United States. The competition remains a key element of U.S. foreign policy today. All indications are that it will remain a key element in American foreign policy far into the future.

Isolationism versus Involvement

Competition between isolationism and involvement was prominent in American foreign policy as early as the late eighteenth century. As we have seen, President George Washington cautioned in his 1796 Farewell Address that the United States should stand apart from Europe because Europe had "a set of primary interests" to which the United States had at most "a very remote relation." Washington did not advocate total isolation and was very aware of the necessity for trade; however, early in his presidency, he found it necessary to become involved in foreign affairs to a degree much greater than he preferred, dispatching John Jay to London to resolve lingering disputes with Great Britain. Political and military isolationism may have been fine, but growing tension with Great Britain required a different response.

Washington's successor, John Adams, also found it impossible to pursue a foreign policy course apart from European affairs, fighting an undeclared naval war with France over France's naval practice of impressment. Nevertheless, Adams understood that isolated naval engagements were considerably different from declaring and fighting a war, so Adams refused to ask Congress to declare war on France.

Throughout the nineteenth century, as we will see in subsequent chapters, even though Americans viewed their country as essentially isolationist, the United States on many occasions sallied fully and openly into the international arena. For example, the Barbary War, the War of 1812, the Mexican War, and the Spanish-American War all witnessed significant American forays into the international arena. Even so, most American citizens and their government generally considered these actions as having been forced on the United States.

During these years, neither U.S. trading nor international economic interests were considered to contradict isolationism. For the most part, activities related to trade were viewed as commercial rather than foreign policy interests. Although the United States relative to European states of the day may have pursued an isolationist policy, American isolationism was far from absolute. To most Americans, however, isolationism was a perceived reality.

Even during the early twentieth century, many Americans advocated isolationism and generally believed that U.S. foreign policy was based on isolationism as a principle. For example, President Woodrow Wilson was reelected in 1916 under the slogan "He kept us out of war," even though the United States while at peace sided more and more with the Allies. U.S. involvement in World War II followed much the same pattern. World War II broke out in Europe in September 1939, but the United States did not become an active combatant until December 1941, fully 27 months after the conflict began. Throughout these 27 months, the United States pursued carefully crafted policies that balanced isolation and involvement, increasingly aiding Great Britain during the period but never initiating a policy during this time that forced it to become an active combatant. And so the competing themes of isolationism and involvement co-existed.

World War II ended the tradition of perceived American isolation, even though the tension between isolationism and involvement remained. Although the United States briefly flirted with a return to isolationism following the war, the war changed the world significantly. During World War II, American power—military, economic, and political—grew immensely. The combination of a changed world and the growth of American power placed the United States in a position where it concluded it had no recourse but to abandon isolationism.

This did not mean that all Americans were pleased with the new dominance of involvement, even interventionism, in American foreign policy. Indeed, during the late twentieth and into the early twenty-first century, a significant number of Americans preferred that the United States return to a more isolationist foreign policy. For example, during the late 1960s and early 1970s, primarily because of the Vietnam War, many Americans questioned why the United States was so actively involved in so many foreign countries.

Similarly, following the collapse of the Soviet Union in 1991, many Americans wondered why the United States, with the threat from the Soviet Union now gone, could not once again stand apart from most foreign issues. Indeed, during the presidential elections of 1992, 1996, and 2000, conservative columnist and presidential candidate Pat Buchanan frequently argued that the United States needed to rethink and reassess its global involvement and adopt a more isolationist foreign policy.[28] Some moderate and liberal American analysts and observers also expressed concern, usually without advocating isolationism, that the United States had overextended itself and would decline as an international power if it did not abandon some foreign commitments.[29]

Even so, despite the post–Cold War attraction of renewed emphasis on isolationism and concerns expressed by others that the United States was overextended, America's post–Cold War presidents, George H. W. Bush, Bill Clinton, and George W. Bush, argued that the United States, because of its economic strength, military power, and global interests, needed to remain deeply engaged in foreign affairs and international issues. Not surprisingly, their administrations charted foreign policy courses that reflected their beliefs.

Much as we saw with the competing themes of realism and idealism, then, the competition between isolationism and involvement is more accurately phrased as a debate over where on an isolationist-to-involvement spectrum an administration's foreign policy should be, as opposed to which polar extreme on the spectrum an administration should adopt. Again, for purposes of analysis and understanding, it is most useful to think of isolationism and involvement as polar extremes on a spectrum, as shown in Figure 2.2.

Since World War II, no American president could even remotely be labeled an isolationist. Nevertheless, the competing themes of isolationism and involvement remain central elements in American political discourse about foreign policy. Even in the twenty-first century, and despite the terrorist attacks of September 11, 2001, many

FIGURE 2.2
The Foreign Policy Spectrum: From Isolationism to Involvement

Americans are not completely convinced that the United States should be involved in much of anything beyond the water's edge. Indeed, even those who strongly support international involvement often differ significantly on when, where, how, and how deeply to become involved.

Unilateralism versus Multilateralism

Unlike the competition between the first two sets of competing themes in American foreign policy, both of which trace their roots to the early years of the American republic, the tension between unilateralism and multilateralism is primarily a post–World War II phenomenon, with the significant exception of the efforts of Woodrow Wilson and other post–World War I idealists to have the United States adopt a multilateral foreign policy. *Unilateralism,* as we saw earlier, is a term used to describe foreign policies that stress independent action, often without consulting others, while *multilateralism* is the belief that foreign policy decisions should be made and actions undertaken with other states.

Except for the Wilson presidency, unilateralism was a dominant element of American foreign policy throughout American history until World War II. However, the war had an immense impact on American views of unilateralism. Undertaking the war as a multilateral effort, and thrust into a position of global leadership by the war and by its own economic and military strength, the United States after the war moved away from unilateralism, working increasingly with other states to restructure post–World War II global society. Reasoning that many of the issues that confronted the postwar world could best be resolved with international cooperation, the United States was one of the primary forces behind the creation of the United Nations, the World Bank, and other multilateral international institutions. After the Cold War began in the late 1940s, the United States also worked with other Western states to present a united front against the Soviet Union in a variety of joint defense and economic venues. For example, the North Atlantic Treaty Organization, formed in 1949, became the first peacetime military alliance that the United States ever joined.

Despite its new emphasis on multilateralism, many Americans throughout the Cold War disagreed with the trend, rejecting the United Nations, the World Bank, and the other multilateral directions that American foreign policy had taken. To them, multilateralism contradicted American tradition, abridged American sovereignty, tied the United States to causes that they viewed as not in American interests, and limited American freedom of action in foreign affairs. Unilateralism remained their preferred way to make foreign policy choices. Nevertheless, multilateralism predominated.

After the Soviet Union broke up in 1991, one of the rationales for multilateralism, presenting a united front to the USSR, disappeared. Thus, the debate reemerged with a vengeance: should the United States act unilaterally or multilaterally in its foreign policy? Some identified the new international environment—with the United States as the only remaining superpower—as a "unipolar moment" and urged the United States to act unilaterally wherever its interests so dictated.[30] Others remained convinced that multilateralism was the best approach to take.[31] The debate raged.[32]

Presidents George H. W. Bush and Bill Clinton opted for multilateralism, believing that many international economic, social, environmental, and other issues could best be resolved via international cooperation. Thus, despite the end of the Soviet threat, the United States continued to work with other states in international institutions to restructure and reshape the international system. Indeed, President George H. W. Bush favored a multilateral approach to helping the newly independent states that emerged from the wreckage of the Soviet Union make the transition from communism to democracy. He also obtained United Nations support to expel Iraq from Kuwait in Operation Desert Storm. Similarly, after a considerable debate within the United States, President Bill Clinton signed the Kyoto Environmental Protocol and the treaty establishing the International Criminal Court, and he deployed U.S. forces overseas in several locations to support UN peacekeeping efforts. Clearly, multilateralism predominated.

The picture under President George W. Bush became more complicated. Despite the predominance of multilateralism under Bush the elder and Clinton, many Americans asked, "Since the United States is economically and militarily the most powerful country in the world, why should it not do what it wants in foreign and military affairs? Why should it limit its actions in foreign and military affairs to those with which other countries and international organizations like NATO and the UN agree?"

Early in his administration, George W. Bush appeared to side with this perspective, renouncing the Kyoto Environmental Protocol and the International Criminal Court and informing Russia that the United States intended to unilaterally abrogate the 1972 Anti-Ballistic Missile Treaty if it were not renegotiated. The September 11, 2001, terrorist attacks slowed the American move toward unilateralism as Bush formed a loose global alliance to fight terrorism. This alliance proved critical in the quick victory the United States achieved in late 2001 and early 2002 in Afghanistan, overthrowing the Taliban government there that provided aid, assistance, and shelter to Osama bin Laden's al Qaeda terrorist network.[33]

As 2002 proceeded, however, many observers concluded that the administration of George W. Bush had returned to its earlier unilateralist tendencies. Indeed, in the eyes of many, Bush's post-9/11 emphasis on coalition building was a temporary aberration from his true unilateralist preferences. Critics of the Bush Administration, both within the United States and outside, concluded that by late 2002 the United States had adopted a unilateralist foreign policy. American leadership in and initiation of the 2003 war against Iraq underlined this belief. Some observers argued that the United States had adopted policies so unilateralist that it had become a "rogue nation."[34]

Once again, then, as with the previous two sets of competing themes we examined, the competition between unilateralism and multilateralism may best be viewed as a debate over where on a unilateralist-to-multilateralist spectrum an administration's foreign policy should be, as opposed to which polar extreme on the spectrum an adminis-

FIGURE 2.3
The Foreign Policy Spectrum: From Unilateralism to Multilateralism

tration should adopt. Once more, then, for purposes of analysis and understanding, it is most useful to think of unilateralism and multilateralism as polar extremes on a spectrum, as shown in Figure 2.3.

Thus, the tension between unilateralism and multilateralism as competing themes in American foreign policy continues. Although multilateralism overshadowed unilateralism in U.S. foreign policy throughout most of the post–World War II era, the post–Cold War era witnessed a resurgence of unilateralist preferences within the United States that the September 2001 attacks may have strengthened.

CHANGE, CONTINUITY, AND OTHER VIEWPOINTS

The foreign policy concepts that we examined in this chapter—mission, interests, principles, and competing themes—play major roles in American foreign policy. As we will see in later chapters, these concepts have often been intertwined in American foreign policy as it unfolded over the almost two and a half centuries of American history. Change and continuity are present in substantial ways in all, and so, too, are differing American and international viewpoints about each.

While specific manifestations of the American mission have changed over time, its core element has not. Whereas Thomas Jefferson asserted that the American mission was to serve as a beacon for those who were repressed, Harry Truman and subsequent American presidents, including George W. Bush, believed that the United States has a much more activist role to play in supporting democratic change overseas. The key is that the sense of mission—promoting democracy in one way or another—remains.

The same is true for American interests. Much has changed, but much remains the same. Americans are no longer concerned about the French or Indians attacking the American frontier, the British burning Washington, D.C., Germans obtaining secret weapons, or Russians launching missiles against the United States, but maintaining military security and advantage remains in America's interest. Similarly, American international economic interest is no longer to sell goods to warring European states, but enhancing U.S. economic strength remains a key foreign policy interest.

Regarding principles, it may be argued that a significant change has occurred. While claims of morality and pragmatism remain underlying principles of American foreign policy even as they have been since colonial days, the changing world situation and the growth of American power have reduced emphasis on the principle of isolationism. Even here, however, there is room for debate, for as we have seen, questions abound about the extent to which isolationism has affected American foreign policy.

As for the three sets of competing themes, Americans will undoubtedly continue to disagree about the extent to which American foreign policy should be based on realism or idealism, isolationism or involvement, and unilateralism or multilateralism. Other competing themes also appear from time to time, but these three doubtlessly will continue to predominate, with the first two being over two centuries old and the third more than 50 years old.

Throughout our study of American foreign policy, mission, interests, principles, and competing themes will appear in one guise and then another. As we decipher what the missions, interests, principles, and competing themes are that influence and determine U.S. foreign policy today, we would do well to remember that not everyone, regardless of whether they are scholars, policymakers, or the general public, see them in the same way. Within the United States, even the experts are often deeply divided about foreign policy missions, interests, principles, and themes. Outside the United States, many people view American foreign policy in ways that make it difficult for Americans to believe that the subject of discussion is American foreign policy. Several examples illustrate the point.

Within the United States, for example, most people agree that American foreign policy has distinct periods, but even the experts disagree on what those periods are. Thomas G. Paterson and his colleagues divide American foreign policy between 1789 and 1914 into six periods. Jerel A. Rosati presents the case for two periods during the same years. Meanwhile, Gene E. Rainey maintains that in the period before World War I alone, U.S. foreign policy had three eras.[35]

The contrast between dominant American views of U.S. foreign policy and the views that many people outside the United States often have about U.S. foreign policy is often even more stark. This should not be surprising, given that the views that a country and its citizens hold are products of the country's history, culture, values, and so on. Thus, it is to be expected that differing perceptions develop. Recognizing that such differences exist, and identifying what they are, is a key task in studying and understanding U.S. foreign policy and, indeed, the foreign policy of all countries. Here, we provide several examples to illustrate the point, concentrating on isolationism and moralism. Mexico, America's closest neighbor to the south, provides an excellent starting point.

"Poor Mexico. So far from God, and so close to the United States." That, as we saw in Chapter 1, is the way Mexican President Porfirio Diaz analyzed his country's situation regarding the United States in the early 1900s.[36] Why and how could a Mexican leader hold a view of the United States that was so much at odds with how most Americans viewed their country?

The history of U.S.-Mexican relations in the nineteenth and early twentieth century provides insight. Following the 1846–1848 Mexican-American War, Mexico lost nearly one-third of its territory to the United States, the present-day states of Arizona, California, Nevada, New Mexico, and Utah. Other U.S. military interventions in Mexico occurred in 1806, 1836, 1842, 1844, 1859, 1866, 1870, 1873, 1876, 1913, and 1914–1917.[37] American investment also played a major role in Mexican affairs, with U.S. citizens owning as much as 40 percent of Mexico's property by 1910. Given this history of American military intervention and economic penetration, it is understandable that the friendship and cordial relations that have marked U.S.-Mexican relations since World War II have not persuaded all Mexicans that U.S. foreign policy toward Mexico has been isolationist or moral.

Mexico's experience is not unique. Between 1900 and 1925 alone, the United States intervened militarily in other Latin American countries dozens of times, for a host of political, economic, and security reasons.[38] It is understandable, then, why U.S. claims of isolationist and moralist foreign policy preferences have been viewed skeptically by many in Latin America.

People beyond the Western Hemisphere are also skeptical about American claims of isolationism and moralism. Examining once again the first 25 years of the twentieth century, U.S. military forces were deployed in 1900 and 1901 in the Philippines; in 1904 and 1905 in Korea; and in 1900, 1911, 1912, 1916, 1917, 1920, 1922–1923, and 1924 in China.[39] Isolationism and moralism? From the American perspective, perhaps. But from the Mexican, Latin American, and Asian viewpoints, the case for American isolationism and moralism is difficult to make. As seen by many throughout the world, the United States is simply a powerful country imposing its will.

Making the case for or against American isolationism and moralism is not our purpose here. Rather, our objective is to illustrate that widely different perceptions of the principles that many Americans believe their country's foreign policy is based on exist, and are ardently believed by those who hold them. Regardless of whether we study American foreign policy via history and diplomatic history, social science methodologies, or policy analysis, the reality of opposed perspectives complicates our study. Thus, in the following five chapters, as we study one view of the evolution of American foreign policy from colonial times to the twenty-first century, we must understand that other people hold other views and other interpretations of these events. Nevertheless, the views presented here will provide the foundation upon which our later study of the politics and policies of contemporary American foreign policy is based.

SUMMARY

Despite differences on foreign policy issues, many Americans agree about U.S. foreign policy missions, interests, and principles. These concepts are rooted in over two centuries of experience, tradition, practice, and political culture. Missions, interests, and principles are intertwined. *Missions* are defined as long-term objectives that a country pursues in foreign policy. *Interests* are more concrete objectives such as national security, economic well-being, and providing a homeland for an identifiable group. *Principles* are the beliefs and premises that underlie foreign policy.

Throughout history, many Americans asserted that the United States was different from other countries. This concept was called *exceptionalism,* and it carried a sense of mission. The American mission changed over time, beginning with the United States serving as a model for others who desired democracy and a freer way of life, and changing by the twentieth century to the United States acting militarily, economically, and politically to provide others such opportunities.

Throughout U.S. history, different individuals and groups have claimed that the policies they preferred were the true U.S. interests. Even so, the president usually defines interests. Policymakers, scholars, and analysts have identified at least six U.S. interests: acquiring and augmenting power, obtaining military security or advantage, developing and maintaining economic strength, furthering an ideology such as "making the world safe for democracy," promoting morality and the rule of law, and maintaining cultural identity.

Historically, most U.S. citizens would probably also agree that four principles underlie American foreign policy. First, they would agree that, until World War II, isolationism was a central principle. Second, they would accept that, with occasional lapses, American foreign policy was moralistic. Third, they would concede that U.S. foreign policy was pragmatic. Finally, they would agree that the United States stressed unilateralism in foreign policy before World War II, but that multilateralism was a key principle of U.S. policy after the war.

American foreign policy missions, interests, and principles sometimes conflict with one another. This has given rise to several conflicting themes in foreign policy, three of which are most important: (1) the conflict between idealism and realism that has troubled foreign policymakers since the United States was founded; (2) the contradiction between isolationism and involvement, which also dates back to America's founding; and (3) more recently, tension between unilateralism and multilateralism.

The competing themes discussed above should make it clear that, within the United States, disagreement continues to exist on foreign policy. It should come as no surprise that people outside the United States also hold considerably different viewpoints about U.S. foreign policy than do Americans. For example, the differences between the U.S. and Mexican views of American isolationism and moralism are so significant that it is sometimes difficult to believe they are perceptions of the same principles.

Given these realities, as we decipher what the missions, interests, principles, and competing themes are that influence and determine U.S. foreign policy today, we must remember that not everyone sees them the same way.

KEY TERMS AND CONCEPTS

missions
interests
principles
competing themes
exceptionalism
power
military security and/or advantage
economic strength
ideological criteria
morality and the rule of law
cultural identity

isolationism
moralism
manifest destiny
Roosevelt Corollary
pragmatism
unilateralism
multilateralism
idealism versus realism
isolationism versus involvement
unilateralism versus multilateralism

THINKING CRITICALLY

1. Identify and explain the concepts of missions, interests, principles, and competing themes in American foreign policy.

2. What is American exceptionalism, and how has it influenced the conduct of American foreign policy?

3. How has the American sense of mission in foreign policy changed over time? Discuss specific examples.

4. Explain the concept of national interest in international affairs. Why is national interest difficult to define? What are six widely accepted primary national interests?

5. Define and discuss four widely accepted principles of American foreign policy.

6. Define and discuss the competing themes of realism and idealism in American foreign policy. Provide at least two concrete examples of occasions when the competition between these themes influenced American foreign policy.

7. Define and discuss the competing themes of isolationism and involvement in American foreign policy. Provide at least two concrete examples of occasions when the competition between these themes influenced American foreign policy.

8. Define and discuss the competing themes of unilateralism and multilateralism in American foreign policy. Provide at least two concrete examples of occasions when the competition between these themes influenced American foreign policy.

9. Why might citizens of other countries have different views of American foreign policy than U.S. citizens have? Provide specific examples of such differing views.

NOTES

1. For an interesting and provocative view of American exceptionalism, see Seymour Martin Lipsett, *American Exceptionalism* (New York: Norton, 1996).
2. For a detailed discussion of Thomas Jefferson and his foreign and domestic policies, see Joseph J. Ellis, *American Sphinx: The Character of Thomas Jefferson* (New York: Vantage Books, 1996).
3. Harry S. Truman, speech before a Joint Session of Congress, March 12, 1947.
4. *Presidential Commission on National Goals* (Washington, D.C.: U.S. Government Printing Office, 1960).
5. For a discussion of Clinton's enlargement policies, see Anthony Lake, "From Containment to Enlargement," *Department of State Dispatch* (September 27, 1993), pp. 658–664.
6. George W. Bush, Address to the Nation, October 7, 2001.
7. For an in-depth treatment of the American mission, see Tony Smith, *America's Mission: The United States and the Worldwide Struggle for Democracy in the Twentieth Century* (Princeton: Princeton University Press, 1995). See also Joshua Muravchik, *Exporting Democracy: Fulfilling America's Destiny* (Washington, D.C.: American Enterprise Institute, 1991).
8. Some experts might disagree with this statement, pointing to the willingness of states that are members of the European Union (EU) to allow the EU to limit their sovereignty and independence. While it is true that member states have given the EU the ability to impose decisions on its members in several areas, EU member states still retain their sovereignty and independence, including the ability to renounce membership in the EU or ignore EU decisions if they so choose.
9. Hans Morgenthau is one of the most articulate defenders of the concept of national interest. See particularly Hans J. Morgenthau, *In Defense of the National Interest,* and Hans J. Morgenthau, "Defining the National Interest—Again," in *Perspectives on American Foreign Policy,* ed. Charles W. Kegley Jr. and Eugene R. Wittkopf (New York: St. Martins, 1983), pp. 32–39. Critiques of the national interest will be provided later, during the discussion of the competing themes of realism and idealism.
10. For a dissenting view on the 2003 Iraq War, see former NATO Supreme Allied Commander in Europe and 2004 presidential candidate Wesley K. Clark, *Winning Modern Wars: Iraq, Terrorism, and the American Empire* (New York: Public Affairs, 2003).
11. See Ellis, *American Sphinx.*
12. See Hans J. Morgenthau, *Politics among Nations* (New York: Knopf, 1948), especially chapter 3.
13. See note 2 in the Introduction for a discussion of the differences between influence and control.
14. Feudalism, a social structure prevalent in Europe and many other locations, had a strict class structure that determined the relationship between a very small and rich noble class and a very large and poor peasant

class. The nobility owned almost all land and other property, while the peasants worked the land the nobility owned. The peasants were beholden to the nobility for practically everything. A very strict code of conduct backed by the government and, in Europe, the church, assured that the peasants were subservient to the nobility.

15. Ralph K. Andrist, ed., *George Washington: A Biography in His Own Words* (New York: Harper and Row, 1972), pp. 373–374.

16. For in-depth discussions of manifest destiny, see Thomas R. Hietala, *Manifest Destiny: Anxious Aggrandisement in Late Jacksonian America* (Ithaca, N.Y.: Cornell University Press, 1985), and Frederick Merk, *Manifest Destiny and Mission in American History* (New York: Vintage Books, 1963).

17. As reported in Norman A. Graebner et al., *A History of the American People* (New York: McGraw-Hill, 1975), p. 572.

18. For more detailed discussion of the Roosevelt Corollary, see Dexter Perkins, *The Monroe Doctrine, 1867–1907* (Baltimore: Johns Hopkins University Press, 1966).

19. Collective security is the concept that if one nation is attacked by another, then other nations will together respond against the state that launched the original attack. The theory is that the certainty of a collective response against an attack will influence the aggressor state not to launch an attack. For an analysis of the role that collective security played in the League of Nations during the years between World Wars I and II, see F. S. Northedge, *The League of Nations: Its Life and Times, 1920–1946* (New York: Holmes and Meier, 1986).

20. For a more detailed analysis of the role of moralism in American foreign policy, see Robert W. McElroy, *Morality and American Foreign Policy* (Princeton: Princeton University Press, 1992), and Gil Loescher Jr., *The Moral Nation* (South Bend, Ind.: University of Notre Dame Press, 1989).

21. For good discussions of the conflict between John Adams and Thomas Jefferson over foreign policy toward Great Britain and France, see David McCullough, *John Adams* (New York: Simon and Schuster, 2001), especially chapters 8 and 9, and Joseph J. Ellis, *Founding Brothers* (New York: Vantage Books, 2000), especially chapters 5 and 6.

22. For several views of Woodrow Wilson and the role of his ideas in creating the post–World War I international system, see H. R. Rudin, *Armistice 1918* (New Haven: Yale University Press, 1944); T. A. Bailey, *Wilson and the Peacemakers* (New York: Macmillan, 1947); A. Lentin, *Lloyd George, Woodrow Wilson, and the Guilt of Germany: An Essay in the Pre-History of Appeasement* (Baton Rouge: Louisiana State University Press, 1984); and Klaus Schwabe, *Woodrow Wilson, Revolutionary Germany, and Peacemaking, 1918–1919* (Chapel Hill: University of North Carolina Press, 1985).

23. For a pre–World War II proponent of what later became realism, see E. H. Carr, *The Twenty Year Crisis, 1919–1939* (London: Macmillan, 1939).

24. See George Kennan, *American Diplomacy, 1900–1950* (New York: New American Library, 1951); George Kennan, *Realities of American Foreign Policy* (Princeton: Princeton University Press, 1954); Hans J. Morgenthau, *Politics among Nations* (New York: Knopf, 1948); Reinhold Niebuhr, *Moral Man and Immoral Society* (New York: Scribner's, 1947); and Kenneth W. Thompson, *Political Realism and the Crisis of World Politics* (Princeton: Princeton University Press, 1960).

25. Kenneth N. Waltz is widely regarded as the father of neo-realism. In his *Theory of International Politics* (Reading, Mass.: Addison Wesley, 1979) and subsequent works, Waltz provided the core of neo-realism by arguing, among many other things, that power remained important, and that states continued to seek power to survive, but that the international system that emerged from their interactions influenced them to take certain actions and constrained them from taking other actions. Neo-realism thus adds the global level of analysis to its explanation of what drives states to act in the ways they do. See also Robert Jervis, "Realism, Neorealism, and Cooperation," *International Security* (Summer 1999).

26. John J. Mearsheimer, in *The Tragedy of Great Power Politics* (New York: Norton, 2001), became the leading proponent of offensive realism, which argues that "great powers seek to maximize their share of world power" because "having dominant power is the best means to ensure one's own survival."

27. Emerging in the 1990s, neo-liberalism embraces a host of different viewpoints on how the international system works and what policies states should adopt to achieve their respective aims. Most analysts who consider themselves neo-liberalists focus on how democratic change, multilateral diplomacy, ethics and human rights, international law, and related multilateral cooperative and humanist enterprises can improve the human condition in international affairs.

28. For Pat Buchanan's views on foreign policy and other issues, see Patrick J. Buchanan, *A Republic, Not an Empire* (Washington, D.C.: Regnery Publishing, 1999).

29. See Chalmers Johnson, *Blowback: The Costs and Consequences of American Empire* (New York: Henry Holt, 2000), and Charles Kupchan, *The End of the American Era: U.S. Foreign Policy and the Geopolitics of the Twenty First Century* (New York: Knopf, 2002).

30. See for example Charles Krauthammer, "The Uni-Polar Moment," *Foreign Affairs* (Number 1, 1991), and William C. Wohlforth, "The Stability of a Unipolar World," *International Security* 24 (Summer 1999): 5–41.

31. See for example Joseph S. Nye Jr., *The Paradox of American Power: Why the World's Only Superpower Can't Go It Alone* (New York: Oxford University Press, 2002), and John Ruggie, *Winning the Peace* (New York: Columbia University Press, 1998).

32. For other perspectives on the debate, see Stewart Patrick and Shepard Forman, eds., *Multilateralism and U.S. Foreign Policy: Ambivalent Engagement* (Boulder, Colo.: Lynne Rienner, 2001), and David Malone et al., eds., *Unilateralism and U.S. Foreign Policy: International Perspectives* (Boulder, Colo.: Lynne Rienner, 2003).

33. For a good tracing of this evolution, see Bob Woodward, *Bush at War* (New York: Simon and Schuster, 2002).

34. Clyde Prestowitz, *Rogue Nation: America's Unilateralism and the Failure of Good Intentions* (New York: Basic Books, 2003).

35. Thomas G. Paterson et al., *American Foreign Relations: A History to 1920,* 4th ed. (Lexington, Mass.: D. C. Heath, 1995); Jerel A. Rosati, *The Politics of United States Foreign Policy,* 2nd ed. (New York: Harcourt Brace, 1999); and Gene E. Rainey, *Patterns of American Foreign Policy* (Boston: Allyn and Bacon, 1975).

36. For an excellent study of the career of Porfirio Diaz, see Paul Garner, *Porfirio Diaz* (New York: Pearson Education, 2001).

37. See Chapters 3 and 4 in this text.

38. American armed forces were deployed in 1901 and 1902 into Colombia; in 1903, 1907, 1911, 1912, 1919, 1924, and 1925 into Honduras; in 1903, 1904, 1914, and from 1916 to 1924 into the Dominican Republic; from 1903 to 1914 and 1918–1920, 1921, and 1925 into Panama; from 1906 to 1909, in 1912, and between 1917–1922 into Cuba; in 1910 into Nicaragua; in 1914 and from 1915 to 1934 into Haiti; in 1920 into Guatemala; and in 1921 into Costa Rica. See Chapters 4 and 5 in this text.

39. See Chapters 4 and 5 in this text.

The Background
and History of
American Policy

Introduction to Part Two

How did the United States grow in slightly more than two centuries from a little remarked and weak country on the fringes of world affairs to its present status as the most powerful country in the world, the central actor in international affairs, coordinating a global war on terrorism—or, in the eyes of others, a country trying to create a global empire? Equally important, what role did American foreign policy have in that transformation, and what does this mean for American foreign policy and the United States today?

The following five chapters help answer these questions by providing the background and tracing the history of American foreign policy from before independence to the present day. It is a history that (1) begins with the United States as a new state trying to find its place in the world during the late eighteenth and nineteenth centuries; (2) continues as the United States evolves into a state that, like most other countries of the late nineteenth and early twentieth centuries, embarks on imperial adventures to expand its influence; (3) follows the United States after World War I as it tries to escape the responsibilities of international involvement only to discover as World War II erupts that such responsibilities cannot be ignored; (4) encompasses the United States' emergence after World War II as one of two superpowers and the end of the decades-long struggle against the Soviet Union known as the Cold War; and (5) finds the United States since the early 1990s as the world's only superpower, trying to build a new world order even as it leads a global war against terrorism.

The key events and major decisions of each of these five periods are detailed in the following five chapters, each of which concentrates on the international level of analysis—that is, what the United States was doing in its foreign policy. As a general rule, each of the following five chapters also examines American foreign policy from the perspective of the rational policy model (Model I) of foreign policy discussed in Chapter 1. Under this model, it will be recalled, a country's foreign policy is viewed, in the words of Graham Allison, as the "more or less purposive acts of unified national governments," designed to "show how the nation or government could have chosen the action in question, given the strategic problem that it faced."[1] Each chapter also examines American foreign policy within a broader international context so students can acquire an understanding of what the United States was doing in its foreign policy relative to other states of each period.

But why study the background and history of American foreign policy in the first place? There are two reasons. First, there is an old but important saying: "Those who do not understand history are condemned to repeat it." Studying the background and history of American foreign policy is thus a learning experience that will help students of American foreign policy better understand the advantages and disadvantages, the successes and failures, of past American foreign policies. The past may not always be prologue, but it can definitely provide lessons for the present and future. The difficult part is identifying the correct lessons.

Second, even though Americans are an ahistorical people, the same is not true of the citizens of many other countries. Thus, even though the nineteenth- and twentieth-century U.S. interventions into and conflicts with Central American states, China, Mexico, and Russia are irrelevant ancient history to many Americans, these and other American foreign policy actions are lenses through which many Central Americans, Chinese, Mexicans, and Russians view the United States. Past events help shape present perceptions, and often have a sizeable impact on the ability to implement present policy.

If the United States is to best formulate and implement its policy toward other states, it must therefore understand how and why other countries hold the views of the United States and its foreign policy that they do. This can only be done if Americans, and others, recognize that the history of American foreign policy provides a window to understanding the ways that others perceive and respond to current American foreign policy.

NOTES

1. Graham Allison, "Conceptual Models and the Cuban Missile Crisis," *American Political Science Review,* 63 (March 1969): 689–718.

CHAPTER 3

Finding a Place in the World: 1756–1865

- What was the world like when the United States gained independence?
- What did the new nation try to accomplish in foreign policy?
- How did the United States expand across North America?
- How did the United states defend itself and its interests?
- How important was trade to the early United States?
- What impact did the Civil War have on U.S. foreign policy?

U.S.S. CONSTITUTION

Throughout the nineteenth century, the United States was a major trading nation, with its trading interests defended by naval vessels such as the U.S.S. Constitution, *shown here under full sail. Today, the* Constitution, *the only remaining U.S. naval vessel from this era, is berthed in Boston.*

In 1783, the British colonies in North America that eventually became the United States finally won independence from Great Britain after a seven-year war. After independence, the former colonies struggled to define who they were and to find their place in the world. Organized into a loose federation governed by a document called the "Articles of Confederation," the newly independent states soon recognized that the confederation was in trouble. By 1786, only three years after independence, several states had economies in a free fall, and rebellion had broken out in Massachusetts.

Understanding that they needed a stronger, better organized, more centralized government to provide economic opportunity and domestic tranquility, the Founding Fathers of the United States met in Philadelphia in 1787 to write the Constitution. Over the next two years, the states ratified the Constitution, and the United States came into existence in 1789.[1]

As a sovereign and independent country, the United States soon faced a series of foreign policy challenges that included naval confrontations with France and Great

Britain, piracy in the Mediterranean Sea, disagreement over trade policy, and renewed warfare with Great Britain. Throughout these early challenges, the new nation struggled to define its interests and to formulate and implement its foreign policy. The early foreign policy struggles that the United States faced were perhaps inevitable, an unavoidable experience for a new country with a new type of government that was trying to find its place in the world.

For the 13 colonies that eventually became the United States, the search for their place in the world did not begin with independence. Even before they gained independence, Great Britain's North American colonies faced a number of external challenges, responding to some in concert with Great Britain, but meeting others alone with little direction or support from London. "If we are British subjects," many colonists must have wondered, "then why are we so independent and self-sufficient?" The story of American foreign policy, and of the challenges it confronted, thus begins with the 13 colonies before they gained independence.

THE AMERICAN COLONIES AND STATES IN A GLOBAL CONTEXT: 1756–1789

Separated from Europe by the great width of the Atlantic Ocean and the several months it took to cross it in the seventeenth and eighteenth centuries, many of North America's early European colonial settlers hoped that European political affairs and conflicts would not intrude on their lives, wanting to be done with European affairs once and for all. They were sadly disappointed, however, as their hope of isolation was often interrupted by European issues that spilled over to the colonies. Even before American independence, then, the competing themes of isolationism and involvement were prominent in North American affairs.

Before Independence

For the future United States, the 1756–1763 **Seven Years' War,** known in North America as the **French and Indian War,** was the most important spill-over. In Europe, the Seven Years' War pitted Austria, France, and Russia against Prussia and Great Britain, with Austria, France, and Russia at first pushing Prussia back. Eventually, superior Prussian organization and the military brilliance of Prussia's ruler Frederick the Great gained Prussia a stalemate on land, while Great Britain used its navy and the mobility that it provided at sea to attack French colonies in Canada, the West Indies, and India. The war ended in 1763 with the Treaty of Paris, which gave Great Britain control of French Canada and the Ohio Valley to the Mississippi River, as well as, of course, the colonies it previously had in North America. Outside North America, the 1763 Treaty of Paris expanded British rule in India. Great Britain also developed a huge national debt during the war, so King George III reduced government expenditures and increased taxes to pay off his war debt. These decisions had immense international implications.[2]

One way to reduce expenditures was to curtail defense spending. Realizing this, and fearing that a westward movement by British subjects living in North America into the territory newly acquired from France might lead to additional warfare and expense, the British Parliament in 1763 decreed that westward migration of British subjects in North America must stop. This dismayed Britain's North American colonial subjects.

Worse, King George's decision to pay off his war debt by raising taxes also applied to the North Americans colonists, many of whom for years had ignored British taxes with little concern expressed by the British Crown. Thus, when Great Britain passed the 1764 Sugar Act, the 1765 Stamp Act, and the 1773 Tea Act[3] to raise revenue to pay off its war debt and tried to enforce payment of those taxes, the colonists grew resentful. "Taxation without representation" was denounced as "tyranny." The seeds of revolution were sown.

The American War of Independence

When warfare erupted in North America in 1775, France saw an opportunity to recoup some of its losses from the Seven Years' War and rearrange the balance of power in Europe.[4] Indeed, without **France's involvement in the American War of Independence,** the colonists could not have won independence. Still smarting from the defeat Britain had inflicted on it in the Seven Year's War, France provided money, munitions, and other war goods to the American rebels even before Benjamin Franklin arrived in Paris in 1776 to seek French support. Franklin concluded with France the first treaty in American history, the **1778 Treaty with France,** in which France promised to help the colonies fight for independence from Great Britain in return for the colonies' support for other French interests.

French support was immensely important. For example, at the Battle of Saratoga in 1777, as much as 90 percent of the arms and ammunition came from France. As telling, when Britain's Lord Cornwallis and his army were cornered on land by the rebels at York-town, Virginia, in 1781, they were prevented from being resupplied or rescued from the sea by a blockading French fleet.

With Cornwallis' defeat, Great Britain concluded that the cost of defeating the rebels was too much. The **1783 Treaty of Paris** that concluded the war recognized American independence, transferred some British colonies outside North America back to France, and retained Canada for Britain.[5]

Foreign Policy under the Articles of Confederation

With overseas involvement having played a major role in the American War of Independence, the 13 new states of North America at first tried to govern themselves under a loose confederation. This, to them, was the ideal solution to the problems caused by the centralized control that existed under British rule. The Articles, they reasoned, would be an ideal governing structure that allowed extensive local control and decision making.

In three years, the new structure proved unequal to the task. The economies of several states went into decline, rebellion erupted in Massachusetts, and tensions grew between states as the different trade and tariff rules that the states created on their own led to a decline in trade. In diplomacy, although the Confederation Congress could declare war, send and receive ambassadors, and conclude treaties, it could do little more. When Great Britain refused to leave forts in what is today western New York, western Pennsylvania, Ohio, and Michigan, it could do nothing. When British officials in Canada in 1786 negotiated with separatist leaders in Vermont about attaching Vermont to Canada, it could do nothing. Relations with Spain, France, and other European states fared no better. Especially perplexing was the inability of the Confederation Congress to do anything when the Barbary states of North Africa[6] in the 1780s captured American merchant ships and held the ships and crews for ransom. By 1789, in foreign policy and domestic affairs, the states of North America were ready for another new beginning.[7]

Even before the United States existed, the newly independent states experienced tension between isolationism and involvement, and between ideal and more realistic solutions to the problems of governance. Many people preferred isolationism, but involvement with the external world proved unavoidable and led directly to the American Revolution. Involvement with the external world, especially France, was also a prerequisite for American independence. Similarly, after independence, many North Americans ideally preferred a loose-knit decentralized government, but that experiment did not work. An approach was needed that placed greater authority in the hands of a central government. And thus the United States was born, with a foreign policy beset by tension between isolationism and involvement, and (even though the terms were not used) between idealism and realism.

THE FOREIGN POLICY OF AN INFANT STATE: 1789–1815

At first, the United States delved gingerly into foreign policy. Torn between the ideals of democracy and freedom and the need for economic strength and military capabilities, most Americans preferred isolationism to international involvement, even though they recognized that total separation from European affairs was unattainable.

Even in the nation's earliest years, many prominent Americans believed that the United States had a mission: to serve as a model for others and as a beacon of hope for people in other countries where governments ruled arbitrarily. As we saw in Chapter 2, Benjamin Franklin hoped that the creation of the United States would "have some effect in diminishing the misery of those, who in other parts of the world groan under despotism," while Thomas Jefferson believed that the United States was "the last best hope of mankind" and a "barrier against the returns of ignorance and barbarism."

Early American leaders also had strong views about the United States' national interests. As James Madison, Alexander Hamilton, and John Jay clearly showed in *The Federalist Papers* (the articles they wrote that in many experts' eyes were the reason the Constitution was eventually approved), attaining military security and developing economic strength were prominent considerations in the arguments for the Constitution.[8] Not surprisingly, attaining military security and developing economic strength were also prominent elements in the foreign policies of early presidents, even though disagreements existed about how the United States could attain security and strengthen its economy.

From the very beginning of the American state, then, American foreign policy was torn between the competing themes of isolationism and involvement, and idealism and realism. American policymakers also confronted a true level-of-analysis problem: should they advocate a foreign policy that was best for the infant country they were creating, or for their long-established home states to which they each had strong ties, or for their own personal and family betterment? Fortunately for the future of the United States, America's founders invariably chose the first.

Washington's Foreign Policy

After independence, protecting trade relations with Great Britain and expanding trade with other European states was the infant nation's leading foreign policy priority. This often brought the United States into conflict with European powers, primarily Great Britain and France, who were locked in a series of wars that continued almost nonstop from 1793 until 1815.

In 1791, most U.S. trade—as much as 90 percent of all imports and 50 percent of all exports—was with Great Britain. However, as the French Revolution evolved between 1789 and 1793 and with France finally declaring war on Great Britain in 1793, Americans saw an opportunity to expand trade with France and other continental European states. Many Americans, including Secretary of State Thomas Jefferson, considered this not only an opportunity but a responsibility, since they believed that the 1778 Treaty with France remained in effect and committed the United States to France's side.

Other Americans, led by Secretary of the Treasury Alexander Hamilton, considered expanded trade with France not an opportunity but a danger. They believed that expanding trade with France would endanger trade with Great Britain, lead to more animosity between the United States and Great Britain, and possibly embroil the United States in a European war. In addition, Hamilton argued, the 1778 Treaty with France was no longer valid because both the French and the U.S. governments had changed several times.[9]

President George Washington solved this dilemma by issuing in 1793 a **Neutrality Proclamation** that declared that the United States sided with neither Great Britain nor France. The Neutrality Proclamation did not address the question of whom Americans could trade with, but it provided a definitive answer about the U.S. position on the war between France and Great Britain. Trying to stay out of European wars while trading with both sides—an effort in essence to mix isolationism with involvement—thus became a hallmark of American foreign policy.[10]

Unfortunately, the Neutrality Proclamation did not end America's foreign policy problems. France's Minister to the United States (the equivalent of ambassador) Edmond Genet precipitated a major crisis later in 1793 when he commissioned 14 privately owned American ships to attack and capture British merchant ships. The American ships took at least 80 British vessels as prizes before Washington, incensed over Genet's activities, demanded that France recall Genet.[11]

Another crisis resulting from the war in Europe led to the United States' first major treaty. Angry over growing American trade with France and seeing expanded U.S.-French trade as American support for the French war effort, Great Britain ordered the Royal Navy to seize U.S. ships trading with the French West Indies. By 1794, the Royal Navy had seized over 250 U.S. merchant vessels. Americans were incensed. With war sentiments rising, Alexander Hamilton convinced Washington to send a mission headed by John Jay to Great Britain to resolve this and other issues.

Jay's mission led to the **Jay Treaty,** which helped resolve U.S.-British boundary disputes along the Canadian border, removed British forces from forts in American territory, settled debts incurred during the Revolutionary War, and improved commerce between the two countries. However, the treaty did not state that Great Britain renounced its claimed right of seizing ships trading with its enemies during wartime. This omission led some Americans to denounce the treaty. Despite this omission and lingering bitterness from the Revolutionary War, the treaty lowered U.S.-British tensions and passed the U.S. Senate by the required two-thirds majority in 1795. The crisis passed.[12]

As the first major U.S. treaty actually concluded by the United States, Jay's Treaty was a milestone in U.S. foreign policy. Even so, the United States did not commit itself to foreign alliances. George Washington emphasized this in his 1796 **Farewell Address** in which he stated that it was the United States' "true policy to steer clear of permanent alliances with any portion of the foreign world." "Europe has a set of primary interests which to us have none or a very remote relation," Washington observed, and the United States should therefore avoid becoming involved in Europe's conflicts.

This did not mean that Washington advocated total isolationism. While he believed that U.S. democracy and security depended on remaining apart from European politics, he accepted the need for "temporary alliances for extraordinary purposes" and for "extending our commercial relations," albeit with "as little political connection as possible" as a result of trade.[13] And trade the United States did. Throughout Washington's presidency, American ships plied the sealanes between Europe and the United States, and elsewhere as well. Trade with European states grew impressively as American ships carried raw materials, war supplies, and other goods to both sides in Europe's ongoing conflicts of the 1790s, bringing handsome profits to American merchants. From the very beginning, then, the United States began to acquire a reputation as a bold and pragmatic trading nation.

Adams's Foreign Policy

Like Washington before him, John Adams, after he became president in 1797, could not steer the United States onto an isolationist course. On several occasions during his presidency, Adams found the United States unavoidably involved in European affairs. Similarly, Adams often took the military strength and economic power of foreign states into account as he made foreign policy decisions, marking himself what later generations would call a realist.

The American willingness to trade with both sides in Europe's ongoing conflicts was a primary reason that foreign policy crises developed under Adams. France, like Great Britain, ordered its warships to seize neutral ships carrying cargo to enemy states. By early 1797, France had seized several hundred American vessels. Trying to avoid a conflict with France, Adams authorized American diplomats to meet with French authorities to find a way to lessen tensions. However, this in itself led to a crisis when French Foreign Minister Talleyrand refused to meet with the diplomats unless they paid a bribe. This incident, known as the XYZ Affair because Talleyrand's demands were communicated to the U.S. diplomats by three unnamed French agents, angered many Americans.

French warships continued to seize American merchant ships in 1797 and 1798. Congress responded by renouncing all treaties with France, building new warships, and authorizing funds for a regular army. Meanwhile, the United States fought an undeclared naval war with France, capturing between 80 and 90 French ships. U.S. naval vessels fought French warships at least nine times, usually emerging victorious.

Despite the XYZ Affair and the undeclared naval war, fighting did not escalate into a declared war. There were two reasons for this. First, France was already embroiled in fighting in Europe and did not want an additional declared enemy. Second, Adams, unlike many in his Federalist Party, believed that war with France was not in the United States' interest. The issue of war or peace with France deeply divided the Federalists and played a major role in Adams's defeat in the election of 1800.[14]

Jefferson's Foreign Policy

Thomas Jefferson became president in 1801, pledging that the United States would seek "peace, commerce, and honest friendship with all nations, entangling alliances with none."[15] Throughout Jefferson's two terms, this proved easier to say than to do. Once again, pressures for involvement in foreign affairs outweighed desires for isolationism.

France presented Jefferson with his first foreign policy challenge. Formerly a strong supporter of France, Jefferson by the time he became president had adopted a more balanced outlook. In 1801, word filtered to North America that Spain had ceded the Louisiana Territory to France and that France was sending 30,000 soldiers to the Caribbean island of Hispaniola (on which the countries of Haiti and the Dominican Republic are today) to subdue a slave rebellion. Hearing this, Jefferson became concerned that Napoleon intended to create a new French empire in North America and warned that if France took possession of New Orleans, the United States "must marry ourselves to the British fleet and nation."[16]

Tensions escalated when the Spanish governor of Louisiana in 1802 withdrew the right, guaranteed in a 1796 Spanish-American treaty, of American farmers and traders to use New Orleans as a trading site. Jefferson and others saw this as Napoleon's handiwork. Frontiersmen in Tennessee and Kentucky depended on access to New Orleans via the Mississippi River for their livelihoods and debated attacking New Orleans before French forces arrived. Alexander Hamilton, never an admirer of France, urged Jefferson to seize not only New Orleans but also Spanish Florida. Jefferson, however, decided to negotiate and sent James Monroe to France and Spain with an offer to buy New Orleans and Florida for $10 million.

By the time Monroe arrived in Paris in 1803, France's outlook on a new empire in the New World had changed. Napoleon's plans for a new North American empire had received a serious setback as yellow fever and guerrilla attacks decimated the French army in Hispaniola. Napoleon was also planning another campaign to expand his European empire and needed money. Monroe was therefore pleasantly stunned when the French government offered to sell the entire Louisiana Territory for $15 million.

France's offer went beyond what Monroe was empowered to accept, but he quickly said yes. Jefferson was pleased with the deal, the Senate ratified the treaty, and by the end of 1803 the United States owned the Louisiana Territory. Jefferson's and Monroe's pragmatism had converted an impending crisis into an immense opportunity that Napoleon himself recognized would "affirm forever the power of the United States."[17] The **Louisiana Purchase** thus extended the United States' territory from the Atlantic to the Pacific and was an immense success for Jefferson and his administration.

Other foreign policy challenges were resolved less successfully. During Jefferson's presidency, the North African Barbary states, as they had since American independence, continued to capture U.S. ships, holding them and their crews for ransom. Intent on stopping this, Jefferson dispatched a squadron of U.S. warships to the Mediterranean to deal with the Barbary states. This led to the undeclared **Barbary War,** which lasted for several years and ended in 1805 when the U.S. squadron and mercenary troops forced Tripoli's ruler to conclude a deal in which he released American prisoners for $60,000. The victory was not complete, however, as other Barbary states preyed on U.S. and other ships until after the War of 1812.

Great Britain also presented problems for Jefferson, primarily because of **impressment,** the naval practice of stopping ships at sea to remove sailors who had deserted from the Royal Navy and were now working on U.S. ships. Other states, especially France, also engaged in the practice, but it was Great Britain that presented the real problem. Engaged in European warfare, Great Britain began this practice in the 1790s, but as the Napoleonic Wars worsened in Europe, it stepped up impressment in the early nineteenth century. Inevitably, not only Royal Navy deserters but American citizens as well were impressed.

Impressment incensed the American public, especially after the Chesapeake-Leopard Affair in 1807 in which the American frigate *Chesapeake* was attacked, defeated, and boarded by the H.M.S. *Leopard.* Four sailors were seized from the *Chesapeake,* three of whom were American citizens. Mobs gathered in American cities and demanded war with Great Britain. Jefferson instead negotiated, securing the return of the three Americans. Despite its error, Great Britain refused to renounce impressment.

In response to impressment and the *Chesapeake* affair, Congress in 1807 at Jefferson's urging passed the **Embargo Act,** which prevented U.S. ships from leaving U.S. ports for foreign ports without governmental approval. Jefferson believed that European states, embroiled in the Napoleonic Wars, depended so much on U.S.-provided supplies and raw materials that Great Britain and France, the two primary offenders, would stop impressment. Jefferson was wrong. Impressment continued, and the Embargo Act drove U.S. exports down 80 percent. The American economy suffered badly, with hundreds of thousands of people out of work. Inflation soared.

Finally, in 1809, an exchange of diplomatic notes between the U.S. secretary of state and the British minister in Washington settled some of the outstanding British-American issues. This was the first important **executive agreement,** a government-to-government accord entered into by the United States and binding on only the administration that concluded it.[18]

Madison's Foreign Policy

U.S.-British relations continued to deteriorate after James Madison became president. Fueled by impressment, a desire to defend American honor, Indian attacks in the western United States that many believed were fomented by the British, American territorial designs on Canada, and economic depression in the South and West, Congress at Madison's request declared war on Great Britain. The **War of 1812** had begun.[19]

As a rule, Americans from the West and South supported war and those from the North and East opposed it. Attitudes toward the war were split on regional and party lines, with Republicans generally supporting war and Federalists for the most part opposing it. Not surprisingly, the vote for the War of 1812 in both houses of Congress was close, 19 to 13 in the Senate and 79 to 49 in the House. All 39 Federalists in both houses of Congress voted against war.

The United States entered the War of 1812 as a divided nation. In the fighting, the United States held a clear edge in naval encounters, but warfare on the ground produced no clear victor even though Great Britain seized and burned Washington, D.C. The war dragged on for two years, ending only after Great Britain decided to concentrate on defeating Napoleon in Europe. In 1814, the United States and Great Britain concluded the Treaty of Ghent, bringing the war to an end. The treaty showed how inconclusive the fighting had been, as Great Britain and the United States agreed to abide by the borders, treaty obligations, and other conditions that existed before the war.

Given the slowness of communications between Europe and North America during this era, it took months for word of the Treaty of Ghent to reach the United States. The delay provided the United States the opportunity to achieve one of its most storied military victories. The Battle of New Orleans was fought after the Treaty of Ghent had been signed, but no one in New Orleans knew the war was over.

By 1815, then, the United States had been in existence for 26 years and had been led by four presidents: Washington, Adams, Jefferson, and Madison. Each had experienced tension between isolationism and involvement, and between idealism and realism, in their foreign policy, and all four had initiated policies that balanced the different sides of the competing themes. Subsequent presidents would frequently follow similar courses of action.

All four presidents had also struggled to find a consensus that would bind the infant nation together during times of crisis, and none had completely succeeded. Indeed, given the internal discord that often prevailed, it may even be said that all except Washington failed. Debate over war or peace with France undermined Adams's presidency, how to respond to impressment and the embargo divided the country under Jefferson, and state and regional interests complicated Madison's conduct of the War of 1812. After 26 years of existence, the United States was still searching for its place in the world.

CONTINENTAL EXPANSION AND HEMISPHERIC INTERESTS: 1815–1848

Having survived although not won another war with Great Britain, the United States for the next 30 years concentrated much of its foreign policy on continental expansion. At the same time, the United States began to assert itself as a power with growing foreign interests, especially in Latin America.

Throughout these years, Americans continued to see their country as different from and better than European states. The American mission thus remained closely connected to ideological interests. Economic prosperity and military security remained important American interests, but in addition, some Americans began to believe that the United States needed to gain a place as a country to be reckoned with among the community of nations. The quest for national power in some circles thus grew in importance as an American interest. As before, isolationism, pragmatism, moralism, and unilateralism remained key principles of U.S. foreign policy.

The competing themes of isolationism versus involvement and realism versus idealism also remained evident, played out especially in U.S. relations with Great Britain, the declaration of the Monroe Doctrine, continental expansion, and relations with Mexico. Between 1815 and 1848, Americans continued to assert that the United States was isolationist, but the United States regularly and frequently became involved with foreign states. Similarly, Americans maintained that the United States followed ideals in its foreign policy, pointing especially to the Monroe Doctrine as proof. At the same time, however, the Monroe Doctrine was enforced by the strength of British arms, and the United States often undertook actions as it expanded westward and went to war with Mexico that caused many to conclude that American foreign policy was based less on idealism than on military power and a quest for economic prosperity. No one called it realism, but many charged that American foreign policy had all the manifestations of what eventually would be called realpolitik.

Relations with Great Britain

Throughout these years, the United States was primarily concerned with Great Britain, and rightly so. Great Britain was the world's most powerful country and presented the greatest threat to American security. Americans had fought two wars against Great Britain in less than 40 years. At the same time, most American trade was with Great Britain, and most Americans (at the time) traced their ancestry there. Understandably, Great Britain attracted, repelled, and struck fear into Americans. Most expected U.S.-British tensions to continue, and to an extent they were right. Disputes over the U.S.-Canadian boundary simmered, a few Americans aided sporadic Canadian efforts to gain independence, and trade rivalry between the United States and Great Britain in Latin America and the Caribbean increased.

Nevertheless, the years after the War of 1812 witnessed a significant change in U.S.-British relations brought about by conscious U.S. and British efforts to avoid conflict and by common trading interests. In 1817, the two countries concluded the Rush-Bagot Agreement, which restricted both sides to no more than four warships on the Great Lakes and Lake Champlain. In 1818, the United States and Great Britain extended the 49th parallel as the boundary between the United States and Canada as far west as the Rocky Mountains, with the Oregon Territory beyond the Rockies remaining "free and open" to U.S. and British citizens. In addition, the two countries signed several trade and fishery agreements, thereby ending other disputes. Also, as we will see later, U.S.-British diplomatic contacts paved the way for the 1823 U.S. declaration of the Monroe Doctrine.

During the 1820s and 1830s, several incidents on the U.S.-Canadian border increased U.S.-British tensions. Thus, the United States and Great Britain renewed efforts to resolve Canadian-American border issues, finally concluding the 1842 Webster-Ashburton Treaty that settled boundary disputes between Canada and Maine. And in 1846, despite American blustering about "54-40 or Fight," the United States and Britain agreed to divide the Oregon Territory at the 49th parallel, extending the U.S.-Canadian border all the way to the Pacific Ocean. By mid-century, then, even though British-American disputes flared during the 1850s, the American Civil War, and thereafter, the chances for renewed conflict between the United States and Great Britain had been reduced.[20]

The Monroe Doctrine

Elsewhere in the Western Hemisphere, empire-shaking events were unfolding. In Latin American between 1808 and 1822, revolutionaries like Simon Bolivar and Jose San Martin led revolts against Spain as one Latin American state after another won independence. The United States did little to aid the revolutions, but most Americans applauded the Latin American struggle for independence. They also displayed their usual pragmatism and expanded trade with their independent neighbors.

Meanwhile, in Europe after Napoleon's final defeat in 1815, Europe's Great Powers—Austria, Britain, post-Napoleonic France, Prussia, and Russia—created an informal alliance system, the **Concert of Europe.** This system was based on a desire to avoid war, maintain the status quo, and, except for Great Britain, keep conservative kings in power. To a great extent, the Concert kept the peace in Europe into the 1850s and beyond. However, the Concert often preserved peace by intervening in other states. For example, Austrian troops marched into Naples and Piedmont in 1821 to put down uprisings, French troops in 1822 crossed into Spain to help Ferdinand VII stay in power, and the Concert in 1821–1822 helped the Ottoman Empire quiet a Greek independence movement.[21]

President James Monroe feared that the Concert's next venture might be into Latin America to restore Spain's empire there. Great Britain was also concerned. Like the United States, British trade had grown in Latin America as the wars of independence proceeded. Britain also feared that a restoration of Spain's colonial empire might strengthen France. Given these coincident interests, the two countries began diplomatic conversations that led Monroe in 1823 to proclaim the **Monroe Doctrine.** Under the doctrine, Monroe announced that "the American continents, by the free and independent condition which they have assumed and maintain, are henceforth not to be considered as subjects for future colonization by any European power." He also declared that the United States viewed any attempt to restore colonies or establish new ones in the New World as "dangerous" to its "peace and safety" and that the United States would not become involved in any European quarrels.[22]

These were fine words, but the United States could not enforce them. Fortunately for the United States, Great Britain could. Since Great Britain believed that its own commercial and strategic interests dictated that it keep other European powers out of the Americas, the British navy protected British interests and helped enforce the Monroe Doctrine. This community of interests was illustrated by the fact that although Great Britain expanded its small colonial presence in Latin America several times after 1823, the United States never invoked the Monroe Doctrine.

Viewed from outside the United States, the Monroe Doctrine was as much a declaration of a U.S. sphere of influence as a statement of U.S. anti-colonialism. To non-Americans, even though the United States put forward the Monroe Doctrine as a statement of idealism, it was a statement about U.S. self-interest and U.S. concern about the possible expansion of European Great Power influence. Viewed differently, Monroe had perfectly balanced the competing themes of realism and idealism.

Continental Expansion

As important as improved relations with Great Britain and the Monroe Doctrine were, the United States devoted most of its attention during the first half of the nineteenth century to an even more momentous activity: continental expansion. When the nineteenth century began, the United States consisted of the original 13 colonies and a few other states that had joined the union in the years thereafter. By mid-century, the United States owned or claimed almost all the land between the 49th parallel and the Rio Grande River, stretching from the Atlantic to the Pacific oceans.

The United States acquired its vast territorial holding in various ways. As we have seen, it bought the Louisiana Territory from France in 1803. It acquired Florida from Spain in 1819 through a combination of military force, pugnacious diplomacy, and money. It took land from Native Americans in wars against the Creeks, Sioux, Seminoles, Comanches, Apaches, and other tribes, exterminating many and forcing others to move from ancestral land to new territory farther west or onto reservations. In 1846, it negotiated with Great Britain to divide the Oregon Territory. It annexed Texas in 1845. Between 1846 and 1848, it fought a war against Mexico, imposing on Mexico at the end of the war the Treaty of Guadalupe Hidalgo in which Mexico ceded to the United States what is now California, Nevada, Utah, and parts of Arizona, New Mexico, Colorado, and Wyoming.

This expansion was accomplished under the concept of **manifest destiny,** the American belief that it was a divinely mandated United States obligation to expand across North America from the Atlantic to the Pacific and acquire all territory in between. Fueled by a complex mix of economics, politics, ideology, strategy, and racism, the concept of manifest destiny permitted Americans to rationalize U.S. expansion as a legitimate and moral undertaking.[23]

Many Americans held another curious view about their country's continental expansion. Although they decried the overseas expansionism of others as colonialism, many did not view the United States' expansion in North America as colonialism. Because it was undertaken in territory that was connected to the United States, they believed that this expansion was different from colonialism. It was, after all, the manifest destiny of the United States to expand from the Atlantic to the Pacific oceans and to acquire, tame, and control all the land in between.

The United State's continental expansion was also aided by war in Europe. During the first half of the nineteenth century, European powers were focused first on the Napoleonic Wars and then on maintaining stability in Europe after Napoleon's defeat. As we have seen, Napoleon's need for money to finance his fighting was one reason that he sold the Louisiana Territory. Then the Concert of Europe concentrated on maintaining the status quo in Europe, avoiding European wars and, except for Great Britain, keeping conservative rulers in power.

After the decades of war unleashed by the French Revolution and Napoleon, the Concert's objectives were understandable. They also worked to the American advantage.

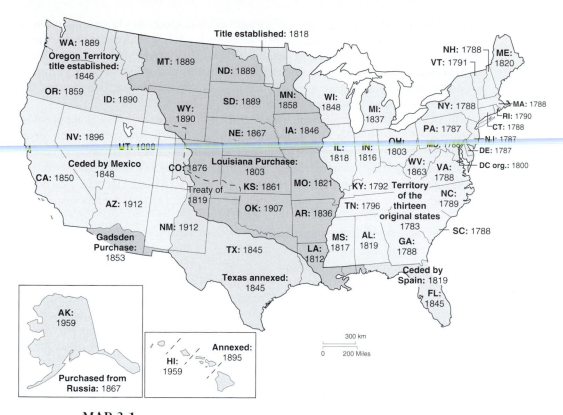

MAP 3.1
The United States' Expansion in North America
*Using manifest destiny as a primary rationale for expansion, the United States
acquired land by war, negotiations, and purchase from France, Great Britain,
Russia, Spain, and Native Americans as it expanded across North America.*

With European powers other than Great Britain focusing on European affairs, the United
States could concentrate on continental expansion with little concern about European
reaction. By mid-century, then, most of what is today the continental United States was
in the United States' hands, even though the United States did not consolidate its control
until after the American Civil War.

Relations with Mexico

Much of America's expansion in the nineteenth century came at the expense of Mexico. Mexico had won independence from Spain in 1821, but twice during its first three
decades of independence it lost significant amounts of territory to the United States.
The first time was the **Texas revolution and annexation.** In 1819, before Mexican
independence, the United States concluded an agreement with Spain in which the
United States accepted Spain's claims to Texas as Mexico's northernmost province.

Soon thereafter, Mexico's Spanish government offered Americans large land grants if they pledged allegiance to Spain and converted to Catholicism. After independence, the Mexican government continued this policy. Up to 20,000 Americans, many of them slave owners, pledged allegiance first to Spain and then independent Mexico, promised to convert to Catholicism, and moved to Texas. Unfortunately for Mexico, most of the immigrants still saw themselves as Americans.

In 1834, General Antonio Santa Anna seized power in Mexico City, determined to assert control over all of Mexico including Texas. By 1835, Texans were in open revolt against Santa Anna, setting up a separatist government and raising an army to defend themselves. Rejecting Texan independence, Santa Anna marched into Texas, defeating the Texans at the Alamo in 1836. Six weeks later, the Texans turned the tables on Santa Anna and routed his forces, capturing him and forcing him to sign a treaty that recognized Texas's independence.

Texas was now an independent country, but most Texans wanted to join the United States. Therefore Texas asked the United States to annex it, but the United States refused, not wanting to upset the delicate balance between slave states and nonslave states that kept political peace in the United States. Thus, for nine years, Texas was an independent country. Finally, in 1846, President John Tyler signed legislation annexing Texas, three days before pro-expansion president-elect James Polk took office. Mexico's minister to the United States left Washington a week later, having previously told the United States that it would break diplomatic relations if the United States annexed Texas.

U.S.-Mexican tensions escalated as Polk supported Texas's claim that the Rio Grande River, not the more northern Nueces River, was its border with Mexico. But Polk's territorial ambitions for the United States extended beyond the land between the Rio Grande and Nueces River. Thus, the American president helped incite American settlers in California, then a part of Mexico, to rise up against Mexico. Polk sent a delegation to Mexico City to buy California and New Mexico, but the Mexican government, incensed by the annexation of Texas, refused to receive it. Polk then ordered General Zachary Taylor to march from Corpus Christi to the Rio Grande River to solidify Texas's claim to the land between the Rio Grande and Nueces rivers. Hoping that Mexican forces would attack Taylor's troops and provide a pretext for war, Polk was not disappointed. Mexican forces crossed the Rio Grande, surprised an American cavalry force, killing 11, and provided the American president the pretext he sought to ask Congress to declare war. Congress obliged, and the **War with Mexico** had begun.[24]

American forces invaded Mexico soon after, marching into Mexico City in 1847. This did not end the war, as a peace settlement proved difficult to conclude. Finally, in 1848, the United States and Mexico signed the Treaty of Guadalupe Hidalgo in which the United States paid Mexico $15 million and Mexico ceded to the United States what is now California, Nevada, Utah, and parts of Arizona, New Mexico, Colorado, and Wyoming. Congress quickly ratified the treaty.

The War with Mexico raised several questions about foreign policy. First, many believed that the president engineered the war so the United States could obtain more land. This troubled many Americans, who asked if the president had too much power.

Second, some noted that even though Congress questioned the war and the peace treaty, it declared war and accepted the treaty with little debate. This led some to ask if Congress too readily abandoned its foreign policy responsibilities. Third, some Americans saw the war as clear territorial expansionism. Where, they asked, had U.S. idealism gone? Others were perplexed that, as during the War of 1812, most Americans did not support the war. This weakened the U.S. ability to conduct the war, they said, and provided comfort to the enemy. In the century and a half since the Mexican War, many Americans at different times have raised these same questions about other U.S. foreign policy undertakings.

Mexicans, too, had questions about their neighbor to the north. Since its 1821 independence, Mexico twice lost large amounts of territory to the United States. First Texas rebelled and won independence, eventually joining the United States. Then the United States defeated Mexico and imposed a humiliating peace with American troops in Mexico's capital. Given that the first three decades of U.S.-Mexican relations were not good, many Mexicans were concerned about what kind of a neighbor the United States was.[25]

Halfway through the nineteenth century, then, after not quite 60 years of existence, the United States had grown from a country confined to a strip of land along the Atlantic coast to a country that owned or claimed territory that stretched from the Atlantic to Pacific. Most Americans were proud of this accomplishment, much of it achieved through force of arms. Others, however, were concerned that the United States in its quest to grow and obtain economic prosperity had abandoned its ideals. Thus, the struggle between realism and idealism continued.

So, too, did the conflict between the competing themes of isolationism and involvement. Most Americans still considered their country isolationist, pointing to the United States' continuing avoidance of European wars as proof. But others looked at Britain's role in enforcing the Monroe Doctrine, the Mexican War, and the entire saga of the United States' westward expansion and concluded that the United States was deeply, and not idealistically, involved in international affairs.

The country was also beginning to find its place in the world. Americans were known everywhere as shrewd and successful traders, and the country's startling territorial growth had marked it as a country on the rise. Even so, there was one major uncertainty regarding America's future as the 1840s ended and the 1850s began, and that was the future of slavery. Slavery was a deeply divisive issue, not only in American domestic politics and policy in the mid-nineteenth century, but also in American foreign policy.

TRADE, HOPES OF EMPIRE, AND CIVIL WAR: 1848–1865

By the mid-nineteenth century, the United States was a growing economic and military power. Although the United States was no match for the major European powers of the day, American power and self-confidence was growing, and the United States was expanding its trading interests. Some Americans, especially southern slave owners, were even beginning to dream of empire.

The Granger Collection, NY

Slavery and the slave trade played a major role in the United States and its foreign policy in the nineteenth century. It divided North from South, led to efforts to acquire territory in the Caribbean and Central America, and was one of the primary causes of the Civil War.

U.S. Trade and Commerce

From its inception, the United States was a trading nation. Although Alexander Hamilton in his 1791 *Report on Manufactures* urged Congress to follow a policy of **economic protectionism**—that is, imposing tariffs, quotas, and other restraints on trade to protect domestic industries from foreign competition—the United States during the early years of the republic usually implemented different policies than those recommended by Hamilton. Instead of protectionism, the United States usually offered **trade reciprocity** and pursued **most favored nation (MFN) status.** Reciprocity meant that the United States treated foreign traders the same way that foreign countries treated U.S. traders, and MFN status meant that U.S. exports faced the lowest tariffs offered to any other country.

For most of the United States' early years, this worked well, in part because U.S. raw materials and products were in great demand in Europe during the Napoleonic Wars. However, when the Napoleonic Wars ended in 1815, this changed. Peace led to increased competition at home and abroad, and the United States adopted **protectionist tariffs** to do what Hamilton suggested years before—keep the home market for domestic products. Congress passed the first truly protectionist tariff in 1816.

Over the next eight years, Congress created the so-called American System of increasingly higher tariffs. Under the American System, tariffs reached 20 to 30 percent of the value of an import and sometimes up to 100 percent. High tariffs protected the American market for U.S. producers and remained in place until the twentieth century, but they cut off foreign markets for U.S. producers as foreign countries retaliated with their own high tariffs. As a result, U.S. trade declined between 1824 and 1830, growing again after then. However, the growth of international trade was slower than the growth of trade within the United States.

During the first half of the nineteenth century, U.S. trading interests also expanded geographically. Concentrating first on trade with Europe and the Caribbean, American traders next turned their eyes to Latin America as countries there achieved independence. In addition, the United States' westward expansion added California and the Pacific Northwest to American trading horizons. Increasingly, U.S. merchant ships plied Pacific trading lanes toward Asia, especially after Great Britain's victory in the First Opium War (1839–1842) opened China to trade. In the wake of Great Britain's victory, the United States concluded a treaty with China that gained the United States most favored nation status. American traders and missionaries began to arrive in China soon after. Indeed, by the early 1850s, one-third of all Chinese trade outside Asia was with the United States.

The United States demonstrated its economic interests elsewhere in East Asia in 1852 and 1854 when Commodore Matthew Perry took the U.S. Navy's East India Squadron into Japanese waters and opened Japan to Western trade.[26] U.S. trade with China and Japan expanded rapidly as first clipper ships and then steam-powered merchant vessels sailed the sea lanes in record time between Asia and the United States' Atlantic coast.

By 1860, Europe remained the United States' most important trading partner, but the United States had global trading interests. The Civil War curtailed these interests for a time, but when the war ended, as we will see, America's global economic interests became even more expansive. Considering trade a commercial need rather than a foreign policy interest, few Americans believed that trade contradicted isolationism. Indeed, many argued that trade could be and should be pursued apart from territorial acquisition and political or diplomatic issues. This, they alleged, showed that American trade confirmed that the United States was isolationist.

Slavery and Southern Hopes of Empire

The competing themes of isolationism versus involvement and idealism versus realism were also played out in American foreign policy in the 1850s in Latin America and the Caribbean as southern politicians, business leaders, and writers searched for ways to expand U.S., and particularly southern, trading and territorial interests there. During the decade, American adventurers sponsored by southern interests launched forays into Cuba, Mexico, Nicaragua, Honduras, and the Dominican Republic to gain profit and to acquire territory into which slavery could expand.[27] Motivated primarily by the desire to find territory into which slavery could expand for economic profit and political advantage, Southerners were at odds with Easterners and Northerners over expansion.

By the 1850s, manifest destiny and territorial expansion had generally fallen out of favor in the U.S. East and North. There were several reasons for this. First, as we have seen, the War with Mexico raised questions about U.S. foreign policy that were difficult to answer. Second, with border disputes with Canada having been resolved and cordial relations with Great Britain in place, few Easterners and Northerners saw either a reason or an opportunity to acquire Canadian territory. Third, most Easterners and Northerners opposed territorial expansion in Latin America and the Caribbean because expansion there would bring more slave states into the Union. If this occurred, the South would gain a majority in the U.S. House of Representatives and Senate and be able to dominate national policy decisions. No Northerner or Easterner wanted that.

Conversely, southern political and business interests saw economic and political advantages to expansion into Latin America and the Caribbean. The economic advantages that slavery provided to slave owners were at the heart of Southerners' desire to expand, but at the same time, Southerners were well aware that adding slave states to the Union had the potential to give states where slavery was legal a majority in the House and Senate.[28] Thus, slavery became a bellwether issue in American foreign policy during the 1850s. Not surprisingly, southern political and business interests supported an array of American adventurers who tried to expand U.S., and specifically southern, interests in Latin America and the Caribbean.

The most notorious adventurer was William Walker, who in the 1850s launched several forays into Central America. In 1853, Walker and his mercenary band invaded Lower California, holding the territorial capital of La Paz for a short time. In 1855, he conquered Nicaragua, declaring himself president. His brutal dictatorial regime fell to forces from other Central American states in 1857 as he plotted to build a Central American empire. Walker tried to return later in the year to regain his rule but was stopped and arrested by the U.S. Navy. Undeterred, Walker invaded Nicaragua twice more, in 1858 and 1860. Captured in Honduras after his 1860 assault failed, he was executed by a Honduran firing squad.[29]

Cuba was also a key target of pro-slavery expansionists. A rich and fertile island astride the Caribbean's main trading lanes, Cuba had not joined the anti-Spanish Latin American revolutions earlier in the century and remained a Spanish possession. Governed by corrupt Spanish administrations that brutally repressed the island's frequent slave revolts, Cuba was seen by many Southerners as a place ripe for acquisition where slavery could prosper.

The United States made several attempts to acquire Cuba, most initiated with southern support.[30] President James Polk in 1848 offered Spain $100 million for the island, but Spain refused because of strong British and French opposition to the sale. Polk's successors, Zachary Taylor and Millard Fillmore, had no interest in acquiring Cuba, but their successors, Franklin Pierce and James Buchanan, both coveted the island, attempting but failing to buy it. The depth of some Americans' desire for the island was illustrated by the 1854 **Ostend Manifesto,** which declared that if Spain rejected a U.S. offer of $120 million, the United States would "by every law, human and divine . . . be justified in wresting [Cuba] from Spain if we possess the power."[31]

Despite these attempts to bring Latin American and Caribbean lands under American control, the United States acquired no holdings in Latin America and the Caribbean in the 1850s. When Abraham Lincoln, a staunch opponent of slavery, won the 1860 presidential election, it was clear that the annexation of Cuba or any other territory in which slavery was legal would not occur during the next four years. Nevertheless, the damage had been done, with many people in Latin America and the Caribbean now viewing the United States not as an idealistic and moral country but as a country bent on territorial expansion.

Foreign Policy during the Civil War

The implications of Lincoln's election went beyond ending possible U.S. expansion into Latin America and the Caribbean. Convinced that Lincoln's election signaled a shift of political power to the national government, and fearing that Lincoln might try to end slavery, South Carolina seceded from the Union and fired on the federal garrison at Fort Sumter. Lincoln, pledged to defend the Constitution and maintain the Union, resolved that southern secession would not stand. The American Civil War had begun.

For four years, warfare raged. Most battles were fought in the South, whose territory was ravaged. Over 600,000 troops died, and hundreds of thousands were wounded. Especially during the early years of the war, even though the North had twice as many people as the South and over 90 percent of the manufacturing capacity, it was far from evident who would win. As one noted historian observed: "Confederate armies did not have to invade and conquer the North; they needed only to hold out long enough to force the North to the conclusion that the price of conquering the South and annihilating its armies was too high."[32]

This had an immense impact on the foreign policies of the Union and the Confederacy, and on the foreign policies of several European states, especially Great Britain.[33] From the Union's perspective, with victory uncertain, keeping the war an American affair and limiting foreign support for the Confederacy were key objectives. Lincoln succeeded in this even though his secretary of state, William Seward, on several occasions threatened to go to war with Great Britain if the British did not see events as the Union saw them and interpret international law as the Union preferred. Thus, tension between the United States and Great Britain increased during the war over issues such as the United States stopping British vessels to search for Confederate diplomats and contraband and Great Britain building commerce raiders for the Confederacy. However, Great Britain remained neutral; Great Britain and other European states recognized the Confederacy's belligerency but not its independence.

From the Confederacy's perspective, enticing Great Britain or other European powers to recognize its independence would have provided more than political prestige. It also might have forced the Union to declare war on Great Britain and other powers. This would have benefited the Confederacy. At the same time, the South reasoned, Great Britain depended on the South for cotton to keep British textile mills operating. Many Southerners believed that since cotton was king, Great Britain would eventually side with them.[34]

Great Britain had different views. From London's perspective, at least during the first year of the war, southern success was almost inevitable. There was therefore no reason to recognize the South too quickly and anger the Union, London reasoned. Also, although southern cotton was important to Great Britain, it did not dominate British policy. In 1860, the bumper southern cotton crop allowed British cotton textile production to exceed demand, so a backlog of goods existed. Since Great Britain believed the war would be short, London expected the backlog would meet demand. At the same time, Great Britain developed other sources of cotton within its empire in Egypt and India. These sources came on line in 1863, reducing British need for southern cotton. Worse for the Confederacy, the Union in 1863 won major victories at Gettysburg and Vicksburg and Lincoln issued the Emancipation Proclamation, liberating slaves in the Confederacy, a move that played well in anti-slavery London. By 1863, then, British recognition of the Confederacy was not likely.[35]

The impact of these calculations was seen in the way American, Confederate, and British foreign policy unfolded over the **Trent Affair** in late 1861. Intending to improve its position with Great Britain, the Confederacy ordered two diplomats, James Mason and John Slidell, to go to London. Thinking their chances of getting to Great Britain were greatest if they sailed on a neutral vessel that the U.S. Navy under the maritime laws of the day should not stop, the two diplomats traveled to Cuba and boarded the *Trent,* a British ship bound for London. Nevertheless, the U.S. Navy stopped the *Trent* and captured Mason and Slidell.

Great Britain was outraged. Stopping a neutral ship, London pointed out, was almost identical to British actions before the War of 1812 over which the United States had gone to war, that Great Britain had later renounced, and that international law had since made illegal. But Great Britain did not want war. Instead, Great Britain sent the United States a carefully worded note that expressed outrage, demanded the release of the Confederate diplomats, and provided the United States a legal loophole of disavowing the actions of the U.S. Navy commander who had boarded the *Trent*. Secretary of State Seward used the loophole, saying the commander had exceeded his authority, praised Great Britain for adopting U.S. views on impressment, and freed Mason and Slidell.[36]

Another crisis loomed over British construction of ships for the Confederacy. Early in the war, the Confederacy contracted with private British interests to build **blockade runners** and **commerce raiders.**[37] Especially during the first years of the war, when the Union blockade of southern ports was a "paper blockade," British-built blockade runners successfully completed the run from Great Britain to the Confederacy, bringing much needed war supplies and earning handsome profits. The Union blockade did not become truly effective until late in the war.[38]

Some British-built commerce raiders were quite successful. Although Union diplomats in 1863 convinced the British government to detain two raiders that were being built near Liverpool, several British-built Confederate commerce raiders were by this time at sea, wreaking havoc with Union shipping. The *Alabama* was the most successful, sailing in 1862 and destroying Union shipping for a year and a half until it was sunk off France by the *Kearsarge* in 1864.

Throughout these episodes, tensions between the Union and Great Britain rose because of actions by each that the other found provocative. Since neither Washington nor London wanted war, however, peace prevailed. The same was true when in 1861 Great Britain, France, and Spain occupied Mexico City to force Mexico to pay interest on a debt. The United States objected to this **European occupation of Mexico,** claiming it violated the Monroe Doctrine. Nevertheless, the Union's response was restrained because it was struggling for survival. This restraint proved justified when in 1862 Great Britain and Spain settled their dispute with Mexico and withdrew.

By late 1862, only France remained in Mexico. In 1863, France sent more troops to Mexico City and proclaimed Mexico a monarchy under Austrian Archduke Maximilian, but the United States refused to recognize his rule when he arrived in 1864. By this time, the Union was winning the Civil War, and Congress passed a resolution condemning France's presence in Mexico. Hoping to avoid confrontation with France, Lincoln disavowed the resolution. Even so, with France facing problems in Europe, and the United States at the end of the Civil War possessing a huge army, France scaled back its presence in Mexico, withdrawing all but 20,000 troops. In the end, France's occupation of Mexico simply faded away when a Mexican firing squad in 1867 killed Maximilian.

WHITHER AMERICA?

With the Civil War over, the United States had surmounted its worst crisis. There no longer was any doubt: the United States was a single country, and slavery had ended. Nevertheless, Americans were faced with the task of rebuilding a shattered country. Hundreds of thousands had died, and over a million had been wounded. Although the North's economic infrastructure had escaped the ravages of war, the South's had been destroyed. In addition, with the emancipation of the slaves, the foundation of the South's social structure and economic strength was eliminated. Animosity ran deep between North and South.

Even though the United States had weathered the crisis, the end of the Civil War raised questions about future American foreign policy. Whereas before the war the country had a sense of mission, the conflict undermined America's ability to serve as the "last best hope of mankind," as Jefferson had described it. How could a country that had just fought a bloody Civil War serve as a "best hope"? Even the emancipation of the slaves lent little credence to the American claim of being a "best hope" or a "superior example," since most European states had ended slavery decades before the United States did.

The Civil War also raised questions about American interests. Enhancing national power, obtaining military security, and building economic strength all remained important, but the chief national purpose inevitably became rebuilding the shattered nation. Neither ideology nor the rule of law loomed large as interests following the Civil War, while maintaining cultural identity presented a new challenge as liberated slaves in theory were provided opportunities for citizenship. Could the United States—which for the first 80 years of its existence had been based almost exclusively on British traditions—begin to become multicultural?

As for American foreign policy, the principles of isolationism, moralism, pragmatism, and unilateralism all remained important. Continued emphasis on isolationism provided the country with an opportunity to lick its wounds and recover from the trauma of civil war. Moralism also remained an important element of the American self-image, at least where people congratulated themselves for ending slavery. Pragmatism remained important, especially in trade and commerce. And as always since independence, the United States intended to act alone and on its own in foreign policy.

As the Civil War drew to a close, the direction that future U.S. foreign policy would take was unclear. Which competing theme would predominate: isolationism or involvement? Would idealism or realism emerge supreme? The need to concentrate on rebuilding the country argued for isolationism, but the need for economic growth and prosperity argued for involvement. Similarly, regaining a sense of mission lent credence to arguments for idealism, but how idealistic could a country shattered by war afford to be? No one knew.

SUMMARY

Even before they gained independence, Great Britain's North American colonies faced external challenges. The 1756–1763 Seven Years' War, also known as the French and Indian War, was the most important. After the war, Great Britain increased taxes to pay off its war debt, but the colonists, used to running their own affairs, revolted. The American Revolution lasted from 1775 to 1783, with France providing the rebels money, munitions, and other goods. In 1783, the Treaty of Paris recognized American independence.

After the Articles of Confederation proved inadequate, the United States was founded in 1789. Most citizens of the new country preferred isolationism to international involvement, and many believed the United States had a mission to serve as a model for others. They also were concerned about military security and economic strength, even though disagreements existed about how to attain either. Protecting trade with Great Britain and expanding trade with other European states was the chief U.S. foreign policy priority.

Trade often brought the United States into conflict with Great Britain and France as these two countries fought in Europe. Thus, George Washington in 1793 issued a Neutrality Proclamation and stated in his 1796 Farewell Address that the United States should "steer clear of permanent alliances." Even so, Americans continued to trade with both sides. Thus, as French warships seized American ships, the United States fought an undeclared naval war with France under John Adams.

Under Thomas Jefferson, the United States bought the Louisiana Territory from France, sent a naval force to the Mediterranean to fight the Barbary pirates, and countered the British policy of impressment with the 1807 Embargo Act. Nevertheless, U.S.-British relations worsened under James Madison. Fueled by impressment, defense of honor, Indian attacks in the west, U.S. designs on Canada, and economic depression, the War of 1812 began, ending in 1815 indecisively. By then, the United States had had four presidents, each of whom had experienced tension between isolationism and involvement, and between idealism and realism. All four initiated policies that balanced the different sides of the competing themes.

After the War of 1812, the United States for 30 years concentrated on continental expansion. The United States also asserted itself, especially regarding Mexico and Latin America. During these years, Americans saw their country as better than European states, with a mission connected to ideology. Economic prosperity and military security also were key interests as some Americans argued that the United States needed to become a world power. The competing themes of isolationism versus involvement, and realism versus idealism, also remained evident, played out between 1815 and 1850 in U.S. relations with Great Britain, the declaration of the Monroe Doctrine, continental expansion, and relations with Mexico.

American strength and self-confidence grew in mid-century as the United States expanded its trade interests in Latin America and Asia. Some slave owners even dreamed of empire in the Caribbean and Latin America, but attempts to gain territory there failed. When Abraham Lincoln won the presidency in 1860, it was clear that no land would be annexed in which slavery might be legal.

Convinced that Lincoln's election meant political power had shifted to the national government, and fearing that Lincoln might end slavery, South Carolina seceded and the Civil War began. From the Union's viewpoint, limiting foreign support for the Confederacy was a key objective. From the Confederacy's perspective, enticing Great Britain to recognize its independence could have led to material support and political prestige. European states for the most part steered clear of the war. Thus, the Union was more successful in achieving its foreign policy objectives.

When the Civil War ended, the course of future U.S. foreign policy was unclear. Would isolationism or involvement, idealism or realism, emerge supreme, and what would the American mission be? No one knew.

KEY TERMS AND CONCEPTS

Seven Years' War (French and Indian War)
American War of Independence
France's involvement in the American
   War of Independence
1778 Treaty with France
1783 Treaty of Paris
Neutrality Proclamation
Jay Treaty
Washington's Farewell Address
Louisiana Purchase
Barbary War
impressment
Embargo Act of 1807
executive agreement

War of 1812
Concert of Europe
Monroe Doctrine
manifest destiny
Texas revolution and annexation
War with Mexico
economic protectionism
trade reciprocity
most favored nation (MFN) status
protectionist tariffs
Ostend Manifesto
Trent Affair
blockade runners and commerce raiders
European occupation of Mexico

THINKING CRITICALLY

1. What factors led American colonists to grow increasingly resentful of Great Britain, and eventually to revolt against Great Britain, in the late eighteenth century?

2. What role did France play in the American Revolution?

3. Use concrete examples to show how the competing themes of isolationism and involvement, and idealism and realism, were evident in American foreign policy during the presidencies of George Washington, John Adams, and Thomas Jefferson.

4. Explain why isolationism was such an important concept in U.S. foreign policy before the American Civil War, and illustrate how isolationism was more an ideal than a reality.

5. Trace the major events in the United States' expansion to the Pacific Ocean, and explain the role that Manifest Destiny played in American expansion.

6. What role did foreign trade play in U.S. foreign policy before the American Civil War? How and where did the United States expand and defend its trading interests?

7. What impact did slavery have on U.S. foreign policy before the American Civil War?

8. What were the primary foreign policy objectives of the North and the South during the American Civil War, and why and how did both sides try to achieve their objectives?

9. Explain why the future of American foreign policy was so uncertain at the conclusion of the American Civil War.

NOTES

1. Rhode Island did not ratify the Constitution until 1790, one year after George Washington became president of the United States.

2. For good discussions of eighteenth-century warfare and rivalry among the great powers of the day, see Michael Howard, *War in European History* (New York: Oxford University Press, 1976); Derek McKay and H. M. Scott, *The Rise of the Great Powers, 1648–1815* (London: Longman, 1983); Paul Kennedy, *The Rise and Fall of the Great Powers* (New York: Random House, 1987); and Jeremy Black, *European Warfare, 1660–1815* (New Haven: Yale University Press, 1994).

3. The 1763 Tea Act led directly to the "Boston Tea Party," in which colonists dressed as Indians dumped tea from British merchant ships in Boston Harbor into the bay.

4. Just as the Seven Years' War led King George to increase taxes on his subjects, the combination of the Seven Years' War and French involvement in the American War of Independence led French King Louis XVI to increase taxes on his subjects. Louis's actions inflamed anti-royal sentiment among the masses in France and contributed directly to the 1789 French Revolution. This in turn led to over two decades of warfare throughout much of Europe, culminating in the rise of Napoleon in 1799 and the Napoleonic Wars that raged across Europe until 1815, ending only with Napoleon's defeat at Waterloo.

5. Samuel Flagg Bemis, *The Diplomacy of the American Revolution* (Bloomington: Indiana University Press, 1957), is probably the classic study of the complex diplomacy of the American Revolution. See also Richard Van Alstyne, *Empire and Independence: The International History of the American Revolution* (New York: Wiley, 1965).

6. The Barbary states were Algiers, Morocco, Tripoli, and Tunis.

7. For good discussions of American foreign policy before, during, and immediately after the Articles of Confederation period, see Lawrence S. Kaplan, *Colonies into Nation: American Diplomacy, 1763–1801* (New York: Macmillan, 1972), and Merrill Jensen, *The New Nation: A History of the United States during the Confederation, 1781–1789* (New York: Knopf, 1950).

8. See again Kaplan, *Colonies into Nation,* and Paul A. Varg, *Foreign Policies of the Founding Fathers* (Baltimore: Penguin Books, 1970).

9. For more on this and other disagreements between Jefferson and Hamilton on American foreign and domestic policies, see Claude G. Bowers's classic *Jefferson and Hamilton: The Struggle for Democracy in America* (Boston: Houghton-Mifflin, 1925).

10. The disagreements between Hamilton and Jefferson over policy toward France and Great Britain, and Washington's declaration of the Neutrality Proclamation, provide an excellent opportunity to use the methodology of levels of analysis discussed in Chapter 1. To what extent did Jefferson's preference that the United States lean toward France in its policies result from his own clear personal preferences (at this time) for things French, and to what extent was it a true reflection of his belief that such policies were in the best interests of the United States? To what extent did Hamilton's preference that the United States lean toward

Great Britain in its policies result from his personal feelings, and to what extent was it a true reflection of his belief that such policies were in the best interests of the United States? The same questions may be asked about George Washington's position. The answers will vary depending on which level of analysis one uses.

11. For more on Genet, see Harry Ammon, *The Genet Mission* (New York: Norton, 1973).

12. Samuel Flagg Bemis, *Jay's Treaty: A Study in Commerce and Diplomacy* (New Haven: Yale University Press, 1962), and Jerald A. Combs, *The Jay Treaty: Political Battleground of the Founding Fathers* (Berkeley: University of California Press, 1970), provide extensive context for and details about Jay's Treaty and its negotiation.

13. George Washington's Farewell Address, as quoted in James D. Richardson, ed., *A Compilation of the Messages and Papers of the Presidents, 1789–1901* (Washington, D.C.: U.S. Government Printing Office, 1896–1914, in 10 volumes), Vol. 1, pp. 221–223.

14. For detailed discussions of foreign policy during John Adams's presidency, see David McCullough, *John Adams* (New York: Simon and Schuster, 2001).

15. Thomas Jefferson's Inaugural Address, as quoted in Richardson, p. 323.

16. Quoted in Robert M. Johnstone Jr., *Jefferson and the Presidency* (Ithaca, N.Y.: Cornell University Press, 1978), p. 69.

17. Quoted in E. W. Lyon, *Louisiana in French Diplomacy: 1759–1804* (Norman: University of Oklahoma Press, 1934), p. 206.

18. For a good discussion of deteriorating U.S.-British relations during Jefferson's presidency, see Bradford Perkins, *Prologue to War: England and the United States, 1805–1812* (Berkeley: University of California Press, 1961).

19. See R. Horsman, *The Causes of the War of 1812* (Philadelphia: University of Pennsylvania Press, 1962), for a deeper analysis of the causes of the War of 1812.

20. For a good survey of U.S.-British relations during this period and beyond, see Charles S. Campbell, *From Revolution to Rapprochement: The United States and Great Britain, 1783–1900* (New York: Wiley, 1974).

21. For a good overview of European politics during this era, see Paul Schroeder, *The Transformation of European Politics 1763–1848* (Oxford: Clarendon Press, 1994).

22. For a more detailed discussion of the origins of the Monroe Doctrine, see Ernest R. May, *The Making of the Monroe Doctrine* (Cambridge, Mass.: Harvard University Press, 1975). See also Dexter Perkins, *The Monroe Doctrine, 1823–1826* (Cambridge, Mass.: Harvard University Press, 1927).

23. For in-depth discussions of manifest destiny, see Thomas R. Hietala, *Manifest Destiny: Anxious Aggrandisement in Late Jacksonian America* (Ithaca, N.Y.: Cornell University Press, 1985), and Frederick Merk, *Manifest Destiny and Mission in American History* (New York: Vintage Books, 1963).

24. For three different views of the War with Mexico and U.S.-Mexican relations, see John H. Schroeder, *Mr. Polk's War* (Madison: University of Wisconsin Press, 1973); Robert A. Pastor and Jorge G. Castaneda, *Limits to Friendship: The United States and Mexico* (New York: Knopf, 1988); and W. Dirk Raat, *Mexico and the United States* (Athens: University of Georgia Press, 1992).

25. See Gene M. Brack, *Mexico Views Manifest Destiny: 1821–1846* (Albuquerque: University of New Mexico Press, 1975).

26. For more on Perry's mission and other aspects of U.S.-Japanese relations, see Charles E. New, *The Troubled Encounter: The United States and Japan* (New York: Wiley, 1975).

27. For greater details of southern hopes for empire, see Robert E. May, *The Southern Dream of a Caribbean Empire, 1854–1861* (Baton Rouge: Louisiana State University Press, 1973).

28. See Eugene D. Genovese, *The Political Economy of Slavery* (New York: Vintage Books, 1967), and David Potter, *The Impending Crisis, 1848–1861* (New York: Harper and Row, 1976), for additional views of the role of slavery in American foreign and domestic policies and politics.

29. For an older assessment of William Walker's forays into Central America, see William O. Scroggs, *Filibusters and Financiers: The Story of William Walker and His Associates* (New York: Macmillan, 1916).

30. See Lester D. Langley, *The Cuban Policy of the United States* (New York: Wiley, 1968); Basil Rauch, *American Interest in Cuba, 1848–1855* (New York: Columbia University Press, 1948); and Gavin B. Henderson, "Southern Designs on Cuba, 1854–1857, and Some European Opinions," *Journal of Southern History* (August, 1939).

31. As quoted in Ruhl J. Bartlett, ed., *The Record of American Diplomacy* (New York: Knopf, 1960), p. 241.

32. James M. McPherson, "American Victory, American Defeat," in *Why the Confederacy Lost*, ed. Gabor S. Boritt (New York: Oxford University Press, 1992), p. 21.

33. David P. Crook has written extensively on Confederate and Union foreign policy during the Civil War. See especially *Diplomacy during the American Civil War* (New York: Wiley, 1975), and *The North, the South, and the Powers: 1861–1865* (New York: Wiley, 1974).

34. See Frank L. Owsley and Harriet C. Owsley, *King Cotton Diplomacy: Foreign Relations of the Confederate States of America* (Chicago, Ill.: University of Chicago Press, 1959).

35. Crook, *The North, the South, and the Powers*.

36. See Gordon H. Warren, *Fountain of Discontent: The Trent Affair and Freedom of the Seas* (Boston: Northeastern University Press, 1981), for an in-depth treatment of the affair.

37. For details of British involvement with the Confederate Navy, see Frank J. Merli, *Great Britain and the Confederate Navy, 1861–1865* (Bloomington: Indiana University Press, 1981).

38. At the beginning of the war, the Union had 42 operational warships, only eight of which were in American waters, to blockade over 3,000 miles of Confederate coast.

CHAPTER 4

Building an Empire: 1865–1914

Teddy Roosevelt, shown here addressing a crowd, was a leading advocate for and architect of American expansion and empire before, during, and after his presidency (1901–1909).

- What foreign policies did the United States initiate after the Civil War?
- What role did foreign trade play in U.S. foreign policy?
- Why did the U.S. Navy become so important?
- Why did the United States begin to acquire possessions overseas?
- How did the United States manage and consolidate its overseas empire?
- What policies did the United States pursue overseas, especially in Latin America and Asia?
- Why did the United States and Great Britain begin a rapprochement?

As the carnage of the American Civil War ended, no one knew what to expect from the United States either domestically or in foreign policy. Would the United States be able to heal its wounds? Once the wounds healed, how bad would the scars be? What policies, domestic and foreign, would the United States implement as it recovered from its national trauma?

Fortunately, the United States prospered in the decades after the Civil War, enjoying unprecedented economic growth as industrialization accelerated, agricultural production expanded, and electricity and other new technologies enhanced living standards. Consolidating its hold on its previously acquired Western territories, the United States added new states as Indian tribes were defeated and removed to reservations. U.S. citizens and foreign immigrants alike flooded into the newly secure lands, aided by railroads.

Slowly at first, but then more rapidly, these trends and events were reflected in American foreign policy. As the economy grew, U.S. trading interests expanded. As the Civil War receded, American nationalism returned. As American capabilities increased, the United States, like European powers of the day, grew comfortable with the expansion of influence and the acquisition of overseas territory. At the same time, the American sense of mission returned, and its foreign policy interests were reclarified, all theoretically based on the same four principles that had underpinned American foreign policy since the Revolution—isolationism, moralism, pragmatism, and unilateralism. As before, the competing themes of isolationism versus involvement and idealism versus realism played central roles in American foreign policy debates and decisions.

TERRITORIAL ACQUISITIONS, FOREIGN TRADE, AND REGIONAL AND GLOBAL INTERESTS: 1865–1895

Territorial expansion was one of the main activities of post–Civil War U.S. foreign policy. Initial **post–Civil War expansion** was substantially the handiwork of Secretary of State William Seward and a few others. It foreshadowed a later period of American expansion that was widely supported as derived from the American mission and morality and widely reviled as abandoning that mission and morality.[1]

Post–Civil War Territorial Acquisitions

Seward had been Lincoln's secretary of state, and he continued under Lincoln's successor, President Andrew Johnson. A committed expansionist, Seward believed the United States should be the seat of power for an empire that stretched into Latin America and into Asia based on commerce and the proclaimed superiority of American institutions. After the Civil War, Seward worked to achieve this.[2]

Seward began his effort in the Danish West Indies, today's U.S. Virgin Islands, attempting to buy the islands in 1865. In 1867, he signed a treaty with Denmark that would have transferred the islands to U.S. control for $7.5 million, but the impeachment trial of President Johnson sidetracked Senate passage of the treaty. Johnson's successor, Ulysses Grant, never submitted the treaty to the Senate, and Denmark retained the islands until the United States obtained them in 1917. Seward also tried to purchase the main port of the Dominican Republic in 1866, but this effort failed as well.

Seward was more successful acquiring Alaska and Midway Island, both in 1867. The secretary of state negotiated Alaska's purchase from Russia for $7.2 million,[3] and a U.S. Navy vessel claimed the mid-Pacific Midway Islands for the United States. Seward left office in 1869, pleased with what he had accomplished but disappointed he had not achieved more.

Seward's departure did not end America's post–Civil War efforts to expand. Soon after Ulysses Grant took office in 1869, Grant's personal secretary, working with American business interests in the Dominican Republic, signed two treaties with the Dominican president. Under the first, the United States would annex the country and assume its national debt. The second said that if the Senate did not ratify the first, the United States could purchase the main harbor in the Dominican Republic for $2 million. Ecstatic, Grant sent a message to Congress lauding the treaty, pointing out that the Dominican Republic had raw materials, provided superb harbors, and offered a market for American products.

The Senate was not convinced, rejecting the first treaty by a 28–28 vote that was well short of the two-thirds majority needed for ratification. The second treaty never came to a vote. Some senators who opposed the treaties believed that they had been improperly negotiated. Others heard rumors of undisclosed personal financial deals. Still others felt pressured to oppose the treaties by anti-imperialists, some of whom opposed the treaties because they were opposed to imperialism on principle and others of whom feared that the treaties would add more nonwhites and Catholics to the United States.[4]

Dominican annexation had failed. For the next decade, with no real champion within senior government circles, territorial expansion took a back seat to domestic issues, especially rebuilding the country, consolidating control over contiguous territory that the United States had already acquired, and economic growth.

Economic Growth, Foreign Trade, and Foreign Policy

American economic growth between 1870 and the end of the eighteenth century was remarkable. U.S. steel production, often seen as a measure of economic strength and vitality, leaped by a factor of 145 between 1870 and 1900, going from 77,000 tons to over 11 million tons. U.S. farmers were unsurpassed in their efficiency and productivity. Overall, the United States gross national product, a measure of the productivity of a country's economy, more than doubled between 1870 and 1900. According to later estimates, the United States passed Great Britain sometime in the 1890s as the world's leading manufacturing country.

The United States experienced economic problems as well, but for the most part they were overlooked. Economic depressions struck from 1873 to 1878 and again from 1893 to 1897. As industrialization proceeded, many Americans also suffered under miserable working conditions. Child labor was also widely accepted, and "robber barons" took advantage of everything they could to increase their wealth. Despite these problems, most Americans were proud of their country's economic successes, and with reason.

The **growth of American foreign trade** played a major role in U.S. economic prosperity. Between 1865 and 1900, American exports increased from just over $200 million to approximately $1.5 billion. Despite the growth of American manufacturing, agricultural products still accounted for over two-thirds of all U.S. exports as late as 1900. U.S. manufacturing exports did not pass agricultural exports in total value until shortly before World War I. Most American exports went to Europe and Canada, but Asia and Latin America were growing in importance as destinations for American exports.

To many Americans, foreign trade meant jobs and prosperity. Tens of thousands of workers were employed by companies that derived their profits from exports. Even though the United States maintained high tariffs through most of the 1865–1895 period, the United States benefited from Great Britain's low tariffs and desire for U.S. raw materials and products. Foreign trade also was a way to dispose of goods that were produced that exceeded domestic consumption.

As American economic strength grew and U.S. confidence returned following the Civil War, many people, especially political leaders, business people, and other opinion leaders, came to see foreign trade as much more than just jobs and prosperity.[5] To many, trade was a way to help "civilize" others, to spread American values and outlooks, and to bring the benefits of the American way of life to others. Foreign trade was thus an adjunct to the religious missionary undertakings that were so prevalent in the late nineteenth century. It also coincided with America's returning sense of mission and the underlying principle of morality.[6] As a consequence, many idealists of the period favored trade.

Others saw foreign trade as a symbol of greatness and proof that the United States was becoming a leading power. With international rivalry and competition being hallmarks of late nineteenth century international life, expanding foreign trade was a profitable and visible way to prove that one's country was a world leader. Those who in later periods would be called realists also therefore favored trade.

Still others saw foreign trade as a way that the United States could extend its political influence without the messiness of occupation, colonization, and control. Influence followed economics, many believed, and if American political influence followed in the wake of foreign trade, so much the better. U.S. influence could therefore be acquired, some reasoned, without the need to control a colonial empire. The United States could enjoy the benefits of empire without the costs of imperial control or compromising morality as a principle. Most Americans, then, idealists and realists alike, saw foreign trade as a good thing, and for many reasons.

Trade also had two other major implications for U.S. foreign policy. The first concerned the U.S. Navy. As American trading interests became increasingly large and global, questions arose about how the United States could defend its shipping. Few U.S. leaders in the late nineteenth century wanted to rely on Great Britain's Royal Navy to police and protect international trading lanes, especially given their mistrust of Great Britain brought about by British neutrality during the Civil War and Great Britain's construction of commerce raiders for the Confederacy. In addition, many Americans accepted the maxim that great nations had great navies. The United States had become a great nation, they argued, and therefore the United States had to build a great navy.

Although the U.S. Navy had been built up during the Civil War, by the 1880s it had atrophied. Many ships had been retired, and few new ones were built. As sentiment grew for a **U.S. naval build-up,** Congress responded, funding over 30 new cruisers and battleships between 1883 and 1889 alone. The new ships were made of steel and powered by steam, designed to provide the United States a global naval capability. Congress and the Department of the Navy strengthened support for the build-up by naming cruisers after cities and battleships after states, a practice that continued until after World War II. By 1893, the U.S. Navy was the seventh most powerful in the world.[7]

The United States was not alone in its naval build-up. In the late nineteenth century, many great powers were influenced by the work of Captain **Alfred Thayer Mahan,** an instructor at the U.S. Naval War College. Mahan's 1890 book, *The Influence of Sea Power upon History,* persuaded many that powerful navies were the source of national power, prestige, and empire.[8] Although the global naval race would doubtless have occurred even without Mahan's book, it laid the intellectual foundation for the naval arms build-up of the late nineteenth and early twentieth century.

The second implication of trade flowed directly from the need for a navy. In the late nineteenth century, most naval vessels were fueled by coal. If naval vessels were to operate far from their home ports, they required fueling stations. Inevitably, then, some Americans began to covet lands remote from the United States because of the need for coaling stations. Like other countries in the 1880s and 1890s, the United States was slowly seduced by the idea of empire.

Regional and Global Interests

The post–Civil War expansion of American regional and global interests began slowly enough. As a general rule, in the 25 years between 1870 and 1895, the United States followed in the wake of European states as they extended their influence in and control of China, carved up Africa, and extended their colonial empires wherever else they could. The United States, interested at first not in extending its own control of territory but in expanding its trade and whatever influence trade brought with it, proceeded cautiously.

For example, in China, the United States "proved" its moralism, idealism, and support for the rule of law by verbally opposing British and French **gunboat diplomacy**— the threat to use naval force to enforce a policy. Even so, the United States followed in the wake of the British and French to expand American trade and influence whenever an opportunity presented itself. American missionaries also played an active role in China, spreading American views of Christianity and Western values.[9] The United States also kept a squadron of warships in the western Pacific, the Asiatic Squadron, to defend American interests.

Despite these activities, U.S. interests in China and the rest of Asia were relatively small. U.S. trade with Asia totaled only 5 percent of the American trade turnover in the late 1890s, and even though U.S. missionaries in China received extensive publicity, no more than a thousand toiled in China in the late 1890s. Africa received even less American interest as European powers carved the continent into colonies.

But this did not mean that the United States was not interested in expanding its influence or obtaining overseas sites for coaling stations. Rather than Asia or Africa, U.S. interest focused on Hawaii, Samoa, and Latin America.

In 1875, the United States concluded a treaty with Hawaii that promised Hawaii could export sugar to the United States without a tariff or duty if Hawaii refused trade concessions to other countries. By this time, much of the Hawaiian sugar industry was controlled by Americans, several of whom were sons of Protestant missionaries who had earlier come to Hawaii to "civilize" Hawaiians. When Congress in 1890 changed the sugar laws to give preference to domestic sugar producers, these Americans revolted against Hawaiian Queen Liliuokalani, deposing her in 1893 so the United States could annex Hawaii and Hawaiian sugar could be subsidized as a domestic product. President Grover Cleveland, although an expansionist, refused to support **Hawaiian annexation,** since he opposed annexation by force. Queen Liliuokalani was released from prison but not restored to her throne, and the American revolutionaries remained in power. Hawaiian annexation was delayed until 1898, when the Spanish-American War increased the strategic value of the Hawaiian Islands.[10]

Samoa experienced a different fate. The United States, Germany, and Great Britain were all interested in the islands, even though the U.S. Senate in 1878 ratified a treaty with a Samoan chief that gave the United States rights to build a naval station and to intercede in Samoan disputes with other countries. A 1887 conference between the three countries failed to resolve lingering disagreements, and Germany landed troops in Samoa. Congress quickly authorized funds to protect American lives and property in Samoa. Fearing that the **Samoan crisis** was out of control, the three countries met again in 1889, this time splitting Samoa into three parts, one each for Germany, Great Britain, and the United States. Although the agreement was later revised to include only Germany and the United States, with Great Britain receiving islands elsewhere in the Pacific, the United States had begun to obtain a permanent presence in the Pacific.[11]

As important as U.S. interests in Hawaii and Samoa were, they paled in comparison to **U.S. interests in Latin America.** After the 1867 fall of French-installed Emperor Maximilian in Mexico, U.S. investment poured into Mexico, especially in mining and railroads, and U.S.-Mexican trade expanded. U.S trade with and investments in Cuba also grew significantly, primarily in sugar and mining. Also, after Great Britain opened the Suez Canal in Egypt in 1869, American interest in building a canal across Central America grew, with Panama and Nicaragua regarded as the most probable sites.

The frequency of American gunboat diplomacy and military intervention in Latin America illustrates the importance of the region to the United States and the extent to which the United States was willing and able to project power there. In 1873 and 1885, the United States landed troops in Panama, at the time part of Colombia, to protect American interests. In 1885, a U.S. warship intimidated Guatemala after Guatemala invaded El Salvador and threatened U.S. economic interests there. In 1891, the United States sent a ship to Chile to protect American lives and property during a civil war there. After the war, shore leave for the ship's crew deteriorated into a brawl that left two sailors dead and threatened to lead to an American-Chilean conflict. In 1893–1894, the United States' South Atlantic Squadron broke a blockade that rebels had imposed on Rio de Janeiro during a civil war in Brazil.[12]

By the mid-1890s, American power had grown steadily for more than two decades. Confident in their prosperity, convinced that their political institutions were superior to those that existed anywhere else in the world, and pleased that the country was again becoming united, most Americans were again confident that their country had a special role in the world and that it served as an example for other countries. It was prosperous, it was confident, and it was democratic, and even though it intervened overseas on occasion, it rarely extended its political control outside its own territory except by treaty.

Meanwhile, economic prosperity and defending U.S. interests remained key U.S. foreign policy concerns. Trade was important to American prosperity, and the combination of expanding trade and changing naval technologies convinced some Americans, especially realists and those supporting international involvement, that the United States needed to acquire coaling stations overseas to protect trade routes. Pragmatically, Americans traded with whomever they could, and few Americans thought that either trade or acquiring coaling stations contradicted either morality or isolationism, especially if coaling stations were acquired via diplomacy. And as before, the United States acted unilaterally, striving to obtain and defend its interests as it saw fit.

These trends in U.S. foreign policy by the mid-1890s divided Americans into three major schools of thought. The first, probably the largest, was proud of these activities and concluded that the United States had not abandoned the principles upon which it had based its foreign policy. Even though the United States was a major trading nation, this school observed, it remained by 1895 isolated from most of the political and diplomatic intrigue found in Europe and elsewhere. And the United States, proponents pointed out, rarely sought colonies or other overseas holdings. As Secretary of State James G. Blaine said, the United States did not seek the annexation of territory, but rather the "annexation of trade."[13] Further, this school argued that American morality was illustrated by the United States' hesitancy to acquire overseas territory, and that when the United States intervened in the Pacific or Latin America, its actions were morally justified. This view in the mid-twentieth century received the name "imperial anti-colonialism."[14]

A second school of thought, which in the 1890s came to be called **anti-imperialism,** was critical of the new assertiveness and acquisitiveness in U.S. foreign policy. It claimed that the United States was abandoning the moral high ground that had marked much of previous U.S. policy, and it believed that the United States' new assertiveness indicated it had abandoned isolationism. Anti-imperialists were not pleased by either direction of policy, but in the 1870s and 1880s, they were few in number.

The third school of thought argued that the United States should adopt an even more aggressive and expansionistic foreign policy than it was already pursuing. This school's advocates were convinced that the United States needed more foreign markets in which to sell surplus products and that the United States needed overseas naval bases rather than coaling stations to defend trading lanes that led to the markets. They knew that other powers of the day were engaged in imperial conquests in Africa, the Middle East, and Asia, and that those conquests were seen as proof of national power. In short, they preferred that the United States adopt a foreign policy that for all practical purposes was classic imperialism.[15]

By the mid-1890s, advocates of the third school of thought increasingly directed U.S. foreign policy, and overseas intervention increasingly became a hallmark of U.S. foreign policy, justified, according to some, by the American mission and morality, and, according to others, by the need for the United States to take its rightful place as a Great Power. As the United States became imperialist in earnest, the domestic debate over American imperialism also heated up.

IMPERIALISM IN EARNEST: 1895–1900

Between 1895 and 1890, the United States initiated a confrontation with Great Britain over Venezuela, defeated Spain in a conflict over Cuba and acquired an overseas empire, fought against an insurrection in one of its new colonies, and declared an "Open Door" policy in China to defend and expand its commercial interests there. As these adventures unfolded, a heated debate erupted between Americans who supported and those who opposed the United States' imperial policies. As a result, the contradictions between the competing themes of isolationism and involvement, and idealism and realism, reached levels of controversy rarely before seen.

The Venezuela Crisis

The United States' 1895 confrontation with Great Britain was over a dispute between Great Britain and Venezuela about the border between Venezuela and Great Britain's colony of British Guiana. Great Britain and Venezuela had disagreed about the border for decades, but in the early 1890s, London became more assertive. When Great Britain landed troops in Nicaragua in 1895, President Grover Cleveland feared that Great Britain's imperial grasp was expanding. Although Great Britain soon withdrew from Nicaragua, the Venezuela situation concerned the president, and not only because of British imperial intentions.

Trade and commerce were also at issue, since British territorial claims included the mouth of the Orinoco River. If Great Britain acquired control of the river mouth, it could close the river, depriving American trading interests of access to northern South America. With the United States mired in an economic depression and with foreign trade seen as a way to stimulate economic growth, Cleveland believed he could not allow this to occur.

The president's political reputation was also on the line. Cleveland's Democratic Party had lost badly in the 1894 mid-term congressional elections, so he needed a political success to restore his credibility. In addition, pro-expansion Republicans criticized him for opposing the annexation of Hawaii, and some chastised him because they believed Great Britain's actions in Nicaragua and pressure on Venezuela compromised the Monroe Doctrine. Congress also pressured Cleveland to act on Venezuela when, in early 1895, it unanimously passed a resolution asking that Great Britain and Venezuela submit their dispute to arbitration.

From Cleveland's perspective, there were many reasons to act. Thus, he ordered Secretary of State Richard Olney to craft a memorandum to Great Britain, the final version of which demanded arbitration, hinted at American intervention if Great Britain refused, and insisted on an answer before the end of the year. Invoking a confrontational interpretation of the Monroe Doctrine, the **Olney Memorandum** declared that:

> The states of America, South as well as North, by geographical proximity, by natural sympathy, by similarities of governmental constitutions, are friends and allies, commercially and politically, of the United States. . . . Today the United States is practically sovereign on this continent, and its fiat is law. . . . [The United States'] infinite resources combined with its isolated position render it master of the situation and practically invulnerable as against any or all other powers.[16]

Underestimating Cleveland's seriousness, Great Britain studied the memorandum for several months before declaring the Monroe Doctrine did not apply. The British response also denied that the United States had any interests in the dispute. Cleveland was livid, delivering a message to Congress in which he declared that the United States intended to establish a commission to determine the true boundary, that the boundary would become fact through arbitration, and that American action would enforce it.[17] To many, this appeared an ultimatum. A mild dispute had escalated into the **Venezuelan Crisis.**

In reality, neither the United States nor Great Britain wanted war. Cleveland's intent was to lay down a marker of U.S. influence and to make sure that he personally appeared assertive.[18] Great Britain wanted to make sure that the United States did not undermine British interests, and was in reality more concerned with Germany's growing naval strength and in resolving a crisis in South Africa than in confronting the United States over a South American colonial boundary. Both sides had miscalculated, so with no one wanting war, the two sides in 1896 began negotiations to resolve the dispute, establishing a commission that in 1899 settled the disagreement for the most part in Venezuela's favor. No Venezuelans served on the commission.

Although the crisis was peacefully resolved, it set several U.S foreign policy precedents. First, the United States exhibited a new boldness that reappeared frequently in future years. Second, the United States declared itself the arbiter of Western Hemisphere issues to an extent far greater than earlier, the Monroe Doctrine not withstanding. What is more, Great Britain, the world's leading power, accepted this. Third, Cleveland thrust the presidency forward as the central actor in foreign policy at the expense of Congress. Finally, American public sentiment rallied behind presidential leadership in foreign policy in a way rarely seen earlier. The statements of nationalism and pride that flourished in support of the U.S. positions were tagged **jingoism,** a term used to describe such sentiments even today.

Cuba and the Spanish-American War

The Venezuelan dispute was not the only crisis in the region in 1895 and 1896. In 1895, after 15 years of exile in the United States, Cuban nationalist **Jose Marti** led a force of revolutionaries back to the island to try to win Cuban independence from Spain. No friend of the United States,[19] Marti set in motion events that led to the 1898 Spanish-American War and the United States' acquisition of a small global empire.

Cuba was no stranger to revolution and warfare. Although the island did not join the revolutionary wave that gained independence from Spain for most of Latin America earlier in the century, sporadic slave revolts erupted in Cuba during the 1830s and 1840s. Then, in 1851, a Spanish military officer gained support from pro-slavery American elements and launched an invasion of Cuba from the United States that failed. Between 1868 and 1878, Cuban-born Spaniards, called **Creoles,** led a bloody but unsuccessful revolt against their motherland. Throughout these years, the United States kept a close eye on Cuban affairs, first driven by pro-slavery southern political and business leaders who saw Cuba as a potential slave state, and then after the Civil War by pro-expansion leaders from all parts of the United States.

Spain's victory in the Creole war did not end the Creoles' desire for independence. When Marti invaded, many joined him, intending to win independence by making the island an economic liability to Spain by burning crops and destroying property. By 1896, the revolutionaries controlled over 60 percent of Cuba. Desperate to maintain control, Spain's governor general initiated his own scorched-earth policy. Worse, he removed most of the population to concentration camps where brutality, suffering, and death reigned supreme. By late 1896, because of both Spanish and insurrectionist activities, once-rich Cuba was a human and economic disaster.

The Cuban revolution and its brutality gave Cleveland no good policy options. If he recognized Cuban independence, Spain might declare war on the United States, a war that Cleveland did not want. Cleveland also opposed recognizing Cuban independence because he did not believe that the Cuban insurgents could rule effectively and because

U.S. recognition of Cuba meant that any Spanish effort to maintain control of Cuba would be a violation of the Monroe Doctrine. Recognizing Cuban independence therefore was not a viable choice.

On the other hand, inaction was not wise. The revolt and Spain's effort to quell it were destroying U.S. property. The brutality of the fighting and the concentration camps also appalled many Americans. In addition, Congress threatened to take matters into its own hands, first passing in 1896 a resolution calling on Cleveland to recognize a state of belligerency between Cuba and Spain and then in early 1897 developing a congressional resolution that recognized Cuban independence.

Faced with no good option, Cleveland had Secretary of State Olney send a memorandum to Spain informing it that the United States preferred continued Spanish control of Cuba with autonomy and home rule for the island. Spain rejected Olney's memorandum. Cleveland in his 1896 end-of-year address to Congress therefore declared that Spain had to grant home rule but not independence to Cuba so that bloodshed would end and so that property and trade would be protected. Cleveland implied that the United States would end its restraint toward the conflict if its demands were not met.[20]

Cleveland left the presidency in early 1897 having avoided war with Spain and having staked out the U.S. position. The new president, William McKinley, held many of Cleveland's foreign policy views despite being in a different party: overseas expansion was desirable but war should be avoided; the United States because of its superior political system, economic strength, and culture had a major role to play in Latin America; the Cuban situation should be resolved according to U.S. wishes but without direct military involvement. Unlike his predecessor, McKinley could not keep the United States out of war.

Throughout 1897, various members of Congress proposed resolutions ranging from condemnation of Spain to recognition of Cuba. McKinley prevented their passage, relying on diplomacy and sending a demand to Spain, insisting that the fighting in Cuba stop. A new Spanish government responded by instituting reforms in Cuba in late 1897 and providing the island some home rule, but fighting continued. Thus, in his 1897 end-of-year message to Congress, McKinley expressed "gravest apprehension" about Cuba. Conversely, he sought to quiet pro-war jingoism by declaring that it would be a "criminal injustice" if the United States annexed Cuba and by advocating that Spain be given time to resolve the situation. Still, McKinley said, all policy options, including intervening "with force," remained open.[21]

In early 1898, three events accelerated the slide toward war. First, Spain's Cuban reforms were failing. Second, the Spanish minister to the United States wrote a letter to a Spanish politician that implied that the Cuban reforms were a ruse and that described McKinley as "weak."[22] Intercepted in Cuba by a supporter of the revolution and sent to the State Department and William Randolph Hearst's jingoistic newspaper *New York Journa'*, the letter infuriated Americans. Third, the battleship U.S.S. *Maine,* sent to Havana in January to show U.S. concern and protect American citizens, blew up and sank in February in Havana harbor. What happened to the *Maine* is debated even today,[23] but most Americans in 1898 believed that it was sunk by Spain.

War sentiment built rapidly, but McKinley still opted for diplomacy, sending an ultimatum to Spain that demanded an armistice and U.S. arbitration of the conflict and that implied only Cuban independence was acceptable. Spain accepted some provisions but rejected U.S. arbitration and Cuban independence. By late April, the United States and

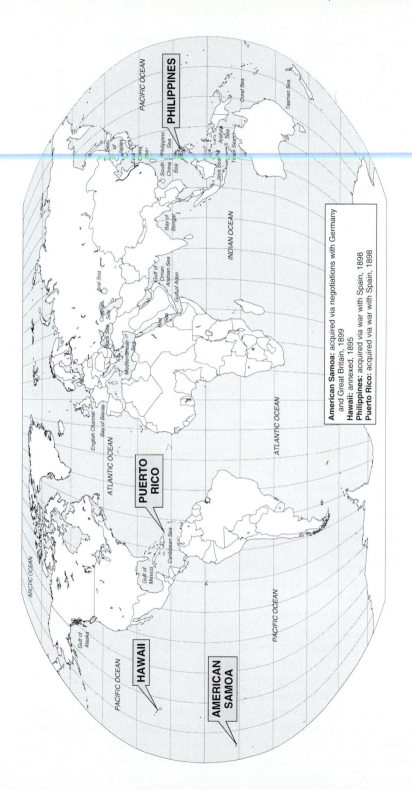

MAP 4.1
American Overseas Territorial Acquisitions: **1889–1899**

Spain were at war, with Congress having passed the **Teller Amendment,** which declared that the United States would not annex Cuba.

The three-and-a-half month **Spanish-American War** was not much of a conflict. In May, the U.S. Asiatic Squadron destroyed the Spanish fleet in Manila harbor in the Philippines. In June, U.S. forces invaded Cuba. By mid-August, Spanish resistance in the Philippines, Cuba, and Puerto Rico, which the United States had also invaded, ended. Meanwhile, in July, the United States annexed Hawaii, still ruled by the same Americans who had tried but failed to convince Cleveland to annex the islands. With war underway in the Pacific, Hawaii was an excellent way station on the sea lane to the Philippines.[24]

After several months of negotiations, Spain and the United States concluded a peace agreement, the Treaty of Paris, in which Cuba received independence and Spain transferred ownership of the Philippines and Puerto Rico to the United States for $20 million. The treaty generated intense debate in the United States, barely winning passage in the Senate by a vote of 57 to 27. The Spanish-American War was over, Cuba was independent, and the United States had imperial holdings in the Caribbean and the Pacific.

Issues in Asia

Like other imperial powers, the United States soon found that empires bring costs as well as benefits. The United States first experienced this truth in the Philippines.

When the United States acquired the Philippines, it ignored the Filipinos' pleas for independence, even though they had borne the brunt of the land fighting in the Philippines during the Spanish-American War. Indeed, the Filipinos had begun fighting for their independence from Spain in 1896. Not surprisingly, Filipino rebels, led by Emilio Aguinaldo, soon turned their ire and weapons against their new overlords, the Americans, most of whom considered Filipinos racially inferior and incapable of governing themselves.

In 1899, Aguinaldo proclaimed the Philippine Republic and took up arms against the occupying American forces. For over two years, U.S. forces fought to put down the **Philippine insurrection,** losing over 5,000 troops. Filipinos suffered far worse as 200,000 people died. American soldiers and Filipino insurgents alike committed appalling atrocities. Although the United States reestablished control by 1902, sporadic guerrilla warfare continued until 1914.

Outside the Philippines, the United States found itself drawn into Chinese affairs. American business people had long seen China as a potentially immense market, and American missionaries had long viewed China as ripe ground for missionary work. By the mid-1890s, these visions were still more dreams than reality, but as European states and Japan partitioned China after China's defeat in the 1895 Sino-Japanese War, the United States became increasingly concerned that its traders and missionaries would be excluded from the new European zones of influence in China.

The U.S. reaction was to appeal in 1899 to France, Germany, Great Britain, Italy, Japan, and Russia to accept and promote equal trade opportunities for all states in their spheres of influence in China. The various states responded to the proposal in various ways, but no one rejected it completely. Thus, the United States proclaimed that an **Open Door policy** was in place in China that enabled all countries to trade in all enclaves in China.

But all was not well in China. In 1900, the Boxers, a secret society whose goal was to throw Westerners out of China and restore Chinese control, rose against Western business people and missionaries, killing hundreds. The Boxers then lay siege to Western embassies in Beijing. Responding to the **Boxer Rebellion,** Western states sent 15,500 troops to Beijing to break the siege, including 2,500 American soldiers. The rationale for the U.S. involvement was to protect "equal and impartial trade" in China and preserve China as a "territorial and administrative entity."[25] The siege was soon broken.

The Debate over Empire

The United States' move toward global empire in the late 1890s was not universally applauded within the United States. The ensuing **debate over empire** revolved around three views that were similar to the views debated in the 1870s and 1880s over expanding American overseas interests. Anti-imperialists opposed overseas expansion, pragmatists supported the growth of America's overseas presence and influence if it was primarily obtained via trade and commerce, and imperialists believed that the United States should strive to develop an overseas empire through almost any means possible to establish its position once and for all as a great power. The conflicts between isolationism and involvement, and between what would later be called idealism and realism, dominated the disagreements between these outlooks.[26]

Anti-imperialists such as writer Mark Twain, politician William Jennings Bryan, labor leader Samuel Gompers, and others in the U.S. Congress and general population protested that the United States had compromised or even abandoned the ideals on which it was founded and the proclaimed morality that had been a basis for American foreign policy. They argued that when the United States subjugated others to its rule as it had in the Philippines, Samoa, and Hawaii, it violated the very principles on which it had been founded. They pointed out that even if it did not take and hold territory, when the United States intervened at will in Latin America and Asia, it was behaving internationally exactly like the European powers that in earlier years it had criticized and condemned. Objecting to the treaty that ended the Spanish-American War and to other U.S. imperial behavior, they organized the **Anti-Imperialist League** in 1898, which argued that the United States had abandoned both moralism and isolationism as underlying principles in its foreign policy. But they never had enough political strength to change U.S. foreign policy.

Still, the influence that anti-imperialists had in domestic politics in the United States in the late 1890s should not be underestimated. For example, as we have seen, the treaty that ended the Spanish-American War and provided the United States with most of its imperial holdings barely received the required two-thirds of the votes required for passage, 57–27.

Others Americans such as Grover Cleveland, industrialist Andrew Carnegie, and other business leaders took a pragmatic view. They were comfortable with expanding American overseas influence and presence through trade and commerce but not through military conquest, war, and subterfuge. This, it will be recalled, was why Cleveland refused to annex Hawaii during his presidency. Similarly, Andrew Carnegie believed that the overseas expansion of U.S. influence through trade was desirable, but he was so opposed to the acquisition of the Philippines through military force that he offered to pay

Spain $20 million himself to assure Philippine independence. This, ironically, was how much the United States paid Spain at the end of the Spanish-American War to acquire the Philippines and Puerto Rico.

Despite these moderate dissenting voices, imperialists such as Theodore Roosevelt and eventually William McKinley determined policy and held sway over public opinion. Even before becoming president, Roosevelt was a bombastic imperialist, believing that it was the United States' destiny to become a world power and that the United States had to act like a world power. McKinley, as we have seen, was more reluctant, seeking first to expand U.S. influence through trade and diplomacy, but then moving into the imperialist camp.

Imperialists based their desire for territorial acquisition and conquest on economics, a belief in national destiny, and pride. Many also applauded the idea of the **white man's burden,** a belief that whites were superior to other races and had a responsibility to "civilize," "educate," and "Christianize" them. Racism thus mixed with a changed sense of mission to play a major role in driving U.S. policy during the late nineteenth and twentieth centuries. In a sense, it may be argued that this new mission and economic interests combined to supplant the principles of moralism and isolationism as they had been traditionally interpreted in the United States.

By the beginning of the twentieth century, the United States was a powerful country with global interests. It produced over 30 percent of the world's manufactured products, more than any other country. Even though most U.S. trade was with Europe, American businesses operated around the world. The American armed forces were sizeable enough to be deployed in the Caribbean, in Latin America, in Asia, and elsewhere. As the twentieth century dawned, the United States was on the verge of becoming a world power that rivaled established European powers, but not many realized it.

EXPANDING AND CONSOLIDATING THE EMPIRE: 1900–1914

By the time Theodore Roosevelt became president in 1901, the United States was well embarked on its journey down the imperial path. No one was more "qualified" than Roosevelt to accelerate America's expansion and consolidate its empire.

Roosevelt was a man of many talents and interests. Born into a wealthy East Coast family, he was a writer, orator, big-game hunter, military leader, international strategist, and politician. As assistant secretary of the navy during the 1890s, he planned naval strategy, lectured at the Naval War College, and became friends with Alfred Thayer Mahan. As governor of New York, he identified with the progressive movement and instituted social reforms because he feared that social and economic inequities within the United States would undermine American strength. A firm believer in the white man's burden, Roosevelt argued that "civilized" countries, particularly the United States, had responsibilities as the world's police and to intervene to establish order.[27] As he told Congress in 1902: "More and more the increasing interdependence and complexity of international political and economic relations render it incumbent on all civilized and orderly powers to insist on the proper policing of the world."[28]

As president from 1901 to 1909, Roosevelt set the tone for twentieth-century U.S. foreign policy before World War I. Even though Roosevelt's successors, William Howard Taft and Woodrow Wilson, were not as flamboyant as Roosevelt, they often pursued interventionist foreign policies reminiscent of him. As Europe slid toward war at the start of the twentieth century, U.S. political, economic, and military interests in Latin America and Asia expanded.

Latin American Interests and Interventions

Nowhere were American interests more sizeable and interventions more frequent than in Latin America. This was especially true in and around the Caribbean Sea, where the United States had several reasons for its interests and interventions.

First, U.S. businesses and private individuals had extensive holdings in Cuba, Mexico, and other countries in the region. By 1913, U.S. investments in Cuba surpassed $200 million. This was dwarfed by the $1.5 billion that Americans invested in Mexico. Sometimes praised and sometimes decried as **dollar diplomacy,** American investments played a major role in U.S. foreign policy toward the region and in furthering U.S. interests.

Second, after Europe, the countries of the Caribbean littoral were collectively the second most important U.S. trading partner. Mexico and Cuba again led the way, with U.S. imports from Cuba totaling over $130 million in 1914. Along with U.S. investments in the region, trade was an integral part of American dollar diplomacy.

Third, the United States' sense of racial and cultural superiority influenced the United States to believe that several regional states such as Cuba, the Dominican Republic, Haiti, Nicaragua, and Venezuela were not able to run their economies or govern themselves. Many Americans therefore concluded that these countries would benefit from American tutelage, presence, and control.

Fourth, the United States was concerned that Germany or another European power might use the inability of countries in the region, especially Venezuela or the Dominican Republic, to pay debts as a pretext for military occupation. If this occurred, many Americans believed, the Monroe Doctrine would be compromised and Germany or another occupying power might present a strategic military threat to the United States from the Caribbean.

Fifth, the United States eyed Panama and Nicaragua as potential sites to build a canal through Central America to join the Atlantic and Pacific oceans. A canal would provide the United States with economic and strategic advantages, cut the cost of shipping between the United States' east and west coasts, and allow the U.S. Navy to move ships between the Atlantic and Pacific without having to go around the southern tip of South America.

Theodore Roosevelt artfully wove his views of how and why the United States might have to intervene in the region to protect its interests into the **Roosevelt Corollary** to the Monroe Doctrine. After early in his presidency accepting the view that European countries could punish irresponsible financial behavior on the part of Western Hemispheric states, Roosevelt became concerned that Germany and Great Britain might have ulterior motives for their actions. Roosevelt's concerns were generated by events in Venezuela and the Dominican Republic between 1902 and 1904.

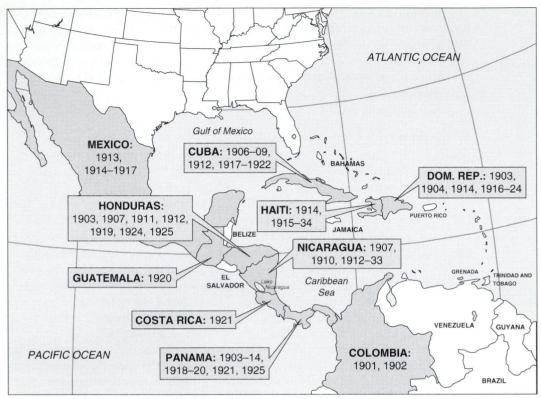

MAP 4.2
American Interventions in Mexico, Latin American, and the Caribbean: 1900–1925

Venezuela owed German and British investors over $15 million and regularly deferred repayment. By late 1902, both European powers had had enough. After first gaining U.S. approval, Germany and Great Britain delivered an ultimatum to Venezuela, bombarded two Venezuelan forts, captured several Venezuelan ships, and imposed a blockade until the money they were due was repaid. In early 1903, German warships attacked two more Venezuelan forts.

The 1903 attacks were more than Roosevelt was willing to accept. He quietly sent a note to Germany, demanding that the attacks cease; he also dispatched an American fleet to the Caribbean for maneuvers. Soon thereafter, Germany and Great Britain lifted the blockade and submitted their dispute with Venezuela to the Permanent Court at the Hague for settlement.

This incident as well as a continuing financial crisis in the Dominican Republic that Roosevelt feared might also lead to German intervention prompted the president in 1904 to proclaim the Roosevelt Corollary to the Monroe Doctrine. According to the Corollary:

> If a nation shows that it knows how to act with decency in industrial and political matters, if it keeps order and pays its obligations, then it need fear no interference from the

United States. Brutal wrong-doing, or an impotence which results in a general loosening of the ties of civilized society, may finally require intervention by some civilized nation, and in the Western Hemisphere the United States might act as a policeman, at least in the Caribbean region.[29]

As important as the Roosevelt Corollary was, the United States even before it was proclaimed practiced many of the policies that it prescribed, most forcefully with Cuba. Cuba had been occupied by American forces at the end of the Spanish-American War and promised independence by the United States as soon as it could put a stable government into place. However, Cuba recovered slowly from the devastation that had been inflicted on it during the 1895–1898 Creole-Spanish war and the ensuing Spanish-American War, even though the U.S. military governor, General Leonard Wood, built highways, improved the health and educational systems, and established a considerable degree of order on the island.

Cuban independence was delayed not only by U.S. concern about stability in Cuba but also by the Philippine insurrection. Uncertain about the Cuban government and fearing that a pro-independence revolution might erupt in Cuba as one had in the Philippines, the U.S. Senate in 1901 passed the **Platt Amendment,** which declared that Cuba could not make a treaty with any country that might weaken its independence. The amendment also gave the United States the right to intervene if "life, property, and individual liberty" were threatened and provided the United States in perpetuity land needed to build a naval station, what is today the Guantanamo Bay Navy Base.[30] Despite Cuban objections to the Platt Amendment, the amendment was added to the Cuban constitution in 1901. It became a treaty between the United States and Cuba in 1903.

Heavily dependent on U.S. investment and trade, and with the United States maintaining the right to intervene in Cuban affairs almost whenever it desired, Cuba had obtained independence, but it was independence in name only. And intervene the United States did, first from 1906 to 1909 when Roosevelt dispatched 5,000 U.S. troops to the island to help support a U.S.-installed government. President Taft returned American troops to Cuba again in 1912 when revolution threatened. In 1917, President Wilson ordered U.S. forces ashore to protect Cuba and American investments in Cuba from the possibility of a feared German attack. Cuba was an American protectorate in fact if not in name, a status that it labored under until 1934, when the Platt Amendment was repealed.[31]

Cuba was not the only country in the region that owed its "independence" to the United States. So, too, did Panama, a part of Colombia until 1903. **Panamanian independence** was a result of a plot initiated by a small group of Panamanians and Americans living in Panama and carried out with the full knowledge and support of the U.S. government. The plot had been hatched earlier in 1903 after the Colombian legislature rejected a proposed U.S.-Colombian treaty that would have given the United States the right to build a canal across the Isthmus of Panama to join the Atlantic and Pacific Oceans.

Displeased that the legislature's action prevented them from benefiting from a canal, the plotters developed a scheme to separate Panama from Colombia. Having communicated their intentions to U.S. representatives, the plotters were pleased when a U.S. naval vessel arrived shortly before the plot was to be initiated. The actual revolution took place without the active involvement of the United States, and American troops were not landed after the Panamanian-American junta had the situation under control and declared independence. Even so, everyone understood that the United States had promoted the plot, supported the plot, and would benefit from the plot.[32]

Pleased with American support and recognizing that a canal through Panama would provide a good source of income, the new Panamanian government created a special canal zone over which the United States received "power and authority" as "if it were the sovereign of the territory," with the U.S. control of the canal zone extending "in perpetuity."[33] The U.S. Senate passed the treaty in 1904, 66 to 14. Construction on the **Panama Canal** began later in 1904 and took ten years. Roosevelt, ever the strategist, considered his support for Panamanian independence and the building of the Panama Canal his greatest foreign policy accomplishment.

With extensive economic and political interests throughout the Caribbean and the countries whose shores bordered its water, the United States used its superior force and sense of righteous purpose to intervene on numerous occasions in numerous other countries in the region. U.S. troops were ashore in Nicaragua from 1909 to 1910, from 1912 to 1925, and again from 1926 to 1933. The United States also supervised the country's financial affairs from 1911 to 1924. American armed forces occupied Haiti from 1915 to 1934, and the United States controlled its finances from 1916 to 1941. In the Dominican Republic, U.S. troops landed in 1916 and stayed until 1924. The United States also financially supervised the country for most of the time between 1905 and 1941. U.S. troops also landed in Honduras in 1924, although they stayed only a year.

Meanwhile, the United States developed naval bases in Puerto Rico and at Guantanamo Bay in Cuba. In 1917, the United States purchased the Danish Virgin Islands. By 1920, with Great Britain accepting American preeminence in the Caribbean and the German navy having been eliminated by World War I, the Caribbean was for all practical purposes an American-controlled lake. With extensive economic and political interests in the region and both the ability and the willingness to intervene amply demonstrated, it is little wonder that, by the 1920s, the countries of the region regarded the United States as the domineering "Colossus of the North."[34]

The United States in Mexico

The United States was also deeply involved in Mexican affairs. After France's venture to install Austrian Archduke Maximilian as emperor of Mexico failed in 1867 with Maximilian's death before a Mexican firing squad, **Porfirio Diaz** seized power and ruled as Mexican dictator from 1876 until 1911. During Diaz's rule, Mexicans had no political freedom, but the country experienced unprecedented stability.

U.S.-Mexican relations were also cordial, and American businesses and private interests poured over a billion dollars of investment into Mexico during these years, especially in mining, railroads, and port development. By the early twentieth century, Americans owned over 40 percent of all Mexican property. Mexican-American trade had grown impressively as well.

The United States in 1904 promoted and protected Panama's independence from Colombia. For its efforts, the United States received the Canal Zone from Panama. In 1914, the Panama Canal opened, linking the Atlantic and Pacific oceans and cutting weeks off the travel time between the east and west coasts of the United States. This reduced the cost of trade and allowed the United States to move naval vessels rapidly from one ocean to another. Here, the U.S.S. Severn transits the Panama Canal in 1914.

In 1910, a revolution broke out in Mexico, and Diaz was overthrown the following year. Eventually General **Victoriano Huerta** emerged as Mexico's leader, but civil war continued in much of the country as many Mexicans refused to accept his rule. American lives were lost and property destroyed during the fighting, but President Taft resolved not to intervene. After assuming the presidency in 1913, Wilson at first followed Taft's non-interventionist policy, observing that his government was "not the servant of those who wish to enhance the value of their Mexican investments."[35]

Despite his non-interventionist preference, Wilson was concerned about Mexico's civil war. Believing that he knew better than the Mexicans how to resolve the fighting, Wilson proposed an armistice between all factions in Mexico to be followed by a free election with Huerta promising not to run for the presidency. Wilson also pledged that if U.S. advice were followed, the United States would recognize the new government and provide aid. Huerta rejected the proposal, observing that if Mexico heeded U.S. advice, future Mexican presidential elections would be subject to a U.S. veto. Incensed by the response, Wilson embargoed U.S. arms shipments to Mexico and warned Americans to leave. As fighting continued and Huerta became more dictatorial, Wilson concluded that if the United States could not force Huerta from power through diplomacy, "it will become the duty of the United States to use less peaceful means to put him out."[36]

This was easier said than done, even though an incident in the Mexican port city of Tampico in 1914 provided a pretext for the United States to invade. Huerta's troops in Tampico arrested several U.S. sailors who were loading supplies to bring to U.S naval vessels anchored offshore. The sailors were soon released and the commander of the Mexican garrison verbally apologized, but the U.S. commander deemed the verbal apology insufficient, demanding instead a full 21-gun salute. Huerta refused. Wilson immediately asked Congress to authorize the use of armed force against Huerta. When Congress approved, Wilson ordered U.S. marines ashore in Veracruz and Tampico, hoping to undermine support for Huerta. Fighting broke out, and 19 Americans and several hundred Mexicans were killed. Instead of undermining Huerta, the **invasion of Veracruz** increased support for him.

Concerned about the U.S. invasion of Mexico and the fighting in Mexico, Argentina, Brazil, and Chile proposed that they serve as mediators. Wilson accepted the proposal, but mediation failed when the United States refused to discuss the evacuation of Veracruz and Tampico and demanded the end of Huerta's rule in Mexico. Ironically, two weeks after the conference ended, Huerta's government fell and Huerta fled to Europe, not because of the United States but because a Mexican faction under one of Mexico's provincial governors, Venustiano Carranza, drove him from power. Hoping to avoid further fighting, Wilson ordered American forces to quit Veracruz and Tampico, even though the United States did not recognize Carranza's regime.

Peace proved elusive as one of Carranza's generals, **Pancho Villa,** revolted against Carranza. By the end of 1914, Villa occupied Mexico City, but Carranza rallied his forces and counterattacked, driving Villa north. With over 2,500 U.S. citizens in the devastated Mexican capital, Wilson considered ordering U.S. marines to occupy the city, but he decided against it as U.S.-German relations deteriorated, especially after the May 1915 sinking of the *Lusitania*. With U.S. businesses backing Carranza and the United States becoming more concerned about World War I in Europe, Wilson granted Carranza's government provisional recognition and permitted weapons shipments to it, but not to other Mexican factions.

This infuriated Villa, still operating in Mexico's north. Influenced by German agents who found their way to his camp and sought to tie the United States down in a conflict in North American so it could not support the Allies in Europe, Villa denounced Carranza as an American vassal. In March 1916, Villa and his troops crossed the U.S.-Mexican border and attacked Columbus, New Mexico. Seventeen Americans and over a hundred of Villa's men died.

Within hours, Wilson ordered General John Pershing to initiate **Mexican Punitive Expedition.** For almost a year, as many as 7,000 U.S. soldiers chased Villa through Mexico, penetrating 350 miles into Mexico but never finding his main force. On one occasion, U.S. troops fought forces loyal to Carranza. Throughout 1916, Wilson ignored Carranza's demands that U.S. forces be withdrawn, in part because Wilson did not want to appear weak during the 1916 presidential election. Finally, in January 1917, with the United States inching closer to entering World War I in Europe, Wilson ordered Pershing's forces home. By February, American troops were back in the United States.

This did not end the American adventure with Mexico. Later in February, British intelligence provided the U.S. Department of State with a captured note from Germany to Mexico, the **Zimmermann Telegram,** in which Germany proposed that Mexico enter an alliance with Germany and possibly Japan. Germany suggested that if such an alliance were formed, Germany might help Mexico reclaim land it lost to the United States during the 1847–1848 Mexican-American War. Thus, to secure the United States' flank and prevent the possibility of a two-front war, Wilson in August 1917 granted Carranza's government full recognition. For the first time since 1911, the United States and Mexico had complete diplomatic relations.

Nevertheless, Wilson's attitude of superiority toward Mexico, the occupation of Veracruz and Tampico, and the Mexican Punitive Expedition damaged U.S.-Mexican relations. These wounds came on top of the scars from the 1847–1848 Mexican-American War and its settlement.[37] Although Mexico and the United States were neighbors, by the early years of the twentieth century, with the exception of the Diaz years, the history of their relationship was far from happy.[38]

Balancing Act in Asia

Even as the United States extended its empire and consolidated its influence in Latin America and the Caribbean during the first years of the twentieth century, it remained active in Asian affairs. By 1902, the anti-American, pro-independence rebellion in the Philippines was under control, but events elsewhere in Asia demanded American attention.

Despite the Open Door policy that the United States proclaimed in Asia at the end of the nineteenth century, Great Power rivalry in China remained sharp. It was particularly intense between Japan and Russia in China's northern province, Manchuria. In 1904, rivalry exploded into war as the Japanese army and navy inflicted defeats on their Russian counterparts. Even so, by 1905, Japan's treasury had run out of money and its army had been depleted by its victories, so Japan asked the United States to convene a peace conference.

Seeing an opportunity to protect American trading interests in Asia and to reemphasize the sanctity of the Open Door, Roosevelt invited Japan and Russia to send representatives to Portsmouth, New Hampshire. By the end of August 1905, the two sides under Roosevelt's tutelage had fashioned the **Treaty of Portsmouth,** which gave Japan control of Korea, divided Sakhalin Island between Japan and Russia, mandated Russian withdrawal from Manchuria, and gave Russia's lease on the Liaodong Peninsula and the Harbin–Port Arthur railroad to Japan.

The U.S. role as peacemaker in the Russo-Japanese War augured well for future U.S.-Japanese relations, but tension rose when in 1906 and 1907 anti-Japanese legislation was passed and anti-Oriental race riots broke out in California. Roosevelt condemned the legislation and the riots, but Japanese resentment and American anti-Japanese sentiment remained.

Recognizing the potential for more crises with Japan, Roosevelt adopted a two-pronged policy toward the country. First, he stressed the importance of a strong navy by asking Congress to build more battleships and by sending 16 battleships, the "Great White Fleet," on a round-the-world cruise that included Japan. Second, Roosevelt accepted that Japan had special interests in China. Roosevelt's policies bore fruit in the 1908 **Root-Takahira Declaration,** which pledged that each side recognized the other's possessions in the Pacific, accepted that the Pacific was an open and free sealane, and respected equal opportunity for all in China.[39] When Roosevelt left office in 1909, U.S.-Japanese relations were again on an even keel.

This soon changed. Whereas Roosevelt leaned toward Japan, President Taft leaned toward China. Roosevelt sided with Japan for strategic reasons, recognizing that even though he mistrusted Japanese intentions, only Japan could challenge U.S. interests in the Pacific. Taft sided with China because of economic interests. He, like many before, during, and after his time, believed China was an immense market that could be cultivated with immense profit to follow. As a result, Taft's policy toward China sought to protect the Open Door, to enhance commercial access to China, and to protect China's political and territorial integrity. Despite alienating Japan, Taft's policies achieved some success before the Chinese Revolution broke out in 1911, eventually toppling the Manchu dynasty and throwing all foreign interests in China open to question.

Woodrow Wilson also tilted American policy toward China, with the United States in 1913 becoming the first country to recognize the newly proclaimed Chinese Republic. In most respects, Wilson's policy toward China resembled Taft's as the United States sought to expand trade with China even as it supported the civil-war-wracked country's political and territorial integrity. Wilson maintained this policy well into his administration, not conceding until after the United States entered World War I in 1917 that "Japan has special interests in China."[40]

In the early years of the twentieth century, then, the United States performed a balancing act in Asia as it sought to defend its strategic and economic interests there. It was a difficult act, but for the most part, the United States succeeded. Even so, seeds of mistrust were sown that had disastrous results less than three decades later.

Anglo-American Rapprochement and the Prelude to World War I

Throughout the nineteenth century, Anglo-American relations went through alternating periods of tension and amity. Following the 1895 Venezuela Crisis, Anglo-American relations again improved, only in 1903 to run aground on a dispute between Canada and the United States over the Canadian-Alaskan boundary. Roosevelt refused a British proposal for arbitration, instead sending 800 soldiers to

Alaska. Since Great Britain was responsible for Canadian foreign relations, it appeared that when it came to Anglo-American relations, the new century would repeat the pattern of the old one.

The original impression was wrong. Rather than fight, Washington and London agreed to establish a mixed U.S.-British commission to resolve the issue. By the end of the year, the commission decided the dispute in the United States' favor. The last territorial issue between Canada and the United States, or for that matter between Great Britain and the United States, was resolved.

The Alaska settlement issued in a period of **Anglo-American rapprochement,** an era in which Great Britain and the United States found common ground on more and more issues and in which both countries recognized and supported the colonial empires and spheres of influence of the other. When issues arose, as in the 1903 Alaska dispute, the 1902–1903 disagreement over Venezuela's debt to Great Britain and Germany, or the 1905 tension over North Atlantic fisheries, they were usually remanded to a commission or the international tribunal sitting in the Hague. Also, although American policies in Latin America and the Caribbean did not always please Great Britain, London increasingly accepted them. Indeed, in the wake of the 1902–1903 Venezuelan debt issue, Great Britain publicly praised the Monroe Doctrine and the British ambassador told Roosevelt that the United States needed to be prepared to "police the whole American continent."[41] The United States and Great Britain had several reasons for developing a new relationship.

First, the United States by the early twentieth century had become a true world power. Its economy was the largest in the world. Its navy, while not yet a match for Great Britain's Royal Navy, was formidable. Both sides recognized these facts and therefore sought to avoid unnecessary confrontations.

Second, faced with an increasingly ambitious and powerful Germany, Great Britain tried to cultivate the United States as a friend. Reasoning that if the United States policed the Western Hemisphere its own forces could be redeployed to protect the British Empire elsewhere, Great Britain after 1902 reduced its naval presence in the Caribbean to a single flotilla of ships that visited only once a year.

Third, the two countries increasingly believed that their common language and similar cultures bound them together rather than separated them. Given the racial chauvinism of the era, this was understandable. Racism also led both countries to conclude that they served as civilizing influences in the colonial world.

Fourth, the United States and Great Britain each accepted the other's colonial holdings as legitimate and encouraged the other to retain its colonies. Admittedly, the United States often declared that independence was the end objective of colonialism, but only after the colonized peoples had been "civilized" and "educated." The U.S. position thus presented no immediate threat to the British Empire. At the same time, the United States, like Great Britain, ignored the nationalist sentiments of other people who wanted to determine their own future, as shown by U.S. policies toward Cuba, Mexico, the Philippines, Colombia, Panama, Nicaragua, and elsewhere.

A partnership was being forged. Given the strained history of Anglo-American relations, how strong would it be? At the time, no one knew, but it would prove to be one of the most important relationships of the twentieth century.[42]

MISSIONS, INTERESTS, PRINCIPLES, AND COMPETING THEMES AT THE START OF THE TWENTIETH CENTURY

By the beginning of the twentieth century, the United States verged on being a world power. In foreign policy, the country had recovered from the Civil War and adopted activist and imperial policies, especially in Latin America and to a lesser extent Asia. Increasingly, the United States under post–Civil War presidents adopted the stance that its self-proclaimed superior values and institutions not only should be examples for others but also should be selectively imposed on others. Teddy Roosevelt's observation that "the United States might act as a policeman" was considerably different from Thomas Jefferson's view that the United States was "a sanctuary for those whom the misrule of Europe may compel to seek happiness in other climes."

This subtle change in mission, as we have seen, led to extensive debate about whether the United States had abandoned the principles upon which it had originally based its foreign policy. No one disputed that the United States acted unilaterally. Rather, the debate centered on isolationism, moralism, and pragmatism. As for competing themes, involvement clearly dominated isolationism, and realism claimed to co-opt the goals of idealism.

Critics of American policies argued that the United States' acquisition of territory in the Caribbean and the Pacific and its frequent interventions in Latin America proved that the United States had cast aside isolationism and that its control of overseas territory and people showed that it had abandoned moralism. In foreign policy, critics charged, the United States no longer held true to the ideals upon which it was founded.

Defenders of U.S. foreign policy rejected these claims, arguing that despite these examples, isolationism and moralism remained underlying principles of U.S. foreign policy. After all, they pointed out, despite its activism in Latin America and Asia, the United States with only a single exception continued its traditional policy of avoiding entanglement in disputes on the European continent.[43] And, they continued, overseas holdings and frequent interventions were simply moral and pragmatic American efforts to bring the advantages of American values and institutions to other people. The United States may have moved somewhat closer to involvement than isolationism than it had been in earlier years, but it had done so as much because of idealistic as for realistic reasons.

"Pragmatism and moralism?" the critics shot back. If controlling foreign land and people was an example of pragmatism and moralism, then the United States in the early twentieth century had fallen to the same level as Great Britain during the years before the American Revolution. And so in the early years of the twentieth century, the debate over American foreign policy principles raged.

As for U.S. interests, some had changed, and some had remained the same. The United States was no longer an isolated and weak country, as it had been a century before; it was now one of the world's most powerful countries, and many American believed it should seek even more power. With the security of the American homeland assured, the United States employed its military as it saw fit in Asia and Latin America. U.S. economic interests stretched from Europe to Latin America to Asia, and many Americans loudly proclaimed the superiority of their values and institutions. Meanwhile, debate continued over American morality and the extent to which the United States followed international law, and despite the liberation of slaves and the arrival of millions of non-Anglo-Saxon immigrants, the country's cultural identity remained primarily Anglo-Saxon.

All things considered, as Americans surveyed the early twentieth-century world, most liked what they saw. Most believed that their country had a bright future. Disagreement over competing themes remained, as did debate over foreign policy missions, principles, and interests. But to most Americans, this disagreement and debate mattered little.

Meanwhile, storm clouds of war were gathering in Europe. For three years, the United States steered clear of the conflict, but eventually, despite its proclaimed intention to remain isolated from European political, military, and diplomatic affairs, it fell into the cauldron of World War I.

SUMMARY

The United States prospered after the Civil War as industrialization accelerated, agricultural production expanded, new technologies enhanced living standards, and new states joined the Union. Foreign policy reflected these trends as trade expanded, nationalism returned, and American international influence grew. A sense of mission returned as foreign policy interests were clarified, based on the principles that had underpinned foreign policy since the American Revolution: isolationism, moralism, pragmatism, and unilateralism. The competing themes of isolationism versus involvement and idealism versus realism also played central roles.

Territorial expansion was a main activity of post–Civil War U.S. foreign policy. The United States acquired Alaska and Midway Island in 1867 and part of Samoa in 1875. It tried but failed to acquire the Danish West Indies and the Dominican Republic in the late 1860s. U.S. interest in building a canal across Central America also grew. The United States often used gunboat diplomacy and military interventions to defend its interests and to project power into Latin America. These actions divided Americans by the 1890s into three schools of thought. The first was proud of and satisfied with U.S. actions, the second criticized expansion, and the third argued that the United States should be even more expansionistic.

Increasingly in the 1890s, the third school directed U.S. foreign policy. Thus, from 1895 to 1900, the United States initiated a confrontation with Great Britain over Venezuela, defeated Spain in a conflict over Cuba, acquired an overseas empire, fought against a rebellion in the Philippines, declared an "Open Door" in China so it could expand trade there, and annexed Hawaii.

As president from 1901 to 1909, Theodore Roosevelt set the tone for twentieth-century U.S. foreign policy before World War I. Presidents William Taft and Woodrow Wilson were less flamboyant than Roosevelt, but they also often intervened overseas.

U.S. interests were most sizeable and interventions most frequent in Central America and the Caribbean, where Roosevelt declared the United States "might act as a policeman." Thus, the United States landed troops in countries in the region frequently, backed Panama's independence so it could build a canal there, developed naval bases in Puerto Rico and Cuba, and purchased the Danish Virgin Islands.

The United States was also deeply involved in Mexico, pouring extensive private investment into the country. In 1910, a revolution broke out in Mexico. The United States did not intervene, but a 1914 incident in a Mexican port led Woodrow Wilson to land troops. They were soon withdrawn, but as fighting between Mexican factions continued, Pancho Villa crossed into the United States in 1916 and attacked a New Mexican town. Wilson ordered U.S. troops back into Mexico, where they remained for almost a year.

The United States also remained actively engaged elsewhere in foreign policy. In Asia, it quelled the rebellion in the Philippines, negotiated a 1905 peace treaty between Russia and Japan, and stayed engaged with China and Japan. In Europe, it significantly improved relations with Great Britain, with which it had had alternating periods of tension and amity throughout the nineteenth century.

By this time, the United States verged on being a world power. Post–Civil War U.S. presidents had adopted the stance that the country's self-proclaimed superior values and institutions should be both examples for others and selectively imposed on others. This was a different mission from Jefferson's belief that the United States was "a sanctuary" for those who sought to escape "the misrule of Europe." As for U.S. interests, the United States was no longer weak and isolated, as it was a century before. It was a world power, and many American believed it should seek more power. With homeland security assured, the United States employed its military as it saw fit in Asia and Latin America. Its economic interests were global, and the country prospered. As Americans surveyed the early twentieth-century world, most liked what they saw.

KEY TERMS AND CONCEPTS

post–Civil War expansion
growth of American foreign trade
U.S. naval build-up
Alfred Thayer Mahan
gunboat diplomacy
Hawaiian annexation
Samoan crisis
U.S. interests in Latin America
anti-imperialism
Olney Memorandum
Venezuelan Crisis
jingoism
Jose Marti
Creoles
Teller Amendment
Spanish-American War
Philippine insurrection
Open Door policy

Boxer Rebellion
debate over empire
Anti-Imperialist League
white man's burden
dollar diplomacy
Roosevelt Corollary
Platt Amendment
Panamanian independence
Panama Canal
Porfirio Diaz
Victoriano Huerta
invasion of Veracruz
Pancho Villa
Mexican Punitive Expedition
Zimmermann Telegram
Treaty of Portsmouth
Root-Takahira Declaration
Anglo-American rapprochement

THINKING CRITICALLY

1. How, where, and why did the United States expand and attempt to expand its overseas territorial holdings after the Civil War and before the Spanish-American War?

2. What role did foreign trade play in American foreign policy after the Civil War and before the Spanish-American War?

3. Explain why and how the U.S. Navy became so important during the late nineteenth century.

4. During the 1890s, how did American imperialists and anti-imperialists use the concepts of an American mission, principles, and interests to support their views of what American foreign policy should be?

5. What factors led to the Spanish-American War? Why do many experts consider this war so important in the history of American foreign policy?

6. Describe Theodore Roosevelt's views of the role that the United States should play in world affairs, and detail how American foreign policy during Roosevelt's presidency reflected these views.

7. Where and why did the United States intervene in Latin America and the Caribbean during the first two decades of the twentieth century? What role did the Roosevelt Corollary to the Monroe Doctrine play in these interventions?

8. Detail the history of U.S.-Mexican relations from the end of the American Civil War to the end of World War I.

9. Describe the evolution of U.S. relations with Japan and China from the end of the American Civil War to the outbreak of World war I.

10. How and why did an Anglo-American rapprochement develop in the years before World War I?

NOTES

1. For several different perspectives on the growth of the American empire during this era, see Walter LaFeber, *The New Empire* (Ithaca, N.Y.: Cornell University Press, 1963); Ernest N. Paolino, *The Foundations of the American Empire: William Henry Seward and U.S. Foreign Policy* (Ithaca, N.Y.: Cornell University Press, 1973); William A. Williams, *The Roots of the Modern American Empire* (New York: Random House, 1969); and Milton Plesur, *America's Outward Thrust: Approaches to Foreign Affairs, 1865–1890* (DeKalb: Northern Illinois University Press, 1971).

2. For a good discussion of William Henry Seward's years as secretary of state, see again Paolino, *The Foundations of the American Empire: William Henry Seward and U.S. Foreign Policy.*

3. For details of the Alaska purchase, see Ronald J. Jensen, *The Alaska Purchase and Russian-American Relations* (Seattle: University of Washington Press, 1975).

4. For details of this episode, see Charles C. Tansill, *The United States and Santo Domingo, 1789–1873* (Baltimore: Johns Hopkins University Press, 1938).

5. For further discussion of these ideas, see David A. Lake, *Power, Protection, and Free Trade* (Ithaca, N.Y.: Cornell University Press, 1988), and Plesur, *America's Outward Thrust.*

6. For a fascinating study of how the conflict between American idealism and American imperialism played out in China, see David L. Anderson, *Imperialism and Idealism: American Diplomats in China, 1861–1898* (Bloomington: Indiana University Press, 1985).

7. For a few of the many studies about the rise of American naval power, especially in the late nineteenth century, see Kenneth J. Hagan, *American Gunboat Diplomacy and the Old Navy, 1877–1889* (Westport, Conn.: Greenwood Press, 1973); Frederick C. Drake, *The Empire of the Seas* (Honolulu: University of Hawaii Press, 1984); and Harold Sprout and Margaret Sprout, *The Rise of American Naval Power, 1776–1918* (1966).

8. Alfred Thayer Mahan, *The Influence of Sea Power upon History, 1660–1783* (Boston: Little, Brown, 1890).

9. See Anderson, *Imperialism and Idealism.*

10. See Merze Tate, *The United States and the Hawaiian Kingdom* (New Haven: Yale University Press, 1965).

11. See Paul M. Kennedy, *The Samoan Tangle* (New York: Barnes & Noble, 1974).

12. These events are explored in detail in Robert L. Beisner, *From the Old Diplomacy to the New: 1865–1900* (Arlington Heights, Ill.: Harlan Davidson, 1986).

13. As quoted in LaFeber, *The New Empire*, p. 106.

14. The so-called Wisconsin School of historians, led by William Appleman Williams, originated the term "imperial anti-colonialism." See especially William A. Williams, *The Roots of the Modern American Empire,* and William A. Williams, *The Tragedy of American Diplomacy* (New York: Norton, 1988).

15. For more details on the growing pressure in the 1890s for the United States to adopt a blatantly imperial foreign policy, see David Healy, *U.S. Expansionism: The Imperialist Urge in the 1890s* (Madison: University of Wisconsin Press, 1970), and Julius W. Pratt, *Expansionists of 1898* (Chicago: Quadrangle Press, 1964).

16. *Foreign Relations 1895: Part 1* (Washington, D.C.: U.S. Government Printing Office, 1896), pp. 545–562.

17. Richard E. Welch Jr., *The Presidencies of Grover Cleveland* (Lawrence: University Press of Kansas, 1988), pp. 184–186.

18. The Venezuelan Crisis provides another excellent opportunity to use the methodology of levels of analysis discussed in Chapter 1. For example, did President Cleveland move toward confrontation with Great Britain over Venezuela to strengthen his own personal political standing, to improve the lot of his Democratic Party, to defend the Monroe Doctrine and defend U.S. trading interests, or to strengthen the United States international position? The answers will vary depending on which level of analysis one uses.

19. Marti considered the United States a country "full of hate" that pursued a "conquering policy" toward Latin American states. See John M. Kirk, *Jose Marti* (Gainesville: University Presses of Florida, 1983), for details on Marti's antipathy toward the United States.

20. James D. Richardson, ed., *A Compilation of the Messages and Papers of the Presidents, 1789–1897*, Vol. 9 (Washington, D.C.: U.S. Government Printing Office, 1896–1899), pp. 716–722.

21. *Congressional Record,* Vol. 31 (December 6, 1897), pp. 3–5.

22. *Foreign Relations 1898* (Washington, D.C.: U.S. Government Printing Office, 1901), pp. 1007–1008.

23. The United States conducted three inquiries into the sinking of the *Maine*. The first, just after the disaster, concluded that a mine had sunk the ship. The second, undertaken in 1911 when the *Maine* was raised and then sunk at sea, concluded simply that an external explosion had destroyed the vessel. The third, conducted in 1976, concluded that an internal accident led to the explosion that caused the sinking of the *Maine*.

24. For more details about the Spanish-American War, see Frank Freidel, *The Splendid Little War* (Boston: Little, Brown, 1958), and David Healy, *U.S. Expansionism.*

25. *Foreign Relations 1901*, Appendix: "Affairs in China" (Washington, D.C.: U.S. Government Printing Office, 1902), p. 12.

26. See LaFeber, *The New Empire;* Williams, *The Roots of the Modern American Empire;* Beisner, *From the Old Diplomacy to the New: 1865–1900;* Healy, *U.S. Expansionism;* and Pratt, *Expansionists of 1898.*

27. For in-depth studies of Theodore Roosevelt, see William H. Harbaugh, *The Life and Times of Theodore Roosevelt* (New York: Oxford University Press, 1975), and Lewis L. Gould, *The Presidency of Theodore Roosevelt* (Lawrence: University Press of Kansas, 1991).

28. As reported in John Morton Blum, *The Republican Roosevelt* (New York: Atheneum, 1973), p. 127.

29. For more detailed discussion of the Roosevelt Corollary, see Dexter Perkins, *The Monroe Doctrine, 1867–1907* (Baltimore: Johns Hopkins University Press, 1966).

30. *Congressional Record*, Vol. 34 (February 26, 1901), p. 3036.

31. For discussions of U.S.-Cuban relations during this period, see David F. Healy, *The United States in Cuba, 1898–1902* (Madison: University of Wisconsin Press, 1963); R. H. Fitzgibbon, *Cuba and the United States, 1900–1935* (New York: Russell and Russell, 1964); and Allan R. Millett, *The Politics of Intervention* (Columbus: Ohio State University Press, 1968). See also Jaime Suchlicki, *Cuba: From Columbus to Castro* (Washington, D.C.: Pergamon-Brassey's, 1986).

32. For details of how Panama won its independence, see Walter LaFeber, *The Panama Canal* (New York: Oxford University Press, 1989), and Stephen J. Randall, *Colombia and the United States* (Athens: University of Georgia Press, 1992).

33. As reported in LaFeber, *The Panama Canal*, pp. 225–226.

34. For more detailed views of how the United States came to be regarded as the "Colossus of the North," see Cole Blasier, *The Hovering Giant: U.S. Responses to Revolutionary Change in Latin America, 1910–1985* (Pittsburgh: University of Pittsburgh Press, 1985), and Robert Pastor, *Whirlpool: U.S. Policy toward Latin America and the Caribbean* (Princeton: Princeton University Press, 1992). See also Thomas Walker, *Nicaragua: The Land of Sandino* (Boulder, Colo.: Westview Press, 1986).

35. See Arthur S. Link, *Wilson: Confusions and Crises, 1915–1916* (Princeton: Princeton University Press, 1964), p. 317.

36. As reported in Arthur S. Link, *Wilson: The New Freedom* (Princeton: Princeton University Press, 1956), pp. 386–387.

37. For details on U.S. military actions in Mexico during Wilson's presidency, see Alan Knight, *U.S.-Mexican Relations, 1910–1940* (San Diego: Center for U.S.-Mexican Studies, 1987), as well as the books by Arthur S. Link cited in the previous two notes.

38. For another view of U.S.-Mexican relations, see Robert A. Pastor and Jorge G. Castaneda, *Limits to Friendship: The United States and Mexico* (New York: Knopf, 1988).

39. For insight on Theodore Roosevelt's dealings with Japan, see Raymond A. Esthus, *Theodore Roosevelt and Japan* (Seattle: University of Washington Press, 1988).

40. *Foreign Relations 1922*, Vol. 2 (Washington, D.C.: U.S. Government Printing Office, 1938), p. 591.

41. As reported in Dexter Perkins, *The Monroe Doctrine, 1823–1826* (Cambridge, Mass.: Harvard University Press, 1927), p. 364.

42. For other views of the developing U.S.-British friendship, see Bradford Perkins, *The Great Rapprochement: England and the United States, 1895–1914* (New York: Atheneum, 1968); C. S. Campbell, *Anglo-American Understanding, 1898–1903* (Baltimore: Johns Hopkins University Press, 1957); and A. E. Campbell, *Great Britain and the United States* (Westport, Conn.: Greenwood Press, 1974).

43. The exception was in 1906, when Germany asked Roosevelt to organize a conference to settle a dispute between Germany and France over Morocco. Roosevelt settled the dispute but was criticized in the United States because his effort had the potential to embroil the United States in a European conflict. Taft and Wilson steered clear of subsequent direct involvement in Europe's affairs until 1917.

CHAPTER 5

Becoming a Global Power: 1914–1945

World War I (1914–1918) caused more death and destruction than any previous war. The United States stayed out of the war until 1917 but eventually joined the Allies and played a major role in winning the war.

- How did the United States avoid entering World War I for so long?
- Why did the United States eventually enter the war?
- What policies did the United States prefer at the end of World War I?
- How did domestic politics affect U.S. policy during and after World War I?
- What foreign policies did the United States follow in the 1920s?
- How did the Great Depression affect U.S. foreign policy?
- How did the United States respond to war and conflict during the 1930s?
- What policies did the United States pursue in the 1930s in Latin America and Asia?
- What policies did the United States implement during World War II?

In 1914, Europe slid into a war that nobody really wanted. Europe's slide toward World War I would have been comic if its results had not been not so tragic. Following the June assassination of Archduke Ferdinand of Austria-Hungary in Sarajevo, Bosnia, Austria-Hungary demanded that Serbia permit Austria-Hungary to enter Serbia to search for the assassins. Serbia refused. Austria-Hungary prepared to march into Serbia anyway, and Russia, committed by secret treaty to Serbia's defense, began to mobilize.

At first, Russia's Czar Nicholas ordered partial mobilization, intending to show Austria-Hungary that Russia would defend Serbia, but Russia's generals urged Nicholas to order a full mobilization, since Russia mobilized more slowly than other European states. The czar agreed.[1] Germany viewed Russia's mobilization with alarm and began to mobilize.

Meanwhile, Austria-Hungary feared that Germany would renege on its "blank check" promise of support for Austria-Hungary in the event of an Austro-Hungarian conflict with Russia. Austria-Hungary therefore refused to respond to urgent diplomatic communications from Germany and marched into Serbia. World War I had begun.[2]

AMERICAN FOREIGN POLICY DURING WORLD WAR I: 1914–1918

The United States and most of the rest of the non-European world watched in horrified amazement as Europeans in August 1914 began to slaughter each other. For four long years, Europe was wracked by the bloodiest fighting that humankind had ever seen. Still shielded by the same ocean that had insulated their new nation from Europe's politics and warfare, Americans, at least in theory, remained neutral and aloof from the conflict for three years.

The attempt to remain disengaged from World War I did not mean that the United States had no foreign policy between 1914 and 1917. As we have seen, the United States maintained an active foreign policy during these years in Mexico and the Caribbean as well as Asia. However, even during these years, the United States more and more focused on the war in Europe.

The Rhetoric of Neutrality

Beneath the surface, neutrality was more rhetoric than reality. Even before World War I, American concerns about Germany had been building. More than one American president was concerned during the early twentieth century about German designs on territory in Latin America and the Caribbean. At the same time, Anglo-American rapprochement proceeded. By 1914, the United States was more aligned with Great Britain than with Germany.

This alignment was bolstered by American economic ties to Great Britain and its allies, especially France. In 1914, U.S. exports to Great Britain and France totaled $754 million. By 1916, U.S. exports to the same two countries had soared to $2.75 billion, much of it in munitions and other war goods. Conversely, U.S. exports to Germany during the same period declined from $345 million to $2 million, both because of the United States' increasingly close liaison with the Allies and Great Britain's blockade of Germany and its allies.

American loans to Europe's warring nations followed a similar pattern. At first, the Wilson Administration asked American bankers not to make loans to European belligerents, but this soon changed. Between 1914 and 1917, U.S. banks and other financial interests loaned the Allies $2.3 billion, while Germany received $27 million.[3]

This did not mean that all Americans favored the Allied Powers during the years of proclaimed U.S. neutrality. Most American citizens of English and Scottish ancestry supported Great Britain and its allies, but many of America's millions of Irish immigrants were anti-British. Similarly, many of the United States' German immigrants tilted toward their former homeland. Importantly, though, most Americans in positions of authority, including President Wilson, sided with Great Britain and its allies.

German actions also undermined pro-German sympathy in the United States. At the beginning of the war, German plans called for an attack through Belgium into France's north, ignoring Belgian neutrality. Executing the plan to near perfection, Germany swept through Belgium in days and almost knocked France out of the war in little more than a month. However, Germany's violation of Belgian neutrality and its brutal occupation of Belgium alienated many Americans. Great Britain exaggerated the stories of German brutality to garner more American sympathy and support.[4]

Germany's adoption of unrestricted submarine warfare and refusal to accept American interpretations of the rights of neutral countries on the high seas drove the United States to enter World War I on the side of the Allies. To be sure, Great Britain also violated the rights of neutral countries on the high seas. For example, Great Britain declared food and cotton to be war materials and subject to seizure, forced U.S. ships bound for Germany to go to British or French ports for inspection, and mined international waters in the North Sea to sink ships bound for German ports. British ships also hoisted the flags of neutral countries, often the United States, to try to avoid Germany's new weapon of war, the submarine. In addition, Great Britain violated prevailing international law by arming its merchant ships, technically making them warships not permitted to receive arms or munitions in neutral ports.

The United States often protested Britain's **violation of neutral rights.** In response, Great Britain generally paid appropriate verbal homage to international law, compensated American businesses for their losses, took out more loans from the United States, and continued its high-handed practices. Germany in turn protested the United States' willingness to accept Great Britain's high-handed practices. German leaders also knew that Great Britain and its allies were importing billions of dollars of munitions and other war materials from the United States. With the Royal Navy blockading Germany's surface fleet into its North Sea and Baltic ports, Germany turned to the submarine to try to stop the flow of supplies from North America to the Allies.

In early 1915, Germany announced that it was retaliating for Great Britain's blockade of Germany by declaring a war zone around the British Isles. Any enemy ship in the war zone would be sunk without warning, Germany declared. Further, Great Britain's practice of allowing its ships to sail under a neutral flag created the danger that a neutral ship might be accidentally sunk, Berlin warned, so neutral ships in the zone were in danger.

Wilson immediately responded that Germany would be held to a "strict accountability" if American lives or property were lost.[5] The United States also tried but failed to arrange a compromise between Germany and Great Britain in which Germany would renounce unannounced attacks in return for Great Britain's pledge to stop arming merchant ships and allowing food shipments to reach Germany. During the first three months that the policy was in place, German submarines sank 90 ships in the war zone. One American was killed, but the United States, hoping to avoid a crisis, did not protest. Then, in May, a German submarine sank the passenger liner ***Lusitania,*** killing 128 Americans. U.S.-German relations deteriorated drastically.[6]

Even so, most Americans still wanted to avoid war. For example, Secretary of State William Jennings Bryan argued that Americans could avoid being killed simply by sailing on American ships rather than ships of countries that were at war. Indeed, he had a point. Between August 1914 when the war started and mid-March 1917, only three Americans had died on an American ship sunk by a German submarine, whereas over 190, including the 128 on the *Lusitania*, had died on ships owned by countries at war.

Wilson also did not want war, but he disagreed with Bryan, maintaining that Germany's unannounced submarine attacks against passenger ships and merchant vessels violated international law even if the attacks were restricted to ships owned by belligerent countries. When a German submarine damaged a French passenger vessel in 1916, injuring several Americans, Wilson threatened to break diplomatic relations with Germany. Not wanting the United States to enter the war, Germany pledged that submarines would not attack passenger vessels or merchant ships without prior warning.

Wilson used this success and the fact that the United States was not at war to mount his successful 1916 reelection campaign. Using the slogan "He kept us out of war," Wilson won an easy victory. After the election, Wilson launched a diplomatic offensive in which he urged Europe's warring countries to accept "peace without victory" based on the "equality of nations."[7] Many Americans applauded Wilson's high-minded rhetoric, but most European leaders thought Wilson hopelessly naive.

With European leaders having rejected Wilson's call for peace without victory, Germany on January 31, 1917, sealed the failure of Wilson's peace offensive and assured American entry into World War I on the side of the Allies by announcing a policy of **unrestricted submarine warfare.** Under this policy, German submarines would sink without warning any enemy or neutral ship found near Great Britain. Germany gambled that even if this brought the United States into the war, its submarines could choke Great Britain into submission before the United States could have an impact on the war. With Great Britain out of the war, Germany reasoned, the United States would have no reason to continue hostilities. Incensed, the United States on February 3 broke diplomatic relations with Germany.

Before the end of the month, U.S.-German relations deteriorated even more as British intelligence provided the U.S. Department of State with a captured note from Germany to Mexico, the **Zimmermann telegram,** in which Germany proposed that Mexico enter an alliance with Germany and possibly Japan. As discussed in Chapter 4, the telegram suggested that if such an alliance were formed, Germany would help Mexico reclaim land it lost to the United States during the 1847–1848 Mexican-American War.[8]

The combination of unrestricted submarine warfare and the Zimmermann telegram made an American declaration of war against Germany inevitable. As submarines sank ship after ship in February and March, Wilson opted for war. Addressing a joint session of Congress on April 2, 1917, Wilson declared that Germany had unleashed "warfare against mankind" with its submarines and that Germany endangered the "very roots of human life." Declaring that "the world must be made safe for democracy," Wilson asked Congress for a declaration of war against Germany.[9]

On April 4, the Senate approved Wilson's request 82–6. The House followed suit two days later 373–50. The United States was at war with Germany. Wilson's rhetoric made it clear that the United States intended to win the war, overthrow autocracy, and impose its view of human rights, self-determination, and democracy on Europe once Germany and its allies were defeated. Idealism, it seemed, was returning to U.S. foreign policy.

Winning the War

But first a war had to be fought and won. Despite Wilson's support for increased defense spending in 1916 and the efforts of other Americans such as Teddy Roosevelt even before then to prepare the United States for war, the United States was not prepared to make a quick major contribution to the war. Germany had counted on exactly this reality when it declared unrestricted submarine warfare in early 1917. What Germany did not count on was how strong U.S. nationalism could become, how quickly the United States could organize for war, and how easily the United States could turn its production to war.

When the United States declared war in April 1917, the Regular Army had only 130,000 officers and men, but the **American military build-up** was rapid and impressive. The first U.S. troops arrived in Europe in June, proclaiming, "Lafayette, we are here!" in reference to the French noble who had gone to the United States to support its revolution against Great Britain almost a century and a half earlier. One million American troops were in Europe a year later, and by the time the armistice was signed in November 1918, 2 million U.S. troops were on the continent.

Not all of the American forces were well trained or equipped. Some never fired a shot until they were in combat, sometimes with weapons that they borrowed from the French. Despite the problems, American soldiers in May and June 1918 played a key role in stopping an offensive that Germany hoped would win the war. A month later over a million U.S. soldiers helped spearhead an Allied offensive that drove Germany to negotiations. By October 1918, U.S. troops held over 20 percent of the Allies' front line, which was advancing slowly toward Germany.[10]

With their armies crumbling and riots breaking out in their cities, Germany and Austria-Hungary in September 1918 exchanged notes with Wilson about the possibility of an armistice. The other Allied powers, uncomfortable with Wilson's views about "peace without victory," were not pleased. Then, in early October, the German chancellor asked Wilson to arrange an armistice. Austria-Hungary left the war on November 3 and Germany capitulated eight days later. World War I was over, and the United States had played a major role in winning it.[11] It remained to be seen if the United States—or the world—could win the peace.

Winning the Peace

Wilson was convinced that the United States could win the peace and that he personally had the perfect plan to construct a peaceful postwar world. Wilson's views on how this could be done, on how the international system needed to be structured to achieve this, on how states had to be internally structured to maximize chances for peace, and on the role the United States would play in this world came to be labeled **Wilsonianism,** or Wilsonian idealism. Wilsonianism dominated U.S. foreign policy throughout World War I and the peace conference that followed.

President Woodrow Wilson's plans for creating a peaceful post–World War I world included national self-determination and the League of Nations, both of which were seen as hopelessly naïve by British Prime Minister Lloyd George and French Premier Georges Clemenceau. Here (from left to right) George, Clemenceau, and Wilson stroll together at the 1919 Versailles Peace Conference.

In simplest terms, Wilsonian idealism opposed imperialism, war, and revolution. Wilson believed he knew how to eliminate all three. Barriers to democracy and to free trade had to be eliminated. An open free-market economic system, Wilson asserted, supported and went hand-in-hand with democracy. Secret diplomacy had to be replaced by open agreements openly negotiated. Militarism would be restrained not only by democracy but also by disarmament programs and arms control agreements. Colonialism would disappear as ethnic groups voted for the government of their choice, exercising **national self-determination** to set up their own democratically elected government in their own country. The United States, Wilson believed, was perfectly suited as the exceptional nation with superior ideals to lead the world toward the new utopian international system.

Wilson discussed his view of what the postwar world would be like with evangelistic zeal. Even before the war was over, he offered the clearest statement of his view in his **Fourteen Points** speech to Congress in January 1918. Wilson argued for a postwar world with "open covenants" that were "openly arrived at," universal freedom of navigation on the high seas, the removal of tariffs and creation of equal trading opportunities for all, smaller militaries and arms reductions, and an end to colonialism. (See Table 5.1.) The Fourteen Points also included self-determination for national minorities throughout Europe. Wilson's final point was the most revolutionary, a call to create an international organization that would assure "political independence and territorial integrity to great and small state alike." Even though the details of many of the Fourteen

TABLE 5.1
WILSON'S FOURTEEN POINTS

1. Open covenants of peace, openly arrived at.

2. Absolute freedom of navigation upon the sea.

3. The removal, so far as possible, of all economic barriers and the establishment of an equality of trade conditions among all nations.

4. Adequate guarantees given and taken that national armaments will be reduced to the lowest point consistent with domestic safety.

5. A free open-minded, and absolutely impartial adjustment of all imperial claims.

6. The evacuation of all Russian territory... [and] independent determination of her own political development and national policy.

7. Belgium ... must be evacuated and restored without any attempt to limit ... sovereignty.

8. All French territory should be freed and the invaded portions restored, and the wrong done to France by Prussia in 1871 in the matter of Alsace-Lorraine ... should be righted.

9. A readjustment of the frontiers of Italy should be effected along clearly recognized lines of nationality.

10. The peoples of Austria-Hungary ... should be accorded the freest opportunity of autonomous development.

11. Rumania, Serbia, and Montenegro should be evacuated; occupied territories restored; Serbia accorded free and secure access to the sea; and the relations of the several Balkan states to one another determined by friendly counsel along historically established lines of allegiance and nationality.

12. The Turkish portions of the present Ottoman Empire should be assured a secure sovereignty, but the other nationalities ... should be assured ... [an] autonomous development, and the Dardanelles should be permanently opened as a free passage to the ships and commerce of all nations.

13. An independent Polish nation should be erected ... [with] political and economic independence and territorial integrity.

14. A general association of nations must be formed under specific covenants for the purpose of affording mutual guarantees of political independence and territorial integrity to great and small states alike.

Source: Excerpted from a speech by President Woodrow Wilson to a Joint Session of the U.S. Congress, *Congressional Record*, January 8, 1918, p. 691.

Points needed to be worked out, Wilson was convinced that his views provided the foundation for a lasting, fair, and nonpunitive peace settlement.[12]

Wilson's Fourteen Points formed an integrated perspective on international affairs that was revolutionary. According to Wilsonian idealism as espoused in the Fourteen Points, countries did not have to go to war with each other. Indeed, Wilson argued, if World War I (at the time called "The Great War," since there was not yet a World War II) proved anything, it was that modern war had become too costly and ways had to be found to prevent countries from going to war. And Wilson believed that he knew how to do this. The key, the American president said, was to understand that states could cooperate, indeed, often wanted to cooperate, if only the right combination of international and domestic political systems could be created that provided incentives for countries to stay at peace. This could be accomplished, Wilson believed, if two crucial elements were in place.

First, countries had to form an international organization called the League of Nations that would have all states act together against any state that got out of line and became aggressive. This concept, called **collective security,** was based on the premise that if one country attacked another, then other countries that belonged to the League would unite against the attacking country. The League of Nations was thus critically important for Wilson's plans, because it provided the needed structure for the international system and served as a tool that provided an incentive for states to be peaceful.

Second, Wilson maintained, democratically elected national governments that led countries that traded freely with each other and that did not fear their neighbors because of collective security would in most cases not want to go to war. The internal structure of states was thus also important to Wilson: each nationality had to have its own country; each nationality had to elect its own government democratically (these two points together were called national self-determination); and each country had to be able to trade peacefully with its neighbors. Wilsonian idealism therefore argued that, together, the right international system and the right internal structure of states would combine to prevent war, or at least make it less likely.[13]

Critics responded that although this was a great theory, it would never work in practice. Ever since the modern system of nation-states came into being in the seventeenth century,[14] Wilson's opponents asserted, nation-states survived on the basis of their own military and economic strength, on the basis of the alliances they could create, and on the basis of defending their own national interest on their own wherever and whenever it was necessary. In the United States, many Americans believed that Wilsonianism, the Fourteen Points, and the president were hopelessly naive. Worse, they feared that policies based on Wilsonianism and the Fourteen Points would squander American resources by involving the United States in foreign adventures in pursuit of an impossible international dream.

European leaders were even more appalled by Wilsonianism and the Fourteen Points. Most wanted to punish Germany for the war, force Germany to pay reparations for war damages, divide Germany's colonies among themselves, and use the old maxim: "To the victors belong the spoils." They considered Wilson both naive and a dangerous zealot. French Premier Georges Clemenceau held a particularly dim view of the American president and his proposals, observing that "God gave us the Ten Commandments, and we broke them. Wilson gave us the Fourteen Points. We shall see."[15] The idealism of the American president and the realism of Clemenceau and other European leaders stood in stark contrast to one another.

Faced by opposition to his programs at home and abroad, Wilson headed the U.S. delegation to the **Versailles Peace Conference,** scheduled to begin in January 1919. When he departed for Paris in December, his credibility had been further weakened by the November 1918 mid-term Congressional elections that returned a Republican majority to both houses of Congress. Undeterred, Wilson left for Versailles, convinced that his plans were the basis for peace.

The **Treaty of Paris** that emerged from the Versailles Peace Conference was not a success for Wilson, but neither was it a failure.[16] France and Great Britain wanted to punish Germany and keep it weak. They therefore inserted a war-guilt clause in the treaty that blamed Germany for the war and required Germany to pay reparations. Germany was also stripped of over 10 percent of its population and territory. Wilson opposed these measures, arguing prophetically that they would ignite a German desire for revenge, but he conceded on all three points.[17] Wilson also lost his appeal to end colonialism, as the victors kept their colonies and divided the losers' colonies among themselves, establishing a mandate system that resembled traditional colonialism in everything but name.

But Wilson triumphed on two key points. The first was national self-determination, under which many of Europe's ethnic groups set up their own democratically elected government in their own country. National self-determination led to a redrawn map of Europe as Austria, Czechoslovakia, Estonia, Finland, Hungary, Latvia, Lithuania, Poland, and Yugoslavia emerged as independent countries.

Convinced of the righteousness of his cause and confident in his ability to convince others that he was right, Wilson believed that his real triumph at Versailles was the creation of the **League of Nations,** an international organization designed to keep peace through collective security. Collective security, as we have seen, was based on the premise that if one country attacked another, then other countries that belonged to the League would unite against the attacking country. The importance of the League, Wilson believed, was underlined by its placement—it was detailed in the first 26 articles of the 440-article Treaty of Paris.

Wilson was so absorbed in creating the League that he failed to build support for it in the United States. A Democratic president with a Republican Senate, Wilson did not court Republican senators by including them in the U.S. delegation to the Versailles conference. He alienated others with his attitude of moral superiority and condescension. Many also feared that U.S. membership in the League would fly in the face of traditional U.S. isolationism from Europe, while others believed that League membership would compromise American sovereignty and force the United States to act in situations when its national interest was not clearly at stake. The League of Nations thus raised, for perhaps the first time in the history of American foreign policy, fears that multilateralism might supplant unilateralism.

With these concerns coupled with his personal animosity toward Wilson, Chairman of the Senate Foreign Relations Committee Henry Cabot Lodge, mimicking Wilson's Fourteen Points, offered a list of 14 reservations about U.S. membership in the League. The most serious reservation challenged the concept of collective security by stating that if the United States joined the League, it was under no obligation to preserve the territorial integrity or political independence of another country unless Congress authorized such action.

Wilson refused to accept any reservations, embarking instead in late 1919 on an around-the-country speaking tour to support the League and the Treaty of Paris. Wilson harshly criticized his opponents during the tour. Pushing himself, Wilson collapsed, returned to Washington, and suffered a massive stroke. Still refusing to consider any reservations to the League or the treaty, Wilson watched helplessly as the Senate several times in late 1919 and early 1920 rejected the League and the entire Treaty of Paris, both with and without reservations. Finally, in 1921, Congress officially ended the war with Germany as the United States accepted the Treaty of Paris without the League of Nations articles.[18]

The American failure to join the League was sometimes viewed in the United States as the reason the League eventually failed. There is no doubt that this was part of the reason, but the fact that no other major country wanted the League to have meaningful military or other coercive capabilities also contributed to the League's failure. The League never received the capabilities it needed to do what it was established to do. As for the United States, it did not join the League for several reasons. Concern about the implications of the League for American sovereignty, Wilson's pride and refusal to compromise, senatorial vanity and resentment, political partisanship, and the desire of the American public to concentrate on domestic affairs and return to isolationism once World War I ended all contributed to the United States' refusal to join the League.

The United States and the Russian Revolution

Even before World War I ended and the debate over the League began, the United States had become involved in another intervention, this time in Russia. In early 1917, a revolution in Russia forced the Russian czar to abdicate and brought a provisional government to power. Most Americans, including Wilson, praised this revolution, seeing it as a blow against dictatorship. Wilson even observed that the overthrow of the czar made it easier for the United States to enter World War I on the Allies' side, because with the czar's removal, the conflict now pitted democratic countries against autocratic countries.

Later in 1917, another revolution, this time led by **V. I. Lenin** and his **Bolshevik Party,** brought a communist government to power in Russia. This concerned many Americans and Western Europeans, since Bolshevism preached world revolution. American and Western European concern changed to anger in early 1918 when the Bolsheviks concluded the Treaty of Brest-Litovsk with Germany, under which Russia lost over a million square miles and, more importantly from the U.S. and Allied perspectives, withdrew from the war.[19] The picture became even more confused when civil war broke out in Russia between the Bolsheviks and anti-Bolshevik forces.

Opposed to Bolshevism and fearing that Russian arms might fall into German hands, Great Britain, France, and the United States sent troops to northern Russia in 1918. Eventually 5,000 U.S. troops deployed there, some of whom fought against the Bolsheviks. Wilson sent another 10,000 troops to Siberia to counter Japanese expansionism and to try to rescue a Czech army unit that had been organized in Russia during World War I to fight Germany. American troops did not leave Russia until 1920, well after World War I ended.

Wilson had mixed motives in sending U.S. troops to Russia. Clearly, he opposed Bolshevism. Indeed, during the **Red Scare** that developed in the United States in 1918 and 1919, the Wilson Administration arrested and deported people on flimsy evidence, sometimes manufactured, that they harbored communist sympathies. But it is less clear that Wilson supported the British and French desire to overthrow the Bolshevik regime. He also feared that Russian arms might fall into German hands and believed that Japan, with 72,000 soldiers on the ground in Russia's far east, had designs on Russian territory.

Whatever Wilson's motives, U.S. troops were on the ground in Russia from 1918 to 1920.[20] Americans have generally forgotten the **American intervention in Russia,** but Russians, especially during the Cold War, remembered it.

AMERICA'S INTERWAR YEARS: 1918–1941

Convinced that they had won World War I for the Allies and desiring to return to "normalcy,"[21] most Americans by 1920 wanted to forget European issues and world affairs; a strong desire for isolationism, at least from European affairs, emerged once again. Americans also wanted to forget that World War I had cost 130,000 U.S. lives and $30 billion, small numbers compared to the costs that European countries had paid, but significant nonetheless.

Despite these desires and the popular perception that the United States returned to isolationism in the 1920s and 1930s, the United States remained involved overseas in numerous ways. At the same time, even though Wilsonian idealism had been rejected, U.S. foreign policy balanced idealism and realism to a surprising degree. On the one hand, American foreign policy during the 1920s concentrated on arms control and disarmament, but on the other, it also stressed foreign trade, investment, and maintaining order in Latin America and the Caribbean. The first activities were new departures brought about by Wilsonianism, a revulsion to the slaughter of World War I, and a hope that a new naval arms race could be contained and war prevented. The last two foreign policy activities were similar to those that the United States pursued with enthusiasm earlier in the century.

After the Great Depression struck in 1929, and with new conflicts erupting in the 1930s, the United States modified many of its policies as it searched for nonmilitary ways to curtail the rising tide of conquest throughout the world. Even as it pursued increasingly futile arms control efforts, it recognized the Soviet Union and adopted a new policy stance toward Latin America and the Caribbean. Despite all this international activity in the 1920s and 1930s, most Americans still believed their country was isolated from world affairs, probably because the United States managed to avoid war and military confrontations.

The Roaring Twenties

By personal preference and as a result of Wilson's unhappy experience with the League of Nations, Wilson's two presidential successors, Warren Harding and Calvin Coolidge, little involved themselves with foreign affairs. Leaving foreign policy to their secretaries of state, Harding and Coolidge presided over a United States whose population wanted to concentrate on domestic affairs.

Nevertheless, with the devastation of World War I in mind, Americans knew that they did not want to experience another world war or engage in an arms race. Not surprisingly, then, the United States became actively involved in efforts to outlaw war and to contain military build-ups. One seeming success was the 1928 **Kellogg-Briand Pact,** negotiated by Secretary of State Frank Kellogg and French Foreign Minister Aristide Briand. Although the French aim was to conclude a Franco-American security agreement to provide France protection from Germany, Kellogg refocused the pact so that signatory countries "condemn[ed] recourse to war for the solution of international controversies, and renounce[d] it as an instrument of national policy."[22] Sixty-two countries signed the pact, which was a high-minded statement of principle. However, without enforcement mechanisms, it bordered on meaninglessness as a statement of policy.

The United States was also actively involved in other arms control and disarmament efforts during the 1920s, most notably the 1921–1922 Washington Naval Conference, which finalized an agreement that forbade the construction of battleships and heavy cruisers for ten years. The conference also established the ratio of permitted tonnage for capital ships at 5 for the United States, 5 for Great Britain, 3 for Japan, and 1.67 each for France and Italy.[23] Meanwhile, the cause of peace advanced elsewhere. France, Germany, Great Britain, and Italy in 1925 concluded the Locarno Treaties, which guaranteed boundaries in Europe.[24] The League of Nations also had occasional successes resolving potential conflicts in Scandinavia and the Balkans during the 1920s. Notably, Germany was admitted to the League in 1926.

Advancing foreign trade and investment were other U.S. foreign policy priorities during the 1920s as the American economy grew rapidly. During the Harding and Coolidge years, the United States produced nearly half of the world's industrial output. U.S. foreign trade more than doubled, even though the United States imposed a high tariff in 1922 to protect domestic production. American foreign investment also expanded extensively, with U.S. investment doubling in Europe and tripling in Latin America. For the United States, most of the decade was indeed the **Roaring Twenties.**

In addition to emphasizing foreign trade and investment, the United States during the 1920s continued to stress maintaining order in Latin America and the Caribbean as U.S. businesses traded and invested throughout the region. In Cuba, Guatemala, Honduras, Mexico, Panama, Venezuela, and elsewhere, they made handsome profits and dominated the local economies. Meanwhile, the **U.S. occupations of the Dominican Republic, Nicaragua, and Haiti,** all initiated before the United States entered World War I, continued.

Marines landed in the Dominican Republic in 1916 to establish order after years of civil strife. To assure financial responsibility and maintain order, the United States controlled the country's finances and established a National Constabulary. After the marines' presence became a political issue in the presidential campaigns of 1920, with the Republicans favoring withdrawal, the marines left in 1924. The United States later cited the withdrawal as an indication of the United States' neighborliness toward Latin American and Caribbean states, but the United States retained control of the Dominican Republic's finances until 1941.

In Nicaragua, marines occupied the country from 1912 to 1925. They were withdrawn in 1925, but Coolidge ordered them to return in 1926 to quell supposed pro-Bolshevik sentiment in the country. Up to 5,000 marines remained until 1933, inciting in Nicaragua an anti-American revolution led by Cesar Augusto Sandino. The United States also created a Nicaraguan National Guard to help maintain order. In the United States, the occupation of and fighting in Nicaragua fomented heated debate about American morality; many Americans, including members of Congress, remained unconvinced about the presence of a communist menace. Congress also resented that the president acted without first consulting it. These disagreements were eerily similar to the ones that unfolded in the 1980s over Nicaragua between the executive and legislative branches during the Reagan Administration.

The worst example of American interventionism was in Haiti, where marines landed in 1915 to protect American interests after a civil war erupted. They stayed until 1934,

CHAPTER 5 *Becoming a Global Power: 1914–1945*

again creating a national guard to maintain order. Despite providing some improvements to the transportation, education, and health infrastructures, the U.S. occupation of Haiti does not have a proud history. The marines carried the racist attitudes that prevailed in the United States with them to Haiti, sometimes using forced labor to help build roads and public works. Brutality and oppression prevailed.

The U.S. occupations of and withdrawals from the Dominican Republic, Nicaragua, and Haiti left weak and unstable political systems that provided fertile soil for dictatorial governments dominated by military strongmen. In the Dominican Republic, General Rafael Trujillo gained power in a fraudulent 1930 election and remained president until 1961, eliminating opposition, favoring U.S. economic interests, and becoming rich. In Nicaragua, General Anastasio Somoza seized power in 1936 and retained it until 1979. He followed Trujillo's pattern of eliminating opposition, favoring American economic interests, and enriching himself and his family. In Haiti, a series of dictators ran the country with political power wielded by the American-trained national guard, which finally seized power for itself in 1946. Another revolution in 1956–1957 brought Dr. Francis "Papa Doc" Duvalier to power. He ruled until 1971, after which his son "Baby Doc" held power until he was overthrown in 1986. Both Papa Doc and Baby Doc brutally oppressed opposition and enriched themselves and their family.[25]

New Approaches in the Thirties

As Herbert Hoover assumed the presidency in 1929, most Americans looked forward to continuing economic growth and prosperity. Their dreams were shattered in October 1929 when the New York stock market crashed, ushering into the United States an economic depression that had already appeared in many other countries. The **Great Depression** worsened political and economic conflicts all over the world as economies collapsed, debtors defaulted, investment disappeared, and international trade went into a tailspin. In the United States, trade declined from $5.4 billion in 1929 to $2.1 billion in 1933. Thirteen million Americans were unemployed.[26]

Increasing international tension accompanied the world's worsening economic condition. This was evident first in the failure of the 1930 London Naval Conference to place limitations on "minor" ships such as submarines. The following year Japan invaded Manchuria, with the United States blandly announcing that it would recognize no territorial gains made by armed force. The League of Nations issued a report that called Japan's action aggression, after which Japan withdrew from the League. In 1932, the League of Nations Geneva Disarmament Conference, which the United States attended, foundered on Germany's demand for equality in weapons with France and France's refusal to accept Germany's demand.

The Great Depression led to new approaches to domestic and foreign policy issues in many countries. The United States was no exception. One of the first new initiatives that the United States undertook to revive its ailing economy was to increase tariffs to protect domestic production. Passed in 1930, the **Smoot-Hawley Tariff** raised taxes on imports to an unprecedented level. It also accelerated the decline in trade and led to retaliatory tariffs by at least 25 other countries against the United States.[27]

Franklin D. Roosevelt took office as president in 1933 determined to set the United States on new domestic and foreign policy courses. In domestic affairs, he proclaimed the **New Deal,** in which the national government played a larger role than ever before in economic affairs and accepted deficit spending in an attempt to recover from the Great Depression. In foreign policy, Roosevelt accepted a mechanism, the Reciprocal Trade Agreements Act, which allowed the president to reduce tariffs by up to 50 percent after understandings were reached with other countries. In 1933, he recognized the Soviet Union, avoiding the issue of debts that the old czarist government owed the United States, and that the Soviet government refused to pay, by agreeing to discuss them in the future.[28]

Roosevelt also changed U.S. policy toward Latin America and the Caribbean by proclaiming the **Good Neighbor policy,** under which Roosevelt promised the United States would "respect the rights of others," that is, Latin American and Caribbean states.[29] Following the proclamation of the Good Neighbor policy, the United States became less likely to use military force to protect American business interests in the region and more willing to discuss rather than impose solutions on Latin American and Caribbean states. Even so, given the history of U.S. relations with states in the region, the reality of American economic clout and military power loomed in the background.

Careening toward Conflict

The Great Depression undermined the economic and social fabric of many countries around the world. Several turned to extremist political parties to solve their problems. This was particularly true in Germany, Italy, and Japan.

In Germany, reparation payments, poor leadership, and the Great Depression devastated the economy, and many Germans looked for strong leadership to find a way out of the crisis. Adolf Hitler's **National Socialist (Nazi) Party** claimed to offer such leadership. As a result, the Nazis won more and more seats in elections to the German parliament held between 1930 and 1933, enabling Hitler to become Germany's chancellor in 1933. Hitler preached that Germans were a superior race destined to rule Europe and the world. He also played on Germany's desire for revenge for the humiliations inflicted on the country in the 1918 Treaty of Paris.[30]

In Italy, the fascist dictator Benito Mussolini promoted ultra-nationalism, advocated Italian expansion, and sought to create a new Roman empire. In Asia, Japan's military gained control and set the island country on a path toward militarism, expansion, and empire. As we have seen, Japan invaded Manchuria, part of northern China, in 1931, annexed it in 1932, and withdrew from the League of Nations in 1933 after the League issued a report that labeled the **Japanese invasion of Manchuria** aggression.

The world was careening down a path toward conflict. After Hitler became chancellor in 1933, Germany withdrew from the League of Nations, two years later announcing that it was rearming. The League condemned Germany's actions, but neither it nor any individual state did anything more. In 1935, Italy invaded Ethiopia. This time the League condemned and invoked economic sanctions against Italy, but the sanctions failed to influence Italy. Never a major player in the international politics of the 1930s, the League was now universally considered ineffective.

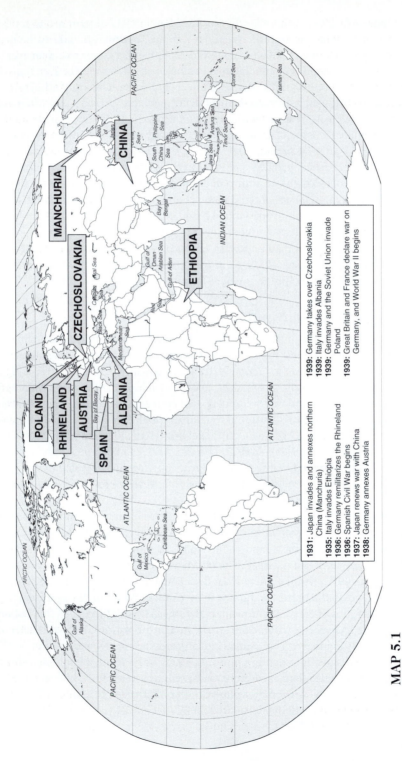

MAP 5.1
Global Hot Spots and Conflicts in the 1930s

The world's descent into war continued in the last half of the 1930s. In 1936, Hitler sent German troops into the Rhineland, an area of Germany bordering France and Belgium that the Treaty of Paris had "permanently" demilitarized. The Spanish Civil War erupted in 1936, with Italy and Germany aiding General Francisco Franco's assault on the Spanish government. After three years, Franco emerged victorious. Italy and Germany also established a formal alliance in 1936, the **Rome-Berlin Axis.** Japan renewed its war with China in 1937, acquiring territory along China's coast as it attempted to subjugate the entire country. In 1938, Germany marched into Austria and annexed it. Later the same year, after fomenting riots in the German-speaking Sudetenland portion of Czechoslovakia, Hitler at the 1938 **Munich Conference** gained British, French, and Italian acceptance of German control over the Sudetenland. This policy of **appeasement** failed. In early 1939, Germany took over the rest of Czechoslovakia and Italy marched into Albania. Throughout these years, Hitler's government persecuted Jews in every territory Germany controlled.[31]

Then, in August 1939, Germany and the Soviet Union signed the **Nazi-Soviet Non-Aggression Pact.**[32] In September, Germany invaded Poland. Two days later, France and Great Britain declared war on Germany. World War II had begun.

American Isolationism and Neutrality before World War II

Meanwhile, the United States, like the rest of the world, did little to oppose German, Japanese, and Italian aggression except write diplomatic notes and complain. Still mired in the Great Depression, the United States tried to stay apart from the building political and military crises in Europe and Asia. Although never officially stated, the prevailing American attitude in almost all sectors of the population seemed to be: "We oppose German, Italian, and Japanese expansion, but it is up to the countries of Europe and Asia to stop it." Most Americans retreated behind the traditional American claims of isolationism to avoid action and responsibility.

Congress expressed its isolationism and desire to avoid conflict by passing a series of **Neutrality Acts** from 1935 to 1937 to keep President Franklin D. Roosevelt and others from involving the United States in foreign conflicts. Roosevelt supported the 1935 Neutrality Act until it became clear that Congress would not give him the ability to decide which country in a conflict an arms embargo should be placed upon. Thus, the president would not be able to discriminate between an aggressor state and a victim state. Instead, Congress in the 1935 Neutrality Act required an arms embargo to be placed on all combatants once the president declared that a state of war existed. Later Neutrality Acts forbade the United States and U.S. banks from extending loans to warring countries, declared American neutrality in the Spanish Civil War, prevented American citizens from traveling on ships sailing under the flag of warring countries, and mandated that U.S. exports to warring countries be shipped in vessels those countries owned.[33]

Until late 1938, Roosevelt was as much an isolationist and supporter of neutrality as anyone. He often implored Americans to conform to the Neutrality Acts and declared in a 1936 speech that he had "pass[ed] unnumbered hours, thinking and planning how war may be kept" from the United States.[34] When Germany annexed Czechoslovakia in 1938, Roosevelt called for negotiations but informed Hitler that the United States had "no political involvement in Europe," thereby removing any chance that Hitler might be deterred by possible U.S. opposition.[35] At first, when the Munich Conference partitioned Czechoslovakia, Roosevelt supported appeasement, even welcoming it as a step toward peace.

Why did Roosevelt and most Americans support isolationism and neutrality in the late 1930s despite the gathering clouds of aggression and war? There were several reasons for American isolationism and neutrality.

First, despite Roosevelt's New Deal, the United States remained mired in the Great Depression, and most Americans saw economic recovery as the primary national objective. Many of Roosevelt's supporters feared that if the United States involved itself more deeply in European and Asian issues, resources would be diverted from the New Deal and it would fail.

Second, most Americans remained convinced that Europe and Asia were far away and should handle their own problems. Having come to Europe's rescue in World War I only 20 years earlier, most Americans saw no reason to do it again. Isolationism once again reigned over involvement, especially when it came to European and Asian affairs, but elsewhere as well.

Third, some Americans were convinced that Germany was partially justified in its efforts to regain land taken from it by the 1918 Treaty of Paris. Some also argued that Great Britain and France were as much to blame for World War I as Germany, and that American involvement in World War I was a mistake not to be repeated, probably precipitated by arms makers and bankers who profited from the war.[36]

Fourth, some Americans remembered how, during World War I, the Wilson Administration curtailed civil liberties to quell dissent and opposition to the war effort. They did not want that to happen again.

Fifth, having substantially disarmed following World War I, the United States was unprepared to respond militarily to overseas aggression even had it so desired. The U.S. Army was undermanned and poorly trained, and although the U.S. Navy had a sizeable presence particularly in the Pacific, it was not prepared for warfare.

From Neutrality to War

Despite the reasons for American isolationism and neutrality, Germany's absorption of Czechoslovakia and Japan's aggression against China troubled Roosevelt. Thus, Roosevelt in late 1938 began preparing the United States for greater involvement. He asked Congress for $300 million for national defense, protested to Germany about its persecution of the Jews, and loaned money to China in its struggle against Japan. He permitted France to purchase over 500 U.S.-made warplanes and developed a program to increase U.S. aircraft production to 10,000 planes per year. Clearly, Roosevelt had experienced a change of heart. He also advocated revising the Neutrality Act so that the United States at the president's discretion could embargo arms sales and shipments to aggressor states while providing arms to states that had been attacked, but Congress refused.

Even after Germany invaded and defeated Poland, the United States did not go to war. As in World War I, the United States remained aloof from the conflict, this time for 26 months. Throughout this time, Roosevelt moved the United States closer and closer to an outright alliance with Great Britain, attempting to provide it with as much assistance as possible without going to war.[37] Roosevelt began this effort shortly after Germany invaded Poland by again asking Congress to revise the Neutrality Act. This time Congress approved Roosevelt's request to give him the ability to permit arms sales and shipments to states that had been attacked but embargo them to aggressor states.

Roosevelt's pro-Allied leanings were further underlined in subsequent weeks when he influenced the Pan-American Conference, an organization that included almost all Western Hemisphere states, to declare a 300-mile-wide neutrality zone along the entire coast of the Americas with the exception of Canada. The U.S. Navy began sending **neutrality patrols** into this zone with the intention of sinking any unidentified warship from a belligerent state that was found in the neutral zone. The only such ships, of course, were German submarines. The neutrality zone and its accompanying neutrality patrols were the precursors to greatly expanded U.S.-British naval cooperation during 1940 and 1941.

The United States also took other steps during 1940 and 1941 to assist Great Britain. After France fell to Germany in June 1940, Roosevelt promised British Prime Minister **Winston Churchill** that the United States would provide Great Britain "the material resources of this nation."[38] He began to do this in September 1940 when he used an executive agreement to transfer 50 destroyers to Great Britain in exchange for the use of eight British bases stretching from Newfoundland in the north to British Guiana in the south. This began the **Lend-Lease Program,** which Congress formally approved—and expanded—in March 1941 when it allowed Roosevelt to "sell, transfer title to, exchange, lease, lend, or otherwise dispose of" arms, munitions, and any other defense materials to "any country whose defense the President deems vital to the defense of the United States."[39] The United States became, in Roosevelt's own phrase, "the great arsenal of democracy."[40] Although the way in which the Lend-Lease Program began via an executive agreement caused considerable resentment in Congress both at the time and later, it was clear that Roosevelt believed the United States needed to act, and act quickly, without entering into a lengthy debate over the wisdom of supplying aid to Great Britain. (See Chapter 10 for details.)

Roosevelt also began to prepare the United States for war. In 1940, he induced Congress to pass the Selective Training and Service Act, the first peacetime draft in U.S. history. He increased military spending and asked prominent Americans to support Lend-Lease, the draft, and larger defense expenditures. In early 1941 he extended the reach of the U.S. Navy's neutrality patrols so that American warships steamed halfway across the Atlantic. In mid-1941, he sent troops to Greenland and Iceland in the interests of hemispheric defense.

As if any more proof were needed that Roosevelt had opted for virtual alliance with Great Britain, the president met with Winston Churchill in August on a British battleship off Newfoundland to discuss the war and determine what additional support the United States could provide. Convinced that war with Germany and probably Japan was inevitable, Roosevelt and Churchill concluded the **Atlantic Charter,** soon regarded as the Anglo-American statement of war objectives. Like Wilson's Fourteen Points, the Atlantic Charter argued for collective security, national self-determination, freedom of the seas, and an open international trading system. In addition, the United States and

Great Britain rejected territorial gains and pledged themselves to economic policies that would lead to "social security." They also agreed to establish a "wider and permanent system of general security" and to respect each other's "existing obligations" (i.e. Great Britain's colonial empire), but Churchill could not convince Roosevelt to include a specific statement on either a new League of Nations or support for colonialism.[41]

The Atlantic Charter sealed Anglo-American collaboration, but it did not guarantee U.S. entry into World War II. Many Americans even in mid-1941 advocated avoiding war. Thus, Roosevelt had to undertake these activities carefully and develop bipartisan support. Despite Roosevelt's care to develop domestic support and the growing urgency of the need for such programs, considerable opposition to the programs and to U.S. involvement with, much less entry into, the war remained. Strong opposition to entering the war remained even after German subs in late 1941 sank two U.S. destroyers, the *Kearny* and the *Reuben James*. Although Roosevelt in November convinced Congress to repeal several Neutrality Act provisions, every poll of the period indicated that while Americans had no sympathy for Germany, Italy, or Japan, they did not want to go to war. As one British participant in the Atlantic Charter meeting observed, "There isn't the slightest chance of the United States entering the war until compelled to do so by a direct attack on its own territory."[42]

Meanwhile, war clouds were gathering in Asia. As we have seen, when Japan resumed its efforts to conquer China in 1937, the United States protested but, for several reasons, did little. Public sentiment remained strongly anti-war, attention was focused on escaping the Great Depression, and U.S. military forces in the Pacific were no match for Japan. As in Europe, however, the United States slowly changed policy to cope with the situation. In July 1939, the United States notified Japan that in six months it would abrogate the 1911 U.S.-Japanese commercial treaty. After the treaty was abrogated, Roosevelt placed an embargo on shipments of aviation fuel and high-grade scrap iron to Japan, later expanding the embargo to include all scrap metal. U.S. oil shipments to Japan continued.

None of this deterred Japan. Japan's assault on China continued in 1940. With France having been defeated in June by Germany, Japan occupied France's colonies in northern Indochina in September. Japan in the same month concluded the **Tripartite Pact** with Germany and Italy in which all three countries agreed to come to the defense of the others if any were attacked by a country not currently in the war. With the United States being the only major power not at war, it was clear against whom the pact was aimed.

Roosevelt recognized that, even though the United States remained at peace, the war had become globalized.[43] Roosevelt chose to concentrate first on Germany and avoid conflict with Japan without appeasing Japan. Thus, the president throughout early 1941 authorized U.S. diplomats to make numerous contacts with their Japanese counterparts to express U.S. concerns about Japan's aggressive policies, insist that Japan respect Chinese sovereignty and territorial integrity, and find a way to avoid war. Several private efforts to these ends were also initiated. None succeeded in restraining Japan's imperialism. When in July the United States discovered Japanese troop transports heading toward France's colonies in southern Indochina, Roosevelt signed an executive order freezing Japan's funds in the United States. This meant that the United States stopped almost all trade with Japan, including oil.

This placed Japan in a difficult position. With a U.S. embargo in place on all strategic materials including oil, metal, and aviation fuel, Japan had two choices. First, it could end its effort to conquer China, but no one in Tokyo preferred that. Second, it could invade the oil-rich Dutch and British East Indies. This would require Japanese military action against the U.S.-controlled Philippines, and that would mean war with the United States. Japan chose the second option.[44]

On December 7, 1941, Japan used a new weapon of war, the aircraft carrier, to initiate an attack against the U.S. naval base at **Pearl Harbor** in Hawaii. Over 300 warplanes launched from six Japanese carriers killed 2,400 Americans and sank seven battleships. On December 8, Roosevelt asked Congress for a declaration of war. Roosevelt's request met with unanimous support in the Senate and only a single negative vote in the House. The United States was at war with Japan. Three days later, in keeping with the Tripartite Pact with Japan, Hitler declared war on the United States. Roosevelt's artful balancing act of suspending the United States between neutrality and war while being the arsenal of democracy had succeeded for over two years, but the United States now was at war on two fronts.

AMERICAN FOREIGN POLICY DURING WORLD WAR II: 1941–1945

After the attack on Pearl Harbor, Americans threw themselves behind the war effort. American workers and the U.S. economy provided the arms, munitions, military equipment, and other war goods that powered the U.S. armed forces as they fought in Africa, Asia, Europe, and at sea. They also provided millions of tons of weapons, equipment, and supplies to America's major allies: Great Britain, China, and Russia. Throughout World War II, there were three key U.S. strategies: maintain a Grand Alliance of Great Britain, the Soviet Union, and the United States; win the war in Europe first; and achieve complete victory and unconditional surrender.[45]

The **Grand Alliance** included U.S. provision of large quantities of aid and assistance to Great Britain and the Soviet Union and frequent conferences to plan wartime and postwar strategy. As Table 5.2 shows, conferences occurred often, especially between the United States and Great Britain. The conferences played a key role in the coalition warfare that led to the defeat of the Axis powers, but they did not prevent disagreements from occurring.

One of the main disagreements within the Grand Alliance was over opening a second front in Europe. Bearing the brunt of the Nazi's armed forces, the Soviet Union and its leader **Joseph Stalin** wanted an Anglo-American invasion across the English Channel as soon as possible to divert some of Germany's forces away from the Soviet Union. After first telling the Soviets that an invasion would occur in 1942, the United States and Great Britain delayed until 1943 and eventually June 1944. The Soviet Union and Stalin resented this delay, refusing to see their allies' North African and Italian campaigns in 1942 and 1943 as true second fronts, since the fighting there diverted few if any German forces from the war in Russia. This caused a serious rift in the Grand Alliance.

TABLE 5.2
MAJOR WORLD WAR II CONFERENCES

Conference	Date	Participants	Major Outcomes
Newfoundland	Aug. 1941	U.S., G.B	Atlantic Charter
Washington	Dec. 1941	U.S., G.B.	War against Germany is top priority: UN Declaration
Washington	June 1942	U.S., G.B.	North African campaign plans
Moscow	Aug. 1942	U.S., G.B., USSR	Delay second front
Casablanca	Jan. 1943	U.S., G.B.	Unconditional surrender is goal; Italian campaign plans
Washington	May 1943	U.S., G.B.	May 1944 target day for cross-channel invasion
Quebec	Aug. 1943	U.S.,G.B.	Confirms cross-channel attack
Moscow	Oct. 1943	U.S., G.B., USSR	UN to be formed after war; USSR to enter Pacific war after Europe war over
Washington	Nov. 1943	44 countries	Creates UN Relief and Rehabilitation Administration
Cairo	Nov. 1943	U.S., G.B., China	Planning for postwar Asia
Teheran	Nov. 1943	U.S., G.B., USSR	Reaffirms UN and Soviet entry to Pacific war; agreement on cross-channel attack
Bretton Woods	July 1944	44 countries	Creates World Bank and International Monetary Fund
Dumbarton Oaks	Aug.–Sept. 1944	U.S., G.B., USSR, China	Planning for UN
Quebec	Sept. 1944	U.S., G.B.	Planning for postwar Germany
Moscow	Oct. 1944	G.B., USSR	Spheres of influence in Balkans agreed to
Yalta	Feb. 1945	U.S., G.B., USSR	Planning for postwar Poland and UN; German reparations; reaffirms USSR to enter Pacific war and get Asian territory.
San Francisco	Apr.–June 1945	50 countries	UN Charter
Potsdam	July–Aug. 1945	U.S., G.B., USSR	German reconstruction and reparations

The Grand Alliance was also divided over Eastern European boundaries and politics. At the 1945 **Yalta and Potsdam conferences,** the three allies discussed boundary issues and Europe's postwar political map. At Yalta, Roosevelt pushed for free elections in Eastern Europe. Stalin seemed to accept this, but no agreement was nailed down. At Potsdam, the allies divided Germany and Berlin into four occupation zones, one each overseen by the United States, Great Britain, France, and the Soviet Union.[46] Other bilateral meetings included discussions of boundaries and postwar governance, with Churchill and Stalin even agreeing at a 1944 conference to establish spheres of influence in Balkan states on a percentage basis.

None of the conferences reached a true accord on Eastern Europe, and the political map of postwar Europe became one of the most divisive and contentious issues in the postwar world.[47] In the years after the war, the Soviet Union was substantially free to establish pro-communist governments in the countries in Eastern Europe where it had troops. Meanwhile in Germany, the American, British, and French zones were united to become West Germany and West Berlin, and the Soviet zone turned into East Germany and East Berlin. The Yalta and Potsdam conferences thus shaped the map of postwar Europe that was in place from 1945 until 1989, when communism collapsed in Eastern Europe.

The second key U.S. strategy during World War II—winning the war in Europe first—flowed out of Roosevelt's decision before the United States entered the war to help Great Britain and attempt to avoid war with Japan. Roosevelt recognized that Germany presented a more serious threat than Japan to the survival of both Great Britain and the Soviet Union.

The third key strategy that the United States and its allies pursued was to achieve complete victory and unconditional surrender. Learning from World War I and the Treaty of Paris, the members of the Grand Alliance intended to remove the governments of Germany, Italy, and Japan as well as the political philosophies of fascism and militarism that had fomented World War II. This meant that new governments had to be constructed based on new political philosophies. Since the United States and Great Britain were democratic states and the Soviet Union was a communist state, the Grand Alliance never agreed on what type of governments would be put into place in the defeated states after World War II. This led to serious problems following the war.

After the United States entered World War II, the war in Europe continued for three and a half years. When the conflict ended in 1945, over 40 million people had been killed, including over 6 million Jews slaughtered by the Nazis. The Soviet Union lost 20–25 million people. Even today, no one is certain how many Soviet citizens died. Europe again lay in ruins. Germany was shattered, occupied by American, British, French, and Soviet troops. Almost every economy in continental Europe was at a standstill. Governments and societies in many countries had to be reconstructed from scratch. No war had ever been as destructive.

Meanwhile, in the Pacific, the United States pursued an island-hopping strategy as it pushed the Japanese empire back toward its home islands. Finally, in August 1945, the United States dropped atomic bombs on the Japanese cities of **Hiroshima and Nagasaki.**[48] Fittingly, the most destructive war in human history ended with the use of the most destructive weapons human beings had ever created.

HOW DO YOU REBUILD A SHATTERED WORLD?

World War II was over, but who would rebuild the shattered world, in whose image would it be shaped, and how would it be done? These were the central questions that faced the Grand Alliance at the end of the war. The questions were serious in Europe, but somewhat less vexing in Japan, where the United States predominated. In China, meanwhile, civil war resumed between the Nationalist Chinese, favored by the United States, and the Communist Chinese.

In Europe, disagreements over the future of Germany, Poland, and other states threatened to tear the Grand Alliance apart. Great Britain and the United States had similar views. Both wanted states with democratic governments and free-market economies, and both wanted Germany to be economically prosperous but not militaristic. Conversely, the Soviet Union wanted pro-Soviet and preferably communist governments with centralized economic and political systems. Moscow also wanted to keep Germany weak and to punish it for the destruction it inflicted on the Soviet Union during the war. As with World War I, then, the war had been won, but the question remained whether peace would prevail.

For the United States, there was a critical difference between the end of World War I and the end of World War II. At the end of World War I, the United States, although the only major state whose homeland was not ravaged by war, was only one of several powerful states. At the end of World War II, the United States was far and away the world's most powerful country both militarily and economically. Its military had won the war against Japan almost single-handedly, and it had played a dominant role along with the Soviet Union in defeating Germany. It was the only country with the ability to build atomic weapons. And once again its homeland and its economy had escaped the worst effects of war.

How would the United States respond to its new position of global preeminence, predominance, and power, and how would its preeminence, predominance, and power affect its mission, interests, and principles? Which competing theme would predominate: isolationism or involvement? Would the United States return to the essentially isolationist policies that it had preferred, at least regarding Europe, for most of its history, or had the experience of World War II convinced American leaders and the American people that isolationism was a policy of the past? Which competing theme would emerge supreme: idealism or realism? Would the United States conclude that peace could best be achieved by cooperation or by power? And would the United States continue the multilateralist policies that it had adopted during World War II, seeking to create a new cooperative international order, or would it return to the essentially unilateralist tendencies that had dominated American foreign policy for most of American history? In the brave new post–World War II world, no one knew, not even the Americans.

SUMMARY

In 1914, Europe slid into a war that nobody wanted. For three years, the United States avoided the First World War, but Germany's use of unrestricted submarine warfare, its refusal to honor rights of neutral countries on the high seas, and its proposal to Mexico that Mexico ally itself with Germany to regain land Mexico lost to the United States convinced President Woodrow Wilson in 1917 to ask Congress to declare war on Germany.

The U.S. military build-up was rapid. When the war ended in late 1918, 2 million U.S. troops were in Europe, having played a major role in winning the war. Wilson also believed he had a perfect plan to build a peaceful postwar world. Called Wilsonian idealism, his plan proposed to eliminate barriers to democracy and free trade; build an open free-market economic system; end secret diplomacy; pursue disarmament; allow ethnic groups to exercise national self-determination by setting up their own democratically elected government in their own country; and create a League of Nations that would use collective security, that is, states acting together against any state that was aggressive, to deter conflict.

Many opposed Wilson's ideas. Many Americans wanted to return to isolationism, and Europeans wanted to punish Germany. As a result, the Treaty of Paris that ended the war blamed Germany for the war, required it to pay reparations, and stripped it of territory, but it also included national self-determination and the League of Nations. However, with many Americans fearing that League membership would end isolationism and force the United States to act when its interests were not at stake, the United States never joined the League.

Despite isolationism, the United States in the 1920s stayed involved in foreign affairs, pursuing idealism via efforts like the Kellogg-Briand Pact to abolish war and the Washington Naval Treaties to reduce the size of navies, and stressing traditional policies such as trade and maintaining order in Latin America and the Caribbean by occupying the Dominican Republic, Nicaragua, and Haiti. When Franklin Roosevelt became president in 1933, the United States undertook new foreign policies like recognizing the Soviet Union and adopting a Good Neighbor policy in Latin American and the Caribbean under which the United States would respect the rights of others. Even so, most Americans saw the United States as isolationist, probably because it stayed out of the Spanish Civil War, Japan's war against China, and other 1930s conflicts. Then, in 1939, World War II began when Germany invaded Poland and France and Britain declared war on Germany.

The United States at first stayed out of the war, but Roosevelt soon asked Congress to pass the first peacetime draft in U.S. history and began the Lend-Lease Program in which the United States gave ships and arms to Great Britain in exchange for naval bases. He also met British Prime Minister Winston Churchill to discuss what other help the United States could provide and to sign the Atlantic Charter, a statement of war objectives.

War clouds gathered in Asia as in 1937, Japan resumed its war against China. The United States embargoed oil and scrap-metal sales to Japan and then froze Japanese funds in U.S. banks. In turn, Japan concluded it had to invade the oil-rich East Indies, which required it to attack U.S. forces in the Pacific. On December 7, 1941, Japan attacked the U.S. naval base at Pearl Harbor in Hawaii. The United States was at war.

Americans threw themselves behind the war effort, providing U.S. forces and American allies immense quantities of war goods. U.S. war strategies included creating a Grand Alliance of Great Britain, the Soviet Union, and the United States; winning the war in Europe first; and achieving complete victory and unconditional surrender. When the European war ended, over 40 million people had died, Europe lay in ruins, and almost every economy was at a standstill. In the Pacific, the United States used an island-hopping strategy, ending the war in August 1945 by dropping atomic bombs on Hiroshima and Nagasaki in Japan.

At the end of World War II, the United States was the world's most powerful country, its homeland almost untouched by war. How would the United States respond to its new position of global preeminence, predominance, and power? No one knew, not even the Americans.

KEY TERMS AND CONCEPTS

rhetoric of neutrality

violation of neutral rights

Lusitania

unrestricted submarine warfare

Zimmermann telegram

American military build-up

Wilsonianism

national self-determination

Fourteen Points

collective security

Versailles Peace Conference

Treaty of Paris

League of Nations

V. I. Lenin

Bolshevik Party

Red Scare

American intervention in Russia

Kellogg-Briand Pact

Roaring Twenties

U.S. occupations of the Dominican
    Republic, Nicaragua, and Haiti

Great Depression

Smoot-Hawley Tariff

New Deal

Good Neighbor policy

National Socialist (Nazi) Party

Japanese invasion of Manchuria

Rome-Berlin Axis

Munich Conference

appeasement

Nazi-Soviet Non-Aggression Pact

Neutrality Acts

neutrality patrols

Winston Churchill

Lend-Lease Program

Atlantic Charter

Tripartite Pact

Pearl Harbor

Grand Alliance

Joseph Stalin

Yalta and Potsdam conferences

Hiroshima and Nagasaki

THINKING CRITICALLY

1. How and why did the United States stay out of World War I for as long as it did, and why did it eventually enter the war?

2. What impact did the U.S. entry into World War I have on the war?

3. What is Wilsonian idealism, and how did it affect the peace settlement at the end of World War I?

4. What role did the United States play in the formation and operation of the League of Nations? How successful was the League, and why?

5. Why did the United States refuse to join the League of Nations? What impact did this have on the League?

6. Using examples to support your position, assess the extent to which the United States retreated into isolationism and pursued idealism in its foreign policy in the 1920s.

7. What were the major events that led to World War II in Europe, and how did the United States respond to them? Why did U.S. policymakers choose these responses?

8. What were the major events that led to World War II in Asia and the Pacific, and how did the United States respond to them? Why did U.S. policymakers choose these responses?

9. What were the three key U.S. strategies in World War II, and how and why did the United States pursue each?

NOTES

1. For details of the Russian fiasco, see David MacKenzie and Michael W. Curran, *A History of Russia and the Soviet Union* (Homewood, Ill.: Dorsey Press, n.d.), pp. 434–436.

2. Historians more or less agree that World War I erupted for seven primary reasons: (1) the growing power of Germany, along with Germany's desire to expand; (2) the changing relative economic strength of Europe's great powers, especially Austria-Hungary, France, Germany, Great Britain, and Russia; (3) colonial rivalries and global imperialism; (4) the growth of nationalism in Europe, and especially its impact in the Balkans on Austria-Hungary and the Ottoman Empire; (5) the rigid alliance system of the early twentieth century that arrayed France, Great Britain, and Russia on one side against Austria-Hungary and Germany on the other; (6) the "cult of the offensive" that led leaders to believe a military conflict would be short and not very costly; and (7) the growing naval rivalry between Great Britain and Germany. For discussions of how and why Europe slid into World War I, see Rene Albrecht-Carre, *A Diplomatic History of Europe since the Congress of Vienna* (New York: Harper and Row, 1973); James Joll, *The Origins of the First World War* (London, England: Longman, 1992); and A. J. P. Taylor, *The Struggle for Mastery in Europe* (Oxford, England: Clarion Press, 1957).

3. See Paul Kennedy, *The Rise and Fall of the Great Powers* (New York: Vintage, 1987), especially pp. 194–249, for discussion of U.S. and European industrial, trade, and financial dealings and their impact on national power before World War I.

4. For details on the American entry into World War I, see Ross Gregory, *The Origins of American Intervention in the First World War* (New York: Norton, 1971).

5. U.S. Department of State, *Foreign Relations of the United States, 1915, Supplement* (Washington, D.C.: U.S. Government Printing Office, 1928), p. 99.

6. See Thomas A. Bailey and Paul B. Ryan, *The Lusitania Disaster* (New York: Free Press, 1975), for a discussion of the sinking of the *Lusitania*.

7. As reported in R. S. Baker and W. E. Dodd, eds., *Public Papers of Woodrow Wilson: The New Democracy*, Vol. 2 (New York: Harper and Brothers, 1926), pp. 407–414.

8. See Barbara Tuchman, *The Zimmermann Telegram* (New York: Viking, 1958).

9. As reported in R. S. Baker and W. E. Dodd, eds., *Public Papers of Woodrow Wilson: War and Peace*, Vol. 1 (New York: Harper and Brothers, 1927), pp. 6–16.

10. For several views of the American role in World War I, see Edward M. Coffman, *The War to End All Wars: The American Military Experience in World War I* (Lexington: University of Kentucky Press, 1998); John S. D. Eisenhower and Joanne Thompson Eisenhower, *Yanks: The Epic Story of the American Army in World War I* (New York: Free Press, 2002); and Anne Cipriano Venzon, ed., *The United States in the First World War: An Encyclopedia*, Military History of the United States (New York: Garland, 1995).

11. For histories of World War I, see James L. Stokesbury, *A Short History of World War I* (New York: Morrow, 1981); B. H. Liddel Hart, *History of the First World War, 1914–1918* (London, England: Faber and Faber, 1938); and Taylor, *The Struggle for Mastery in Europe*.

12. For discussions of Wilson's Fourteen Points, see Robert H. Ferrell, *American Diplomacy: A History* (New York: Norton, 1975), pp. 482–492; and Arthur S. Link et al., eds., *The Papers of Woodrow Wilson*, Vol. 45 (Princeton: Princeton University Press, 1964), p. 529. See also Lloyd E. Ambrosius, *Wilsonianism: Woodrow Wilson and His Legacy in American Foreign Policy* (New York: Palgrave Macmillan, 2002).

13. Wilson's arguments laid the intellectual foundation for the "democratic peace" viewpoint that became prevalent following the end of the Cold War, which argues that democracies do not go to war with each other. This view of international politics as it applies to American foreign policy will be covered in greater depth in Chapter 7.

14. The 1648 Treaty of Westphalia, which ended the Thirty Years War, is widely perceived as the father of the modern international system of sovereign nation-states. For the text of the treaty, see the Yale School of Law's Avalon Project at http://www.yale.edu.lawweb/avalon/westphal.htm.

15. As reported in Henry Blumenthal, *Illusion and Reality in Franco-American Relations, 1914–1945* (Baton Rouge: Louisiana State University Press, 1986), p. 48.

16. For several views of the Versailles Peace Conference, see H. R. Rudin, *Armistice 1918* (New Haven: Yale University Press, 1944); T. A. Bailey, *Wilson and the Peacemakers* (New York: Macmillan, 1947); A. Lentin, *Lloyd George, Woodrow Wilson, and the Guilt of Germany: An Essay in the Pre-History of Appeasement* (Baton Rouge: Louisiana State University Press, 1984); and Klaus Schwabe, *Woodrow Wilson, Revolutionary Germany, and Peacemaking, 1918–1919* (Chapel Hill: University of North Carolina Press, 1985).

17. Wilson was not alone in his concern. A British observer noted that, "After the 'War to end War,' they seem to have been pretty successful in Paris at making a 'Peace to end Peace.'" Archibald Wavell, as quoted in David Fromkin, *A Peace to End All Peace: The Fall of the Ottoman Empire and the Creation of the Modern Middle East* (New York: Avon, 1989).

18. For details on the American debate over the League of Nations and the Treaty of Paris, see Robert H. Ferrell, *Woodrow Wilson and World War I, 1917–1921* (New York: Harper and Row, 1985), and D. F. Fleming, *The United States and League of Nations, 1918–1920* (New York: Russell and Russell, 1968).

19. For details of these events, see Mackenzie and Curran, pp. 435–467; and John M. Thompson, *Russia, Bolshevism, and the Versailles Peace* (Princeton: Princeton University Press, 1966).

20. For details of the American intervention in Russia, see Robert L. Willett Jr., *Sideshow: America's Undeclared War, 1918–1920* (Brassey's, 2003).

21. "Normalcy" was a term that President Harding used to indicate that he intended to concentrate on domestic affairs. For one view of American foreign policy under Harding, see chapter 3 of Benjamin D. Rhodes, *United States Foreign Policy in the Interwar Period, 1918–1941: The Golden Age of American Diplomatic and Military Complacency* (New York: Praeger, 2001).

22. *The General Pact for the Renunciation of War* (Washington, D.C.: U.S. Government Printing Office, 1928).

23. For a good discussion of the Washington Naval Treaty and other naval events of the early twentieth century, see Phillips Payson O'Brien, *British and American Naval Power: Politics and Policy, 1900–1936* (New York: Praeger, 1998).

24. For the text of the Locarno Pact, see League of Nations, *Treaty Series, 1926–1927*, Vol. 54, pp. 291–297.

25. For more details on these events, see Cole Blasier, *The Hovering Giant: U.S. Responses to Revolutionary Change in Latin America, 1910–1985* (Pittsburgh: University of Pittsburgh Press, 1985). See also Robert Pastor, *Whirlpool: U.S. Foreign Policy toward Latin America and the Caribbean* (Princeton: Princeton University Press, 1992).

26. See Charles P. Kindleberger, *The World in Depression 1929–1939* (Berkeley: University of California Press, 1986), for a global view of the Great Depression.

27. See Joseph M. Jones, *Tariff Retaliation: Repercussions of the Hawley-Smoot Bill* (New York: Garland, 1983).

28. For a discussion of some of the issues and events surrounding Roosevelt's recognition of the Soviet Union, see M. Wayne Morris, *Stalin's Famine and Roosevelt's Recognition of Russia* (Rowman and Littlefield, 1994).

29. As reported in Samuel I. Rosenman, ed., *Public Papers and Addresses of Franklin D. Roosevelt*, Vol. 2 (New York: Macmillan, 1938–1950, in 13 volumes), p. 14. Also see Blasier, *The Hovering Giant*, and Pastor, *Whirlpool*, for discussion of the Good Neighbor policy.

30. For details of Hitler's rise to power, see Konrad Heiden, *The Führer: Hitler's Rise to Power* (New York: Carroll and Graf, 1999).

31. For the Nazi role in the world's slide to war, see Christian Leitz, *Nazi Foreign Policy 1933–1941: The Road to Global War* (New York: Routledge, 2003). See also Lloyd C. Gardner, *Spheres of Influence: The Great Powers Partition Europe, from Munich to Yalta* (Chicago: Ivan R. Dee, 1990).

32. See Anthony Read, *Deadly Embrace: Hitler, Stalin, and the Nazi-Soviet Pact, 1939–1941* (New York: Norton, 1988), and Frances A. Ierace, *America and the Nazi-Soviet Pact* (New York: Vantage Press, 1978).

33. See Robert Dallek, *Franklin D. Roosevelt and American Foreign Policy, 1932–1945* (New York: Oxford University Press, 1995), and Rhodes, *United States Foreign Policy in the Interwar Period*, chapter 6

34. As reported in Rosenman, *Public Papers and Addresses of Franklin D. Roosevelt*, Vol. 5, p. 289.

35. *Foreign Relations of the United States, 1938*, Vol. 1 (Washington, D.C.: U.S. Government Printing Office, 1955), p. 685.

36. For a discussion of this view, see Wayne S. Cole, *Senator Gerald P. Nye and American Foreign Relations* (Minneapolis: University of Minnesota Press, 1962).

37. For another view of these events, see Waldo Heinrichs, *Threshold of War: Franklin D. Roosevelt and American Entry into World War II* (New York: Oxford University Press, 1990).

38. As reported in Rosenman, *Public Papers and Addresses of Franklin D. Roosevelt, 1940*, Vol. 9, p. 263.

39. *Congressional Record*, 77 (March 8, 1941), p. 2097.

40. As reported in Rosenman, *Public Papers and Addresses of Franklin D. Roosevelt, 1940*, Vol. 9, p. 640–643.

41. For the text of the Atlantic Charter, see *Foreign Relations of the United States, 1941*, Vol. 1 (Washington, D.C.: U.S. Government Printing Office, 1958), pp. 368–369. For details of the meeting that led to the charter, see Theodore A. Wilson, *The First Summit: Roosevelt and Churchill at Placentia Bay, 1941* (Boston: Houghton Mifflin, 1969).

42. Wilson, *The First Summit*, p. 260.

43. As Roosevelt wrote in January 1941, "We must recognize that hostilities in Europe, in Africa, and in Asia are all parts of a single world conflict." See Arnold A. Offner, *The Origins of the Second World War* (New York: Praeger, 1975), p. 193.

44. For a view of Japanese-American relations before World War II that is relatively sympathetic to Japan, see Roland H. Worth, *No Choice but War: The United States Embargo against Japan and the Eruption of War in the Pacific* (Jefferson, N.C.: McFarland, 1995).

45. For good accounts of World War II, see J. F. C. Fuller, *The Second World War* (New York: Meredith, 1968); and B. H. Liddel Hart, *History of the Second World War* (New York: Putnam, 1971).

46. For different views of the Yalta and Potsdam conferences, see Richard F. Fenno, *The Yalta Conference* (New York: D.C. Heath, 1972); Russell H. Buhite and Russell D. Buhite, *Decisions at Yalta: An Appraisal of Summit Diplomacy* (Scholarly Resources, 1992); Herbert Feis, *Between War and Peace: The Potsdam Conference* (Princeton: Princeton University Press, 1960); James L. Gormly, *From Potsdam to the Cold War: Big Three Diplomacy, 1945–1947* (Scholarly Resources, 1997); and W. R. Smyser and Paul H. Nitze, *From Yalta to Berlin: The Cold War Struggle over Germany* (New York: Palgrave Macmillan, 2000).

47. For additional discussion of the strained relations between the Soviet Union on the one hand and the United States and Great Britain on the other, see John Lewis Gaddis, *Strategies of Containment* (New York: Oxford, 1982), pp. 3–24; and Walter LaFeber, *America, Russia, and the Cold War 1975–1990* (New York: McGraw-Hill, 1991), pp. 8–28.

48. For discussion of the decision to drop the atomic bomb, see Martin J. Sherwin, *A World Destroyed: The Atomic Bomb and the Grand Alliance* (New York: Random House, 1989).

CHAPTER 6

Fighting the Cold War: 1945–1989

The mushroom cloud of nuclear weapons presented a terrifying backdrop to the Cold War. Nuclear weapons were never used during the Cold War, but hundreds were tested. The only time nuclear weapons were used in war was at the end of World War II, against the Japanese cities of Hiroshima (August 6, 1945) and Nagasaki (August 9, 1945). The Nagasaki explosion is shown here.

- How did the victors try to shape the world after World War II?
- Why did the Cold War begin?
- How did U.S. foreign policy change after World War II?
- How did different presidents implement the policy of containment?
- What impact did Vietnam have on the United States and U.S. foreign policy?
- What was détente, and why did it begin and end?
- After détente ended, what foreign policies did the United States pursue?

World War II ended with American fighting forces spread across the world. Never before had one country had the ability to project so great a power into every part of the globe. The United States was also the only industrialized country whose homeland had avoided the ravages of war. The era of the global **superpower** had arrived, and the United States, with its unrivaled economic and military capabilities, headed by its nuclear monopoly, had become the first superpower, without consciously seeking those capabilities.[1]

The United States' ability to project military power around the world may or may not have implied that it had the desire to do so. Differences of opinion exist even today about American intentions at the end of World War II. Sometimes the debate is quite heated, pitting so-called traditionalists against revisionists.

Traditionalists assert that, except in the area of trade, the United States was generally isolationist following the war. They point to the demobilization of U.S. conventional forces and the withdrawal of U.S. forces from Europe as proof. Often, they also point to the American desire to create the United Nations and to establish a stable international economic system as proof that the United States had only peaceful intentions and that the beginning of the Cold War was not the United States' fault. Rather, traditionalists point to the Soviet Union and its expansionist policies after World War II as the cause of the Cold War as the Soviet Union placed communist parties in power in Eastern and Central Europe, pressured Turkey, and refused to withdraw from Iran.[2]

Conversely, **revisionists** dismiss most of the traditionalists' arguments and argue instead that the United States was the primary cause of the Cold War. As the only country with nuclear weapons, they charge, the United States did not need a large conventional force to exert its influence and control. With its economic base intact, they continue, the United States could exert its economic strength wherever it desired without relying on conventional military power. Most revisionists assert that American post–World War II intentions were to continue to be involved, but at a distance, and to exert U.S. economic influence and expand U.S. political control globally, much as the United States had done in Latin America in the early years of the twentieth century. Further, they argue that the Soviet Union was not a serious threat to peace, and that its leaders responded to a perceived American threat.[3]

Whatever the reality, hopes for peace, prosperity, and security following World War II were high but not easily realized. As discussed in Chapter 5, the cooperative relationship that existed between the United States and Great Britain on the one hand and the Soviet Union on the other was strained even during the war. Relations grew even more tense after the war. U.S.-Soviet disagreement erupted over the Soviet creation of communist governments in Eastern Europe; communist subversion in France and Italy; Soviet pressures on Turkey; communist-led revolutions in Greece, Malaya, the Philippines, and Indochina; and the resumption of the communist-nationalist civil war in China.[4]

These issues led to the **Cold War,** a political-military-economic confrontation between the United States and its allies on the one hand and the Soviet Union and its allies on the other. The confrontation did not explode into full-scale war, but both sides armed themselves with thousands of nuclear weapons and large conventional forces. Conflicts and small wars occasionally erupted that involved one of the superpowers or its allies. In addition, numerous crises that did not escalate to fighting developed.[5] There were also periods during which tensions between the superpowers and their allies abated.

The Cold War began in the late 1940s and lasted until, depending on one's point of view, either the collapse of communism in Eastern Europe in 1989 or the dissolution of the Soviet Union itself in 1991. Throughout the Cold War, the United States, its leaders, and the American people saw their mission as defending democracy, promoting U.S./Western values, and preventing the spread of communism. "The free peoples of the world look to us for support in maintaining their freedoms," President Harry Truman observed in a March 12, 1947, speech before Congress that later became famous as the "Truman Doctrine speech." Continuing, Truman observed, "Great responsibilities have been placed upon us by the swift movement of events." The United States had no choice, he believed, but to support and aid foreign nations and individuals who desired political freedom as defined by the United States.

Subsequent Cold War era presidents—both Republican and Democratic—and their foreign policies followed in Truman's mission-oriented footsteps. Thus, in 1960, the Eisenhower Administration's *Presidential Commission on National Goals* postulated that U.S. foreign policy objectives should be "to extend the areas of freedom throughout the world" and "help build a world in which every human being shall be free to develop his capacities to the fullest." President John Kennedy soon after this in his inaugural address declared that the United States would "go anywhere" and "pay any price" to defend freedom, a message echoed in a somewhat different tone over two decades later by President Ronald Reagan, who in a speech on March 1983 labeled the Soviet Union an "evil empire" and declared that the United States would "rise to the challenge" to assure that communism was a "chapter in human history whose last pages even now are being written."

To America's Cold War presidents, then, the mission was clear, to defend democracy, promote U.S./Western values, and prevent the spread of communism. Different presidents pursued the mission in different ways, sometimes using different tools of policy to pursue U.S. national interests, but every president during the Cold War accepted that the United States was locked in a monumental global struggle for influence, and possibly survival, with the Soviet Union—all carried out under the specter of nuclear war.

Not surprisingly, then, with only a few years of exception, American presidents throughout the Cold War emphasized realism over idealism. Military might and economic strength, of pragmatic necessity, took precedence over morality and ideals. Only Jimmy Carter during the first years of his presidency stressed idealism over realism, and his outlook shifted late in his presidency because of the capture of American hostages in the U.S. embassy in Iran and the Soviet invasion of Afghanistan. No American president, not even Richard Nixon, rejected or abandoned American morality and ideals, but often during the Cold War these principles took a back seat to realpolitik.

Similarly, every American president during the Cold War stressed involvement over isolation. Only after the Vietnam War, when the United States suffered through its "Vietnam Syndrome" of self-doubt, did the United States exhibit a desire to return to a degree of isolationism. To be sure, debates often raged in the United States among American leaders and the American people about the wisdom of a specific overseas commitment or policy and about whether the United States had become overcommitted, but seldom during the Cold War was the necessity of overseas involvement questioned.

So, too, with multilateralism, always emphasized during the Cold War by American presidents over unilateralism. During the Cold War, American involvement in alliances, international institutions, and other international cooperative ventures reached levels unprecedented in American history. At the same time, every American Cold War president strongly defended and utilized, some more than others, the sovereign American right to act unilaterally when American national interests, in their views, required independent action.

When World War II ended, however, few Americans predicted a future world in which American foreign policy would be dominated by realism, international involvement, and multilateralism. Indeed, in 1945, most Americans hoped that victory would lead to a future of peace and prosperity, with few foreign or military worries. For a few short years—some would say months—after World War II, this hope indeed appeared a possibility.

THE POSTWAR WORLD BEFORE THE COLD WAR: 1945–1947

The post–World War II American hope for a future of peace and prosperity with few foreign or military worries was of course the result of the resounding Allied victory in World War II. With Germany and Japan having been defeated, the immediate military threat to the United States and its Allies was over. As a result of the end of the military threat and the American hope for the future, the United States between 1945 and 1947 returned most of its armed forces that had been deployed overseas to the United States. Thus, in May 1945, the United States had 3.5 million troops in Europe, but by March 1946, only 400,000 remained. Much the same thing happened in Asia. As American troops returned home, they were demobilized. As a result, the United States had 11.5 million men under arms in 1945, and only 2 million in uniform by 1947. One expert called the American action the "most rapid demobilization in the history of the world."[6] Many Americans saw this as proof that the United States had no desire to be a global power and that the American love for isolationism had returned.

The reality, however, was somewhat different. Even before World War II had ended, President Franklin Roosevelt and most American policymakers recognized that the United States, because of its immense military power and economic strength and because of the devastation that World War II had visited on most of the rest of the world, inevitably had to play a major role in building the post–World War II international system. Thus, Roosevelt recognized, the United States had to remain involved in world affairs in substantial ways. And the United States, Roosevelt believed, had to blend realism and idealism in its foreign policy, striving to create a better world even as it recognized that military capabilities and economic strength remained critical to its foreign policy.

Further, Roosevelt believed, if peace was to be obtained and a better and safer world created, the United States had to be involved in multilateral international organizations in ways that it never before had been. Although Roosevelt did not live to see the end of World War II, his beliefs and his handiwork appeared in many of the international organizations and agreements that came into being after the war. The United Nations, a "new and improved" League of Nations, and the Bretton Woods Agreements, a set of accords that structured the postwar international economic system, were among the most important. Conceptually created during Roosevelt's presidency and implemented during the presidency of Harry S. Truman, the United Nations and the Bretton Woods agreements became crucial parts of the United States' immediate post–World War II foreign policy.

New International Institutions

Having experienced the ravages of two world wars within 30 years, the victorious powers understandably believed it necessary to somehow keep the peace once it was won. The advent of nuclear weapons made it all the more important to find a way to do this.

One way to accomplish this, Roosevelt believed, was to create a new and improved League of Nations, this time with the participation of all of the world's great powers, including the United States. Thus, even before the war ended, the United States and 51 other countries met in San Francisco in 1945 to create a new international governmental organization, the **United Nations.**[7] The UN's primary purpose was to guarantee the security of member states and to promote economic, physical, and social well-being around the world. Successful UN operations depended on the postwar cooperation of members of the Grand Alliance as well as China and France, the states that had the five permanent seats on the UN Security Council. The United States was one of the primary supporters of the creation of the United Nations.

U.S. and Western European leaders also believed that the collapse of the international economic system and the decline of international trade in the 1930s had helped create conditions that led to the rise of dictators and the beginning of World War II. To prevent this from happening again and to help maintain international economic stability, aid economic development, and encourage trade, the victorious powers led by the United States also intended to create new international economic organizations.

Thus, 44 countries sent representatives to Bretton Woods, New Hampshire, in 1944 to finalize the **Bretton Woods Agreements.**[8] These agreements established the **International Monetary Fund (IMF)** to stabilize exchange rates among major currencies and set their value in terms of the dollar and gold, and the International Bank for Reconstruction and Development, also called the **World Bank,** tasked to help the world recover economically from the destruction of World War II. These organizations remain in place today and play a major role in current international affairs.

The United States and its allies also hoped to create an international trade organization at Bretton Woods, but the U.S. Congress feared that such an organization would lead to international control of the U.S. economy. Given this fear, the most that could be achieved was a **General Agreement on Tariffs and Trade (GATT),** a set of agreements that over the years led to negotiations that substantially reduced tariffs. GATT remained in place until the present World Trade Organization was created in 1995.

The American intention to participate in these institutions signaled a significant shift in U.S. attitudes away from isolationism and unilateralism and toward international involvement and multilateralism. To participate in these institutions, the United States had to be more involved in international organizations than before the war. The United States also had to be more willing to accept multilateral solutions to international problems than it had earlier been. Gradually, then, the United States after World War II moved away from isolationism and unilateralism and toward internationalism and multilateralism.

Why Did the Cold War Happen?

With new international organizations on the horizon and high hopes for postwar cooperation, why did the Cold War happen? At least six reasons have been advanced for why the Cold War began: (1) the history of U.S.-Soviet relations, (2) different national objectives, (3) opposed ideologies, (4) the personalities of decision makers, (5) differing perceptions of the international environment, and (6) specific post–World War II Soviet actions.[9]

U.S.-Soviet relations before World War II ranged from openly hostile to coolly formal. In the Soviet Union, memories of the 1918–1920 American intervention in Russia and the United States' refusal to recognize the Soviet regime until 1933 lingered. In the United States, the Red Scare of the early 1920s, fears of international communism during the 1930s, and Soviet unwillingness to pay czarist debts created an equally pallid climate for good relations. As we saw in Chapter 5, mistrust continued during World War II.

Differing postwar objectives also helped cause the Cold War. Regardless of whether the Soviet Union established governments in its own image in Eastern Europe after the war for expansionist reasons or out of a desire to defend its own western boundaries, American policymakers saw Soviet actions as a conscious and well-thought-out thrust into the European heartland. Conversely, as the United States argued for free elections and free trade, Soviet leaders believed the United States was acting as Marxism-Leninism decreed it must, as an expansionistic political-economic system. Opposed perceptions of national objectives thus played a major role in causing the Cold War.

The opposed ideologies of Soviet Marxism-Leninism and American capitalist democracy also helped cause animosity. Most Americans considered communism an expansionistic, atheistic, dictatorial, militaristic form of social organization. To many Soviets, capitalist democracy presented a threat to the survival of the Soviet state. Each side was predisposed to view the other as the enemy, and that is exactly what happened as U.S. foreign policy became an anti-Soviet crusade, thereby proving to the Soviet leadership the accuracy of Marxist-Leninist ideological preconceptions.

In addition, the leaders' personalities contributed to hostility. Winston Churchill, the British prime minister during most of the 1940s, advocated spheres of influence and a realist view of international relations concentrating on power. He did not trust Soviet leader Joseph Stalin or the wisdom of U.S. leaders. Meanwhile, Stalin feared that his own domestic power base was eroding and was paranoid regarding U.S. and British intentions. Stalin and Franklin Roosevelt had had a degree of grudging respect for each other, but the new U.S. president, Harry Truman, had no use for Stalin and trusted him even less than did Churchill.

Perceptually, U.S. and Soviet leaders chose selectively from the historical record, real and imagined objectives, ideological beliefs, and their own personal biases to arrive at an image of the other side that was malevolent and evil. Events were interpreted in light of expectations, and both sides had ample evidence to "prove" the worst intentions of the other. Given these different perspectives, the Cold War may not have been inevitable, but only an inordinate amount of fortuitous circumstances could have prevented it.

Post–World War II Soviet actions also helped cause the Cold War. Despite tensions from the five causes already discussed, the Cold War did not begin immediately after World War II. It took two years for the skeptical cooperation that existed between the two sides during World War II to disappear. Soviet policies in Eastern Europe, Soviet pressures on Iran, and disagreements at the United Nations over the control of nuclear weapons all played key roles.

By the end of 1945, the Soviet Union had become the dominant power in Eastern Europe. It had no intention of reducing its influence or loosening its political control, regardless of agreements reached at the 1945 Yalta and Potsdam conferences. Two foreign ministers conferences in London and Moscow in late 1945 and an early 1946 Paris Peace Conference failed to slow the growth of Soviet influence and control in Eastern Europe. Indeed, as the Soviets solidified their hold over Poland, Bulgaria, and other Eastern European states, Winston Churchill in a 1946 speech in Fulton, Missouri, warned that an **Iron Curtain** had descended across the European continent.[10] Soviet-controlled states were behind the curtain, Churchill said, and Western democracies were in front of it.

Soviet policies in Iran also contributed to deteriorating East-West relations. The British and the Soviets agreed in 1942 to occupy Iran to protect the country from Germany and to secure supply lines to Russia. Both countries also agreed to withdraw their troops after the war. In keeping with the agreement, Great Britain pulled out in 1945, but Soviet forces remained into 1946. Concerned by the Soviet presence, the United States sent a warning to Moscow and deployed an aircraft carrier to the eastern Mediterranean Sea. The Soviets then withdrew. Truman and most of his administration concluded that when the United States confronted perceived Soviet expansion with the possible use of force, the Soviet Union would withdraw.

Meanwhile, at the United Nations, the United States and the Soviet Union squabbled over how to control nuclear weapons. In 1946, the United States submitted a proposal to the UN called the Baruch Plan, which proposed a new international authority to oversee nuclear research, institute inspections to assure compliance, end the production of nuclear weapons, and destroy existing weapons. The destruction of existing weapons, all of which were owned by the United States, would be the last stage. Not trusting the United States, the Soviets rejected the plan, proposing instead that the United States should destroy its nuclear weapons first. Deadlock ensued, with the inability to reach agreement contributing to the growth of U.S.-Soviet tension.

The Truman Doctrine, the Marshall Plan, and Containment

Two situations in southern Europe in 1946 and 1947 accelerated the decline in U.S.-Soviet relations. In Turkey, the Soviet government sought to control passage of ships through the Dardanelles, the straits that connect the Black Sea to the Mediterranean Sea. When Turkey refused, the Soviet Union threatened to take action. Great Britain backed Turkey.

Meanwhile, in Greece, a civil war raged between the royalist government supported by Great Britain and communist insurgents supported by communist Yugoslavia. The United States considered this Great Britain's problem until early 1947, when London told Washington that, because of its war-weakened economy, it no longer could aid Greece or provide assistance to Turkey.

Britain's pronouncement shocked the Truman Administration. Without outside support, the Turkish government might accede to Soviet demands. Without military aid, the Greek government would surely fall to the insurgents. After considerable internal discussion about what to do, the United States stepped into the breach.[11] On March 12, 1947, President Truman delivered a speech to Congress in which he outlined the world situation as he saw it and stated how he believed the United States should respond to the world situation:

> At the present moment in world history nearly every nation must choose between alternative ways of life. The choice is too often not a free one. One way of life is based upon the free will of the majority, and is distinguished by free institutions, representative government, free elections, guarantees of individual liberty, and freedom of speech and religion and freedom from political oppression. The second way of life is based upon the will of a minority forcibly imposed upon the majority. It relies upon terror and oppression, a controlled press and radio, fixed elections, and the suppression of personal freedom. I believe that it must be the policy of the United States to support free peoples who are resisting attempted subjugation by armed minorities or by outside pressure. I believe that we must assist free peoples to work out their destinies in their own ways.[12]

Truman's declaration that "it must be the policy of the United States to support free peoples who are resisting attempted subjugation by armed minorities or by outside pressure" became known as the **Truman Doctrine.** To be sure, questions existed about the doctrine. Did it apply only to Greece and Turkey, or did it apply anywhere? Were there limits to American assistance, and if so, what were they? Even though these and other questions were not answered, Congress supported Truman's request for $400 million of aid for Greece and Turkey. For all practical purposes, the almost two-century-old U.S. tradition of remaining aloof from European affairs except during wartime had been abandoned.

Another indication of the United States' new resolve to play a larger role in Europe followed. Recognizing that Europe's economy was in a shambles, understanding that without external aid there was little hope of recovery, and fearing that Europe's plight provided fertile grounds for communist expansion, Secretary of State George Marshall in June 1947 called on European states to draw up a plan for continent-wide economic assistance to be provided by the United States[13] After several meetings, the first of which was attended by the Soviet Union and its allied states, European states presented their request to the United States. By this time, the Soviet Union and its allies had withdrawn.

Despite doubts, Congress supported the idea. In its first year of operation (1948–1949), the **Marshall Plan** provided more than $13 billion to European states to rebuild.[14] The Marshall Plan provided the basis for European economic recovery, which improved the lives of millions of Europeans and enhanced both European and American security by preventing communist parties from winning elections throughout Western Europe.

The Truman Doctrine and the Marshall Plan were the first two linchpins of what became the U.S. strategy of **containment.** As U.S. diplomat George Kennan postulated in his famous "X Article," which became the central intellectual argument for containment, the Soviet Union wanted to dominate Europe as well as the rest of the world. Therefore, to contain the Soviet Union, the United States needed to apply counterpressure wherever the Soviet Union applied pressure: "The Soviet pressure against the free institutions of the Western World is something that can be contained by the adroit and vigilant application of counterforce at a series of constantly shifting geographical and political points, corresponding to the shifts and maneuvers of Soviet policy."[15]

Kennan argued only that American counterpressure would contain the Soviet Union, but he predicted that counterpressure would force the Soviet Union to change its policies or break up. In a sentence that was truly prescient in light of events 44 years later, Kennan came close to foreseeing the future. The United States, he asserted, "has it in its power to increase enormously the strains under which Soviet policy must operate, to force upon the Kremlin a far greater degree of moderation and circumspection than it has had to observe in recent years, and in this way to promote tendencies which must eventually find their outlet in either the breakup or the gradual mellowing of Soviet power."[16]

For Kennan, the issue was not whether the United States had enough power to contain the Soviet Union. It did. The question was whether the United States had the patience, the desire, and the wisdom to contain the Soviet Union in the right way and in the right places. With the Truman Doctrine and the Marshall Plan, then, President Truman began to implement containment. Every American president from Truman through George H. W. Bush followed Kennan's prescription. World War III never happened, the Soviet empire collapsed, and in 1991 the Soviet Union broke up. But in many of the years between 1947 and 1991, it was far from clear what the outcome would be.[17]

Europe Divided

By 1948, Europe was divided. In Eastern Europe, the Soviet Union exercised growing control. The Soviet Union itself ran East Germany, removing the few industries that survived World War II and transporting them to the Soviet Union as reparations for the war. Soviet-supported communists were consolidating power in Bulgaria, Hungary, Poland, and Rumania.

But Soviet control of Eastern Europe was not complete. Czechoslovakia in early 1948 remained democratic, and in Yugoslavia a communist government under Josip Broz Tito regularly disagreed with Soviet preferences. The split between the two communist countries became public in 1948, and the United States soon began to provide economic and military assistance to Tito's government to help it maintain independence from Moscow.[18]

In the United States, these trends strengthened anti-Soviet sentiment. From the American perspective, the Soviet Union had broken promises made at Yalta to allow democratic elections in Eastern Europe and had expanded its imperial control. Responding to Soviet expansion, Congress passed the **1947 National Security Act,** which created the Department of Defense to oversee U.S. defense, the Central Intelligence Agency to collect and analyze intelligence, and the National Security Council to advise the president. Meanwhile, democratically elected governments ruled in Western Europe, often influenced by the United States. In addition, in 1948, Belgium, France, Great Britain, Luxembourg, and the Netherlands concluded the Brussels Treaty for collective self-defense. The U.S. Senate passed a resolution 64–4 that praised it and suggested U.S. participation.

Two 1948 events drove the wedge between East and West deeper and finalized the division of Europe that existed until 1989. The first was the **communist coup in Czecho slovakia.** Governed since World War II by a democratically elected socialist-oriented

MAP 6.1
The Division of Europe During the Cold War
Western and Eastern Europe: Before the 1989 Eastern European revolutions, all the countries to the left of the heavy line were considered part of Western Europe, and all the countries to the right were part of Eastern Europe, except for Greece.

government, the country in 1948 fell victim to a communist coup. The second event was the **Berlin blockade,** which began in 1948 as the Soviet Union cut off Western access to the divided city and tried to prevent the Western powers from issuing a new currency in their zones of Germany. The United States responded with the **Berlin airlift,** during which American military planes supplied all the needs of the residents of Berlin until the blockade was finally lifted in 1949.[19]

By 1948, then, Europe was divided. Debate continued in the United States and Western Europe about what had gone wrong and over who caused the Cold War, but the Cold War was in full swing.

TRUMAN, EISENHOWER, AND THE COLD WAR: 1948–1961

After winning the 1948 presidential election, Harry Truman used his 1949 inaugural address to draw the outlines of the foreign policy he intended to follow during the next four years. He made four key points. First, he praised the United Nations and guaranteed U.S. support for it. Second, he promised continued Marshall Plan aid to Europe. Third, he revealed that the United States was planning to create a military alliance of states in Europe and North America. Fourth, he advocated that the United States extend foreign aid to "underdeveloped areas" of the world for humanitarian reasons and as a way to prevent the expansion of communism.[20] Truman's first two points were not surprises, since they continued policies that were in place before the presidential election, but his third and fourth points marked significant new departures for American foreign policy.

NATO, Foreign Aid, and Korea

In keeping with Truman's third point, the United States and 11 other countries in 1949 signed the North Atlantic Treaty, which stated that all signatory states considered "an armed attack against one or more . . . an attack against them all." This was the first time the United States joined a peacetime political military alliance. Then, in 1950, treaty members created the **North Atlantic Treaty Organization (NATO),** a regional defense alliance to implement the treaty and deter Soviet aggression.[21] NATO became a central piece of the United States' containment strategy and remains a central piece of U.S. defense policy today, even though its reason for existing has changed.

Truman's fourth point, that the United States should extend foreign aid to underdeveloped areas of the world, became the basis for U.S. economic assistance to areas of the world beyond Europe, and the beginning point for U.S. economic assistance to the underdeveloped world. Here, three points must be made. First, U.S. economic assistance to the underdeveloped world has never been large. Second, most American economic assistance has been given to a few strategically important states such as Israel and Egypt. Third, American military assistance to foreign states has almost always far exceeded U.S. economic assistance.[22]

The Truman Administration faced several security challenges in 1949. In China, **Mao Zedong** and his Chinese Communist Party triumphed over Chiang Kai-shek and his Kuomintang Nationalist Party in the long-running Chinese Civil War. Suddenly, as seen from Washington, one-fifth of humankind had fallen under communist rule. Equally foreboding, the Soviet Union in 1949 exploded an atomic weapon, ending the four-year-long American monopoly on nuclear weapons.

Concerned about the direction of world events, Truman in early 1950 asked the State Department and Defense Department to undertake a joint review of American security policy. This report, called **NSC-68,** pointed to Mao's victory in China and postulated that since the Soviet Union had just acquired nuclear weapons, communist military aggression around the world would be relentless. Further, it argued that the only way the United States could deter communist aggression was to develop its own large conventional and nuclear forces.[23] Even so, most Americans and their Western European allies at first were not willing to significantly increase defense spending.

This attitude changed in September 1950 when North Korea invaded South Korea. At the end of World War II, Korea had been divided into two zones to facilitate Japanese surrender, the northern one occupied by the Soviets and the southern one by the Americans. This division remained until North Korea invaded South Korea, initiating the **Korean War.**

Taken by surprise, South Korean forces fell back. The United States then sent troops under UN auspices to South Korea. When U.S. forces arrived, they pushed the North Korean forces back, but the United States changed its war aims from defending South Korea to unifying all of Korea. As U.S. forces advanced north and approached Korea's border with China, China entered the war and drove the Americans back. Fighting dragged on for months. Finally, the warring parties agreed to a truce, dividing the peninsula almost exactly where it had been divided before the North Korean invasion. It remains divided today, with U.S. troops still deployed along the demilitarized zone between the two Koreas.[24]

Truman and other American leaders were firmly convinced that the Soviet Union was behind the North Korean assault. This heightened the urgency of providing NATO with effective military forces. More and more American troops were therefore dispatched to Europe during the 1950s, with U.S. force levels there reaching over a half million. Many crises occurred in Europe during the Cold War, but throughout the Cold War, NATO helped deter war in Europe.

Eisenhower and Containment

The growth of U.S.-Soviet tensions and the frustrations of the Korean War played a significant role in the 1952 presidential election, in which former General Dwight D. Eisenhower emerged victorious. Eisenhower was the first Republican president since Herbert Hoover left office in 1931.

Republicans, especially Eisenhower's Secretary of State John Foster Dulles, condemned Truman's containment policy as immoral, arguing that it "condemned half the world" to live under communism.[25] Dulles called for the "rollback of communism," the "liberation" of Eastern Europe and China, and the implementation of a policy of **massive retaliation** under which the United States would employ nuclear weapons against the Soviet Union if the Soviets attempted to expand territories under their control.

Eisenhower, however, adopted more moderate rhetoric and policies than those of his secretary of state.

Eisenhower's intent was to counter and contain the Soviet Union. Thus, during the 1950s, Eisenhower and Dulles created alliances additional to NATO to contain the Soviet Union. Eventually, the **U.S. alliance system** included the Southeast Asian Treaty Organization, the Central Treaty Organization, the Australia–New Zealand–United States (ANZUS) pact, and bilateral security agreements with Japan and Taiwan.[26] U.S. policy generally supported the UN, but the UN could do little because it was tied up by procedures that allowed any of the five permanent members of the Security Council to veto any action with which they disagreed.

Throughout the Eisenhower era, U.S.-Soviet relations were on a roller coaster. During the first three years of the Eisenhower Administration, U.S.-Soviet tension eased, substantially because an armistice ended fighting in Korea. In 1955, Eisenhower and Soviet leader Nikita Khrushchev met at a **summit meeting** in Geneva to improve relations between the two superpowers. This was the first meeting between leaders of the two countries since 1945. The meeting was friendly, and even though it accomplished little, the world breathed a sigh of relief.

In 1956, however, the "Spirit of Geneva" vanished when Soviet tanks rolled into Hungary to quell an anti-communist uprising there. At the same time, British, French, and Israeli forces invaded Egypt. The United States was in a difficult situation, unable to help a revolution in Hungary that it favored and critical of its own allies for initiating an invasion that it opposed.[27] Tensions escalated further in 1957 when the Soviet Union launched the world's first earth satellite, *Sputnik*, and threatened to use its missiles if it had to.[28]

The Soviet Union in 1958 also increased pressure on Berlin in the first of several **Berlin crises.** West Berlin, deep within and surrounded by hundreds of thousands of Soviet troops in Soviet-occupied East Germany, was vulnerable to Soviet pressure, as had been conspicuously shown during the Berlin blockade. Khrushchev now issued an ultimatum that he intended to sign a peace treaty with communist East Germany, thereby formalizing the division of Germany into two states.[29]

East-West tension escalated as confrontational rhetoric increased and armed forces were placed on high alert. However, with the specter of nuclear weapons in the background, nobody wanted war, and tension dissipated as careful diplomacy removed the edge from U.S.-Soviet relations. Indeed, East-West relations improved so much that, in 1959, Khrushchev visited the United States.

Improved relations were short-lived. In 1960, an American U-2 spy plane was shot down over the Soviet Union just before Eisenhower and Khrushchev held a summit meeting in Paris. The summit collapsed, rhetoric escalated, and tension remained high throughout the remaining months of Eisenhower's presidency.[30]

Throughout this time, nuclear weapons and deterrence played major roles in U.S strategy. The theory behind **deterrence** was that if a potential enemy intended to attack but knew he would in turn be attacked, he would not attack. As the United States and the Soviet Union developed large nuclear arsenals during the 1950s and 1960s, a new version of deterrence developed, **mutual assured destruction (MAD).** The theory underlying MAD was that both the United States and the Soviet Union were deterred from launching a nuclear attack because each knew that if they attacked first, the other would still have enough nuclear weapons remaining to destroy the attacker as a functioning society.[31]

The Cold War, Power, and American Foreign Policy Principles

By the beginning of the 1960s, the world was divided into two hostile camps. This **East-West conflict** pitted one group of states called the **First World,** led by the United States, against a second group of states, the **Second World,** led by the Soviet Union.

The two superpowers and their allies not only confronted each other but also tried to increase their influence in and control over a third group of states, the **Third World,** which consisted primarily of African, Middle Eastern, and Asian states that were former colonies of European powers. Most Third World countries were poor and economically underdeveloped. Most also preferred to remain part of the **Nonaligned Movement,** that is, allied to neither superpower, even though many received economic and military assistance from anyone who would offer it. Latin American states were often considered part of the Third World even though most were allies of the United States and within the American sphere of influence.

Containment remained the core of U.S. foreign policy, implemented via a combination of the Truman Doctrine, the Marshall Plan, NATO, the worldwide American alliance system, U.S. conventional and nuclear armed forces deployed at forward positions around the world, and other U.S. economic and military assistance programs. As a concept, containment fit well with moralism and pragmatism, which remained key principles of U.S. policy. Most Americans despised communism as morally wrong, a dangerous, godless, and dictatorial philosophy, and accepted that the United States had to adopt pragmatic policies and even support authoritarian governments to contain communism.

Meanwhile, the growth of American power and exigencies of the Cold War forced changes to two other principles on which Americans believed their country's foreign policy had been based. Most Americans accepted the need to discard isolationism and unilateralism as principles of foreign policy. Some people called for their return, but most agreed that if the United States and the West were to counter the Soviet Union and communism successfully, involvement and multilateralism must be accepted as the order of the day.

Thus, by the early 1960s, two old sets of competing themes, isolationism versus involvement and idealism versus realism, remained prominent in American foreign policy, and a new set of competing themes, unilateralism versus multilateralism, had appeared. Americans generally accepted the need for involvement over isolationism, and realism dominated idealism even though idealism was far from dead. Indeed, with the struggle between the United States and the Soviet Union often seen as a struggle between good and evil that could be decided by military force, many Americans saw idealism and realism as opposite sides of the same coin. Meanwhile, American leaders accepted that the Soviet threat could only be met by multilateral policies. For the first time in history, multilateralism therefore became a key element of American foreign policy. Even so, supporters of unilateralism remained vocal and influential.

KENNEDY, JOHNSON, AND THE CRISES OF THE 1960s

When John Kennedy was inaugurated in 1961, he brought a sense of optimism and activism to American foreign and domestic policy that captivated many Americans. "Ask not what your country can do for you," Kennedy urged Americans, "but what you can do for your country."

Balancing realism with idealism, the new president's foreign policy agenda emphasized containing the Soviet Union while at the same time establishing cordial relations with the USSR to lessen the danger of nuclear war. Thus, in 1961, Kennedy met Khrushchev for the Vienna Summit. The meeting did not go well as Khrushchev attempted to intimidate Kennedy. Both leaders returned to their respective countries and increased military spending.[32]

The Cuban Missile Crisis and Its Aftermath

In 1962, the Soviet Union began to deploy intermediate-range ballistic missiles in Cuba, only 90 miles from Florida. After American intelligence flights over Cuba discovered the Soviet missiles, the United States invoked the Monroe Doctrine, placed a naval blockade around Cuba, and warned the Soviet Union to withdraw the missiles or suffer the consequences. The ensuing **Cuban Missile Crisis** plunged the world into what is still regarded as the most dangerous crisis of the entire Cold War.

The crisis developed slowly. When the missiles were discovered but before the discovery became public knowledge, President Kennedy formed an Executive Committee of the National Security Council (ExComm) to debate policy options and implement policy. The 16 ExComm members held widely different views of appropriate policy, some arguing for a full-scale invasion, some for bringing the issue to the United Nations, and others for placing a naval blockade or quarantine around the Caribbean island. Eventually, Kennedy and his advisers settled on the last option, and the world held its breath as Soviet freighters thought to have missiles on board sailed closer to the American naval ships surrounding Cuba. Eventually the Soviet ships reversed course. The world breathed a sigh of relief.

But the crisis was not over. The Soviet Union still had missiles in Cuba, and Kennedy insisted that they be removed. Kennedy and Khrushchev exchanged a series of messages directly and through intermediaries in which both leaders tried to find a solution to the dilemma. Throughout, Kennedy remained firm that the missiles be withdrawn, and eventually Khrushchev yielded. At the same time, the United States pledged not to invade Cuba, and the Americans eventually withdrew some obsolete missiles from Turkey that they had deployed there years earlier. The Cuban Missile Crisis was over, the Monroe Doctrine remained in place, and the United States retained its strategic nuclear superiority.[33]

Perhaps surprisingly, the end of the missile crisis led to another period of improved U.S.-Soviet relations. During the crisis, the United States and the Soviet Union had marched to the edge of nuclear confrontation, and neither liked what it had seen. Thus, in 1963, the two superpowers concluded a partial nuclear test ban treaty and installed a "hot line" between Washington and Moscow to allow the leaders of the two countries to talk directly during crises.

The Cuban Missile Crisis also underlined to American leaders and the American public the continued need for containing the Soviet Union. The Cuban Missile Crisis proved that the Soviet Union remained an expansionist power, most Americans believed. Therefore, despite the dangers and costs that went with containment, containment was the correct strategy, and the United States remained the morally correct defender of liberty and justice, acting pragmatically but with restraint to prevent Soviet expansion. Few questioned the morality of containment, the necessity for pragmatism, or the need for internationalism and American-led multilateralism.

The United States aid program to developing states was a good example of how morality, pragmatism, internationalism, and multilateralism combined during the 1950s and 1960s—and of how involvement dominated isolationism, realism balanced idealism, and multilateralism took precedence over unilateralism. In the 1950s, Truman and Eisenhower assisted countries in Asia, Africa, Latin America, and elsewhere out of humanitarian concern and to build a bulwark against Soviet influence. Encouraged by success in rebuilding Europe under the Marshall Plan, most American policymakers idealistically saw foreign aid and international economic institutions as ways to transform poor countries into prosperous anti-communist states. While U.S. aid programs to developing states never grew to the size of the Marshall Plan, most Americans were pleased that the United States had such programs. U.S. involvement overseas was good, most thought, especially if it both helped people and contained communism.[34]

Vietnam

Then came U.S. involvement in **Vietnam.** Divided by the 1954 Geneva Accords, Vietnam was ruled in the north by Ho Chi Minh and his Communist Party and in the south by Ngo Dinh Diem, who headed an autocratic anti-communist South Vietnamese government supported during the 1950s and early 1960s by the presence of a few U.S. military advisers.[35] Few Americans were aware of the U.S. military presence in South Vietnam, and those who were accepted it as necessary to counter North Vietnam's threat to South Vietnam.

By the time Kennedy took office in 1961, the situation in South Vietnam was dire. Kennedy, acting on his belief that the United States should "go anywhere and pay any price" to contain communism, gradually increased the number of American advisers in Vietnam from under 1,000 when he took office to almost 16,000 by the time he was assassinated in 1963. Although disagreement exists over what he would have done in Vietnam had he lived, it is clear that the U.S. commitment to Vietnam expanded under Kennedy.

The situation in South Vietnam continued to deteriorate in late 1963 and 1964 as government replaced government and as the Vietcong and North Vietnamese expanded their control of South Vietnamese territory. Early in 1964, the United States began clandestine operations against North Vietnam. In the eyes of some, these operations led to the August 1964 North Vietnamese attacks against two American destroyers, the *Maddox* and the *C. Turner Joy,* on patrol in the Gulf of Tonkin off the Vietnamese coast. Debate continues to the present day about what really happened during these attacks, and about whether the attacks really occurred.[36] Nevertheless, the Johnson Administration used the attacks to convince Congress to pass the Gulf of Tonkin resolution, which authorized

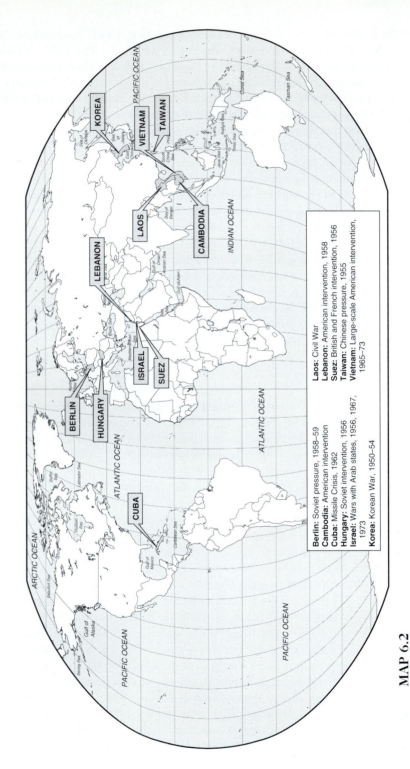

MAP 6.2
Major Cold War Hot Spots and Crises from the 1950s Through the Early 1970s

Berlin: Soviet pressure, 1958–59
Cambodia: American intervention
Cuba: Missile Crisis, 1962
Hungary: Soviet intervention, 1956
Israel: Wars with Arab states, 1956, 1967, 1973
Korea: Korean War, 1950–54

Laos: Civil War
Lebanon: American intervention, 1958
Suez: British and French intervention, 1956
Taiwan: Chinese pressure, 1955
Vietnam: Large-scale American intervention, 1965–73

President Johnson to take "all necessary steps, including the use of armed forces," to assist American allies in Southeast Asia.

The Tonkin resolution was notable for several reasons, but perhaps most importantly in that Congress gave the president the power to conduct military operations in Vietnam as he saw fit. And Johnson used this power, ordering first in late 1964 retaliatory attacks against North Vietnam and raids against North Vietnamese supply lines running through Laos, followed in early 1965 by "Operation Rolling Thunder," a series of almost daily large-scale bombing attacks against North Vietnam to try to convince it to stop its support of and involvement in the insurgency in South Vietnam. When in early 1965 the United States introduced ground combat units to South Vietnam, it was clear that the United States had changed both the size and the nature of its commitment to South Vietnam. The war had become Americanized.[37]

By the late 1960s, 500,000 U.S. troops were in Vietnam, and the fighting escalated. As U.S. deaths mounted—over 58,000 Americans died there—and costs grew, more and more Americans asked questions about U.S. foreign policy that they had rarely asked before. Was the United States on the side of justice in Vietnam, or had it replaced France as a colonial power? Was the United States pursuing a respectable and honorable objective with dishonorable and unjustified means? How much killing and how great a cost would the United States bear to prevent the expansion of communism? Was communism still the enemy it had been during the preceding 25 years?

Increasingly, Americans questioned their conviction that the U.S. presence in Vietnam was moral and that communism presented a threat to "true" American interests. Indeed, by late 1967, more Americans opposed the war in Vietnam than supported it, and by late 1969, almost 60 percent of the American population opposed the war, with about 30 percent supporting it and 10 percent remaining undecided. The realization that minorities had been suppressed within the United States also challenged the basis of a moral crusade against communism. As Americans asked these questions and riots tore many U.S. cities apart in the late 1960s, Americans were not as sure of their moral superiority as they had once been, and they were not as sure that containment was the right strategy upon which to base foreign policy.[38]

U.S. economic preeminence also declined in the 1960s. Vietnam was partially to blame, since billions of dollars were squandered there, but U.S. economic preeminence also declined for other reasons. For example, other states had rebuilt their economies following World War II, often with technologies more advanced than those the United States used. Also, U.S. investment lagged as excessive consumerism began to take its toll.

By the end of the 1960s, U.S. optimism had waned. What some had touted as "the American century" appeared to have become "the American decade." Even though the United States had no military and economic equal, the optimism that marked the U.S. world outlook for most of the 1950s and 1960s had faded.

GRAND STRATEGY UNDER NIXON AND FORD: 1969–1977

When Richard Nixon became president in 1969, he was convinced that the United States was in crisis, and he had a grand strategy in foreign policy to rectify the situation. **Nixon's grand strategy** revolved around détente with the Soviet Union, improved relations with

China, and withdrawal from Vietnam.[39] The ultimate realist, Nixon was praised by his supporters for claiming to understand the way the world worked, and condemned by his critics for ignoring idealism and, some said, morality.

Détente

Declaring that it was time to move from "an era of confrontation" to "an era of negotiation" with the USSR, Nixon had several reasons for pursuing **détente,** that is, improved East-West relations especially between the United States and the Soviet Union. First, Nixon recognized that a U.S.-Soviet nuclear war would destroy life on earth. Such a war therefore had to be avoided, and this could best be achieved through improved relations. Second, Nixon believed that improved U.S.-Soviet relations could help the United States get out of Vietnam. Third, Nixon concluded that improved U.S.-Soviet relations would limit Soviet expansionism by giving the Kremlin a stake in improved relations with the United States and the West. With these objectives in mind, Nixon initiated policies that gradually eased tensions between East and West.[40]

The changed nature of U.S.-Soviet relations brought about by détente was best illustrated by the frequency of summit meetings. Between 1945 and 1971, U.S. and Soviet leaders met three times, at Geneva in 1955, in the United States in 1959, and at Vienna

Improving relations with the Soviet Union under the policy of détente played a major role in President Richard Nixon's grand strategy. Nixon met Soviet Premier Leonid Brezhnev at summit meetings three times in three years (1972, 1973, and 1974), greatly easing U.S.-Soviet tensions. Here, the two leaders exchange pleasantries after signing a nuclear arms control agreement at one of the summit meetings.

in 1961. Under détente, Nixon and Soviet leader Leonid Brezhnev met three times in three years, in 1972, 1973, and 1974, alternating between Moscow and Washington. Nixon's successor, Gerald Ford, met with Brezhnev in 1974 in Vladivostok and then in 1975 in Helsinki. In 1979, Brezhnev met another U.S. president, Jimmy Carter, in Vienna.

Détente was more than summitry. It also included increased U.S.-Soviet trade, arms control agreements such as the Strategic Arms Limitation Treaty and the Anti-Ballistic Missile Treaty, and cultural exchanges. Détente improved East-West relations in Europe as well. West Germany and East Germany improved relations, and the heads of government of almost every state in Europe and North America attended a meeting in Helsinki, Finland, in 1975.[41]

Relations with China

Improving U.S-Chinese relations also played a critical role in Nixon's grand strategy. U.S.-Chinese relations had been hostile ever since the Korean War, with a key point of tension being U.S. support for the Nationalist Chinese government on Taiwan. Vowing to improve U.S.-Chinese relations but not abandon Taiwan, Nixon surprised the world in 1972 by journeying to China. The trip was a resounding success. U.S.-Chinese relations improved greatly after Nixon's trip. Diplomatic contacts were expanded, strategic outlooks shared, and trade increased. The two sides also issued the Shanghai Communique, in which the communist Chinese government stated that it was the "sole legal government of China" and the United States reaffirmed its interest in "a peaceful settlement of the Taiwan question by the Chinese themselves."[42]

Vietnamization and the Nixon Doctrine

Part of Nixon's grand strategy was to withdraw American forces from Vietnam while maintaining South Vietnam's independence. Nixon tried to do this with **Vietnamization,** a policy under which the United States equipped and trained South Vietnam's armed forces to defend their country by themselves as U.S. forces withdrew. To buy time for this equipping and training to proceed, Nixon expanded the U.S. bombing of North Vietnam and of North Vietnamese and Vietcong forces in the south.[43]

Internationally, détente with the Soviet Union and improved relations with China provided Nixon the maneuvering room he needed to expand the bombing. Soviet and Chinese protests about the bombing were generally muted. Domestically, however, expanded bombing led to more anti-war protests, at least until American ground forces began to be withdrawn in large numbers and the American casualty count dwindled to near zero. In 1973, the last American combat troops left Vietnam, and the United States' direct military involvement in the Vietnam War was over.

Throughout these years, even as Nixon calculated how to implement his grand strategy, some Americans criticized his approach to foreign policy as coldly cynical. Claiming that Nixon emphasized pragmatism to the exclusion of moralism, they charged that Nixon's foreign policy was similar to old-style European power politics that the United States had rejected since the early days of the Republic. Critics pointed especially to the **Nixon Doctrine** as evidence of Nixon's cynicism. Under the Nixon Doctrine, the United States expanded its military aid to South Vietnam and accelerated its bombing in Vietnam even as negotiations for withdrawal proceeded. This, to many, showed that Nixon ignored morality in foreign policy. Others supported Nixon's approach, arguing that it would get the United States out of Vietnam and at the same time allow the country to defend itself.

The Middle East

Nixon faced foreign policy challenges additional to those related to the Soviet Union, China, and Vietnam. One of the most serious was in the Middle East, where the **Arab-Israeli conflict** boiled over into open warfare.

In Israel and Jordan were both created by the United Nations in 1948 when the UN partitioned the Palestinian Mandate, land that Great Britain received at the end of World War I from what had been the Ottoman Empire. Warfare soon broke out as Egypt, Iraq, Jordan, Lebanon, and Syria attacked, rejecting the presence of a Jewish state formed from land that they claimed belonged to Palestinian Arabs. Israel won the war, in the process acquiring land that the UN intended for Palestinians. By the time Nixon became president, two other Arab-Israeli wars had been fought, in 1956 and 1967, with Israel winning both.[44]

In 1973, the fourth major Arab-Israeli war erupted as Egypt and Syria launched a surprise attack. Taken off guard, Israel suffered heavy losses and was almost defeated. The United States, always a close Israeli ally, initiated a massive airlift to rearm Israel's armed forces and avert disaster. After an Israeli counteroffensive drove Egyptian and Syrian forces back, U.S. diplomacy constructed a cease-fire. An uneasy peace fell over the Middle East, and Nixon dispatched U.S. Secretary of State Henry Kissinger to the Middle East to try to arrange a more lasting peace. For months, Kissinger and other U.S. diplomats engaged in shuttle diplomacy, flying from capital to capital, achieving a few successes and keeping the situation under control, but not resolving the Arab-Israeli conflict.[45]

Economic Issues

Nixon also faced serious international economic problems. As already related, U.S. economic preeminence by the late 1960s had declined. The Vietnam War, excessive American consumerism, and growing American dependence on external sources of energy all contributed to a seemingly unstoppable outflow of dollars into the international economy and equally uncontrollable domestic inflation.

Nixon responded to the growing balance of payments deficit in 1971 by levying a 10 percent surcharge on all dutiable imports to the United States and by suspending the convertibility of the dollar to gold. He also put a wage and price freeze in place domestically. As necessary as these steps may have been for the United States, they nevertheless shocked the international community, since the United States for all practical purposes had unilaterally abandoned the Bretton Woods system. The international monetary system was in disarray.[46]

The United States' own economic situation deteriorated further following the 1973 Arab-Israeli War when the Organization of Petroleum Exporting Countries (OPEC) cut back its oil production, embargoed oil exports to the United States in retaliation for U.S.

support of Israel, and quadrupled oil prices. Although the embargo was eventually lifted, the United States had become well aware of its dependence on foreign energy and on its economic interdependence with the rest of the world.

The Ford Interregnum

In 1974, abuses of presidential power collectively known as the Watergate Affair forced Nixon to resign as president. His successor, Gerald Ford, adopted most of Nixon's foreign policies. Indeed, Ford journeyed to Helsinki in 1975 to attend the Helsinki Conference on Security and Cooperation in Europe, widely regarded as the high-water mark for détente. But détente's euphoria was short-lived. Even as European and North American leaders met in Helsinki, events were unfolding in Vietnam and in Angola that weakened détente.

In 1975, North Vietnam invaded South Vietnam. Glad to be out of Vietnam, neither Ford nor the American military nor the American public seriously sought to expand U.S. aid to South Vietnam or use American armed force to counter the invasion. Vietnam was thus united under a communist government.

Also in 1975, civil war broke out in Angola as Portugal ended its colonial presence there. The following year, the Soviet Union helped Cuba deploy 20,000 troops to Angola, swinging the war toward the pro-Soviet faction, the MPLA. Although the United States criticized Soviet and Cuban actions in Angola, it did nothing to respond politically, economically, or militarily. Once again, neither Ford nor the American military nor the American public wanted to become involved. Indeed, Congress so feared another Vietnam that it passed a bill that prevented the United States from providing aid to any party involved in the Angolan conflict.[47]

These events weakened détente. How serious could Soviet leaders be about peaceful coexistence and friendship, more and more Americans asked, if they helped one state invade another and if they provided military assistance and transportation to help Cuban troops support a pro-Soviet government in Africa? Even so, détente remained the watchword in U.S.-Soviet relations until the end of the Ford Administration.

FROM DÉTENTE TO RENEWED CONFRONTATION: 1977–1989

When Jimmy Carter was inaugurated in 1977, he intended to pursue détente, but he rejected what many saw as Nixon's excessive realism and abandonment of moralism. Carter emphasized idealism and morality, and the defense of **human rights** became a centerpiece of his foreign policy.[48] Carter also stressed the need for peaceful resolution of conflict. All this found a sympathetic ear among Americans. Still weary from the Vietnam War, many, like the new president, believed that once again the United States should be idealistic and strive for morality and peace in its foreign policy. Carter believed that the United States could have "a foreign policy that is democratic; that is based on fundamental values, and that uses power and influence that we have for humane purposes." He also declared that American foreign policy should be "based on constant decency in its values and an optimism in our historical vision."[49]

At the same time, Carter was neither an isolationist nor a unilateralist. While he was more skeptical than his several presidential predeccesors of the need for the United States to intervene overseas, he by no means believed that the United States should disengage from the international community. And he strongly believed that the United States needed to remain deeply involved in multilateral diplomacy and international organizations. While Carter would return the United States to a more idealistic foreign policy, he would abandon neither the international involvement nor the multilateralism that his several predecessors has pursued in their foreign policies.

Carter's Early Presidency

During his first two years as president, Carter concentrated on human rights and empha-sized détente. For example, as anti-government sentiment built in Iran in 1977 and 1978 against the pro-American but repressive shah, the United States, concerned about the shah's human rights record, advised him to become less repressive. As anti-shah senti-ment crystallized into street demonstrations, the United States did not come to the shah's defense. When full-scale revolution broke out against the shah, the United States in 1979 advised him to leave and seek asylum elsewhere as a fundamentalist Islamic government came to power in Iran.[50]

Carter also emphasized human rights and peaceful resolution of conflict in the Arab-Israeli conflict. Thus, in 1978, he invited Israel's Prime Minister Menachem Begin and Egypt's President Anwar Sadat to Camp David in Maryland to try to work out a peace settlement. Carter used the force of his personality and his arguments to craft an agree-ment between the two Middle Eastern leaders under which Israel would, among other things, recognize the "legitimate rights of the Palestinians" and return the Sinai Penin-sula to Egypt. Perhaps most importantly, Sadat and Begin also committed their countries to sign a peace treaty within three months. Even though problems developed with other parts of the Camp David Accords, both men followed through on the peace treaty, which was concluded in 1979.[51]

Despite the seeming success at Camp David, some Americans argued that a foreign policy based on human rights and peaceful resolution of conflict was hopelessly naive and even dangerous. They pointed to the overthrow of the shah to buttress their argu-ment, asserting that emphasis on human rights had undermined a key American ally in a critical part of the world. Others critics of Carter's foreign policy chastised détente, arguing that North Vietnam's takeover of South Vietnam and Cuba's presence in Angola showed that détente was a concept whose time had passed.[52]

Concerns about human rights and détente as the bases for American foreign policy escalated in 1978 as the Soviet Union again helped Cuba deploy troops to Africa, this time to support a pro-communist government in Ethiopia. Carter criticized the Soviet and Cuban action but, like Ford before him in Angola, did little. Once again, neither the president nor the American military nor the American public wanted to become involved in another conflict.

Carter's critics also attacked him for his 1979 recognition of the communist gov-ernment in Beijing as the legitimate government of China. Although the transfer of American recognition from the Taiwan government to the Beijing government was the logical next step in the process set in motion by Nixon's 1972 visit to Beijing, some Americans saw Carter's recognition of Beijing as another proof of the weakness of Carter's foreign policy.

Despite criticism, Carter pushed forward with human rights, the peaceful resolution of conflict, and détente. Additionally, in 1979, he met Soviet leader Leonid Brezhnev at a summit and concluded another strategic arms limitations agreement, SALT II, with the Soviet Union. However, concerns over Soviet adventurism delayed Senate passage of SALT II. Then, in late 1979, two crises erupted that ended détente and changed Carter's foreign policy.

Carter's Crises: 1979–1981

In November 1979, radical students with the support of Iran's fundamentalist Islamic government that had replaced the shah overran the U.S. embassy in Teheran and held the American embassy staff captive. The **Iran hostage crisis** continued for over a year, with the United States seemingly powerless to gain the hostages' release. A failed rescue attempt added to the American humiliation. Domestically, the hostage crisis undermined Carter's credibility and his political support. Even more embarrassing for Carter, the hostages were not released until the day that he left office in 1981.[53]

Carter's second crisis began in December 1979 when the Soviet Union invaded Afghanistan. Described by Carter as "the most serious strategic challenge since the Cold War began," the **Soviet invasion of Afghanistan** led to an immediate increase in U.S. defense spending. Carter also declared that the United States would fight to prevent any further Soviet movement toward the Persian Gulf and its nearby oil fields. This policy, labeled the **Carter Doctrine,** was essentially a return to containment. Indeed, under the Carter Doctrine, the United States during the last two years of the Carter presidency began to arm Afghan tribesmen called the mujahadeen, who were fighting against Soviet occupation forces in Afghanistan. Détente was dead.[54]

During the last year of his presidency, Carter devoted an immense amount of time and attention to resolving the Iran hostage crisis and responding to the Soviet invasion of Afghanistan. With an economy beset by double-digit inflation precipitated in part by another round of oil price increases, it is doubtful if Carter could have won the 1980 presidential election even in the absence of the Iran hostage crisis and the Soviet invasion of Afghanistan. There is no doubt, however, that with the United States unable to respond effectively to either crisis, Carter's foreign policy crises sealed his defeat in the 1980 presidential election.

Reagan and Renewed Containment

When Ronald Reagan became president in 1981, the United States was beginning to overcome its "Vietnam hangover." Goaded by Soviet adventurism in Africa, the hostage crisis in Iran, and the Soviet invasion of Afghanistan, Americans favored a more assertive foreign policy. Carter moved in this direction during his last year as president, but it was Ronald Reagan who defined a new foreign policy that fit the emerging mood of national assertiveness.

As much a realist in foreign policy as Richard Nixon, Reagan entered office arguing that even though the United States had to build its military power and economic strength to cope with the Soviet Union, the United States was also both idealistic and moralistic. Reagan was also deeply committed to international involvement, rejecting isolationism as a relic of the past. Reagan's position on the competing themes of unilateralism versus multilateralism was particularly instructive; although he was prepared to cooperate internationally whenever possible, he was also prepared to act unilaterally whenever necessary. Throughout his two terms, Reagan emphasized rebuilding U.S. military strength, countering Soviet adventurism in the Third World, the fundamental morality of U.S. policies, and the importance of free trade. For eight years, then, these four precepts were the pillars of U.S. foreign policy.

The Reagan Administration's arms build-up was the largest increase in American defense spending since the beginning of the Cold War. Planning to spend $1.6 trillion on defense between 1981 and 1986, Reagan intended to strengthen U.S. military forces across the board.[55] At the strategic nuclear level, he initiated or accelerated development and deployment of MX intercontinental missiles, Trident II submarine-launched ballistic missiles, B-1 bombers, and cruise missiles. He also accelerated programs to improve the American ability to command and control nuclear weapons. These programs were designed to eliminate the "window of vulnerability" that Reagan feared was developing between U.S. and Soviet strategic nuclear forces. Reagan also decided to move forward with the 1979 NATO decision to deploy Pershing II intermediate-range missiles and cruise missiles if an agreement could not be reached with the Soviet Union to limit these weapons.[56]

As under previous administrations, the United States also pursued arms control efforts with the Soviet Union. Some progress was achieved, but no agreements were at first reached. Reagan maintained that the lack of success was due to Soviet intransigence and the complexities of the issues.[57] Reagan's critics asserted that the real cause of the lack of progress was U.S. intransigence, especially over the "Star Wars" strategic defense program and the opposition of some U.S. officials to arms control.

Reagan's military build-up proceeded at the conventional level as well. The purpose of the conventional build-up was both to deter Soviet aggression and to enable the United States to respond better and more quickly to regional military challenges. The conventional military build-up included building a 600-ship navy, positioning more military supplies and equipment overseas in and near areas where they might be needed, and buying more aircraft and tanks. It also included maintaining equipment better, training forces better, and increasing U.S. military presence overseas.

As U.S. defense spending climbed, debates about national priorities erupted. No program generated as much debate as Reagan's **Strategic Defense Initiative (SDI),** called "Star Wars" by its detractors. There were several proposed versions of SDI, ranging from a land-based system that used high-speed rockets to a space-based system that used lasers. All had the same purpose: to defend the United States against a missile attack launched by an enemy. An expensive experimental program, SDI rejected the 30-year-old belief that deterrence should be based on vulnerability, retaliation, and mutual assured destruction and asserted that it would soon be technologically feasible to defend the American homeland.[58]

A willingness to use military force accompanied Reagan's military build-up. In 1981, U.S. carrier-based fighters shot down two Libyan planes over the Mediterranean Sea after Libya stated it intended to attack U.S. interests. In 1983, U.S. forces invaded Grenada following a coup on that Caribbean island. In 1983 and 1984, U.S. naval guns and aircraft pounded Syrian and fundamentalist Islamic positions in Lebanon in retaliation for attacks against U.S. marines on a peacekeeping mission there. From 1981 through 1986, a U.S. military build-up in Central America and the Caribbean sent a message to Cuba and Nicaragua that the United States would not accept adventurism in the region. In 1985, U.S. fighters forced an Egyptian airliner carrying terrorists who hijacked an Italian ocean liner and killed an American passenger to land. In 1986, the United States twice struck military targets and terrorist training camps in Libya. And in 1987 and 1988, the United States retaliated for Iranian actions in the Persian Gulf.[59]

Many Americans viewed these uses of military force favorably. Others were less sure, criticizing the Reagan Administration as being too willing to use military force. Other critics noted that none of the incidents pitted American forces against opponents that had sizeable military capabilities. There were also strong indications that sizeable segments of the American public had grown wary both of U.S. overseas activism and of the American arms build-up. For example, in mid-1982, over half a million Americans turned out in Manhattan to protest the American nuclear build-up, and in early 1983, a *Newsweek* poll reported that 64 percent of the American public supported a freeze on nuclear weapons.[60] Nevertheless, as far as capabilities were concerned, the American military resurgence by the mid-1980s was real.

A second key thrust of Reagan's foreign policy was containing Soviet expansionism in the Third World. During the 1970s, the Soviet Union played a major role in helping North Vietnam defeat South Vietnam, armed and deployed Cuban troops in Angola and Ethiopia, provided extensive military aid to many Third World states, and invaded Afghanistan. Reagan believed that the Soviet Union had taken advantage of the United States' "Vietnam hangover," weak U.S. leadership, and the Soviet Union's military strength to expand its presence and influence in the Third World. Reagan concluded that the United States had to stop Soviet expansionism. Reagan summed up his view of the Soviet Union in 1981 when he asserted that the Soviets "reserve unto themselves the right to commit any crime, to lie, to cheat," and had undertaken "the most brazen imperial drive in history" during the 1960s and 1970s.[61] Later, Reagan condemned the Soviet Union as an "evil empire" and the "focus of evil" in the world, and declared that the Cold War was a "struggle between right and wrong, good and evil."[62]

The combination of the U.S. defense build-up and Reagan's criticisms of the Soviet Union worsened U.S.-Soviet relations. The year 1983 was particularly tense as Reagan announced plans for SDI and the Soviet Union shot down a Korean airliner that flew into Soviet airspace, killing over 250 people. The United States also invaded Grenada and stepped up support for the Contras, the insurgency attempting to overthrow the pro-Soviet Sandinista government in Nicaragua. Meanwhile, the Soviet Union used carpet bombing and chemical warfare in Afghanistan, and NATO deployed intermediate-range ballistic missiles in Europe, leading to a Soviet walkout from arms talks in Geneva. The Reagan Administration also condemned **state-supported terrorism,** under which the

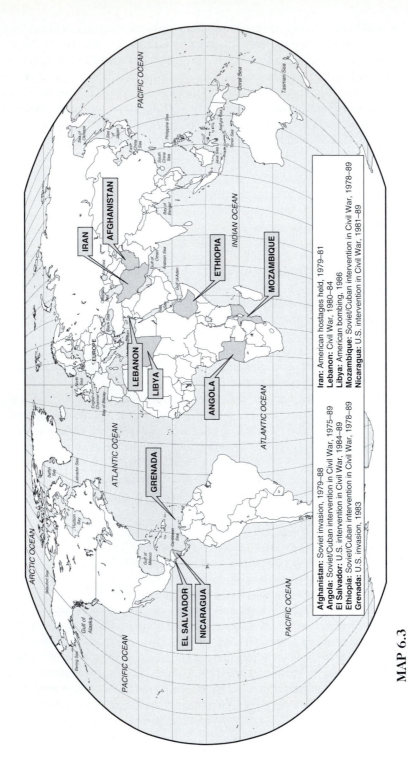

MAP 6.3
Major Cold War Hot Spots and Crises During the Late 1970s and 1980s

Afghanistan: Soviet invasion, 1979–88
Angola: Soviet/Cuban intervention in Civil War, 1975–89
El Salvador: U.S. intervention in Civil War, 1984–89
Ethiopia: Soviet/Cuban intervention in Civil War, 1978–89
Grenada: U.S. invasion, 1983

Iran: American hostages held, 1979–81
Lebanon: Civil War, 1980–84
Libya: American bombing, 1986
Mozambique: Soviet/Cuban intervention in Civil War, 1978–89
Nicaragua: U.S. intervention in Civil War, 1981–89

Soviet Union and its allies supplied weapons and training to terrorists from other countries that could not be directly traced to the Soviet Union.

In addition to its arms build-up and its rhetoric, the United States also implemented the **Reagan Doctrine** to try to contain the expansion of Soviet influence in the Third world. Under the Reagan Doctrine, the United States provided military support to anti-Soviet movements fighting pro-Soviet governments in Afghanistan, Angola, Mozambique, and Nicaragua. This, it was believed, would increase the cost of Soviet involvement in the Third World and lead Soviet leaders to refrain from more adventures there.[63]

Reagan also changed his position on China, in part to help contain the Soviet Union. During the 1980 presidential campaign, Reagan had declared that he would reverse Carter's recognition of Beijing and restore diplomatic ties with Taiwan. However, after he became president, Reagan dropped the issue and U.S.-Chinese relations recovered in 1982 and 1983 as trade expanded and military-to-military ties were discussed. In 1984, Reagan visited China even though U.S. support for Taiwan remained an irritant in U.S.-Chinese relations. The grand design that Nixon had initiated with China and that had been furthered by Carter thus became part of Reagan's strategy for containing the Soviet Union.

Throughout the first three years of Reagan's administration, U.S.-Soviet tensions ran high. Surprisingly, however, relations improved in 1984 as the two superpowers upgraded the hotline between Washington and Moscow and agreed to expand arms control talks, meeting throughout 1985 in Geneva. As important was the deescalation in rhetoric from both capitals. What happened?

First, the 1984 U.S. presidential election constrained U.S. rhetoric. Although Americans at first supported the U.S. arms build-up, they grew increasingly concerned about confrontation, especially nuclear confrontation, with the Soviet Union. Recognizing this, Reagan moderated his public statements. This drew a favorable response from Moscow.

Second, the American arms build-up and the Reagan Doctrine both began to have an impact on Soviet decision makers. SDI and the Soviet Union's quagmire in Afghanistan had particularly strong impacts on Soviet outlooks. So, too, did Reagan's willingness to rethink his position on China and maintain close Washington-Beijing relations.

Finally, the Soviet Union had serious internal problems. Its economy was performing poorly, with agricultural production down and industrial production stagnant. It was also in a leadership crisis: three general secretaries of the Communist Party, roughly equivalent to the U.S. president, died between 1982 and 1985. These and other problems had to be addressed. To do this, the USSR needed a less confrontational relationship with the United States.[64]

Morality and Economics

Even though he emphasized an arms build-up and containing the Soviet Union, Reagan also claimed that his foreign policy stressed morality. Many Americans rejected Reagan's claims, believing that Reagan generally ignored morality and human rights.

The president, however, argued that the United States supported human rights by meeting with the South African government to discuss why apartheid should be abolished rather than by breaking relations with South Africa. Calling his policy constructive engagement, Reagan argued that diplomatic pressure applied by discussions and warnings had a greater chance of dismantling apartheid in South Africa than diplomatic pressure applied by breaking relations.

Most African Americans and Democrats considered constructive engagement proof that Reagan cared little for moral considerations or human rights in his foreign policy, but Reagan countered that his policy would succeed. Meanwhile, throughout the 1980s, more and more American companies divested themselves of business interests in South Africa.[65]

Reagan also asserted that morality in foreign policy meant more than majority rule. It also meant that other American policies and beliefs such as open and free elections, freedom of the press and speech, and support for private enterprise were fundamentally correct. Thus, Reagan argued, it was moral for the United States to support the Contras against the Sandinistas in Nicaragua and it was proper to criticize Soviet human rights violations.

As for the criticism that the United States ignored human rights violations in countries that were friendly with the United States, the Reagan Administration replied that a fundamental difference existed between authoritarian dictatorships of the right, with which the United States was more likely to be friends, and totalitarian dictatorships of the left, which were pro-Soviet. Authoritarian dictatorships could change over time of their own volition if the United States applied subtle pressure to them, the Reagan Administration argued. Totalitarian dictatorships could not.

These arguments divided the American body politic, with some people accepting them, and others seeing them not as proof of morality but as conservative ideology. Few disputed that morality and human rights should be central tenets of U.S. foreign policy, but disagreement existed over what morality and human rights meant and over which policies should be implemented to achieve them. And disagreement existed over which of the foreign policy themes, idealism or realism, predominated. Reagan's critics claimed that his foreign policy was based totally on realpolitik; his supporters claimed that both realism and idealism existed in Reagan's foreign policy if only one took the time to look for them.

A final key thrust of Reagan's foreign policy was the creation of an open international economic system based on free trade.[66] Free trade, as we have seen, had long been a theme of American foreign policy, dating back to the nineteenth century and the "Open Door" policy in Asia. From Reagan's perspective, such a system had all the benefits of competition. At first, this strategy appeared to be working: the U.S. economy expanded, inflation went down, and economic growth accelerated in other industrial states. Developing states also benefited as their economies grew faster than their debts.

In 1985, however, American economic problems began to multiply as the U.S. trade deficit increased and more U.S. jobs were lost to foreign competition. Reagan's critics charged that the president's emphasis on free trade led to the export of American jobs and capital and favored the wealthy at the expense of the worker. Reagan and his supporters countered that even though some short-term dislocations were inevitable, in the long run everyone would be better off.

The battle was thus joined as conflict developed between the Democratic-controlled Congress and the Reagan Administration over trade policy. Congress several times passed legislation during 1985 and 1986 to protect U.S. jobs and industry from foreign competition. Meanwhile, the Reagan Administration continued its efforts to reduce trade barriers. Disagreements between Congress and the executive branch over trade and the creation of an open economic system continued into the administration of George H. W. Bush.

Trade relations with Japan also troubled the Reagan Administration. Throughout the 1980s, Japan compiled large trade surpluses with the United States, and many people believed that the United States and Japan were locked in a trade war that Japan was winning. Even though the island country remained a staunch American ally, many Americans believed that Japanese firms enjoyed unfair trade advantages, such as the Japanese government's creation of barriers to imports and its provision of guaranteed low-interest loans to Japanese corporations. Other Americans believed that Japan's low level of defense spending also provided Japan unfair economic advantages. These trade tensions complicated but did not undermine U.S.-Japanese political, diplomatic, and military relations throughout the Reagan years and into the Bush Administration.

Revolution and Democratization in Latin America and Asia

The Reagan years witnessed extensive revolutionary and democratic change in Latin America and Asia. On occasion, the United States was directly involved, but in other instances, revolution and democratization were the result of local, regional, and global political, economic, and social forces beyond the direct control or influence of the United States or any other international actor. The Reagan Administration argued that these forces and the revolutionary and democratic trends that they unleashed favored the United States and its allies in the ongoing Cold War conflict with communism.

The Reagan Administration was particularly concerned about revolution in the Caribbean and Central America. After intervening in the Caribbean island of Grenada in 1983 to overthrow a Marxist movement that had initiated a coup and proclaimed itself the government, the United States turned its attention to Nicaragua, where the **Sandinistas** in 1979 had overthrown the pro-American dictator Anastasio Somoza. The Carter Administration at first had supported the Sandinista regime, but as the Sandinistas became increasingly more authoritarian domestically and moved closer politically and diplomatically to the Soviet Union and Cuba, the United States increasingly distanced itself from the new Nicaraguan government.

The Reagan Administration considered the Sandinista regime a Marxist dictatorship and a Soviet-Cuban client and also believed that it supported Marxist revolutions in other Central American states. The United States therefore helped anti-Sandinista Nicaraguans form an opposition group, the **Contras,** and began arming and training them. Based in Nicaragua's neighboring state Honduras, the Contras launched numerous forays into Nicaragua to harass and try to undermine the Sandinistas. Many Americans opposed Reagan's pro-Contra policies. Indeed, from 1984 to 1986, the U.S. Congress expressly forbade funding the Contras.

The United States also was directly involved in a civil war in El Salvador. Placing the conflict into a Cold War context, the Reagan Administration legitimized U.S. involvement there by proclaiming that the Sandinistas were providing the El Salvador rebels arms and munitions furnished by Cuba and the Soviet Union. Other Americans viewed the situation differently, proclaiming that El Salvador's civil war was the result of domestic dictatorship and inequitable distributions of wealth in El Salvador.

Much of the debate over the Reagan Administration's El Salvador policy ended in 1985 when Napoleon Duarte, a wealthy conservative who favored democratic political reforms, won the presidential election. Reagan logically argued that even though fighting continued in El Salvador, the United States now provided economic and military support to the moderate center.

The Reagan Administration was not as fortunate in Nicaragua. Despite the congressional ban on funding to the Contras, the Reagan Administration secretly funneled money to them by diverting funds obtained from a secret arms sale to Iran. The Reagan Administration also ran the Contra operation from the National Security Council to keep it secret from Congress and the public. In 1987, however, the operation lost its cover and became public. This episode, known as the **Iran-Contra affair,** undermined the credibility of the Reagan Administration and Reagan personally, who declared that he did not know anything about it. Many Americans concluded that Reagan was either lying or not in control of his foreign policy.[67]

The United States also was involved in a revolution in Haiti. Haiti had been ruled for years by the brutal Duvalier family, first "Papa Doc" and then his son "Baby Doc." Since the Duvaliers were also anti-communist, the United States for the most part had turned a blind eye to them. In 1986, however, protests broke out against Baby Doc. The United States advised him not to resort to violence and, as demonstrations grew, provided him a plane to leave Haiti. Reagan declared that the new U.S. position was because "the American people believe in human rights and oppose tyranny in whatever form, whether of the left or the right."[68]

On the other side of the world, the United States adopted a new stance toward the Philippines, where the United States had long supported dictator Ferdinand Marcos. When in 1986 Marcos claimed victory in a fraudulent election over Corazon Aquino, and Filipinos took to the streets, the United States advised him to step down. He did, Aquino became president, and democracy came to the Philippines. Similarly, in South Korea, street demonstrations had flared up against the pro-American military government for years. As anti-government sentiment built again in 1987, the United States pressured the military to allow free presidential elections. It did, and a civilian government came to power. The same thing happened in Chile, where the United States pressured the dictatorial government of General Augusto Pinochet to hold elections. Eventually it did, and democracy came to Chile as well.

Moving toward an End to the Cold War: 1987–1989

As important as these events were, and as significant as the change in U.S. attitudes toward dictatorships of the right was, Reagan's foreign policy remained focused on U.S.-Soviet relations. After **Mikhail Gorbachev** became the Soviet leader in 1985, U.S-Soviet relations improved dramatically. Gorbachev introduced reforms in Soviet domestic, foreign, and military policies that transformed the USSR and U.S.-Soviet relations. The reforms were intended to address the problems that the Soviet Union faced, but they led to the end of the Cold War and the demise of the Soviet Union.

Even before Gorbachev's reforms took hold, Gorbachev and Reagan laid the groundwork for a transformation in U.S.-Soviet relations. Reagan and Gorbachev met first in Geneva in 1985, next in Reykjavik in 1986, and for a third time in Washington in 1987. They eventually held five summits before Reagan left office in 1989.

Significant changes in the U.S.-Soviet relationship began at the 1987 Washington summit when Reagan and Gorbachev agreed to eliminate intermediate nuclear forces. The Intermediate Nuclear Forces Agreement was a significant breakthrough, the first time that the two sides agreed to do away with an entire class of nuclear weapons.[69] In addition, Gorbachev promised the Soviet Union would reduce the size of its armed forces.

Changes in U.S.-Soviet relations became even more pronounced in 1988 and early 1989 as Gorbachev redefined long-held Soviet outlooks on international relations, arms control progressed, and negotiations on resolving Third World conflicts moved forward. Notably, U.S.-Soviet conversations were devoid of the confrontational rhetoric that had periodically emerged from Washington and Moscow in earlier years. Importantly, the Soviet leader on several occasions declared that the time had passed for military intervention outside one's own country and that the countries of Eastern Europe had the right to choose whatever type of government they wanted.

A WORLD TRANSFORMED?

As 1988 faded into 1989 and Reagan prepared to leave office, U.S.-Soviet relations and East-West relations had been transformed by changes in foreign and military policy initiated both in Washington and Moscow. It was a different world than it had been at any time since the Cold War started in earnest with the declaration of the Truman Doctrine and the Marshall Plan and the implementation of containment 42 years earlier. Some experts and analysts declared the Cold War over.

The dimensions of change were evident during Reagan's last weeks in office. In early December 1988, Soviet President Mikhail Gorbachev addressed the United Nations, announcing that his country would reduce its military by half a million troops, withdraw six tank divisions from Eastern Europe and disband them, pull forces out of the western USSR thereby reducing the threat to Western Europe, and withdraw forces from Mongolia. Two weeks later, Cuba, South Africa, and Angola signed an agreement at the UN under which Cuba withdrew its forces from Angola and Namibia received independence from South Africa, thereby cooling a Cold War hot spot. In January 1989, Vietnam agreed to withdraw its troops from Cambodia before the end of the year, reducing tensions in another hot spot. When on January 20, 1989, President Ronald Reagan received his final national security briefing from General Colin Powell, Powell said simply, "The world is quiet today, Mr. President."[70]

American public opinion agreed with Powell. A December poll indicated that 54 percent of the public believed that the Soviet Union was no threat or a minor threat to the United States. Also, 65 percent of the respondents said that they believed the Soviet Union was primarily concerned with protecting its own security.[71] The old Cold War consensus on which the United States had based its foreign policy had changed. The world—and American foreign policy—had truly been transformed between the time Reagan took office in 1981 and when he left it in 1989. But as amazing as these changes were, they were nothing compared to what soon was to come.

SUMMARY

World War II ended with American fighting forces spread across the world. Never before had one country projected so much power around the globe. The United States had become the first superpower.

The United States' ability to project power may or may not have implied that it desired to do so. Differences of opinion exist even today about U.S. intentions when the war ended. The debate pits traditionalists, who say the United States returned to isolationism after the war as evidenced by the return to the United States of most of its military forces, against revisionists, who claim the United States caused the Cold War.

The Cold War was a political-military-economic confrontation between the United States and its allies on one hand and the Soviet Union and its allies on the other. Both sides armed themselves with many nuclear and conventional weapons. Small wars occasionally erupted that involved one of the superpowers or its allies. Numerous crises that did not escalate to fighting also occurred. The Cold War began in the late 1940s and lasted until Eastern European communist regimes fell in 1989. During this era, Americans saw their mission as defending democracy, promoting U.S./Western values, and preventing the spread of communism. The United States emphasized realism over idealism, involvement over isolation, and multilateralism over unilateralism.

Why did the Cold War happen? Six reasons have been advanced: past U.S.-Soviet relations, different national objectives, opposed ideologies, the personalities of decision makers, differing perceptions, and specific post–World War II Soviet actions like the expansion of Soviet power into Eastern Europe and Soviet policies toward Iran and Turkey.

The Cold War had several distinct periods. The first extended from 1948 to 1961, during which time the United States under Presidents Truman and Eisenhower initiated containment, declared in the Truman Doctrine that the United States would aid countries fighting for their freedom, provided Marshall Plan aid to Europe, helped form the North Atlantic Treaty Organization, sent troops to South Korea to counter a North Korean invasion, declared it would retaliate against Soviet aggression by using nuclear weapons, and had several confrontations with the Soviets over Berlin.

The second period was during the 1960s, when the United States under Presidents Kennedy and Johnson again confronted the Soviet Union over Berlin, faced down the Soviets in the Cuban Missile Crisis, and deployed troops to Vietnam in a war that soon became a quagmire.

The next Cold War period extended from 1969 to 1977 under Richard Nixon and Gerald Ford, both of whom pursued Nixon's strategy of détente with the Soviet Union, improved relations with China, and withdrawal from Vietnam.

The final Cold War period stretched from 1977 to 1989 and included the policies of détente and human rights preferred by Jimmy Carter and the renewed confrontation and containment followed by Ronald Reagan. Under Carter, the United States continued with détente even as Carter rejected Nixon's excessive realism and emphasized human rights.

However, when in 1979 radical Iranian students held the American embassy staff as captives and the Soviet Union invaded Afghanistan, Carter reinitiated containment. When Reagan became president in 1981, the United States emphasized rebuilding U.S. military strength, countering Soviet adventurism in the Third World, stressing the morality of U.S. policies, and striving for free trade.

Even so, Reagan's foreign policy was focused on the Soviet Union. After Mikhail Gorbachev became the Soviet leader in 1985, U.S-Soviet relations improved dramatically as Gorbachev introduced reforms in Soviet domestic, foreign, and military policies. Reagan and Gorbachev in 1987 agreed to eliminate intermediate nuclear forces. Arms control also progressed, and negotiations on resolving Third World conflicts moved forward.

By 1989, U.S.-Soviet relations and East-West relations had been transformed by changes in foreign and military policy initiated both in Washington and Moscow. It was a different world than it had been at any time since the Cold War began. As amazing as these changes were, they were nothing compared to what soon occurred.

KEY TERMS AND CONCEPTS

superpower
traditionalists
revisionists
Cold War
United Nations
Bretton Woods Agreements
International Monetary Fund
World Bank
General Agreement on Tariffs and
   Trade (GATT)
Iron Curtain
Truman Doctrine
Marshall Plan
containment
1947 National Security Act
communist coup in Czechoslovakia
Berlin blockade
Berlin airlift
North Atlantic Treaty Organization
   (NATO)
Mao Zedong
NSC-68
Korean War
massive retaliation
U.S. alliance system
summit meeting
Sputnik

Berlin crises
deterrence
mutual assured destruction (MAD)
East-West conflict
First World
Second World
Third World
Nonaligned Movement
Cuban Missile Crisis
Vietnam
Nixon's grand strategy
détente
Vietnamization
Nixon Doctrine
Arab-Israeli conflict
human rights
Iran hostage crisis
Soviet invasion of Afghanistan
Carter Doctrine
Strategic Defense Initiative (SDI)
state-supported terrorism
Reagan Doctrine
trade relations with Japan
Sandinistas
Contras
Iran-Contra affair
Mikhail Gorbachev

THINKING CRITICALLY

1. Whose arguments regarding American foreign policy in the years after World War II are most persuasive, those of the traditionalists or those of the revisionists? Why?

2. What was the Cold War, and what were its causes?

3. How did American views on idealism versus realism, isolationism versus involvement, and unilateralism versus multilateralism change following World War II?

4. American and other Western leaders believed that the United Nations and the Bretton Woods Agreements would help create a peaceful post–World War II world. Explain their reasoning, and assess the extent to which they were correct or incorrect.

5. What was containment, and how was it operationalized during the 1940s and 1950s?

6. What was the theory behind deterrence and mutual assured destruction, and to what extent did these policies contribute to world peace and American national security?

7. Why were Berlin and Cuba so important during the Cold War? How did tensions in both locations escalate and deescalate?

8. Assess the impact that Vietnam had on American foreign policy.

9. What was Richard Nixon's grand strategy, and how did he implement it?

10. Contrast Richard Nixon's foreign policy, with its emphasis on realism, with Jimmy Carter's foreign policy, with its emphasis on idealism.

11. Describe and explain the impact that the Iran hostage crisis and the Soviet invasion of Afghanistan had on U.S. foreign policy and Jimmy Carter's worldview.

12. What were the four pillars of U.S. foreign policy under Ronald Reagan, and how did Reagan implement and pursue each?

13. Contrast Jimmy Carter's views of human rights with Ronald Reagan's views of human rights.

14. Explain the arguments in support of an open international economic system and free trade. Explain the arguments against an open international system and free trade. Which position is better for the United States?

15. What role did summitry play during the Cold War, and in ending the Cold War?

16. What factors led to the improvement in U.S.-Soviet relations in the late 1980s, and to what extent did each contribute to that improvement?

NOTES

1. The Soviet Union by the early 1950s was also regarded as a superpower because of its nuclear weapons and large standing army. However, it never had an ability to project military power globally, nor did it have an economy that ever rivaled that of the United States.

2. For the work of some of the more noted traditionalists, see Stephen E. Ambrose, *Rise to Globalism: American Foreign Policy since 1938* (New York: Penguin, 1993); Louis J. Halle, *The Cold War as History* (New York: Harper and Row, 1967); Henry Kissinger, *Diplomacy* (New York: Simon and Schuster, 1994); and John Spanier and Steven W. Hook, *American Foreign Policy since World War II* (Washington, D.C.: Congressional Quarterly, 2000).

3. For the work of some of the more noted revisionists, see Gar Alperovitz, *Atomic Diplomacy* (New York: Vintage Books, 1967); Gabriel Kolko, *The Roots of American Foreign Policy* (Boston: Beacon Press, 1969); Walter LaFeber, *The New Empire* (Ithaca, N.Y.: Cornell University Press, 1963); and William Appleman Williams, *The Tragedy of American Diplomacy* (New York: Norton, 1988). The collapse of the Soviet Union and the release of a significant number of Soviet-era documents by the new Russian government has given rise to what might be called a second wave of revisionist analysis as scholars and analysts begin to understand the thinking that took place within the Kremlin. One of the earliest and best of this ilk is John Lewis Gaddis, *We Now Know: Rethinking Cold War History* (New York: Oxford University Press, 1997).

4. These disagreements are traced, often with different explanations as to why they occurred, by the traditionalists and revisionists identified in the preceding two notes.

5. The terms "confrontation," "crisis," "conflict," and "war" as used in this chapter require clarification. "Confrontation" is the most general term, referring to the existence of political, military, diplomatic, or other tension between two or more international actors. "Crisis" refers to the sudden growth of such tension, with the possibility that such tension may escalate to a conflict. "Conflict," in turn, refers to a situation in which fighting takes place, although not necessarily large-scale fighting, which is considered "war" or "guerrilla war" regardless of whether it is formally declared. The demarcation lines between these four terms are more often than not vague and imprecise.

6. Ambrose, p. 79.

7. For a good description of the UN and its early years, see Ruth B. Russell, *A History of the United Nations Charter: The Role of the United States 1940–1945* (Washington, D.C.: Brookings Institution, 1958).

8. See W. M. Scammell, *The International Economy since 1945* (New York: St. Martin's Press, 1980), and Richard N. Gardner, *Sterling-Dollar Diplomacy in Current Perspective: The Origins and Prospects of Our International Economic Order* (New York: Columbia University Press, 1980).

9. For a few more of the many views and interpretations of who caused the Cold War, in addition to the traditionalists and revisionists listed in notes 2 and 3, see Seyom Brown, *The Faces of Power* (New York: Columbia University Press, 1969); Herbert Feis, *From Trust to Terror: The Onset of the Cold War, 1945–1950* (New York: Norton, 1970); William L. Gaddis, *The United States and the Origins of the Cold War, 1941–47* (New York: Columbia University Press, 1972); Lloyd C. Gardner, *American Foreign Policy: Present to Past* (New York: Free Press, 1974); John Herz, *Beginnings of the Cold War* (Bloomington: Indiana University Press, 1966); David Horowitz, *The Free World Colossus* (New York: Hill and Wang, 1965); George F. Kennan, *American Diplomacy, 1900–1950* (New York: New American Library, 1951); Walter Lippman, *The Cold War: A Study in U.S. Foreign Policy* (New York: Harper and Row, 1947); Vojtech Mastny, *Russia's Road to the Cold War* (New York: Columbia University Press, 1979); James A. Nathan and James K. Oliver, *United States Foreign Policy and World Order* (Boston: Little, Brown, 1976); Thomas G. Paterson, *On Every Front: The Making of the Cold War* (New York: Norton, 1979); and Daniel Yergin, *Shattered Peace: The Origins of the Cold War and the National Security State* (Boston: Houghton Mifflin, 1978).

10. Winston Churchill, "The Sinews of Peace," March 5, 1946, in *Vital Speeches of the Day*, Vol. 12 (March 15, 1946), p. 332. At the time of his speech, Churchill was not prime minister.

11. For an insider's view of these and subsequent critical decisions, see Joseph Marion Jones, *The Fifteen Weeks* (New York: Harcourt Brace Jovanovich, 1964).

12. "Text of President Truman's Speech on New Foreign Policy," *New York Times* (March 13, 1947).

13. *Department of State Bulletin*, 16 (July 15, 1947): 1159–1160.

14. Corrected for inflation, this is about $100 billion in 2003 dollars.

15. George F. Kennan ("X"), "The Sources of Soviet Conduct," *Foreign Affairs* (July 1947): 566–582.

16. Kennan, "The Sources of Soviet Conduct."

17. For more detailed discussions of containment, see Terry L. Deibel and John Lewis Gaddis, *Containment: Concept and Policy*, Vols. 1 and 2 (Washington, D.C.: National Defense University Press, 1986).

18. See Milovan Djilas, *Tito: The Story from Inside* (New York: Harcourt Brace Jovanovich, 1980), for an excellent study of the Yugoslav leader written by one of his erstwhile lieutenants.

19. For good studies of the Berlin blockade and airlift, see Richard Collier, *Bridge across the Sky: The Berlin Blockade and Airlift, 1948–1949* (New York: McGraw-Hill, 1978); Michael D. Haycock, *City under Siege: The Berlin Blockade and Airlift, 1948–1949* (Dulles, Va.: Brassey's, 2000); and Roger G. Miller, *To Save a City: The Berlin Airlift, 1948–1949* (University Press of the Pacific, 2002).

20. *Public Papers of the President, Truman, 1949* (Washington, D.C.: U.S. Government Printing Office, 1964), p. 114.

21. *Department of State Bulletin*, 20, (March 20, 1949): 340. The North Atlantic Treaty's original signatory states were Belgium, Canada, Denmark, France, Great Britain, Iceland, Italy, Luxembourg, the Netherlands, Norway, Portugal, and the United States. As of 2003, NATO had 19 members, with more soon to join.

22. See Sergei Y. Shenin, *The United States and the Third World: The Origins of Postwar Relations and the Point Four Program* (Commack, N.Y.: Nova Science Publishers, 1999).

23. NSC-68 can be found in Thomas Etzold and John Lewis Gaddis, eds., *Containment: Documents in American Policy and Strategy, 1945–1950* (New York: Columbia University Press, 1978).

24. For good studies of the Korean War and the accompanying Truman-MacArthur controversy, see William W. Stueck, *The Korean War: An International History* (Princeton: Princeton University Press, 1995), and John Spanier, *The Truman MacArthur Controversy and the Korean War* (Cambridge, Mass.: Belknap, 1959).

25. See Townsend Hoopes, *The Devil and John Foster Dulles: The Diplomacy of the Eisenhower Era* (Boston: Little, Brown, 1973).

26. For discussions of various treaties within the U.S. alliance system, see Ruth C. Lawson, *International Regional Organizations: Constitutional Foundations* (New York: Praeger, 1962); Robert E. Osgood, *NATO* (Chicago: University of Chicago Press, 1962); and Malcolm McKinnin, *Independence and Foreign Policy: New Zealand in the World Since 1935* (Auckland, New Zealand: Auckland University Press, 1993).

27. See Roger Louis and Roger Owen, eds., *Suez 1956* (New York: Oxford University Press, 1989), and Diane B. Kunz, *The Economic Diplomacy of the Suez Crisis* (Chapel Hill: University of North Carolina Press, 1991).

28. See Paul Dickson, *Sputnik: The Shock of the Century* (New York: Penguin Putnam, 2003); Asif A. Siddiqi, *Sputnik and the Soviet Space Challenge* (Gainesville: University of Florida Press, 2003); and Robert A. Divine, *The Sputnik Challenge* (New York: Oxford University Press, 1993).

29. See William Burr, "Avoiding the Slippery Slope: The Eisenhower Administration and the Berlin Crisis, November 1958–January 1959," *Diplomatic History* 18 (Spring 1994): 177–205; and Gaddis, *We Now Know*, pp. 138–143. For Nikita Khrushchev's view of the Berlin crises, see Nikita Khrushchev, *Khrushchev Remembers* (Boston: Little, Brown, 1970), pp. 452–460.

30. See Michael R. Beschloss, *Mayday: Eisenhower, Khrushchev, and the U-2 Affair* (New York: Harper and Row, 1986).

31. For good discussions of nuclear strategy, see Lawrence Freedman, *The Evolution of Nuclear Strategy* (New York: St. Martin's Press, 1981); Fred Kaplan, *The Wizards of Armageddon* (New York: Simon and Schuster, 1983); and Gregg Herken, *Counsels of War* (New York: Oxford University Press, 1987).

32. For Nikita Khrushchev's view of the 1961 Vienna Summit with John Kennedy, see Khrushchev, *Khrushchev Remembers*, p. 458. For Dean Rusk's view of the summit, see Dean Rusk, *As I Saw It* (New York: Norton, 1990), pp. 220–222.

33. The Soviet Union had several reasons for placing missiles in Cuba, the most likely of which was to reduce the United States' strategic nuclear advantage. At the time, the United States had about 180 intercontinental ballistic missiles, and the Soviet Union had about 20. Placing missiles in Cuba would have eliminated much of this strategic American advantage. Other reasons that Khrushchev may have placed missiles in Cuba include to prevent an American invasion of Cuba and to allow the Soviet Union to ratchet up the pres-

sure it could apply to Berlin. For insider views of the Cuban Missile Crisis, see Robert F. Kennedy, *Thirteen Days: A Memoir of the Cuban Missile Crisis* (New York: Norton, 1968), and Rusk, *As I Saw It*, pp. 229–245. For transcripts of tapes made in the White House during the Cuban Missile Crisis, see Ernest R. May and Philip Zelikow, *The Kennedy Tapes: Inside the White House during the Cuban Missile Crisis* (Cambridge, Mass.: Harvard University Press, 1997). For a detailed analysis of the crisis using the three models discussed in Chapter 1, see Graham Allison and Philip Zelikow, *Essence of Decision: Explaining the Cuban Missile Crisis*, 2nd ed. (New York: Longman, 1999).

34. Contrary to popular American beliefs, the United States at no time provided more than $7 billion of combined economic and military assistance per year between 1945 and 1970. In most years during this period, economic aid was greater than military aid. See *The Statistical History of the United States from Colonial Times to the Present* (New York: Basic Books, 1976).

35. See Ellen J. Hammer, *The Struggle for Indochina, 1940–1955* (Stanford, Calif.: Stanford University Press, 1966), and Melvin Gurtov, *The First Vietnam Crisis* (New York: Columbia University Press, 1967).

36. See George C. Herring, *America's Longest War: The United States and Vietnam* (New York: Knopf, 1986), pp. 119–123, for a synopsis of this debate.

37. For detailed discussions of the United States in Vietnam, see George McTurnan Kahin and John W. Lewis, *The United States in Vietnam* (New York: Delta, 1969); Stanley C. Karnow, *Vietnam: A History* (New York: Viking Press, 1983); Paul Kattenburg, *The Vietnam Trauma in American Foreign Policy, 1945–1975* (New Brunswick, N.J.: Transaction Books, 1980); Daniel S. Papp, *Vietnam: The View from Moscow, Beijing, Washington* (Jefferson, N.C.: McFarland, 1981); Rusk, *As I Saw It*, pp. 415–506; U.S. Department of Defense, *United States-Vietnam Relations 1945–1967* (Washington, D.C.: U.S. Government Printing Office, 1971).

38. John E. Mueller, *War, Presidents, and Public Opinion* (New York: Wiley, 1973), pp. 54–55.

39. For Richard Nixon's own conception of the state of international relations during the late 1960s and early 1970s, see Richard M. Nixon, *U.S. Foreign Policy for the 1970s,* Vols. 1–3 (Washington, D.C.: U.S. Government Printing Office, 1970–1972).

40. See Michael Froman, *The Development of the Idea of Détente* (New York: St. Martin's Press, 1992).

41. For details of U.S.-Soviet summitry and détente under Nixon, see Raymond L. Garthoff, *Détente and Confrontation: American-Soviet Relations from Nixon to Reagan* (Washington, D.C.: Brookings Institution, 1985). For an insider's view of the summits as well as a much broader study of diplomacy in the Western World, see Henry A. Kissinger, *Diplomacy* (New York: Touchstone, 1994).

42. *Peking Review*, March 3, 1972, pp. 4–5. See also Gene T. Hsiao, *Sino-American Détente and Its Policy Implications* (New York: Praeger, 1974).

43. See those sources listed in note 37.

44. In 1956, Israel, Great Britain, and France attacked Egypt in a dispute over the Suez Canal. The three easily defeated Egypt, but the United States and the Soviet Union insisted that Great Britain and France withdraw and Israel return the land that it acquired in the war to Egypt. All three complied. Another war erupted in 1967, which Israel won in a stunningly short six days. In this war, Israel acquired the Gaza Strip and the Sinai Peninsula from Egypt, the Golan Heights from Syria, and Jerusalem and the West Bank of the Jordan River from Jordan.

45. See Frank Aker, *October 1973: The Arab-Israeli War* (Hamden, Conn.: Archon, 1991). See also George W. Gawrych, *The Albatross of Decisive Victory: War and Policy between Egypt and Israel in the 1967 and 1973 Arab-Israeli Wars* (Westport, Conn.: Greenwood, 2000).

46. See Fred L. Block, *Disorder: A Study of United States International Monetary Policy from World War II to the Present* (Berkeley: University of California Press, 1977); Alfred E. Eckes Jr., *A Search for Solvency: Bretton Woods and the International Monetary System, 1941–1971* (Austin: University of Texas Press, 1975); and Arthur Lewis, *The Evolution of the International Economic Order* (Princeton: Princeton University Press, 1978).

47. For accounts of the Angolan conflict, see Arthur Jay Klinghoffer, *The Angolan War: A Study in Soviet Policy in the Third World* (Boulder, Colo.: Westview Press, 1980); John Marcum, *The Angolan Revolution:*

Exile Politics and Guerrilla Warfare, 1962–1967 (Cambridge, Mass.: 1978); and Daniel S. Papp, "Angola, National Liberation, and the Soviet Union," *Parameters* 8 (June 1978): 57–70.

48. For discussions of Carter's human rights policy, see Arthur Schlesinger Jr., "Human Rights and the American Tradition," *Foreign Affairs: America and the World 1978*, Vol. 57, pp. 503–526; and G. D. Loescher, "Carter's Human Rights Policy and the 95th Congress," *World Today* 35 (April 1979): 140–159.

49. Jimmy Carter, "Humane Purposes in Foreign Policy," commencement address at the University of Notre Dame, Department of State news release, May 22, 1977.

50. For a discussion of U.S. policy toward Iran under the shah, see Mark J. Gasiorowski, *U.S. Foreign Policy and the Shah: Building a Client State in Iran* (Ithaca, N.Y.: Cornell University Press, 1991); Barry M. Rubin, *Paved with Good Intentions: The American Experience and Iran* (New York: Viking, 1981); and Gary Sick, *All Fall Down: America's Tragic Encounter with Iran* (New York: Viking, 1986).

51. See Department of State Publication 8954, *The Camp David Summit* (Washington, D.C.: Office of Public Communications, Bureau of Public Affairs, September 1978).

52. See J. Rees, "Disastrous Foreign Policy of Jimmy Carter," *American Opinion* 23 (May 1980): 33–39; and J. J. Kirkpatrick, "Establishing a Viable Human Rights Policy," *World Affairs* 143 (Spring 1981): 323–334.

53. For a view of the hostage crisis from the perspective of one of the hostages, see William J. Daugherty, *In the Shadow of the Ayatollah: A CIA Hostage in Iran* (Annapolis, M.D.: Naval Institute Press, 2001).

54. For more details on Afghanistan and Soviet policies there, see J. Bruce Amstutz, *Afghanistan: The First Five Years of the Soviet Occupation* (Washington, D.C.: National Defense University Press, 1986); Henry S. Bradsher, *Afghanistan and the Soviet Union* (Durham, N.C.: Duke University Press, 1985); and Rosanne Klass, ed., *Afghanistan: The Great Game Revisited* (New York: Freedom House, 1990).

55. *Congressional Quarterly Almanac 1981* (Washington, D.C.: Congressional Quarterly, Inc., 1982), pp. 240–241; Stephen Webbe, "Defense: Reagan Plans Largest U.S. Defense Buildup since Vietnam," *Christian Science Monitor* (May 1, 1981): 8–9.

56. See Colin S. Gray, "Strategic Forces," in Joseph Kruzel, ed., *1986–87 American Defense Annual* (Lexington, Mass.: Lexington Books, 1986).

57. See Alexander Haig, "Arms Control and Strategic Nuclear Forces" (Washington, D.C.: Bureau of Public Affairs, Department of State, November 4, 1981); and Strobe Talbott, *Deadly Gambits* (New York: Vintage Books, 1985).

58. For perspectives on SDI, see John Pike, *The Strategic Defense Initiative* (Washington, D.C.: Federation of American Scientists, 1985), and Office of Technology Assessment, *Ballistic Missile Defense Technologies* (Washington, D.C.: Office of Technology Assessment, 1985).

59. For general discussions of foreign policy under Ronald Reagan, see William G. Hyland, ed., *The Reagan Foreign Policy* (New York: New American Library, 1987); Congressional Quarterly Staff, *U.S. Foreign Policy: The Reagan Imprint* (Washington, D.C.: CQ Press, 1986); Alexander M. Haig, *Caveat: Realism, Reagan, and Foreign Policy* (New York: Macmillan, 1984); and George P. Shultz, *Turmoil and Triumph: My Years as Secretary of State* (New York: Scribner, 1993).

60. *New York Times,* June 13, 1982; and *Newsweek*, January 31, 1983.

61. *New York Times*, January 30, 1981.

62. For the full text of Reagan's March 8, 1983, speech to an evangelical fundamentalist convention in Orlando, Florida, see Strobe Talbott, *The Russians and Reagan* (New York: Vintage, 1984), pp. 105–118.

63. For a discussion of the Reagan Doctrine, see Mark P. Lagon, *The Reagan Doctrine: Sources of American Conduct in the Cold War's Last Chapter* (New York: Praeger, 1994).

64. For more details on these and other explanations of the changing state of Soviet-American relations under Reagan, see Raymond L. Garthoff, ed., *The Great Transition: American-Soviet Relations and the End of the Cold War* (Washington, D.C.: Brookings Institution, 1994); Don Oberdorfer, *From the Cold War to a New Era: The United States and the Soviet Union, 1983–1991* (Baltimore: Johns Hopkins University Press, 1998), pp. 1–327; Seweryn Bialer, *Gorbachev's Russia and American Foreign Policy* (Boulder, Colo.: Westview Press, 1988); and David Holloway, "Gorbachev's New Thinking," and Robert Legvold, "The Revo-

lution in Soviet Foreign Policy," both in William P. Bundy, *Foreign Affairs: America and the World 1988/89*, Vol. 68 (1989), pp. 66–98.

65. See Pauline H. Baker, *The United States and South Africa: The Reagan Years* (New York: Ford Foundation, 1989).

66. For a discussion of Reagan's early international economic policies, see Jeffrey E. Garten, "Gunboat Economics," *Foreign Affairs: America and the World 1984*, Vol. 63, pp. 538–599; and Robert D. Hormats, "World Economy Under Stress," *Foreign Affairs: America and the World 1985*, Vol. 64, pp. 455–478.

67. See Clyde R. Mark, "Iran-Contra Affair: A Chronology," Report 86-190F (Washington, D.C.: Congressional Research Service, April 2, 1987), and *Report of the Congressional Committees Investigating the Iran-Contra Affair* (Washington, D.C.: U.S. Government Printing Office, November 1987).

68. *New York Times*, March 15, 1986.

69. For the text of the INF Agreement, see *Arms Control and Disarmament Agreements: Texts and Histories of the Negotiations* (Washington, D.C.: United States Arms Control and Disarmament Agency, 1990), pp. 345–444.

70. This paragraph is derived from Oberdorfer, pp. 316–325.

71. Oberdorfer, p. 323.

CHAPTER **7**

Shaping the Post–Cold War World: 1989–Today

The men who ended the Cold War: soon-to-be President George H. W. Bush (1989–1993), President Ronald Reagan (1981–1989), and Soviet President Mikhail Gorbachev (1985–1991), stand, left to right, in front of New York's World Trade Center at the 1988 Reagan-Bush-Gorbachev summit.

- How and why did the Cold War end?
- Why did the United States react so strongly to Iraq's invasion of Kuwait?
- How has the United States responded to economic globalization?
- What policies did the United States initiate after the end of the Cold War to try to shape the international system?
- What impact did the September 11, 2001, terrorist attacks have on U.S. foreign policy?
- What are the main challenges for U.S. foreign policy today?

George H. W. Bush campaigned for the presidency pledging to follow President Reagan's foreign policy directions. However, by the time he became president in 1989, so many changes had taken place in Eastern Europe and the Soviet Union that the entire direction of U.S. foreign policy toward these states had to be revised. Other aspects of U.S. foreign policy also required revision as crises erupted in China, Latin America, and the Middle East. And after the Soviet Union collapsed in 1991, Bush faced the challenge of shaping a post–Cold War world and defining an appropriate American foreign policy for that world.

As president of the world's only remaining superpower, Bush began these efforts but did not complete them. The task was immense, and Bush's successors, Bill Clinton and George W. Bush, continued the effort. All three post–Cold War presidents struggled to answer the questions: "After the Cold War, what is America's foreign policy mission?" "What are its post–Cold War interests, and upon which principles should its post–Cold War foreign policy be based?" "Which is more important, realism or idealism? involvement or isolationism? multilateralism or unilateralism?"

Even today, in a world substantially changed by the September 11, 2001, terrorist attacks, answering these questions is a difficult task. Nevertheless, the uncertainty of the present-day world and the difficulty of answering these questions should not obscure several verities of post–Cold War American foreign policy discussed in this chapter.

First, despite concerns that the collapse of communism and the dissolution of the Soviet Union would deprive the United States of a foreign policy mission and set American foreign policy adrift, America's post–Cold War presidents all pursued a foreign policy mission that was similar not only to each other's but also to their Cold War predecessors'. Admittedly, preventing the spread of communism was no longer part of the American mission, but defending democracy and promoting U.S./Western values— whether it be in Eastern Europe and the former Soviet Union as under George H. W. Bush, in Haiti and Kosovo as under Bill Clinton, or in Afghanistan and Iraq as under George W. Bush—provided a consistency and continuity to post–Cold War American foreign policy, as well as a link to American foreign policy during the Cold War, even if the policy tools used by the respective post–Cold War presidents differed.

Second, two principles upon which American foreign policy has been historically based, pragmatism and moralism, remain enshrined in post–Cold War U.S. foreign policy, while a third principle, unilateralism, has been reemphasized by George W. Bush. The fourth principle, isolationism, abandoned since World War II, remains an historical artifact. Despite the end of the Soviet threat and sporadic calls to reemphasize isolationism, no post–Cold War president has given serious consideration to abandoning the United States' international involvement.

Third, how to achieve the United States' national interests is as much a topic of debate and disagreement as ever, even if a broad consensus exists on mission and principle. For example, even though strengthening the American economy is widely accepted as an American national interest, American leaders, including both Bushes and Clinton, endorsed globalization, while much of the American public preferred to protect American jobs.[1] Similarly, even though virtually every American supports the war on terrorism in one way or another, some, including President George W. Bush, believed the best way to prosecute it was to eliminate Saddam Hussein as leader of Iraq, while others, such as retired NATO commander and 2004 presidential candidate Wesley Clark, argued that finding Osama bin Laden and destroying al Qaeda would do more to enhance American security.[2]

Fourth, the competing themes of realism versus idealism, isolationism versus involvement, and unilateralism versus multilateralism remain as much a part of the dialogue over twenty-first-century American foreign policy as in preceding centuries. Realism and involvement continue to hold sway over idealism and isolationism, but both idealism and isolationism continue to have their proponents. Indeed, the debates between realists and idealists and between isolationists and internationalists are less about which extreme to adopt in foreign policy as about where on a spectrum between the extremes

American foreign policy should be. The same is true of the debate between unilateralists and multilateralists, with multilateralism holding sway during the Cold War and during the post–Cold War presidencies of George H. W. Bush and Bill Clinton, and unilateralism holding sway under George W. Bush. But under all three post–Cold War presidents, neither multilateralism nor unilateralism predominated to the exclusion of the other. Thus, as we will see, despite their multilateralist preferences, George H. W. Bush refused to commit the United States to most of the agreements reached by the Rio de Janeiro Environmental Summit and Bill Clinton acted unilaterally to launch cruise missile strikes against Sudan and Afghanistan. Conversely, despite his unilateralist preferences, George W. Bush sought to assemble a "coalition of the willing" before the United States launched the 2003 war against Iraq. Post–Cold War presidents, like most of their Cold War predecessors, have sought to achieve a balancing act between the extremes of all three pairs of competing themes.

As we will see in this chapter, American foreign policy in the post–Cold War era is determined, as in earlier periods of American history, by U.S. policymakers on the basis of the policies that they formulate and implement and by America's people on the basis of the leaders that they elect. In the post–Cold War era, American foreign policy remains a work in progress. Little is written in stone.

GEORGE H. W. BUSH AND A NEW WORLD ORDER: 1989–1993

George H. W. Bush assumed the presidency in 1989 with more foreign policy experience than any other recent new occupant of the White House. A committed internationalist and multilateralist, Bush had served as U.S. ambassador to the United Nations, ambassador to China, director of the Central Intelligence Agency, and Ronald Reagan's vice president. During his presidency, one foreign policy challenge unfolded after another. A realist who believed that American foreign policy was both moral and idealistic, President Bush needed all his foreign policy experience as the world went through a dynamic period of change.

Many challenges were unexpected. Few people expected communism to collapse in Eastern Europe. Given the Chinese government's economic reforms and increasingly relaxed domestic policies during the 1980s, few believed that it would massacre its citizens to maintain power. Iraq's 1991 invasion of Kuwait caught everyone by surprise. Few predicted that the Soviet Union would break up later in 1991. Conversely, the unrest in the Philippines and the hostility of an anti-American government in Panama were not entirely unexpected. Bush also faced economic, environmental, drug, and immigration issues.

The Collapse of Eastern European Communism

Few events changed the world in the second half of the twentieth century as much as the 1989 **collapse of Eastern European communism.** Ever since the late 1940s, the Soviet

Union dominated Eastern Europe politically, economically, and militarily. On two occasions, during the 1956 Hungarian revolution and the 1968 Czechoslovakian uprising, the Soviet Union used military force to maintain its dominance; Soviet leaders ordered their troops based in Eastern Europe to subdue the revolts. In 1980, Poland's communist government declared martial law to bring a growing anti-communist labor movement under control.

The possibility that this pattern of Soviet intervention might change emerged in 1988 as Soviet leader Mikhail Gorbachev declared that Eastern European countries could determine their own future. In 1989, he went further, declaring that the time for military intervention outside one's country had passed. These statements had great implications for Eastern Europe, and Eastern Europeans realized it. Thus, in 1989, anti-communist sentiment swelled in every Eastern European state.[3] In Poland, the non-communist trade union Solidarity won a free election and took power. In Hungary, the government abandoned the term "communist," held free elections, and opened its border with Austria. Thousands of East Germans used this route to defect to the West. Street demonstrations erupted in Czechoslovakia, East Germany, and Bulgaria, leading to the fall of communist governments. In Romania, the communist government called out the army in an attempt to retain power, but failed. Meanwhile, Gorbachev was as good as his word, ordering Soviet troops to remain in their barracks.

By the end of 1989, no communist government except Yugoslavia's remained in Eastern Europe. One of the chief causes of the Cold War—the division of Europe into East and West—was gone. The collapse of Eastern European communism was complete, and the political map of Europe was transformed.

The United States and its Western European allies played no direct role in this. The revolutions were unexpected, and the United States had no policies ready to put into place. U.S. involvement was limited to a 1989 visit by Bush to Poland and Hungary to show support for their democratic movements. The United States also said little about Eastern European events, not wanting to provide an excuse for the Soviet Union to intervene. A tacit agreement existed between Gorbachev and Bush, with Gorbachev allowing events to proceed and Bush not making too much of the crises in Eastern European communism.

Faced with a new situation in Eastern Europe, the United States and Western Europe responded slowly. Following the revolutions, the United States and other democratic states provided economic aid, technical assistance, and political advice to the new non-communist Eastern European governments, most of which tried to establish democratic political systems and free-market economies. The task was difficult. All struggled as they found old ways difficult to abandon and new ways difficult to embrace. This continued throughout the 1990s and into the twenty-first century, with the Czech Republic, Hungary, and Poland making the most progress toward remaking their societies.

East Germany had a different fate. Divided into four zones at the end of World War II, Germany evolved into two states, democratic West Germany formed out of the U.S., British, and French zones and communist East Germany formed from the Soviet zone. With communism gone, many East and West Germans wanted to unite. In early 1990, East Germany held an election in which new East German political parties tied to West German parties emerged victorious. Their victory strengthened West German Chancellor Helmut Kohl's argument that the two Germany's should unite.

German unification posed a problem for Europe, the Soviet Union, and the United States. The problem was immediate for European and Soviet leaders: a unified Germany had the potential to be the most powerful state in Europe. Europeans and Soviets also had not forgotten that Germany had initiated the most destructive conflict in history, during which the Soviet Union alone suffered at least 20 million deaths. While many Europeans believed that Germany had become a peace-loving state during nearly half a century of democratic governance, others, especially in the Soviet Union, feared that German expansionism could reemerge.

In the wake of the collapse of Eastern European communism, U.S. and European leaders were faced with the question of whether they could construct a security system for Europe that accounted for Eastern Europe's transformation and German unification. They proved equal to the task, helped by Gorbachev's acceptance of a unified Germany within NATO. With the Soviet Union and other European states having concluded that a unified Germany within NATO did not present a threat to security, East and West Germany were united in late 1990 to form a single Germany.[4]

At the same time, NATO at American urging developed the **North Atlantic Coordination Council (NACC)** to give former communist countries in Eastern Europe a forum in which they could join NATO members to discuss Europe's evolving security situation. Few concrete policies emerged from NACC, but it served as an effective way to develop communication between NATO countries and the emerging non-communist governments of Eastern Europe.[5]

Crises in Asia and Latin America

Bush's 1989 foreign policy challenges were not limited to Eastern Europe. Crises also erupted in Asia and Latin America during his first year in office.

U.S.-Chinese relations began well under Bush as he traveled to China just after taking office. However, soon after, riots broke out in Tibet, China sent in troops, and many Tibetans were killed. A few weeks later, Chinese students and workers took to the streets in Beijing and other Chinese cities, demanding political reform. Over 100,000 people occupied Beijing's Tiananmen Square alone. At the same time, Gorbachev visited China, ending 30 years of Sino-Soviet tension. Students and workers, still in the streets, lauded Gorbachev for the reforms he had instituted in the Soviet Union. At first, the Chinese government did not respond, appearing indecisive. Then in June, just after Gorbachev left, it dispatched troops into Tiananmen Square and killed several thousand demonstrators.

The **Tiananmen Square massacre** shocked the world. The United States condemned China and suspended diplomatic, military, trade, and other contacts. Americans of all political persuasions were repulsed by the massacre. Many advocated breaking diplomatic relations with Beijing and restoring ties with Taiwan. On the whole, however, the U.S. response was restrained. Within a month, Bush dispatched National Security Adviser Brent Scowcroft to Beijing. After the visit, relations edged back to where they were before the massacre as pragmatic state interests took precedence over human rights. As revolution unfolded in Eastern Europe and the Soviet Union later in 1989, maintaining stable relations with China in the wake of the Tiananmen massacre was a high American foreign policy priority.[6]

The massacre had barely left the headlines when a crisis unfolded in the Philippines. Three years earlier, the Filipino people had overthrown the dictatorial Marcos regime, bringing Corazon Aquino to power. Well-liked but politically untested, Aquino survived five coup attempts in her first three years in power. Then, in late 1989, units of the Philippine military launched a sixth attempt to overthrow Aquino. This time the United States provided air cover to military units loyal to Aquino as they restored order.[7]

Meanwhile, in Panama, the U.S. stalemate with Panamanian leader General Manuel Noriega continued. For several years, the United States had been displeased with Noriega's anti-Americanism and had attempted to force him out of power using diplomatic pressure and economic sanctions. Despite this pressure, Noriega retained power.

At first, the United States was unwilling to use military force against Noriega, not acting even in August 1989 when dissidents in the Panamanian Defense Force (PDF) revolted against the general. U.S.-Panamanian relations deteriorated further later in 1989 when Noriega declared that a state of war existed between the United States and Panama and a PDF soldier killed a U.S. serviceman. Bush concluded that it was time to act. Thus in December, American forces invaded Panama and overthrew Noriega, bringing him to the United States for trial.[8]

The Persian Gulf War

To optimists and idealists, the peaceful revolutions in Eastern Europe indicated that the world was moving toward an era in which domestic disputes and international disagreements would be solved by political discourse. Conversely, events in China, the Philippines, and Panama illustrated that military force still had utility. This became even more evident in 1990 when Iraq invaded Kuwait and in 1991 when the United States assembled a coalition of states to expel Iraq from Kuwait.

During the 1980s, Iraq fought a bloody eight-year war with Iran. Iraq had been drained by the conflict, and few expected Iraq's dictator, Saddam Hussein, to invade Kuwait, Iraq's oil-rich neighbor to the south that years earlier had been part of the Persian empire. Saddam, however, dreamed of recreating the empire. Thus, in mid-1990, he ordered Iraqi forces to invade Kuwait. Kuwait's outmatched armed forces were overwhelmed in hours.

The Bush Administration likened Iraq's invasion to Hitler's 1939 invasion of Poland, when a powerful country launched an unprovoked attack and conquered a weaker neighboring state. The United States and other countries also feared that Iraq's action foreshadowed an Iraqi invasion of Saudi Arabia. Bush and others feared that Iraqi control of Saudi Arabia, Kuwait, and Iraq's own considerable oil reserves would permit Saddam to dictate world oil prices.

Concerned by Iraqi expansionism, repulsed by a strong state invading and conquering a weaker neighbor, and fearing that Iraq was positioning itself to dictate world oil prices, the United States responded in three ways. First, it deployed naval, air, and ground forces to the region to deter further Iraqi aggression. Second, it built a political-military alliance of over 30 states and urged them to deploy forces to the region. Third, it led efforts to install economic sanctions against Iraq, especially through the UN.

For several months, the United States and its allies built a massive military presence in and around Saudi Arabia as the UN passed resolutions condemning Iraq, authorizing economic sanctions against Iraq, and authorizing the use of forth to expel Iraq from Kuwait. The U.S. Senate also voted to support the use of force against Iraq. With international support, economic sanctions, and military presence in place, the **Persian Gulf War** began in January 1991.

For a month, U.S. and other allied aircraft pounded Iraqi targets, using new laser-guided and other highly accurate bombs. Then the U.S. Army and the armies of allied states launched a tank assault into Iraq and Kuwait. In 100 hours, Iraq was defeated. **Operation Desert Storm,** the U.S. name for the operation, was a success. The war's original objective—expelling Iraq from Kuwait—had been achieved with few casualties. Most U.S. armed forces were withdrawn from Saudi Arabia, but a sizable contingent of American troops and planes remained deployed in the desert kingdom.[9]

But Saddam was still in power. Why did Bush not order U.S. forces to invade Iraq to topple Saddam? There were four reasons. First, the international coalition assembled to pursue the war was fragile, and Bush feared it would unravel if war aims changed. Second, within the United States, Bush had built political support for the war on the basis of expelling Iraq from Kuwait, and he feared that support would not continue if war aims changed. Third, the United States hoped that anti-Saddam sentiment in Iraq would topple Saddam. Even before the allied assault ended, revolts had broken out in Iraq's north and south, and U.S. intelligence believed the same thing could happen in Baghdad, Iraq's capital. Finally, militarily, turning one's forces completely around and initiating an attack in the direction from whence one had come was difficult. All things considered, U.S. military operations stopped after 100 hours.

The Collapse of the Soviet Union

As these events occurred in the Mideast, earth-shaking events unfolded in the Soviet Union.[10] As Gorbachev instituted more and more reforms, the Soviet Union's domestic fabric unraveled and its foreign and military policies posed less a threat to the United States and the West.[11] At the same time, the Soviet Union and the United States forged an increasingly close relationship. Summitry played a key role. Bush and Gorbachev met in New York in December 1988 even before Bush became president. They met again in Malta in 1989 and twice more in 1990 in Washington and Helsinki. Superpower summitry had become institutionalized.[12]

Progress in arms control also helped improve U.S.-Soviet relations. At the nuclear level, the two sides concluded the Intermediate Nuclear Forces (INF) Treaty in 1987. During the next three years, U.S. and Soviet inspectors journeyed to each other's country to watch INF weapons be destroyed. Strategic arms limitations talks continued during Bush's presidency, with the **Strategic Arms Reduction Treaty (START I)** being signed in 1991. START I was the first treaty under which the two sides agreed to reduce the number of strategic nuclear warheads in their inventories from about 10,000 warheads apiece to about 6,500. In 1993, the United States and Russia signed **START II,** which slashed the warheads each side could have to about 3,000.[13] However, neither the United States nor Russia ratified START II until much later.

At the conventional level, two negotiations to strengthen European security by 1990 had succeeded. The first led to the Two Plus Four Treaty between East and West Germany, the United States, the Soviet Union, France, and Great Britain. This treaty finalized details of German unification and Soviet withdrawal from East Germany. The second led to the **Conventional Forces in Europe (CFE) Treaty,** under which the Soviet Union would withdraw most of its military forces based west of the Ural Mountains to locations deeper within the Soviet Union. Simultaneously, NATO states had to reduce their armed forces based in Western Europe.[14]

The two sides also defused Third World issues.[15] After years of discussion, the United States and Soviet Union fashioned a 1988 agreement under which Cuban troops withdrew from Angola, South African troops left Angola and Namibia, and Namibia gained independence from South Africa. This agreement removed a major source of tension from U.S.-Soviet relations. More importantly, the Soviet Union in 1989 withdrew from Afghanistan. The Soviet Union also applied behind-the-scenes pressure that influenced Vietnam in 1989 to end its occupation of Cambodia.

The depth of U.S.-Soviet cooperation was illustrated by the U.S. response to the 1991 coup in Moscow that threatened to topple Gorbachev. Bush condemned the coup, praised Russian President Boris Yeltsin for his stand against it, and supported Gorbachev's return to the Soviet presidency.

MAP 7.1
The Fifteen States That Became Independent When the Soviet Union Collapsed

Following the coup's failure, Bush faced a dilemma. Should the United States continue to support Gorbachev and the Soviet Union, or should it support Boris Yeltsin, who despite his support for Gorbachev's return to the presidency sought to dissolve the Soviet Union? At first, Bush opted for Gorbachev and the Soviet Union. However, as events rushed onward, it became clear that the Soviet Union would not survive, and the United States switched its support to Yeltsin.

Weakened by the coup, its economy in shambles, and torn by internal dissent and the desires of its many nationalities for independence, the Soviet Union at the end of 1991 collapsed. The United States and Russia in early 1992 formally declared an end to hostility. Even the skeptics who doubted that the Cold War had ended in 1989 when Eastern Europe's communist governments were overthrown now had to agree that the Cold War was over.

So, too, was the need for containment, and again Americans asked questions. What would U.S. strategy now be? What should U.S. policy be toward Russia and the 14 other new countries that had been Soviet republics but were now independent states? How much aid should the United States send to help them survive the collapse of their economies? Should the United States cut defense spending? If so, how much? With the Soviet Union gone, there clearly had to be a new order, as George H. W. Bush called it, but what would it be?

Whatever the final answers to these questions, constructing a **new world order** would clearly be a Herculean task. Bush pledged that the United States would lead the world toward a new and more peaceful era. Foreign policy problems erupted in China, the Philippines, Panama, and Iraq, but the American public decided that the end of the Cold War meant it was time to pay more attention to domestic issues, and even a return to isolationism.[16] Bush never succeeded in completing the task of constructing a new world order. Indeed, the task proved so complex that neither of his two successors completed it either.

The Western Hemisphere

The Bush Administration also dealt with Western Hemispheric issues. Bush had inherited an unsettled situation in Central America that could not be ignored. Cuba continued to supply arms to Nicaragua, some of which were shipped on to El Salvador, and the Bush Administration believed that the Soviet Union remained involved in the arms traffic as well, although at a significantly lower level.

The Sandinista regime in Nicaragua was under pressure from other Central American states, the Organization of American States, and the UN to hold elections. Concerned about future Soviet support, wanting to confirm its legitimacy, and confident of its popularity, the Sandinistas agreed to hold elections under international supervision in early 1990. To most peoples' surprise, the Sandinistas lost. To even more surprise, they stepped down peacefully as Violeta Chamorro became president.

Chamorro's victory had several impacts. First, U.S.-Nicaraguan relations improved. Second, the rebels in El Salvador no longer could acquire arms from external sources, and within months, UN-led negotiations ended the conflict. Third, one of the few remaining irritants to U.S.-Soviet relations emanating from the Third World was eliminated.[17]

The Politics of International Economics

Even as Central America's civil wars wound down, the United States negotiated and implemented major economic agreements that had the potential to change the way the world worked economically. This had begun under Reagan, whose administration had negotiated the U.S.-Canada Free Trade Agreement, which took effect in 1989, intending to eliminate most tariffs and duties on U.S.-Canadian trade by 1999.

Bush, like Reagan, was a proponent of free trade. Thus, he used the U.S.-Canadian treaty to set the foundation for negotiations that led to the **North American Free Trade Agreement (NAFTA),** which sought to eliminate tariffs and other barriers to trade between Canada, Mexico, and the United States. Concluded in 1992, NAFTA was controversial and therefore not ratified until 1993 and not operationalized until 1994. NAFTA's critics feared that it would speed the movement of American capital to Mexico as owners took advantage of lower Mexican labor costs and environmental standards. American jobs would be lost, NAFTA's critics charged. Conversely, NAFTA's supporters argued that, over time, NAFTA would increase trade and improve living standards.[18]

Besides NAFTA, the Bush Administration dealt with other international political economic issues, including the U.S. trade deficit, Japanese trade surpluses and trading practices, Third World debt, and the European Community's plan for unity. Each presented different challenges.

During the 1980s, the U.S. trade deficit skyrocketed, reaching $170 billion in 1986. By 1989, it had declined, but Americans still bought much more overseas than they sold. This did not deter Bush from emphasizing free trade as the United States continued multilateral trade discussions under the auspices of the General Agreement on Tariffs and Trade and other forums. Even so, in the absence of a change in behavior on the part of American consumers or a change in government views on free trade, there was little likelihood that the U.S. trade deficit would disappear or be significantly reduced.

Much of the trade deficit was the result of U.S.-Japanese bilateral trade. The U.S. trade deficit with Japan alone in 1989 was over $50 billion. Like Reagan, Bush held bilateral trade negotiations with Japan, but no solutions to the deficit with Japan were in sight.

Few people agreed on why the deficit with Japan was so intractable. Some blamed Japan's trading practices, asserting that Japan dumped products on overseas markets, undercutting foreign competition to get market share. Others criticized Japan's non-tariff barriers to trade, saying that Japan found ways to prevent imports from entering the Japanese market. Still others believed that the structure of Japan's internal market made it difficult for foreign goods to reach the Japanese market. Still others said that non-Japanese firms did not make products that appealed to the Japanese, Japanese companies were better run, and Japanese workers worked harder. Whatever the causes of the deficit, Americans continued to buy more and more Japanese products.[19]

Bush also dealt with growing Third World debt, which by 1989 reached over half a trillion dollars. Several states, such as Argentina and Brazil, nearly defaulted on loans. Bush proposed several ways to cope with the situation, including Third World austerity programs, debt refinancing, debt forgiveness, and debt swaps. To one extent or another, all these solutions were implemented. By the end of George H. W. Bush's term in office, Third World debt remained sizeable, but the crisis had receded.[20]

The Bush Administration also formulated policies to respond to the changing situation in Europe, where the 12-state **European Community (EC)** had set 1992 as the date for European economic integration: the removal of tariffs and other barriers to trade between member states. The United States supported this but was concerned that the EC might close its external borders to imports as it opened its internal borders to internal trade. Close contacts between the Bush Administration and the EC assured that this did not occur.

The EC in 1992 also concluded the Maastricht Treaty, under which the EC would become the **European Union (EU).** The EU was seen as a United States of Europe that would be a political and economic union with a common currency, shared social and domestic policies, and a common foreign and defense policy. The United States also supported this initiative, recognizing that it had great implications not only for Europe but also for the transatlantic relationship.[21]

The Environment, Drugs, and Immigration

Other issues such as the environment and drugs also moved near the top of George H. W. Bush's foreign policy agenda even as immigration, an old issue that had long been dormant, reemerged.

The Bush Administration accepted that the world's environment was deteriorating, but it insisted on additional study before taking action. Arguing that too much emphasis on environmental protection cost jobs and hurt economic growth, Bush also refused to commit the United States to most of the proposals put forward at the 1992 **UN Earth Summit** in Rio de Janeiro, Brazil.[22]

Regarding drugs, the United States in the early 1990s moved to a three-part anti-drug program. First, the United States sought to lower drug production at its source by helping Colombia, Bolivia, and Peru reduce coca production and combat drug cartels. Second, the United States increased its use of its military, Coast Guard, and Drug Enforcement Agency to reduce the drug flow into the United States. Third, the United States tried to reduce demand for drugs with domestic programs.[23]

The United States also faced immigration issues. For years, the United States accepted political refugees but not economic refugees, even though it was difficult to differentiate between them. Thus, many Mexicans entered the United States illegally, most seeking jobs or to be reunited with family. The United States returned some to Mexico, but many remained. Similarly, many Haitians fled to the United States following the 1991 coup there. Many were political refugees, but the United States said most were economic refugees and returned them to Haiti. Cuban immigration to the United States continued as well, accelerating as Cuba's economy deteriorated. In contrast to Mexicans and Haitians, most Cubans were considered political refugees and allowed to stay in the United States.

Despite efforts to come to grips with immigration, the Bush Administration never resolved the complex issues that caused the problem.[24] Immigration, like the environment and drugs, were foreign policy problems that continued into Bill Clinton's presidency.

The Bush Presidency

Having pledged to create a new world order, George H. W. Bush left office with the task incomplete. The American mission, so clear during the Cold War when the United States used its military forces, economic strength, and democratic example and rhetoric to contain communism, was no longer as clear-cut. In the era emerging after the Cold War, what would America's mission be? Bush had tried to provide an answer to the question, but when he left the presidency, the answer remained incomplete.

Significantly, Americans increasingly wanted to pay attention to domestic problems, particularly the economy, rather than foreign policy issues. The prevailing American attitude in 1992 was best captured in a phrase used by Bill Clinton, Bush's opponent in the 1992 presidential election: "It's the economy, stupid!" It was a phrase Clinton would use to Bush's detriment and eventual defeat.[25]

Despite the American public's growing inattention, U.S. national interests in foreign policy were easy to identify. Bush's foreign policy recognized national security, economic prosperity, ideological criteria, and morality and the rule of law as critical foreign policy interests, but during his presidency no consensus had emerged on how they should be pursued in the post–Cold War world. Cold War national security concerns had almost disappeared from the foreign policy agenda, but other security concerns emerged: dealing with the problems that former communist states faced, containing terrorism, and restraining the proliferation of weapons of mass destruction. At the same time, events during the presidency of George H. W. Bush showed that military force was still needed, but with the Cold War over, it was no longer clear when it should be used. Other questions about how best to pursue American foreign policy interests also loomed large as the international economic system moved toward globalization. And other issues ranging from the environment, immigration, and human rights emerged on the U.S. foreign policy agenda.

As for foreign policy principles, Bush's foreign policy had demonstrably been based on international involvement, claims of American moralism, multilateralism, and pragmatism. Even so, other Americans, even in Bush's own Republican Party, preferred policies other than those Bush had adopted. Some called for a return to what they saw as the more traditional principles of isolationism and unilateralism, while others urged the United States to take advantage of the "uni-polar moment" and use America's now unrivaled military and economic strength to push for a position of international primacy and even hegemony.[26]

With uncertainty existing about America's post–Cold War mission, debate raging over how best to pursue American interests, and disagreement at hand over American foreign policy principles, it was not too surprising that conflict continued in the early 1990s between the three sets of competing American foreign policy themes. As George H. W. Bush left office, realism predominated in American foreign policy, but desires for idealism remained. International involvement and multilateralism also had the upper hand, but appeals for a return to isolationism and unilateralism were gaining strength. As Bill Clinton assumed the presidency, a host of foreign policy challenges confronted him.

THE CLINTON PRESIDENCY: 1993–2001

As he became president in 1993, reflecting public opinion, Bill Clinton promised to "focus like a laser beam" on domestic economic issues. The new president soon discovered, however, that foreign policy could not be ignored. He thus devised strategic concepts to replace the now irrelevant containment.

New Strategies

Even though he at first intended to concentrate on domestic affairs, Clinton was not an isolationist, declaring in the 1992 campaign that the United States should "lead a global alliance for democracy as united and steadfast as the global alliance that defeated communism."[27] This intention to remain involved in world affairs in support of democracies crystallized during the Clinton presidency into the strategies of engagement and enlargement. Involvement as opposed to isolationism thus remained preeminent throughout the Clinton years, with a tendency to side with foreign policy idealism as opposed to realism also apparent. During his two terms as president, it also became evident that Clinton preferred multilateralism, although he was not averse to unilateral action if he believed American interests required it.

Engagement meant that the United States would not retreat into isolationism as after World War I and for a short time after World War II. With the Cold War over and communism gone from Eastern Europe and the former Soviet Union, engagement meant that U.S. policies toward these states would be based on cooperation, assistance, and negotiation rather than confrontation. Engagement was linked to **enlargement,** a concept under which the United States promoted democracy, open markets, and other Western political, economic, and social values. As National Security Adviser Anthony Lake declared in 1993: "The successor to a doctrine of containment must be a strategy of enlargement—enlargement of the world's free community…. We must counter the aggression—and support the liberalization—of states hostile to democracy…. The United States will seek to isolate [non-democratic states] diplomatically, militarily, economically, and technologically."[28]

In many respects, then, enlargement was a synonym for democratization. By pursuing enlargement of those territories of the world that were governed by democratic governments, the Clinton Administration hope to create not only a more democratic world but also a more peaceful world. According to the **democratic peace theory,** democracies rarely if ever went to war with other democracies.[29] Thus, any increase in the number of democracies around the world decreased the chances of war and conflict. The democratic peace theory had numerous proponents within the Clinton Administration.

Together, then, engagement and enlargement provided Clinton a rationale under which the United States promoted democracy around the world, assisted former communist states, intervened in Third World crises, pushed for an open international economic system, and tried to counter terrorism and the proliferation of weapons of mass destruction. As with containment, neither engagement nor enlargement defined limits to action. Thus, throughout Clinton's two terms, critics asserted that the United States lacked strategic purpose even though it was engaged everywhere and intervened frequently.

Engagement and enlargement continued throughout Clinton's presidency, but another concept, sustainable development, did not. Sustainable development asserted that "peace, development, and environmental protection are indivisible" and that economic development must "meet the needs and aspirations of the present without compromising the ability of future generations to meet their own needs."[30] The Bush Administration had rejected sustainable development, along with other proposals put forward at the Rio Earth Summit, but Clinton intended to formulate policies in line with sustainable development's multilateral and idealistic preferences to protect the environment, control population growth, improve world health, extend humanitarian assistance, and encourage economic growth.[31] However, the Republican Party won control of Congress in the 1994 congressional elections and adopted a policy agenda that emphasized U.S. interests over international concerns, and unilateralism over multilateralism. As a result, sustainable development disappeared from the foreign policy agenda.

Political and Economic Policies toward Former Communist States

Engagement and enlargement assured American involvement with the former communist states of Eastern Europe and the one-time Soviet Union. In conjunction with its European allies, the United States under Clinton expanded economic assistance to many former communist states, tried to stabilize their political situations, and implemented a "Partnership for Peace" program in which most entered into a close relationship with NATO.

Russia was the center of Clinton's policies to the region, but Russia had immense problems. Trying to overturn decades of communist practices, President Boris Yeltsin instituted extensive but contradictory reforms, many of which accelerated Russia's economic decline. Facing strong opposition from communist, fascist, ultra-nationalist, and other sources, Yeltsin also often appeared unstable and out of control. By 1993, even though Russia relied on Western advice and developed close relations with the West, Russia appeared likely to implode.

Even so, Clinton believed the United States had to support Yeltsin. When they met at the 1993 Vancouver Summit, Clinton promised Yeltsin $1.6 billion, and the two leaders pledged a "new democratic partnership" between Washington and Moscow.[32] Within weeks, the United States and the other six members of the **G-7 industrialized states** pledged over $30 billion of aid to Russia.[33] However, as Russia struggled to implement its economic reforms, aid flowed to Russia slowly. The United States also supported Yeltsin politically, siding with him in 1993 when dissident Russian legislators tried to remove him from office. During the standoff, Yeltsin ordered the military to fire on the Russian parliament building. Throughout the crisis, the United States strongly backed Yeltsin.

After 1993, the United States continued to side with Yeltsin as he weathered one crisis after another. During Russia's military action in Chechnya in 1994 and 1995 as Russia tried to repress a separatist movement, the United States criticized Russian brutality but never wavered in supporting Yeltsin. In 1996, the United States backed Yeltsin in his presidential campaign and provided him technical advice and financial support.

As Russia experienced another financial crisis in 1998, Clinton stood by the beleaguered Russian leader. Finally, as Yeltsin became more erratic, the United States expanded contacts with other Russian leaders. For example, although Yeltsin was hospitalized in early 1999, U.S. Secretary of State Madeline Albright went ahead with a scheduled trip to Moscow, meeting with others in Yeltsin's government and even opposition leaders.

By 1999, the bloom had disappeared from U.S.-Russian relations as Russian arms sales to Iran, ballistic missile defense, NATO expansion, and fighting in the Balkans made it clear that U.S. and Russian interests were far from identical. U.S. and Russian leaders rarely mentioned the "partnership" between the two countries that marked their rhetoric earlier in the decade. Fortunately, however, while the two sides disagreed on numerous issues, the relationship remained free from tension.[34]

Meanwhile, as other former Soviet republics took different paths and implemented different policies, the Clinton Administration developed different policies toward them. For example, as Latvia, Lithuania, and Estonia pursued Western-style political and economic reform, the United States became favorably disposed toward them even as it tried not to arouse Russian concerns. Meanwhile, as Ukraine struggled with reforms, the United States encouraged pro-democratic, pro-market Ukrainian policies and criticized other Ukrainian efforts. In central Asia, the United States encouraged political and economic reform as it tried to enhance its own access to the region's energy resources. Conversely, as Belarus lapsed into Stalinism, the United States ignored it.

Much the same was true of U.S. policy toward the former communist states of Eastern Europe, by the middle 1990s called "Central Europe" because of the recognition that the Baltic states, Belarus, Ukraine, and Russia were "Eastern Europe." Here, too, the United States developed differentiated policies, close and cordial with the Czech Republic, Hungary, Poland, and other states that pursued democrat political and market-oriented economic reform, and restrained with less democratic and less market-oriented states.

Security Policies toward Former Communist States

Although the Cold War was over, security issues still played a major role in U.S. policy toward former communist states. Nuclear issues, NATO expansion, and the bilateral security relationship with Russia were central concerns.

At the nuclear level, START II was signed before Clinton took office, but a major problem existed. Before the Soviet Union broke up, Soviet strategic nuclear weapons were based in four Soviet republics: Russia, which had the most, Belarus, Kazakhstan, and Ukraine. This meant that after the Soviet Union broke up, nuclear weapons were in four independent countries, only one of which, Russia, had signed the Nuclear Non-Proliferation Treaty (NPT).

The Bush administration had begun to address this problem, but its resolution occurred under Clinton. In 1993, Belarus and Kazakhstan pledged to turn over their weapons to Russia and sign the NPT. Ukraine did the same in 1994. These were key actions because they meant that the United States and Russia could implement START I. Meanwhile, START II remained stalled in the U.S. Senate, which finally ratified the agreement in 1996. Russia's parliament was even slower in accepting START II, not ratifying it until 2000.

A second key area of U.S.-Russian nuclear cooperation was in managing surplus nuclear materials. As nuclear weapons were dismantled, significant quantities of pluto-nium and enriched uranium became available. The danger existed that this surplus nuclear material would be purchased by other states intent on developing nuclear capabilities, or it could fall into the hands of terrorists.

Recognizing this, the U.S. Congress under the leadership of Senators Sam Nunn and Richard Lugar passed the **Nunn-Lugar Bill,** under which the United States provided Russia over $1 billion to enhance the security of surplus Russian nuclear materials. Nunn-Lugar funds also paid Russian nuclear scientists in an effort to keep them gainfully employed in Russia instead of going to work in other countries to help them develop nuclear weapons.[35]

NATO expansion also became a central part of U.S. policy toward several former communist states. As we have seen, NATO created the North Atlantic Coordination Council (NACC) upon the overthrow of communism in Eastern Europe. Even so, from the perspective of many former communist states and some Westerners, NACC was not enough, and pressure for NATO expansion mounted. Consequently in 1994, NATO under U.S. leadership created the cooperative arrangement known as the **Partnership for Peace (PFP).**[36]

Almost every Central European state and former Soviet republic, including Russia, joined the PFP. Under the PFP, guidelines were established for military cooperation between PFP members and NATO. The PFP also provided the basis for joint maneuvers between NATO forces and PFP members, including between U.S. and Russian troops. The PFP even established performance guidelines for states that wished to move toward NATO membership.

In 1996, NATO decided to expand and, in 1997, invited the Czech Republic, Hun-gary, and Poland to join. All three accepted, becoming NATO's seventeenth, eighteenth, and nineteenth members at NATO's fiftieth anniversary celebration in 1999. NATO promised other PFP states that this was not NATO's final expansion and that a second round would follow. This encouraged some PFP states, but Russia strongly opposed any NATO enlargement.

Before NATO expanded, Russia had cooperated with NATO in several areas, join-ing NACC, becoming a PFP country, and sending 2,500 troops to Bosnia in cooperation with the NATO-led peacekeeping effort there. Cooperation was sometimes difficult, but on the whole it succeeded. NATO expansion was different. It displeased Russia in every respect. Many Russians saw it as a U.S. effort to embarrass Russia. Others considered it a threat to Russia, since NATO's military might was now nearer to Russia. Even Clin-ton's 1997 assurance that NATO expansion was not directed against Russia and his promise that NATO would not deploy forces in new NATO countries did not assuage Russian fear and anger.

Russia made the best of a bad situation. Negotiations between Russia and NATO led to the 1997 signing of the **NATO-Russia Founding Act** on Mutual Relations, Cooper-ation, and Security. Although not a formal treaty, the Founding Act established a NATO-Russian Joint Council to consider issues such as terrorism, nuclear safety, military doctrine, and peacekeeping.[37] The Founding Act papered over U.S.-Russian disagree-ments, but as the Kosovo situation, examined later, deteriorated in 1998, NATO-Russian relations grew stormy. The U.S.-led NATO air assault against Serbian forces in Kosovo in 1999 raised U.S.-Russian tensions higher than at any time since the Cold War ended. Tensions eased once the bombing ended, and Russia even deployed peacekeeping troops in Kosovo, but the deployment almost foundered over who would command Russian troops and where they would be deployed.

Throughout the Clinton presidency, Russia loomed large in U.S. security interests, but not as large as during the Cold War. Although Russia was no longer an enemy, Russia could not be ignored, and it was clear that Russian and U.S. interests did not always coincide.

Trouble in the Balkans

The United States also found it had security interests in the Balkan Peninsula. Home to diverse nationalities, religions, and cultures, the Balkans had long been a flash point. World War I began in the Balkans, and the United States proclaimed the Truman Doctrine because of a Balkan crisis, the Greek civil war.

After the Cold War began, the Balkans remained calm, with Yugoslavia at the center of Balkan stability. Many hoped that the region had moved beyond its turbulent past. Unfortunately, this hope proved ill founded. In the late 1980s and early 1990s, Yugoslavia unraveled and its diverse peoples, driven by ethnic nationalism, religious animosity, economic decline, and centuries-old memories, went to war against each other. Hundreds of thousands died, millions became refugees, and fighting threatened to spread.

The **Bosnian civil war** was the opening scene for American involvement.[38] Almost half of Bosnia's population was Muslim Slav, but as fighting escalated in the late 1980s, Yugoslavia's Serbian-led government under Slobodan Milosevic and Bosnian Serbs tried to expel them, using murder and rape as policy tools, calling it **ethnic cleansing.** As fighting escalated and deaths mounted in 1992, UN peacekeepers entered Bosnia. The United States did not become involved until 1993, when Clinton ordered U.S. planes to air-drop food and supplies to Bosnian Muslims.

Despite the presence of UN forces, fighting continued. From March 1992 to December 1995, the period of the UN deployment, over half a million people were killed. Serb forces often ignored and overran UN-established safe areas. Ethnic cleansing, rape, and mass executions of civilians continued, primarily but not exclusively by Serbs. UN peacekeepers were sometimes taken hostage.

In late 1995, the U.S. brokered the **Dayton Accords** between Croats, Bosnian Muslims, and Serbs, a peace agreement that divided land along ethnic lines enforced by NATO, which took over peacekeeping responsibilities from the UN.[39] NATO deployed an "Implementation Force" (IFOR) to Bosnia consisting of 20,000 U.S. troops, 43,000 French and British soldiers, and several thousand forces from other countries, including 2,500 from Russia under the auspices of the Partnership for Peace. IFOR in 1997 transitioned into a 30,000-person NATO "Stabilization Force" (SFOR) whose mission was— and is—to separate the one-time warring parties, map minefields, and destroy heavy weapons that remained in the area. Warfare stopped, but the situation in Bosnia remains unsettled even today.

Ethnic cleansing, warfare, and American involvement in the Balkans did not end in Bosnia. In 1997, Albanian Muslims in Kosovo, another Yugoslavian province, began to push for increased autonomy. Radical elements agitated for independence and took up arms against Serb troops and police in Kosovo. Milosevic, still in power, responded again with repression and ethnic cleansing.

As fighting and ethnic cleansing escalated, diplomatic efforts to resolve the situation failed. NATO, having warned Yugoslavia that it would not stand by, in 1999 launched massive air strikes against Yugoslavia. U.S. planes flew most of the missions. Hundreds of thousands of refugees from Kosovo flooded into Albania, Macedonia, and Montenegro, destabilizing all three. After three months of air raids, Milosevic conceded and a peacekeeping force led by NATO with significant numbers of U.S. troops moved into Kosovo.

The **Kosovo conflict** was different from earlier wars. It was the first conflict fought to defend human rights and to prevent one ethnic group from beating, murdering, and raping another. It was a conflict in which U.S. policy sought to prevent U.S. casualties: pilots were ordered to fly above 15,000 feet to make sure no American planes were shot down. Clinton also declared that no U.S. ground troops would be used. Undertaken on a multilateral basis under NATO auspices but with UN support, the Kosovo conflict was technically not a war, since Congress never declared war.[40]

By the end of Clinton's second term, fighting had stopped, but the situation remained unsettled. Was the end of fighting permanent? How long would peacekeepers stay in Bosnia and Kosovo? Could the region rebuild? Would ethnic nationalism and religious animosity ever permit peace and stability in the Balkans? Kosovo remains tense today.

Despite the end of the Balkan wars, the Balkans remain important for the United States. Renewed conflict could draw in Greece, Russia, Turkey, what is left of Yugoslavia, and other states, and refugees from the wars have settled in many European states, straining the ability of Germany and other states to provide aid and destabilizing Albania and Macedonia. The dangers are real.

Intervening Overseas

The Balkan conflicts were one part of a larger issue that confounded the United States once the Cold War ended, namely, when should the United States intervene overseas? Between the end of World War II and the demise of the Soviet Union, U.S. military intervention usually was tied to containing communism and the Soviet Union. With communism discredited and the Soviet Union gone, this easy benchmark no longer existed.

George H. W. Bush had grappled with the problem, sending U.S. troops to Panama to overthrow Noriega, to the Persian Gulf to expel Iraq from Kuwait, and to Somalia to provide humanitarian assistance. When Clinton assumed the presidency, U.S. forces were still deployed in the latter two locations.

In 1991, **Somalia** descended into civil war between clans following the overthrow of longtime President Siad Barre. In 1992, the UN sent troops into Somalia to aid in humanitarian efforts. Later in 1992, Bush deployed 28,000 U.S. troops to Somalia, also for humanitarian purposes. Clinton supported the deployment and kept U.S. forces in Somalia. Gradually, however, the purpose of the UN and U.S. presence changed from

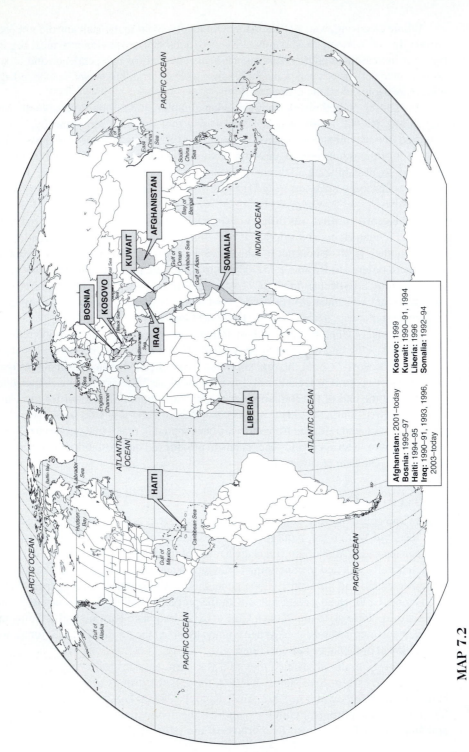

MAP 7.2
Major Post-Cold War American Military Interventions: 1990–Today

creating a secure environment in Somalia so that humanitarian aid could be distributed to enforcing peace and arresting those responsible for unrest. U.S. forces became deeply involved in the fighting. In 1993, 18 Americans were killed in a firefight and Congress called for the withdrawal of U.S. forces. By early 1994, almost all U.S. forces had left the country. A small contingent remained and was finally withdrawn in late 1994.[41]

Meanwhile, in the Persian Gulf, American forces remained arrayed against Iraqi forces. Following the Persian Gulf War, small contingents of American air, ground, and naval forces remained in the region. Adopting a policy it called "dual containment," the Clinton Administration tried to prevent both Iraq and Iran from increasing their influence and expanding their power in the region.[42]

The United States' concern with Iran was its effort to obtain nuclear know-how and material from Russia. U.S. concern with Iraq included Iraqi efforts to obtain nuclear, chemical, and biological weapons, but it also was more immediate. Thus, throughout Clinton's presidency, the United States enforced no-fly zones: areas in northern and southern Iraq where Iraqi planes could not fly. It also launched a 1993 cruise missile attack against Iraq in retaliation for an Iraqi plot to kill former President Bush, deployed 36,000 troops to Kuwait in 1994 in response to an Iraqi build-up near Kuwait, and in 1996 attacked Iraqi missile sites and expanded the no-fly zones.

Closer to home, the **Haitian crisis** also raised the question of where and when to intervene militarily overseas. In 1991, Jean-Bertrand Aristide was elected President of Haiti in a democratic election. The following year, he was overthrown by the military. The coup increased the flow of Haitian refugees who attempted to reach the United States by sea. President Bush ordered the U.S. Coast Guard to return the refugees, if picked up at sea, to Haiti.

When Clinton took office, in keeping with enlargement, he pledged to increase U.S. efforts to return Aristide to power. In 1993, the UN with U.S. support placed economic sanctions on Haiti. Later in 1993, following an agreement between the military government and Aristide to allow Aristide to return, the UN lifted sanctions. The military government reneged, and the UN reimposed sanctions.

In 1994, as the tide of refugees fleeing Haiti continued, Haiti expelled UN human rights observers. Clinton then announced the United States would intervene in Haiti unless democracy were restored, and he sent former President Jimmy Carter, Senator Sam Nunn, and former U.S. Chief of Staff Colin Powell to Haiti to underline his seriousness and, if possible, arrange a peaceful restoration of Aristide. Carter, Nunn, and Powell were successful, the military government resigned, and 15,000 American troops occupied Haiti to maintain order as Aristide returned. The U.S. forces remained in Haiti until 1995, when they were replaced by a UN force.[43]

In addition to Somalia, Bosnia, the Persian Gulf, Haiti, and Kosovo, the United States under Clinton also deployed armed forces or used military force overseas in other locations. For example, U.S. marines in 1996 rescued Americans and other Westerners from Liberia during fighting there. The same year, U.S. aircraft carrier battle groups entered the Taiwan Straits to signal China that the United States supported the island. And in 1998, the United States launched cruise missiles against terrorist and suspected terrorist targets in Sudan and Afghanistan.

After the Cold War, the United States intervened overseas numerous times for a variety of purposes under Presidents George H. W. Bush, Bill Clinton, and George W. Bush. Here, a U.S. soldier patrols a street in Cape Haitien, Haiti, in 1994.

Equally notable, in several instances fighting erupted and tensions escalated but U.S. forces were not used. In Africa, the United States ignored genocide and warfare in Rwanda and Zaire throughout much of the 1990s, even though millions died. In Korea, as tensions ran high between North and South, the United States negotiated an end to North Korea's nuclear program and pledged support to its energy security. In the Middle East, Clinton nurtured the Arab-Israeli peace process that Bush initiated after the Persian Gulf War, though with little success.

The **Arab-Israeli peace process** was particularly arduous. The United States mediated agreements between Israel and the Palestine Liberation Organization (PLO) in 1993 and Israel and Jordan in 1994 that at the time were seen as significant breakthroughs. Clinton went to Syria in 1994 to try to improve relations between Syria and Israel. Little came of the Syria trip, but U.S. efforts to move the peace process along continued in 1995 as the Israeli-PLO accord was strengthened. Later in the year, a right-wing Israeli extremist assassinated Israel's Prime Minister Yitzhak Rabin. In early 1996, Arab-Israeli tensions increased as Rabin's successor, Benjamin Netanyahu, ignored parts of the Israeli-PLO accords that he believed compromised Israeli security. Violence broke out, and scores of Arabs and Israelis died. The United States continued to try to bring the two sides together, but with little success. The United States remained engaged in the peace process throughout Clinton's presidency, but by the time Clinton left office, Arabs and Israelis remained deadlocked.[44]

The frequent American overseas deployments and use of force viewed in conjunction with the occasions when the United States did not use force raised the question: "When and under what conditions should the United States intervene militarily overseas?" To a great extent, Clinton—and Bush before him—intentionally avoided identifying specific criteria on which to base intervention. Each situation was examined individually. Since interventions were undertaken for purposes including peacekeeping and providing humanitarian assistance that were outside the realm of traditional military activities, Clinton's critics charged that he asked the military to undertake missions for which it was ill suited. Since interventions were frequent and undertaken during a time of decreasing defense budgets and personnel, critics also charged that the operational tempo of the U.S. armed forces was too high. Put differently, critics claimed that with fewer people in the military and the defense budget down, too few people were being asked to do too many things in too short a time.[45]

The World Economy

Despite extensive use of the military, the Clinton Administration was not fixated on military affairs. It also focused on international economic policy, especially on trade with the European Union (EU), trade with Asian states, and the creation of four international economic agreements that had extensive implications for the U.S. and the world economy.

The EU was a major U.S. international economic concern, with the United States fearing that the EU, having opened it internal markets, would put in place high tariffs and other barriers to trade. The United States pointed to high-tech products in aerospace and telecommunications as key issues, as well as to agriculture, where the EU's Common Agriculture Policy acted as a barrier to imports. Although U.S.-EU economic disagreements never reached crisis proportions, enough issues were on the table so that they could not be described as cordial.

U.S. policies on sanctions were other points of contention. In 1996, Congress passed two bills, the Iran-Libya Sanctions Act and the Helms-Burton Cuban Liberty and Democratic Solidarity Act, which applied sanctions to businesses, regardless of where they were incorporated, for trading with or investing in Iran, Libya, or Cuba. The EU objected to this, maintaining that the U.S. Congress had no right to try to determine how non-U.S. businesses and governments should conduct their business or policy. After two years of negotiations, the two sides agreed that the United States would waive sanctions on European firms in exchange for European promises to deter investments into illegally expropriated assets and for stepped-up cooperation against terrorism.[46]

U.S. trade with China and Japan also requires commentary. Under Clinton, the United States continued negotiations with Japan to resolve outstanding trade issues. After three years, the negotiations showed little progress. Frustrated, Clinton in 1995 threatened to place a 100 percent tariff on Japanese luxury automobiles. Last-second negotiations averted the tariff, but tensions remained in U.S.-Japanese economic relations until the late 1990s, when Japan's economy went into a downward spiral.

U.S.-Chinese trade relations were also important because of the magnitude of trade, Chinese human rights violations, and the strategic implications of China's growing economy. When Jimmy Carter recognized China in 1979, total U.S.-China trade turnover was just over $2 billion. By Clinton's second year, it had leaped to over $44 billion, with a U.S. deficit of $7 billion.[47]

Clinton's predecessors had tied favorable trade relations with China to improved Chinese human rights practices, but China's human rights practices improved little. Nevertheless, the United States blinked at them and approved favorable trading relations. When in the early 1990s China insisted that its domestic human rights policies were its own business, Clinton was in a difficult situation. He could follow his predecessor's policies of connecting trade to human rights, thereby endangering trade, or he could disconnect trade from human rights, thus protecting trade but marginalizing human rights. Calling his policy "comprehensive engagement," Clinton chose the latter path. Human rights groups condemned it, trade continued to grow, and a crisis was averted as economic pragmatism took precedence over moralism. Meanwhile, the United States and China walked a thin line between cooperation and confrontation over China's copyright infringements, its efforts to intimidate Taiwan, and Chinese nuclear technology sales to Pakistan. Many Americans wondered if conflict between China and the United States was inevitable.[48]

The United States between 1993 and 2001 also played a major role in creating four multilateral economic institutions and agreements. The first was the North American Free Trade Agreement (NAFTA). Forged by the administration of George H. W. Bush, NAFTA had not been passed by Congress when Bush left office. After shaping an alliance with Republican congressional leaders that included compromises desired by both parties, Clinton and a bipartisan group in Congress shepherded NAFTA into law in 1993.

The second accord, concluded in 1994, created the **World Trade Organization (WTO)** and negotiated tariff reductions estimated to be worth over $750 billion during the agreement's first ten years. The WTO was charged with overseeing world trade, adjudicating trade disputes, and lowering tariffs even more. When it became operational in 1995, it superceded the General Agreement on Tariffs and Trade.[49]

The third accord was the **Asian-Pacific Economic Cooperation (APEC) agreement,** approved by 18 countries, including the United States, at the 1994 APEC meeting in Indonesia. The APEC agreement committed all signatory states to dismantle barriers to trade between member states by 2020. Since the United States' transpacific trade was about 50 percent larger than its transatlantic trade, the implications of APEC were immense.

The fourth agreement was the **Free Trade Area of the Americas (FTAA),** concluded in 1994. Under FTAA, 34 Western Hemisphere states pledged to eliminate trade barriers between them by 2010. For the United States, the implications were sizeable: U.S. exports to Latin America, even in the absence of FTAA, were projected to surpass exports to Europe early in the twenty-first century.

Even though the Clinton Administration favored an open international economic system, many other Americans opposed free trade. The best example of this was the rioting that took place in Seattle in 1999 against the World Trade Organization. People from throughout the United States descended on Seattle, complaining that the WTO's policies of reducing tariffs and removing other trade barriers allowed U.S. jobs to go overseas, permitted companies to operate internationally without regard to the environmental damage they caused, and let businesses exploit women and children overseas.

Weapons of Mass Destruction and Terrorism

Preventing the spread of weapons of mass destruction and containing the terrorist threat were also important items on Clinton's foreign policy agenda. Both became increasingly important throughout Clinton's presidency.

Weapons of mass destruction include nuclear, chemical, and biological weapons. Especially after the Soviet Union broke up in 1991, U.S. concern mounted that rogue nations or terrorist groups might obtain Soviet nuclear, chemical, or biological weapons, materials, components, or know-how. To counter these dangers, the Clinton Administration used Nunn-Lugar funds to help Russia dismantle some of its nuclear weapons and missiles, purchase excess Russian fissionable material, improve security at nuclear sites, and pay Russian scientists and engineers so they would not emigrate to Iraq, Iran, or other countries that might use their expertise to develop nuclear weapons or other weapons of mass destruction.

In addition, the United States grew increasingly concerned that Iraq, Iran, or North Korea might develop weapons of mass destruction, especially nuclear weapons. Following the 1991 Persian Gulf War, International Atomic Energy Agency (IAEA) inspectors found that Iraq was only a few years away from developing nuclear weapons. Thus, Clinton supported UN inspections of Iraq and continuation of sanctions against the country. Iraq eventually forced IAEA inspectors to leave, but sanctions remained in place. Clinton also warned that the United States would destroy Iraqi facilities intended to produce weapons of mass destruction.[50]

In Iran, the danger of nuclear proliferation came both from indigenous Iranian nuclear research and development and from Russian-supplied nuclear assistance for allegedly civilian development. Although the Clinton Administration expressed concern about Russia's policies on several occasions, Russia rejected U.S. concerns, and the disagreement was not resolved. Indeed, the problem continued into the administration of George W. Bush.

North Korea also proceeded with a nuclear program during the 1990s that most observers believed had military purposes. Greatly concerned, the United States in 1994 concluded an agreement with North Korea under which the communist state "froze" its nuclear program in return for the construction by the United States, Japan, and South Korea of two nuclear power plants that would not use or produce weapons-grade nuclear materials. The agreement also provided up to ten years of free oil and promoted diplomatic relations. The price of nonproliferation was high, but perhaps not as high as the price of what might occur if proliferation proceeded.[51]

The Clinton Administration also pursued multilateral efforts to prevent the proliferation of weapons of mass destruction. In 1995, it signed an agreement to extend the 1968 Nuclear Non-Proliferation Treaty (NPT) and in 1996 agreed to the **Comprehensive Test Ban Treaty** (CTBT) under which signatory states renounced nuclear tests. Proponents of the NPT and CTBT regard the agreements as needed steps in the right direction toward controlling nuclear weapons, but critics assail them as insufficient, unenforceable, and undermining U.S. security. Indeed, neither India nor Pakistan had signed the NPT or the CTBT, and their 1998 tests of nuclear devices illustrated just how limited the utility of the agreements were if a country truly intended to develop nuclear capabilities.

The growth of the **terrorist threat,** both domestic and international, also vexed Clinton. The United States had faced terrorism before, for example state-supported terrorism during the 1980s as evidenced by the destruction of Pan American Flight 103 over Lockerbie, Scotland, in 1986. In several respects, though, the Clinton Administration faced two new kinds of terrorist threats.

The first came from domestic sources, as illustrated by the 1995 bombing of the U.S. Federal Building in Oklahoma City, which killed over 200 people. Home-grown terrorism struck again a year later when a bomb exploded at the Atlanta Olympics. Although only one person was killed, the Olympic bombing drove home the reality that Americans were not immune to terrorism even within the United States.

The second new type of terrorist threat came from an international terrorist network called **al Qaeda,** masterminded by one-time Saudi Arabian businessman **Osama bin Laden.** Bin Laden's network conducted several attacks against U.S. targets during Clinton's presidency, including the 1993 bombing of the World Trade Center in New York City, the 1995 and 1996 bombings of U.S. military facilities in Saudi Arabia, the 1998 bombings of U.S. embassies in Kenya and Tanzania, and the 2000 attack in Yemen against a U.S. Navy frigate, the U.S.S. *Cole*.

In 1998, Clinton ordered cruise missile attacks against al Qaeda training sites in Afghanistan and a suspected al Qaeda biological weapons production facility in the Sudan. He also authorized a covert operation against bin Laden that did not succeed in capturing him or crippling his operations.[52] Several terrorist plots were foiled during the Clinton years, including a plan to destroy 11 American airliners over the Pacific and an attack against Los Angeles during the millennium celebrations.

The Environment, Drugs, and Immigration

The environment, drugs, and immigration remained high on the U.S. foreign policy agenda under Clinton, even as they had under Bush. Although sustainable development had disappeared from the agenda because of opposition from the Republican majority in Congress, Clinton was still deeply concerned about the environment. Under Clinton, the United States strongly supported a treaty passed at the 1997 **Kyoto Environmental Summit** designed to reduce the emission of greenhouse gases that contribute to global warming. However, many in Congress and U.S. business interests claimed the protocol would be too costly to implement.[53] Despite this opposition, official U.S. policy remained committed to the Kyoto accords.

The Clinton Administration also continued the war against international drug trafficking, but as with the previous administration's efforts, success was mixed. Military cooperation between the United States and several foreign governments, especially Columbia, Peru, and Bolivia, grew significantly, with U.S. forces for the most part providing information and acting as advisers to local militaries in crop eradication, processing-plant destruction, and drug-route interdiction efforts. The U.S. Drug Enforcement Agency also played a major role in these efforts. In 2000, Clinton traveled to Colombia to announce the United States was providing Colombia with more military assistance and a $1.3 billion grant for the war on drugs.[54]

Immigration issues also plagued the Clinton Administration as tens of thousands of undocumented foreign nationals entered the United States, especially from Haiti, Mexico, and Cuba. The main thrust of U.S. policy continued to be that the United States accepted political refugees but not economic refugees. As we have seen, U.S. concern over refugees fleeing Haiti after the 1992 military coup there helped influence the United States to force the military junta out of power in 1994. Meanwhile, throughout Clinton's presidency, U.S. and Mexican officials tried to develop policies that both countries found acceptable, but the challenge was difficult. Meanwhile, even though most Cuban immigrants were deemed political refugees and permitted to stay in the United States, the difficulty of defining who was and was not a political refugee was illustrated in 2000 by the case of Elian Gonzalez, a six-year-old boy found adrift at sea alone after his mother and others who had attempted to flee Cuba by boat had died. For months, a legal battle raged in the United States about whether the boy should be returned to his father in Cuba or be allowed to remain with relatives in the United States. Eventually, the boy was returned to his father.[55]

By the time he left office in 2001, Bill Clinton, like George H. W. Bush before him, had crafted a complex foreign policy agenda. Both Bush and Clinton conducted strongly internationalist foreign policies despite sentiment in some quarters that the United States, with the Cold War over, should reemphasize isolationism. Both Bush and Clinton also pursued multilateralist foreign policies, although neither was averse to acting unilaterally when they believed American interests demanded it. And although Clinton was more of an idealist than Bush, both presidents conducted foreign policies that blended the two competing themes of idealism and realism. Both also believed that the U.S. mission remained much as it was in previous years, to defend and promote democracy, capitalism, and other Western values such as human rights, but neither had forged a consensus over foreign policy around which Americans rallied. American foreign policy was not adrift, but neither democratization nor human rights nor environmental and drug and immigration issues had the urgency that containment had had.

GEORGE W. BUSH'S FOREIGN POLICY: 2001–2005

George W. Bush, son of former President George H. W. Bush, assumed the presidency in 2001. Recognizing his own inexperience in foreign and defense matters, he chose an experienced team to formulate and implement foreign and defense policy. Bush appointed retired General Colin Powell, chairman of the Joint Chiefs of Staff during Operation Desert Storm, as secretary of state, and he asked Donald Rumsfeld, secretary of defense under Gerald Ford, to return to his former position. In addition Bush's vice president was Richard Cheney, who had been secretary of defense under Bush's father.

When Bush assumed the presidency, he faced the same range of issues and questions with which his two predecessors had grappled. How should the United States help Russia and other former communist states develop democratic political systems, form free-market economies, and reduce security concerns? How should the United States handle China's emergence as a world power? What could the United States do to help the Mideast peace process? What should the United States do to counter the proliferation of weapons of mass destruction and the threat of terrorism? When should the United States intervene militarily overseas? What policies should the United States implement to deal with international environmental, drug, and immigration concerns? Slowly, the new president formulated and implemented policies to cope with these issues. No one expected that, within the first year of the Bush presidency, the issue of how to respond to the threat of terrorism would dominate all other foreign policy issues.

The First Eight Months

During his first eight months in the White House, George W. Bush ordered several changes to U.S. foreign and defense policies. As a Texan, Bush placed a high priority on U.S. relations with Mexico and other Latin American states. His first trip outside the United States as president was to Mexico to discuss cooperation on immigration issues, anti-drug policies, economic development, and other U.S.-Mexican border issues. Bush also journeyed to the 2001 Summit of the Americas in Canada.[56]

During his first months in office, Bush also often met with European leaders. For example, British Prime Minister Tony Blair and German Chancellor Gerhard Schroeder visited Washington, with Schroeder and Bush issuing a joint statement on a transatlantic vision for the twenty-first century.[57] Bush also visited Europe twice, the first time going to NATO headquarters in Belgium as well as four other countries, and the second time to Italy to the meeting of the **G-8 industrialized states** (the new name for the G-7, given the inclusion of Russia). On both trips, Bush met with Russian President Vladimir Putin, who had replaced Boris Yeltsin as Russia's president in 2000.

On the other side of the world, the United States and China navigated their way out of a dangerous incident in early 2001 after a Chinese fighter plane and a U.S. reconnaissance aircraft collided off China's coast. The importance of U.S.-Japanese relations was also underscored as two different Japanese prime ministers visited Washington during Bush's first eight months in office.

Bush also instituted several policy changes that signaled a renewed emphasis on unilateralism. Secretary of Defense Rumsfeld began an extensive review of U.S. defense policy as Bush made it clear that he intended to pursue ballistic missile defense, thereby signaling he intended to abandon the 1972 U.S.-Soviet Anti-Ballistic Missile Treaty. This was one of the issues that Bush and Putin discussed during their European meetings. Bush also announced that the United States no longer would abide by agreements on the Kyoto Environmental Summit and the International Criminal Court, and he pushed Congress to expand presidential authority to negotiate preferential trade agreements.[58]

By September 2001, the Bush Administration had a full foreign policy agenda. Relations with Latin America, Europe, Russia, and China all loomed large, as did security, international economics, immigration, drugs, and the environment. The Bush Administration appeared as committed to international involvement as its post–Cold War predecessors but was also moving toward a more realist and unilateralist foreign policy than either George H. W. Bush or Bill Clinton. Even so, after eight months, the new administration had not sorted through its considerable foreign policy agenda to determine which items it considered most important. To some, it appeared American foreign policy was in disarray, while others believed the new administration simply needed more time to become oriented in the complex terrain of the twenty-first century.

September 11 and the War on Terrorism

Suddenly and unexpectedly, on the morning of September 11, 2001, the Bush Administration's foreign policy priorities became clear when 19 members of Osama bin Laden's al Qaeda terrorist network hijacked four jetliners, flying two into the twin towers of New York's World Trade Center, destroying them and killing almost 3,000 people.[59] Another hijacked plane slammed into the Pentagon, killing 189. The fourth plane plummeted into a field in western Pennsylvania after passengers, realizing what happened to the other three planes, charged the hijackers and forced them to lose control of the plane. Everyone on board died.

The United States immediately closed its civilian air system and ordered all planes to land. Unsure of the size of the assault, Vice President Dick Cheney, congressional leaders, and other senior government officials moved to undisclosed locations until the situation was clarified. The New York Stock Exchange closed, sending shivers through a world economy already struggling. In the following months, fallout continued as the United States created an Office of Homeland Security and Americans became more security conscious.

These steps failed to prevent unknown terrorists from mailing anthrax spores to media members and prominent politicians. At least five people died. The anthrax attacks raised the specter that terrorist groups or rogue states might employ weapons of mass destruction—biological, chemical, or nuclear weapons—against the United States

After the September 11 attack, Bush organized a coalition of states to combat terrorism. He also demanded that the **Taliban** government of Afghanistan, which had provided safe haven for bin Laden and al Qaeda's terrorist training camps, turn bin Laden over to the United States. When the Taliban refused, the United States in October 2001 initiated massive air strikes against Taliban and al Qaeda targets. The United States also began providing military assistance to anti-Taliban Afghans who had been fighting the Taliban. U.S. Special Forces and Ranger units also began operating against the Taliban and al Qaeda and providing intelligence and training to anti-Taliban forces. Eventually U.S. Marine and Army personnel were introduced as well.

By the end of 2001, the Taliban were overthrown. By early 2002, 16,500 troops from 17 countries were deployed in Afghanistan in the **war on terrorism.** U.S. Department of State sources reported that 136 countries had offered some form of military assistance to the United States for the war against terrorism. Meanwhile, the international community pledged $1.8 billion for 2002 to help rebuild Afghanistan, with another $2.7 billion for subsequent years. This was a small total in comparison to the need, but it was a start.

Outside Afghanistan, a broader war on terrorism began soon after the September 11 attacks. Many countries shared intelligence about terrorists, and Interpol and other security agencies stepped up their surveillance of known and suspected terrorists. Albania, Belgium, France, Germany, India, Italy, Morocco, Singapore, Spain, the United Kingdom, the United States, and other countries detained suspected al Qaeda members, over 500 in the United States and at least 100 in the United Kingdom. Over 1,000 people were detained around the world because of their ties to al Qaeda or other terrorist groups. The United States also orchestrated an international effort to end al Qaeda's use of banks and other international financial institutions to finance terrorist activities.

These steps did not win the war on terrorism. The Central Intelligence Agency estimated that 5,000–10,000 al Qaeda operatives remained in 68 countries, including the United States. Anti-terrorist efforts therefore continued, and the United States provided anti-terrorist training around the world. In 2002, over 200 American military personnel arrived in Georgia to train Georgian anti-terrorist personnel. Georgia, which bordered

A

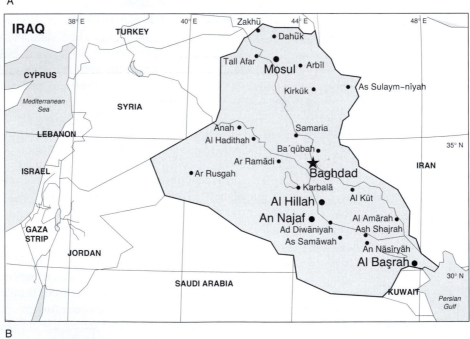

B

MAP 7.3
Afghanistan and Iraq: Theaters of Conflict in the War on Terrorism

Russia's breakaway province of Chechnya, was a main transit route for Chechen fighters to join the Taliban and al Qaeda. Also in 2002, 700 U.S. troops went to the Philippines to help the military there combat terrorist groups, especially Abu Sayyaf, which had ties to al Qaeda. American forces also deployed to Yemen in 2002 to help Yemeni security forces counter al Qaeda elements that had taken refuge there.

The Bush Administration declared that the United States would take the war to states that aided or sheltered terrorists. Iraq, Iran, and North Korea dominated American attention, with Bush referring to these states as the "axis of evil" in his 2002 State of the Union message.[60] Other officials pointed to Cuba, Djibouti, Libya, Somalia, Syria, and Sudan as states that either assisted or shielded terrorists. Also, U.S. concerns over Iraq's efforts to develop weapons of mass destruction led the United States in late 2002 to threaten that it would attack Iraq, alone if necessary but preferably in concert with other states.

By late 2002, the combination of American concern over terrorism and rogue states that had weapons of mass destruction caused the Bush Administration to reassess the United States' reliance on the policy of deterrence that had served the United States so well during the Cold War. Terrorists who were willing to die and leaders of rogue states who used weapons of mass destruction against their own people could not be deterred by traditional deterrence, Bush reasoned, so new policies that did not rely on deterrence would have to be fashioned to prevent terrorism and frustrate the ability of rogue states to obtain weapons of mass destruction.

Thus, in late 2002, the Bush Administration crafted a new strategic doctrine called **preemptive defense,** declaring that "the United States can no longer solely rely on a reactive posture as we have in the past…. We cannot let our enemies strike first…. As a matter of common sense and self-defense, America will act against emerging threats before they are fully formed."[61] Supporters of the doctrine praised it as necessary to counter the threats that terrorism and rogue states posed. Critics believed that the United States intended to do whatever it wanted to do in international affairs. Critics also feared that other countries might invoke preemptive defense for their own purposes and charged that the doctrine undermined sovereignty and international law and would lead to a more dangerous world.[62] (See Chapter 13 for details of the debate over preemptive defense.)

By late 2002, then, the war on terrorism was a multifaceted global undertaking no longer free of controversy. It included military action overseas, security measures at home, intelligence sharing with allies, cooperative diplomacy with a number of countries, eliminating terrorist access to financial institutions, and preemptive American military action. Bush Administration spokespersons cautioned that the war on terrorism would be long and costly. They also promised that it would be won.

Unilateralism, Imperialism, or Both?

The September 11 terrorist attacks gave the United States three clear and overarching foreign policy priorities: defending the homeland, prosecuting a global war against terrorism, and preventing rogue states and terrorist groups from obtaining weapons of mass destruction. Few Americans disagreed with these priorities or the policies that were implemented to achieve them, at least at first. Indeed, in the days immediately after the attacks on the United States, polls indicated that almost 90 percent of the American public supported retaliation, and as the war on terrorism unfolded in Afghanistan and elsewhere, support for the way in which the war was being conducted remained high, often above 70 percent.[63]

However, as the United States increasingly pursued military dimensions of the war on terrorism on its own and declared under preemptive defense that it would "act alone, if necessary, to exercise [its] right of self-defense,"[64] questions developed within the United States about the extent to which the United States should pursue these objectives unilaterally. These questions were mirrored by growing concern overseas that the United States had abandoned multilateralism, adopted unilateralism, and "place[d] little stock in the needs and opinions of other countries."[65] In addition to the war on terrorism and preemptive defense, there was a considerable body of evidence—U.S. relations with Russia and the Middle East, the U.S. position on the International Criminal Court, U.S. hostility toward international environmental agreements, and U.S. trade and aid policies—that lent credence to claims that the Bush Administration had reverted to unilateralism.

Charges of American unilateralism in its relations with Russia focused on the U.S. intent to deploy a ballistic missile defense system, which required revision of the 1972 Anti-Ballistic Missile Treaty. At first, the United States and Russia were deeply divided over the issue, with the United States declaring that it would move ahead with missile defense regardless of whether Russia accepted a revised treaty, and Russia strongly opposing both revising the treaty and U.S. deployment. Gradually, however, Russian President Putin shifted positions and indicated a willingness to modify the treaty, thereby removing missile defense as a stumbling block in U.S.-Russian relations.[66]

Other U.S.-Russian negotiations proceeded with less tension. Thus, after September 11, Putin played a major role in helping the United States gain access to former Soviet military bases in central Asia. In return, the United States muted its criticism of Russian policies in the breakaway Russian province of Chechnya. Perhaps more importantly, the United States and Russia made so much progress on strategic arms discussions that during Bush's May 2002 trip to Moscow, Bush and Putin signed a Strategic Offensive Arms Reduction Treaty under which both sides agreed to cut their strategic nuclear arsenal to 1,700 and 2,200 warheads, the lowest total in decades.[67] Putin also indicated that Russia would lessen its opposition to NATO expansion if Russia gained a more significant role in NATO discussions. This played a major role in the NATO deliberations that led to the creation in mid-2002 of the NATO-Russia Council, a forum in which NATO's 19 members and Russia met at least monthly to discuss security issues, including terrorism, arms control, and crisis management.

All was not perfect in U.S.-Russian relations. The two countries disagreed over the danger presented by Russian trade with and aid to Iran, Iraq, and North Korea. Russia maintained that its policies presented no threat to American interests, while the United States feared that all three states could divert Russian trade and aid to programs to develop weapons of mass destruction. Russia also opposed unilateral U.S. action against Iraq, but despite these disagreements and lingering Russian concerns, the U.S.-Russian relationship by 2003 had reached a degree of strategic stability not seen in decades.

Many observers also believed that American foreign policy toward the Middle East was unilateralist. Israeli-Palestinian tensions rose in 2001 and 2002 as Palestinian radicals launched suicide attacks that killed many Israeli civilians and Israel retaliated against Palestinian targets. At first, the United States stayed aloof from the escalating conflict. In 2002, however, Bush decided only U.S. diplomacy had a chance to stop the violence and dispatched Secretary of State Colin Powell to the Middle East to deescalate the crisis, but to no avail. As violence continued, the United States sided with Israel, finally cutting communications with Palestinian leader Yasser Arafat in a move that surprised European and Arab states.[68]

The Bush Administration's position on the **International Criminal Court** (ICC) also raised concerns that the United States had opted for unilateralism. Conceptualized in a 1998 UN treaty that gave the ICC international jurisdiction over crimes against humanity, war crimes, and genocide, the ICC became operational in 2002 after 139 states signed the treaty and 78 ratified it. The United States at first was not one of them, as conservative Americans argued that the court had powers that might lead to politically motivated prosecution of U.S. military personnel involved in peacekeeping missions.

In 2000, the United States under Clinton signed the treaty. However, the Senate never ratified it, and when George W. Bush took office, he renounced it. As the court neared operational status in 2002, Bush threatened to have the United States oppose all UN peacekeeping missions if the ICC began operations. The United States also initiated an extensive diplomatic offensive to conclude one-on-one agreements between the United States and other countries that declared the other countries would not prosecute or bring charges against U.S. peacekeepers.[69] To many observers, it appeared the United States was acting unilaterally, attempting to place itself outside and above international law.

The United States also moved on its own track in international environmental issues. As already related, George W. Bush renounced U.S. adherence to and participation in the 1997 Kyoto Environmental agreements. Similarly, the United States played a minor role in the 2002 UN Summit on Sustainable Development even though it proclaimed it supported the summit's goals of protecting plants and wildlife, reducing pollution, and bringing more water, electricity, and housing to poor countries. The best measure of American aloofness was that Bush, almost alone among the leaders of developed states, did not attend the summit.

Aspects of the American stance on trade also were contrary to prevailing international law and practice. For example, to gain congressional passage of a Trade Promotion Authority bill that for the first time since 1994 gave the president authority to negotiate preferential trade agreements, Bush in early 2002 approved tariffs and subsidies to protect American farmers and steel producers even though this was contrary to his own free-market preferences as well as prevailing international law and practices that favored reduced subsidies and tariffs as determined by the World Trade Organization. The WTO ruled against the U.S. tariffs and subsidies and determined that the European Union could impose $4 billion in penalties against the United States because it provided tax breaks to exporters, an action considered an illegal subsidy under international law.

U.S. claims that it intended to expand aid to developing countries were also sometimes criticized. When in early 2002 Bush called for a "new compact for global development" in which the United States would increase its foreign aid by 50 percent, or $5 billion, between 2002 and 2005, domestic and foreign critics assailed it as too little, too much tied to a conservative economic agenda, and too narrowly focused on America's own interests because the Bush Administration intended to direct it toward countries where there was "good governance, attention to health and education, and sound economic policies that fostered the free-market."[70] Despite this criticism, Bush in late 2003 expanded U.S. official development assistance by over $2 billion, the largest single increase in U.S. foreign aid since the Kennedy Administration.

Even with the trend toward unilateralism, occasional American policies emphasized multilateralism. For example, when in 2002 North Korea announced that it intended to abrogate the agreement it had made with the Clinton Administration to abandon its nuclear weapons programs in exchange for U.S. assistance, the Bush Administration reacted with a surprising degree of equanimity, declaring that it intended to pursue multilateral diplomacy to convince North Korea that developing weapons of mass destruction was not in its own best interest.[71]

By 2003, then, homeland defense, the war on terrorism, and curtailing threats posed by weapons of mass destruction were the central elements of the U.S. foreign policy agenda, but critics both inside and outside the United States labeled American actions in pursuit of these policies, as well as other American policies, unilateralist. Critics charged that the United States had a dismissive attitude toward international treaties and agreements and that the United States refused to pay attention to the views and policies of other countries.[72] U.S. officials dismissed these claims, asserting that since the United States had more "influence, power, prestige, and clout" than "any nation in the history of the world," a "certain amount of envy" was inevitable.[73]

Other critics of American foreign policy argued that the United States had gone far beyond unilateralism and had in fact become a new imperial power, constructing a new American empire based on American military strength, economic clout, and the absence of any other state or coalition of states that could balance American power. Pointing to the expanded American military presence around the world and the clear U.S. willingness to use it in the name of the war on terror, critics saw in the Bush Administration's actions a grand design that intended to place the United States in a position of global dominance that neither other states nor nonstate actors could challenge. Some critics labeled the United States "imperial America" and others believed the United States had become a "rogue nation," but all were convinced that the United States under Bush intended to act as it saw fit, whenever it so chose.[74] And this was even before the war in Iraq.

The Iraq War and Its Aftermath

The Bush Administration's actions toward Iraq and its ruler Saddam Hussein were at the center of many of the charges that unilateralism and imperialism had become the order of the day in U.S. foreign policy. Denounced by Bush in his 2002 State of the Union Address as one of three states that formed an "axis of evil" (the others were Iran and North Korea), Iraq became the focus of American concern about rogue-state development of weapons of mass destruction and support for terrorism. Throughout 2002, the United States increased pressure on Iraq, urging the UN to insist that Iraq readmit inspectors to look for weapons of mass destruction and warning Iraq, and the rest of the world, that it would take unilateral military action against Iraq if UN inspections did not occur.[75]

Finally, Iraq accepted UN inspectors, who by early 2003 concluded that Iraq had not provided the full truth about its biological, chemical, and nuclear programs. They believed Iraq had not fully accounted for components it had acquired that could be used to build weapons of mass destruction, but they found no concrete evidence that such weapons existed. Most members of the UN wanted to provide the inspectors more time to conduct their search and Iraq more time to provide required information, but the United States was adamant: Iraq had had enough time, the United States insisted, and military action was required.

Thus, in March 2003, the United States, heading what President Bush called a "coalition of the willing," unleashed an aerial and ground assault against Iraq, beginning the **Iraq War.** The United States had two primary war aims: to assure that Iraq had no weapons of mass destruction and to end Saddam's brutal rule. The United States provided by far the largest share of military forces and weaponry, but Great Britain also provided substantial ground and air forces. After three weeks of sometimes fierce fighting, American forces rolled into Baghdad. Attacks launched by Saddam loyalists on U.S. forces continued in the weeks and months after the occupation of Baghdad, but the war was won, Saddam ruled no more, and the United States had sustained few casualties.[76]

But where were Iraq's weapons of mass destruction? The United States claimed that they would be found after further investigation. Some people feared that they had found their way to the international arms market and possibly terrorists. Still others claimed that they never existed in the first place. With Iraq's alleged weapons of destruction unaccounted for, the United States increasingly emphasized the overthrow of Saddam Hussein, the end of his brutality, and the democratization of Iraq as its chief war aims.[77]

Rebuilding Iraq also became a crucial U.S. objective. Having suffered through the 1991 Persian Gulf War, the decade-long UN embargo that followed the war, the 2003 war, and years of Saddam's misrule and plundering of the economy, Iraq's economy was in dire straights. The U.S. set about the task of rebuilding Iraq, complicated throughout 2003, 2004, and on into 2005 by suicide bombings, abductions and beheadings, and other attacks by Saddam loyalists, Islamic fundamentalists, and other anti-American actors against U.S. and Allied troops, humanitarian and reconstruction personnel, and Iraq's economy and government.[79]

The Iraqi war was a central part of the Bush administration's activist foreign policy, with Bush declaring that the U.S. would continue to defend its freedom, and the freedom of others, by acting before its enemies could act. This was a new version of the American mission, necessitated, Bush maintained, by new terrorist threats that endangered American security and the security of other civilized states. And if others would not act cooperatively to preemptively eliminate threats, the U.S. would act unilaterally. Realism, involvement, and unilateralism were the order of the day for American foreign policy as seen by Bush.

Others saw things differently. Thus, the Iraqi war became a major issue in the 2004 presidential election, with Democratic challenger John Kerry declaring that Bush had alienated American allies, acted too unilaterally, diverted attention from the real war on terror against al Qaeda, and mishandled Iraqi reconstruction efforts. Other American and overseas critics were more extreme, charging that the U.S. had become an imperial power that was using its military to build an empire, dismantle threats to its power, and assure access to oil and other resources.

So the debate over American foreign policy continues.

THE FUTURE OF AMERICAN FOREIGN POLICY

During its more than two centuries of existence, the United States has risen from a small, weak, and inconsequential player on the margins of world affairs to become the central actor in international affairs. Today, the United States is the world's only superpower, with the world's largest economy, most powerful military forces, and most influential social and cultural outlooks.

These realities raise immense questions for the future of American foreign policy. What missions and interests will the United States pursue? How will the United States use its unrivaled power and influence to pursue its missions and interests? Will it seek to dominate or cooperate, to persuade or to impose? How will the United States respond to and cope with threats to its missions and interests, especially nontraditional threats such as terrorism and weapons of mass destruction?

The answers to many of these questions are subjects of intense debate. Indeed, the U.S. mission has in fact changed over time. As we have seen, Thomas Jefferson in the eighteenth century believed that the U.S. mission was to be a "sanctuary" for those who sought to flee "the misrule of Europe." How different Jefferson's view was compared to Harry Truman's twentieth-century proclamation that "the free peoples of the world look to us for support in maintaining their freedoms" or George W. Bush's twenty-first-century view that the United States had to "defend not only our precious freedoms, but also the freedom of people everywhere to live and raise their children free from fear."[79] To Harry Truman and George W. Bush, the United States was a sanctuary no more, but an activist defender of freedom around the world. Similarly, as we have seen, some U.S. national interests have changed over time, with Americans defining those interests in different ways. These disagreements have often given rise to intense debates about American foreign policy interests.

What of principles? Some of them, too, have changed over time. Initiating in the eighteenth century a foreign policy based in part on the seemingly contradictory principles of moralism and pragmatism, the United States and probably most Americans remain wedded to these principles today. How else to explain American willingness during the Cold War pragmatically to be an ally of some of the most repugnant dictators in the world in the pursuit of the moralistic greater good of combating communism? How else in the wake of the destruction of the World Trade Center to explain the United States' willingness once again pragmatically to seek alliance with repressive regimes to moralistically combat the evil of international terrorism? Moralism and pragmatism, as contradictory as they may be, remain core principles of U.S. foreign policy.

Isolationism and unilateralism are different matters. As American power grew and the world changed following World War II, the United States abandoned isolationism as a key principle of foreign policy. Not all Americans agreed with this, and some even today call for a return to this principle upon which American foreign policy was initiated in the eighteenth century. Realistically, however, there is little chance of this occurring. As for unilateralism, it was substantially overshadowed following World War II by a new U.S. multilateralism manifested in American willingness to join a military alliance for the first time during peace and to participate extensively in a host of multilateral international organizations such as the UN, the World Bank, and the International Monetary Fund.

Even so, American multilateralism was far from complete. Indeed, throughout the Cold War, American allies often criticized the United States for acting unilaterally. And as we have seen, with the United States today having far more military and economic might than any other international actor and at the same time facing new types of threats to its security, the United States has reemphasized unilateralist foreign policy principles, with some observers charging that the United States had opted for an imperial strategy.

Meanwhile, the conflicts between the three sets of competing themes that have so dominated American foreign policy—realism versus idealism, isolationism versus involvement, and unilateralism versus multilateralism—continue unabated. Realists argue that only military power and economic strength can defend American interests and build a better world, while idealists argue that transnational institutions, international law, and morality have as important or an even more important role to play in U.S. foreign policy. Isolationists argue that American interests can best be served by substantially withdrawing from world affairs, while those advocating international involvement assert that isolationism is a relic of a bygone era and that American interests can best be served by active foreign involvement. And unilateralists and multilateralists continue to argue about whether American interests can best be pursued by acting alone or by forging policies and programs in cooperation with other international actors.

Recent presidents have charted foreign policy courses between the polar extremes of these competing themes, leaning one way or another, sometimes strongly, but for the most part balancing realism with idealism, isolationism with involvement, and unilateralism with multilateralism. This difficult and artful balancing act will likely continue as the United States reexamines, redefines, and then pursues its foreign policy mission and interests, based on principles that themselves are often the subjects of debate and disagreement.

To reiterate, then, American foreign policy throughout history has been a work in progress, determined by America's policymakers on the basis of the policies that they formulate and implement and by America's people on the basis of the leaders that they elect. It remains a work in progress today. With our understanding of the history of U.S. foreign policy well in hand, we now turn to the way that American foreign policy is made.

SUMMARY

George H. W. Bush pledged to follow Ronald Reagan's foreign policy, but by the time he became president in 1989, the world had changed so much that U.S. foreign policy had to be revised. The chief change was the 1989 collapse of Eastern Europe communism, which ended the main cause of the Cold War, the division of Europe into East and West. Also in 1989, crises erupted in China, where the Tiananmen Square massacre shocked the world, and Panama, which the United States invaded to overthrow Manuel Noriega. When in 1990 Iraq invaded Kuwait, the United States assembled a coalition to expel Iraq from Kuwait in 1991. Meanwhile, the Soviet Union became less stable, collapsing in 1991 and being replaced by Russia and 14 other new states. This ended the need for containment. What would U.S. foreign policy strategy now be? No one knew.

The United States under George H. W. Bush also grappled with international economic issues ranging from the North American Free Trade Agreement (NAFTA), a large trade deficit, and Third World debt to coping with Japanese trade surpluses and facing the European Community's plan for unity. Environmental issues, the drug trade, immigration, and civil war in Somalia, to which the United States deployed military forces, were also challenges.

When Bill Clinton became president in 1993, he focused foreign policy on engagement, meaning that the United States would not become isolationist, and enlargement, an idea under which the United States promoted open markets, democracy, and Western values. The bloom disappeared from U.S.-Russian relations during the Clinton years as Russian arms sales to Iran, ballistic missile defense, NATO expansion, and fighting in the Balkans showed divergent U.S. and Russian interests. The Bosnian civil war and the 1999 Kosovo conflict saw U.S. forces deployed to Europe in fighting for the first time since World War II.

These conflicts were part of a larger issue, namely, when should the United States intervene overseas? In addition to Bosnia and Kosovo, the United States under Clinton sent military forces to Haiti, Liberia, the Taiwan Straits, and elsewhere. In several cases where fighting erupted and tensions escalated, the United States did not deploy forces: Zaire, Rwanda, and Korea. In the Middle East, Clinton nurtured the Arab-Israeli peace process, but with little success. Clinton also focused on international economics, finalizing NAFTA, the Asian-Pacific Economic Cooperation pact, the Free Trade Area of the Americas, and the World Trade Organization. Stopping the spread of weapons of mass destruction and countering terrorism were also key issues, as were the drug trade, the environment, and immigration.

When George W. Bush became president in 2001, he faced the same range of issues with which his two predecessors grappled. This changed when on September 11, 2001, Osama bin Laden's al Qaeda terrorist network hijacked four jetliners, flying two into the World Trade Center, killing almost 3,000. A war on terrorism soon became the chief U.S. foreign policy priority, which began with the United States overthrowing Afghanistan's Taliban government, which had provided safe haven for bin Laden and al Qaeda. The war on terrorism also included security measures at home, intelligence sharing with allies, cooperative diplomacy with many countries, eliminating terrorist access to banks, and preemptive U.S. military action.

As the United States increasingly pursued the war on terrorism on its own, critics charged the United States was acting unilaterally. There was a considerable body of evidence: U.S. relations with Russia and the Middle East, U.S. opposition to the International Criminal Court, U.S. hostility toward international environmental agreements, and U.S. trade and aid policies, and U.S. actions toward Iraq.

In 2002, the United States warned it would act unilaterally against Iraq if UN inspections for weapons of mass destruction did not occur. When inspectors reported Iraq did not fully cooperate, the United States in 2003 launched the Iraq War. U.S. forces rolled into Baghdad but found no weapons of mass destruction in Iraq, so the United States emphasized overthrowing Saddam, democratizing Iraq, and rebuilding Iraq as its war aims.

By 2004, the United States had an activist foreign policy, declaring it would continue to act before its enemies could. This was a new version of mission, necessitated, George W. Bush maintained, by the terrorist threat. Realism, involvement, and unilateralism were the order of the day. Others disagreed with these policy choices, arguing that the United States had become an imperial power. Thus, the debate over U.S. foreign policy continues.

KEY TERMS AND CONCEPTS

collapse of Eastern European communism	NATO-Russia Founding Act
German unification	Bosnian civil war
North Atlantic Coordination Council (NACC)	ethnic cleansing
Tiananmen Square massacre	Dayton Accords
Persian Gulf War	Kosovo conflict
Operation Desert Storm	Somalia
Strategic Arms Reduction Treaty (START I)	Haitian crisis
START II	Arab-Israeli peace process
Conventional Forces in Europe (CFE) Treaty	World Trade Organization (WTO)
new world order	Asia-Pacific Economic Cooperation (APEC) agreement
North American Free Trade Agreement (NAFTA)	Free Trade Area of the Americas (FTAA)
European Community (EC)	weapons of mass destruction
European Union (EU)	Comprehensive Test Ban Treaty (CTBT)
UN Earth Summit	terrorist threat
engagement	al Qaeda
enlargement	Osama bin Laden
democratic peace theory	Kyoto Environmental Summit
G-7 industrialized states	G-8 industrialized states
Nunn-Lugar Bill	September 11, 2001
Partnership for Peace (PFP)	Taliban
	war on terrorism
	preemptive defense
	International Criminal Court
	Iraq War

THINKING CRITICALLY

1. The text asserts that post–Cold War presidents "have sought to achieve a balancing act" between realism and idealism, involvement and isolation, and unilateralism and multilateralism. Do you agree or disagree? Why?

2. What impact did the collapse of communist governments in Eastern Europe have on U.S. foreign policy, and how did the United States respond to the collapse?

3. Why did the United States see the 1990 Iraqi invasion of Kuwait as a serious challenge, and how did the United States respond to it?

4. What impact did the collapse of the Soviet Union have on U.S. foreign policy, and how did the United States respond to the collapse?

5. What international economic challenges confronted President George H. W. Bush between 1989 and 1993, and what policies did he put in place to respond to them?

6. Explain the concepts of engagement and enlargement, and detail how the Clinton Administration pursued both.

7. How and why did the North Atlantic Treaty Organization change after the Cold War?

8. Using specific examples, analyze why deciding whether, how, and where to intervene overseas has been a perplexing problem for the United States in the post–Cold War era.

9. How and why did the Clinton Administration deepen U.S. involvement with free trade areas and international organizations devoted to free trade?

10. Detail American responses to international terrorism before September 11, 2001, and explain why the United States did not attach higher priority to combating terrorism.

11. Use environmental issues, trade issues, and the International Court of Justice to illustrate the differing approaches to multilateralism and unilateralism preferred by Bill Clinton and George W. Bush.

12. What foreign policy initiatives were begun by George W. Bush before the attacks on the World Trade Center and Pentagon?

13. How did the United States respond to the September 11, 2001, terrorist attacks?

14. Assess the pros and cons of preemptive defense, and analyze the role this doctine has played in American foreign policy since it was proclaimed in 2002.

15. Why has the administration of George W. Bush been accused of unilateralism and imperialism? To what extent to you accept or reject these charges? Support your positions.

NOTES

1. The fifth Chicago Council on Foreign Relations study of American foreign policy attitudes, conducted by the Gallup Organization between October 23 and November 15, 1990, found that 65 percent of the American public thought that "protecting American jobs" was a "very important" foreign policy goal, while only 39 percent of American leaders thought the same goal was "very important."

2. See Wesley K. Clark, *Winning Modern Wars: Iraq, Terrorism, and the American Empire* (New York: Public Affairs, 2003).

3. For several studies of events in Europe during this period, see Lawrence Freedman, ed., *Europe Transformed* (New York: St. Martin's Press, 1990); Glennon J. Harrison, *Europe and the United States* (New York: M. E. Sharpe, 1994); Walter Laquer, *The Dream That Failed* (New York: Oxford University Press, 1994); Gale Stokes, *The Walls Came Tumbling Down* (New York: Oxford University Press, 1993).

4. See Konrad H. Jarausch, *The Rush to German Unity* (New York: Oxford University Press, 1994), and J. K. A. Thomaneck and Bill Niven, *Dividing and Uniting Germany* (New York: Routledge, 2001).

5. For discussions of the North Atlantic Cooperation Council, see John Borawski and Thomas-Durell Young, *NATO after 2000: The Future of the Euro-Atlantic Alliance* (Westport, Conn.: Praeger, 2001), pp. 89–91; and Gerald B. H. Solomon, *The NATO Enlargement Debate, 1990–1997: Blessings of Liberty* (Westport, Conn.: Praeger, 2001), pp. 16–18.

6. For discussion of Chinese foreign policy including U.S.-Chinese relations during George H. W. Bush's presidency, see John W. Garver, *Foreign Relations of the People's Republic of China* (Englewood Cliffs, N.J.: 1993), and Samuel S. Kim, *China and the World: Chinese Foreign Relations in the Post-Cold War Era* (Boulder, Colo.: 1994).

7. For insights on how the United States' chief foreign policy architects saw the Philippines during George H. W. Bush's presidency, see George Bush and Brent Scowcroft, *A World Transformed* (New York: Knopf, 1998), pp. 160–161, 165–167; and James Addison Baker III, *The Politics of Diplomacy: Revolution, War, and Peace, 1989–1992* (New York: Putnam, 1995).

8. See John Dinges, *Our Man in Panama: How General Noriega Used the United States and Made Millions in Drugs and Arms* (New York: Random House, 1990); and Richard M. Koster and Guileermo Sanchez, *In the Time of Tyrants: Panama: 1968–1990* (New York: Norton, 1991).

9. For analysis of different aspects of the Persian Gulf War, see William Head and Earl H. Tilford Jr., eds., *The Eagle in the Desert: Looking Back on U.S. Involvement in the Persian Gulf War* (Westport, Conn.: Praeger, 1996); James Blackwell, *Thunder in the Desert: The Strategy and Tactics of the Persian Gulf War* (New York: Bantam Books, 1991); and Bob Woodward, *The Commanders* (New York: Simon and Schuster, 1991).

10. For good discussions of the events that led to the decline and fall of the Soviet Union, see Geoffrey Hosking, *The Awakening of the Soviet Union* (Cambridge, Mass.: Harvard University Press, 1990); David Remnick, *Lenin's Tomb: The Last Days of the Soviet Empire* (New York: Random House, 1993); and Jeffrey T. Checkel, *Ideas and International Political Change: Soviet/Russian Behavior and the End of the Cold War* (New Haven: Yale University Press, 1997).

11. American leaders and the general public recognized that the Soviet Union presented less of a threat to the United States. Comparing the results of the 1986 Chicago Council on Foreign Relations study of American foreign policy attitudes with the 1990 study reveals that American leaders in 1986 considered U.S.-Soviet relations the most important foreign policy issue for the United States, but by 1990 considered it only the third most important issue, with a decline of 25 points between 1986 and 1990. Meanwhile, the general public rated U.S.-Soviet relations the most important U.S. foreign policy issue in 1986, but by 1990 it did not even make the list of top ten issues.

12. For an excellent account of the evolution of U.S.-Soviet relations under both Ronald Reagan and George H. W. Bush, see Don Oberdorfer, *From the Cold War to a New Era: The United States and the Soviet Union, 1983–1991* (Baltimore: Johns Hopkins University Press, 1998).

13. See *The Defense Monitor* 22 (1) (1993) for the projected impact of START II on U.S. and Russian nuclear weapon inventories.

14. See Arms Control and Disarmament Agency, *Treaty on Conventional Armed Forces in Europe* (Washington, D.C.: U.S. Information Agency, 1990).

15. W. Raymond Duncan and Carolyn McGiffert Ekedahl, *Moscow and the Third World under Gorbachev* (Boulder, Colo.: Westview Press, 1990), and Melvin A. Goodman, ed., *The End of Superpower Conflict in the Third World* (Boulder, Colo.: Westview Press, 1992), discuss U.S. and Soviet efforts to resolve regional conflicts.

16. See John E. Rielly, "Public Opinion: The Pulse of the '90s," in *The Future of American Foreign Policy*, ed. Charles W. Kegley Jr. and Eugene R. Wittkopf (New York: St. Martin's Press, 1992), pp. 124–132.

17. For reviews of events in Nicaraguan and Central America, see Jack Child, *The Central American Peace Process, 1983–1991* (Boulder, Colo.: Lynne Rienner, 1992).

18. For discussions of NAFTA and the issues that it raised, see William A. Orme, *Understanding NAFTA* (Austin: University of Texas Press, 1996), and Ralph Nader, ed., *The Case against Free Trade: GATT, NAFTA, and the Globalization of Corporate Power* (New York: North Atlantic Books, 1993).

19. For more on U.S.-Japanese trade relations under Bush, see C. Fred Bergsten and Marcus Noland, *Reconcilable Differences? United States-Japan Economic Conflict* (Washington, D.C.: Institute for International Economics, 1993).

20. For discussions of the debt crisis, see Miles Kahler, ed., *The Politics of International Debt* (Ithaca, N.Y.: Cornell University Press, 1985), and Gianni Vaggi, ed., *From the Debt Crisis to Sustainable Development: Changing Perspectives on North-South Relations* (New York: St. Martin's, 1993).

21. See Brian Nelson, David Roberts, and Walter Veit, eds., *The European Community in the 1990s: Economics, Politics, Defense* (Herndon, Va.: Berg, 1992); John Pinder, *European Community: The Building of a*

Union (New York: Oxford University Press, 1995); and Carolyn Rhodes and Sonia Mazey, eds., *The State of the European Union, Vol. 3: Building a European Polity?* (Boulder, Colo.: Lynne Rienner, 1995).

22. For discussions of the Rio Earth Summit, see Caroline Thomas, *Rio: Unraveling the Consequences* (Ilford, Essex, England: Frank Cass, 1994), and Lawrence E. Susskind, *Environmental Diplomacy: Negotiating More Effective Global Agreements* (New York: Oxford University Press, 1994).

23. For extensive discussions of the international drug trade and U.S. responses to it, see Peter Dale Scott and Jonathan Marshall, *Cocaine Politics: Drugs, Armies, and the CIA in Central America* (Berkeley: University of California Press, 1998); Alexander Cockburn et al., *Whiteout: The CIA, Drugs, and the Press* (New York: Verso, 1998); and Alfred M. McCoy, *The Politics of Heroin: CIA Complicity in the Global Drug Trade* (Lawrence Hill, 1991).

24. For good discussions of U.S. immigration policy, see Nicolaus Mills, ed., *Arguing Immigration: The Debate over the Changing Face of America* (New York: Touchstone, 1994).

25. See Rielly, pp. 124–132.

26. See Patrick J. Buchanan, *A Republic, Not an Empire* (Washington, D.C.: Regnery Publishing, 1999), for a discussion of neo-isolationism. For discussions of the debate that later emerged over U.S. grand strategy and the concept of a uni-polar world, see Barry R. Posen and Andrew L. Ross, "Competing Visions of U.S. Grand Strategy," *International Security* 21 (Winter 1996/97): 5–53; and William C. Wohlforth, "The Stability of a Unipolar World," *International Security* 24 (Summer 1999): 5–41.

27. Bill Clinton, "A Strategy for Foreign Policy," *Vital Speeches of the Day* (May 1, 1992), p. 421.

28. Anthony Lake, "From Containment to Enlargement," *Department of State Dispatch* (September 27, 1993), pp. 658–664.

29. Michael E. Brown, Sean M. Lynn-Jones, and Steven E. Miller, eds., *Debating the Democratic Peace* (Cambridge, Mass.: MIT Press, 1997); Michael Doyle, "Liberalism and World Politics," *American Political Science Review* 80 (December 1986): 1131–1169; and Joe D. Hagan, "Domestic Political Systems and War Processes," *Mershon International Studies Review* 38 (October 1994): 183–207.

30. United Nations Conference on Environment and Development, *Agenda 21* (New York: United Nations, 1992); and World Commission on Environment and Development, 1987.

31. U.S. Agency for International Development, *Strategies for Sustainable Development* (Washington, D.C.: U.S. Department of State, 1994), p. 4.

32. *New York Times*, April 5, 1993.

33. The G-7 states were Canada, France, Germany, Great Britain, Italy, Japan, and the United States. Russia has since been added, making the G-7 the G-8. The leaders of these states have met more or less annually since the 1980s to discuss world economic and political issues.

34. For details on U.S.-Russian relations under Clinton, see Strobe Talbott, *The Russia Hand: A Memoir of Presidential Diplomacy* (New York: Random House, 2002).

35. For Senator Richard Lugar's views of the Nunn-Lugar Cooperative Threat Reduction Program, see http://lugar.senate.gov/nunn_lugar_program.html.

36. For an overview of the Partnership for Peace, see http://www.nato.cz/english/partneri.html.

37. For the text of the NATO-Russia Founding Act, see http://nato.int/docu/basictxt/fndact-a.htm.

38. For more on the Bosnian civil war and other conflicts in the Balkans, see James Gow, *Triumph of the Lack of Will: International Diplomacy and the Yugoslav War* (New York: Columbia University Press, 1997), and Sabrina P. Ramet, *Balkan Babel: The Disintegration of Yugoslavia from the Death of Tito to the War for Kosovo* (Boulder, Colo.: Westview Press, 1998).

39. For details about the Dayton Peace Accords and NATO's occupation of Bosnia, see Jane M. O. Sharp, "Dayton Report Card," *International Security* (Winter 1997/98): 101–137.

40. For a critical view of NATO in the Kosovo conflict, see Ted Galen Carpenter, ed., *NATO's Empty Victory: A Postmortem on the Balkan War* (Washington, D.C.: Cato Institute, 2000). See also Elizabeth Pond, "Kosovo: Catalyst for Europe," *Washington Quarterly* (Autumn 1999): 77–92.

41. For more details on the American and UN interventions in Somalia, see John R. Bolton, "Wrong Turn in Somalia," *Foreign Affairs* 73 (January–February 1994), and Jonathan Stevenson, *Losing Mogadishu: Testing U.S. Policy in Somalia* (Annapolis, M.D.: U.S. Naval Institute, 1995).

42. For a critique of dual containment, see F. Gregory Gause III, "The Illogic of Dual Containment," *Foreign Affairs* 73 (March–April 1994): 56–66.

43. For more details on Haitian events, see "A Haitian Chronology," *Congressional Quarterly Weekly Report* (September 17, 1994): 2579; and Pamela Constable, "Haiti: A Nation in Despair, a Policy Adrift," *Current History* (March 1994): 108–109.

44. For an interesting treatment of America's Mideast policy under Bill Clinton, including the Oslo Accords, see William G. Hyland, *Clinton's World* (Westport, Conn.: Praeger, 1999), chapter 12.

45. For one example of such criticism of American military policy under Clinton, see Jack Spencer, "The Facts about Military Readiness," which declared that, "Under the Clinton Administration, the U.S. military has suffered from a dangerous combination of reduced budgets, diminished forces, and increased missions," as reported in Heritage Foundation, *Building a Better Military,* Web Memo #8, March 21, 2001, at http://www.heritage.org/Research/NationalSecurity/WM8.cfm.

46. See Stephen D. Cohen, *Fundamentals of U.S. Foreign Trade Policy: Economics, Politics, Law, and Issues* (Boulder, Colo.: Westview Press, 2003), especially chapter 11, pp. 259–280.

47. International Monetary Fund, *Direction of Trade Statistics*, various editions and pages.

48. See for example Richard Bernstein and Ross H. Munro, "The Coming Conflict with America," *Foreign Affairs* 76 (March–April 1997).

49. Jeffrey J. Schott, *The WTO after Seattle* (Washington, D.C.: Institute for International Economics, 2000), and Bhagirath L. Das, *World Trade Organization: A Guide to New Frameworks for International Trade* (New York: St. Martin's Press, 2000).

50. See Hyland, chapter 13, for an informative treatment of U.S. policy toward Iraq under Bill Clinton.

51. See Michael J. Mazarr, *North Korea and the Bomb: A Case Study in Nonproliferation* (New York: St. Martin's Press, 1996).

52. For details of the effort that have become public, see Barton Gellman, "Clinton's Covert War," *Washington Post Weekly Edition* (January 7–13, 2002): 6–8.

53. For results of the Kyoto Summit, see R. Coppock, "Implementing the Kyoto Protocol," *Issues in Science and Technology* (Spring 1998): 66–74; B. Bolin and A. P. Loeb, "Act Now to Slow Climate Change," *Issues in Science and Technology* (Fall 1998): 18–22; and U.S. Department of State, "The Kyoto Protocol," Fact Sheet Released by the Bureau of Oceans and International Environmental and Scientific Affairs (November 2, 1998).

54. For discussions of Bill Clinton's policies toward Colombia on combating the international flow of drugs, see Russell Crandall, *Driven by Drugs: United States Policy Toward Colombia* (Boulder, Colo.: Lynne Rienner, 2002), and Russell Crandall, "Clinton, Bush, and Plan Colombia," *Survival* 44 (Spring 2002): 159–172.

55. For the Immigration and Naturalization Service's decision on the Elian Gonzalez case, see http://www.sackskolken.com/court/Egonzal_case.html.

56. "President George W. Bush's Address to the Summit of the Americas," White House, April 21, 2001.

57. George W. Bush and Gerhard Schroeder, "Joint Statement on a Trans-Atlantic Vision for the Twenty First Century," White House, March 29, 2001.

58. "Statement on an International Trade Agenda," White House, May 10, 2001.

59. For just a few of the many studies of the impact on American of the September 11, 2001, terrorist attacks, see Daniel S. Papp, *The Impact of September 11 on Contemporary International Relations* (New York: Longman, 2002); Jean Bethke Elshtain, *Just War against Terror: The Burden of American Power in a Violent World* (New York: Basic Books, 2003); Wladyslaw Pleszczynski, ed., *Our Brave New World: Essays on the Impact of September 11* (Stanford, Calif.: Hoover Institute Press, 2002); and Dean C. Alexander and

Yonah Alexander, *Terrorism and Business: The Impact of September 11, 2001* (Transnational Publishers, 2002).

60. George W. Bush, "State of the Union Message," *New York Times* (January 2002).

61. *The National Security Strategy of the United States of America* (Washington, D.C.: U.S. Department of Defense, September 2002).

62. For criticisms of preemptive defense, see "The Use of Force, Legitimacy, and the UN Charter: The Bush Doctrine," *UNA-USA Global Issues Survey 2003*, at http://www.unausa.org/mewindex.asp?place; "Bush Doctrine Fatally Flawed, Dean Says," *Boston Globe* (December 11, 2003); and "Preemptive War Strategy: A New U.S. Empire?" transcript of a foreign policy forum with Joel S. Beinen, Ivan Eland, and Edward A. Olsen, Independent Institute, June 25, 2003, at http://www.independent.org/tii/forums/0625ipf2.html.

63. See "Public Agenda Special Edition: Terrorism," October 23, 2001, and December 17, 2001, found respectively at http://www.publicagenda.org/specials/terrorism/102301terror_pubopinion.htm and http://www.publicagenda.org/specials/terrorism/121701terror_pubopinion.htm.

64. *The National Security Strategy of the United States of America* (Washington, D.C.: U.S. Department of Defense, September 2002).

65. *International Herald Tribune*, September 2, 2002.

66. For different views on ballistic missile defense, see Ivo H. Daalder et al., "A Consensus on Missile Defense?"; Steven E. Miller, "The Flawed Case for Missile Defense"; and Richard Sokolsky, "Imagining European Missile Defense"; all in *Survival* 43 (Autumn 2001): 61–128.

67. "Strategic Offensive Arms Reduction Treaty," U.S. Department of State, May 24, 2002.

68. For a critique of George W. Bush's policies toward the Arab-Israeli conflict, and an interesting comparison of his policies with those of his father, see Milton Viorst, "The Road Map to Nowhere," *Washington Quarterly* 26 (Summer 2003): 177–190. See also Jeremy Pressman, "The Primary Role of the United States in Israeli-Palestinian Relations," *International Studies Perspectives* 4 (May 2003): 191–194.

69. *International Herald Tribune*, July 3, 2002.

70. *New York Times*, March 15, 2002.

71. Gary Samore, "The Korean Nuclear Crisis," *Survival* 45 (Spring 2003): 7–24; and Michael O'Hanlon and Mike Mochizuki, "Toward a Grand Bargain with North Korea," *Washington Quarterly* 26 (Autumn 2003): 7–19.

72. *International Herald Tribune*, September 2, 2002. See also Alexander T. J. Lennon, ed., *What Does the World Want from America? International Perspectives on U.S. Foreign Policy* (Cambridge, Mass.: MIT Press, 2002).

73. *International Herald Tribune*, September 2, 2002.

74. See for example John Newhouse, *Imperial America: The Bush Assault on the World Order* (New York: Knopf, 2003), and Clyde Prestowitz, *Rogue Nation: America's Unilateralism and the Failure of Good Intentions* (New York: Basic Books, 2003). See also Juan A. Alsace, "In Search of Monsters to Destroy: American Empire in the New Millennium," *Parameters* 33 (Autumn 2003): 122–129.

75. Following the 1991 Gulf War, the UN placed weapons inspectors in Iraq to search for weapons of mass destruction and assure that Iraq was not producing biological, chemical, or nuclear weapons. In the mid-1990s, Iraq expelled the UN inspectors. For examples of the building American sentiment in 2002 to go to war with Iraq to remove weapons of mass destruction, see "Remarks by the President to the 2002 Graduation Exercise of the United States Military Academy, West Point, New York June 1, 2002," at www.whitehouse.gov; and Peter Yost, "Prominent Democrats Endorse Administration Plan to Remove Iraqi Leader," Associated Press release, June 17, 2002.

76. For details of the Iraq War, see Williamson Murray and Robert H. Scales Jr., *The Iraq War: A Military History* (Cambridge, Mass.: Harvard University Press, 2003), and Anthony H. Cordesman Jr., *The Iraq War: Strategy, Tactics, and Military Lessons* (Westport, Conn.: Praeger, 2003).

77. Discussions of U.S. war aims may be found at Andrew J. Bacevich, "Don't Get Greedy! For Sensible Limited War Aims in Iraq," *National Review* (February 10, 2003), and Carol Giacomo, "U.S. War Aims Clear,

Regional Aims Murky," Reuters, March 20, 2003, as reported by the Richard Nixon Center, at http://www.nixonfoundation.org/nrc/030320cBombing.shtml.

78. For speculation about what may happen in Iraq, see Daniel L. Bynam and Kenneth M. Pollack, "Democracy in Iraq?," *Washington Quarterly* 26 (Summer 2003): 119–136; and Daniel Bynam, "Constructing a Democratic Iraq," *International Security* 28 (Summer 2003): 47–78.

79. George W. Bush, Address to the Nation, October 7, 2001.

The Politics and Process of American Policy

Introduction to Part Three

In Part II, we examined the background and history of American foreign policy primarily from the perspective of the international level of analysis. For the most part, Part II viewed U.S. foreign policy as "the more or less purposive acts of [a] unified national government" responding to strategic problems. But who makes U.S. foreign policy? How is it made? And what factors do America's policymakers consider when they make foreign policy?

Almost always, American foreign policy—and the foreign policy of many other countries as well—is the end result of a complex, complicated, and even confusing political process. The process, rarely well ordered, takes into account the outlooks and interests of a significant number of government officials, ranging from the president on down, who may hold widely different views about what appropriate policy should be, and equally divergent views about the appropriate way to conduct policy. These disparate foreign policy decision makers debate alternative policies, disagree over cause and effect, and jockey for position to try to have their own preferences determine policy. More perplexingly for those who desire to find a rational and predictable process, U.S. policymakers often take into account the outlooks and interests of a range of nongovernmental interest groups and pressure groups, as well as public opinion, as they formulate and implement U.S. foreign policy.

Concentrating on the national level of analysis, and using a combination of the rational policy, organizational process, and bureaucratic politics models discussed in Chapter 1, the first two chapters in Part III, Chapters 8 and 9, tell the tale of the individuals, the executive departments, significant participants from Congress and the judiciary, and other actors involved in the American foreign policy process. These chapters provide an understanding both of how these players in the American foreign policy process interact with one another as U.S. foreign policy is formulated and implemented, and how each player views his or her individual or organizational interests.

Chapters 10 and 11 examine the tools of American foreign policy. Using an approach rarely seen in American foreign policy textbooks, Chapter 10 explores the open instruments of policy, and Chapter 11 then delves into the secret instruments of policy. This approach provides a unique perspective on how American foreign policy is actually implemented.

After studying the four chapters in Part III, students should have a good grasp of how complex, complicated, and even confusing the political process is that lies behind the scenes of American foreign policy. This understanding, combined with the methodological expertise that students developed in Part I and the historical understanding they acquired in Part II, will well prepare students to take on the intricacies of the critical American foreign policy issues that are laid out in Part IV of this text.

CHAPTER 8

The Presidency and the Executive Branch in American Foreign Policy

The president and executive branch have the lead in the formulation and implementation of U.S. foreign policy. One key executive branch player in foreign policy is the national security adviser. President George W. Bush and National Security Adviser Condoleezza Rice are seen here in the Oval Office discussing U.S. policy toward China.

- What are the president's foreign policy powers?
- Is the president able to command the large foreign policy bureaucracy of the executive branch?
- What role does the rest of the executive branch have in foreign policy?
- In a world of weapons of mass destruction and terrorism, can the United States afford to have a decentralized foreign policy process in which power is shared?

In the minds of those who crafted the U.S. Constitution, efficiency was not the cardinal virtue for good government. If efficiency had been their goal, they would have placed greater authority in the hands of the president. On the contrary, as one constitutional specialist has emphasized, "the framers were unwilling to give the President anything resembling royal prerogative."[1] Through their rejection of sweeping executive powers, they sought to protect themselves—and posterity—against the risks of autocracy.

By rejecting royal prerogative, however, the constitutional framers created a government that often displays signs of sluggishness, parochialism, and disarray. The premium placed by the Constitution on power sharing drives hierarchists to distraction, turns proponents of tidy organizational charts grim faced, and sends twitching those who believe that policymaking should be carried out with the precision of a Swiss watch. The founders had established what Winston Churchill later said a democracy would always be: the very worst possible form of government—except for all the others.

Foreign policy can magnify the slowness and uncertainty with which policy decisions are often made in a democracy. With domestic policy, one can arguably afford to muddle through, moving incrementally for the most part, with slight changes at the margins of existing policy when necessary—an approach that many political scientists have argued is the hallmark of domestic policymaking in the United States.[2] With foreign policy, though, the dangers from abroad may be too dire for politics as usual. Protection against thermonuclear annihilation, terrorist attacks, oil embargoes, and other potential calamities may require sudden and bold initiatives by the executive.

Events overseas often appear to move more rapidly than those at home, in part no doubt because they are farther away and, therefore, less familiar to the American people and less closely watched. This potential for surprise from abroad may require the government to react with greater speed than normal. The need for quick response to a crisis is nothing new. The nation's founders drafted the commander-in-chief clause of the Constitution as a means for providing the president with authority to repel a sudden attack against America without having to wait for a congressional declaration of war. During the Cold War, the ten-minute flight time to Washington, D.C., of Soviet submarine-launched missiles off the American coastline added an exclamation point to the need for speed.

Such reasoning leads some reformers to advocate an approach to foreign policy quite different from what they would tolerate for domestic policy. For foreign affairs, because of the acute dangers and the need for rapid decision, they turn to hierarchy, secrecy, and deliberations by the few, chiefly the president and his or her close advisers. They advocate sacrificing the hallowed traditions of democracy—openness, debate, the careful consideration of a wide range of options, the gauging of public opinion—on the altar of national security.[3]

Others argue, in contrast, that the debate and openness characteristic of domestic policy must be maintained for foreign policy, too, with the exception of a few necessary secrets such as the blueprints of new weapons systems and the names of foreign agents working for the CIA. To surrender foreign policy to an elite group of officials in the executive branch, they argue, is to risk making decisions that are contrary to the will of the people and thereby undermining, in the name of national security, the very essence of democracy and the American form of government.[4]

MODELS OF PRESIDENTIAL POWER

A central issue in any appraisal of American foreign policy is the degree to which it ought to be an executive function—maybe even narrowly defined to encompass only the top officials in the executive branch—or whether, as in domestic policy, it should extend to a wider range of participants, including representatives of the American people in Congress.

Presidents versus Lawmakers

From an institutional point of view, consider two extreme approaches to foreign policy: first, a **presidential model** in which global decisions are left exclusively to the president and his or her top aides—an "imperial president"[5]; and, second, a **legislative model,** in which these decisions would be left primarily to members of Congress—an "imperial Congress."[6] (The judicial branch is seldom a player in foreign policy, although as explored in the next chapter, its periodic involvement in foreign policy issues can sometimes have lasting consequences.)

The presidential model enjoys widespread support for the reasons of urgency mentioned earlier, and because of the far-flung intelligence apparatus within the executive branch that presumably provides the president with better information about foreign affairs than available to the Congress. Moreover, a strong sense exists that, to be taken seriously in the world, the United States must speak with one voice. And some lawmakers have been more than happy to pass on responsibility to the White House for knotty and controversial problems overseas that could spell trouble for them in the next election.

Not everyone, though, has been enthusiastic about foreign policy conducted by executive fiat. Even before the Watergate scandal and the war in Vietnam raised serious doubts about a reliance on presidential power, a pro-Congress viewpoint could be frequently heard—especially from the conservative side of the political spectrum, which argued in favor of the legislative model of foreign policy. Economic conservatives lamented the centralism that Franklin D. Roosevelt had brought to the marketplace. States-rightists fretted over international agreements signed by presidents that might lead indirectly to a further strengthening of authority in Washington. Southerners worried that the federal government might establish new civil rights regulations by way of executive agreements with African nations.[7] Isolationists looked upon the presidency as an agent of intervention abroad that would drain American resources or even sell out American interests, as conservatives argued Franklin Roosevelt had done in 1945 via executive agreements negotiated with Stalin at Yalta.

In more recent times, with three of their own presidents in the White House—Ronald Reagan, George H. W. Bush, and George W. Bush—many conservative Republicans began to see things differently. During these administrations, they favored broader authority for the president in foreign policy. For example, they argued that President Reagan should have wide leeway to carry out whatever policies were necessary to halt communist aggression in Central America, even if that meant rising above laws like the Boland amendments that had placed limits on secret military assistance to the CIA-backed anti-communist *contras* in Nicaragua. The Boland legislation was "unconstitutional," argued arch-conservative Senator Barry Goldwater (R-Arizona). "It's another example of Congress trying to take away the constitutional power of the President to be Commander in Chief and to formulate foreign policy."[8] A majority of lawmakers in both chambers disagreed with Goldwater, however, and steadily tightened the Boland restrictions on covert action in Nicaragua throughout the early 1980s.

Regardless of political leanings, some students of democratic theory argue that lawmakers are closer to the grass roots, especially members of the House of Representatives with their perpetual reelection pressures. As a result, members of Congress have a better comprehension of what the people in Pocatello and Homerville really want with respect to America's role in the world. Were the citizens back home willing to send their sons and daughters into combat in Nicaragua during the Reagan years? Into Iraq and Afghanistan during the two Bush administrations? Were they prepared to support costly defense programs with tax increases or deficit spending? Lawmakers, continues this argument, are like raw nerve endings that reach into each of the 50 states and the 435 congressional districts across the land, sensing the likely response of the American people to vital foreign policy and national security issues. The president cannot possibly visit each district; however, members of Congress do, usually every week, and some every day if their districts are close to Washington, D.C. This makes Congress a unique, continuous forum of timely public opinion.

An example bears this out. During his second term, President Reagan was inclined initially to resist, on ideological grounds, the subsidized shipment of U.S. wheat to the Soviet Union. In response, lawmakers complained vociferously that the president ought to spend more time listening to the plight of American farmers in the congressional districts and less time playing Cold War politics. In light of this criticism from Capitol Hill, led by majority leader Robert Dole (R-Kansas), Reagan allowed the wheat to be sold to the Soviets. By authorizing the sale of wheat, the president mollified farm-state legislators, but in the process he irritated hawkish Republicans who frowned on any trade deals that might help the Soviet economy. Moreover, this decision undercut the sale of Australian wheat to the USSR, triggering angry protests by Australian farmers in front of the U.S. embassy in Canberra.

A Foreign Policy Compact?

In between the presidential and legislative models of foreign policymaking lies a third, the **constitutional balance model,** which is the perspective favored in this book. This model emphasizes cooperation between coequal branches—in other words, an engine with all its cylinders at work. A classic example of cooperation occurred in 1954 when Secretary of State John Foster Dulles, a strong proponent of the domino theory, proposed to President Eisenhower the introduction of a U.S. military presence into Vietnam to assist French troops surrounded by communist forces at the city of Dien Bien Phu.

Before making his decision, Eisenhower asked Dulles to consult with leading members of Congress regarding their opinions on how the United States should proceed. Invited to the White House for a meeting with Dulles and other top officials, the lawmakers asked probing questions that uncovered an important fact: neither the Joint Chiefs of Staff nor key allies abroad supported the plan. Among members of the congressional delegation, some of whom were normally strong supporters of the administration, this discovery caused much skepticism regarding the proposed U.S. intervention, and they advised against it. According to the minutes of the meeting: "discussion developed a unanimous reaction of the Members of Congress that there should be no congressional action until the Secretary had obtained commitments of a political and material nature from our allies. The feeling was unanimous that 'we want no more Koreas with the United States furnishing 90% of the manpower.'"[9] Eisenhower backed away from Dulles's recommendation to use military force in Indochina.[10]

Two incidents during George H. W. Bush's presidency also demonstrated the value of close executive-legislative cooperation. During his first months in office in 1989, Bush patiently and quietly negotiated with Congress an interbranch agreement favoring non-lethal aid for the *contras* in Nicaragua, successfully defusing one of the most controversial foreign policy issues of that decade. In June 1989, when Chinese troops attacked pro-reform students in Beijing, Bush called top lawmakers to the White House and worked out with them a strategy of criticism and sanctions against the Beijing government in punishment for its murder of hundreds of peaceful demonstrators.

President Jimmy Carter's undersecretary of state, Warren M. Christopher (later secretary of state in the Clinton Administration), cast the argument for interbranch cooperation in terms of an executive-legislative compact. "As a fundamental precept," he wrote, "the compact would call for restraint on the part of the Congress—for Congress to recognize and accept the responsibility of the Executive to conduct and manage foreign policy on a daily basis." He stressed that, in return, the executive branch must be prepared to provide Congress "full information and consultation," and "broad policy should be jointly designed." For its part, Congress should attempt only in extreme circumstances "to dictate or overturn Executive decisions and actions."[11] Employing a different image, Senator J. William Fulbright (D-Arkansas) often suggested while chairman of the Foreign Relations Committee that the Congress and the president should jointly chart the desired global routes for the American ship of state. Then it would be up to the president to take command as an able captain and steer the ship safely to port, making periodic adjustments as necessary in consultation with the experienced hands in the Congress.

Real life, though, falls outside the confines of tidy theoretical models. Prescriptions like Christopher's can sound platitudinous in light of the divided institutional relations and fragmented power that actually characterize U.S. foreign policymaking. Still, models do serve to highlight a sense of where, in the opinion of various observers, the institutional "center of gravity" ought to be when decisions are made: with the president, with the Congress, or balanced between the two.

What ought to be is often a different matter from what is. As this chapter attempts to illustrate, something resembling each of these models can be observed at different times as one looks at the institutional side of foreign policy. Sometimes the president is able to gather together enough fragments of power to achieve control over a decision, sometimes the Congress gains control, and sometimes they share power. The challenge is to understand why no single model is sufficient to explain the formulation and conduct of foreign policy by the United States. In the first chapter of this book, we examined the constitutional wellsprings of institutional tension over foreign policy coming from the theory of separate institutions sharing power. In this chapter, we will explore the practice of that theory in the modern era, beginning with the presidency.

THE PRESIDENCY

As we saw in Chapter 1, the Constitution provides the president with a number of powers in foreign affairs. Over time, presidents have expanded these powers. Indeed, throughout most of America's history, but especially during the late twentieth and early twenty-first centuries, the president has enjoyed preeminence in foreign policy. This does not mean that the president has unlimited power with respect to U.S. relations abroad; there are significant limits to what the chief executive can do in this domain, just as with domestic policymaking.

Sources of Presidential Power

Beyond the authority granted in the Constitution, the president enjoys preeminence in American foreign policy for several reasons. The president has greater access than any elected official to information, including classified intelligence. And while anyone can try to speak to the American people about foreign affairs, the president appears on television and radio more frequently than any official, and most citizens tend to place their faith in the White House on foreign policy pronouncements.

The president's control over the resources of the executive branch contributes to the ability of the White House to act alone. A classic illustration occurred during the administration of Teddy Roosevelt. He wanted to send the American navy armada, "the Great White Fleet," around the world to show the flag of the United States and display America's sea power. Members of Congress considered the idea silly and expensive, and refused to appropriate funds for the venture. Roosevelt dispatched the fleet anyway, declaring that it could steam half way around the world on current Navy funding; if the legislative branch wanted the ships to return to America, lawmakers would have to appropriate more money.

More recently, American presidents have regularly used their authority to order U.S. armed forces into foreign operations without seeking approval from others. For example, on their own authority as president, Ronald Reagan ordered air strikes against Libya and the invasion of Grenada; George H. W. Bush initiated an invasion of Panama; Bill Clinton approved cruise-missile attacks against Afghanistan, Iraq, and Sudan; and George W. Bush sent American armed forces and paramilitary intelligence officers on raids against the Taliban regime in Afghanistan after the September 11, 2001, terrorist attacks against the United States, only later receiving congressional approval for an expansion of the war on global terrorism.

Access to information is one of the president's greatest advantages. Often the White House has exclusive sources of information acquired by State Department diplomats, military attachés working for the Defense Department, CIA assets in almost every country, and surveillance satellites and reconnaissance aircraft operated by the National Reconnaissance Office (NRO). Private citizens, companies, interest groups, the media, or even members of Congress cannot match the president's storehouse of information on issues such as Iraq's programs to obtain weapons of mass destruction or the inner workings of decision councils in closed societies like North Korea. However, George W. Bush's information proved wrong with respect to weapons of mass destruction in Iraq.

Limits on Presidential Power

Often high school and college textbooks give the impression that the chief executive has almost superhuman authority.[12] One college text widely used in the 1950s and 1960s referred to Abraham Lincoln as "the martyred Christ of democracy's passion play" and declared that "there is virtually no limit to what the President can do if he does it for democratic ends and by democratic means."[13] Even renowned journalist Theodore H. White lapsed into adulation in his best-selling book *The Making of the President 1960*. "So many and so able are the President's advisors of the permanent services of Defense, State, Treasury, Agriculture," he wrote, "that when crisis happens all necessary information is instantly available, all alternate courses already plotted."[14]

Despite a common belief that the president is (as Vice President Nelson Rockefeller once said, overheatedly) "the unifying force in our lives," scholarly studies of the White House underscore the president's limited ability to overlook or ignore the views of other important officials in government, the media, and pressure groups.[15] However strong a president may appear as the leader of American foreign policy, there are sharp **limits on presidential power.** These include the nature of the international setting, information problems, time constraints, issues of permissibility, the availability of resources, and bureaucratic barriers on the exercise of power.

The International Setting

One of the primary limitations on the president—and for neo-realists the only significant limitation—is the **international setting.** Regardless of how skilled a chief executive may be, the events and conditions a president faces can be unmanageable. Zbigniew Brzezinski, President Carter's national security adviser, expressed dismay at the inability of the United States to control events abroad. Particularly vexing had been the Iranian hostage crisis that lasted from November 1979 until the end of the Carter Administration, a total of 14 months during which Iranian insurgents held Americans captive in the U.S. embassy in Tehran. "History is much more the product of chaos than of conspiracy," observed Brzezinski. "The external world's vision of internal decision-making in the Government assumes too much cohesion and expects too much systematic planning. The fact of the matter is that, increasingly, policy makers are overwhelmed by events and information."[16]

The ill-fated rescue mission attempted by the Carter Administration to free the hostages is replete with further examples of events that defied careful planning, including a crash of rescue helicopters in the Iranian desert and military communication snafus. Similarly, in the war against global terrorism led by George W. Bush's administration, U.S. intelligence assets and military forces were unable to corral all of the al Qaeda leaders in Afghanistan, even with the use of America's sophisticated intelligence capabilities and impressive armaments. Nor was the president able to convince allies in Europe to join the United States in condemning Iraq, Iran, and North Korea as an "axis of evil" or to join the "coalition of the willing" to invade and disarm Iraq.

Information Problems

Presidents often face foreign policy difficulties because of **information problems.** The information they have about world affairs can be tantalizingly incomplete. Paradoxically, too much information can be just as paralyzing to a president as too little. The early warning predicting a Japanese attack on Pearl Harbor in 1941 illustrates the point. America's intelligence agencies had intercepted coded Japanese messages about the impending attack, but this information was lost in the "noise" of several conflicting reports from other sources. The key messages floundered in the lower bureaucracy and President Roosevelt never received the warning.

The problem of insufficient information is more common. Research on surprise military attacks makes it plain that, all too often, nations are caught unprepared because of a lack of information about their enemies, or because that information is ambiguous.[17] Intelligence regarding the possible existence of weapons of mass destruction (WMDs) in Iraq remained ambiguous in the lead-up to the Iraq War in 2003. Surveillance satellites and other sophisticated intelligence-gathering equipment have reduced the level of uncertainty, but no administration possesses a crystal ball, and states have become clever at hiding their weapons programs from satellite surveillance.[18]

Time Constraints

Another limitation faced by those who make foreign policy decisions is **time constraints.** Information and time are intimately related. Without sufficient time to gather data and comprehend their meaning, the decision maker must act with an incomplete understanding of events and conditions. Reflecting on the 1962 Cuban missile crisis, President Kennedy said, "If we had had to act in the first twenty-four hours, I don't think … we would have chosen as prudently as we finally did."[19] We now know from archival research in the United States and Russia that a precipitous U.S. military invasion of Cuba could have been repelled by Cubans and their Soviet military advisers armed with over 200 Soviet tactical nuclear warheads, which the Kennedy Administration did not know were in place on the island at the time. The use of nuclear weapons against American troops might well have triggered a full-scale nuclear war between the United States and the Soviet Union.[20]

Issues of Permissibility

A top aide to President Kennedy, Theodore C. Sorensen, adds **permissibility** to the list of constraints. The Constitution, statutes, court decisions, and international law all define what the president is allowed to do, but ambiguities certainly exist. The Constitution, for example, provides only a vague definition of the commander in chief's duties (Article II, Section 2). Presidents are further hemmed in by what others within the government and in other nations are prepared to let them do. Kennedy's use of a naval quarantine during the Cuban missile crisis was facilitated by formal support from the Organization of American States (OAS), comprising most of the governments in the Western Hemisphere, which voted to endorse the military blockade. Thus, Kennedy's decision was sanctioned by international law through the required two-thirds vote of the OAS for such actions. This support lent authority to Kennedy's actions in the eyes of the world. "What is clear is that a President's authority is not as great as his responsibility," concludes Sorensen, "and that what is desirable is always limited by what is possible or permissible."[21]

Available Resources

How would you complete the following statement? "The official most likely to loom largest in the president's thinking when a key decision must be made is ＿＿＿＿＿＿＿."

Sorensen offers this answer: the director of the Office of Management and Budget (OMB), the top financial officer in the executive branch and an administration's expert on **available resources.**

Almost all government programs cost money. Yet a president faces limits on how much money can be spent, or how high taxes can be raised without wreaking havoc on the economy or stirring opposition among voters. For each program, a president must consult closely with the budget director and will always feel pressure to control spending. Lyndon Johnson's simultaneous attempt to rebuild the cities of American and fight a war in Vietnam proved too costly, fueling inflation and leading to the unpopularity that drove him from office. The unprecedented deficit spending by Presidents Ronald Reagan and George H. W. Bush, equivalent to the combined deficits of every president who served before them, was sharply criticized for the potentially devastating effects the debt could cause when the bills came due. When the Cold War ended in 1991, the Clinton Administration focused on eliminating the debt and managed to bring the budget into balance. Large tax cuts and the war against terrorism increased the debt once again during the administration of George W. Bush, raising fears that valued domestic programs would be displaced by a new defense build-up.

Money is only one governmental resource. Others include the number of soldiers available to fight a war; the quantity and quality of weapons in a nation's ordnance; the will or determination of a populace to pursue a difficult course like the war in Vietnam, the current war against terrorism, or the occupation of Iraq; the credibility of a president; the frequency of television appeals the president can make directly to the public without losing its attention; a nation's industrial output; and the supply of talented military and civilian leaders.

As with money, presidents are unlikely to feel they ever have enough of these resources. During the Johnson years, media experts concluded that the president had used television appeals too often in his efforts to muster support for the Vietnam War. The media saturation, combined with the president's lack of candor about the poor progress of the war, led the public either to tune him out or to view his remarks with increasing skepticism, producing what was called a "credibility gap" between the White House and the people.

Previous Commitments

Sorensen reminds us that "no President starts out with a clean slate before him."[22] A new president will attempt to honor not only many of the statements made in the election campaign, but also the policies put in place by earlier presidents and other top officials. Any president faces a long list of **previous commitments** entered into by prior administrations. It would be difficult, for example, for any new president to decide suddenly to withdraw from NATO; too many predecessors have promised America's commitment to this defense pact, which continues to uphold a symbolic sense of U.S.-Canadian-European unity even in the aftermath of the Cold War, however strained by disagreements over issues such as the war against Iraq in 2003. Nor could a president easily abandon a major weapons system placed into production by an earlier administration, for it would be hard to justify the waste of money that had been invested in the weapon's early development.

Bureaucratic Limits

Another limitation on the presidency is well illustrated by President Harry S. Truman's prediction about the experience his successor, General Dwight Eisenhower, would have in the Oval Office. "He'll sit here," foresaw Truman, "and he'll say, 'Do this! Do that!' And nothing will happen. Poor Ike—it won't be a bit like the Army. He'll find it very frustrating."[23] Expressing his own consternation, President Lyndon Johnson once exclaimed: "Power? The only power I've got is nuclear—and I can't use that."[24]

The reality of **bureaucratic limits** was illustrated during the Cuban missile crisis when President Kennedy decided it would be prudent to move his naval blockade closer to Cuba, thereby giving Kremlin leaders more time to evaluate the danger as Soviet ships steamed across the Atlantic toward the island. Kennedy hoped this might buy time until cooler heads prevailed in Moscow and the Soviets ordered vessels nearing the blockade to return to Russia. The U.S. Navy had different ideas, however, about how to conduct this operation, as Secretary of Defense Robert S. McNamara soon discovered.

When McNamara and his deputy met with Navy officials in a heavily guarded inner ring of the Pentagon, McNamara raised incisive questions about the management of the blockade. Finally, the chief of naval operations (CNO) waved the *Manual of Navy Regulations* in the secretary's face and shouted: "It's all in there!"

"I don't give a damn what John Paul Jones would have done," McNamara responded. "I want to know what you are going to do, now."

At the end of this angry exchange, the CNO concluded brusquely: "Now, Mr. Secretary, if you and your deputy will go back to your office, the Navy will run the blockade."[25]

Executive bureaucrats also sometimes have their own agendas, which may be quite distinct from White House objectives. "No matter who is Secretary of Defense, [the Pentagon] is not a rational decision-making organization," concludes a secretary of the Navy from the Reagan Administration. "It is too big. It is big, big, big … it makes any management person laugh out loud."[26] Even mundane matters can be bogged down in bureaucratic resistance. It took two weeks—and presidential intervention—for the Kennedy Administration to convince intelligence officials that the sign "Central Intelligence Agency" should be removed from alongside the George Washington Parkway in Virginia, after the president's brother, Attorney General Robert Kennedy, decided it was indiscreet to advertise the location of America's foremost secret agency. (The sign is now back up.)

The View from the Oval Office

The picture is mixed, then, when the powers of the presidency in foreign policy are evaluated. The president has both constitutional and evolved foreign policy powers, but these are often offset by a host of formal and informal limitations. When it comes to dealing with Congress, the president has a strong constitutionally based stick, the veto power, to halt congressional initiatives that run contrary to presidential preferences. Lawmakers have to muster a two-thirds majority in both chambers to override a veto. Such an extraordinary majority is difficult to achieve. For example, only a small fraction of the vetoes exercised by President George H. W. Bush were overridden by Congress, and only one dealing with foreign policy. By using the veto, Bush was able to strike down many congressional foreign policy initiatives, including the opposition of lawmakers to the joint development of the FSX fighter jet with Japan, as well as congressional efforts to set conditions on the renewal of China's most favored nation trade status.

The president's constitutional right to recognize foreign regimes, stated in Article II, gives the president additional formal powers of importance. Flowing from that authority is the president's prerogative to appoint ambassadors, though with confirmation by the Senate. The president, by custom, has also established the right to choose the nation's national security adviser without Senate confirmation. Section 2 of Article II in the Constitution further names the president as commander in chief, allowing the chief executive considerable discretionary authority over the use of armed intervention abroad. This is the most disputed of all the president's powers. In recent decades, many lawmakers have argued that modern presidents have gone too far in their claims to nearly exclusive control over the use of overt military force by the United States, an allegation examined later in this book.

Nevertheless, these centralizing prerogatives for presidential control over foreign policy are few in number in the Constitution and are largely overshadowed by the constraints on the office, even when coupled with the advantage of ready access to the media enjoyed by the White House. As President Kennedy once remarked, "The President … must wield these powers under extraordinary limitations—and it is these limitations which so often give the problem of choice its complexity and even poignancy."[27] A closer look at the foreign policy bureaucracy in the executive branch corroborates this observation.

THE FOREIGN POLICY BUREAUCRACY

Perhaps nothing so impresses a student of government who tours the nation's capital as the vastness of its public institutions. The Department of Agriculture, which has its own foreign service division, spreads out over several large city blocks, reaching across busy streets with skywalks to connect its various parts. The Department of Commerce, an important player in the shaping of U.S. foreign trade policy, takes a half hour to circumnavigate by foot. The Department of State, home of America's diplomats, has a seemingly endless number of windows in its many-storied complex. The Department of Defense, the giant of them all, is a vast honeycomb of corridors that would present a challenge to even the most accomplished orienteer. These are merely a few of the large government buildings that dominate the streets of Washington and its suburbs like so many feudal fortresses, none with moats but all nonetheless difficult for the White House and the Cabinet to command.

A Bureaucratic Behemoth

Although the president is theoretically in charge of some 3 million workers in the executive branch and responsible for seeing that they obey the thousands of laws and regulations that guide their departments, agencies, bureaus, and offices, in reality the White House has direct control over very few people. The president appoints only a thin layer of officials at the top. These include the highest positions in a department: the secretary, under secretaries, assistant secretaries, deputy assistant secretaries, and some other top

Built in the 1940s to be a military hospital, the Pentagon for the last several decades has been the headquarters for the U.S. Department of Defense. About 30,000 people work here every day.

officials, like the nation's chief trade negotiator (the United States Trade Representative, or USTR)—altogether some 1,500 Schedule C jobs, out of about 9,000 upper-level slots. The president must rely on these Schedule C appointees to imbue their subordinates in the permanent bureaucracy with a sense of loyalty to the foreign policy positions taken by the White House. Often the submerged mass of the iceberg refuses to support those perched on the top.

Within the bureaucracy, the fragmentation of power advocated by the nation's founders has been carried out to an extreme, some critics argue. Beneath the president sprawls a multiplicity of organization charts that easily fill a volume. The *United States Government Manual,* the official handbook of the federal government that contains organization blueprints and the *raisons d'être* for most agencies, is over 800 pages long. The "wiring diagrams" in these pages are static depictions of what in reality are offices that compete with one another for support from their department chiefs, the White House, and the Congress. The size of the departments, along with their differing cultures and complicated array of bureaucratic rivalries, makes them difficult for presidents to manage.

The difficulties of presidential control over the bureaucracy, with respect to foreign or domestic policy, have long been observed by political scientists. In addition to the bureaucracy's internal organizational complexity, bureaucrats often form alliances with committees on Capitol Hill and groups outside government. These **subgovernments** or **iron triangles,** comprising bureaucrats, lawmakers, and lobbyists, are formidable political forces in Washington, D.C. Presidents come and go, but the bonds of subgovernments endure.

For example, many powerful interest groups have a stake in new weapons systems. In the defense industry, that stake is shared as well by corporate managers, stockholders, and labor organizations. During the Reagan years, the United Auto Workers lobbied vigorously on behalf of the MX missile (a land-based ICBM) because it meant jobs for blue-collar workers. Further, defense contracts bring jobs to the home districts and states of lawmakers, and members of Congress also receive substantial campaign contributions from defense industry political action committees (PACs). Upon retirement, generals and admirals often seek employment with the same corporations they provided with contracts while in the Pentagon. Thus, even though presidents have their own views on which weapons systems they prefer, the White House must contend with these other components of the policy process who have their own ideas about desirable weapons (the Pentagon), who seek as many military contracts as possible (labor and corporate management), and who have their eye on increasing the number of jobs back home and PAC money in their campaign till (lawmakers). This is a powerful combination, labeled the "military-industrial complex" by President Eisenhower in his farewell address.

According to sociologist C. Wright Mills in his influential book *The Power Elite*,[28] this triangle of generals, CEOs, and politicians represents the most dominant force in American government for foreign and domestic policy. While Mills's view is too simplistic, this **power elite** sometimes does represent a formidable barrier to presidential preferences. In times of war, presidents give great deference to the judgment of their generals in the field and weapons manufacturers at home. Even in times of peace, the generals and corporate leaders have easy access to officials in high places. Their skills, expertise, and service to the nation are understandably sought by the White House. And lawmakers value both defense contracts that lead to jobs (and votes) in the home district as well as the political backing of affluent corporate leaders. As a result of these close ties they enjoy with lawmakers, if the military and the CEOs fail to gain presidential support for their projects, they have another chance of winning support from Congress, which controls the nation's purse strings.

The sheer size and intricacy of government institutions in Washington throws up another barrier to the president's ability to achieve his preferred policy objectives. An examination of key elements in the foreign policy bureaucracy—the NSC, the Department of Defense, and the Department of State—provides a sense of this complexity. With the exception of the Department of State, which traces its history back to George Washington's administration, the core structure of today's foreign policy establishment has roots in the National Security Acts of 1947 and 1949. These laws brought about an overhaul of America's entire national security apparatus. They consolidated the Army, the Navy, and the newly created Air Force into a single executive department called the Department of Defense (which replaced the Department of War, whose history was as old as the State Department's); set up the CIA, primarily to collate and analyze information deemed necessary for national security; and created the National Security Council. The end result was a significant improvement in the coordination of national security policy, along with an enhancement of White House control over key foreign policy organizations in the government. A major casualty of the reforms was the primacy of the State Department, as the new NSC began to play an increasingly important role in the shaping of American foreign policy.

The National Security Council

The **National Security Council** or **NSC** consists of three key groups of officials: the statutory principals (the president, the vice president, the secretary of state, and the secretary of defense), the statutory advisers (the director of the CIA and the chair of the Joint Chiefs of Staff), and a professional staff. The tie that binds all three groups is the "special assistant to the president for national security affairs," a job title established in the Eisenhower Administration to designate the person who would be the overall director of the NSC's activities. (During the Truman and early Eisenhower years, this position was known as the "executive secretary," in accordance with the 1947 National Security Act.) This cumbersome formal title was shortened under President Richard M. Nixon to "the assistant for national security affairs" or, in today's common usage, "the national security adviser."

The position of national security adviser has become one of great importance in the government of the United States. Initially, officials in Washington viewed the post of national security adviser as little more than a neutral coordinator of information prepared for the president by those government departments and agencies with foreign policy responsibilities. Now, however, as Elizabeth Drew has accurately noted, the national security adviser resides "at the center of the system for making foreign and defense policy."[29]

Clark M. Clifford, a former top White House aide to President Truman and one of the principal drafters of the 1947 National Security Act, once recalled in congressional testimony:

> Senator, your first question had to do with whether or not those of us who drafted the Act contemplated the creation of a position like the national security adviser and did we have in mind that it would become as important as it did.
>
> We had no such thought in mind. It was not even conceived that there would be such a position. After the Act was passed in 1947, an assistant and I for the balance of the time I was there performed that function. We performed it mainly because of relationships that already had been established with State, with [Secretary of State] Dean Acheson in State, and with [Secretary of Defense] Jim Forrestal…. It worked well. The government was not quite as complicated then as it is now, but I think it worked well. As time went on, apparently a need was felt for such a position … each of the presidents felt that they needed this role.[30]

By the 1960s, the office had undergone a metamorphosis into a number of complicated—and sometimes contradictory—roles. As General Colin L. Powell, who served as national security adviser under President Ronald Reagan, once put it: "I was to perform as judge, traffic cop, truant officer, arbitrator, fireman, chaplain, psychiatrist, and occasional hit man."[31] The job had stretched from the original task of paper-coordinator to one of policy adviser and advocate for the president.

The individuals who have served as national security adviser have exhibited a variety of approaches to the job. Some have been engaged only minimally, if at all, in policy advocacy (the early advisers); others have been active policy entrepreneurs and advocates (Kissinger, Brzezinski, and the most recent advisers). Two incumbents in this office during the Reagan years—Robert C. McFarlane and Vice Admiral John M. Poindexter—strayed into questionable foreign policy and intelligence operations. Some national security advisers have become internationally known, none more than Kissinger, who in 1973 combined the job for two years with his position as secretary of state; others, like Gordon Gray and William P. Clark, have been as obscure as museum curators.

Crowding the NSC's agenda is a constant flow of committee and subcommittee meetings, covering everything from budget reviews and crisis management to policy evaluations of specific topics like arms control or regions of the world. The adviser is steadily on the telephone with other top officials, or meeting with them, and occasionally will host foreign representatives in the adviser's West Wing office. In addition, an activist national security adviser faces many managerial tasks: assigning studies for the NSC staff or other experts to prepare for the president; reading and commenting on completed studies, then distilling the findings and recommendations into a report for the president; serving as traffic cop for the constant flow of paper to the Oval Office on security and foreign policy matters from Cabinet officers and other officials; monitoring the implementation of decisions made by the president to ensure they are properly interpreted and carried out by the bureaucracy; and meeting periodically with newspaper, magazine, and television reporters.

According to former adviser Samuel ("Sandy") R. Berger of the Clinton Administration, the principle role of the adviser is to provide the president with information that "he needs to know in addition to what he wants to know … and to keep the process moving in a direction that he wants it to move." Berger stresses, too, that the purpose of the NSC and, therefore, its adviser, lies in "trying to have a coherent decision-making process" and "determining what [the] priorities are and what is important for the rest of the government to focus on."[32]

Another former adviser, Walt W. Rostow of the Johnson Administration, laid out five basic duties for the man or woman who holds the office:

- Gathering information.
- Presenting, sympathetically, the point of view of each relevant Cabinet member.
- Stating his or her own opinion, without becoming domineering.
- Helping to hold together the president's foreign policy team.
- Implementing the president's decision.

Of these duties, the "biggest job" (according to Rostow) is the gathering or "mobilization" of information.[33]

Another former national security adviser, Brent Scowcroft, has advanced a series of "axioms" about the adviser's responsibilities. He or she has to be a policy integrator and an honest broker, and must be willing to concentrate mainly on offering counsel to the president, not making public pronouncements. Further, the adviser should be prepared to defer to the secretary of state as the chief "explicator" of foreign policy. The adviser also has to guard against the temptation of running foreign policy from the White House. He or she must carefully husband the president's time as well, and sharply limit the operational role of the NSC staff. The adviser has to engage only sparingly in diplomacy with foreign nations—and always in tandem with the secretary of state. The adviser must be able to organize the NSC staff to suit the president's "habits, needs, and proclivities." Lastly, the adviser has to work in a close partnership with the director of the Office of Management and Budget, "instead of allowing OMB to make policy by default by dint of its control over money."[34]

A primary obligation of the adviser is to make sure that the president hears from a broad spectrum of opinions before making a decision. For this purpose, Alexander George once proposed the creation of a White House Special Assistant for Multiple Advocacy, who would be responsible for ensuring that presidents hear a full range of policy options.[35] The NSC adviser, if performing properly, already has this responsibility when it comes to national security. The adviser is expected to keep the channels of communication open between the White House and the departments and agencies; to provide a voice for weaker advocates; to dredge new channels, if necessary, in the persistent search for information and policy options to assist the president; and to be alert constantly for malfunctions in the flow of information to, and the implementation of orders from, the White House. This may have been what President George W. Bush had in mind when he described in an October 28, 2003, press conference the role of Condoleezza Rice as the "un-sticker." Her job, the president said, is to "help unstick things that may get stuck."

The adviser position evolved rapidly into an office of considerable authority during the Kennedy years, prodded by President John F. Kennedy's unhappiness about the Bay of Pigs fiasco.[36] The exceptional energy and intellectual abilities of adviser McGeorge Bundy and his successors (well-regarded scholars like Rostow, Kissinger, and Brzezinski), along with the backing of Presidents Kennedy, Johnson, Nixon, and Carter, allowed an expansion of the initial boundaries of the office.

With Henry Kissinger, the adviser position achieved the zenith of its influence. President Nixon relied heavily on his judgment, and Kissinger proved skillful in nurturing a close relationship with his powerful patron. Kissinger took the office of NSC adviser public, becoming a leading spokesman for foreign policy and appearing frequently on television talk shows. When Brzezinski came into that office with the Carter Administration, he created an office of press secretary as part of the NSC system. At times, Brzezinski seemed to exercise as much sway over American foreign policy as Kissinger had achieved. "I'm a synthesizer, analyzer, coordinator," he declared to an interviewer. "I might also be alerter, energizer, implementer, mediator, even lightening rod. All of these roles I play at different times, depending on the issues."[37]

When Ford replaced Nixon as president in 1974, he kept Kissinger on as both his secretary of state and NSC adviser. In 1975, though, the president decided to split these offices back into the hands of two individuals, with Kissinger as secretary of state and Brent Scowcroft (who had been Kissinger's deputy national security adviser) as national security adviser. At the time, Kissinger recalls that he "resented the decision bitterly," but he came to view the division as wise, realizing that a determined secretary of state "cannot fail to have his view heard"—regardless of who is chairing interdepartmental security committees, the secretary or the adviser.[38] Both by personality and philosophy, Scowcroft settled into a less dominant role than Kissinger had displayed as adviser. "I bent over backwards," he remembers, "not to appear to be repeating, frankly, what Henry Kissinger did."[39]

In hopes of toning down the tension and competition between the national security adviser and the secretary of state that occurred most prominently during the Nixon and Carter years, the Reagan Administration vowed to carry on in the style of Scowcroft, not Kissinger or Brzezinski. The first two advisers in this administration, Richard V. Allen and William P. Clark, stuck to the script, and the third and fourth, Robert C. McFarlane and John M. Poindexter, seemed by all accounts destined to continue the trend. The Iran-Contra scandal of 1986, however, pushed the boundaries of the office into a region of dubious propriety, if not outright illegality, especially under Poindexter. To this day Poindexter maintains that the NSC staff never violated the law during the Iran-Contra affair.[40] This interpretation puts him at odds with a number of lawmakers and legal scholars who criticized the NSC staff for violating the Boland amendments prohibiting covert action in Nicaragua and the Hughes-Ryan Act requiring the reporting of covert action to Congress.[41]

During the Clinton Administration, Sandy Berger converted the NSC into what one senior official outside the White House referred to as "by far, the most dominant entity in foreign policy making in [that] administration."[42] President George W. Bush's choice for NSC adviser was Condoleezza Rice, a former provost at Stanford University and an academic specializing in Soviet affairs. Rice proved to be an important go-between in the administration, arbitrating disputes among the principals and weighing in on policy. With the leverage that comes with close ties to the president and proximity to the Oval Office, she assumed an active role as adviser.

Political scientists Cecil V. Crabb and Kevin V. Mulcahy have devised a classification of adviser roles: the administrator, the coordinator, the counselor, and the agent.[43] The adviser as "administrator" is highly deferential to the secretary of state, unwilling to enter into policy advocacy, and—serving as a conveyer belt—devoted to the day-to-day chores of moving national security papers in and out of the Oval Office. The adviser as "coordinator" takes on the added dimension of defining policy options for the president. The category of "counselor" points to an adviser's entry into the world of policy advocacy in the public arena. The counselor presents his or her personal views to the president, then helps the White House articulate its policy initiatives to the media. As "agent," the adviser steps up the level of activism a notch, dominating the national security process and acting as the chief spokesperson for the president on foreign affairs.

Published in 1991, the Crabb-Mulcahy framework does not account for the most recent advisers: Anthony Lake and Sandy Berger of the Clinton Administration, and Condoleezza Rice of George W. Bush's administration. The fluctuations in adviser roles are illustrated in Figure 8.1. From the National Security Act of 1947 through today, the NSC adviser's performance has swung between passive and active stages. During the NSC's first two decades, the advisers moved steadily toward a more assertive stance, as measured by their internal NSC managerial responsibilities and advocacy of administration policy in public forums. This trend reached a high point under Kissinger.

In reaction to Kissinger's dominance over the policymaking process, the high level of adviser activism gave way to a more behind-the-scenes approach under Scowcroft during the Ford Administration. The role of adviser began to rise again under the aggressive leadership of Brzezinski, experienced another decline with the more passive Allen and Clark, and took a disastrous turn upward on the aggressiveness scale with the questionable

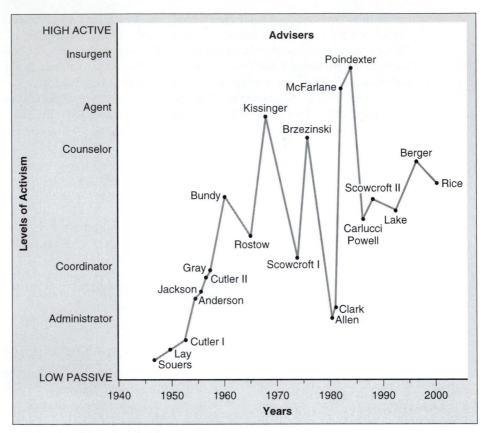

FIGURE 8.1

Fluctuations in the Roles of NSC Advisers

Source: Karl F. Inderfurth and Loch K. Johnson, *Fateful Decisions: Inside the NSC* (New York: Oxford University Press, 2004).

operations carried out under McFarlane and Poindexter—the "insurgent role," in Crabb-Mulcahy terminology. As the Tower Commission investigation into the Iran-Contra affair made clear, the NSC staff had assumed an improper operational role in seeking assistance for the *contras* in Nicaragua in violation of the Boland amendments.[44] When this scandal came to light in 1986, Senator John Glenn (D-Ohio) concluded that the NSC had become a "rogue elephant out of control."[45] Subsequently, the strong personalities of Frank C. Carlucci and Colin L. Powell (who would become secretary of state under George W. Bush) helped to slow a full swing back into an administrator or coordinator role in the wake of the Iran-Contra excesses. With Lake, Berger, and Rice, the role of national security adviser leveled off in the activist counselor mode.

Following a long process of trial and error, and a narrowing oscillation between the extremes of administrator and insurgent, the position of national security adviser has settled into the **counselor role.** The administrator and coordinator roles failed to assist the president effectively in grappling with policy choices, and the insurgent role was dangerous in its lack of accountability to the law and legislative overseers. The goal is an adviser who can provide three vital services: duty as an honest broker, faithfully representing the views and recommendations of the various foreign policy departments; sound and candid advice to the president on national security issues; and skillful public advocacy of the administration's policies—a challenging job description.

The Department of Defense

The **Department of Defense** (DOD), whose headquarters building—the Pentagon—is located in Virginia near the nation's Capital, is responsible for providing the military strength required to deter war and protect the security of the United States. It employs some 2 million men and women in uniform, including 50,000 at sea and 434,000 on foreign soil, as well as 1 million civilians. Seven out of ten workers in the federal government are employed by the DOD. The Department is organized according to functional responsibilities, such as airlift and sealift, intelligence, and research and engineering. Within the Pentagon, the world's largest office building, are layers upon layers of administrative organization, topped by the secretary of defense (who must be a civilian). According to one defense authority, the "Pentagon is choking on bureaucracy."[46] Thirty thousand employees work there, with another 120,000 staff people in nearby buildings.

At times, the secretary of defense has been the most prominent member of the president's Cabinet, as during the war in Vietnam when Robert S. McNamara proved a forceful proponent of U.S. intervention in Southeast Asia, or when Donald Rumsfeld guided America's 2003 Iraq War with a strong hand. The secretary of defense is assisted by a deputy secretary, undersecretaries, assistant secretaries, and a host of other directors, chiefs, and assistants (see Figure 8.2).

The office of the **Joint Chiefs of Staff (JCS)** comprises the principal military advisers to the president, headed by a chairperson selected from one of the military services. The JCS is responsible for the preparation of strategic planning. In addition to the chair, the JCS consists of the chief of staff, United States Army; the chief of naval operations; and the chief of staff, United States Air Force. The commandant of the Marine Corps is an equal participant of the JCS when it addresses subjects germane to the marines. The JCS is assisted by a Joint Staff comprising 400 officers selected in equal numbers from the Army, the Navy (including the Marine Corps), and the Air Force.

The four services tend to be parochial and resistant to effective interservice coordination, and they busily cultivate alliances on Capitol Hill. Yet some important reforms have taken place. During the Carter years, for example, women were fully integrated into the Army. Additionally, Senators Barry Goldwater (R-Arizona) and Sam Nunn (D-Georgia) joined forces with Representative William E. "Bill" Nichols (D-Alabama) to tackle the problem of interservice coordination. Following several years of legislative jockeying, they succeeded in passing a law in 1986, labeled the Goldwater-Nichols Act, that made the JCS chair a more powerful figure and improved coordination among the services. As one historian writes: "The act made the JCS chairman the principal military adviser [to the president], transferred to him the duties previously performed by the corporate JCS, and added new duties. To assist the chairman, Congress created the position of vice chairman as the second-ranking officer. Last, Congress gave the chairman full authority over the Joint Staff."[47] The new law also clarified the chain of command in

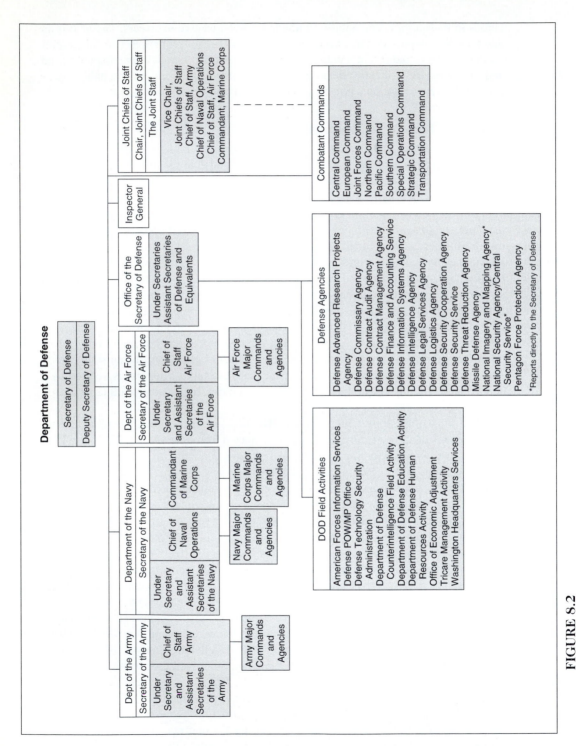

FIGURE 8.2
Organization Chart for the Department of Defense

times of combat, which would run from the president to the secretary of defense to the combatant commander in the field. The JSC and the chair were explicitly removed from this chain. As a result of the law, some 30 levels of authority between the president and the field commander were removed, allowing much swifter military operations.

Despite these important reforms, the DOD continues to display a go-it-alone attitude, with minimal efforts to coordinate policy with the Department of State and other organizations in the foreign policy establishment, or with international organizations like the Red Cross. As one historian emphasizes, "The Pentagon's change-resistant culture represents its greatest organizational weakness."[48]

The Department of Defense absorbs a major portion of the federal budget each year. In 2003, the total obligational authority for DOD equaled about $449 billion, excluding special appropriations for the wars in Iraq and Afghanistan. This accounts for almost 19 percent of the total federal budget and, except for Social Security, is the largest single item. DOD's share of the gross domestic product (GDP) stood at about 5 percent in 1980, approached 6 percent in 1983, and stayed close to that level through 1987. The percentage then declined throughout the rest of the Cold War and after, reaching a nadir of about 3 percent of GDP in 1999. The war against terrorism will bring about a rise again in the percentage when all supplemental spending is added in.

According to recent projections by the Congressional Budget Office (CBO), current defense plans could require an average of $472 billion a year through 2009 and an average of $533 billion a year between 2010 and 2022.[49] Even in 2003, the defense expenditures of the United States surpassed the combined defense expenditures of all the other countries in the world. In current dollars, the Reagan Administration spent over $1 trillion in its first five years in office, nearly equaling the total spent by Presidents Nixon, Ford, and Carter over their combined 12 years in office.[50] George W. Bush's administration is on course to break Ronald Reagan's defense spending records.

Historically, the Army spends more of its budget on troops than on arms and other equipment. As a result, the Army has received the smallest share of the investment funding among the services: about $22 billion a year from 1980 to 2003, compared with $43 billion for the Department of the Navy (which excludes the Marine Corps) and $48 billion for the Air Force. The budget for the Army is projected to increase, though, with more spending on new helicopters, missile defense programs, computers, and combat vehicles. Navy spending on procurement will focus in the future primarily on expanding its fleet from about 300 ships today to 375 by 2022, with an emphasis on smaller littoral combat ships (LCSs). The Navy and Marine Corps plan to integrate their tactical aircraft forces more fully, which will allow a cutback in the number of new planes required. Typically, the Air Force has the largest investment budget of any of the services. Costs will rise as the Joint Strike Fighter (JSF) moves from development into production and as intelligence as well as command-and-control capabilities are enhanced in the war against terrorism. New systems are being developed to replace America's reliance on bombers and land-based intercontinental ballistic missiles (ICBMs).

In addition to funding for the Departments of the Army, Navy, and Air Force, the DOD's budget provides money for a variety of specialized agencies engaged in advanced research, the development of missile defenses, overseeing special operations, and developing and managing information systems. George W. Bush's administration placed a high priority on further development of a ground-based interceptor (GBI) system, designed to protect against incoming ballistic missiles—the "Star Wars" program initiated by President Reagan. The GBI system has had its critics, though. In 2004, a group of 49 retired generals and admirals issued a statement critical of the program, calling for its abandonment and a redirection of the billions of dollars invested in the program each year, roughly $53 billion planned for the next five years. They advocate shifting funds to more immediate homeland defense projects, such as improving harbor and railroad security against terrorist attacks. Overseas, Russia expressed concern about the Star Wars strategy pursued by the United States and vowed to develop "hypersonic" missiles that could pierce the GBI umbrella.

The growth of the Department of Defense over the years was a result of the perceived Soviet threat to U.S. security during the Cold War, which seemed to require American intervention in the Korean War and the conflict in Vietnam as a way of warding off communist global expansion. The fear of global communism led the United States to maintain a large standing military force, much of it dispersed across Western Europe and Asia. Since the end of the Cold War, the Pentagon has been called upon to depose heinous regimes in Afghanistan and Iraq, fight small regional wars in such places as Bosnia and Kosovo, and undertake a global campaign against terrorism—missions used by the military to argue successfully for another dramatic build-up of arms by the United States. The most poignant question related to defense has long been: "How much is enough?" That debate continues into the twenty-first century, as the United States faces increasing opposition around the world (even among friends) to its burgeoning military might and, at home, growing concern about spiraling deficits fueled by military spending. Critics have been particularly concerned that America's generals and admirals overseas—"proconsuls"—are now taking on the role of diplomacy once reserved for seasoned diplomats in the Department of State.[51]

The Department of State

The **Department of State,** the oldest Cabinet-level department in the executive branch, is intricate in spite of its small size (about 10,000 personnel in Washington, D.C., and another 7,000 abroad). The secretary of state is, at least officially, the chief foreign policy adviser to the president, but as we have seen, the reality of foreign policy decision making is sometimes different as national security advisers have risen in prominence since the Kennedy Administration.

The task of the Department of State, as loftily stated by two scholars, is "nothing less than to try, until all efforts are proven in vain, to find a path through which the United States and the rest of the world can be led to security and peace."[52] Toward this noble objective, the secretary of state is assisted by a deputy secretary and four under secretaries: one each for political affairs, economic affairs, security assistance, and management. The secretary also has on call one or more ambassadors at large, who may be dispatched to conduct special negotiations anywhere around the world. In addition, five assistant secretaries direct geographic bureaus for African Affairs, European Affairs, East Asian and Pacific Affairs, Western Hemisphere Affairs, and Near Eastern and South Asian Affairs (see Figure 8.3). They are assisted by country desk officers, who serve as

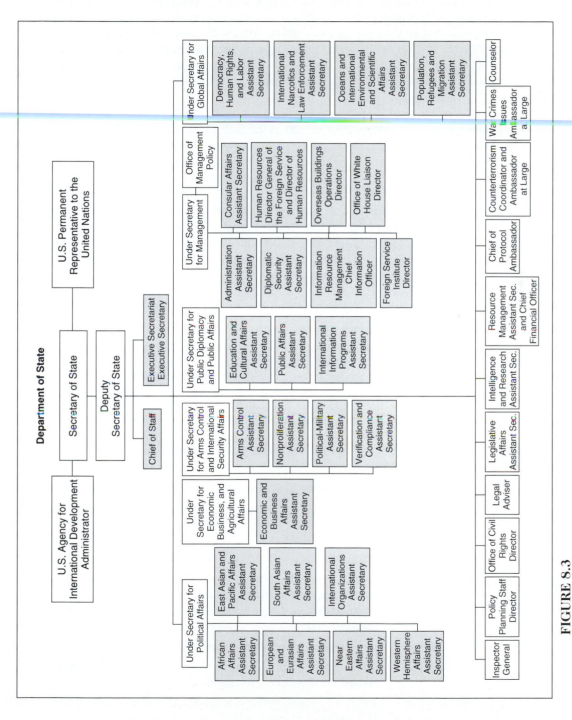

FIGURE 8.3

Organization Chart for the Department of State

the key point of contact in Washington for U.S. ambassadors and the rest of the "country teams" in American embassies abroad. The department also has several functional bureaus, including Educational and Cultural Affairs; Economic and Business Affairs; Intelligence and Research; International Organization Affairs; Public Affairs; Security and Consular Affairs; Political-Military Affairs; and Oceans and International Environmental and Scientific Affairs. The Department's budget hovers around a relatively paltry $5 billion.

The foreign service, with responsibilities for the day-to-day conduct of America's relations with other countries, is the heart of the State Department. The 8,000 men and women of this elite cadre, selected through perhaps the most rigorous entrance examinations in the government, serve in over 134 embassies, 10 missions, 68 consulates general, and a few other offices, as well as within the department's headquarters building in a section of Washington, D.C., known as "Foggy Bottom." Their reports filed from overseas provide valuable information that informs the making of foreign policy decisions.

Inside headquarters, country desk officers keep daily watch over all the countries in the world, reading the secret and unclassified cables and other documents that stream into the Department of State from U.S. embassies in all corners of the globe. Although low on the organizational totem pole, the country desk officer plays a vital role as the person with first contact between the department and its envoys abroad. He or she must make the initial response to incoming information from foreign service officers. As Snyder and Furniss note:

> The desk officer spends a good part of his time talking personally with others in the department and elsewhere within the government. He consults his immediate superiors to receive instructions on policy matters, to relay orally information of importance, to maintain proper coordination of action within the same geographic area. This last function may require formal staff meetings, but more likely it will be handled on an informal level without prior arrangement. Finally, the desk officer usually attends at least one but sometimes three or four committee meetings, either intra- or interdepartmental, possibly in his own right, but more often as representative of his office or bureau, or even of the Secretary of State.[53]

A typical day in the life of a country desk officer looks something like the following:[54]

8:00–9:00 a.m.	reads mail and cables from foreign service officers overseas; reads newspapers.
9:00–10:00 a.m.	staff conference with other desk officers.
10:00–12:00 a.m.	conferences with representatives from other government departments and agencies, such as Agriculture and the U.S. Trade Representative to review pending legislation or policy implementation.
12:00–1:00 p.m.	lunch with colleagues or foreign officials.
1:00–2:00 p.m.	drafts messages for U.S. embassies overseas, walks the drafts around the department for clearance.
2:00–3:00 p.m.	writes a personal, informal letter to a chargé d'affaires in the U.S. embassy in Paris.

3:00–4:00 p.m.	attends conference to brief the under secretary of commerce about an approaching international trade fair in Punta del Este.
4:00–4:30 p.m.	briefs a university researcher going abroad to teach on a Fulbright scholarship.
4:30–5:30 p.m.	reads cables and memoranda that have arrived during the day; writes responses and seeks clearance.
5:30–6:30 p.m.	reads intelligence and other reports relevant to his or her country.

A U.S. **ambassador** is the personal representative of the president to a foreign country. During the 1800s, America's diplomatic corps fell prey to the spoils system that was a part of the government at the time, and the quality of its representation abroad plummeted. Regardless of temperament or training for diplomatic work, wealthy people could essentially buy ambassadorships by contributing large sums of money to the campaigns of would-be presidents. Often the results were less than satisfactory. One American ambassador to Persia had a habit of spitting tobacco juice on the expensive Persian carpets of his hosts; another assigned to a Latin American nation "made a practice of walking around the house naked, continually trailed by a native girl bearing a tray of Scotch whisky, soda, and ice."[55]

The Foreign Service Act of 1915 finally introduced a merit system into the diplomatic corps, and the Rogers Act of 1924 turned the foreign service into a respected professional operation, with an improved merit system, better pay, and sounder administrative practices. Given the modest salary of government officials, private wealth is still necessary to serve as ambassador in the largest diplomatic posts—London, Paris, Berlin. But for the most part, today's State Department is able to assign overseas many of the nation's best minds (and best manners) to represent the United States, regardless of the personal affluence of the individual.

Tensions between the Departments of Defense and State

The Departments of Defense and State make life all the more complicated for presidents by often holding quite separate views of the world and how to respond to foreign threats. The Department of Defense has traditionally (although not always) been predisposed toward the use of military action; here is the home of the warriors. The Department of State, in contrast, has traditionally been inclined—as one might guess—to advocate the power of diplomacy; here is the home of peacemakers.

The Cuban missile crisis provides an illustration of this dichotomy. The pressures for an air strike against Cuba came from the DOD, while the Department of State advocated a more cautious approach that relied on diplomatic channels in the UN and elsewhere. With respect to the war against global terrorism proclaimed by George W. Bush in 2001, leaders in the DOD argued for extending the military attacks against terrorists from the initial battlefield in Afghanistan into other nations, like the Philippines, Yemen, and—a much more far-reaching proposal—Iraq. The State Department was less inclined to rush into further military commitments beyond the one already underway in Afghanistan. During the Reagan Administration, however, these departmental views were sometimes reversed, with State advocating the use of force from time to time and Defense moving more cautiously—an apparent reaction by the armed services to the war in Vietnam and their unwillingness to become involved in military ventures again without the full and clear support of America's political leaders in both the executive and legislative branches.

During the Nixon and Carter administrations, the Department of State served as a greenhouse for nurturing détente with the Soviet Union. In contrast, the DOD was notorious for its "worst-case" analysis of Soviet military intentions, projecting a much more negative view of future U.S.-Soviet relations.

Over the next three chapters, we will examine additional aspects of how the Defense and the State Departments influence the making of American foreign policy. First, though, we examine the contributions of some other departments and agencies.

Bureaucratic Balkanization

The foreign policy programs and operations conducted by the Departments of Defense and State would, alone, be enough to keep a conscientious president burning the midnight oil. Yet these leviathans represent only a fraction of the leadership challenge. Almost every major agency in the government has some sort of international component, involved in negotiations of one kind or another with other nations, often with little or no guidance or control from the White House, the State Department, or Congress. As one observer noted over 25 years ago, before globalization lead to an even greater involvement by U.S. government agencies in international activities: "With over 700 international conferences a years, transnational collegiums of professionals in agriculture, atomic energy, meteorology, satellites, and health tend to work directly with one another with little supervision by the foreign-policy agencies (basically State) in staff conferences, drawing up technical guidelines or reaching consensual decisions."[56] James Madison may well wonder if the seeds of institutional division he and his colleagues sowed in 1787 have borne too much fruit.

Frequently executive agencies pursue their own agendas, not necessarily those of the president or Congress. "Career officials, including those who will come to head organizations such as the Joint Chiefs of Staff, often develop their position largely by calculating the national interest in terms of the organizational interests of the career service to which they belong," writes Morton Halperin.[57] The Air Force, for instance, steadfastly resisted efforts to develop ICBMs at the expense of manned bombers, which are considered the heart and soul of the Air Force mission. "Sitting in [missile] silos just cannot compare to flying bombers," Halperin notes, summing up the Air Force view. The priorities of the White House and the Secretary of Defense be damned; the Air Force generals wanted to *fly*!

Advocacy of narrow bureaucratic interests can lead to considerable strife within the executive branch. Another experienced observer of American policymaking during the Cold War saw what she termed a **Balkanization** of the foreign policy establishment, "with little groups putting as much energy into planning against each other as into planning how to deal with the Soviet Union."[58] As true as this is in the Departments of State, Defense, and elsewhere, it is perhaps even more true in the nation's intelligence community.

The U.S. intelligence community provides a vivid illustration of the organizational divisions that have plagued the president's efforts to guide the nation toward a unified foreign policy. The problems begin inside the CIA itself, the premier U.S. intelligence agency, established in 1947 in hopes of preventing the United States from being taken by surprise as it was by the Japanese attack against Pearl Harbor in 1941. At "the Agency," as insiders refer to the CIA, a variety of cultural enclaves resist cooperation with one another and battle transitory presidents and directors of central intelligence (DCIs) for control over the Agency.

Fissures within the CIA

Admiral Stansfield Turner, DCI from 1977 to 1981, compared running the Central Intelligence Agency to "operating a power plant from a control room with a wall containing many impressive levers that, on the other side of the wall, had been disconnected."[59] When Turner assumed office, he began telling CIA officers what he wanted done. Nothing happened. "I would *order* them to do things," he says, "and nothing would happen." The Directorate of Operations (DO) proved to be the entity most resistant to higher management inside the Agency.

In desperation, Turner asked his top CIA deputy, an up-through-the-ranks DO officer, for help in implementing the orders. The deputy's response was to convene 500 of the Agency's top officials in the CIA's main auditorium, known as "the Bubble." His counsel to the assembled leaders was: be patient, Turner will soon wise up to how the CIA works. When the DCI learned about this meeting, he was livid. Turner viewed himself as the boss and the president's spymaster; the CIA would have to come around to him, not the other way around. As he recalls, "The Agency's attitude was: 'Only we know how to do this.' The intelligence professionals just wanted a figurehead on the seventh floor and that was not my style."[60]

The DO was consistently his biggest headache. Even in his third year at the helm, Turner sensed that the DO rarely kept him adequately informed of its operations in the field. "I wasn't going to try to tell them how to spy," he recalls, "but, in order to pass judgment on an operation, I did want to know: what's the probability you'll get caught, and what's the product you're going to get?" The DO preferred to keep him in the dark— or, at least, so Turner felt. Particularly exasperated by one instance of insubordination, he took steps to discipline a couple of DO officers. Rather than support his efforts, the CIA closed ranks against him, sharply resisting intrusion by this outside military man and his uniformed aides. As Turner recalls, "Not one CIA professional concurred with my instant reaction to fire the two men."[61]

A subsequent DCI reflected on how the CIA had intentionally obstructed Turner's attempts to gain control of the permanent intelligence bureaucracy. "I had learned a valuable lesson working for him," remembered Robert M. Gates, a career CIA analyst. "I now knew that I never wanted to be DCI—anyone who wanted the job clearly didn't understand it."[62] Despite these misgivings, Gates eventually did become director, but his memoirs are a portrait of frustration. Even with this CIA professional in charge, the intelligence bureaucracy—again, chiefly the Directorate of Operations—resisted direction from the DCI's office on the Agency's seventh floor.

President Clinton's first DCI, James Woolsey, had his troubles with the DO, too. After cracking down on the lax security that had permitted DO officer Aldrich H. Ames to sell secrets to the Kremlin, he found to his amazement that the DO's own leaders had decided to confer medals on the very officers he was attempting to punish—a clear signal from the DO to back off its turf. Retreating from his initial impulse to dismiss the officers, as recommended by the Agency's inspector general, Woolsey elected merely to reprimand 11 senior DO managers. When Woolsey's successor, John Deutch (1995–1997), attempted to penalize another group of DO officers for improper activities in Guatemala (they failed to report to Congress and the Justice Department on the CIA's ties to a Guatemalan colonel believed linked to two murders), he became the first DCI ever booed by Agency officers gathered in the Bubble. Three years later, as Deutch, then retired, found himself under investigation for having improperly taken classified intelligence documents home to work on when he was director, the DO bestowed a prestigious CIA medal on one of the officers Deutch had disciplined.

Fissures within the Intelligence Community

The problems of intelligence leadership go beyond the internal workings of the CIA to include the other fourteen agencies in the U.S. intelligence community. Only a Yugoslavian definition of "community" could apply to this sprawling establishment (see Figure 8.4), which in addition to the CIA includes the Defense Intelligence Agency (DIA), the National Security Agency (NSA), five armed services intelligence units, the National Reconnaissance Office (NRO), the new National Geospatial-Intelligence Agency (NGA), the Bureau of Intelligence and Research (in the State Department), the Federal Bureau of Investigation (FBI), and intelligence units in the Treasury, Homeland Security, and Energy Departments.

These agencies have been largely resistant to guidance from the DCI, even though President Truman established a *Central* Intelligence Agency precisely to overcome the institutional fragmentation that had plagued U.S. intelligence before and during the Second World War. Former Representative Lee H. Hamilton (D-Indiana), former chair of the House Intelligence Committee, states: "We don't really have a Director of Central Intelligence. The DCI at CIA controls only a very small portion of the assets of the intelligence community, and there are so many entities you don't have any Director."[63]

Over several administrations, the secretary of defense has stepped into this intelligence vacuum and tilted intelligence increasingly toward support of military operations (SMO, in the inevitable Pentagon acronym), at the expense of the DCI's more civilian orientations, such as the gathering of information on international economic opportunities and support to diplomatic activities—trying to prevent the outbreak of war in the first place. As a recent staff director of the House Intelligence Committee warned, "There is a need to rebuild a strategic, or what we sometimes call the national, capability to end what has been an absolute and total fixation on near-term, tactical [read military] intelligence."[64] This perspective is shared by Representative Porter Goss (R-Florida), the former chair of the House Intelligence Committee appointed DCI in 2004. "The DCI needs greater capability, since he is the chief intelligence architect," he argues. "We have a management problem designed for failure, and it's amazing it works as well as it does. We need more comprehensive management."[65]

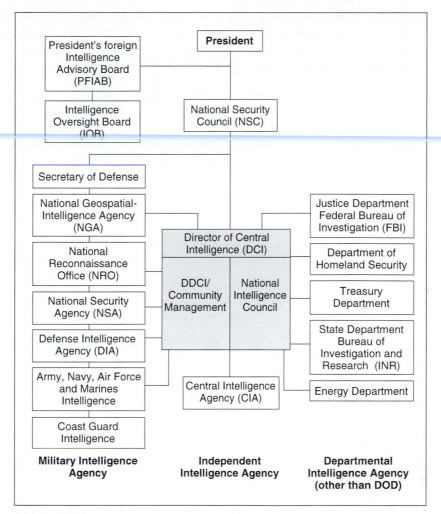

FIGURE 8.4
The U.S. Intelligence Community

Source: Adapted from Loch K. Johnson, *Bombs, Bugs, Drugs and Thugs: Intelligence and America's Quest for Security* (New York: New York University Press, 2002), p. 3.

In the wake of the September 11, 2001, terrorist attacks in the United States, the CIA and the rest of the intelligence community came under fire for their failure to provide specific and timely information about the activities of the terrorist group al Qaeda. The FBI and the CIA proved unable or unwilling to share information with one another about al Qaeda operations around the world, or even about the entry into the United States prior to September 11 of two known al Qaeda operatives. The attacks were not only a U.S. intelligence failure; they were a policy failure too, because the CIA had warned the president and other officials as early as 1995 that America could become a victim of "aerial terrorism," with terrorists filling airplanes with explosives and flying them into skyscrapers.[66] Yet nothing was done to tighten airport security. The terrorists, it turned out, had cunningly calculated that explosives were unnecessary; the volatile high-octane jet fuel would suffice.

In an effort to improve America's defenses against attack, George W. Bush's administration established in 2003 a Department of Homeland Security, which is explored in Chapter 12. As with all new departments, DHS has experienced growing pains and is still a long way from defining and effectively carrying out its responsibilities. Its main mission is to pull together the lines of communications and intelligence necessary to achieve a rapid sharing of information among threat defenders, as well as first responders, at the federal, state, and local levels.

EXECUTIVE COMMAND AND CONTROL OVER FOREIGN POLICY

The looseness in the chain of command within the intelligence agencies—and, indeed, the executive branch as a whole—has alarmed many observers. "In action after action, responsibility for decisions is as fluid and restless as quicksilver, and there seems to be neither a person nor an organization on whom it can be fixed," writes Roger Hilsman, who served as a senior official in the Department of State. "At times the point of decision seems to have escaped into the labyrinth of governmental machinery, beyond layers and layers of bureaucracy."[67]

Operations carried out by the CIA provide an example. In 1983, Representative Edward P. Boland, chairman of the House Intelligence Committee, stressed that the CIA was "almost like a rogue elephant, doing what it wanted to."[68] This harsh judgment came from a deep sense of exasperation over CIA efforts to circumvent his legislation that limited secret paramilitary operations in Nicaragua.

Within the CIA, instances have occurred in which units have planned and implemented aggressive operations abroad without the approval or even the awareness of authorities outside the Agency. In one example, James Angleton, chief of CIA counterintelligence from 1954 to 1974, is reported to have doctored the famous "secret speech" of Soviet premier Nikita Khrushchev. By adding deceptive paragraphs to the speech, then circulating it throughout Eastern Europe, Angleton evidently hoped to stimulate an uprising against the Soviet regime by painting an even more venal portrait of the Stalinist era than did the unadulterated speech itself.[69] The risk in Angleton's scheme lay in the possibility that, if the CIA's hand were discovered, the entire secret speech might have been dismissed as an American fabrication—a U.S. "disinformation" operation.

Moreover, as in any organization, individuals working for the CIA may simply ignore properly authorized policies, guidelines, directives, orders, and laws promulgated by officials. A CIA manual advocating assassinations in Nicaragua in 1984—apparently never approved by the president or even the managers of the CIA and in violation of a 1976 executive order prohibiting assassinations—is a well-known illustration.[70] Another is the secret sale of arms to Iran in exchange for hostages in 1986, an operation never reported to Congress and leading to the Iran-Contra scandal. The Director of Central Intelligence at the time, William J. Casey, advised against informing Congress, despite a law (the Hughes-Ryan Act) to the contrary.[71]

McGeorge Bundy, who as national security adviser chaired the 303 Committee, the NSC panel responsible for the approval of CIA operations during the Kennedy years, has testified that "it can happen, and I think it has happened, that an operation is presented in one way to [the 303 Committee] and executed in a way that is different from what the committee thought it had authorized."[72] The hiring of a mobster by a middle-rank CIA officer in the 1960s as a means for killing Fidel Castro is striking evidence of this possibility. According to sworn testimony before a Senate investigative committee in 1975, members of the Kennedy NSC knew nothing of the CIA's alliance with the underworld.[73]

A constant quandary with respect to the foreign policy bureaucracy is how to control overzealousness or plain unlawfulness, not just at the apex of an organization but at lower echelons even less visible to the public, to overseers in Congress, to the president, or even to agency managers themselves. This difficulty is magnified in the national security apparatus, whose activities are virtually invisible to the public. Commenting on this problem during the Carter years, a senior CIA official said in anguish with reference to his officers trained in paramilitary operations: "What do you do with the fire hoses when there's no fire!"[74] Ruthless former Nicaragua National Guard members in the *contra* army, underworld figures, and ideologically fervent Cuban exiles have numbered among the CIA agents who have proved difficult—sometimes impossible—for even the CIA to control, not to mention more distant White House officials.

SUMMARY

This chapter has emphasized the limitations of presidential power, noting that executive departments and career bureaucrats are often anything but allies of the White House. Their ability to resist the blandishments of even the most charming chief executives is widely recorded. This is frustrating for presidents; after all, bureaucrats are on the president's side—or, at any rate, they are at least in the same branch of government. More foreboding still to the president is the fact that foreign policy authority lodged in the White House is often subject to checks and balances by Congress and the courts, which have an historical obligation to be skeptical about the objectives and methods of the executive branch. By virtue of the Constitution, Congress and the courts stand separate from the bureaucracy and, even more than the bureaucrats, can thwart the foreign policy of the mightiest of presidents.

Those who crafted the U.S. Constitution did not believe efficiency was the cardinal virtue for good government or foreign policy. If efficiency was their goal, they would have given greater authority to the president, but they rejected broad executive powers to protect against autocracy.

There are three primary models of foreign policy decision making. The first argues that decisions should be made by the president and executive branch because of the urgency of many foreign policy decisions and because the intelligence apparatus in the executive branch provides the president with better information. The second asserts that Congress should make most decisions, a view supported by conservatives, isolationists, and democratic theorists who hold that members of the House are closer to the people because of reelection pressures. The third model argues for constitutional balance, which emphasizes foreign policy cooperation between coequal branches. Each model can be observed operating at different times.

Beyond constitutional authority, the president enjoys preeminence in foreign policy because of greater access than any elected official to information, control over resources, and the simple ability to act. Limits on presidential power include the nature of the international setting, information problems, time constraints, issues of permissibility, the availability of resources, previous commitments, and bureaucratic barriers on the exercise of power, including the sheer size and intricacy of government institutions.

The key executive branch bureaucracies involved in foreign policy are the National Security Council, operationally headed by the president's national security adviser; the Department of Defense, under the secretary of defense; and the Department of State, headed by the secretary of state. The office of the Joint Chiefs of Staff comprises the principal military advisers to the president, headed by a chairperson selected from one of the military services. In addition to these key players, almost every major agency in the government has an international component, involved in negotiations of one kind or another with other nations, often with little or no guidance or control from the White House, the State Department, or Congress. Frequently executive agencies pursue their own agendas, not necessarily those of the president or the Congress, with narrow bureaucratic interests sometimes leading to considerable strife within the executive branch. This has been especially true within the national security departments and agencies.

The looseness in the chain of command within the intelligence community and, indeed, the executive branch as a whole has alarmed many observers. Within the Central Intelligence Agency, instances have occurred in which units planned and implemented aggressive operations abroad without the approval or even the awareness of authorities outside the Agency.

Clearly, executive departments and career bureaucrats are not necessarily allies of the White House. Their ability to ignore the authority of even the most charming chief executive is widely recorded. This is frustrating for presidents, but more foreboding to the president still is the fact that presidential foreign policy authority is often subject to checks and balances by Congress and the courts, to which we turn in the next chapter.

KEY TERMS AND CONCEPTS

presidential model of foreign policy
legislative model of foreign policy
constitutional balance model of foreign
   policy
limits on presidential power
international setting
information problems
time constraints
permissibility
available resources
previous commitments

bureaucratic limits
subgovernments (iron triangles)
power elite
National Security Council (NSC)
national security advisor roles
Department of Defense (DOD)
Joint Chiefs of Staff (JCS)
Department of State
ambassador
Balkanization of foreign policy

THINKING CRITICALLY

1. What are the advantages and drawbacks to the model of constitutional balance in foreign affairs, in which both the executive and legislative branches have strong involvement in the making of foreign policy?

2. How would you evaluate the consequences of greater congressional involvement in foreign affairs since the 1960s?

3. Providing concrete examples, assess the extent to which Congress has undermined the ability of the president to act with speed and efficiency in foreign affairs.

4. From your perspective, what is the proper role for the national security adviser in foreign affairs? Why?

5. From your perspective, what is the proper role for the Director of Central Intelligence in foreign affairs? Why?

6. To what extent has institutional gridlock gripped the foreign policy decisionmaking process in the United States?

7. To what extent do the personalities of individual presidents and cabinet members affect the shaping of foreign policy decisions? Provide examples to support your case.

NOTES

1. Professor Laurence H. Tribe, Harvard Law School, quoted by Stuart Taylor Jr., "Reagan's Defenders Arguing He Can Defy Congress's Ban," *New York Times* (May 17, 1987): 1A.
2. Charles E. Lindblom, *Intelligence of Democracy* (New York: Free Press, 1965).
3. See, for example, Harold Laski, *The American Presidency* (New York: Harper and Row, 1949).
4. See, for example, Ernest S. Griffith, *Congress: Its Contemporary Role* (New York: New York University Press, 1961).
5. See Arthur M. Schlesinger Jr., *The Imperial Presidency* (Boston: Houghton Mifflin, 1973).
6. Gordon S. Jones and John A. Marini, eds., *The Imperial Congress: Crisis in the Separation of Powers* (New York: Pharos Books, 1989).
7. Loch K. Johnson, *The Making of International Agreements* (New York: New York University Press, 1984).
8. Quoted in *U.S. News & World Report* (May 2, 1983): 29.
9. John P. Burke and Fred I. Greenstein, *How Presidents Test Reality: Decisions on Vietnam, 1954 and 1965* (New York: Russell Sage Foundation, 1989), p. 51.
10. Chalmers M. Roberts, "The Day We Didn't Go to War," *Reporter* 11 (September 14, 1954): 31–35. See also Melanie Billings-Yun, *Decision against War: Eisenhower and Dien Bien Phu, 1954* (New York: Columbia University Press, 1988); Fred I. Greenstein, *The Hidden-Hand Presidency: Eisenhower as Leader* (Baltimore: Johns Hopkins University Press, 1994); and George C. Herring and Richard H. Immerman, "Eisenhower, Dulles and Dienbienphu: 'The Day We Didn't Go to War' Revisited," *Journal of American History* 71 (1984): 343–363.
11. Warren M. Christopher, "Ceasefire between the Branches: A Compact in Foreign Affairs," *Foreign Affairs* 60 (Summer 1982): 999.
12. Thomas E. Cronin, "Superman, Our Textbook President," *Washington Monthly* 2 (October 1970): 47–54.
13. Clinton Rossiter, *The American Presidency*, rev. ed. (New York: New American Library, 1960), pp. 69, 108.
14. Theodore H. White, *The Making of the President 1960* (New York: Atheneum, 1961), p. 441.
15. See, for example, Richard E. Neustadt, *Presidential Power: The Politics of Leadership from FDR to Carter* (New York: Wiley, 1980).

16. Quoted in the *New York Times* (January 18, 1981): 3.

17. Richard K. Betts, *Surprise Attack: Lessons for Defense Spending* (Washington, D.C.: Brookings Institution, 1982).

18. Loch K. Johnson, "The CIA's Weakest Link," *Washington Monthly* 33 (July/August 2001): 9–14.

19. Theodore C. Sorensen, *Decision-Making in the White House: The Olive Branch or the Arrows* (New York: Columbia University Press, 1963), p. 30.

20. Robert S. McNamara, remarks, University of Georgia (February 21, 1987), Athens, Georgia. For an overview, see John Lewis Gaddis, *We Now Know: Rethinking Cold War History* (New York: Oxford University Press, 1997).

21. Sorensen, *Decision-Making in the White House,* p. 27.

22. Sorensen, *Decision-Making in the White House,* p. 33.

23. Quoted by Neustadt, *Presidential Power,* p. 9.

24. Comment by Senator Hubert H. Humphrey (D-Minnesota), Congressional Fellows Program, American Political Science Association, Washington, D.C. (February 7, 1977).

25. Elie Abel, *The Missile Crisis* (Philadelphia: Lippincott, 1966), pp. 154–156.

26. John F. Lehman Jr., quoted by John H. Cusman Jr., "Ex-Insider Who Elects to Remain on Outside," *New York Times* (January 6, 1989): A11.

27. President John F. Kennedy, remarks in the preface to Sorensen, *Decision-Making in the White House*, p. xii.

28. C. Wright Mills, *The Power Elite* (New York: Oxford University Press, 1959).

29. Elizabeth Drew, "A Reporter at Large: Brzezinski," *New Yorker* (July 1, 1978): 90.

30. Hearings, Senate Foreign Relations Committee (1980), cited in Karl F. Inderfurth and Loch K. Johnson, *Fateful Decisions: Inside the National Security Council* (New York: Oxford University Press, 2004), pp. 132–133.

31. Colin Powell, with Joseph E. Perisco, *My American Journey: An Autobiography* (New York: Random House, 1995), p. 352.

32. *A Forum on the Role of the National Security Advisor,* cosponsored by the Woodrow Wilson International Center for Scholars and the James A. Baker III Institute for Public Policy of Rice University, Washington, D.C. (April 12, 2001), p. 3.

33. *A Forum on the Role of the National Security Advisor,* p. 3.

34. Inderfurth and Johnson, *Fateful Decisions,* p. 135.

35. Alexander L. George, "The Case for Multiple Advocacy in Making Foreign Policy," *American Political Science Review* 66 (September 1972): 751–795; and Alexander L. George, *Presidential Decisionmaking in Foreign Policy* (Boulder, Colo.: Westview, 1980), pp. 153–154.

36. Anthony Lake, remarks, *The National Security Council Project,* Center for International and Security Studies at Maryland and the Brookings Institution, College Park, Maryland (2001), p. 4.

37. Drew, "A Reporter at Large: Brzezinski," p. 96.

38. Henry A. Kissinger, *Years of Upheaval* (Boston: Little, Brown, 1982), p. 435.

39. *The National Security Council Project,* p. 9.

40. *The National Security Council Project,* interview conducted by Ivo H. Daalder and I. M. Destler (March 29, 2000), pp. 61–74.

41. William S. Cohen and George J. Mitchell, *Men of Zeal: A Candid Inside Story of the Iran-Contra Hearings* (New York: Penguin, 1988); Laurence H. Tribe, "Reagan Ignites a Constitutional Crisis," *New York Times* (May 20, 1987): A31.

42. John F. Harris, "Berger's Caution Has Shaped Role of U.S. in War," *Washington Post* (May 16, 1999): A1.

43. Cecil V. Crabb and Kevin Mulcahy, *American National Security: A Presidential Perspective* (Pacific Grove, Calif.: Brooks/Cole, 1991), p. 177.

44. *Report,* President's Special Review Board (Tower Commission), February 26, 1987, pp. C1–C14.

45. Quoted in Karl F. Inderfurth and Loch K. Johnson, *Decisions of the Highest Order* (Pacific Grove, Calif.: Brooks/Cole, 1988), p. 196.

46. James R. Locher III, *Victory on the Potomac: The Goldwater-Nichols Act Unifies the Pentagon* (College Station: Texas A&M University Press, 2002), p. 449.

47. Locher, *Victory on the Potomac,* p. 440.

48. Locher, *Victory on the Potomac,* p. 448.

49. Douglas Holtz-Eakin, director, Congressional Budget Office, "The Long-Term Implications of Current Defense Plans," statement, Committee on the Budget, U.S. House of Representatives (October 16, 2003), p. 3.

50. Daniel Wirls, *Buildup: The Politics of Defense in the Reagan Era* (Ithaca, N.Y.: Cornell University Press, 1992), p. 36.

51. See, for example, Dana Priest, *The Mission: Waging War and Keeping Peace with America's Military* (New York: Norton, 2003).

52. Richard C. Snyder and Edgar S. Furniss Jr., *American Foreign Policy: Formulations, Principles, and Programs* (New York: Rinehart, 1954), p. 308.

53. Snyder and Furniss, *American Foreign Policy*, p. 307.

54. Modified from Robert Ellsworth Elder, *The Policy Machine* (Syracuse: Syracuse University Press, 1960); see also Willard Beaulac, *Career Ambassador* (New York: Macmillan, 1951).

55. Both of these examples are from J. Rives Childs, *American Foreign Service* (New York: Henry Holt, 1948), pp. 5–6.

56. Raymond Hopkins, "The International Role of 'Domestic' Bureaucracy," *International Organization* 30 (1976): 424.

57. Morton H. Halperin, "Organizational Interests," in *U.S. National Security: A Framework for Analysis,* ed. Daniel J. Kaufman, Jeffrey S. McKittrick, and Thomas J. Leney (Lexington, Mass.: D. C. Health, 1985), pp. 201–232.

58. Elizabeth Drew, *New Yorker* (February 14, 1983): 104.

59. Stansfield Turner, *Secrecy and Democracy* (Boston: Houghton Mifflin, 1985), p. 185.

60. Loch K. Johnson, interview with Stansfield Turner, McLean, Virginia (May 1, 1991).

61. Johnson, interview with Turner, p. 57.

62. Robert M. Gates, *From the Shadows* (New York: Simon and Schuster, 1996), p. 140.

63. Quoted in John H. Hedley, "The Intelligence Community: Is It Broken? How to Fix It," *Studies in Intelligence* 39 (1996): 17.

64. John Millis, speech, Central Intelligence Retirees Association, Virginia (October 5, 1998).

65. Remarks, National Intelligence and Technology Symposium, CIA, Langley, Virginia (November 6, 1998).

66. Loch K. Johnson, "Aspin-Brown Commission," *Studies in Intelligence* (September 2004): 1–20.

67. Roger Hilsman, *To Move a Nation* (New York: Delta, 1967), p. 7.

68. Quoted by Don Oberdorfer, *Washington Post* (August 6, 1983): A13.

69. Seymour M. Hersh, "The Angleton Story," *New York Times Magazine* (June 5, 1978): 13ff.

70. Entitled *Psychological Operations in Guerilla Warfare*, the document has been published by Random House (New York, 1985); on this manual, see the *New York Times* (December 6, 1984): A1.

71. Senate Select Committee on Secret Military Assistance to Iran and the Nicaraguan Opposition and House Select Committee to Investigate Covert Arms Transactions with Iran (Inouye-Hamilton Committees), *Report on the Iran-Contra Affair,* S. Rept. 100-216 and H. Rept. 100-433 (Washington, D.C.: U.S. Government Printing Office, November 1987).

72. Quoted by Norman Kepster, *Washington Star* (November 12, 1975): 21.

73. "Alleged Assassination Plots Involving Foreign Leaders," *Interim Report,* Church Committee, S. Rept. No. 94-465 (Washington, D.C.: U.S. Government Printing Office, November 1975).

74. Remarks to Loch K. Johnson during an interview, CIA Headquarters, Langley, Virginia (February 24, 1978).

Congress, which plays a major role in U.S. foreign policy formulation and implementation, asserted its position in foreign policy in 2004 when it created the National Commission on Terrorist Attacks upon the United States, shown hear swearing in Rudolph Giuliani, mayor of New York in 2001, when the terrorist attacks on the World Trade Center occurred.

CHAPTER **9**

Congress, the Courts, and the Public in American Foreign Policy

■ What powers does Congress have in foreign policy?

■ Why is Congress less likely to defer to the president in foreign policy today than in the past?

■ Should Congress act as an equal partner to the executive branch in the making of foreign policy?

■ What role does the judicial branch played in foreign policy?

■ What roles do interest groups and public opinion play in foreign policy?

Despite the limitations on presidential and executive power examined in the previous chapter, the president remains preeminent in the formulation and implementation of U.S. foreign policy, with the executive branch of government outside the presidency being next in importance. Nevertheless, Congress and the judiciary also play a role in foreign policymaking, as do public opinion and interest groups (foreign and domestic). Much to the distress of presidents, Congress, the judiciary, public opinion, and interest groups do not always fall in line behind the preferences of the White House. This chapter develops an understanding of the role played by these other actors in American foreign policy, a domain that is hardly the exclusive preserve of the executive branch.

CONGRESS AND FOREIGN POLICY

The ability of Congress to influence foreign and military policy lies in several areas. Foremost among them are congressional leadership, oversight powers, authority to approve treaties and executive appointments, the power of the purse, and the war power.

Congressional Leadership

Normally in foreign policy, the president proposes (as in domestic policy) and the Congress deposes—that is, lawmakers accept, modify, or reject a president's initiatives. Even though members of Congress rarely use their foreign policy powers to initiate new directions for the United States in the world, they have that prerogative.

For example, when the Soviet Union launched *Sputnik* in 1957, President Eisenhower did not see it as a threat to U.S. security, but some lawmakers did. In the absence of action by the president, a subcommittee of the Senate Armed Services Committee (prodded by Majority Leader Lyndon B. Johnson, D-Texas) held hearings on the challenge presented to the United States by the Soviet space program. Concluding that there was a danger, Congress created the National Aeronautics and Space Administration (NASA) to run a space program, and passed the National Defense Education Act to provide funding for science and foreign-language education. Although technically civilian programs, they were very closely connected to and perceived as vital to national security.

Congressional Oversight

Lee H. Hamilton, a former House member (D-Indiana) and director of the Woodrow Wilson Center in Washington, D.C., offers a strong case for **legislative oversight**—the review of executive branch programs by lawmakers. "Congress must do more than write the laws," he observes; "it must make sure that the administration is carrying out those laws the way Congress intended." By means of oversight, members of Congress "can help protect the country from the imperial presidency and from bureaucratic arrogance" Hamilton asserts, and "help keep federal bureaucracies on their toes."[1] Adds former Senator Wyche Fowler (D-Georgia): "Oversight keeps bureaucrats from doing something stupid."[2] More formally, political scientist Joel D. Aberbach defines legislative oversight as a "review of the actions of federal departments, agencies, and commissions, and of the programs and policies they administer, including review that takes place during program and policy implementation as well as afterward ... a significant facet of congressional efforts to control administration and policy."[3]

The general consensus is that lawmakers have often ignored or overlooked this responsibility. Political scientist John Bibby, for instance, referred to oversight in the 1960s as "the neglected function."[4] In 1974, an internal study concluded unanimously that Congress was "just barely making a scratch on the oversight of the executive branch in any one year."[5] Another academic study concluded two decades later with respect to legislative supervision of the intelligence community that "oversight" was "an aptly chosen figure of speech."[6] Lawmakers slighted oversight for a number of reasons. They preferred to concentrate on lawmaking, since it was easier to claim credit—and impress voters back home—by passing a law with the representative's name on it. Moreover, by avoiding involvement in oversight, a member of Congress could sidestep blame when the executive branch blundered, as when the CIA's secret plan to invade Cuba in 1961 ended in disaster at the Bay of Pigs.

For most of the period from World War II until the late 1960s, Congress deferred to presidential recommendations and military advice regarding U.S. foreign policy and rarely exercised its oversight responsibilities, outside appropriations reviews. The Watergate scandal, the controversial Vietnam War, and charges of CIA spying at home stirred lawmakers into greater scrutiny of executive branch activities. Since then, despite an overall spotty record of maintaining accountability, members of Congress have occasionally played an important supervisory role—although often more in response to the "fire alarms" of a scandal or policy failure rather than careful "police-patrolling" before mistakes are made in the executive branch.[7] In the mid-1960s, the Senate Foreign Relations Committee, led by J. William Fulbright (D-Arkansas), held extensive oversight hearings on the war in Vietnam, helping to educate citizens about the complexities of that conflict and raising doubts about the wisdom of the war. In 1975, a Senate committee led by Frank Church (D-Idaho) revealed improper activities of the CIA and other intelligence agencies. More recently, in 2003, a congressional Joint Committee on Intelligence examined the failure of the intelligence agencies to warn the American people about al Qaeda's plans to attack New York City and Washington, D.C., in 2001.

Treaties and Other International Agreements

The Constitution gives the Senate explicit power to give its advice and consent on treaties. The Senate rarely rejects a major treaty, however—only 16 times in U.S. history. Still, this does not mean that the Senate's treaty power is inconsequential; some of the 16 rejections were important. For example, the Senate rejected the Versailles Treaty of 1919, and thus the League of Nations. Because presidents prefer to avoid the embarrassment of a Senate rejection of a treaty, delay caused by a filibuster, or a Senate refusal to hold hearings on a treaty, the White House is often willing to modify the language of treaties according to the wishes of important senators.

For example, in 1996, Senator Jesse Helms (R-North Carolina), the chair of the Foreign Relations Committee, believed that the terms of the Chemical Weapons Convention (CWC) Treaty were unverifiable—that is, it would be difficult to know if other signatories were honoring the provisions, or violating them through the secret development of chemical weapons programs. Helms therefore kept the Senate from voting on the treaty until it was amended to take into account his criticisms. In 1997, the Senate finally approved the treaty. Even so, questions remained and the necessary implementing legislation was not enacted until 1998. During these years, the Senate's treaty power enabled lawmakers to significantly shape the role of the United States in the Organization for the Prohibition of Chemical Weapons, the new international institution created by the treaty to supervise the destruction of chemical weapons and prohibitions against their production, stockpiles, transfer, and use.

Congress sometimes places restraints on the ability of a president to negotiate a treaty as quickly as the White House might like. Several presidents have urged Congress to approve commercial treaties with few or no amendments, so that bargains struck with foreign countries during the negotiation phase of a treaty will not come unglued during the Senate approval process. This procedure, much desired by the executive branch, is called **fast-track legislation.** While Congress has often been willing to agree to this approach, sometimes lawmakers have refused. For example, congressional opposition to fast-track legislation undermined the Clinton Administration's effort to expand the North American Free Trade Agreement (NAFTA) to include Chile and other countries of the Western Hemisphere. Congress delayed granting George W. Bush fast-track authority until well into his presidency in 2002.

Presidents can avoid the treaty process altogether by using other forms of international agreement-making, such as the executive agreement. Unlike treaties, executive agreements do not require two-thirds approval by the Senate, just the president's signature or sometimes just the approval of a senior official in one of the foreign policy departments.[8] Prior to enactment of the 1972 Case-Zablocki Act, a president did not even have to inform lawmakers about the use of an executive agreement. Normally, presidents take up this instrument of foreign policy only for routine business, such as purchasing the land for a U.S. embassy site overseas.

As America's role in world affairs expanded after World War II, however, presidents turned to executive agreements as a way to conduct foreign affairs efficiently and without the frustration of long debates on Capitol Hill. Executive agreements have become controversial, though, because sometimes they can involve significant policy initiatives. Several executive agreements have been the foundation for the establishment of American military bases overseas, as in Spain, Thailand, and the Philippines, having the effect of committing the United States to a military relationship with other countries without the benefit of Senate review—one of the main reasons the Case-Zablocki Act was passed.

Appointments

Although the Constitution gives the president the power to appoint ambassadors and other individuals involved in the formulation and implementation of foreign and military policy, it also gives the Senate a responsibility for providing advice and consent on the qualification of the individuals nominated for these posts. Frequently, as in the domestic arena, important appointees to these foreign policy posts benefit from close connections to Congress, as in the case of President Reagan's appointment of Richard Perle as assistant secretary of defense. A proponent of a hard-line anti-Soviet policy, Perle previously had worked for many years as a staff adviser to conservative Senator Henry Jackson (D-Washington). Perle's knowledge of Congress, Soviet and defense issues, and Reagan's policy objectives, coupled with the clout wielded by his mentor in the Senate, made him a powerful figure in Washington circles.

Senators can put a hold on the confirmation process to express concern about issues or a specific appointee. In 1994, for example, Senator Jesse Helms used the hold privilege to delay the appointment of Robert Pastor as ambassador to Panama. Helms disliked

Pastor's earlier role in fashioning the Carter Administration's policy toward the Marxist regime in Nicaragua. His appointment to Panama was never approved. In 1997, Governor William Weld (R-Massachusetts) experienced a similar fate. He supported the medical use of marijuana, a position that Helms opposed, and the Senator refused to hold hearings on the Weld appointment as ambassador to Mexico. The nomination collapsed.

Appropriations

Congress can exercise strong influence over foreign policy through the power of the purse. With their control over the budget, lawmakers can even influence when and where the United States goes to war, as when in 1970 the Senate voted to shut off funding for military operations into Cambodia that might have led to an expansion of the war in Vietnam. The war power is shared by Congress and the executive branch, but Congress alone has the authority to appropriate funds to pay for military operations. Sometimes, though, members of Congress approve more for foreign and military affairs than the president requests. This happened frequently during the Clinton presidency, as lawmakers typically appropriated more funds for the Defense Department and the intelligence agencies than Clinton requested, usually earmarking the additional monies for the purchase of new weapons or spy satellites. For instance, in 1999, Congress approved approximately twice as much as President Clinton requested for combat in Kosovo, with much of the added amount spent on weapons systems.

The War Power

The war power may be broadly defined as the actual or threatened use of overt military force. According to the Constitution, this power is shared between the president and Congress, with lawmakers having the power to declare war and the president expected to act as commander in chief of the armed forces. Ideally, this sets up a system of checks and balances that curbs the ability of either branch of government to go to war on its own volition. For several reasons, however, the power of war resides more in the hands of the president and the executive branch than with members of Congress. The executive branch has the ability and responsibility to defend the United States and its interests abroad. While Congress has on occasion attempted to restrict this ability, lawmakers have found that the establishment of limits and forcing the executive branch to honor them is much easier said than done, as attested to by the history of the War Powers Resolution examined later in this chapter.

Further, even though the United States has used military force many times since the Second World War, this nation has never been formally at war during this period. Rather, it has "intervened," fought "police actions," and conducted other "low-intensity military operations" that fell short of a declared war. The actions in Korea, Vietnam, and Iraq were not "wars" in the classic sense because Congress never made a formal declaration. The same is true for the America's military interventions during the 1980s and 1990s in Grenada, Panama, Somalia, the Balkans, and Afghanistan. In each case, the initiative for using military power resided with the president. Some argue that Congress has surrendered its oversight responsibility, while other maintain that lawmakers have simply bowed to the reality that the executive branch has greater access to information and, therefore, a better understanding of the world situation.

As the Vietnam War and the Watergate affair in the early 1970s raised more and more questions about presidential credibility, congressional willingness to follow meekly in the president's footsteps began to wane. As questions emerged about the Watergate cover-up, rising U.S. casualties in Indochina, the questionable dispatch of marines into the Dominican Republic (1965), and CIA domestic spying and questionable involvement in the politics of Chile (a democracy), Congress began to reassert itself. The reasons behind this legislative resurgence must be closely examined if one is to understand contemporary American foreign policy.

THE RESURGENCE OF CONGRESS IN FOREIGN POLICYMAKING

Despite widespread agreement among scholars and practitioners of U.S. foreign affairs that Congress has traditionally trailed in the wake of the president in this policy domain, presidents are often awed by the authority that lawmakers have in the American government. "The Congress looks more powerful sitting here [in the White House] than it did when I was … one of a hundred in the Senate," President Kennedy recalled. Kennedy reflected on "the collective power of the Congress," observing, "there are different views, different interests [and] perspectives … from one end of Pennsylvania Avenue to the other…. There is bound to be conflict."[9]

Other presidents and executive branch officials have shared this lament, often expressing exasperation over the "outside interference" of Congress in the making of foreign policy, a phrase used by John M. Poindexter, President Reagan's national security adviser, during hearings into the Iran-Contra scandal.[10] An irritated President Eisenhower once referred to lawmakers as "those damn monkeys on the Hill."[11] Most presidents probably think this (or worse) from time to time, but usually keep their feelings concealed to avoid retaliation against White House initiatives by aggrieved members of Congress.

Soon after entering office, President Jimmy Carter found his administration's intelligence activities placed under a microscope on Capitol Hill. Battle scarred from fights with the Georgia state legislature, he realized that as president he would have to reckon with another set of elected representatives who might not always agree with him, including Edward P. Boland, an important member of the House of Representatives (D-Massachusetts). How Representative Boland changed his views about the role of Congress in the foreign policy process provides a sense of why lawmakers have become more involved in this policy domain over the past few decades.

In December 1977, the new U.S. House Permanent Select Committee on Intelligence (HPSCI), known informally as the House Intelligence Committee or the Boland Committee (after its chairman), convened for its first briefing on a CIA covert action. Three years earlier, Congress had passed the **Hughes-Ryan Amendment** to the 1947 National Security Act. The new law required the president to approve all important covert actions through a "finding," that is, a formal White House endorsement of such operations. The law further required the president to report the finding to the "appropriate committees" of Congress, which at the time (1974) meant the House and Senate committees on appropriations, armed services, and foreign relations. With the creation of the Senate Select Committee on Intelligence (SSCI) in 1976 and its House counterpart, HPSCI, a year later, the director of Central Intelligence (DCI) began reporting to the two new intelligence oversight committees on most activities, with briefings to other lawmakers on request. Whenever the president authorizes a finding, the DCI is expected to report exclusively to the two intelligence oversight panels (SSCI and HPSCI), a custom made into law by the 1980 Intelligence Oversight Act.

At this first important meeting of HPSCI, Chairman Boland welcomed President Carter's DCI, Stansfield Turner, to the committee's secure hearing room, nestled near the Capitol Rotunda.[12] Silver-haired, stocky, ruggedly handsome, a former Rhodes scholar and middle guard on the Naval Academy football team, Turner smiled at the committee members as they sat along the curvature of a U-shaped mahogany bench. Following an exchange of pleasantries, the DCI read the brief finding statement signed by the president and waited for a response.

Only seven of the committee's 13 members had bothered to attend the meeting: six Democrats and one Republican. Last-minute duties on the more established committees—panels that controlled money for district projects—held a greater attraction for them than HPSCI's first briefing on a top-secret covert action. After a minute of silence, Roman Mazzoli (D-Kentucky) cleared his throat and began criticizing the vagueness of the finding. Turner clenched his teeth, the muscles in his jaw flexing, then replied with a spirited defense of the operation.

Mazzoli was unimpressed. To Turner's irritation, Mazzoli laid out a series of further objections. Soon Chairman Boland raised his hand to end the exchange. "I'd like to have a serious debate," he said, "but this is not the place." Staff aides, seated behind the committee members, looked at each other in dismay. If this was not the place to have a debate with the DCI, in a closed meeting guarded by Capitol Hill police within the inner sanctum of HPSCI's suite of offices near the Capitol Dome, then where was?

"I don't want any adversary proceedings between this committee and the intelligence agencies," Boland said flatly. Mazzoli sank back into his chair, stunned by the chair's decision to end the discussion. A few of the other members turned toward Boland with surprised looks, but no one came to Mazzoli's rescue. Crossing swords with a committee chair was unwise, and doubly so when the chair was also the second-ranking member of the Appropriations Committee and a close friend of the Speaker of the House. In minutes, the meeting was over. Turner and his aides left the room draped in smiles, pleased no doubt to have Boland as an ally on Capitol Hill.

Weeks later, Turner returned with a second finding. Mazzoli immediately showed that he was unwilling to accept Boland's tight control over questioning the DCI. He peppered Turner with questions about the latest covert action approved by President Carter. This time Representative Les Aspin (D-Wisconsin), who had missed the first meeting, joined in. A magna cum laude history graduate of Yale University with a doctorate in economics from MIT, Aspin possessed an incisive analytic mind and a zest for any opportunity to debate issues of foreign and defense policy. (He would later serve as President Clinton's first secretary of defense.)

For this second meeting, the committee's staff director had requested the presence of a transcriber in the room, known on Capitol Hill as a "recorder," to keep a verbatim record of what was said. Employed by Congress for such purposes and cleared by the FBI, the transcriber repeated what was said into a device that covered his face, his voice activating a tape recorder. After observing the recorder, Turner abruptly stopped his briefing and insisted that the man be dismissed in order to maintain secrecy. The room fell silent. Boland finally nodded his head in agreement with the DCI. An aide slipped a note to Aspin: "We must have a record of these briefings! How else are we going to have any memory of what the DCI said, and whether the CIA is living up to his assurances? It'll be his recollection against ours." In a politically risky move, Aspin spoke forcefully against Boland, with Mazzoli joining in.

With the grim look of a headmaster before disobedient school boys, Boland attempted to mollify Aspin and Mazzoli with assurances that a verbatim record was unnecessary, since the committee would have a copy of the finding on file. Aspin insisted, however, that the finding itself was insufficient; the DCI's dialogue with committee members, in which he explained in greater detail the objectives and methods of the operation, was equally important. Glowering at Aspin, the chair repeated in his deep baritone voice that he saw no reason for a transcription of the entire session. He ordered the recorder to desist.

Unbowed, Aspin thrust his head and shoulders forward and stared along the curve of the bench toward Boland. "I call for a roll-call vote on this, Mr. Chairman," Aspin said coldly. Mazzoli offered a crisp second. His face darkening, Boland pushed his chair back from the bench in disgust and ordered the committee clerk to call the roll.

It was gut-check time on the Boland Committee. The chair was unlikely to forget who voted against him in this challenge to his authority. The clerk called out the names of those present: 11 of the 13. When the tally came to an end, Les Aspin had won the right—by a one-vote margin—for HPSCI to keep a word-for-word transcript of the entire covert action briefings and discussions. With this vote, the committee had endorsed a more serious form of accountability for covert actions, one that would allow members to monitor the ongoing performance of the secret agencies in light of promises made by intelligence officials during the committee's closed hearings.

Throughout the first years of the Boland Committee, the tug-of-war continued between the chair and the more outspoken members of his panel. Sometimes Chairman Boland had a majority on his side, and sometimes Aspin and Mazzoli prevailed. Then came the Reagan Administration and the beginning of a dramatic transformation in Boland's attitude toward accountability. President Reagan's DCI, William J. Casey, proved unwilling to keep Boland informed, let alone the full committee, and relations between the CIA and HPSCI (as well as SSCI) deteriorated. Worse still, the executive branch elected to ignore Boland's efforts to curb covert action in Nicaragua through a series of statutory prohibitions passed during 1982–1986, each more stringent than the other and known collectively as the **Boland Amendments.**[13] This White House and CIA arrogance pushed the HPSCI chair toward the view that the executive branch required close monitoring after all—and perhaps even sharp admonishment. The eruption of the Iran-Contra scandal in 1987 drove Chairman Boland far away from his early spirit of camaraderie with DCI Turner and into a deep and abiding distrust of "Wild Bill" Casey and the CIA's Operations Directorate. Boland had joined the ranks of many other law-makers who had grown wary of executive-branch arrogance displayed during the Vietnam War, Watergate, and now Bill Casey's dismissal of congressional accountability over the CIA.

TAKING THE NATION TO WAR

Just as some legislators sought greater congressional accountability over the CIA, others hoped to chain down what the nation's founders called the "dog of war." The decision to go to war is the most solemn action a nation can take, and increasingly during the 1960s, Congress grew reluctant to leave this fateful judgment to the president alone.

Questioning Presidential Authority over the War Power

Troubling to members of Congress in 1965 was President Johnson's invasion of the Dominican Republic. Initially, he stated publicly that the attack had been necessary for the "protection and rescue of Americans." Soon, though, the argument changed: the objective of the 24,000 marine force was to thwart the imminent threat of a communist takeover on the island. This quick reversal, coupled with the president's lack of candor with lawmakers throughout the operation, had the effect of eroding Johnson's credibility within the Congress, where he had once been a popular Senate majority leader. His friendship with the chair of the Senate Foreign Relations Committee, J. William Fulbright (D-Arkansas), who had gone out on a limb to support what at first appeared to be a rescue operation in the Dominican Republic, rapidly soured.

During 1965 as well, key members of Congress began to express doubts about the facts of the Tonkin Gulf incident that had led lawmakers to pass the **Gulf of Tonkin Resolution** in August 1964. The resolution was essentially a blank check for Johnson to pursue the war in Vietnam as he saw fit. With their support for this resolution, members of Congress had essentially voted (by a margin of 533–2) to relinquish control over the war power, giving the president almost unlimited authority to use military force in Indochina. Later, Undersecretary of State Nicholas Katzenbach pointed to the resolution as the "functional equivalent" of a declaration of war by Congress, even though, according to a senior member of the Foreign Relations Committee who participated in the 1964 debate, "Congress neither expected nor even considered at the time of the debate on the resolution that the President would later commit more than half a million American soldiers to a full-scale war in Vietnam."[14]

Senators also became increasingly suspicious of earlier reports from the executive branch that claimed the North Vietnamese had attacked an American destroyer in the Tonkin Gulf in August 1964—the event precipitating passage of the resolution. According to an investigation carried out by the staff of the Senate Foreign Relations Committee, the executive branch might have misinterpreted, exaggerated, or even fabricated the facts. The cauldron of distrust on Capitol Hill began to boil over. In 1966, Senator Fulbright and his committee conducted hearings—nationally televised and highly critical—on America's involvement in the Vietnam conflict.

By 1969, early in Nixon's presidency, the Senate was ready to take stronger action, passing by a vote of 70–16 the **National Commitments Resolution** that called for greater consultation between the executive and legislative branches before the president entered into military and other commitments abroad. The Foreign Relations Committee described this resolution as "an invitation to the executive to reconsider its excesses, and to the legislature to reconsider its omissions, in the making of foreign policy."[15] On its heels came the repeal of the Gulf of Tonkin Resolution in 1970 and, bolder still, passage by the Senate of the **Cooper-Church Amendment** to force withdrawal of U.S. forces from their May 1970 "incursion" into Cambodia.

With the Cooper-Church Amendment, the Senate for the first time in American history threatened to use its penultimate power (short of impeachment) against the president to block his use of military force: the power of the purse. Senators worded the amendment to cut off all funding for support of U.S. troops in Cambodia if the president failed to withdraw them by July 1, 1970. President Nixon did withdraw the troops from Cambodia, as he claimed he had intended all along. The larger war in Vietnam, however, lingered on.

The War Powers Resolution

The struggle between the branches for control over the power to make war reached a climax in 1973 with the enactment of the **War Powers Resolution.** This statute, referred to by then Speaker of the House Carl Albert (D-Oklahoma) as one of the two most important laws passed in his long tenure on Capitol Hill,[16] placed obstacles in the way of presidential authority to commit American forces abroad without congressional approval. The message from Congress was clear: no more blank checks like the Gulf of Tonkin Resolution.

The tension between the branches over the war power stems from the sharing of war-making authority between the Congress (Article I, Section 8) and the president (Article II, Section 2). A former staff director of the Senate Foreign Relations Committee, Pat Holt, has written: "Where to draw the line between the power of Congress to declare war and the power of the president as commander in chief is one of the most controversial issues relating to the Constitution." The two articles set up the perfect conditions for a tug of war between the branches. When the war in Vietnam went badly and the presidency was further weakened by the Watergate scandal, Congress tightened its grip on the rope and yanked. "The War Powers Resolution, in essence," Holt notes, "is an effort by Congress to give itself more leverage in the tug of war with the executive branch."[17]

The War Powers Resolution, as it finally emerged for a vote in 1973 following draft after draft, was, in the words of two close observers, "a complicated law in which a number of disparate strands of congressional thought were woven together."[18] The proposed law required that the president "in every possible instance shall consult with Congress" before introducing armed forces "into hostilities or into situations where imminent involvement in hostilities is clearly indicated by the circumstances." The legislation further required the president to report to the Congress within 48 hours regarding the deployment of troops in three types of situations: when forces are sent into a zone of "hostilities" or into a region where hostilities were imminent; when forces "equipped for combat" are sent into any foreign nation; and when forces are deployed that "substantially enlarge" the number of combat-equipped U.S. troops in the foreign nation. In the first instance, the presidential report starts a 60-day clock ticking. Once that time expires, the White House has to obtain congressional approval for continuation of the military involvement. Reporting under the other two provisions does not set a clock ticking. Every president but Gerald R. Ford and Ronald Reagan has chosen to report under those other two options, thereby denying the presence of "hostilities."

Moreover, the War Powers Resolution allowed Congress to force the withdrawal of U.S. troops from a region at any time by a **concurrent resolution**—a simple majority vote in both chambers without the president's signature or possible veto. This provision amounted to a **legislative veto,** a technique subsequently invalidated by the Supreme Court in a 1983 immigration case known as *U.S. Immigration and Naturalization Service v. Chadha.* The *Chadha* decision was far reaching and, with respect to the War Powers Resolution, crippled the ability of lawmakers to terminate a war quickly, regardless of the president's view.

The War Powers Resolution stipulated, moreover, that if Congress refused to endorse the continued presidential use of force within 60 days of the initial report, the U.S. troops *had* to be withdrawn, though Congress could grant a 30-day extension if necessary to assure an orderly and safe exit. The constitutional authority of the Congress to declare war or to enact authorizations for specific combat operations, according to normal legislative procedures, remained intact.

That the War Powers Resolution took two years to pass indicates the difficulty lawmakers faced in their attempt to modernize the war power. Those in favor of the proposal argued for a return to a system of constitutional balance, rather than warmaking by the president alone. "Recent presidents," complained a report of the Senate Foreign Relations Committee, "have relied upon dubious historical precedents and expansive interpretations of the President's authority as Commander-in-Chief to justify both the initiation and perpetuation of foreign military activities without the consent—in some instances without even the knowledge—of Congress."[19]

In 1973, the chair of the House Committee on Foreign Affairs (now called the Committee on International Relations) said the central purpose of the War Powers Resolution was "to restore the balance between the President and the Congress in the war-making authority by limiting the power of the President to send American Armed Forces to combat in foreign lands without congressional approval. It would restore the rightful role of Congress under the Constitution."[20] Added another lawmaker: "If we have learned but one lesson from the tragedy in Vietnam, I believe it is that we need definite, unmistakable procedures to prevent future undeclared wars. 'No more Vietnams' should be our objective in setting up such procedures."[21]

The proposed law had formidable opponents. Senator Barry Goldwater (R-Arizona) thought it would undermine relations with America's allies, who might perceive the statute as a restraint on a timely response to threats against NATO.[22] The president, Richard Nixon, argued that the resolution "would seriously undermine this Nation's ability to act decisively and convincingly in times of international crisis."[23] He warned further that it "would give every future Congress the ability to handcuff every future President merely by doing nothing and sitting still." Especially odious to the president was the 60-day time limit, which he said would "work to prolong or intensify a crisis."[24] Nor did he view the legislative veto provision as rightful and, indeed, declared it unconstitutional. The Supreme Court would eventually agree in the *Chadha* case. "The only way in which the constitutional powers of a branch of the government can be altered," the president declared, "is by amending the Constitution—and any attempt to make such alterations by legislation alone is clearly without force."[25]

Most worrisome to liberals was the 48-hour provision. At first a leading advocate of a war powers resolution as a means for preventing future Vietnams by executive fiat, Senator Thomas Eagleton (D-Missouri) turned against the measure because of this provision. The two-day leeway given to the president made the proposal, Eagleton said, "a dangerous piece of legislation which, if enacted, would effectively eliminate Congress' constitutional power to authorize war." The resolution had become, he feared, "an undated declaration of war."[26] At the height of the congressional debate, Eagleton cautioned that "every president of the United States will have at least the color of legal authority, the advance blessing of Congress, given on an open, blank-check basis, to take us to war. It is a horrible mistake."[27] Scholar David Gray Adler agrees: "Bluntly stated, the resolution unconstitutionally delegates the power to make war to the president."[28]

This odd collection of conservative and liberal opponents of the resolution formed as a result of the reactions by the two groups to different sections of the bill. Conservatives in Congress, as well as President Nixon, had no objection to the 48-hour discretionary clause, giving the president unprecedented authority to begin a war, but they recoiled from the restrictions on presidential power embodied in the 60-day limit and the option of a concurrent resolution to force an immediate troop withdrawal. For the liberals, the likes and dislikes were exactly reversed. Despite the left-right coalition against the resolution, the proponents were far more numerous—enough even to override in November 1973 President Nixon's veto of the proposal.

Senator Jacob Javits (R-New York), the chief architect of the legislation, observed that "with the war powers resolution's passage, after 200 years, at least something will have been done about codifying the implementation of the most awesome power in the possession of any sovereignty and giving the broad representation of the people in Congress a voice in it. This is critically important, for we have just learned the hard lesson [in Vietnam] that wars cannot be successfully fought except with the consent of the people and with their support." In his opinion, "At long last ... Congress is determined to recapture the awesome power to make war."[29]

The War Powers Resolution in Practice

Since its enactment in 1973, the War Powers Resolution has been dogged by controversy. Sam Nunn (D-Georgia) declared in 1987, when he was chair of the Senate Armed Services Committee, that the resolution "has not worked."[30] In 1983, the *Chadha* decision seemed to prohibit the use of a concurrent resolution to withdraw troops at any time before the 60-day limit expired. A former counsel to the Senate Foreign Relations Committee concluded that, even though the *Chadha* case dealt with a quite separate immigration matter, this section of the resolution had become "clearly invalid."[31] Thus, Congress would have to pass a **joint resolution** (a majority vote in both chambers, susceptible to presidential veto) if lawmakers wished to withdraw U.S. troops from foreign hostilities before the 60-day time expiration.

The ambiguous language of the statute has called into question the meaning of the phrase **zone of hostilities.** As constitutional expert Louis Henkin has noted: "Above all, the resolution suffers gravely from a lack of any definition of 'hostilities.'"[32] This flaw became a source of great consternation to some members of Congress in 1987–1988 when the Reagan Administration placed American warships in the Persian Gulf without reporting under the provisions of the War Powers Resolution. Officials in the executive branch claimed that no report was necessary, since the ships were merely on patrol protecting U.S.-flagged Kuwaiti oil carriers. Yet, as lawmakers pointed out, U.S. ships had been fired on and had fired back, and sailors on these ships were being paid dangerous-duty pay. If this situation failed to signify the presence of hostilities, what did?

In 1987, 115 members of Congress filed suite in U.S. District Court to invoke the War Powers Resolution and start its 60-day clock. The court dismissed the suit, however, on grounds that it was a "by-product of political disputes within Congress" and, therefore, beyond the purview of the judiciary. A Court of Appeals upheld this decision in 1988.[33]

Events in the Persian Gulf were not the first instance of controversy regarding the proper application of the War Powers Resolution. On several earlier occasions since 1973, presidents had been inconsistent in their willingness to report to Congress when American troops had entered a region of hostilities, as stipulated by section 4[a][1] of the resolution, thereby starting the 60-day clock. It is in itself a weakness in the law that the president gets to start (or not start) the clock, rather than Congress. The inconsistency in the president's willingness to report (and therefore start the clock) rendered, according to a legal authority, "largely pyrrhic the widely hailed victory of Congress in 'recapturing' its share of the war-making power."[34]

Congress and the executive branch have continued to engage in a wrestling match over when the provisions of the War Powers Resolution should be honored, with presidents periodically pronouncing that the law is unconstitutional. Three cases illustrate the nature of the ongoing dispute: the *Mayaguez* rescue, peacekeeping in Lebanon, and the invasion of Grenada.

The *Mayaguez* Rescue

In an attempt to rescue American merchant sailors aboard the vessel ***Mayaguez***, captured by the Cambodian navy in May 1975, President Ford reported under section 4[a][1] of the War Powers Resolution (the "hostilities" section) and thus started the 60-day clock. Contrary to the spirit of the law, the president did not consult with a single member of Congress in advance of sending in marines for the rescue operation. Key lawmakers were merely "briefed" beforehand through a short presidential notice. Representative Clement Zablocki (D-Wisconsin) stated at the time: "Clearly it was not the intention of the Congress [in the War Powers Resolution] to be merely informed of decisions made."[35] Senator Eagleton complained bitterly that "all the President has to do is make a telephone call … and say, 'The boys are on the way. I think you should know' … Consultation!"[36]

Moreover, the official reports from President Ford and his successors in compliance with the War Powers Resolutions were skimpy at best. "The reports," according to scholar

Barbara Craig, "are one- to two-page letters that proffer less information than might be gleaned from reading newspaper coverage of the events. Indeed, the report on the *Mayaguez* operation made no mention of the number of casualties (forty-one lives lost in an attempt to rescue thirty-nine merchant marines) nor the fact that bombing of a military airfield occurred after the ship and crew were in U.S. custody."[37] For journalist I. F. Stone, "the most important casualty of the *Mayaguez* crisis was the War Powers Resolution."[38]

Peacekeeping in Lebanon

Another contentious series of events occurred between 1982 and 1984. In response to a request from the Lebanese government, President Reagan in August 1982 sent U.S. marines to participate in a multinational operation to assist the evacuation of members of the Palestine Liberation Organization (PLO) from Lebanon's civil war. In this successful mission, 800 marines joined forces with 800 French soldiers and 400 Italian troops. The president reported this use of the marines under the provisions of the War Powers Resolution.

A month later, the president sent 1,200 troops back into Lebanon. Their assignment this time was much more vague. They were to help the prospects for peace by maintaining a physical presence in Lebanon. Since the marines were bivouacked in a supposedly secure location away from the direct fighting in Beirut, the Reagan Administration argued that the hostilities provision in the War Powers Resolution did not apply. No report—and, therefore, no time clock—was necessary. When sniper fire killed several marines, the credibility of this argument was eroded and congressional pressure mounted to invoke the War Powers Resolution. The Reagan Administration steadfastly refused to send a report to Capitol Hill, however, hoping to avoid any possible infringement of the president's flexibility as commander in chief. "We want to cooperate with the President," said Senate Democratic leader Robert C. Byrd (West Virginia) in response, "but this is the law, and the law cannot be winked at."[39]

Yet wink the Congress did. Lawmakers decided in June 1983 to pass a joint resolution on Lebanon, the **Lebanon Emergency Assistance Act,** which gave the president 18 months to keep the troops where they were. In signing the law, President Reagan said, "I do not and cannot cede any of the authority vested in me under the Constitution as President and Commander-in-Chief of the United States Armed Forces. Nor should my signing be viewed as any acknowledgment that the President's constitutional authority can be impermissibly infringed by statute."[40] With this measure, Congress proclaimed that the clock had started, even though the War Powers Resolution requires *the president* to start the clock with the issuance of a presidential report. "Congress drove a hard bargain," concludes a constitutional scholar sarcastically. "One wonders how its leaders emerged from the negotiations without agreeing to apologize for enacting the War Powers Resolution."[41]

In October 1983, the "peacekeeping mission" in Lebanon unraveled when a terrorist killed 241 U.S. marines in a suicide truck bombing of their headquarters. This tragedy, coupled with subsequent newspaper disclosures on the poor security arrangements for the American troops and a revelation that the Joint Chiefs of Staff had unanimously opposed sending the marines to Lebanon in the first place, raised cries on Capitol Hill to tear up the 18-month blank check offered by the Emergency Assistance Act. When the president ordered the battleship *New Jersey* to fire on suspected enemy installations in Lebanon, the absence of hostilities claimed by the administration become even more farcical. Faced with rising public criticism and, more tangibly, the prospect of a new congressional resolution calling for the "prompt and orderly withdrawal" of U.S. forces in Lebanon, Reagan withdrew the marines in February 1984.

The Grenada Invasion

Almost as controversial as the Lebanese mission was America's invasion of Grenada in October 1983, just two days after the suicide bombing of the marine headquarters in Beirut. The purpose of this operation was ostensibly to rescue American students studying at the medical school on this Caribbean island, where conflict between rival political factions had broken out. After the U.S. invasion, media interviews with the school's students and administrators indicated that they had never felt threatened. Critics of the operation contended that the mission's real purposes were threefold: to prevent a Cuban-backed Marxist takeover of the government; to demonstrate, against however humble an opponent, that the United States was not the impotent giant that some foreigners alleged in the aftermath of the Beirut fiasco; and to divert public attention from the death of the marines in Lebanon.

Like the *Mayaguez* rescue, this display of force against a weak target proved good politics. It boosted the president's standing in the public opinion polls at the precise moment when, given the loss of so many marines placed by a presidential order in a dangerous location with an ambiguous mission, it might have been expected to plummet. In addition, the president's homespun charm in television appearances helped save him from public opprobrium.

In the Grenada invasion, 19 Americans were killed and 144 wounded. The Reagan Administration reported the use of force as required by the War Powers Resolution but did not acknowledge that a 60-day clock had begun to run. Kenneth W. Dam, the deputy secretary of state, expressed the view of the executive branch in congressional hearings. Since it was "highly unlikely" that U.S. troops would be in Grenada longer than 60 days, he said, evocation of the War Powers Resolution was unnecessary.[42]

This assurance failed to satisfy some members of Congress. "Frankly, I don't trust them," said Senator Gary Hart (D-Colorado). "We are dealing with an Administration that is not inclined to obey the law. They can always find an excuse to stay in Grenada, and they very clearly do not want to be bound by the 60-day limit."[43] Through a rider to a budget bill, the Senate passed a resolution in October 1983, by a vote of 64–20, stating that the War Powers clock had indeed started running on Grenada as of October 25. The House soon followed suit, by a vote of 403–23. The budget bill failed, however, and along with it the Grenada rider—by then something of a moot point anyway, because the administration had begun to withdraw U.S. troops from the island.

Reforming the War Powers Resolution

Attempts by Congress to play a stronger role in decisions regarding the use of the war power have met with mixed results. The reports mandated by the War Powers Resolution have been inconsistent and substantively thin, and presidents have been reluctant to acknowledge that Congress has the right to place a time limit on the use of force abroad. Congress itself has often allowed the president to bend the rules of the resolution. In the Lebanese case, Congress gave the president virtual *carte blanche*, at least until the attack against the marines in 1983. Concludes one authority: "In the absence of the Executive's good faith adherence to the spirit of the resolution, which the sponsors also had mistakenly expected … the whole procedural edifice turned out to be a house of cards."[44] Senator Mark O. Hatfield (R-Oregon) blamed the failure of the War Powers Resolution on a lack of "political will" in the Congress—an unwillingness by lawmakers to insist that presidents adhere to the law.[45]

In 1988, Senators Robert Byrd and Sam Nunn declared the War Powers Resolution "broke" and offered measures to fix it. They urged their colleagues to remember that "under the Constitution the Founding Fathers gave Congress the power to declare war." Nonetheless, they acknowledged that the resolution went too far in some respects and recommended abandonment of the 60-day clock, seen as allowing foreign governments and terrorist groups too much leverage over U.S. policy. ("The jerks can jerk us around," they said in a joint press release.) Instead, the **Byrd-Nunn reforms** advocated the creation of a legislative panel for consultation with the executive branch prior to a president's use of overt force abroad. The six-member group would include the majority and minority leaders in both houses, as well as the House Speaker and the Senate president pro tempore.

If so requested by a majority of this panel, the president would also have to consult with a wider group of 18 legislators, including the key foreign policy leaders in both chambers. Further, if Congress decided to limit or halt the use of force, a joint resolution would be the appropriate instrument, according to the Byrd-Nunn prescriptions (and the *Chada* case). Some critics denounced this retreat from a fixed time clock. Others viewed the Nunn-Byrd procedure, which would force Congress to come up with a difficult two-thirds majority to override a possible president veto of a joint resolution, a capitulation that would give the executive branch too much control over war-making—precisely the complaint that had led to the enactment of the War Powers Resolution in the first place.

A new round of discussions about the War Powers Resolution started early in 1989, with the advent of George H. W. Bush's administration. Secretary of State James Baker III proposed that Congress and the executive branch "agree to disagree" over the constitutionality of the resolution and move on to a "gentleman's agreement" that the branches would consult together on proposed military operations. In a mood of conciliation, congressional leaders acknowledged flaws in the resolution and seemed willing to explore fresh approaches.

This spirit of comity came to a sudden stop, however, as the president moved toward the use of military force against Iraq, which had invaded Kuwait in 1990. He claimed inherent constitutional authority for the use of force, as well as authority from the United Nations—as if the UN, not the U.S. Congress, could declare war on behalf of the United States. In a heated debate on the war powers, Congress insisted in December 1990 that force could be used only after a formal declaration of war by Congress, or at least a less solemn but still formal authorization by a majority of legislators. Lawmakers chose the second option and authorized the use of force against Iraq, though by only a four-vote margin in the Senate. Critics soon pronounced the War Powers Resolution an "irrelevancy."[46] And, indeed, it played no role in the Iraq War in 2003.

Death Knell of the War Powers Resolution?

Not everyone agrees that the War Powers Resolution is dead. The American Civil Liberties Union, for instance, argued in 1992 that the deployment of U.S. troops in Somalia should have triggered the 60-day clock. "In this type of situation, the Constitution under no circumstances intended that the President could decide alone to deploy tens of thousands of U.S. troops into a foreign country with the authorization to engage in military combat (even if such a confrontation does not actually occur)," concluded the ACLU. "Rather, the Constitution requires explicit congressional authorization for the use of such force prior to the actual deployment." The ACLU asserted that President George H. W. Bush should have submitted a report regarding the Somalia intervention and argued that Congress had to approve the action within 60 days.[47]

In 1993, concerned about possible use of U.S. military force in Haiti and the Balkans by the Clinton Administration, Senate Minority Leader (and later GOP presidential candidate) Bob Dole (R-Kansas) proposed legislation to amend the War Powers Resolution. The **Dole Amendment** required congressional approval *before* the president could send troops to these locations. This initiative drew little support in the Senate once the Clinton Administration vowed to keep U.S. intervention in Haiti limited and promised to send no ground troops into the Balkans. The Dole proposal did lead senators to call for a sweeping review of the war powers, though, and Majority Leader George Mitchell (D-Maine) assigned a group of colleagues to work on reform proposals for the War Powers Resolution.

These efforts went nowhere, and the resolution fell deeper into disregard. It was all but ignored in President George W. Bush's declaration of war against global terrorism, which was supported by a strong majority vote in both chambers of Congress. As for the war against Iraq, in October 2002 lawmakers turned over the power to decide on the scope of that intervention to the president. "They decided only that he should decide," writes constitutional authority Louis Fisher. Disappointed by the legislative willingness to yield on the war power, Fisher concludes that "it looks to me like an elected monarchy, something the framers thought they had put behind them."[48] He and other leading scholars have concluded that the time has come to scrap the enfeebled War Powers Resolution.[49] Lawmakers, though, were reluctant to call for outright repeal of the law. Robert A. Katzmann suggests that repeal is "unlikely, if for no other reason than it would symbolize to many in Congress a surrender of its role in war-making decisions."[50]

A MORE COMPLICATED FOREIGN POLICY

Other reforms in Congress have further complicated executive-legislative relationships in foreign policy. During the 1960s, several new subcommittees gave lawmakers a greater opportunity for participation in important decisions. This led to the demise of what former Secretary of State Dean Rusk described as the phenomenon of whales and minnows. "When I was a young assistant secretary of State in the 1950s," he recalled in 1980, "the

Department had only to consult five 'whales' on the Hill to gain an accurate reading on how Congress would react to our foreign policy initiatives." The five whales included Senators Everett Dirksen, the minority leader (R-Illinois); Lyndon Johnson, the majority leader (D-Texas); Hubert H. Humphrey (D-Minnesota), the leading liberal in the Senate; and Richard B. Russell (D-Georgia), a conservative expert on military affairs; and, in the House, Speaker Sam Rayburn (D-Texas). "Today, in contrast," Rusk concluded, "you have 535 minnows."[51]

Lobbying five individuals on behalf of the president's foreign policy is clearly a much simpler task than trying to persuade virtually every member in both chambers of Congress, necessary today because of the dispersal of power away from party leaders and committee chairs and more into the hands of rank and file members of Congress. One result of this fragmentation of power on Capitol Hill has been to reduce the effectiveness of lawmakers, who have trouble building legislative coalitions in this fractured setting. Presidents have also responded unevenly to this challenge. President Carter's conception of lobbying Congress was often limited to inviting 125 representatives for breakfast at the White House. President Reagan, more adept in the ways of Washington, paid attention to the needs of individual legislators, periodically providing the Democratic Speaker of the House with a box of his favorite cigars and plying even junior members with special invitations to social galas at the White House.

President Johnson used intimidation against recalcitrant legislators. Once after Frank Church (D-Idaho) criticized his Vietnam War policies, Church received an invitation to visit Johnson at the White House. "Who helped you write that speech on Vietnam?" Johnson inquired, as he wrapped an arm around Church's shoulder as they strolled through the White House Rose Garden. "Walter Lippmann [a prominent journalist at the time] gave me some ideas," Church replied. "Why?"

"Listen, Frank," said the President, "the next time you need a dam out in Idaho, you go see Walter Lippmann."[52]

Despite this thinly veiled threat, Church stepped up his criticism of the war. The State of Idaho seemed to survive, and the Senator was reelected, although Johnson's pork barrel tactics sometimes intimidated more timid members of Congress.

Lawmakers as Foreign Policy Watchdogs

In recent years, Congress has passed several laws that require the executive branch to report to legislators on anticipated foreign policy initiatives. The new **reporting requirements,** like the provision in the Hughes-Ryan Amendment that mandates a report on every important covert action intervention, are designed to shed light on the intentions of the president and the foreign policy bureaucracy.

Congress's insistence on a robust role for itself in foreign policy has led to the development of its own bureaucracy on Capitol Hill. The Senate has over 1,100 staff aides serving on committees, the House over 2,000—roughly double the number before the reformist mood set in during the late 1960s and early 1970s. A study carried out during the 1980s calculated that Congress employs over 450 foreign policy experts,[53] far fewer than the executive branch but enough to keep the bureaucrats and White House aides on their toes.

This growth in Capitol Hill staff has been a mixed blessing. Posing the question, "Is anyone in charge on Capitol Hill?", journalist Gregg Easterbrook makes a compelling case for a resounding "No!" According to a congressional aide interviewed by Easterbrook, "The staffs are so large everybody wants to have his say and leave his own little stamp. Pretty soon the weight of people wanting attention becomes greater than the force moving the legislation, and the whole things grinds to a halt."[54] Zbigniew Brzezinski, President Carter's national security adviser, also criticized the institutional fragmentation on Capitol Hill. "Almost every congressman sees himself as a putative secretary of State," he writes, "surrounded by personal staffers who make it their business to make the life of the secretary of state as miserable as possible. . . ."[55]

Investigations have become one of the chief means used by Congress to review the foreign policy initiatives of the executive branch. "You see, the way a free government works," President Truman once remarked, "there's got to be a housecleaning every now and then."[56] That is the purpose of a congressional inquiry: when it becomes clear that the government house has fallen into disarray, Congress reacts in an effort to restore lawfulness and propriety. At least, that is the ideal. Sometimes, however, Congress abuses the investigative power, as with Senator Joseph McCarthy's witch hunt against the Truman Administration for its foreign policy setbacks in China and Korea.

Members of Congress have on other occasions misused the power of legislative oversight; power may be misused wherever it is placed. In 1995, for example, HPSCI member Robert Torricelli (D-New Jersey) disclosed information related to CIA activities in Guatemala that should not have been released by an individual representative. Fortunately, though, this was the only significant leak by either of the two intelligence oversight committees in Congress since their creation in the mid-1970s, a remarkably good record that refutes the popular image of Congress as a sieve.

Oversight can mean, too, an expensive surcharge on the time of busy officials in the executive branch. During the Reagan years, the secretary of state appeared before one committee of Congress or another every other week.[57] Moreover, even well-intentioned oversight can lead to a meddlesome, excessive involvement by lawmakers and staff in the executive branch's day-to-day conduct of international affairs, bringing cries of **micro-management**—a damning phrase that has become a favorite of bureaucrats opposed to virtually any congressional review of foreign policy decisions.

Frequently, Congress simply proves unable or unwilling to engage in serious efforts at maintaining accountability over the executive branch. A seasoned Hill observer described the House of Representatives as "a large, slow-witted, thin-skinned, defensive composite that wants to stay out of trouble. Its real passion is reserved for its creature comforts: salaries, recesses, office space, allowances, ever more staff to help it reach its timid decisions."[58]

At their best, though, lawmakers can play an indispensable role in the defense of democracy in the United States and in the improvement of this nation's foreign policy decisions. Stephen K. Bailey has stated the possibilities:

> Congress defends freedom by asking rude questions; by stubbornly insisting that technology be discussed in terms of its human effects; by eliciting new ideas from old heads; by building a sympathetic bridge between the bewildered citizen and the bureaucracy; by acting as a sensitive register for group interests whose fortunes are indistinguishable

from the fortunes of vast numbers of citizens and who have a constitutional right to be heard. Congress defends freedom by being a prudent provider; by carefully sifting and refining legislative proposals; by compromising and homogenizing raw forces in conflict; by humbling generals and admirals—and, on occasion, even Presidents.[59]

The capacity of Congress to examine the programs and proposals of the executive branch through independent means, coupled with its grip on the purse strings, makes it the strongest legislative branch not only in the world today, but since the golden days of the Roman Senate. As James Madison envisioned, it can provide an essential check on the abuse of power by the executive branch, even in foreign policy.

THE JUDICIARY IN FOREIGN POLICYMAKING

The third branch of government, the judiciary, infrequently becomes involved in foreign affairs. Its first major venture into this domain in the modern era came in the case ***United States v. Curtiss-Wright Export Corporation*** (1936). A lower court convicted Curtiss-Wright, an American weapons manufacturing company, for the sale of machine guns to Bolivia. The verdict was based on grounds that the sale violated a presidential embargo of arms and munitions to both Bolivia and Paraguay, which were at war against one another at the time. President Franklin D. Roosevelt based his embargo on authority derived from a congressional joint resolution, which permitted the use of this trade instrument by the president if such action might "contribute to the re-establishment of peace between [the warring] countries." On appeal to the Supreme Court, Curtiss-Wright argued that the wording of the resolution was too vague and represented an unconstitutional delegation of legislative power to the president. Writing the majority opinion for the Court, Justice George Sutherland rejected the appeal. Congress could delegate its own power to the president, if it wished, the Court ruled.

At the heart of the case stood the prerogatives of Congress, not whether the president possessed independent powers in foreign affairs. Sutherland added to the majority opinion his own *obiter dicta* (a legal term from the Latin meaning "incidental comments," and therefore not binding) in which he opined that the president had an inherent right to exercise authority in foreign affairs, over and above existing statutory inhibitions. Quoting Justice Marshall in 1800, Sutherland noted that "the President is the sole organ of the nation in its external relations, and its sole representative with foreign nations."[60] In 1987, Iran-Contra conspirators turned to Sutherland's remark as a legal justification for bypassing Congress. Conveniently overlooked by them, and muddled by Sutherland, is the fact that Justice Marshall was referring to the president as the sole *spokesperson* for the nation, not its sole foreign policy *decision maker*.

A legal specialist has referred to Sutherland's *dicta* as "the most extreme interpretation of the powers of the national government. It is the farthest departure from the theory that the United States is a constitutionally limited democracy."[61] Louis Fisher provides the key rebuttal to Sutherland and the Iran-Contra lawbreakers. It is not the *dicta* of an individual justice that matters but rather this central fact: "the Constitution effectively provides that the power of foreign affairs is allocated between Congress and the president."[62]

Another important foreign policy court case arose during the Carter years, relating to the president's decision to terminate in 1979—without consultation with the Senate—a mutual defense treaty with Taiwan. The Supreme Court rejected the view of many senators, including Barry Goldwater (who filed the suit against the president), that the Senate's advice and consent should have been sought. By a vote of 7–2, the Court held in *Goldwater v. Carter* that the president did in fact have the constitutional right to abrogate a treaty, even if it did take two-thirds of the Senate's support to approve the treaty in the first place. Recall, too, that the *Chadha* case in 1983 represented another setback for the Congress, voiding the legislative veto.

Occasionally, though, the courts have trimmed back the president's authority. In the **Pentagon Papers** case (*New York Times Co. v. United States*), for example, the Supreme Court held in 1971 against the president. President Nixon had filed suit to prevent the *New York Times* and other newspapers from publishing the Pentagon's classified history of the Vietnam War, filled with embarrassing revelations about mistakes made during the Johnson and Nixon Administrations in Indochina. In the Court's majority opinion, nothing in these documents would have lead to "irreparable harm" to the United States if published.

The judiciary, then, has been a significant player in American foreign policy only infrequently. This reality should not hide the fact, though, that on those infrequent occasions when the courts are involved in foreign policy areas, their rulings can have a far-reaching influence on the conduct of U.S. relations overseas.

PUBLIC OPINION AND INTEREST GROUPS

Public opinion and interest groups play a curious role in the formulation and implementation of American foreign policy. Sometimes they have a significant influence and sometimes little influence at all. To understand why this is so, we must first explore the way that the public forms its opinions about foreign affairs; then we will examine the international issues of greatest concern to interest groups in the United States.

Public Opinion

There are several hypotheses regarding the way that public opinion forms on foreign policy issues. For example, the **rally-round-the-flag hypothesis** posits that a perceived threat to the United States, or an actual attack, will result in strong patriotic support from the public for presidential leadership, sending the standing of the incumbent commander in chief sharply upward in the public opinion polls.[63] During the *Mayaguez* incident in 1975, Ford's approval rating rose 11 points; the Grenada invasion in 1983 boosted Reagan by four percentage points. Another upward surge in a president's standing occurred in 2001, as ratings for George W. Bush spiked in response to the terrorist attacks on the World Trade Center and the Pentagon. Yet dramatic military action sometimes fails to result in a rallying effect, as in Nixon's invasion of Cambodia in 1970.

Another theory, the **opinion-leadership hypothesis,** maintains that the public will rally to the president's side when citizens have only incomplete or inaccurate information about the details of a foreign policy event.[64] At the time of the *Mayaguez* incident, most people—even members of Congress—were unaware that the mission had ended in disaster. The White

House shaped public opinion through self-serving press releases, putting a favorable spin on the outcome of the "rescue" and reaping the benefits of a rise in the public opinion polls. In contrast, Nixon was unable to conceal from the media his invasion of Cambodia; details became public knowledge, leading to a decline in the polls for the President.

Without reliable information, individuals who might be critical of the president—say, congressional leaders in the opposition party—are in a weak position to offer countervailing views. Therefore, they are inclined to be supportive, or at least quiescent. In turn, the general public has no source of information or guidance from respected officials regarding why, or in what manner, they should question a presidential foreign policy action. Safe from criticism, at least for the time being, the president rises in public esteem as the White House maintains a monopoly over information about unfolding events.

"The point isn't that the heads of 'We the People' are full of Jell-O and that they should be ignored," concludes political scientist Everett C. Ladd. "The public brings to the controversy some basic values and expectations that are firm enough."[65] The hard lesson learned by President Johnson during the war in Vietnam was that, most of the time, the public's views on foreign affairs will be as invisible as the castle ghost, but when officials go beyond the boundaries of what the public finds acceptable—especially in terms of the nation's loss of blood and treasure—the ghost can suddenly become quite real for presidents and lawmakers who must stand for reelection.

Public opinion can play a major role in U.S. foreign policy, as shown here in a 1982 rally in New York City against nuclear weapons attended by well over 100,000 people.

As Richard Sobel concluded, policy officials are constantly aware of public opinion and are by necessity "constrained in the timing, extent, and direction of their actions."[66] Looking into the future, Holsti suggested that as the United States and other states focus more on nonmilitary issues, such as trade, immigration, and the environment—subjects that do no require as much secrecy and speed of action, "it may also be an era in which public opinion plays a more autonomous role…. The relationship between public opinion and foreign policy may take on an added rather than diminished significance during the post–Cold War period."[67]

Domestic Interest Groups

On most occasions, the foreign policy views of the general public are less likely to be taken into account than those of citizens who have organized themselves in cohesive **interest groups,** or **pressure groups,** for the purpose of protecting and promoting their own special interests. The Department of State, like other government agencies, conducts few public opinion polls, but its officials meet regularly with a wide range of interest groups, like Amnesty International, the American Israel Public Affairs Committee (AIPAC), and the U.S.-Japan Trade Council. Oil companies, textile industries, veterans groups, arms control advocates, trade associations, shipping interests, airline companies, ethnic affiliates, farmers, human rights activists, and many other interest groups make their way through Washington's corridors of power to assure that their viewpoints on foreign policy are heard.

Especially influential in recent years has been the Family Steering Committee for the 9/11 Independent Commission, a group of people who lost loved ones in the September 11, 2001, terrorist attacks against the United States. They have been instrumental in keeping the pressure on the White House and the 9/11 Commission to find out as many facts as possible about why the United States failed to thwart the attack and what can be done to prevent another catastrophe like the one that visited New York City and Washington, D.C., on that fateful day. Without this pressure, it is widely believed that the White House would have succeeded in stonewalling the 9/11 Commission's request for access to top-secret documents related to pre-9/11 counterterrorism activities and to the testimony of leading White House officials, including the president, the vice president, and the national security adviser.

Here is just a small sample of some groups in the United States that attempt to shape foreign policy decisions in the nation's Capital:

Emergency Committee for American Trade	United Auto Workers
AFL-CIO	Council for a Livable World
Physicians for Social Responsibility	Committee for a Sane Nuclear Policy
Union of Concerned Scientists	Americans for Democratic Action
American Conservative Union	Environmental Defense Council
Amnesty International	Polish American Congress
Cuban American National Foundation	U.S.-Japan Trade Council
Chamber of Commerce	Business Roundtable
Council on Foreign Relations	Armenian Assembly of America

Organized groups may hope to convince decision makers that they should support policies designed to help the economic needs of the group members. In the case of Detroit auto workers, that might mean seeking relief from the competition of foreign automobile and steel imports; or for American farmers, assistance in locating overseas markets for wheat, corn, and potatoes. Some groups may attempt to fulfill political and ideological goals, be they support for the existence of Israel, funds for rebuilding Afghanistan, or freedom for political dissenters in Venezuela. The range of goals and the lobbying methods are as diverse as the groups themselves.

Not only do legitimate lobbyists and the people they represent have a right to be heard in a democracy, but many of them bring to the government useful information and opinions that often elevate the quality of decisions. Most scholarly studies of lobbyists conclude that they are an excellent source of information for policymakers trying to understand the problems that confront the United States and its citizens.

Think tanks—nonprofit organizations that conduct research on public policy issues—can be influential too. Several hundred of these research organizations exist, such as the American Enterprise Institute (AEI), the Brookings Institution, the Carnegie Endowment for International Peace, the Heritage Foundation, and the Hoover Institution on War, Revolution, and Peace. Many, if not most, are located in and around the Beltway that encircles Washington, D.C. Several think tanks have significant budgets. For example, the RAND Corporation, an influential defense think tank with close ties to the Pentagon and the intelligence community, has an annual budget exceeding $100 million. Others struggle to pay the rent on their offices. Some have a reputation for taking liberal positions, such as the Brookings Institution; others, such as the Heritage Foundation and the AEI, are conservative. Still others, like the Cato Institute, are libertarian.

Some altruistic groups are concerned with the well-being of needy people around the world. At times, their goals can run counter to the official policy of the U.S. government. Such a conflict occurred in 1986 with the Boston-based private relief organization Oxfam America. This group wanted to ship to nongovernmental organizations in Nicaragua some $41,000 worth of supplies, including hammers, chainsaws, water pipes, shovels, wrenches, rakes, seeds, and books on agriculture. The purpose was to alleviate food shortages in a country ravaged by civil war. A year earlier, however, the Reagan Administration had instituted a trade embargo against Nicaragua as part of its squeeze on the Sandinista regime. The administration refused permission for Oxfam to ship the materials.

With respect to defense funding, a Harvard-MIT roundtable agreed that laboratories engaged in the design of weapons, such as the Livermore labs in California and the Los Alamos labs in Nevada, may represent a stronger influence in Washington, D.C., over increased levels of expenditures than even defense corporations like Lockheed-Martin and Boeing themselves.[68]

Global corporations are also effective at lobbying—sometimes secretly. International Telephone and Telegraph (ITT) demonstrated its influence over the White House during the Nixon years by applying strong direct pressure on the administration to intervene on its behalf in Chile. The corporation wanted the government to overthrow the Allende regime in Chile, for fear that it might expropriate ITT's holdings there, and secretly offered the Nixon Administration $1 million to help the CIA carry out the plan. The administration turned down the money, but took up the operation with secret public funds and ultimately succeeded in toppling Allende.

Even individual American states and cities sometimes adopt their own foreign policies. For example, the California State Assembly passed a law in 1986 that required the state pension system to dispose of stocks in companies with business ties in South Africa, a policy called divestment. At the time, this law was one of the strongest blows inflicted by Americans against apartheid (racial segregation) in South Africa, involving some $11.3 billion worth of investments.

Moreover, mayors of American cities can be found pursuing their own brand of international affairs. According to one report, "more than one thousand cities in the Untied States are now establishing their own relations with local communities in foreign countries, including those designated as adversaries, making it possible to deal city to city on issues of trade, technical assistance, immigration, and refugees…. [Further], the radical reduction in the costs of transportation and communication is democratizing international relations."[69]

Sam Yorty, mayor of Los Angeles during the 1960s, spent much of his time traveling abroad, seeking markets for California goods and singing the praises of those nations willing to enter into economic relations with his city. Mayor Andrew Young of Atlanta, the U.S. ambassador to the UN during the Carter Administration, also traveled overseas frequently, dabbling in foreign policy. In 1986 on a visit to Angola, Mayor Young proclaimed his undying friendship to the Marxist regime there, causing conservative interest groups in the United States to ask the mayor in newspaper letters to the editor: "Which side are you on?"[70]

Foreign Lobbies

Some of the groups that descend on the government with foreign policy demands represent the interests of other nations toward which the group members may feel a strong identification and sympathy. The American Jewish community, for instance, has been successful in pressuring the U.S. government for large sums of money earmarked for Israel. The U.S. aid package to Israel, some $3 billion per annum, is the largest for any country.

Not all this success is attributable to the Jewish community's chief lobbying arm, the American Israel Public Affairs Committee (AIPAC). Many lawmakers support Israel because it is the only democracy in the Middle East. Still, AIPAC is renowned for its access to members of Congress and often enjoys favorable vote outcomes—though not always. In 1980, for example, the United States sold a sophisticated military airplane to Saudi Arabia, an Israeli rival, over AIPAC's loud objections. Subsequently, AIPAC was influential in blocking the sale of F-15 jet fighters and 800 Stinger missiles to the Saudis, who then took their lucrative business to Great Britain, where the pro-Israeli lobby is weaker.[71]

Other significant foreign lobbies in the nation's Capital include Greek American, Irish American, and Japanese American organizations. Powerful, too, is the Turkish lobby, as demonstrated by Turkey's spot as No. 3 in the U.S. foreign aid program (after Israel and Egypt). The Turkish embassy in Washington coordinates with Turkish American groups to host lavish parties for lawmakers and officials from the executive branch at its magnificent mansion on "Embassy Row" in northwest D.C. Political scientist James David Barber has pointed to a downside of such influence peddling: "Turkey pays its public-relations company hundreds of thousands of dollars to brighten its image and to obscure its continuing practice, documented in detail, of secret arrest and systematic torture of men and women [in Turkey].... Americans ought not permit themselves to be distracted by hired propagandists."[72]

International Interest Groups

In addition to the formidable array of interest groups within the United States, the world has over 300 intergovernmental organizations **(IGOs),** that is, international organizations created by the governments of two or more states, as well as some 2,400 international nongovernmental organizations **(NGOs),** that is, organizations operating internationally without formal ties to governments. Some IGOs and NGOs have a considerable effect on the conduct of U.S. foreign policy.[73]

Examples of IGOs include the UN, NATO, the Organization of American States (OAS), the League of Arab States, the World Health Organization (WHO), the International Labor Organization (ILO), and the International North Pacific Fisheries Commission. NGOs comprise about 90 percent of all international organizations and include sporting associations like the International Olympic Committee and the International Rugby Board; religious groups such as the Roman Catholic Church; professional organizations such as the global network of Physicians for Social Responsibility; a broad range of groups established to foster trade relations between nations; political parties such as the Social Democrats in Western Europe, where parties reach across national boundaries in an attempt to maintain financial and policy ties based on shared ideological interests; and even terrorist groups, like al Qaeda.

The extent to which IGOs and NGOs influence U.S. foreign policy varies widely. Their ability to affect the course of policy is a function of the resources available to the groups, the extent to which they can elicit support for their cause, and the access that they have to American foreign policy decision makers. While many IGOs and NGOs have only marginal influence on the formulation and conduct of American foreign policy, occasionally—as demonstrated by al Qaeda's attacks against the United States in 2001—they can have a profound effect.

THE CHALLENGE OF A DEMOCRATIC FOREIGN POLICY

The intricate institutional arrangements for arriving at foreign policy decisions within the United States present a picture far different from the one suggested by simplistic organizational charts. Presidents, bureaucrats, lawmakers, and citizens must work with the fragments of power given to them by law, custom, and the Constitution to piece together workable foreign policy initiatives. Sometimes they succeed, and sometimes they do not.

Much depends on the circumstances facing the nation. In times of crisis, greater deference is shown to the president. Much depends, too, on the skills of lawmakers and their interest in foreign policy. Moreover, the liberty of Americans will continue to depend on the understanding that, while a free government must maintain security from foreign threats, it must also protect liberty at home by maintaining close accountability over those individuals in high office entrusted with positions of power.

SUMMARY

Despite the limitations on presidential and executive power, the president remains pre-eminent in U.S. foreign policy, with the executive branch being next in importance. Nevertheless, Congress and the judiciary also have roles in foreign policymaking, as do public opinion and interest groups.

Congress influences foreign policy in several ways. With its leadership capability, lawmakers accept, modify, or reject a president's initiatives. Congress also has oversight power in which it reviews the actions of departments, agencies, and commissions, and the programs and policies they administer. Moreover, Congress has Constitutional authority to approve treaties and executive appointments, but it has used its authority in the case of major treaties rarely, only 16 times in history. It also has the power of the purse, through which it exercises influence over foreign policy, as well as the war power: the ability to declare or threaten to declare war.

Congress's war power has been much debated throughout U.S. history. On occasion, for example with the 1973 War Powers Resolution, Congress has attempted to rein in the president's ability to use military force without a declaration of war. Even so, the war power remains the subject of considerable debate today.

Congress traditionally trails in the wake of the president in foreign policy, but presidents are sometimes concerned by the authority lawmakers have. One reason that recent presidents have developed such concerns is the passage of several laws that require the executive branch to report to legislators on anticipated foreign policy initiatives. Reporting requirements, like the provision in the Hughes-Ryan Amendment that mandates a report on important covert actions, are designed to shed light on the intentions of the president and the foreign policy bureaucracy. Congressional investigations are another way that Congress reviews executive foreign policy initiatives.

Congress's ability to examine the foreign policy of the executive branch through independent means, coupled with its grip on the purse strings, makes it the strongest legislative branch in the world. As James Madison envisioned, it provides an essential check on the power of the executive branch, even in foreign policy.

The third branch of government, the judiciary, rarely is involved in foreign affairs. Occasionally, though, the courts have trimmed presidential authority. For example, in the 1971 Pentagon Papers case, the Supreme Court held against the president. That the judiciary is infrequently a significant player in U.S. foreign policy should not hide the fact that, on infrequent occasions, its rulings can have a significant impact on U.S. foreign policy.

Public opinion and interest groups sometimes play a major role in American foreign policy decisions, but in other instances, they play no role. Foreign policy views of the general public are less likely to be taken into account than those of citizens who organize into pressure groups to promote special interests. Think tanks—organizations that conduct research on public policy issues—are influential, too, as are global corporations. Individual U.S. states, and even cities, sometimes adopt their own foreign policies as well. In addition to U.S. interest groups, the world has over 300 intergovernmental organizations and 2,400 nongovernmental organizations, some of which can have considerable effect on U.S. foreign policy.

The way in which U.S. foreign policy decisions are made presents a picture far different from the one suggested by organizational charts. Presidents, bureaucrats, legislators, and citizens must work with the fragments of power given to them by law, custom, and the Constitution to piece together workable foreign policy. Sometimes they succeed, and sometimes they do not. The liberty of Americans will continue to depend on understanding that, while a free government must maintain security from foreign threats, it must also protect liberty at home by maintaining accountability over individuals in high office.

KEY TERMS AND CONCEPTS

legislative oversight

fast-track legislation

Hughes-Ryan Amendment

Boland Amendments

Gulf of Tonkin Resolution

National Commitments Resolution

Cooper-Church Amendment

War Powers Resolution

concurrent resolution

legislative veto

U.S. Immigration and Naturalization Service v. Chadha

joint resolution

zone of hostilities

Mayaguez

Lebanese Emergency Assistance Act

Byrd-Nunn reforms

Dole Amendment

reporting requirements

micro-management

United States v. Curtiss-Wright Export Corporation

Goldwater v. Carter

Pentagon Papers

rally-round-the-flag hypothesis

opinion-leadership hypothesis

interest groups or pressure groups

IGOs and NGOs

THINKING CRITICALLY

1. What are the strengths and weaknesses of lawmakers when it comes to crafting U.S. foreign policy?

2. Explain the effect of the September 11, 2001, terrorist attacks on U.S. public opinion and foreign policy.

3. Why did public opinion in other countries turn against the United States soon after the 9/11 attacks?

4. How do lawmakers decide which foreign policies to support and which to oppose?

5. Explain how interest groups make their views known to decision makers in the Washington foreign policy community.

6. What role did foriegn policy play in the 2004 presidential election?

7. Can you identify examples where specific pressure groups in the United States have been able to shape foreign policy decisions to benefit themselves that may have harmed broader U.S. foreign policy interests?

NOTES

1. Lee H. Hamilton, with Jordan Tama, *A Creative Tension: The Foreign Policy Roles of the President and Congress* (Washington, D.C.: Woodrow Wilson Center Press, 2002), p. 56.

2. Remarks, interview with Loch K. Johnson, Washington, D.C., February 8, 2003.

3. Joel D. Aberbach, *Keeping a Watchful Eye: The Politics of Congressional Oversight* (Washington, D.C.: Brookings Institution, 1990), p. 2.

4. John F. Bibby, "Congress' Neglected Function," in *The Republican Papers*, ed. Melvin R. Laird (New York: Anchor, 1968), p. 477.

5. Committee on Committees (the Bolling Committee), *Committee Reform Amendments of 1974,* H. Rept. 93-916, 93rd Cong., 2d Sess. (1974), p. 62.

6. William H. Jackson Jr., remark, book review, *Intelligence and National Security* 5 (July 1990): 254.

7. On this distinction, see Matthew D. McCubbins and Thomas Schwartz, "Congressional Oversight Overlooked: Police Patrols and Fire Alarms," *American Journal of Political Science* 28 (February 1984): 165–179.

8. Loch K. Johnson, *The Making of International Agreements: Congress Confronts the Executive* (New York: New York University Press, 1984).

9. Quoted by Theodore C. Sorensen, *Kennedy* (New York: Harper and Row, 1965), p. 346.

10. Senate Select Committee on Secret Military Assistance to Iran and the Nicaraguan Opposition and House Select Committee to Investigate Covert Arms Transactions with Iran (the Inouye-Hamilton Committees), *Report,* U.S. Congress (July 24, 1987).

11. Quoted by James David Barber, *The Presidential Character: Predicting Performance in the White House* (Englewood Cliffs, N.J.: Prentice-Hall, 1972), p. 157.

12. This account is drawn from Loch K. Johnson, *America's Secret Agencies: U.S. Intelligence in a Hostile World* (New Haven: Yale University Press, 1996), pp. 89–94.

13. Inouye-Hamilton Committees; Henry A. Kissinger, "A Matter of Balance," *Los Angeles Times* (July 26, 1987): E1.

14. Katzenbach's remark is in "U.S. Commitments to Foreign Powers," Hearings, Committee on Foreign Relations, U.S. Senate (1967), p. 82; the senator cited is Frank Church (D-Idaho), "Of Presidents and Caesars: The Decline of Constitutional Government in the Conduct of American Foreign Policy," *Idaho Law Review* 6 (Fall 1969): 10.

15. The committee's language is quoted in Pat Holt, *The War Powers Resolution: The Role of Congress in U.S. Armed Intervention* (Washington, D.C.: American Enterprise for Public Policy Research, 1978), p. 4.

16. Loch K. Johnson, interview with Speaker Carl Albert, Washington, D.C. (July 15, 1975). The other key statute, in Albert's opinion, was the Budget and Impoundment Control Act of 1974, another effort by Congress to rein in presidential power—this time in the area of federal spending.

17. Holt, *The War Powers Resolution,* p. 39.

18. Cecil V. Crabb, Jr. and Pat M. Holt, *Invitation to Struggle: Congress, the President and Foreign Policy* (Washington, D.C.: Congressional Quarterly, 1984), p. 143.

19. Committee of Foreign Relations, U.S. Senate, Report No. 220, *Senate Reports* 161 (1973): 4.

20. Clement Zablocki (D-Wisconsin), *Congressional Record* (October 4, 1973): 33038.

21. Senate Spark Matsunaga (D-Hawaii), "War Powers Legislation: Practical and Constitutional Problems," *Department of State Bulletin* 28 (June 1971): 834.

22. *Congressional Record* 119 (1973): 24532.

23. "President Nixon's Veto of War Powers Measure Overridden by the Congress," *Department of State Bulletin* 26 (November 1973): 662.

24. Quoted by Holt, *The War Powers Resolution,* p. 8.

25. Quoted in the *Congressional Quarterly Almanac,* 29 (1973): 916.

26. Thomas F. Eagleton, *War and Presidential Power: A Chronicle of Congressional Surrender* (New York: Liveright, 1974), pp. 221, 223.

27. *Congressional Quarterly Almanac* 29 (1973): 916.

28. "War Powers Resolution," in *Encyclopedia of the American Presidency*, Vol. 4, ed. Leonard W. Levy and Louis Fisher (New York: Simon and Schuster, 1994), p. 1587.

29. "Congress Overrides Nixon's Veto of War Powers Bill," *Congressional Quarterly Weekly Report* 31 (November 10, 1973): 2985; and the *Congressional Record* (1973): 36187.

30. Quoted in the *Atlanta Constitution* (November 10, 1987): A8.

31. Michael J. Glennon, "The War Powers Resolution Ten Years Later: More Politics Than Law," *American Journal of International Law* 78 (July 1984): 577.

32. Louis Henkin, "Foreign Affairs and the Constitution," *Foreign Affairs* 66 (Winter 1987–1988): 300.

33. See William P. Agee, "The War Powers Resolution: Congress Seeks to Reassert Its Proper Constitutional Role as a Partner in War Making," *Rutgers Law Journal* 18 (Winter 1987): 405–435.

34. Glennon, "The War Powers Resolution Ten Years Later," p. 571.

35. John Y. Sullivan, *The War Powers Resolution: A Special Study of the Committee on Foreign Affairs, Committee on Foreign Affairs,* U.S. House of Representatives (1982), p. 219.

36. *Congressional Record* (November 7, 1975): 36177.

37. Barbara Hinkson Craig, "The Power to Make War: Congress' Search for an Effective Role," *Journal of Policy Analysis and Management* 1 (1982): 324.

38. Quoted in Sullivan, *The War Powers Resolution,* p. 218.

39. *New York Times* (September 16, 1983): A1.

40. Quoted in Crabb and Holt, *Invitation to Struggle,* p. 147.

41. Michael J. Glennon, "Some Compromise!" *Christian Science Monitor* (October 24, 1983): 21. See also Glennon's *Constitutional Diplomacy* (Princeton: Princeton University Press, 1990), and Harold Hongju Koh, *The National Security Constitution: Sharing Power after the Iran-Contra Affair* (New Haven: Yale University Press, 1990).

42. Quoted in the *New York Times* (October 28, 1983): A1.

43. *New York Times* (October 28, 1983): A1.

44. Glennon, "The War Powers Resolution," p. 573.

45. Remarks, "Focus on the War Powers Act," 2 *Newsletter*, Center on National Policy, Washington, D.C. (1988), p. 6.

46. For example, Richard E. Cohen, "United Front on War Powers—For Now," *National Journal* (January 23, 1993): 208.

47. An ACLU letter to Speaker of the House Tom Foley and Senate Majority Leader George Mitchell, reprinted in *First Principles,* Center for National Security Studies, 17 (December 1992): 1–2.

48. Louis Fisher, "The Way We Go to War: The Iraq Resolution," in *Considering the Bush Presidency,* ed. Mark Rozell and Gary Gregg (New York: Oxford University Press, 2003), p. 28.

49. See, for example, Louis Fisher, *Congressional Abdication on War and Spending* (College Station: Texas A&M University Press, 2000).

50. Robert A. Katzmann, "War Powers: Toward a New Accommodation," in *A Question of Balance: The President, the Congress, and Foreign Policy,* ed. Thomas E. Mann (Washington, D.C.: Brookings Institution, 1990), p. 67.

51. Loch K. Johnson, interview with Dean Rusk, Athens, Georgia (May 22, 1980).

52. Loch K. Johnson, interview with Frank Church, Boise, Idaho (October 22, 1974).

53. Gregg Easterbrook, "What's Wrong with Congress?" *Atlantic Monthly* (December 1984): 59.

54. Easterbrook, "What's Wrong with Congress?" p. 59.

55. Zbigniew Brzezinski, "Reagan May Be a Great Leader, but His Foreign Policy Is a Shambles," *Washington Post* (national weekly edition, October 20, 1986): 23.

56. Quoted by Merle Miller, *Plain Speaking: An Oral Biography of Harry S Truman* (New York: Berkley, 1963), p. 420; on congressional investigations, see Loch K. Johnson, Erna Gelles, and John C. Kuzenski, "The Study of Congressional Investigations," *Congress and the Presidency* 19 (Autumn 1992): 137–156.

57. Easterbrook, "What's Wrong with Congress?" p. 65.

58. Mary McGrory, *Washington Star* (March 9, 1976): 14.

59. Stephen K. Bailey, *Congress in the Seventies,* 2nd ed. (New York: St. Martin's Press, 1970), p. 109.

60. Justice Marshall, *Annals,* 6th Congress (1800), col. 613.

61. D. M. Levitan, "The Foreign Relations Power: An Analysis of Mr. Justice Sutherland's Theory," *Yale Law Journal* (April 1946): 493.

62. Louis Fisher, "Foreign Policy Powers of the President and Congress," *Annals of the American Academy of Political and Social Science* 499 (September 1988): 152.

63. John Mueller, *War, Presidents and Public Opinion* (New York: Wiley, 1973), pp. 208–213.

64. Richard A. Brody and Catherine R. Shapiro, "A Reconsideration of the Rally Phenomenon in Public Opinion," in *Political Behavior Annual* 2, ed. Samuel Long (Boulder, Colo.: Westview Press, 1989), pp. 77–102.

65. Public lecture, University of Georgia, April 28, 1999.

66. Richard Sobel, *The Impact of Public Opinion on U.S. Foreign Policy Since Vietnam* (New York: Oxford University Press, 2001), p. 238.

67. Ole R. Holsti, "Public Opinion," in *Encyclopedia of U.S. Foreign Relations,* Vol. 3, ed. Bruce W. Jentleson and Thomas G. Paterson (New York: Oxford University Press, 1997), pp. 446–447.

68. "Assessing Strategic Arms Control," Roundtable, MIT-Harvard Summer Program on Nuclear Weapons and Arms Control (June 27, 1985).

69. Richard J. Barnet, *The Rockets' Red Glare: When America Goes to War* (New York: Simon and Schuster, 1990), pp. 411–412.

70. Letter to the editor, *Atlanta Constitution* (September 7, 1986): A12.

71. Jeffrey Record, "AIPAC's Extremism Serves Israel Badly," *Los Angeles Times* (August 8, 1988): 2:13.

72. James David Barber, "Lobbies Can't Erase Rights Violations," *New York Times* (June 9, 1986): 19.

73. See Charles W. Kegley Jr. and Eugene R. Wittkopf, *World Politics: Trends and Transformation* (New York: St. Martin's Press, 1981), p. 104.

CHAPTER 10

The Open Instruments of American Foreign Policy: War, Diplomacy, Trade, Aid, and Reputation

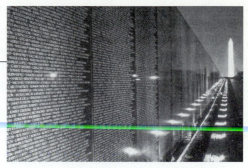

War brings death, a fact vividly shown by the Vietnam War Memorial in Washington, D.C., upon which are inscribed the names of over 58,000 Americans who lost their lives during the Vietnam War. No one knows for sure, but it is estimated that over 2 million Vietnamese were killed during the conflict.

- How and when should the United States resort to the use of armed force abroad?

- What weaponry does the United States rely on for protection against foreign threats?

- To what extent is the treaty power an important instrument of foreign policy?

- What roles do economic statescraft, trade, and aid play in American foreign policy?

- How important are moral suasion and soft power in America's external relations?

ROY W. PEAGLER • FRANK M. RHODES • LAVLE J. HALL •
ROBERT J. ROBERTSON • THOMAS QUICHOCHO SABLAN • ROBERT V. THOMAS •
RICHARD V. THOMPSON • LAWRENCE S. VOGEL • JOHN S. WOOLHEATER

These are a few of the more than 58,000 names on the Vietnam War Memorial in Washington, D.C. The death roster, carved in sleek, black marble, stirs a strong emotional response in most visitors old enough to remember the war in Southeast Asia. Reading or touching the row after row of names brings back painful media images of GIs being evacuated from the battlefield on armored halftracks, bandages over their eyes, their legs twisted and bloodied, plasma tubes jabbed into their arms.

The war went badly for the United States. The Vietnam jungle terrain was alien, and America's South Vietnamese allies in the Army of the Republic of Vietnam (ARVN) were confusingly similar in appearance to the North Vietnamese and Vietcong (VC) enemies. Moreover, guerrilla warfare was still something of a novelty for the United States, not at all like the head-on clashes and distinguishable fronts of the Second World War and the Korean War. Here was combat in which an innocent-looking 70-year-old woman in a rice paddy might have a hand grenade tucked under her clothing, where every turn on the jungle trail might hold a booby trap, where VC would appear and disappear like deadly phantoms in the thick underbrush.

In addition to those who lost their lives, some 200,000 more Americans required hospitalization from battle wounds. Among these, thousands were badly maimed, physically and mentally.[1] Many soldiers returned to the United States with serious drug additions, for the stress in Vietnam was great and drugs were plentiful. The soldiers were youngsters for the most part, with worried parents back home, romances put on hold, jobs to resume, schooling to continue, careers and families ahead—the American Dream disrupted or, for those with names now etched in marble on the Vietnam War Memorial, lost forever. The memorial, the most visited site in the nation's capital, stands above all as a reminder of the human costs that accompany war.

The use of overt force to achieve the foreign policy objectives of the United States is a drastic but sometimes necessary option. This chapter first explores its ramifications, then turns to America's use of diplomacy to settle disputes peacefully through negotiations—"jawing instead of warring," as Winston S. Churchill put it. This chapter also examines a range of economic options (the instruments of trade and aid), as well as this nation's reliance on the evocation of moral principles and "soft power."

THE WAR POWER

The **war power**, defined broadly in the preceding chapter to mean the actual or threatened use of overt military force, represents the most extreme and hazardous means for pursuing foreign policy goals. The importance of the war power stems from the fundamental fact that international politics remains in a primitive state, with force the final arbiter between sovereign nations. From time to time, nations find it in their best interests to use military force, turning to the uniformed services to secure their objectives—especially after the quieter approaches of diplomacy or covert action have failed. In March 2003, after unsuccessful attempts through diplomacy and covert action to stop Iraq's program to develop **weapons of mass destruction** (**WMD**)—nuclear, biological, and chemical arms, sometimes referred to as "NBC weapons"—George W. Bush's administration decided that it would take a military invasion and the toppling of Saddam Hussein's regime to guarantee an end to the threat.

Many others disagreed with the president's intention to go to war. They believed that UN weapons inspectors, back in Iraq after several years' absence, should be given more time to search for WMDs, and that Congress should have a full-fledged debate on the wisdom of military intervention. "There was no need for Congress to act when it did," wrote Louis Fisher. "Instead of passing legislation to authorize war, members of Congress agreed to compromise language that left the decisive judgment with the President. Placing the power to initiate war in the hands of one person was precisely what the Framers hoped to avoid when they drafted the Constitution."[2]

Arguments over how the United States should enter into war aside (discussed in Chapter 9), whatever instruments of foreign policy a nation selects, success often depends on having a convincing backstop of military power—an ability to change the behavior of another state through the threat or application of armed force. The security of America's citizens is the government's first obligation and, in the final analysis, this security rests on a nation's capacity to defend its citizens with weapons and warriors.

One use of a military backstop can be seen in the idea of what Alexander George refers to as "coercive diplomacy" or "forceful persuasion." Military force is presented as a threat to an adversary to persuade him to change unwanted behavior—speaking softly to opponents, but carrying a big stick, as Teddy Roosevelt advised. Of course, as George notes, the success of this maneuver depends upon having a rational adversary. "In some cultures," he cautions, "leaders respond very negatively indeed to being threatened or are constrained by domestic pressures from backing down in the face of an ultimatum. Then, too, there is the possibility that the opponent will misperceive and miscalculate."[3]

The war power is significant as well because high stakes attend its use, as the names on the Vietnam War Memorial attest. Whether to take up arms has always been the most fateful decision a nation can make and may call for, as President Abraham Lincoln expressed so movingly in the Gettysburg Address, a citizen's "last full measure of devotion."

With the dawning of the nuclear age in 1945, the dangers of military conflict have dramatically escalated. Modern WMDs hold the prospect of widespread death and even the possible extinction of whole societies. As two authorities have noted, "the central fact of life in the nuclear age is the unquestioned and unambiguous ability of nations possessing nuclear weapons to destroy each other."[4] Terrorists who fly airplanes into buildings, or who spread smallpox virus in the streets of a metropolis, disseminate anthrax by letter or from the valves of a crop duster, or release toxic chemicals like the nerve gas sarin into subway systems, are perils that can no longer be dismissed as fanciful science fiction.

The Dimensions of Warfare

The war power involves more than the threat or application of force against the enemy. **Military strategy,** the overt use of armed force to achieve foreign policy goals, depends on a complex interplay of operational, logistical, social, and technological considerations.[5] American policymakers—indeed, the policymakers of any country—must take into account all four dimensions of military strategy before they decide to use war, or the threat of war, as a policy instrument.

The **operational dimension** consists of the skill displayed by a nation's battlefield commanders and Pentagon war planners, particularly the flexibility and imagination with which they handle their troops and arms. Having a Robert E. Lee, a Ulysses S. Grant, a Duke of Wellington, or a Vo Nguyen Giap (the commander of the North Vietnamese during

America's war in Vietnam) at the helm clearly can be of enormous importance when a nation goes to war.

Yet as reflected in the experiences of the American Civil War, the presence of a Robert E. Lee does not guarantee victory. The Union Army won in part because the North was able to deploy overwhelming physical force against the South. The superior roads and riverways enjoyed by northern generals, along with the North's greater industrial capacity to produce rifles and cannonballs—the **logistical dimension** of military strategy—relegated the South's often brilliant operational abilities to a level of secondary importance.

But efficient transportation systems and factories are in themselves insufficient to ensure battlefield success. Political will, as the famous military theorist Karl von Clausewitz (1780–1831) emphasized, is indispensable for victory in war. When it came to the massive production of weapons, North Vietnam had no hope of matching the United States during the war in Vietnam, even with the help of the Soviet Union and China. Missing from the American side, however, was a resolute desire to stay the course regardless of time, cost, and loss of life. In contrast, the North Vietnamese and their Viet Cong (VC) allies in South Vietnam seemed prepared to fight on indefinitely. During the American Civil War, leaders in the South had hoped the Northerners would tire of the conflict and quit. Lyndon Johnson's administration hoped the same of the North Vietnamese and the VC. In both cases, wishful thinking led to a fatal miscalculation.

As military historian Michael Howard has noted with respect to the American Civil War, once both sides displayed equal degrees of steadfastness—the **social dimension** of strategy—"the capacity of the North to mobilize superior forces ultimately became the decisive factor in the struggle."[6] The terrorist group al Qaeda may have similarly miscalculated that the attacks on the World Trade Center and the Pentagon in September 2001 would undermine American will and cause the United States to retreat from the Middle East and South Asia, as it had from Somalia in 1993.

Moreover, **weapons technology,** the fourth dimension of military strategy, can be a significant factor in some instances—although not in the American Civil War, where both sides had arms of comparable strength. The longbow, the breech-loading rifle, steel breech-loading artillery, and the atomic bomb are examples of weapons that gave one nation a decided edge over another in past military struggles. A more recent example is the use of precision bombing in the 1991 Persian Gulf War, the war against al Qaeda and the Taliban regime in Afghanistan in 2001–2002, and the Iraq War in 2003.

America's Modern Weapons of War

The United States, like other major powers, has a military arsenal filled with strategic nuclear, tactical nuclear, and conventional weapons. The most fearful are the **strategic nuclear weapons**, which are able to strike the enemy from afar with massive levels of destructive power caused by a release of nuclear energy. These weapons include intercontinental ballistic missiles (ICBMs), submarine-launched ballistic missiles (SLBMs), and long-range bombers equipped with nuclear warheads. **Tactical nuclear weapons** also rely on a nuclear reaction for their force, but one of more limited explosive yield designed to eliminate relatively small targets on a battlefield. Some of these "theater nuclear weapons" can deliver a larger punch, however, than the bombs dropped on Hiroshima and Nagasaki.

Both strategic and tactical nuclear weapons continue to attract interest and funding in Washington. In a December 2003 memo to the nation's weapons laboratories, the head of the National Nuclear Security Administration commented on the recent congressional repeal, at the urging of George W. Bush's administration, of a 1994 ban on U.S. research and development into low-yield nuclear weapons. "We are now free," read the memo, "to explore a range of technical options that could strengthen our ability to deter, or respond to new or emerging threats, without any concern that some ideas could inadvertently violate a vague and arbitrary limitation."[7] The congressional action set the stage for the administration's pursuit of a new generation of nuclear weaponry.

Conventional weapons rely on nonnuclear technology: everything from M-16 rifles to the blast effect of chemical reactions. This distinction is somewhat artificial, though, since the destructive force of some advanced, high-yield conventional weapons such as the "Daisy Cutter" bomb used in 2001–2002 against the Taliban regime in Afghanistan

Submarines that launch nuclear-tipped ballistic missiles with ranges of thousands of miles were key elements of U.S. deterrence strategy, based on the triad—submarines, bombers, and land-based missiles—during the Cold War, and remain major parts of the U.S. defense establishment today.

are barely distinguishable from low-yield tactical nuclear weapons in terms of the damage they can inflict.

The Effects of Nuclear Weapons

The world continues to bristle with nuclear weapons, even though some nations like the United States and Russia have sought to reduce their enormous stockpiles through arms control negotiations. Moreover, the prospects for the proliferation of nuclear weapons in the developing world remain worrisome, despite an occasional renouncement of advanced programs by some nations such as Libya's declaration in the closing days of 2003 that it would eschew further development of NBC weapons. Given this situation, it is important for students of foreign policy to understand the potential **effects of nuclear weapons.**

Upon detonation, they produce intense heat, strong blast and high winds, radiation (which can be long lasting), and severe atmospheric disturbances. The immediate consequence of a nuclear explosion is widespread devastation around the target center. The figures in Table 10.1, based on the assumption of a normal, clear day (12-mile visibility) and 80 percent of the nuclear fireball dissipated, provide a sense of the relationship between a bomb's yield and the thermal, blast, and radiation effects. In a nuclear attack against a city, about 50 percent of the deaths would come from the release of thermal energy, 35 percent from the blast wave, and 15 percent from the ionized radiation.[8] The larger the yield of the weapons, the more important the thermal effect becomes. As shown in the table, thermal radiation is the greatest danger to human beings, even at a considerable distance from the center of the explosion (ground zero). Nations with nuclear weapons have targeting plans that revolve around two major options: an attack against military weapons and facilities (a **counterforce** targeting strategy) or against industrial and communications centers (a city-oriented **countervalue** targeting strategy). In both cases, the blast effect is important. Indeed, the destructive radius of the blast wave is an even more important calculation for war planners than a bomb's thermal effects.

Nuclear weapons also emit gamma rays, a type of radiation that literally tears apart the molecules of human tissues as the particles penetrate the body. If gamma rays enter the testes or ovaries, they can cause genetic alterations. The effects of radiation are often delayed, with cancers appearing five or even 40 years after the initial exposure. The **rad** is the unit used to measure how much gamma energy is absorbed by a human. A dental x-ray is equivalent to about 0.1 rads. Following an exposure to 450 rads, an individual has a 50–50 chance of dying—that is, about 50 percent of those exposed to this level of radiation will succumb.

Electromagnetic pulses (EMPs) are also a product of nuclear explosions. According to a weapons expert, "gamma rays will cause electrons to be ejected from atoms in the air, thus ionizing the atmosphere around the burst. This will result in disturbances of electromagnetic waves transmitted by radar and communications equipment."[9] All communications and radar operations, along with the microchips in the ignition of automobiles and computers, would be disrupted or destroyed.

Scientists worry, too, about the prospect of a **nuclear winter.** Using computer modeling, some have predicted catastrophic effects on the earth's climate if several cities were targeted in a nuclear war. The soot from burning buildings would rise into the

TABLE 10.1
THE EFFECTS OF NUCLEAR WEAPONS

Yield	Radius in miles of third-degree burns	Radius in miles of 165-mph winds	Radius in miles of 500 rads of radiation
2 KT	0.58	0.55	0.57
13 KT	1.40	1.00	0.80
1 MT	8.00	4.30	1.60
20 MT	25.00	11.80	3.00

Yield in kilotons (KT) and megatons (MT). 165-mph winds are equivalent to about 5 pounds per square inch (psi) pressure above normal atmospheric pressure. (An overpressure of 3 psi is sufficient to collapse a frame house.)

Source: George Rathjens, Harvard-MIT Summer Program on Nuclear Weapons and Arms Control, Cambridge, Mass., June 17, 1985.

atmosphere and block out the sun's rays, bringing about a rapid drop in earth temperatures. The surface of the planet might freeze to a depth of a meter, making if difficult if not impossible to bury the dead. Food supplies would diminish and drinking water would freeze. Looking into the nuclear winter hypothesis in the event of a nuclear exchange between the United States and the Soviet Union, a research team concluded: "It is clear that the ecosystem effects *alone* resulting from a large-scale thermonuclear war could be enough to destroy the current civilization in at least the Northern Hemisphere.... The possibility of the extinction of *Homo sapiens* cannot be excluded."[10]

No one really knows with certainty what the ecological effects of a nuclear war would be. Even without a nuclear winter, however, the post-attack conditions would be grim. Radiation would linger, medical supplies (including antibodies) would be destroyed, and a sizable proportion of the total number of physicians and nurses would be killed or incapacitated. In the case of a 6,500 megaton attack against the United States (the baseline normally used by analysts during the Cold War in estimates on the effects of a nuclear war between the two superpowers), about half of America's grain supply would be immediately destroyed. Further, the distribution of food would be enormously difficult and, in the filthy, garbage-strewn post-attack environment, a recrudescence of the rat population would occur. The United States would be thrown back into a "medieval setting."[11] So would the nation that initiated the attack, for it would soon experience the full retaliatory effects of an American response.

Conventional Weapons

While the biggest bang remains in the nuclear arsenal, the biggest bucks are spent on conventional weapons. During the Cold War, Secretary of Defense Robert S. McNamara explained why. "The fact that the Soviet Union and the United States can mutually destroy one another regardless of who strikes first narrows the range of Soviet aggression which our nuclear forces can effectively deter," he wrote. "We, and our allies as well, require substantial non-nuclear forces in order to cope with levels of aggression that massive strategic forces do not, in fact, deter."[12] The United States could not use nuclear weapons to settle the conflicts in Vietnam, Somalia, the Balkans, the Persian Gulf, or Afghanistan, for instance, without the world viewing Americans as despicable monsters. Instead, the United States appropriately relied on convention weapons to fight in these conflicts.

The Dangers of Chemical and Biological Weapons

Nuclear weapons are not the only means of mass destruction. **Chemical and biological weapons** could also be used by unscrupulous nations or nonstate actors. While the United States eschews the use of such weapons, some dictators have released these substances against their enemies, most recently Iraq in a war against Iran during the 1980s. Americans must be on guard against their use against the homeland or U.S. troops abroad. Imagine, for example, these plausible scenarios[13]:

- An al Qaeda member leases or steals a Twin Otter airplane from a small airport in the Virginia countryside. He heads for Washington, D.C., then drops a fine rain of anthrax spores out the window from a suitcase while flying at low altitude along the Smithsonian Mall in the nation's capital. The attack would prove fatal within 48 hours to almost everyone inside the Washington Beltway.[14]

- A White House science adviser informs the president that North Korea is probably developing biological weapons, most likely using smallpox, a disease thought to have been responsible for the deaths of at least 300 million people in the twentieth century alone and more people through the ages than any other infectious disease, including the Black Death of the Middle Ages.[15] The adviser suggests that the leaders of North Korea, known to have resorted in the past to risky acts of brinkmanship in their dealings with other nations, may have in mind loading a missile with hundreds of small bomblets filled with smallpox virus and firing the projectile at the United States. At least some of the bomblets would likely slip through any missile defense program the United States might develop in the near future, and the disease would be disseminated over a wide area.[16]

One does not have to be a Chicken Little to have some concern about scenarios like these. Two authorities noted in 1993, for example, that the likelihood of terrorists using biological agents as weapons is "probably increasing, as biological weapons proliferate and the stability of the cold war balance of power passes."[17] Similarly, an analyst in the Canadian Security Intelligence Service concluded that "the likelihood of future terrorist use of CB [chemical-biological] agents is both real and growing."[18] In 2004, a study by the Center for Strategic and International Studies in Washington, D.C., concluded that the United States is woefully ill prepared to detect and respond to a bioterrorist assault, warning that "biological weapons have the potential to cause casualties equal to, or far greater than, nuclear weapons."[19]

In 1999, the chairman of the National Intelligence Council stated that the peril of chemical and biological terrorist operations against the United States is rising, and former intelligence director James Woolsey pointed to biological terrorism as "the single most dangerous threat to our national security in the foreseeable future."[20] President Bill Clinton came to the conclusion, based on CIA reports, that a terrorist group would try a chemical or biological attack against this nation within a few years.[21]

Experts consider smallpox the greatest biological threat facing the United States— "far more deadly than a nuclear weapon"—since 42 percent of the American public have never been vaccinated against the disease.[22] During the Cold War, the Soviet Union evidently made tons of smallpox virus, and designed special warheads to deliver the lethal scourge to the United States in long-range missiles, should a war have broken out between the superpowers.[23] Next in the hierarchy of dangers is an anthrax attack. In light of these threats, political scientist Richard K. Betts called for "standby programs for mass vaccinations and emergency treatment with antibiotics" to increase the protection or recover from biological attacks.[24]

Military Power and Deterrence as Policy Instruments

The array of military forces available to American policymakers is large and diverse. It must be understood, though, that not every military capability can be used in every situation. A Delta Force team could not have stopped a Soviet invasion of Europe during the Cold War; tanks are not much good for sneaking up on terrorists bivouacked in the desert; nuclear bombs are excessive in a guerrilla war; aircraft carriers have no relevance in defending against cyberwarfare (attacks against America's computer infrastructure). Different weapons have different roles. As Donald M. Snow explains, the uses of military force vary according to the nature of specific threats faced by the United States. "The *military instrument of power*," he writes, "is not *an* instrument at all but a series of instruments of various sizes and natures that can be applied to a panoply of situations."[25]

During the Cold War, the United States concentrated on deterring a U.S.-Soviet conflict, since a nuclear war would have been devastating to both societies. While all of America's weapons—conventional, tactical nuclear, strategic nuclear, and (when the United States had them) chemical and biological—played a role in deterrence, most of the nation's deterrence posture relied on strategic nuclear weapons.

What exactly is deterrence? **Deterrence** is the ability to convince an enemy not to attack because of the certainty of a devastating retaliatory attack. Soviet leaders understood that the superpowers were like two scorpions in a jar: if one stung the other, the attacker would be stung in return and both would die. In a different metaphor, the superpowers were like two men in a cellar standing in gasoline up to their necks, with their arms aloft and matchboxes in their hands; if either struck a match, both would be consumed in the conflagration. The dire consequences that stemmed from the doctrine of deterrence—or "mutually assured destruction," with its memorable acronym, MAD—kept both sides at bay and discouraged the outbreak of a nuclear World War III.

John Foster Dulles, secretary of state during the Eisenhower years, took the doctrine of deterrence to an extreme, declaring that the United States would pursue a strategy of "massive retaliation" against Soviet territorial expansion—a daring assertion that became known as "brinkmanship." The economist Thomas C. Schelling referred to this threatened use of nuclear weapons as a means for gaining political influence over the Soviets as "diplomacy of violence."[26]

The Kennedy Administration became convinced that it was foolhardy—and dangerous—to rely on nuclear saber-rattling to protect America's global interests. It developed a military strategy of "flexible response," developing lower levels of weaponry that could be used to respond to threats of guerrilla warfare in the jungles of Southeast Asia and other contingencies around the world. If it had to, America would be prepared to fight "limited wars" and "low-intensity conflicts." Officials in Washington made sure that the United

States deployed more than enough nuclear weapons to keep the Soviets honest and for targeting their larger number of ground troops, should the Red Army prove brazen enough to pour through the Fulda Gap in an assault against Western Europe. But America would also have tanks and missiles, as well as aircraft carriers and Green Berets, attack helicopters and bombers, to fight lesser wars, if necessary, or to rescue Americans overseas caught in hostile situations that involved foreign mobs, armies, or guerrilla forces.

The Triad

During the Cold War, the United States developed different ways to deliver American nuclear weapons against the Soviet Union, as a means of protecting its ultimate deterrent—strategic nuclear weapons—against a surprise attack ordered by the Kremlin. This system is known as the **triad** and consists of ICBMs (intercontinental ballistic missiles), SLBMs (submarine-launched ballistic missiles), and intercontinental bombers armed with nuclear bombs.

The ICBMs are poised ready for launch in underground silos, located chiefly in the West and Midwest regions of the United States. They are capable of hitting targets halfway around the world in 30 minutes with a high degree of accuracy. The submarine leg of the triad is the least vulnerable to an enemy's first-strike capability. Hiding deep beneath the ocean's surface, each American nuclear submarine is armed with 16 or more SLBMs that together can inflict more destructive power on an enemy than the aggregate total of every weapon ever used in the history of warfare. Moreover, the submarines are difficult to track and, if found, even harder to attack. The major shortcoming of this leg of the triad is the difficulty the Pentagon faces in communicating with a submarine that is deeply submerged. The bomber leg of the triad has some special advantages. This is the only system that can be redirected, or even recalled, after being set on its flight path. Critics believe, however, that bombers, even those with radar-elusive Stealth technology, have become the dinosaurs of the nuclear age: large, slow-moving targets, easy for enemy fighter planes and surface-to-air missiles (SAMs) to destroy. The figures in Table 10.2 display the distribution of strategic warheads across the triad for both the United States and Russia as of 2002.

TABLE 10.2
STRATEGIC WARHEADS: A U.S. AND RUSSIAN COMPARISON, 2002

	Number of Strategic Warheads	
Weapon system	*U.S.*	*Russia*
Land		
ICBMs	1,701	3,364
Sea		
SLBMs	3,120	1,868
Air		
Bombers	1,128	626
Totals	5,949	5,858

Source: Adapted from the U.S. Arms Control Association Fact Sheets, 2002.

Ballistic Missile Defense

Not wishing to rely on the triad alone for protection against attack, the Reagan Administration conceived of an imaginative proposal to shield the United States against a nuclear missile assault during the Cold War. The plan, which envisioned shooting down the missiles with space-based laser technology, was known within the administration as the Strategic Defense Initiative (SDI), but it was labeled "Star Wars" by the media, after a popular science fiction film at the time loaded with laser-beam weapons. Whether such a **ballistic missile defense (BMD)**—presently referred to as a **ground-based interceptor (GBI)** system—would actually work remains a topic of intense debate. Many scientists are skeptical. They calculate that it would be relatively easy for a well-armed adversary to overwhelm a BMD/GBI system by firing nuclear-tipped missiles at the United States, accompanied by thousands of decoy missiles to confuse ground interceptors.

Proponents of ballistic missile defense, including President George W. Bush, speak more of knocking down with a limited BMD system small numbers of incoming missiles fired at the United States by terrorists or rogue nations, rather than trying to counter a massive onslaught of missiles fired by a major adversary. This more feasible objective is more persuasive, especially in light of the terrorist attacks of September 2001. Ironically, though, the terrorists who attacked the World Trade Center and the Pentagon needed only box-cutters to take over four U.S. commercial airliners to use as weapons. A GBI system would have been of no use against this type of threat, just as it would fail to guard against a nuclear weapon on a cargo ship steaming into an American harbor, on a train passing through a city, or hidden inside a truck or an SUV in an underground parking lot beneath a towering building.

The Doctrine of Preemptive Defense

Even though the Cold War is over, the nuclear deterrent presumably continues to cause adversaries (new and old) to think twice before attacking the United States with large-scale force. Similarly, the lower range of weaponry has a deterrent effect against some nonnuclear nations and factions, since an armed retaliation by the United States with conventional forces can be, for all practical purposes, just as lethal as a nuclear response.

What happens, however, when deterrence fails? At the nuclear level, the assumption is that the United States, if attacked with nuclear weapons, would immediately launch a devastating strategic nuclear counterattack. Fortunately, this assumption has never had to be tested. At the conventional level, however, history provides some recent examples of failed deterrence. Iraq's Saddam Hussein thought in 1991 that the United States would not respond to his invasion of Kuwait, perhaps in part because the U.S. ambassador in Iraq at the time may have given the dictator a false impression that the United States would remain idle. In 2003, he again believed that the United States would not attack his country to stop whatever WMD programs he might have had underway. Wrong both times. The terrorist group al Qaeda seemed impervious to deterrence, too, apparently motivated to attack the United States in 2001 by an ideology that espouses the virtue of death to al Qaeda fighters in a holy war *(jihad)* against the American Satan. At the conventional level, then, the answer in recent years to the question "What happens if deterrence fails?" is clear: America's armed services shift from a state of potential energy to kinetic energy, striking back at the attackers with swift and overwhelming force, as Iraq and al Qaeda have recently experienced.

The 2001 terrorist attacks against the United States, coupled with the danger that rogue nations or terrorists might acquire WMDs and use them against the American homeland or U.S. troops abroad, led George W. Bush's administration to conclude that deterrence might no longer be effective against potential enemies. The United States needed to adopt an additional—and more aggressive—policy tool to enhance American security. On June 1, 2002, Bush unveiled in a commencement address at the United States Military Academy the outlines of a new American defense strategy. Declaring that in the war against terrorism "deterrence—the promise of massive retaliation against nations—means nothing against shadowy terrorist networks with no nation or citizens to defend," the president said that henceforth the United States would "confront the worst threats before they emerge" through a policy of **preemption.**

Three months later, the Bush Administration formally changed U.S. defense strategy to embrace this new doctrine.[27] The United States would "no longer solely rely on a reactive posture as we have in the past…. We cannot let our enemies strike first…. As a matter of common sense and self-defense, America will act against emerging threats before they are full formed."[28]

This major departure from earlier practice was legitimate, in the eyes of the Bush Administration, because of the destruction of the World Trade Center and the attack on the Pentagon in 2001. An important consideration, too, was the fear expressed later in the year by the president's national security adviser, Condoleezza Rice. She warned that we would see a mushroom cloud from a nuclear weapon over an American city, unless the U.S. acted in a preemptive manner against rogue states and terrorist groups.

Critics were quick to reject the preemptive approach to foreign threats. They reasoned that deterrence worked against most enemies, and that al Qaeda could be handled by tracking down the terrorists with the CIA or Special Forces. Critics also feared that preemption opened a Pandora's box in which a state could use force against any neighbor, claiming that it had to resort to warfare in order to preempt an attack the other side was allegedly planning. Should Pakistan attack India preemptively because the latter might attack it, or vice versa? Surely this would lead to a nuclear war in South Asia. What kind of world would it be where nations launched surprise attacks against other nations for fear that the same thing could happen to them? It seemed a recipe for chaos. "The campaign for war [in Iraq]," Louis Fisher argued, "was dominated more by fear than facts, more by assertions of what might be, or could be, or used to be, than by what actually existed."[29]

Yet the smoldering ruins of the World Trade Center on the afternoon of September 11, 2001, and the mushroom cloud that Rice speaks of are images difficult to dismiss; they lend some credence to the argument in favor of preemption, at least in times of a clear and present danger. Thus, a new foreign policy debate was joined. The doctrine of preemption will remain an important and controversial subject in the coming years.

How Much Is Enough?

The same question that has plagued every American president from George Washington to the present will continue to perplex future chief executives: "How much should the United

States spend on weapons and troops to defend itself?" Clearly, the president and other decision makers have an immense military establishment at their disposal. At the same time, as September 11, 2001, made abundantly clear, the United States faces an uncertain and dangerous international situation. Answers to the question of military spending have varied from administration to administration. Indeed, the same president sometimes answered the question in different ways, as shown by Jimmy Carter before and after the Soviet invasion of Afghanistan in 1979, and George W. Bush before and after the 9/11 attacks.

Specific numbers help illustrate the point. The U.S. investment in conventional forces during the Reagan Administration was unprecedented in peacetime: 8–9 percent real growth in defense expenditures per annum (in 1986 constant dollars)—the highest growth rate since the Second World War. Annual military spending neared $400 billion in 1987; it was $144 billion in 1980. After the Cold War ended in 1991, Presidents George H. W. Bush and Bill Clinton reduced U.S. defense spending in search of a "peace dividend" to spend on domestic programs. In the aftermath of the 2001 terrorist attacks against the United States, however, President George W. Bush proposed a $379 billion defense budget in 2002—an increase of $48 billion over the previous year. The defense budget of George W. Bush's administration has exceeded the annual military expenditures of all the rest of the nations of the world combined.[30]

A further consideration is that warfare, preemptive or otherwise, can be a highly unpredictable venture. As Snow notes, "once we get in, we find that the situation is more intractable than we had realized, that our involvement is more open ended than we had thought, and that long-term success is much more difficult to attain than we had calculated."[31] Not the least of the challenges is to repair the damage caused by war. This involves the physical reconstruction of the territory where the war has been waged and, more complicated still, the creation of order, stability, and justice in the area—in a word, state-building, a task that has proven to be enormously difficult and expensive in places like Afghanistan and Iraq.

Moreover, the costs of war are not only monetary. At the beginning of the twentieth century, the young Winston Churchill, who would become prime minister of Great Britain during the Second World War, participated in a cavalry charge by the 21st Lancers against the fearsome, scimitar-wielding Dervish warriors in Egypt. "Nobody expected to be killed," he later recalled. "Here and there in every regiment or battalion, half a dozen, a score, at the worst thirty or forty, would pay the forfeit; but to the great mass of those who took part in the little wars of Britain in those vanished light-hearted days, this was only a sporting element in a splendid game."[32] Modern weaponry and terrorism have brought an end to war as a genteel pursuit for the professional military. Now, as the attack on the World Trade Center and the Pentagon reminded us, each one of us could be a target.

Ideally, the outbreak of war or other forms of violence between states and factions might be avoided through a peaceful negotiation of disputes. This is the goal of diplomacy, a vital instrument of American foreign policy.

THE POWER OF DIPLOMACY

Diplomacy (from the Greek *diplomata*, meaning "folded documents") may be defined as "the formalized system of procedures or the process by which sovereign states, usually through ambassadors or other diplomatic representatives but sometimes through executive agents, conduct their official relations."[33] Former U.S. ambassador George Kennan put it more simply: diplomacy is "the business of communicating between governments."[34] Ideally, the United States would like to settle disputes with other nations and groups without the use of military force and loss of life; diplomacy holds that promise. As former Secretary of State Henry Kissinger has written, "[the statesman's] instrument is diplomacy, the art of relating states to each other by agreement rather than by the exercise of force."[35]

In the view of international relations scholar Hans J. Morgenthau, diplomacy is one of the most important powers a nation has—second only to military strength (the *sine qua non* for state survival in the realist's perspective on world affairs). Morgenthau considered diplomacy an "art" whose purpose was nothing less than to bring "the different elements of national power to bear with maximum effect upon those points in the international situation which concern the national interest most directly." When carried out with competence, diplomacy managed to "bring the ends and means of foreign policy into harmony with the available resources of national power."[36]

The American ambassador David D. Newsom stressed that once a sound foreign policy is crafted by a nation's leaders, "diplomacy can then add the needed skills of implementation in the knowledge of other cultures, the skill of negotiation, the art of persuasion, and the power to observe and report." He continued: "The policies the United States pursues … must, to be acceptable, be expressed and explained and defended to skeptical, distracted, and occasionally unfriendly governments and peoples abroad. This becomes the task of the American diplomat who, in a mediating role, must also explain the realities that confront America to those in Washington who may be unready to accept the anomalies of an outside world."[37]

Entering into International Agreements

The United States uses three major forms of agreement making in its diplomatic negotiations: the treaty, the statutory agreement, and the executive agreement. As discussed in Chapter 9, the **treaty power** is based on Article II, Section 2, of the Constitution, which states that the president "shall have power by and with the advice of the Senate to make treaties, provided two-thirds of the Senators present concur." On any important treaty, all 100 members are likely to be present, so the executive branch must count on mustering at least 67 votes for a treaty to pass.

The **statutory agreement** also involves legislative authority, but instead of two-thirds approval in the Senate, which can be difficult to achieve on contentious issues, this procedure requires an easier majority vote—although in *both* chambers of Congress. With this approach, Congress authorizes a formal relationship with another country by passing a law to that effect. The simplest way for a president to make an international agreement, however, is to bypass Congress altogether, avoiding debate, criticism, and perhaps defeat on Capitol Hill. That is a major attraction of the **executive agreement,** whereby the executive branch enters into a diplomatic understanding with another nation without the advice and consent of the Senate or the counsel of the House of Representatives. Use of this instrument amounts to diplomacy by executive fiat.

Originally designed as the solemn means by which the United States would enter into commitments with other nations, in the modern era the treaty has been largely abandoned by presidents in favor of statutory and executive agreements. For example, from 1946 through the 1970s, a scant 6 percent of the total number of international agreements entered into by the United States were approved by way of the constitutional treaty procedure, although a few like the Panama Canal Treaty of 1978 were of substantial importance. The overwhelming percentage (87 percent) of all U.S. international pacts during this period were statutory agreements, and only about 7 percent were executive agreements. Within this 7 percent, however, were some far-reaching pacts, such as the establishment of a new and expensive U.S. military base in South Korea.[38] These figures, which have remained fairly steady in more recent years, indicate that Congress has been involved in international agreements, but chiefly through the instrument of normal lawmaking—not the treaty procedure.

Controversy over Executive Agreements

Even though Congress remains a participant in the making of international agreements, the use of executive agreements has evoked extensive controversy between the executive and legislative branches of government. President Franklin D. Roosevelt's use of an executive agreement to provide destroyers to Great Britain in 1940 was one of the main reasons the debate was joined. In the summer of 1940, Great Britain faced an imminent German invasion. France had already fallen and the English Channel no longer seemed an adequate barrier in light of the formidable military capabilities of the Nazi war machine. To help stem a German invasion of the British Isles, Roosevelt authorized a major military agreement with the United Kingdom. The United States would lend the British 50 somewhat antiquated American destroyers in exchange for leasing rights to certain naval bases in the Western Hemisphere that belonged to the U.K. This **"Lend-Lease" Agreement** provided legal grounds for a possible declaration of war against the United States by the Germans.

While one might have expected such a serious commitment to be the subject of a formal treaty, Roosevelt instead used an executive agreement. By his own signature—without even the slightest nod to Congress, let alone a request for a two-thirds vote of support within the Senate—the president moved the United States closer to entering the Second World War. Although Congress later in March 1941 formally approved and even expanded the Lend-Lease Program, allowing Roosevelt to "sell, transfer title to, exchange, lease, lend, or otherwise dispose of" arms, munitions, and any other defense materials to "any country whose defense the President deems vital to the defense of the United States," it was clear that a major watershed had been passed in American foreign policy.

President Roosevelt's motives were no doubt of the highest order. He quite properly hoped to turn back the totalitarian tide that was flowing against the Western democracies, and he felt he had to move quickly before it was too late. A debate in the Senate might have prolonged—or even thwarted—an American response, just as Senate debate had undermined America's entry into the League of Nations in 1920 even though President Woodrow Wilson was the leading international spokesman for the organization. London might have fallen before the British received the ships they needed to defend themselves.

Critics of Roosevelt's bypassing of the treaty procedure contend, however, that he exceeded his constitutional authority. In a study of the treaty process, the Senate Foreign

Relations Committee concluded in 1969: "More serious in the long run than the President's action [the lend-lease agreement] was the preparation of a brief by the Attorney General contending that the action was constitutional. Had the President publicly acknowledged his incursion on the Senate's treaty power and explained it as an emergency measure, a damaging constitutional precedent would have been averted. Instead, a spurious claim of constitutionality was made, compounding the incursion on the Senate's authority into a precedent for future incursions."[39]

The destroyers-for-bases agreement ushered in an era that witnessed the rapid erosion of the treaty power in favor of statutory and executive agreements. Roosevelt's deal with the British by way of an executive agreement, reached in a time of emergency, came to be seen by officials in the executive branch as a precedent to draw upon following the Second World War.

Executive agreements remained controversial during the Cold War, as the executive branch continued to use them to undertake actions that it deemed appropriate but feared Congress might derail. For example, in 1962, Secretary of State Dean Rusk joined with the foreign minister of Thailand to issue a statement in which Rusk announced "the firm intention of the United States to aid Thailand, its ally and historic friend, in resisting Communist aggression and subversion." This pledge went far beyond the language of the Southeast Asia Treaty Organization (SEATO) Treaty, signed in 1954, which provided only that member nations would "consult" in times of military peril and act to meet the common danger in accordance with their own "constitutional processes." The communique and the new executive agreements transformed the collective security arrangement established under SEATO into a bilateral U.S.-Thai defense pact.[40]

There was precedent for Rusk's action. Earlier, during the Eisenhower Administration, the United States had entered into a similar arrangement with the Philippines. The Philippines already enjoyed (since 1952) a formal military alliance with the United States, based on the Philippines Mutual Defense Treaty. This treaty ensured consultation and, if necessary, military protection, in accordance with America's constitutional processes—that is, approval by Congress and the president. Yet these assurances were evidently insufficient for Philippine President Magsaysay, who in 1954 requested additional guarantees of an American military shield. In response, Secretary of State John Foster Dulles forwarded to Magsaysay a diplomatic communique that said, since U.S. military forces were already stationed in his country, "an armed attack on the Philippines could not but be also an attack upon the military forces of the United States." In place of "constitutional processes," Dulles had substituted assurances of a quick American military response. President Eisenhower and a new president of the Philippines (Garcia) reaffirmed this "further bilateral assurance" (the State Department's euphemism) through a joint communique in 1958, and by a more formal executive agreement the following year, the Bohlen-Serrano Agreement.[41]

The stationing of U.S. troops in the Philippines had been far more telling about America's military intentions than the language of a formal treaty. As a Senate inquiry into U.S. military commitments abroad concluded in 1970: "Overseas bases, the presence of elements of U.S. armed forces, joint planning, joint exercises, or extensive military assistance programs represent to host governments more valid assurances of U.S. commitment than any treaty or agreement."[42] The executive branch was willing to provide these assurances, without public debate on their merits.

Whether or not the military alliances with Thailand and the Philippines were appropriate is a separate question. What concerned constitutional experts was the procedure selected to establish the commitments. The original intent of military alliances, approved through the rigorous and solemn treaty procedure laid out in the Constitution, had been altered by communique and follow-up secret executive agreements. In the eyes of international law, executive agreements carry the weight of treaties, as do statutory agreements. All three forms of agreements represent official commitments by the United States to other countries. Given their importance, the realization that executive agreements are sometimes made in secret—without debate in the Congress—has made them a subject of controversy.

Lawmakers accept the value of executive agreements when used for minor commitments, such as the purchase of strawberries from Mexico or the protection of migratory birds from Canada. The principles of good management argue against congressional involvement in the hundreds of routine understandings reached each year between the United States and other nations. Congress balks, though, when new and consequential commitments are pursued through this instrument of diplomacy. "In some instances," members of the Senate Foreign Relations Committee have complained, "we have come close to reversing the traditional distinction between the treaty as the instrument of major commitment and the executive agreement as the instrument of a minor one."[43]

The point of the complaint is underlined by a series of secret understandings reached with Spain in 1963 regarding military base rights on the Iberian Peninsula. An official in the executive branch assured the Spanish government at the time that U.S. troops stationed in Spain would represent "a far more visible and credible security guarantee than any written document."[44] From the vantage point of the Senate Committee on Foreign Relations, though, this pronouncement epitomized the abandonment of constitutional procedure. "The making of such a commitment by means of an executive agreement, or a military memorandum," argued the committee, "has no valid place in our constitutional law, and constitutes a usurpation of the treaty power of the Senate." The committee considered the Spanish bases agreement a "quasi-commitment, unspecified as to exact import but, like buds in springtime, ready, under the right climatic conditions, to burst into full bloom."[45]

How Commitments Expand

Sometimes America's diplomatic initiatives are stretched far beyond their original intent via so-called creeping commitments. This happens as executive-branch officials seek to "fill in the details" once a broad agreement is reached. As with Dulles's interpretation of the Philippines Mutual Defense Treaty, the expansion of a relationship can be considerable. These "auxiliary arrangements"—executive agreements following in the wake of treaties and statutory agreements—take on a bewildering variety of forms, including memoranda of understanding, exchange of notes, exchange of letters, technical arrangements, protocols, the *note verbale*, the *aide mémoire,* agreed minutes, joint communiques, joint military plans, military assistance, and the stationing of troops.

The executive branch has also used secret agreements to carry out diplomacy. Chiding Secretary of State Henry Kissinger for "obsessive secrecy," Senator Henry Jackson (D-Washington) once accused him of withholding from Congress for two years secret "understandings" reached with the Soviet Union during the initial negotiations over SALT

(Strategic Arms Limitation Talks). Jackson further alleged that Kissinger had withheld from Congress "crucial communications" on the faltering U.S.-Soviet trade talks in 1974.[46] Diplomatic correspondent Tad Szulc drew a similar conclusion about the secretary of state. "The fact is that virtually nobody—possibly not even [Presidents] Richard Nixon and Gerald Ford—knew precisely what promises and commitments Kissinger made to foreign leaders during his eight years in power," Szulc charged, "to Mao Tse-tung and Chou En-lai, Brezhnev and Dobrynin, Le Duc Tho, Sadat and King Faisal, Golda Meir or any number of other foreign presidents, foreign ministers and ambassadors."[47]

One of the controversial "understandings" reached by Kissinger was with Israel and Egypt in 1975 over the question of a Sinai disengagement. These negotiations included the commitment of U.S. personnel to serve as monitors in a region where military hostilities might have easily resumed with little warning. The Department of State declared the "understanding" a proper exercise of executive authority, not a commitment requiring the treaty procedure. President Ford, however, backed away from this position as congressional criticism mounted; he eventually sought legislative authority, by way of a statutory agreement, to implement the provisions of the accord.

Placing Limits on Executive Agreements and Creeping Commitments

Ever since disputes erupted between the executive and legislative branches in the 1960s and 1970s over the Vietnam War and the Watergate scandal, Congress has struggled to restore a more meaningful role for lawmakers in the making of international agreements. At a hearing held by the Senate Foreign Relations Committee in 1971, Senator J. William Fulbright (D-Arkansas) observed: "We have discovered that the President does not always know best, and that, indeed, the country would be far better off today if the Congress had been more assertive in the exercise of its constitutional role, which consists as least as much in assertion and criticism as it does in subservience."[48] A member of the Committee argued further: "The President of the United States alone decides what is to be sent up as a treaty. The Senate has no choice in that whatsoever…. The President can dispense with Senate advice and consent merely by calling a treaty an executive agreement. I do not see that as a fair balance."[49]

Congress has had a mixed record in its efforts to limit the use of executive agreements, creeping commitments, and other executive actions designed to bypass the Congress in the making international pacts. For example, as we saw in the *Goldwater v. Carter* case of 1979 (discussed in Chapter 9), Congress has been unsuccessful in its attempt to prevent presidents from unilaterally terminating treaties. Lawmakers, though, were more successful in their efforts to prevent presidents from reinterpreting treaties by changing their original meaning by presidential decree without Senate approval. During the Reagan years, the Department of State's legal adviser, Abraham Sofaer, claimed that the administration could pursue development of the Strategic Defense Initiative without approval from the Senate for a reinterpretation of the Anti-Ballistic Missile (ABM) Treaty with the Soviet Union, which SDI would contravene. When the Senate balked at this bold attempt to strengthen the president's grip over treaties, President Reagan retreated. Later during the Reagan Administration, the Senate emphasized its concern about presidential treaty reinterpretation by insisting in the language of the Intermediate Range Nuclear

Forces (INF) Treaty in 1987 that presidents did not have unilateral authority to subsequently alter the original meaning of this or any other treaty approved by the Senate.[50]

The Value of Opportune Civilities

Most disputes between nations are resolved through diplomatic negotiations. Whatever the disagreements between the branches over how international agreements ought to be struck, one can thank the diplomats for using their negotiating talents to seek a reduction in the frequency of wars fought on this hostile globe. Diplomatic successes are most often achieved in a piecemeal manner, painstakingly fashioned and sometimes conducted through hidden "back channels," as when Henry Kissinger turned to secret diplomacy to improve U.S.-Sino relationships in the 1970s.

The British statesman Lord Salisbury (1830–1903) observed that the victories of the diplomat "are made up of a series of microscopic advantages: of a judicious suggestion here, of an opportune civility there, of a wise concession at one moment and a farsighted persistence at another; of sleepless tact, immovable calmness and patience that no folly, no provocation, no blunders can shake."[51] The opportune civilities and other advantages that diplomacy provides are critical tools that American foreign policymakers use to advance the foreign policy objectives of the United States.

INSTRUMENTS OF TRADE AND AID

Securing international trading opportunities to enhance the economic prosperity of the United States is high on the list of priorities for any American diplomat. "Aside from war and preparations for war, and occasionally aside from migration," writes economist Thomas C. Schelling, "trade is the most important relationship that most countries have with each other."[52]

The instrument of international commerce—economic statecraft—has long been an important consideration in America's relations with the world. Thomas Jefferson ordered military action against the Barbary pirates for their disruption of U.S. shipping in the Mediterranean. The Carter and Reagan Administrations consistently wrangled with the Japanese over their flooding of U.S. markets with Toyotas and Hondas while Japan constructed high tariff walls against American-made products. George W. Bush's administration has fought its own trade battles, including disputes with the Europeans over U.S. steel tariffs.

In Search of Commercial Opportunities

In pursuit of its economic goals, the United States has drawn on a range of foreign policy instruments. An important argument over the years for the establishment of a powerful navy, for example, has been to keep the sealanes open for U.S. commercial shipping. Now and then the United States has sent in the marines or the CIA to protect American business interests abroad, as in Kuwait (oil), Guatemala (bananas), and Chile (copper). Mostly, though, the United States has relied on diplomatic negotiations to establish trading partnerships.

Over 50 percent of America's exports and imports are with the industrialized nations of the West. Canada and Mexico are America's primary trading partners in this hemisphere, and Germany and Japan beyond. Canada exports more to the United States than to any other country and, in return, takes in 20 percent of all American exports—the largest two-way trading relationship in the world. Mexico is America's fourth largest export market, following Canada, the European Community, and Japan. The developing world, home of three-quarters of the world's population, is significant as well to the United States as a growing market. And it is the site of such essential resources as tin, rubber, bauxite, and oil.

Free-trade areas, such as the one established under the North American Free Trade Agreement (NAFTA), are also critical to America's international economic activity. Even so, as we saw in Chapter 7, NAFTA became a subject of national debate. President George H. W. Bush argued that NAFTA would "bring together the energies and talents of three great nations," Canada, Mexico, and the United States, and "create jobs and promote growth in the United States." Yet many Americans, especially labor unions, feared that U.S. companies might move south of the border in search of cheap labor, taking away jobs from this country. Some critics complained, too, that Mexico would ignore America's strong environmental standards, as well as its laws regulating labor conditions and the rights of workers. The debate spilled over into the Clinton Administration. Finally, in 1994, President Clinton was able to bring about passage of the trade agreement on Capitol Hill, opening up new commercial opportunities among the three nations.

From the perspective of a decade, evaluations of NAFTA are mixed, with some experts pointing to the loss of U.S. jobs to Mexico but others pointing to increased profits in both nations as a result of the improved flow of goods, services, and investment among the three signatory nations. In addition to NAFTA, in conjunction with other nations, the United States helped to develop an Asia-Pacific Economic Cooperation (APEC) forum and is working toward the establishment of a Free Trade Area of the Americas (FTAA).

Protectionism versus Free Trade

Sometimes the United States registers an imbalance in commerce with other nations. These negative trade statistics, which primarily reflect a loss of sales and jobs in domestic manufacturing, can lead to a rising tide of **protectionism,** that is, support for the use of government tariffs and quotas against imports to protect U.S. industries from foreign competitors. In 1988 and again in 2004, presidential contender Representative Richard Gephart (D-Missouri) ran on a protectionist platform. Although he never won his party's nomination, Gephart's message had substantial support in some sections of the country hit by foreign competition. As the Democratic leader in the House of Representatives, he was well known for his steady drumbeat against what he perceived as unfair Japanese trading practices. Manufacturers and trade unions in the United States have sought protection against many other products, too, such as machine tools from Germany and Switzerland.

In contrast, President Ronald Reagan steadfastly defended a policy of **free trade,** a phrase used to describe the removal of government tariffs or other restrictions on international commerce. Behind the scenes, though, the Reagan White House—like every other recent administration—pressured the Japanese and other governments to buy more U.S. products and cut back on their own flow of goods into the American market. George

W. Bush also espoused free-trade principles, but responding in 2002 to pressure from U.S. steel companies and their unions located in politically important states like Pennsylvania and West Virginia, he imposed tariffs on imported steel. Brazil criticized the tariffs, noting that they contradicted the spirit of improving free trade in the Western Hemisphere. Russia retaliated by banning imports of poultry from the United States, harming the economy of states like Georgia, which sells 80 percent of its poultry production to the Russians. The World Trade Organization ruled against the American position in most of these cases, and in 2003 the Bush Administration phased out the steel tariffs, despite strong pressure from the U.S. steel lobby to keep them in place.

Imports and Exports

Although experiencing a relative decline in recent decades, the United States is still by far the single largest international trader. America's imports consist primarily of consumer goods, automobiles, and fuels. Petroleum imports are always large and, in some years, they have accounted for as much as one-third of total U.S. imports—the largest single deficit commodity in U.S. trade. The United States has recorded significant deficits with other products as well, including motor vehicles; wearing apparel; iron and steel; consumer electronics; nonferrous metals; footwear; coffee, tea and spices; natural gas; diamonds; paper; telecommunications equipment; alcoholic beverages; toys and sporting goods; and fish.

American exports consist primarily of food, chemicals, and machinery, and the United States has enjoyed significant trade surpluses in several products, including cereals and grains; aircraft equipment and spacecraft; music CDs; films; oilseeds; computers; coal; scientific and engineering equipment; skateboards and snowboards; military arms and vehicles; construction equipment; plastic and rubber; cotton; animal feed; tobacco; power generating equipment; organic chemicals; and pharmaceutical products. Nonetheless, the United States in the 1980s imported more than it exported for the first time since 1914, and in 2004 chalked up new record trade imbalances—notably with China. This shift has been attributable mainly to a steady deterioration in America's merchandise trade performance, along with oil import costs and unfair protectionist practices in certain countries. During some months in recent decades, the United States—once the "bread-basket of the world"—has even imported more food than it exported.

The Multinationals

As if disputes between nations over exports and imports were an insufficient complication, the international economic system is made all the more complex by the existence of **multinational corporations (MNCs):** over 37,000 firms "with foreign subsidiaries which extend the production and marketing of the firm beyond the boundaries of any one country."[53] The MNCs, a driving force behind the globalization of the economy, grew up in the decades following the Second World War as a result, in part, of the international revolution in transportation and communications that made it technically possible for businesses to have ties that stretched around the world.

The effects of the MNCs have been much debated. Some observers view them as benign contributors to world trade; others see them as a spearhead of a new form of imperialism. In market economies like Canada, France, and Great Britain, American-owned MNCs seem to have produced positive results in the host economy, especially with respect to capital formation, export promotion, balance of payments, and improved access to advanced technology and management skills.

But MNCs have also cast a shadow. As Stiglitz notes, "Soft drinks manufacturers around the world have been overwhelmed by the entrance of Coca-Cola and Pepsi into their home markets."[54] Once a multinational corporation drives out the local competition, it can use its monopoly status to raise prices for its product. Some MNCs have displayed extreme predatory behavior against the governments of developing nations, as exemplified by the efforts of the International Telephone and Telegraphy Company (ITT) to undermine the Allende regime in Chile during the 1960s.

A few experts also argue that the MNC is rapidly replacing the nation as the key entity in the crafting of international economic policies. According to this view, marketing decisions by corporate executives can be more important to world affairs than the political decisions of elected representatives within a nation. The end result is the gradual subservience of state sovereignty to corporate power, as global profit considerations trump international politics and diplomacy.

The most sanguine perspective on MNCs anticipates that they will turn increasingly toward the developing world in search of raw materials and lower labor costs, leading to a mutually beneficial partnership between global corporations and poor nations; by providing better working conditions, the MNCs will boost worker productivity, bringing about a decrease in product costs.[55] A less optimistic perspective emphasizes the exploitative side of the MNCs, in which aggressive and powerful corporations dominate the developing nations.[56] A third outcome is the continuing preeminence of the nation, a condition Robert Gilpin refers to as mercantilism, that is, "the priority of *national* economic and political objectives over considerations of *global* economic efficiency."[57] In this model, which Gilpin thinks is the most probably outcome, the MNCs remain accountable to the foreign policies set by national governments. Whether these governments are benign or predatory toward the poor nations depends, though, on the philosophy of their leaders.

The Use of Trade Sanctions

Trade sanctions are another instrument of economic power available to the United States. **Most favored nation (MFN) rights,** for example, bestow upon another country the best trading relationship for their imports that the United States has to offer—a form of economic reward for nations friendly toward America and who are willing to offer reciprocal trading rights. When Chinese leaders used force against pro-democracy demonstrators in the Tiananmen Square Massacre of 1989, some U.S. lawmakers called for the termination of MFN privileges for China. President George H. W. Bush was unwilling to go that far, but he did cut off the sale of all American military equipment to Beijing.

Embargoes, which are prohibitions on exports, provide another instrument of economic statecraft. So do **boycotts,** or prohibitions against imports or other forms of business cooperation with another country. Both represent forms of economic punishment.

When the Soviet military invaded Afghanistan in 1979, President Carter instituted a grain embargo against the USSR. The Reagan Administration subsequently lifted the embargo in response to complaints from American farmers that the policy's primary effect was to harm the sales of their crops overseas. The United States has maintained a boycott against Cuban sugar ever since Cuba's communist leader, Fidel Castro, came to power in 1959. Iraq's invasion of Kuwait in 1991 provoked a worldwide boycott of Iraqi oil sales, depriving the nation of an estimated $17 billion a year in revenues. Economic analyst David Baldwin divides these and other economic instruments into positive and negative inducements, as displayed in Table 10.3.

While the array of economic "carrots and sticks" in Table 10.3 may seem potent, in fact, economic inducements have had only modest success over the years. Embargoes and boycotts often fail because other nations refuse to honor them. For example, when the United States stopped shipping grain to the Soviet Union, the farmers of Canada and Argentina were happy to accommodate the Soviet demand for grain. One authoritative study on embargoes concludes that they have "not been notably successful except as a direct adjunct of war."[58] Economic punishments have been criticized, too, for hurting not so much dictators like Saddam Hussein of Iraq as the innocent poor people who suffer beneath them.

TABLE 10.3
INSTRUMENTS OF INTERNATIONAL ECONOMIC POWER:
TRADE SANCTIONS AND INDUCEMENTS

Positive Inducements	*Negative Sanctions*
Trade	**Trade**
Favorable tariffs	Embargo
Most favored nation (MFN) rights	Boycott
Tariff reduction	Tariff discrimination
Direct purchase	Withdrawal of MFN rights
Subsidies to exports or imports	Blacklist
Granting of export and important licenses	Quotas
	License denial
	Dumping
Capital	Preclusive buying
Providing of aid	
Investment guarantees	
Encouragement of private capital	**Capital**
Favorable tax measures	Freezing assets
	Import and export controls
	Suspension of aid
	Expropriation
	Unfavorable taxation
	Withholding of dues to IMF

Source: Adapted from David A. Baldwin, *Economic Statecraft* (Princeton: Princeton University Press, 1985), pp. 41–42.

Foreign Aid as an Instrument of Foreign Policy

Foreign aid may be defined as "economic and military assistance on a government-to-government level, or through government-supported agencies or programs."[59] Economic assistance, referred to by one expert as "an obvious weapon in the contest for global influence,"[60] includes direct grants, technical cooperation, and loans that are either "hard" (offered at commercial bank interest rates) or "soft" (concessional, meaning at low interest rates). Most U.S. economic aid to the developing world has been in the form of soft loans. Military assistance—often called "security assistance"—includes the use of military advisory groups, equipment, and defense-oriented economic support, such as funding for the construction of dock facilities and railroads.

In the 1980s, Secretary of State George P. Schulz noted that "the total cost in tax dollars for all our security and economic assistance programs in the developing countries is $43.91 per person. In contrast, we Americans spend $104 per person a year for TV and radio sets, $35 per person per year for barbershops and beauty parlors, $97 per person per year for soap and cleaning supplies, and $21 per person per year for flowers and potted plants."[61] In the aggregate, the United States spends more on foreign aid than any other country except Japan, but as a percentage of gross domestic product (GDP), it has the smallest aid budget of any affluent nation—about 0.1 percent of GDP, or half of what it spent in 1990.[62] This amounts to less than a penny of every dollar spent in the FY 2003 budget. Among the industrialized nations, only tiny Denmark spends more than 1.0 percent of GDP on foreign aid.

The Marshall Plan, named after Secretary of State George C. Marshall, remains the shining jewel among America's foreign aid programs since the end of World War II. Between 1948 and 1952, America provided over $13 billion via the Marshall Plan, known more formally as the European Recovery Program, to revive the economies of Western Europe. A comparable program would cost about $90 billion today. American business leaders, aware of the possibility of profits if Europe could become a healthy market and understanding as well the need to bolster Europe's strength against the anti-capitalist influence of the Soviet bloc, supported the Marshall Plan. The result was a full recovery for Western Europe.

What might have happened in the 1990s if the United States had initiated an economic recovery program like the Marshall Plan in Afghanistan, helping the people there build schools and hospitals, instead of abandoning the nation once the Soviet invasion in the 1980s had been repelled? Perhaps Afghanistan would have been less inclined to fall into the hands of the extremist Taliban regime or serve as a sanctuary for al Qaeda. Today that abandonment continues to haunt American foreign policy in the region. In 2004, a U.S. government-relief official in Afghanistan told a reporter that the local people constantly pose this question to him about the United States: "Are you going to stay?" They say, "You guys are going to leave us, like you did in 1992. If we had confidence in the staying power of America, we'd deal with you."[63] Looking back at the positive effects of the Marshall Plan, two defense policy specialists conclude that "although the specific circumstances and challenges are quite different, the security of the United States now depends on achieving throughout the Arab and Islamic world what the Marshall Plan achieved in Europe … [a] robust and focused foreign assistance program is one of the weapons we must have to prevail."[64]

Foreign aid has had its problems and critics, though, especially because of the waste and ineffectiveness of some programs. In the 1980s, a few foreign dictators, such as Somoza of Nicaragua, amassed great wealth by stealing from U.S. aid programs. Ferdinand Marcos, the Philippine dictator, received enormous sums of U.S. assistance during the first half of the Cold War. After he was deposed in 1986, media images of the 3,000 pairs of shoes purchased by his wife, Imelda Marcos, soured many Americans toward the use of foreign aid. "Compared to Imelda, Marie Antoinette was a bag-lady," complained a leading member of Congress."[65]

Observes a foreign aid expert: "In the final analysis, all aid donors must grapple with an inescapable dilemma: government-to-government resource transfers permit the leaders of the recipient government to pursue their preexisting intentions with fewer constraints, no matter what those preexisting intentions may happen to be."[66] Foreign aid must be carefully monitored to prevent waste and corruption, but one former ambassador's counsel is wise, too: "We need officials who care about these poor, weak nations and their peoples, officials who will show up occasionally to ask, 'What are your special problems? What can we buy from you, and what can we sell? What is it in medicine, food, education, technology that we can provide?' When the automatic rifles are being fired, and artillery shells are exploding, as in El Salvador and Nicaragua, it is a bit late for the U.S. to fashion a policy."[67]

And it was too late in Afghanistan, too, when war broke out in 2001. As the war on terrorism progressed in 2002, George W. Bush's administration appeared to have an appreciation for this perspective. The president acknowledged that foreign aid may be an important instrument in the war against terrorism, which finds a fertile breeding ground in nations plagued by poverty and a sense of desperation. He announced a 50 percent increase in the U.S. foreign aid budget over the next four years, to $15 billion by 2006. This represented a large increase in U.S. aid, but a percentage of GDP still small by the standards of other industrialized nations.

MORAL SUASION AND SOFT POWER: THE IMPORTANCE OF REPUTATION, IDEOLOGY, AND CULTURE

The United States is accepted as a leader in many parts of the world not simply because of its economic strength or its imposing military weapons, but because of its commitment to democracy, freedom, and human rights around the world. As Supreme Court Justice William O. Douglas once observed, America is admired abroad not "so much for our B-52 bombers and for our atomic stockpile, but … for the First Amendment and the freedom of people to speak and believe and to write, have fair trials."[68] Here, in his view, was "the great magnet" that made the United States a great world leader: the power of **moral suasion**—the pursuit of high ideals such as democracy and human rights. Indeed, in the eyes of many, moral suasion and the related concept of **soft power**—the notion that a nation's cultural appeal can attract the support of other nations—are important tools at the disposal of American foreign policymakers.

Morality versus Pragmatism

As seen in earlier chapters, American foreign policy has long emphasized morality, and officials in Washington, D.C., have long understood that morality, or moral suasion, has provided the United States with an advantage in foreign affairs. The Founding Fathers sought to establish a more open and representative government than those found in Europe. In that same spirit, in the early 1900s, President Woodrow Wilson called for open diplomacy. More recently, revulsion against CIA assassination plots led President Ford to sign an executive order in 1976 that prohibited this option except in times of war authorized by Congress. Indeed, Inis L. Claude Jr., an international relations scholar, pointed out that Americans "undoubtedly place a high value on having—not merely on being thought to have—clean hands and a pure heart; the discomfort of a guilty conscience, or even of nagging uncertainty about one's virtue, is not an easy thing to bear." He attributed the unwillingness of the United States to participate in global politics before the twentieth century, in part, to "the dread of dirty hands."[69]

The desire of the United States for an ethical approach to foreign policy has not eliminated by any means the tension between morality and pragmatism in the conduct of America's international affairs. This tension has existed throughout America's history. Put simply, the issue revolves around the question: "Which actions are proper for the United States in its conduct of foreign policy, and which are not?" On some occasions, American officials seemed to abandon moral principles. For example, in 1954, a top-secret document prepared for President Eisenhower warned: "We must learn to subvert, sabotage and destroy our enemies by more clever, more sophisticated and more effective methods than those used against us."[70]

Many Americans object to such a harsh philosophy of international relations. For example, in 1976, the chairman of a special investigative committee looking into the activities of the CIA asked why the United States had to engage in secret wars against "leaders of small, weak countries that could not possibly threaten the United States?" He remarked in dismay that "no country was too small, no foreign leader too trifling to escape our attention."[71] In a similar vein, the Nobel Prize-winning German author Günter Grass asked with respect to America's involvement in Nicaragua during the 1980s, "How impoverished must a country be before it is not a threat to the U.S. government?"[72]

The Carter Administration was well known for its stress on morality in world affairs. More than ever before, the government of the United States shifted its attention toward relations with the poorer countries, instead of the usual fixation on the wealthy industrial nations of the world. Carter and his advisers often spoke of the dignity that should be accorded the former colonial states, and underscored the importance of majority rule for South Africa, a relationship of greater political equality between large and small nations, and a fairer sharing of the world's economic wealth. "Human rights has been a special concern of this Administration," stated Secretary of State Edmund S. Muskie. "We stand for the right of people to be free of torture and repression, to choose their leaders, to participate in the decisions that affect their daily lives, to speak and write and travel freely." In Muskie's view, military arms were insufficient to defend America's vital interests abroad: "We must also arm ourselves with the conviction that our values have increasing power in today's world."[73]

As with the three major sets of competing themes of American foreign policy set down in this book, the tension between morality and pragmatism rarely presents officials with a clear black-and-white choice. The U.S. government must balance these values. As Henry Kissinger has written, "Our cause must be just, but it must prosper in a world of sovereign nations and competing wills." Emphasizing that sound policy has to "relate ends to means," he argues that "neither moralistic rhetoric nor obsession with pure power politics will produce a foreign policy worthy of our opportunity—or adequate for our survival."[74]

Hard Power versus Soft Power

The distinction that foreign policy specialists make between "hard" and "soft" power is related to the conflict between moralism and pragmatism in foreign policy.[75] The use of military and economic instruments are examples of **hard power,** in which direct inducements are employed by the United States against another nation or group as a means for encouraging compliance with American objectives. In contrast, a more indirect (soft) way to bring about compliance is to urge others to adopt U.S. objectives because they are laudable in themselves and should be pursued for their intrinsic value, not because the United States is applying pressure of some sort.

Soft power refers to the idea that a nation's cultural appeal, coupled with its pursuit of high ideals (moral suasion), can bend other nations toward its aim of influence without the use of military, diplomatic, or commercial coercion.[76] The cultural attributes of the United States—pop music, film, television shows, literature, or (stretching the word "culture" to the breaking point) even savory fast foods—often attract adherents to America and its lifestyle. Sometimes such identification with American culture can influence others to be more accepting of U.S. foreign policy objectives.

But there is a downside to soft power as well. Sometimes "creeping American commercialism" strains U.S. relationships around the globe, robbing other nations of their sense of national identify in the face of ubiquitous U.S. brand names. The violent and crude lyrics of some American rock music often offend foreigners, just as they do many Americans. Nor does the violence and explicit sexual content of many of America's film and television exports, as well as revealing fashion styles for women that run counter to traditional dress in many countries, assist the goal of winning friends for the United States overseas. Thus, America's soft power is a double-edged sword, both attracting and repelling the international community, and Americans themselves.

Nevertheless, moral suasion and soft power can have considerable influence on America's standing in the world, however difficult this relationship may be to measure quantitatively. For example, many analysts who have studied the collapse of communism in the Soviet Union and Eastern Europe argue that, as important as hard power was in deterring Soviet military aggression, it was actually the moral suasion and soft power of Western democratic institutions and practices that won the ideological struggle between the East and the West.[77]

As significant as they may be, moral suasion and soft power are elusive instruments for officials to grasp and use. Moreover, their results are often unclear. Thus, policy-makers are more inclined to take up the more tangible instruments of hard power—military and economic initiatives that can be directly applied to solving, or at least managing, America's problems in the world. A largely hidden yet important feature of U.S. hard power is its use of secret intelligence agencies, the subject of the next chapter.

SUMMARY

The United States uses a number of different foreign policy instruments as it pursues its foreign policy goals. These include the war power, diplomacy, economic statecraft including trade and aid, moral principles, and other elements of soft power.

The war power is the actual or threatened use of overt military force. It is the most extreme means of pursuing foreign policy goals. The use or threatened use of military force intends to persuade an adversary to change behavior. High stakes attend the use of the war power. Indeed, when the nuclear age dawned in 1945, the dangers of military conflict dramatically escalated.

The United States has a large military, filled with conventional, tactical nuclear, and strategic nuclear weapons. Conventional weapons include everything from rifles and tanks to bombs and missiles; tactical nuclear weapons use nuclear energy to destroy their targets but yield small explosions; and strategic nuclear weapons are delivered by intercontinental ballistic missiles, submarine-launched ballistic missiles, and bombers, together called the triad. In 2003, the United States spent more on defense than the rest of the world combined.

One purpose of military forces, especially nuclear forces, is to deter an enemy. Deterrence is the ability to convince an enemy not to attack because of the certainty of a devastating retaliatory attack. During the Cold War, the United States and the Soviet Union understood that if either attacked the other, both would be destroyed.

 The threat that rogue nations or terrorists might use weapons of mass destruction against the United States led President George W. Bush to conclude in 2002 that deterrence was no longer effective. He unveiled the doctrine of preemptive defense, in which the United States will attack potential enemies before they can attack the United States. Critics claim this doctrine allows the United States, or any nation, to attack whomever it wants to.

Diplomacy, defined as the business of communicating between governments, is another U.S. foreign policy instrument. The United States uses three major forms of international agreements in diplomacy: treaties, statutory agreements, and executive agreements. On occasion, U.S. diplomatic initiatives stretch beyond their original intent via creeping commitments as officials fill in the details when a broad agreement is reached. The executive branch has also used secret agreements to carry out diplomacy.

International trade is also a U.S. priority. Free trade is important in current U.S. trade policy, but the loss of jobs as a result of increased imports has led to calls for protectionism, that is, using tariffs and quotas against imports to protect U.S. industries from foreign competitors. The United States also uses other instruments of economic statecraft such as granting most favored nation rights, which bestow upon a country the best trading relationship for its imports that the United States offers; embargoes, which prohibit exports; and boycotts, which prohibit imports or other forms of business with another country. These instruments may appear potent, but they have had only modest success over the years.

Foreign aid, defined as economic and military assistance on a government-to-government level, or through government-supported agencies or programs, is another tool of economic statecraft. It includes direct grants, technical cooperation, and loans that are either hard (offered at commercial bank interest rates), or soft (offered at low interest rates). Foreign aid has its problems, though, especially because of the waste and ineffectiveness of some programs.

Finally, the United States is accepted as a leader in many parts of the world not because of its economy and military, but because of moral suasion: its commitment to democracy, freedom, and human rights. To many, moral suasion and the idea that a nation's cultural appeal can bend other nations toward its aims without coercion, an approach called soft power, are important foreign policy tools.

As significant as they are, moral suasion and soft power are elusive instruments for officials to use, and they yield unclear results. Thus, policymakers are often more inclined to take up the more tangible instruments of hard power that can be directly applied to solving, or at least managing, America's problems in the world.

KEY TERMS AND CONCEPTS

war power
weapons of mass destruction (WMD)
military strategy: operational, logistical,
   social, weapons technology
strategic nuclear weapons
tactical nuclear weapons
conventional weapons
effects of nuclear weapons
counterforce/countervalue targeting
rad
electromagnetic pulses (EMPs)
nuclear winter
chemical and biological weapons
deterrence
triad
ballistic missile defense (BMD)
ground-based interceptor (GBI)

doctrine of preemption
diplomacy
treaty power
statutory agreement
executive agreement
"Lend-Lease" Agreement
free-trade areas
protectionism
free trade
multinational corporations (MNCs)
most favored nation (MFN) rights
embargoes
boycotts
foreign aid
moral suasion
soft power
hard power

THINKING CRITICALLY

1. Evaulate the war in Iraq initiated in 2003, using the various dimensions of strategy discussed in this chapter.

2. Would you have voted for the 1973 War Powers Resolution? Why, or why not?

3. Would you leave the 1973 War Powers Resolution as it is, improve it through amendments, or repeal it? Why?

4. Explain what the strategic weapons triad is, and discuss its relevance now that the Cold War is over.

5. Why did the Cold War end? Is the world safer now, or more dangerous, for the United States?

6. Evaluate the success of the global war against terrorism to date.

7. What are the most dangerous global threats to the United States today? Establish a threat hierarchy.

8. What tools would you use to counter global threats to American security, and how would you use them?

NOTES

1. See Charles Figley and Seymour Levintman, eds., *Strangers at Home: Vietnam Veterans since the War* (New York: Viking, 1983), p. 472.

2. Louis Fisher, "Deciding on War against Iraq: Institutional Failures," *Political Science Quarterly* 118 (2003): 410.

3. From "Speaking with Alexander George about 'Coercive Diplomacy,'" interview, *United States Institute of Peace Journal* 4 (October 1991): 1–2.

4. Paul P. Craig and John A. Jungerman, *Nuclear Arms Race: Technology and Society* (New York: McGraw-Hill, 1986), p. 8.

5. Michael Howard, "The Forgotten Dimensions of Strategy," *Foreign Affairs* 57 (Summer 1979): 975–986.

6. Howard, "The Forgotten Dimensions of Strategy," p. 977.

7. Linton F. Brooks, quoted by Ian Hoffman, *Oakland Tribune* (December 11, 2003), as cited by Steven Aftergood in *Secrecy News*, the electronic newsletter of the Federation of American Scientists, Vol. 2003 (December 17, 2003).

8. L. W. McNaught, *Nuclear Weapons and Their Effects* (London: Brassey's, 1984), p. 27.

9. McNaught, *Nuclear Weapons and Their Effects,* pp. 30, 96.

10. P. R. Ehrlich et al., "The Long-Term Biological Consequences of Nuclear War," *Science* 222 (December 23, 1983): 1299, original emphasis.

11. Dr. Jennifer Leaning, remarks, Harvard-MIT Summer Program on Nuclear Weapons (June 17, 1985); see also Jonathan Schell, *The Fate of the Earth* (New York: Knopf, 1974).

12. Robert S. McNamara, *The Essence of Security* (New York: Harper and Row, 1968), p. 59.

13. Drawn from Loch K. Johnson, *Bombs, Bugs, Drugs, and Thugs: Intelligence and America's Quest for Security* (New York: New York University Press, 2000), pp. 78–79.

14. See "Proliferation of Weapons of Mass Destruction: Assessing the Risks," *Report OTA-ISC-559* (Washington, D.C.: U.S. Government Printing Office, August 1993), p. 53.

15. Richard Preston, "The Demon in the Freezer," *New Yorker* (July 12, 1999): 44, 47.

16. This scenario is based on remarks by physicist Richard L. Garwin in William J. Broad, "After Many Misses, Pentagon Still Pursues Missile Defense," *New York Times* (May 24, 1999): 23.

17. Robert H. Kupperman and David M. Smith, "Coping with Biological Terrorism," in *Biological Weapons: Weapons of the Future?* ed. Brad Roberts (Washington, D.C.: Center for Strategic and International Studies, 1993), p. 45.

18. Ron Purver, "Understanding Past Non-Use of C.B.W. by Terrorists," presentation to the conference on ChemBio Terrorism: Wave of the Future? sponsored by the Chemical and Biological Arms Control Institute, Washington, D.C. (April 29, 1996).

19. See Judith Miller's report on the study in "U.S. Ill-Prepared for Bioterrorism," *International Herald Tribune* (March 29, 2004): 7.

20. Both cited by William J. Broad and Judith Miller, "The Threat of Germ Weapons Is Rising," *New York Times* (December 27, 1999): E1, E5.

21. Judith Miller and William J. Broad, "Clinton Describes Terrorism Threat for 21st Century," *New York Times* (January 22, 1999): A1.

22. See William J. Broad and Judith Miller, "Government Report Says 3 Nations Hide Stocks of Smallpox," *New York Times* (June 13, 1999): A1; and Judith Miller and William J. Broad, "Clinton to Announce That U.S. Will Keep Sample of Lethal Smallpox Virus," *New York Times* (April 22, 1999): A12.

23. Ken Alibek with Stephen Handelman, *Biohazard* (New York: Random House, 1999).

24. "Weapons of Mass Destruction," *Foreign Affairs* 77 (January/February 1998): 37.

25. Donald M. Snow, *When America Fights: The Uses of U.S. Military Force* (Washington, D.C.: Congressional Quarterly Press, 2000), p. 82, original emphasis.

26. Thomas C. Schelling, *Arms and Influence* (New Haven: Yale University Press, 1966). For a more charitable assessment of the Eisenhower Administration's approach, see Fred I. Greenstein, *The Hidden-Hand Presidency: Eisenhower as Leader* (Baltimore: Johns Hopkins University Press, 1994).

27. See Ivo H. Daalder and James M. Lindsay, *America Unbound: The Bush Revolution in Foreign Policy* (Washington, D.C.: Brookings Institution, 2003).

28. The administration and others often used the phrase "preemption" as though it were interchangeable with the phrase "preventive war," although in fact the two are distinct strategic concepts. The doctrine of preventive war assumes that war with another nation is inevitable; therefore, it is better to begin the war straight away rather than wait until the adversary grows stronger. Despite its use of the term preemption, the planning by George W. Bush's administration about Iraq appeared to be dominated by preventive war thinking. Used more precisely, preemption refers in contrast to a nation's decision to conduct a quick strike against another threatening nation, based on reliable intelligence that the adversary is about to launch an attack. See James J. Wirtz and James A. Russell, "U.S. Policy on Preventive War and Preemption," *Nonproliferation Review* (Spring 2003): 113–123.

29. Fisher, "Deciding on War against Iraq," p. 389.

30. Lawrence J. Korb, testimony, Hearings, Budget Committee, U.S. House of Representatives (February 12, 2002).

31. Snow, *When America Fights,* p. 112.

32. Winston S. Churchill, *My Early Life: A Roving Commission* (New York: Scribner's, 1930), p. 180.

33. Alan K. Henrikson, "Diplomatic Method," in *Encyclopedia of U.S. Foreign Relations,* Vol. 2, ed. Bruce W. Jentleson and Thomas G. Paterson (New York: Oxford University Press), p. 23.

34. Both of these definitions are quoted in Norman J. Padelford and George A. Lincoln, *The Dynamics of International Politics* (New York: Macmillan, 1962), p. 340.

35. Henry Kissinger, *A World Restored* (Boston, Houghton Mifflin, 1957), p. 326.

36. Hans J. Morgenthau, *Politics among Nations: The Struggle for Power and Peace*, 4th ed. (New York: Knopf, 1967), pp. 135–136.

37. David D. Newsom, *Diplomacy and the American Democracy* (Bloomington: Indiana University Press, 1988), pp. 23, 219. Newsom notes another valuable service of the diplomat: assisting citizens who are traveling overseas. In this capacity, he or she "is a combination of parish priest and city clerk, helping to get fellow citizens out of jail, issuing replacement passports, settling citizenship problems, handling the effects of the deceased, seeking to reunite families, and registering births" (p. 199).

38. Loch K. Johnson, *The Making of International Agreements: Congress Confronts the Executive* (New York: New York University Press, 1984).

39. "National Commitments," Committee on Foreign Relations, Report No. 91-129, U.S. Senate (April 16, 1969), p. 27.

40. "U.S. Security Agreements and Commitments Abroad: Laos and Thailand," Hearings, Committee on Foreign Relations, part 6, U.S. Senate (1969–1970).

41. "Philippines," Committee on Foreign Relations, *Report* (December 21, 1970), p. 5.

42. "Philippines," p. 20.

43. "Philippines," p. 28.

44. "U.S. Security Agreements and Commitments Abroad: Spain and Portugal, Hearings, Committee on Foreign Relations, U.S. Senate (1969–1970).

45. "National Commitments," pp. 28–29.

46. Quoted in the *Washington Post* (April 9, 1975): A1.

47. Tad Szulc, *The Illusion of Peace* (New York: Viking, 1979), p. 212.

48. "Transmittal of Executive Agreements," Committee on Foreign Relations, Report No. 92-591, U.S. Senate (1971), p. 3.

49. Dick Clark (D-Iowa), *Congressional Record* (June 28, 1978): S10010.

50. Joseph R. Biden Jr., and John B. Ritch III, "The Treaty Power: Upholding a Constitutional Partnership," *University of Pennsylvania Law Review* 137 (1989): 1529–1557.

51. Quoted in correspondence to the authors from British scholar-researcher Frank Adams (December 21, 1988).

52. "National Security Considerations Affecting Trade Policy," Report, Williams Commission, Vol. 1 (1974), p. 737.

53. Joan Edelman Spero, *The Politics of International Economic Relations,* 2nd ed. (New York: St. Martin's, 1981), p. 103.

54. Joseph E. Stiglitz, *Globalization and Its Discontents* (New York: Norton, 2003), p. 68.

55. See, for example, Raymond Vernon, *Sovereignty at Bay: The Multinational Spread of U.S. Enterprises* (New York: Basic Books, 1971); Stiglitz, *Globalization and Its Discontents*, p. 69.

56. Johan Galtung, "A Structural Theory of Imperialism," *Journal of Peace Research* 2 (1971): 81–98.

57. "Three Models of the Future," *International Organization* 29 (1975): 44, original emphasis.

58. Joan Hoff Wilson, "Economic Foreign Policy," in *Encyclopedia of American Foreign Policy,* Vol. 2, ed. Alexander DeConde (New York: Scribner's, 1978), p. 320.

59. Ian J. Bickerton, "Foreign Aid," in *Encyclopedia of American Foreign Policy,* p. 372.

60. Newsom, *Diplomacy and the American Democracy,* p. 161.

61. Quoted by Bernard Gwertzman, "A Citizen Pays $43 for Aid, Schultz Says," *New York Times* (February 25, 1983): A1.

62. John Cassidy, "Helping Hands," *New Yorker* (March 18, 2002): 62, 64.

63. Quoted by Seymour M. Hersh, "The Other War: Why Bush's Afghanistan Problem Won't Go Away," *New Yorker* (April 12, 2004): 47.

64. Quoted by Cassidy, "Helping Hands," p. 64.

65. Representative Stephen Solarz (D-New York), quoted on *Washington Week in Review,* Public Broadcasting System (March 14, 1986).

66. Nicholas Eberstadt, "Foreign Aid," in Jentleson and Paterson, Vol. 2, p. 149.

67. Quoted in "American Ignorance," *Atlanta Constitution* (November 4, 1979): A14.

68. Interview with William O. Douglas, *CBS Evening News* (January 19, 1980).

69. "The Common Defense and Great-Power Responsibilities," *Political Science Quarterly* 101 (1986): 731.

70. From the General Doolittle Report, Hoover Commission (1954), cited in "Foreign and Military Intelligence," *Final Report,* Select Committee on Intelligence, U.S. Senate (April 26, 1976), p. 9.

71. Senator Frank Church (D-Idaho), "Covert Action: Swampland of American Foreign Policy," *Bulletin of the Atomic Scientists* 32 (February 1976): 9.

72. Günter Grass, "Solidarity with the Sandinistas," *Nation* 236 (March 12, 1983): 301.

73. "Human Freedom: America's Vision," *Current Policy,* No. 208, Department of State (August 7, 1980), p. 3.

74. Quoted by Anthony Lewis, "Morality in Foreign Policy," *New York Times* (October 21, 1976): 39.

75. Joseph S. Nye Jr., *Understanding International Conflicts,* 2nd ed. (New York: Longman, 1997), pp. 52–53.

76. Joseph S. Nye Jr., *The Paradox of American Power* (New York: Oxford, 2002), pp. 67–69.

77. See, for example, John Lewis Gaddis, *We Now Know: Rethinking Cold War History* (New York: Oxford, 1997).

CHAPTER 11

The Secret Instruments of American Foreign Policy: Espionage, Counterintelligence, and Covert Action

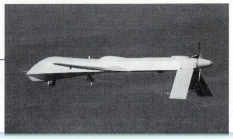

Intelligence is crucial to American foreign policy, and it can be gathered in many ways, ranging from spies and satellites to electronic eavesdropping and unmanned aerial vehicles such as the Predator, shown here. The Predator not only collects intelligence but also can fire weapons such as the Hellfire missile.

- In what sense is reliable information the foundation of an effective foreign policy?
- How does the United States gather and assess information from around the world?
- Why is counterintelligence an important dimension of foreign policy?
- To what extent has covert action played a significant role in America's foreign affairs?
- Have the CIA's secret operations been an asset or a liability to the United States?

Early one morning in October 1994, Secretary of Defense William J. Perry rose from the oversized desk in his office within the Pentagon's E Ring, the outermost of the building's five concentric corridors, to greet General John Shalikashvili, chairman of the Joint Chiefs of Staff (JCS).[1] Under his arm, the general carried a portfolio of photographs recently taken by a U.S. surveillance satellite scanning Iraq, a nation about the size of California. He spread the "imagery," as government officials refer to satellite photography, across a conference table in the bunker-like room whose drabness is relieved only by a bank of windows that face out to the Potomac River and, off in the distance, the Washington Monument.

Using a pointer, Shalikashvili directed Perry's attention to a disturbing set of photographs. Improbable as it might have seemed, coming just three and a half years after Iraq suffered a humiliating defeat in the 1991 Persian Gulf War, elements of the Republican Guard, Saddam's elite troops, supported by mechanized infantry, armor, and tank units, were moving at a rapid clip southward toward Al Basrah, a city in Iraq just 30 miles from the Kuwaiti border. The force aimed like an arrow at the Al Jahra heights overlooking Kuwait City, in an apparent repeat of the same maneuver that led to the Iraqi conquest of Kuwait in 1990. At its current rate of speed, the Republican Guard would be pouring across the Kuwaiti border in a couple of days.

Faced with this startling evidence, Perry quickly ordered to the Iraqi border a U.S. armored brigade stationed in Kuwait, as a check against a possible invasion. With a rising sense of uneasiness, the secretary of defense and the top Pentagon brass awaited fresh satellite photographs of the Iraq-Kuwaiti border. Over the next 24 hours, young captains and lieutenants brought new batches of imagery into Perry's office and arrayed them on the table. In an area near Al Basrah, upwards of 10,000 Iraqi troops had amassed. Steadily the number rose to 50,000, some bivouacking within 12 miles of the border. The American brigade had arrived in defense, but it consisted of only 2,000 lightly armed marines.

While the United States also had 200 warplanes in the area on standby alert, the Iraqi armored forces dwarfed the U.S. presence on the ground. President Bill Clinton ordered 450 more warplanes to Kuwait, along with the 24th Mechanized Infantry Division and a marine contingent from Camp Pendleton. The aircraft carrier *George Washington* steamed toward the Red Sea. None of these forces, though, would arrive in time to halt an invasion of Kuwait. The secretary of defense and the JCS chair faced the strong possibility of a rout that would quickly wipe away the small American brigade assembled at the border.

But when the next set of photos arrived, Perry and Shalikashvili could finally breathe a sigh of relief. The Iraqi troops had suddenly stopped, and some elements were already turning back toward Baghdad.

Here was the good news: photographic intelligence may well have prevented the outbreak of another war in the Persian Gulf. In the absence of the satellite imagery, the United States would never have known about the march toward Kuwait by the Republican Guard. "Had the intelligence arrived three or four days later, it would have been too late," recalls a high-ranking civilian official who followed the events in the Pentagon during those tense autumn days.

Yet the episode carried with it some bad news, too. Even though vital intelligence had arrived in time to allow Secretary Perry a chance to put up some semblance of defense at the border, the single marine brigade would have been unable to stop the thousands of troops in the Republican Guard. The best the secretary of defense could hope for was that the marines would intimidate Saddam. Fortunately, the bluff worked. The

American troops, though, could just as well have been overrun. To field a larger force capable of standing up to the Iraqis, the Defense Department needed more advanced warning than had been provided by the initial batch of photographs.

Retrospective studies of the satellite imagery taken of Iraq before the crisis ("walking back the cat," in spytalk) disclosed the presence of palpable clues indicating that, for weeks, the Iraqis had been gathering an invasion force near Baghdad. Intelligence analysts in the National Photographic Intelligence Center had missed these signs. Intelligence had succeeded, but it had also failed. The fault lay less in the realm of technical intelligence than in the lack of a sufficient number of well-trained experts to interpret earlier satellite findings. Moreover, a few relatively cheap reconnaissance airplanes in the region might have provided even better, and more easily analyzed, coverage of the Iraq-Kuwait border than had the periodic orbiting of a surveillance satellite.

INTELLIGENCE: THE NATION'S FIRST LINE OF DEFENSE

The ability of the United States to defend and advance its interests in the world often depends on having good information.[2] This chapter examines the value to the United States of collecting and interpreting information acquired through secret means from around the world, as a supplement to reporting by the media and the diplomatic corps. America's diplomats also engage in secrecy from time to time, but these activities are normally limited to behind-the-scenes negotiations with the diplomats of other nations. And sometimes the CIA conducts overt diplomacy, as during the Clinton years when Director of Central Intelligence George J. Tenet negotiated between Israeli and Palestinian security forces.

The purpose of information gathering is to guard against dangers to America's security by providing early warnings about possible attacks, like those that took place against New York City and Washington, D.C., in 2001, or the Japanese bombing of Pearl Harbor in 1941—both examples of how inadequate information can lead to great harm to the American people. Information is valuable, too, as a means for alerting the United States to diplomatic and economic opportunities abroad.

As this chapter reveals, gathering information overseas and assessing its significance is easier said than done. So are two other secret activities carried out by America's intelligence agencies and examined in this chapter. One is counterintelligence, America's efforts to thwart the clandestine operations of hostile intelligence services and terrorist factions directed against the United States. The other is covert action, the attempt to secretly manipulate world events in a manner favorable to the interests of the United States.[3] First we look at how the CIA collects and interprets information.[4]

The Origins of Modern Intelligence Gathering

On the morning of December 7, 1941, almost 100 U.S. ships and some 300 aircraft were based at Pearl Harbor in Hawaii.[5] In a surprise attack, the Japanese hit all eight battleships moored at the naval base, sinking five, along with two destroyers and several other ships. Over 200 planes suffered damage. Luckily, the two aircraft carriers in the Pacific fleet happened to be at sea; less fortunate were 2,330 service personnel killed and 1,145 wounded, along with 100 civilian casualties.

The blow stunned the nation. Officials in Washington, D.C., did not realize the Japanese had developed aerial torpedoes. Once dropped into the sea from fighter airplanes, these new weapons were able to navigate the shallow waters of Pearl Harbor. Officials had considered a Japanese assault against the Philippines much more likely. Some fragments of evidence suggesting that an attack against Pearl Harbor might occur were stuck within the bowels of the government, without ever being coordinated and distributed to the president or other senior policy officials. Some intelligence officers kept this vital information bottled up, for fear that "Operation Magic," the U.S. intelligence program that cracked the Japanese military codes, might be revealed if the information were shared too widely.[6]

Once World War II ended, President Harry S Truman vowed to improve the way in which the United States collected, assessed, and disseminated within the government information about global events. As he recalled, "I got a couple of admirals together and they formed the Central Intelligence Agency for the benefit and convenience of the President of the United States." Thus, "instead of the President having to look through a bunch of papers two feet high, the information was coordinated so that the President could arrive at the facts."[7] The goal was to provide useful facts and insights to the nation's decision makers as a means for clarifying the range of foreign policy options before them. The CIA defines this information, or **intelligence,** as "knowledge and foreknowledge of the world around us—the prelude to Presidential decision and action."[8]

The Intelligence Cycle

The means by which intelligence is gathered from around the world and channeled to the desks of policymakers may be viewed as a multiphased process, often referred to as the **intelligence cycle.**[9] (See Figure 11.1.) The cycle consists of a period of preliminary planning, followed by the collection, processing, analysis, and dissemination of information. The ultimate purpose, as a senior intelligence official has put it simply, is to "find the best minds available to produce the best one-page report on subject x."[10]

Planning.   The initial planning phase involves deciding what nations and groups warrant intelligence surveillance. At the beginning of every administration, the **Director of Central Intelligence (DCI),** who heads the CIA and supervises America's fourteen other secret agencies, works with the White House to prepare a "threat assessment," a priority listing of the most dangerous perils faced by the United States.[11] These officials then determine how much money from the annual intelligence budget, reportedly about $40 billion in 2004, will be spent tracking the activities of each target on the list.

This planning stage is critical. Unless a target is taken seriously during this setting of priorities, it is unlikely to receive much attention by those responsible for collecting information in the field. During the Cold War, the United States concentrated mainly on gathering intelligence about the Soviet Union and other communist powers, neglecting lesser targets like Afghanistan, India, and Iraq. This region of the world—the Mideast

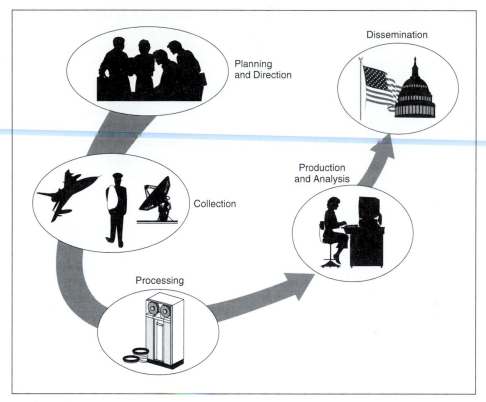

FIGURE 11.1
The Intelligence Cycle

Source: Adapted from *Fact Book on Intelligence,* Office of Public Affairs, Central Intelligence Agency (September 1991), p. 13.

and South Asia—would take the United States by surprise after the Cold War, as displayed in the hostility toward Americans exhibited by the Taliban regime in Afghanistan, the unanticipated Indian nuclear tests in 1998, and the outbreak of two wars against Iraq.

Terrorism has risen steadily on the list of intelligence priorities since the end of the Cold War, but until September 2001 it remained just one of several demands on the resources of the U.S. intelligence agencies. High among these demands were unpredictable ("rogue" or renegade) regimes like North Korea, Iraq, and Iran, which together comprised an "axis of evil," according to President George W. Bush in his 2002 State of the Union Address. Russia's massive nuclear arsenal also kept the attention of Washington officials, as did the growing military might of China. As a result of the attacks against the World Trade Center and the Pentagon in 2001, however, terrorism attained a position of preeminence on America's threat list, resulting in a greater concentration of intelligence resources against Osama bin Laden and his al Qaeda network, as well as other terrorist organizations in over 60 countries.

Collection.   The collection phase became skewed as well during the Cold War, in a manner that further harmed America's preparedness to comprehend and address terrorism and other challenges in the developing world. Understandably awed by the dazzling technological capabilities of satellites and reconnaissance airplanes (U-2s, SR-71s, and unmanned aerial vehicles, or UAVs, such as the "Predator"), officials in Washington poured most of the intelligence budget into machines capable of photographing Soviet tanks and missile silos and eavesdropping on telephone conversations in communist capitals. Surveillance machines are known as technical intelligence, or simply **techint**.[12] In light of this infatuation with spy machines ("hardware"), the development of espionage or human intelligence—**humint**—became a neglected instrument of America's secret foreign policy.[13] This lack of emphasis on global humint harmed America's ability to comprehend and address terrorism and other challenges that developed in the world after the Cold War ended.

Machines certainly have their place in America's spy defenses, and they played an important role in Afghanistan in 2001–2002, as satellites hovered over its rugged mountains, taking photographs of likely Taliban encampments, and UAVs swooped into its valleys in search of al Qaeda terrorists. But machines cannot peer inside caves nor see through the canvas tents or roofed mud huts where terrorists gather to plan their lethal operations. A secret agent in the enemy's camp is necessary to acquire this kind of information, the only kind likely to give the United States an accurate and advanced warning of future attacks. Humint remains the key to protecting the United States against a range of future treats, especially acts of terrorism, even though foreign agents often prevaricate to make themselves seem more important to their CIA paymasters or are otherwise unreliable and must be handled with caution. During the Cuban missile crisis in 1962, CIA humint reports from the island were mostly inaccurate and useless. However, a few among the total provided indispensable tipoffs that the Soviets had introduced missiles into Cuba. This initial humint warning was then confirmed by U-2 overflights, an example of humint and techint working together synergistically, as they should.

Espionage networks take time to develop, and only recently has the DCI launched a major recruitment drive to hire more Arab Americans and others who have language skills and knowledge about Afghanistan, Iraq, and other parts of the world largely ignored by the United States during the Cold War. Intelligence officers with these skills are needed to recruit local agents overseas, who in turn do the actual spying for the CIA. The September 2001 attacks against the United States accelerated these efforts, although finding American citizens who speak Pasto, Dari, Arabic, and Farsi and want to work for the intelligence agencies—living overseas in less than luxurious (and sometimes dangerous) conditions at a modest government salary—has been difficult. The candidate must be driven by a strong sense of patriotism and a desire to join the war against terrorism on the front lines.

Especially challenging is the task of convincing CIA officers to operate abroad under nonofficial cover (NOC), rather than within the comfort and safety of official cover within a U.S. embassy. In the first instance, the officer pretends to be an American businessperson abroad or perhaps a student. This provides the officer with a good excuse to mingle in the local society. In the second instance, the officer pretends to be a diplomat inside the embassy, but in some countries the local society would shun a U.S. government worker.

Most countries use the NOC approach, and they may have their intelligence officers develop long-term residencies in another country. These "sleepers" can be activated to spy or conduct covert action after years of working innocently as, for example, a local proprietor or foreign-language teacher. American intelligence officers who stay within the confines of an embassy will meet fellow diplomats from other countries on the cocktail circuit, but they are unlikely to meet a member of al Qaeda in that setting. Yet giving up official cover means also giving up diplomatic immunity if one is caught overseas engaging in espionage—a dangerous proposition. Moreover, how many young Americans are willing to live in a place like rural Afghanistan, with little contact with fellow Americans, none of the enjoyment of embassy social life, and warlords threatening the countryside? Recruiting men and women to assume the NOC life is a hard sell, however vital it may be for acquiring information about what is really going on in a country.

Processing.   The National Security Agency (NSA) collects electronic information, chiefly telephone conversations, globally for the United States. When one NSA director was asked about the major challenges facing his organization, he replied, "I have three: processing, processing, and processing."[14] In this daunting phase of the intelligence cycle, information must be converted from "raw" (unevaluated) intelligence—such as a message in Farsi, a secret code, or the obscure markings in a satellite photograph—into an explanation in plain English. The chief difficulty is the sheer volume of information that pours into the secret agencies, especially from machines around the globe. A former intelligence manager recalls that he often felt as though a fire hose was being held to his mouth.[15]

Hundreds of photographs from satellites stream back to the United States each day, along with thousands of untranslated telephone intercepts. The curse of intelligence is that inevitably the overwhelming percentage of information gathered abroad consists of "noise"—useless chatter—in the midst of which vital bits of information may be embedded. Those who face the task of sorting through this floodtide of information have sometimes failed to pinpoint key information in a timely manner. In 2001, for example, the NSA intercepted an al Qaeda message on September 10, a day before the terrorist attacks, but it was not translated until September 12. The message read: "Tomorrow is zero hour"—a palpable clue that, had it been interpreted in time, might have helped prevent the attacks by leading to tightened airport security on September 11.

Analysis.   Once information is processed, it must be studied for insights into the intentions of America's adversaries. This effort to interpret intelligence is called **analysis** (or "assessment" in Great Britain) and lies at the heart of the intelligence process.[16] If the CIA is unable to provide reliable insights into what all the information means, all the preceding stages are for nought. It is one thing to discover that a group of terrorists have convened in Kuala Lumpur (as al Qaeda members did prior to the 9/11 attacks), but what policymakers really want to know is what schemes the terrorists may have hatched at the meeting. The key questions are: "What are the specific implications for America's security?" "If the United States is going to be attacked, then when, where, how, and by whom?"

Good analysis depends on assembling the best brains possible to evaluate global events and conditions, drawing on a blend of mainly public knowledge augmented by secrets purloined from a nation's inner government council or a terrorist's desert tent or remote cave in Afghanistan. The chief problem once again is recruiting into the intelligence service well-educated Americans who have knowledge about the politics, economics, culture, and military affairs in places like Afghanistan, Iraq, and Sudan. The CIA and the other secret agencies have been scrambling to redirect their resources from the communist world to the world of Islam and other parts of the globe largely ignored by the United States during the Cold War. But, like the establishment of new espionage rings, hiring and training outstanding analysts takes time.

Each day, the intelligence agencies produce a number of analytic documents known as "current intelligence." The **President's Daily Brief** (**PDB**) is the most prominent, arriving early each morning at the White House and a few Cabinet offices, accompanied by an armed guard and a CIA briefer.[17] This top-secret document, printed in a newspaper-like format with four-color graphics, informs the president and other top officials about major global developments that have taken place in the last 24 hours, and it often sets the agenda for early morning discussions among foreign policy officials.

Officials also receive from the intelligence agencies longer, in-depth "research intelligence" reports. The showpiece in this category is the often hefty **National Intelligence Estimate (NIE)** on a country or subject. The purpose of an NIE is to present "a statement of what is going to happen in any country, in any area, in any given situation, and as far as possible into the future."[18] An NIE might probe the likely activities of leading terrorist groups over the next five years, the global aspirations of the Chinese, or the efficiencies of Russian rocket fuel.

Dissemination.   Intelligence must be distributed to those who make decisions on behalf of the United States. This may seem simple enough, but it is a phase rife with opportunities for error.[19] "Good packaging is vital," stresses an intelligence professional. "We used to throw things over the transom [to policymakers]. Now we *market.* You must focus the policymaker's attention. They are busy."[20]

Ideally, the information will meet six essential standards: relevance, timeliness, accuracy, breadth, lack of bias, and specificity. Relevance is vital. If intelligence fails to help put out the fires that have flared up in the policymaker's in-box, it will be ignored. Incisive reports on political elections in Poland have their place, but what the White House wants above all is knowledge about global "hot spots," like Somalia in 1993, Afghanistan in 2001–2002, and Iraq in 2003–2004. Often intelligence reports are out of sync with the main issues before policymakers, because analysts become wedded to their own research interests—say, the state of the Mongolian People's Army—at the expense of topics currently more pressing to decision makers. In 2001, the White House's open declaration of war against al Qaeda, the Taliban, and global terrorism, all backed by a vote of Congress, helped focus the work of the intelligence agencies on the president's top foreign policy priorities.

Timeliness is equally vital. An acronym that every intelligence analyst shudders to see scrawled across his or her report is OBE, short for "overtaken by events." Reports on the whereabouts of terrorists are especially perishable, as the United States discovered in 1999 when the Clinton Administration ordered the Pentagon to fire cruise missiles at bin Laden's encampment in the Zhawar Kili region of Afghanistan's Paktia Province, only to learn that he had departed hours earlier.

Similarly, the accuracy of information is critical. One of this nation's worst intelligence embarrassments came in 1999 when the CIA misidentified the Chinese embassy in Belgrade as a weapons depot, leading to a NATO bombing of the building and the death of Chinese diplomats.

Intelligence must be comprehensive as well, drawn from all of the intelligence agencies and coordinated into a meaningful whole: what intelligence officers refer to as **all-source intelligence.** Here one runs into the vexing problem of fragmentation among the secret agencies, which in a misnomer are often called the "intelligence community." These agencies often act more like separate medieval fiefdoms than a cluster of organizations all working together to provide the president with the best possible information about world events. As things stand presently, the DCI has neither budgetary nor appointment powers over any of the intelligence agencies, except the CIA. As a result, the "all-source" goal dreamed of by President Truman when he created a Central Intelligence Agency in 1947 remains unfulfilled.

Intelligence must also be unbiased and free of political spin. An analyst is expected to assess the facts in a dispassionate manner. Usually intelligence officers maintain this ethos, but occasionally they succumb to White House pressure for **intelligence to please,** that is, data that support the president's political agenda rather than reflect the often unpleasant reality that an administration's policy has failed or is wrong minded.[21] In 2003–2004, critics accused both the CIA and MI6 (British intelligence) of providing information selectively to President George W. Bush and Prime Minister Tony Blair in support of their claims that Iraq was developing weapons of mass destruction. Armed with this information, the two leaders could argue more persuasively in favor of invading Iraq. Others claimed that, on the contrary, the intelligence agencies were not to blame; it was the leaders, or at least their aides, who selectively chose ("cherry picked") only those fragments of intelligence that supported the WMD hypothesis, rejecting other intelligence that downplayed the Iraqi weapons threat. The controversy spawned several investigations on both sides of the Atlantic as lawmakers and parliamentarians sought the truth.

Intelligence must also exhibit a certain amount of specificity to be useful. Through a technique called "traffic analysis," intelligence agencies may report that terrorists are suddenly communicating more often with one another by cellphone or e-mail, but such reports are not helpful unless they include something about what the terrorists are actually saying. Warnings that indicate a terrorist attack may occur against Atlanta or Chicago next week are of little help unless they can provide more detail about when and where. In other words, intelligence needs to be "actionable."

The Challenges for Intelligence

Much can go wrong with intelligence.[22] If intelligence is to function properly in the new global war against terrorism, the planning phase must identify the most threatening targets and direct adequate resources against them. Collection must be riveted on tracking terrorists as well as other adversaries, and it must employ the most effective mix of machines and human spies. Processing must move faster and with greater skill in discriminating the wheat from the chaff. Analysts must possess a deeper understanding of foreign countries that harbor terrorist cells and other enemies of the United States, as well as a comprehension of what motivates their hatred toward Americans. At the end of the intelligence cycle, intelligence officers must present policymakers with information that is pertinent, on time, reliable, all-source, unbiased, and sufficiently detailed to act upon.

On their side of the equation, policymakers must also have the courage to hear the truth rather than brush it aside because it fails to support preconceived policy positions, as President Lyndon B. Johnson consistently did with respect to intelligence reports that brought him bad news about the progress of the war in Vietnam.[23] He didn't want to hear bad news; he wanted to win the war. Paul Wolfowitz, George W. Bush's deputy secretary of defense, offered this telling observation: "Policymakers are like surgeons. They don't last long if they ignore what they see when they cut an issue open."[24] Nevertheless, in 2004, critics accused him of failing to follow his own advice when bad news began to mount over America's war in Iraq.

How well did the intelligence cycle operate in the months before al Qaeda's attacks against the United States in 2001? Obviously, not well enough.[25] Insufficient attention was paid to the terrorist threat, despite the attack against the World Trade Center in 1993 and subsequent attacks against U.S. embassies and a Navy ship overseas. Moreover, information about terrorists was collected in a spotty manner, in part attributable to the lack of good intelligence officers abroad with Mideast and South Asian language skills, and without adequate coordination among the intelligence agencies. Two FBI agents, one stationed in Phoenix and another in Minneapolis, came up with data about suspicious local commercial airline flight training by Mideast visitors to the United States, but their reports fell on deaf ears at FBI Headquarters in Washington. The CIA tracked two al Qaeda operatives as they entered San Diego in early 2001. The men would eventually join 17 others in the 9/11 attacks. However, the CIA reported to the FBI the sighting of these men as if it were merely a routine matter. The FBI, in turn, conducted a desultory search for them, with no sense of urgency, and never found them. Neither agency did much to coordinate their counterterrorist efforts with one another, face to face or electronically; indeed, the FBI's computer system was antiquated and incompatible with other intelligence agencies.[26]

The events of 9/11 reflected not only a series of intelligence failures but also policy failures. Both the Clinton and the George W. Bush Administrations did little to respond to intelligence reports that pointed to the likelihood of catastrophic terrorist events in the United States. A top-secret alert, issued as early as 1995 and since declassified, concluded that "'aerial terrorism' seems likely at some point, filling an airplane with explosives and dive-bombing a target."[27] The report was wrong only about the need for explosives. On August 6, 2001, a now declassified top-secret CIA memo to the president, entitled "Bin Laden Determined to Strike in US," warned that al Qaeda wanted to hijack a U.S. aircraft, had conducted surveillance of buildings in New York, and "was in the U.S. planning attacks with explosives."[28] This report, given to the president over a month before the 9/11 attacks, was not detailed enough to reveal the precise modus operandi of the al Qaeda terrorists. However, coupled with the 1995 alert, repeated periodically from 1995 through 2001, it should have led to tighter airport security and a more focused manhunt for the al Qaeda operatives.

Each step in the intelligence cycle presents many challenges to intelligence officers and policymakers. Despite flaws and mistakes, the United States is fortunate to have the largest and most effective intelligence agencies in world history. They have achieved many successes. Among them: tracking down and capturing terrorist Carlos the Jackal in Sudan, as well as the ringleader of the World Trade Center bombing in 1993, the two Libyan intelligence officers convicted in the bombing of Pan Am 103, the leaders of the Shining Path in Peru, the Pakistani Mir Aimal Kansi (who murdered two CIA officers near the CIA's headquarters in 1993), Saddam Hussein in 2003, and many top al Qaeda members throughout 2001–2004. Even so, Americans must brace themselves for intelligence failures from time to time. Neither this nor any other nation possesses a crystal ball with perfect information about the machinations of every state adversary and terrorist thug around the world.[29]

COUNTERINTELLIGENCE: A WILDERNESS OF MIRRORS

Although it was never directly mentioned in the National Security Act of 1947, America's secret agencies quickly adopted a second mission in support of their primary one of intelligence collection and analysis, namely, the protection of America's secrets from espionage by hostile (and sometimes even friendly) foreign powers. This mission is known as **counterintelligence.**[30] Defined more formally, counterintelligence is the "knowledge needed for the protection and preservation of the military, economic, and productive strength of the United States, including the security of the Government in domestic and foreign affairs against or from espionage, sabotage, and all other similar clandestine activities designed to weaken or destroy the United States."[31]

Counterintelligence specialists wage nothing less than a secret war against antagonistic intelligence services and terrorist organizations—the latter task a subsidiary of counterintelligence known as counterterrorism. As an expert testified before a Senate committee: "In the absence of an effective U.S. counterintelligence program, [adversaries of democracy] function in what is largely a benign environment."[32]

The Concerns of Counterintelligence

Over the years, the United States has faced numerous adversaries, from British redcoats and Barbary pirates in the early days to the Soviet Red Army and al Qaeda terrorists in the modern era. In the midst of the Cold War, over 1,000 Soviet officials were on permanent assignment in the United States, according to FBI figures released by a Senate committee in 1976.[33] Among these, the FBI identified over 40 percent as members of the KGB or GRU, the Soviet civilian and military intelligence units. Estimates on the number of unidentified intelligence officers (so-called illegals) residing in the United States raised this figure to over 60 percent of the Soviet "diplomatic" representation. Some defector sources have estimated that 70 percent to 80 percent of Soviet embassy officials in Washington, D.C., or Soviets assigned to the United Nations in New York City, had intelligence connections of one kind or another.

The opening of America's deep-water ports to Russian ships in 1972 gave the Soviet intelligence services "virtually complete geographic access to the United States," testified a counterintelligence specialist before the Church Committee in 1975. For example, over 200 Soviet ships, with crews totalling 13,000, called at 40 deep-water ports in the United States during 1974. Various exchange groups provided additional opportunities for Soviet intelligence gathering within the United States. Some 4,000 Soviets entered the United States as commercial or exchange visitors on an annual basis during the later decades of the Cold War; the FBI estimated that a sizeable percentage of these visitors were likely engaged in espionage. Moreover, the FBI identified over 100 intelligence officers among the approximately 400 Soviet students who attended American universities during this period. As well, the United States experienced during the 1970s a sharp increase in the number of Soviet immigrants to the United States, along with a rise in East-West commercial exchange visitors—some of whom were suspected KGB and GRU agents. Recently, the co-chair of a joint investigative committee on intelligence noted that the FBI had warned Congress that a large number of suspected al Qaeda terrorists and sympathizers continued to move about inside the United States after the 9/11 attacks.[34]

Counterintelligence as a Product and an Activity

Counterintelligence is both a product and an activity. The product is reliable information about all hostile foreign intelligence services and other threats, such as al Qaeda cells within the United States. It is necessary to understand the organizational structure of the enemy, its key personnel, its methods of recruitment and training, and the details of specific operations. The efforts of intelligence services and terrorist cells through the world to conceal such information from one another, through various security devices and elaborate deceptions, creates what a CIA chief of counterintelligence, James Angleton, referred to as a "wilderness of mirrors" (borrowing a line from the poet T. S. Eliot).

As an activity, counterintelligence consists of two matching halves: counterespionage and security. Counterespionage is the offensive, or aggressive side of counterintelligence. It involves the identification of specific adversaries and the development of detailed knowledge about the operations they are planning or conducting. Counterespionage personnel must then attempt to block these operations by infiltrating the hostile service and by using sundry forms of manipulation. Security is the passive, or defensive, side of counterintelligence. It entails the establishment of static defenses against all hostile and concealed operations aimed at the United States. Security defenses include the screening and clearance of personnel and the establishment of programs to safeguard sensitive intelligence information.

Among the specific defensive devices used for information control by counterintelligence officers are: security clearances, consisting of thorough inquiries into the backgrounds of job candidates; polygraphs; locking containers; security education; document accountability; censorship; camouflage; and codes. Grim-faced uniformed guards with German shepherds patrol the electrified fences at the CIA's headquarters. Inside, polygraph experts administer tests of loyalty on all new recruits and, periodically, seasoned intelligence officers, cross-examining them on whether they have had any associations with foreigners. The polygraph has produced uneven results. Several traitors have been able to fool the machines, among them Aldrich H. Ames, who worked at the heart of the CIA and passed along its secrets to Russia; his deception was discovered in 1994 and he is now in prison for life. On occasion, though, polygraph sessions have uncovered treason. Beyond armed guards and watchdogs, devices for physical security include fences, lighting, alarms, badges, and passes. The control of a specific area relies on curfews, checkpoints, and restricted zones.

Counterintelligence as Organization

At the CIA, the Office of Security is responsible for protection of the agency's personnel and installations, while counterespionage operations are largely the preserve of the Operations Directorate and its Counterintelligence Staff, which has personnel overseas using official or nonofficial cover). In order to combat terrorism more effectively, DCI William J. Casey established a Counterterrorism Center (CTC) in 1986. Despite its preponderance of CIA personnel, the CTC has 24 officers from a dozen other agencies, including the FBI and the Department of State the two most important links.

In growing frustration over the failure of the CTC and the FBI to share counterterrorism information with one another both before and after the 9/11 attacks on the United States, President George W. Bush established a new Terrorist Threat Integration Center (TTIC) in 2003. As the president said in his State of the Union Address that year, the purpose of the TTIC is "to merge and analyze all threat information in a single location…. In order to better protect our homeland, our intelligence agencies must coexist like they never had before." The TTIC incorporates CIA and FBI counterterrorism units, as well as representatives involved in counterterrorism from throughout the government. The precise structure and mission of the TTIC remain foggy, however, and riven with bureaucratic bickering—much like the new Department of Homeland Security, with its obvious interest in counterintelligence matters.

The Penetration and the Double Agent

Several kinds of operations exist within the rubric of counterespionage. One, however, transcends all the others in importance: the **penetration** or, in the common vernacular, the "mole." The penetration is an operation that either plants or recruits an agent inside a targeted organization. Since the primary goal of counterintelligence is to contain the intelligence services and saboteurs of the enemy, it is desirable to know an enemy's plans in advance and in as much detail as possible. This logical, but challenging, objective may be achieved through a high-level infiltration of an adversary's intelligence service or government, or burrowing into a terrorist cell. Moreover, a well-placed infiltrator in a hostile intelligence service or terrorist camp may be better able than anyone else to determine whether one's own service has been penetrated by an outsider.

The methods of infiltrating an adversary's organization take several forms. Usually the most effective and desirable penetration is the recruitment of an agent-in-place, someone already in the employment of an enemy intelligence service or a terrorist group. Ideally, the agent-in-place will be both highly placed and susceptible to recruitment by the United States. The prospective recruit, say, a Pakistani diplomat at the UN with suspected ties to remnants of the Taliban regime in Afghanistan (and therefore possible ties to al

Qaeda), is approached and asked to work for "the government" of the United States (in fact, the CIA or the FBI). Various inducements may be used to entice the recruit. Money has been the most effective bait since the Cold War. During the Cold War, however, foreigners—notably disaffected individuals inside the intelligence services of the Soviet bloc—would sometimes spy for the United States purely out of a sense of anti-communist ideology or disenchantment over the misdirection of communism under the leadership of Joseph Stalin and other Soviet dictators.[35] The continuing importance of money as a trigger for treason in the post–Cold War era was illustrated recently in the United States. In 2003, Brian P. Regan, an intelligence analyst with access to spy satellite technology and facing $100,000 in credit-card debt, was convicted of plotting to sell to Iraqi officials the coordinates of U.S. satellite surveillance in the Persian Gulf region.

If the recruitment is successful, an agent-in-place operation can be highly productive, since the agent is presumably already trusted within his or her organization and will have unquestioned access to key secret documents. Jack E. Dunlap, who worked at and spied on the National Security Agency in the 1960s, is a well-known example of a Soviet agent-in-place within the U.S. intelligence service during the Cold War. His handler was a Soviet Air Force attaché at the Soviet embassy in Washington. A single penetration can be an intelligence gold mine. Soviet successes were the recruitment of Kim Philby (in British intelligence), Aldrich H. Ames (in the CIA), and Robert P. Hanssen (in the FBI). The United States recruited Col. Oleg Penkovsky, a KGB expert on Soviet weaponry.[36]

Another method of infiltration is the double agent: an individual engaged in espionage for two or more intelligence services. Double agents are costly, time consuming, and risky. The loyalty of a double agent remains a question mark, and double-crosses are commonplace. Running double agents involves much pure drudgery, with few dramatic results, as new information is constantly and painstakingly checked against existing files. For example, the extraordinary staffing requirements of double-agent operations restricted the capacity of the British to operate many of them during the Second World War. The British ran only approximately 150 for the entire period of the war, and no more than about 25 at any one time—even though the task was eased significantly by the ability of the British to read German secret ciphers throughout most of the war.[37] Many of these agents—some say all—ended up double-crossing the British.

The Defector

Almost as good as the agent-in-place, and less troublesome to manage than the double agent, is the **defector**—a person who has access to important information in a nation or terrorist organization and is prepared to give or sell it to another nation. In this case the challenge consists of a skillful interrogation and validation of the defector's credentials *(bona fides)*. Some defectors are in fact decoys, equipped by their countries with a credible mix of false and genuine documents along with other logistical support.

Although an agent-in-place is preferable because of the ongoing useful information he or she can provide, often such an agent does not want to accept the risk of staying in place—especially in nations where the security is sophisticated and the execution of traitors swift and often painful. The agent's usual preference is to defect to safety in the United States. As a result, agents-in-place are harder to come by in tightly controlled totalitarian regimes with robust counterintelligence services of their own; defection is more likely. Agents-in-place are more easily recruited in the developing nations, where sophisticated security that might discover them is often lacking.

Defectors who are recruited overseas by the CIA are occasionally brought to the United States and resettled, if the defector is considered highly important, that is, someone likely to provide valuable, ongoing information, or someone who has already provided vital information to the United States and now seeks exfiltration to avoid capture and execution. The FBI is notified of the exfiltration and, after the CIA completes its interrogation, FBI counterintelligence officers may further interrogate the defector.

Sometimes the *bona fides* of a defector remain in dispute for many years, as in the case of Yuri Nosenko, who defected from the USSR soon after the assassination of President John F. Kennedy in 1963. His major message was to bring word that Moscow had nothing to do with the president's murder. The FBI viewed Nosenko as a legitimate defector; however, James Angleton, the CIA's chief of counterintelligence, worried that he was really a "false defector," sent into the United States to sow disinformation.

Counterintelligence Interrogation

The matter of counterintelligence interrogation methods has been controversial, raising the question of what techniques should be permissible in a democracy. In 2003, the CIA captured in Pakistan Kahlid Sheikh Mohammed, the suspected mastermind of the Pentagon and World Trade Center attacks two years earlier. Immediately, media accounts around the world (including the United States) speculated that he might be mistreated—even tortured—by his CIA handlers. Officials within the CIA responded that no brutal force would be used, not the least because psychological pressure was considered more effective. Former CIA officers speculated that the al Qaeda strategist would be subjected to sleep deprivation; in contrast, if he cooperated, he would be given rewards, such as good food, rest, and a television. They conceded, though, that while there would be no stretching on the rack, captured terrorists might be forced to sit or stand in awkward or painful positions for hours at a time—"torture lite."

The line between acceptable and unacceptable interrogation techniques is not well defined, and apt to be smudged by interrogators who may be angry about past attacks as well as concerned about the possibility of another sudden strike against the United States unless warning information is extracted quickly from a captured terrorist. "There was a before 9/11 and there was an after 9/11," Cofer Black, the head of the CIA's Counterterrorism Center, has said. "After 9/11, the gloves came off."[38]

Counterintelligence and Accountability

The counterintelligence mission is among the most secretive of all intelligence activities—the heart of the onion. Its tight compartmentalization makes proper supervision a challenge for lawmakers and executive overseers. The most disquieting chapter in U.S. counterintelligence occurred during the 1960s and early 1970s when America's secret agencies began to spy at home, against the very people they had sworn to protect.[39] The CIA generated a databank on 1.5 million U.S. citizens, almost all of whom were simply exercising their First Amendment rights to dissent against the war in Vietnam. Many had their mail intercepted and read, their telephones tapped, their day-to-day activities monitored. The NSA intercepted every cable that was sent overseas or received by Americans. The FBI carried out 500,000 investigations of so-called subversives (mainly Vietnam War dissenters, but civil rights activists and Ku Klux Klan members were added to the "enemies list"), without a single case ending up in a court conviction.

During this period, FBI agents wrote anonymous letters meant to incite violence among African Americans. The bureau's counterintelligence program, labeled **cointelpro,** involved not only spying on but the harassment of civil rights activists and Vietnam War dissidents. The purpose was to fray or break family, friendship, and workplace ties as punishment against those Americans who disagreed with key foreign and domestic policies of the Johnson and Nixon Administrations.[40] The overzealous pursuit of counterintelligence threatened the very foundations of American democracy, undermining basic U.S. laws and the constitutional right to free expression. Only when the CIA's transgressions leaked to the press in 1974, triggering a congressional inquiry, did these illegal operations by the CIA, the FBI, the NSA, and military intelligence units come to a halt. As this experience illustrates, a democracy cannot remain free without having strong accountability over its counterintelligence services.

COVERT ACTION: THE THIRD OPTION

The CIA also carries out covert actions, some of which have been controversial.[41] **Covert action** (CA) can be defined as secret activities conducted by the United States to influence and manipulate events abroad. The emphasis is on indirect, unattributed, clandestine operations; the role of the U.S. government is meant to be neither apparent nor publicly acknowledged. This approach to advancing the nation's interests overseas is sometimes referred to as the "Third Option" between sending in overt military force, on the one hand, and relying on the diplomatic corps to achieve national objectives, on the other hand.

Since the use of military force is "noisy" and likely to draw a quick reaction from adversaries, as well as stir widespread debate and criticism, and since diplomacy can be notoriously slow and often ineffectual, covert action has been a beguiling alternative for presidents. With this instrument, a president can move rapidly and in relative quiet, avoiding lengthy policy debates with Congress and journalists. Hence, another insider euphemism for covert action is the "quiet option." Moreover, covert action has the advantage of usually costing less money than a substantial military build-up—although any major intervention abroad will usually entail both covert action and an overt military presence as in Afghanistan in 2001–2002 and Iraq in 2003–2004.

The Evolution of Covert Action in the United States

The use of covert action by the United States is as old as the nation itself, having been employed extensively by the colonial insurgents during the Revolutionary War against Great Britain in 1776.[42] The revolutionaries secretly urged France to aid the war effort and covertly provide troops with weapons, and General George Washington ordered a campaign of secret propaganda against his British military adversaries. Soon after the founding of the new nation, President Thomas Jefferson secretly supplied arms to insurgents in Tripoli to ferment a coup against the unfriendly throne of the bashaw, and President James Madison authorized paramilitary operations against the Spanish in Florida. During America's Civil War, the North and South both resorted to covert action for spreading propaganda and supplying arms to sympathizers.

Not until World War II, though, did the United States begin to carry out covert actions in a concerted manner. President Franklin Roosevelt established the Office of Strategic Services (OSS) to engage not only in espionage but the sabotage of bridges and railroads in Germany, the dissemination of propaganda, and the support of resistance groups. Although the OSS was disbanded after the war, President Truman insisted that the statutory language of the National Security Act of 1947, which created the CIA, provided for the possibility that the new agency might be called upon to engage in operations beyond the collection of intelligence. Without mentioning covert action explicitly, the law stated in an open-ended fashion that the CIA would have authority to "perform such other functions and duties related to intelligence affecting the nation as the National Security Council may from time-to-time direct."

The immediate challenge presented by the Soviet Union was its avowed intent to spread its communist system far and wide. This threat turned the Truman Administration toward the ambiguous passage in the National Security Act. The administration interpreted the language broadly as an invitation to unleash the CIA to fight against global communism. In the late 1940s and early 1950s, secret funding went to pro-Western labor unions, political parties, and publishers in Europe; anti-communist dictators in Latin America; and pro-Western factions in Asia, Africa, and the Middle East. The CIA succeeded in toppling with ease regimes in Iran (1953) and Guatemala (1954) that seemed to threaten American interests. Despite the failure of covert action to depose Cuba's Fidel Castro in 1961 (the disastrous Bay of Pigs operation), by the end of the 1960s the CIA had hundreds of operations underway in every corner of the globe. During major overt wars in Korea (1950–1953) and Vietnam (1964–1975), CIA paramilitary operations were an important element of the U.S. military campaigns.

When the United States withdrew from the unpopular war in Vietnam, funding for covert action began a downward slide, accelerated further by the misuse of the CIA by the Nixon Administration during the Watergate affair in 1973–1974 and by investigative disclosures in 1975 that the CIA had spied on American citizens and tried to subvert the democratically elected president of Chile (Salvador Allende). When President Jimmy Carter entered office in 1977, the CIA's covert action budget had plummeted to a small percentage of the Agency's funding. President Carter kept the funding at that level for most of his administration, but following the Soviet invasion of Afghanistan in 1979, the covert action budget began to grow again. When the Reagan Administration came to power, this secret approach to foreign policy entered a golden age. The so-called **Reagan Doctrine,** a term coined by the media, entailed a set of covert programs led by the CIA under which the U.S. provided extensive military and other assistance to groups and movements fighting against communist governments and their allies throughout the world. The Reagan Doctrine focused especially on Nicaragua and Afghanistan but also provided support for substantial covert operations in El Salvador, Angola, Cambodia, Eastern Europe, and against the Soviet Union itself.

The illegal aspects of the Iran-Contra scandal of 1987 discredited the CIA generally and covert action in particular, and the budget for these operations fell to its lowest level since the opening months of the Cold War in 1947. The funding remained at this level throughout George H. W. Bush's administration, rising modestly as the Clinton Administration turned to the CIA for help with its foreign policy woes in Haiti, Africa, and the Balkans. It would take the attacks against the United States in September 2001, though, to bring about a major infusion of new funds for covert action in the name of combating global terrorism.

The use of CIA paramilitary operations against the Taliban regime in Afghanistan opened a new chapter in America's use of covert action. Events in Afghanistan in 2001–2002 pointed to a successful triple-threat formula for the accomplishment of U.S. foreign policy objectives: precision bombing by the U.S. Air Force, support from local allied insurgents (Afghani warlords in the Northern Alliance), and paramilitary operations conducted jointly by CIA operatives and the Pentagon Special Forces. The CIA also launched two new UAVs during the war in Afghanistan, the Global Hawk and the Predator, capable of taking close-range photographs of the enemy and transmitting them quickly to attack helicopters, fighter planes, artillery units, and nearby U.S. troops. Further, some Predators carried Hellfire missiles—"the latest covert action tool"[43]—which gave the Third Option a new lethal dimension in the war against terrorism. In 2003, a Predator hovering over Yemen's desert at 30,000 feet launched a Hellfire missile at an automobile with suspected al Qaeda operatives inside, killing all six people in the vehicle, including an American citizen.

The Methods of Covert Action

Covert action takes four major forms, often used in conjunction with one another: propaganda (psychological warfare operations or "psy-ops"), along with political, economic, and paramilitary (PM) operations. During the Cold War, these activities are estimated to have accounted respectively for roughly 40, 30, 10, and 20 percent of the total number of covert actions. Paramilitary operations, however, were by far the most expensive and controversial.[44]

Propaganda

During the Cold War, the United States Information Agency (USIA) served as the main instrument of U.S. overt propaganda, releasing through the auspices of American embassies abroad a vast amount of information about the United States, its society, and its international objectives. As a supplement to this open flow of information, the CIA secretly inserted, under the authority of presidential directives, comparable, often identical, themes into media outlets in nations around the world. As with the USIA press releases, the CIA's **covert propaganda** was in almost all cases accurate, if partial to the policies of the United States. Only about 2 percent was false ("black"), usually dealing with military operations.

Indigenous agents known as "media assets" located in foreign countries—journalists, radio and television commentators, op-ed and magazine writers, book authors—expressed "their" views through local media channels, although the material was often written for them in their native tongue by propaganda specialists in the Operations Directorate at CIA headquarters in Langley, Virginia. Unsuspecting local audiences understandably looked upon these indigenous sources of information in their own media as far more credible than USIA press releases. In return for their services, the media assets would receive cash payments and travel stipends from a CIA "case officer," the agent handler who normally operates out of the American embassy in a nation's capital. During the height of the Cold War, the CIA placed 70–80 media insertions each day into foreign media outlets, a great tidal wave of information flowing secretly from Agency headquarters in Virginia into hundreds of media channels in almost every foreign country.

Against tightly controlled totalitarian regimes where it was difficult, if not impossible, to recruit local media assets, the CIA relied on infiltrating propaganda into the country. These efforts could be quite primitive, including the lofting of balloons into the skies to carry speeches, magazines, books, and transistor radios into forbidden territories where, thanks to these airborne deliveries, a deprived citizenry might have the opportunity to read about the outside world. Most of the balloons aimed at the USSR during the Cold War crash landed in that empire's vast expanse, with unknown but probably negligible effects. The CIA also dispatched airplanes to drop leaflets over hostile regimes or transmitted radio broadcasts, sometimes from makeshift stations in remote jungles. Most successful were the radio transmissions directed toward the Soviet Union and Eastern Europe, especially those conducted by Radio Free Europe (RFE) and Radio Liberty (RL), operating in Munich initially under the auspices of the CIA until their secret ties with the intelligence agency were leaked to the media in the early 1970s. These radio stations are credited with having helped to sustain hope behind the Iron Curtain among dissident groups and slowly but steadily contributing to the erosion of internal support for communist regimes.

While the CIA's secret propaganda operations against the communist bloc during the Cold War have been praised by elites and the general public in the United States, the Agency's operations in the developing world have been subjected to widespread criticism.[45] The best known and most controversial example was Chile during the 1960s. In the Chilean presidential election of 1964, the CIA spent $3 million to blacken the reputation of Salvador Allende, the socialist presidential candidate with suspected connections to Moscow. On a per capita basis, this amount of money was equivalent to the secret expenditure of $60 million in a U.S. presidential election at the time. The CIA managed to thwart Allende's bid for his country's presidency in 1964, but he persevered and was finally elected to that office in a free and open election in 1970.

The CIA then turned to a range of propaganda and other covert actions designed to destroy his regime. The Agency poured another $3 million worth of secret propaganda into the country between 1970 and 1973, in the form of press releases, radio commentary, films, pamphlets, posters, leaflets, direct mailings, paper streamers, and vivid wall paintings conjuring images of communist tanks and firing squads that would supposedly soon become a part of life in Chile. The CIA also flooded the predominantly Catholic country with hundreds of thousands of copies of an anti-communist pastoral letter written many years earlier by Pope Pius XI. The effect was to substantially weaken the Allende government.

Years earlier, the CIA had carried out a particularly successful operation in Central America.[46] In 1954, Agency operatives set up a radio station in the mountains of Guatemala. Local media assets began to broadcast the fiction that a revolution had erupted and that the people of Guatemala were joining the movement in large numbers, marching against the pro-communist dictator Jacobo Arbenz. With a speed that astonished even the CIA instigators, the hapless Arbenz panicked over the prospect of the masses storming his palace and resigned before a shot was fired. This bloodless coup was a heady experience for advocates of covert action, coming only seven years after the establishment of the CIA and on the heels of a similar victory in Iran in 1953 (though one that relied as much on clandestine political maneuvering as covert propaganda). It began to seem as though the world could be transformed toward a pro-Western orientation by Madison Avenue public relations techniques secretly applied by the CIA.

The CIA's use of propaganda has had its share of critics. Early in the Cold War, the CIA funded the National Student Association inside the United States as part of its propaganda operations. The purpose was to encourage young Americans to travel abroad and counter Soviet efforts at manipulating international student conferences. Critics were enraged, though, by the CIA's trespassing into the activities of groups within the United States, strictly prohibited by the 1947 founding statute.

The specter of influencing American audiences, not just foreign countries, arose again when it became public that the CIA was sponsoring the publication of anti-communist books written by Soviet defectors as well as U.S. authors. The idea of American writers on the payroll of a secret intelligence agency struck critics as beyond the pale, at least in a democracy. So did the revelation that the CIA had American journalists on its payroll. Estimates of the numbers ranged from three dozen, conceded by the Agency, to over 400.[47] Furthermore, it came to light that the Agency had secretly encouraged its U.S. media assets to write negative reviews of books published by American authors critical of the CIA. George Orwell's fears of Big Brother government appeared to have come to roost in the United States.

Troublesome, too, was the notion of "blowback" or "replay," the phenomenon of inserting propaganda abroad only to have it waft back to U.S. audiences by way of American correspondents innocently reading CIA media insertions in foreign newspapers and reporting this information to American readers. Critics raised doubts as well about the propriety of placing secret propaganda into the media outlets of fellow democracies. The USSR and communist China, yes, because their citizens had no access to accurate information about the world, their masters had no compunction about manipulating their own media, and the regimes were hostile toward the United States. But places like Denmark, France, and Germany were, for the critics, a different story. Here were robust democracies with free presses where the CIA, according to critics, had no right to manipulate the reading public, any more than Americans would like reporters for the *New York Times,* the *Washington Post,* or any other American newspaper to be on the secret payroll of Russian or Chinese intelligence agencies.

Sometimes the CIA's propaganda operations seemed at though they had been crafted by an imaginative descendent of Franz Kafka. As a means for discrediting Fidel Castro of Cuba, one CIA plan consisted of spreading the word that the second coming of Christ was imminent and that Christ was against Castro. As a former CIA officer told a Senate investigative committee: "You would spread this word around Cuba, and then on whatever date it was, that there would be a manifestation of the thing. And at that time—this is absolutely true—and at that time just over the horizon there would be an American submarine which would surface off of Cuba and send up some starshells. And this would be the manifestation of the Second Coming and Castro would be overthrown."[48] The CIA called this operation "Elimination by Illumination." Fortunately, someone in the higher reaches of the Agency had the good sense to bring down the curtain on this theater of the absurd before it was acted out, just as they did another crazy scheme later in the Cold War that called for "filling a captured Soviet transport plane—Soviet markings and all—with live pigs and dropping them over Mecca, Islam's most holy city."[49]

Political Covert Action

Governments also carry out **political covert actions,** or "special activities," as the United States likes to clothe the concept euphemistically in its official—and rare—public references to the subject. In this form, covert action may involve secret payments to friendly foreign politicians and bureaucrats. Critics scorn this method as nothing less than bribery to nurture America's national interests abroad. Advocates prefer a more sanguine interpretation: stipends for the advancement of global democracy—what British intelligence officers in Her Majesty's Secret Service refer to affectionately as "King George's cavalry."

According to the public record, during the Cold War the CIA's political sponsorships included political parties, individual politicians, and dictators in such places as Italy, Jordan, Iran, Ecuador, El Salvador, Angola, Chile, West Germany, Greece, Egypt, Sudan, Suriname, Mauritius, and the Philippines. Secret funds were used to win the favor of influential government officials; to help win elections for pro-Western factions, as in Italy during the early days of the Cold War; to recruit and build parties and regimes opposed to communism; and to strengthen labor unions against Communist Party takeovers.

Propaganda and political covert action are meant to work hand in glove, and sometimes both are subsumed under the "political" label. Some offices in the CIA's Operations Directorate, where covert actions are planned and managed, resemble a presidential campaign headquarters, with intelligence officers engaged in the mass production of brochures, speeches, placards, campaign buttons, and bumper stickers. Never mind that campaign buttons look a little out of place on tribal warlords, or that some of the developing countries where the material is sent have only a few automobiles. Their common purpose during the Cold War was to persuade important foreign officials to turn a favorable eye toward the United States and away from the Soviet Union—or more recently, away from adversaries like the Baath Party in Iraq or al Qaeda. In this sense, the Cold War and the era since may be thought of as a subterranean political struggle between the United States and its adversaries, in which the CIA has waged a secret war to win the hearts and minds of people around the world and to place into positions of power in foreign countries men and women with ideological views compatible with American values and objectives.

Economic Covert Action

An additional weapon in America's arsenal of clandestine operations is the use of subversion against an adversary's means of economic production, an approach known as **economic covert action.** During its campaign to ruin Allende, the CIA provided financial support to factions within Chile for the purposes of encouraging strikes, especially against the trucking industry, that would roil the regime in commercial chaos. Previously, at the time of the Kennedy Administration, the CIA planned to undermine Soviet-Cuban relations by lacing 14,125 bags of sugar bound from Havana to Moscow with an unpalatable, though harmless, chemical substance. At the eleventh hour, a White House aide learned of the proposal and, deeming it excessive, brought it to a halt.[50]

In the conduct of economic covert action, foreign currencies may be counterfeited; the world price of trading commodities depressed, which is especially harmful to one-crop economies, as in the case of Cuban's reliance on sugar cane; harbors and piers mined to discourage commercial shipping, as carried out by the Johnson and Nixon Administrations against North Vietnam and by the Reagan Administration against the Marxist regime in Nicaragua; electrical power lines and oil-storage tankers dynamited, as in North Vietnam and Nicaragua; oil supplies contaminated, as in North Vietnam; and clouds seeded in an effort to disrupt weather patterns over the enemy's territory, attempted without success during the Vietnam War.

Today, a prime target of economic dislocation is an adversary's computer systems, a *modus operandi* known as "cyber-warfare." With skillful hacking, a nation or terrorist group's financial transactions can be left in disarray, its bank assets stolen, its communications hopelessly tangled, and its military command-and-control capabilities frozen. America's counterintelligence officials worry about these methods being used against the United States—an electronic Pearl Harbor, perhaps aimed at Wall Street, that could be at least as disrupting as a direct terrorist or military attack.

Paramilitary Covert Action

While some of the covert actions examined earlier such as the mining of foreign harbors can be quite violent, **paramilitary (PM) operations** are usually the most extreme and controversial manifestations of a nation's secret foreign policy. They can involve a small-scale assassination plot against a foreign leader or large-scale "secret" warfare against an entire nation. The latter idea is something of an oxymoron, since the extensive use of military force against an adversary does not stay secret for long.

The CIA's Special Operations Group (SOG), a unit in the Operations Directorate, sponsored several guerrilla wars during the Cold War. From 1963 to 1973, for example, the Agency backed the Mhong (Meo) tribes of North Laos in a war against the communist Pathet Lao, who served as puppets of North Vietnam. The two sides fought to a draw before the United States finally withdrew from the struggle. According to the public record, the CIA also supported pro-Western insurgents in such places as Ukraine, Poland, Albania, Hungary, Indonesia, China, Oman, Malaysia, Iraq, the Dominican Republic, Venezuela, North Korea, Bolivia, Thailand, Haiti, Guatemala, Cuba, Greece, Turkey, Vietnam, Afghanistan, Angola, and Nicaragua.

In these operations, the CIA's main role was to provide advice and weaponry. During the early stages of the Cold War, anti-communist dissidents became the beneficiaries of a wide range of arms shipments from the United States, compliments of the CIA. These shipments included high-powered rifles, suitcase bombs, fragmentation grenades, rapid-fire machine guns, 64-mm antitank rockets, .38-caliber pistols, .30-caliber M-1 carbines, .45-caliber submachine guns, tear-gas grenades, and full supplies of ammunition. When the Reagan Administration came into office, it funneled through the auspices of the CIA a reported $3 billion worth of weaponry to anti-Soviet fighters in Afghanistan: the *mujahadeen*, or "soldiers of god." Among the weapons were sophisticated shoulder-held Stinger and Blowpipe missiles capable of bringing down Soviet planes and helicopters. This "secret" supply of armaments to the *mujahadeen* is widely thought to have been an important consideration in Moscow's decision to withdraw from its losing "Vietnam" war in Afghanistan.

Since the end of the Cold War, the CIA has provided substantial amounts of arms and financial support to a new list of pro-U.S. factions, especially in the Middle East, the Balkans, and South Asia. Recipients have included the Iraqi National Congress, an umbrella group of insurgents opposed to Saddam Hussein's regime; opponents of Serbian expansion in Bosnia and Kosovo; and Afghanistan's Northern Alliance, along with other anti-Taliban factions, following the 2001 terrorist attacks against the United States.

As part of its paramilitary operations, the CIA is also extensively involved in the training of foreign soldiers to fight on behalf of U.S. and democratic interests. These programs have entailed the training of foreign soldiers for guerrilla warfare, as well as counterterrorism. The CIA's military advisers for such purposes are often borrowed from the Department of Defense (DOD) and given nonofficial battlefield gear, a conversion known colloquially as "sheepdipping." The CIA's paramilitary program includes support to the Department of Defense in the development of the Pentagon's own unconventional warfare capability, known as "Special Operations" (Special Ops) and carried out by elite Special Forces. The CIA, for instance, has provided weapons to the DOD for covert sales aboard. Some of the weapons sold to Iran by the Defense Department in the notorious arms-sale scandal of 1986–1987, the Iran-Contra affair, had their origin in the CIA's paramilitary arsenal.

Moreover, the CIA provides training for military and police units in the developing world, particularly security personnel responsible for the protection of a nation's leaders. Among the skills taught at Camp Perry, the Agency's training facility in Virginia, are lessons in how to protect communications channels and the techniques of "executive driving," designed to impart nimble, spin-away steering skills for maneuvering an automobile through terrorist roadblocks. Some critics have claimed that the CIA teaches foreign security forces how to torture their dissidents, but in fact such practices do not need to be taught and are not taught by the CIA; unfortunately, any thug can conceive of brutal interrogation methods and does not need outside tutoring.

During those infrequent moments when the United States is not involved in the support of paramilitary wars in one place or another, as during the first year of the Carter Administration, the CIA's Special Operations Group bides its time by conducting training operations for its own personnel and by keeping up its military hardware, which includes a small navy and air force. Above all, SOG is kept busy in its added responsibilities to provide support for intelligence collection operations, especially in remote regions like the mountains of Afghanistan, where CIA paramilitary officers have recently developed geographic expertise and contacts with local warlords.

Assassination Plots

The murder of individual foreign leaders—the **assassination option**—is a special category within the domain of paramilitary operations. This option has gone by a variety of euphemisms, such as "executive action," "termination with extreme prejudice," and "neutralization." At one time during the Cold War, proposals for assassination were screened by a special unit within the CIA called the "Health Alteration Committee." Its counterpart in the Soviet Union was the KGB's "Department of Wet Affairs."

For such purposes, the CIA developed a lethal storehouse of chemical and biological materials as well as high-tech delivery systems. Though small in total volume, these poisons included shellfish toxin and cobra venom, and they were plentiful and deadly enough to kill the population of a small city. One delivery system entailed the application of poison to a slender dart the size of a sewing needle ("a nondiscernible microbioinoculator"). An electric dart gun (a "noise-free disseminator"), resembling an oversized .45 pistol with a telescopic sight, propelled the dart silently toward the victim, with reliable accuracy up to 100 meters.

Senator Frank Church (left), displaying a CIA poison-dart gun with Senator John Tower (right), led a 1975 investigation into covert intelligence activities, discovering that the CIA initiated and carried out a large number of assassination plots around the world. These revelations led President Ford to sign an executive order forbidding assassination as an instrument of U.S. foreign policy.

The Cuban Plots

Fidel Castro was America's prime target for assassination during the Kennedy Administration, although whether the planned murder was officially sanctioned by President John F. Kennedy is disputed by historians and insiders. The CIA emptied its medicine cabinet of drugs and poisons in various attempts to kill or debilitate the Cuban leader. The CIA's agents—"assets," in Agency lingo—planned to dust his combat boots with depilatory powder, in hopes the chemical would enter his bloodstream through his feet and cause his charismatic beard to fall off. This plot had to be abandoned, since Castro's boots were not so accessible. Next, agents tried (but failed) to inject his cigars with the hallucinogenic drug LSD or with the deadly botulinum toxin.

CIA assets persevered, placing Madura foot fungus in an underwater diving suit that was to be presented to Castro through an intermediary on his birthday. The suit was never used by the Cuban leader. In another plot, assets placed beautiful seashells filled with explosives near coral reefs in Castro's favorite diving lagoon. They were to be detonated from a small submarine nearby as soon as the Cuban President came close to the shells. He never did. Castro seems to have been the world's luckiest man—or, with Soviet counterintelligence officers at his side, perhaps one of the best informed and best guarded. The public record now indicates that *every* CIA agent sent into Cuba to collect information was discovered and "doubled" (turned back) against the United States. Perhaps Castro learned about every assassination plot as well, with the help of the KGB and GRU.

Undeterred, the CIA equipped yet another asset with a special ballpoint pen filled with the poison Blackleaf-40. With its needle point, the pen was a perfect disguise for a hypodermic syringe, suitable for injecting the poison into Castro's skin. This required, however, that an asset come close enough to the target to inject the fluid, which proved impossible. The CIA also contacted the Mafia in the United States for help in murdering the elusive Cuban leader. The mob still had contacts in Havana from pre-Castro days, when that city flourished as a center for gambling, and was able to recruit assassins inside Cuba; however, these efforts failed, too.

Another prime target for "health alteration" during the Kennedy years was Patrice Lumumba, the Congolese leader. Relying on the protected use of a State Department diplomatic pouch, the Special Operations Group forwarded to the CIA's chief of station (COS) in Congo a peculiar set of diplomatic instructions, which were accompanied by rubber gloves, a gauze mask, a hypodermic syringe, and lethal biological toxin. The purpose was clear. As the COS wryly recalled in subsequent congressional testimony: "I knew it wasn't for somebody to get his polio shot up to date."[51] In case there was any misunderstanding, an enclosed coded message ordered the COS to inject the toxin into Lumumba's food or toothpaste at the earliest opportunity. His death would come quickly. The COS initially protested, via return coded message, arguing that it would be more suitable to eliminate the African leader by more direct means. "Recommend hqs pouch soonest high powered foreign make rifle with telescopic scope and silencer," he suggested in a top-secret cable back to CIA headquarters. Overruled, the COS proceeded to carry out his orders. However, members of a rival Congolese faction beat the CIA to the punch and murdered Lumumba for their own political reasons having to do with an internal power struggle.

During the Cold War, the CIA had close ties to factions who "neutralized" a number of other foreign leaders, including Rafael Trujillo of the Dominican Republic, Ngo Dinh Diem of South Vietnam, and General Rene Schneider of Chile. While the Agency did provide weapons to these groups, a Senate investigation in 1975 could find no indication that the CIA was actually behind the murders.[52] Indeed, the factions were no longer controlled by the United States at the time of the assassinations. Similarly, the CIA provided weapons to dissidents who may have then plotted the death of President Sukarno of Indonesia and Francois "Papa Doc" Duvalier of Haiti, but again the plots appear to have gone forward without the Agency's imprimatur.

The CIA has been involved in assassinations below the level of high leadership as well. An obstreperous Iraqi colonel with Soviet connections was one target during the Cold War. The Operations Directorate sent orders to the field that the colonel should be disabled for several months by exposing him to an incapacitating chemical placed on his handkerchief. "We do not consciously seek subject's permanent removal from the scene," the secret cable advised. "We also do not object should this complication develop."

The most widely reported CIA operation to eliminate large numbers of lower-level officials from the scene arose in the context of the Vietnam War. Codenamed the "Phoenix Program," the intention was to subdue the influence of the communist Viet Cong (VC) in the South Vietnamese countryside. Some 20,000 VC officials were killed as a result of this operation, though mostly in the context of military or paramilitary combat with South Vietnamese or U.S. troops.

The Senate investigation in 1975 into these assassination plots disclosed that the United States had become a kind of "global Godfather," carrying out murder plots around the world.[53] The public revulsion stemming from these findings led President Ford to sign an executive order prohibiting assassination as an instrument of U.S. foreign policy. The order, which states that "no person, employed by or acting on behalf of the United States Government, shall engage in, or conspire to engage in assassination," has been endorsed by subsequent presidents.

Nevertheless, in 1984 during the Reagan Administration, CIA personnel distributed a manual in the northern provinces of Nicaragua that instructed pro-U.S. *contra* insurgents in the arts of "neutralizing" local government officials. It had all the hallmarks of a Phoenix-like program to systematically assassinate village representatives of the ruling Sandinista regime. Moreover, in 1986 the Reagan Administration ordered an overt U.S. Air Force F-111 bombing of Muammar Qaddafi's home in Libya, claiming that this was not an assassination attempt but rather a military operation against the leader of a nation suspected of sponsoring terrorism. During the Persian Gulf War in 1991 and the Iraq War in 2003, both Bush presidents hoped that the Iraqi leader Saddam Hussein would be a victim of the extensive bombing of Baghdad. Indeed, during both wars, the White House authorized bombing attacks against selected targets with the specific intention of killing Saddam, who was eventually captured in 2003.

The Ford executive order prohibiting assassination remains in effect, but with two important exceptions: when America employs overt force in a short-term military strike, as in Libya, or when the United States is engaged in a more formal and protracted war, as in Iraq in 2003–2004, and in Afghanistan during 2001–2002. In a recent review of the executive order, Congress has provided leeway for another exception: if a terrorist were known to be driving a truck laden with explosives toward a U.S. facility, the CIA would be expected to kill him or her if there were no other way to prevent the attack.

The war-related exception has proved controversial. The Predator strike against the al Qaeda automobile in the Yemen desert in 2003 raised serious questions about where the battlefield is in the war against terrorism. President George W. Bush said that some 60 nations have harbored terrorists. Did that mean that the CIA had authority from the president to hunt down alleged terrorists in each one of these nations, launching Hellfire missiles at suspects from 30,000 feet without any due process or other judicial proceedings? What about the rights of the people targeted, such as the U.S. citizen in the car in Yemen, to prove their innocence before the death penalty was inflicted swiftly by a hovering Predator? In 2003–2004, the Special Forces created an assassination group called Task Force 121 to hunt down and capture or kill Baathist insurgents in Iraq associated with the fallen Hussein regime, raising serious questions about the extent of proper accountability over this group.[54] The operations of Task Force 121 seemed to slip by the system of congressional oversight established to supervise CIA covert actions as discussed in Chapter 9.

A Covert Action Balance Sheet

Since the outbreak of the Cold War and the establishment of the CIA in 1947, covert action has exercised a fascination on most presidents and their national security advisers. But what have been the results? This question may be answered according to both practical outcomes and ethical considerations. With respect to practicalities, a further distinction must be made between the short-term and long-term consequences of covert action.

The practical results have been mixed. Sometimes covert action has led to stunning successes for the United States, at least over the short term. In Europe in the immediate aftermath of the Second World War (particularly in Greece and Italy), in Iran (1953), in Guatemala (1954), and less spectacularly throughout Latin America in the 1950s, covert action played a significant role in thwarting communist and Marxist political leaders, who were often sponsored openly or covertly by the USSR. Over the short run, the CIA also chalked up notable successes in Laos (1963–1973) and Afghanistan (1982–1988 and 2001–2002).

Yet the lasting value of some of these "victories"—the long-term consequence—has been questionable.[55] Iran is hardly a close friend of the United States today; Guatemala and Panama are as poor and repressive as ever; the first Afghanistan intervention brought the Taliban regime to power, which gave safe haven to al Qaeda; and the second Afghanistan intervention is unlikely to have brought global terrorism to a halt, although it took a useful step in that direction. Moreover, there have been spectacular failures of covert action, from the Bay of Pigs to the inability of the Iraqi National Congress to dislodge the regime of Saddam Hussein from 1991 to 2003.

On practical grounds, perhaps the best conclusion one can draw based on the empirical record is to say that, like overt economic sanctions or bombing, covert action sometimes works and sometimes does not. Its chances seem best when the objectives are limited; when strong opposition groups already exist within the target nation or group;

and, in the case of paramilitary operations, when aided and abetted by overt precision bombing and elite Special Forces on the ground—the prescription for success in Afghanistan in 2001–02.

From a moral point of view, proponents of covert action argue that the defeat of such venal powers as the communists during the Cold War or terrorists today justifies the use of covert action, even in the extreme forms of political bribery, severe economic disruptions, secret wars, and assassination plots. When a barroom brawl breaks out, they reason, adherence to polite rules makes little sense.

Those taking a more ethical view of foreign policy balk, though, at the "anything goes" approach to America's security—the unsavory "ends justify the means" argument.[56] In their minds, realism should be tempered with idealism. "When we choose our weapons, let's choose ones we are good at using—like the Marshal Plan—not ones that we are bad at—like the Bay of Pigs," maintains Harvard University law professor Roger Fisher. "To join some adversaries in the grotesque world of poison dart-guns and covert operations is to give up the most powerful weapons we have: idealism, morality, due process of law, and belief in the freedom to disagree, including the right of other countries to disagree with us."[57]

It is one thing for other nations simply to disagree with the United States, and quite another for terrorists to fly airplanes into America's buildings. Trying to kill Fidel Castro or Patrice Lumumba because they oppose U.S. policies may be viewed as excessive, but using covert action assets to hunt down al Qaeda members who embrace suicidal attacks against U.S. urban population centers is more palatable to most Americans. Even then, though, the United States should attempt to understand and address the underlying sources of terrorism, which often springs from conditions of desperate poverty.[58] Similarly, critics of covert action balk at manipulating the media in fellow democracies, intervening in free elections, or tampering with open economic systems.

Debate within the United States over the practical and moral implications of covert action and other intelligence activities will continue to ebb and flow.[59] What will remain constant is the nearly irresistible tug of the Third Option on America's leaders, as they search for effective instruments to achieve the policy objectives of the United States around the globe.

SUMMARY

The ability of the United States to defend and advance its interests in the world often depends on having good information. Gathering information overseas and assessing its significance is easier said than done, as are two other activities carried out by U.S. intelligence agencies: counterintelligence, that is, efforts to thwart the clandestine operations of hostile intelligence services and terrorist factions directed against the United States, and covert action, the attempt to secretly manipulate world events in a manner favorable to U.S. interests.

The means by which intelligence is gathered from around the world and channeled to the desks of policymakers is a multiphased process, often referred to as the intelligence cycle, consisting of a period of planning, followed by the collection, processing, analysis, and dissemination of information.

Each step in the intelligence cycle presents challenges to intelligence officers and policymakers. Despite flaws and mistakes, many of which should be corrected in light of the inquiries into the errors preceding the September 2001 terrorist attacks, the United States has the most effective intelligence agencies in world history. Even so, Americans must brace themselves for intelligence failures, since no nation possesses a crystal ball with perfect information about the machinations of every state and terrorist around the world.

U.S. intelligence agencies have a second mission in support of their primary one of intelligence collection and analysis: counterintelligence. Counterintelligence specialists wage a secret war against antagonistic intelligence services and terrorist organizations. Efforts against the latter are known as counterterrorism.

Counterintelligence is both a product and an activity. The product is reliable information about hostile foreign intelligence services. As an activity, counterintelligence consists of two matching halves, counterespionage and security. Counterespionage involves the identification of specific adversaries and the development of detailed knowledge about the operations they are planning or conducting. Security entails the establishment of defenses against hostile and concealed operations aimed at the United States. Security clearances, consisting of thorough inquiries into the backgrounds of job candidates, and the use of polygraphs, locking containers, security education, document accountability, censorship, codes, and camouflage are some of the defenses counterespionage uses.

The Central Intelligence Agency also carries out covert actions. The emphasis is on indirect, unattributed, clandestine operations, with the role of the United States neither apparent nor publicly acknowledged. Sometimes called the "Third Option," existing between the use of overt military force, on the one hand, and relying on the diplomatic corps on the other, covert action is often quite controversial.

Covert action takes four major forms, often used together: propaganda, and political, economic, and paramilitary operations. In the Cold War, these activities are estimated to have accounted respectively for 40, 30, 10, and 20 percent of all covert actions. Paramilitary operations were the most expensive and controversial, but the practical results were mixed. Sometimes covert action leads to stunning successes for the United States, at least over the short term, but the lasting value of some successes has been questionable.

Perhaps the best conclusion one can draw is that, like overt economic sanctions or military action, covert action sometimes works and sometimes does not. Debate over the practical and moral implications of covert action and other intelligence activities will continue to ebb and flow. What will remain constant is the tug of the Third Option on U.S. leaders as they search for a quiet means to achieve U.S. objectives around the globe.

KEY TERMS AND CONCEPTS

intelligence	analysis
intelligence cycle	President's Daily Brief (PDB)
Director of Central Intelligence (DCI)	National Intelligence Estimate (NIE)
techint	all-source intelligence
humint	intelligence to please

counterintelligence
penetration
defector
cointelpro
covert action
Reagan Doctrine

covert propaganda
political covert actions
economic covert actions
paramilitary (PM) operations
assassination option

THINKING CRITICALLY

1. Explain the role of intelligence in the making of U.S. foreign policy.

2. Why did America's intelligence agencies fail to warn the nation of the terrorist attacks of September 11, 2001?

3. What steps have been taken to address these failures, and how successful do you believe they have been?

4. Have covert actions advanced the interests of the United States in the world, or hurt the nation's reputation? Provide evidence to support your position.

5. What can be done to improve U.S. intelligence agencies, so that failures are less likely?

6. To what extent has the system of accountability over covert operations established in the 1970s reduced the effectiveness of the intelligence agencies?

7. What ethical limits do you think should be placed on the use of secret operations by the United States overseas?

NOTES

1. This account is drawn from Loch K. Johnson, "The CIA's Weakest Link," *Washington Monthly* 33 (July/August 2001): 9–14.

2. See the Aspin-Brown Commission, *Preparing for the 21st Century: An Appraisal of U.S. Intelligence,* Report of the Commission on the Roles and Capabilities of the United States Intelligence Community (Washington, D.C.: U.S. Government Printing Office (March 1, 1996); Loch K. Johnson and James J. Wirtz, *Strategic Intelligence: Windows into a Secret World* (Los Angeles: Roxbury, 2004).

3. See Loch K. Johnson, *America's Secret Power: The CIA in a Democratic Society* (New York: Oxford University Press, 1989), and Mark M. Lowenthal, *Intelligence: From Secrets to Policy,* 2nd ed. (Washington, D.C.: CQ Press, 2003).

4. On the CIA, see Rhodri Jeffreys-Jones, *The CIA and American Democracy* (New Haven: Yale University Press, 1989); Loch K. Johnson, *Bombs, Bugs, Drugs, and Thugs: Intelligence and America's Quest for Security* (New York: New York University Press, 2002); and John Ranelagh, *The Agency: The Rise and Decline of the CIA* (New York: Simon and Schuster, 1986).

5. Roberta Wohlstetter, *Pearl Harbor: Warning and Decision* (Stanford: Stanford University Press, 1962).

6. Alvin D. Coox, "Pearl Harbor," in *Decisive Battles of the Twentieth Century,* ed. Noble Frankland and Christopher Dowling (New York: McKay, 1976), p. 148.

7. Cited by Merle Miller, *Plain Speaking: An Oral Biography of Harry S. Truman* (New York: Berkeley, 1973), p. 420, note.

8. *Fact Book on Intelligence,* Office of Public Affairs, Central Intelligence Agency (April 1983), p. 17.

9. Arthur S. Hulnick, "The Intelligence Producer–Policy Consumer Linkage: A Theoretical Approach," *Intelligence and National Security* 1 (May): 212–233.

10. Remark, Conference on Intelligence, U.S. Air Force Academy, Colorado Springs, Colorado (June 6, 1984).

11. For the memoirs of some recent DCIs, see William E. Colby and Peter Forbath, *Honorable Men: My Life in the CIA* (New York: Simon and Schuster, 1978); Richard Helms with William Hood, *A Look over My Shoulder* (New York: Simon and Schuster, 2003); Robert M. Gates, *From the Shadows* (New York: Simon and Schuster, 1996); and Stansfield Turner, *Secrecy and Democracy* (Boston: Houghton Mifflin, 1985).

12. On techint, see Jeffrey T. Richelson, *The U.S. Intelligence Community,* 4th ed. (Boulder, Colo.: Westview Press, 1999).

13. Loch K. Johnson, *Secret Agencies: U.S. Intelligence in a Hostile World* (New Haven: Yale University Press, 1996).

14. Loch K. Johnson, *Secret Agencies,* p. 121.

15. Loch K. Johnson, *A Season of Inquiry: The Senate Intelligence Ivestigation* (Lexington: University Press of Kentucky, 1985), p. 24.

16. Percy Cradock, *Know Your Enemy* (London: Murray, 2002).

17. Christopher Andrew, *For the President's Eyes Only: Secret Intelligence and the American Presidency from Washington to Bush* (New York: Harper Collins, 1995).

18. Harry Howe Ransom, *The Intelligence Establishment* (Cambridge, Mass.: Harvard University Press, 1970), p. 147, citing an intelligence professional's observation published in *Military Review* (May 1961): 20.

19. Gregory F. Treverton, *Reshaping National Intelligence for an Age of Information* (New York: Cambridge University Press, 2001).

20. Remarks, Conference on Intelligence, U.S. Air Force Academy, Colorado Springs, original emphasis.

21. See Harry Howe Ransom, "The Politicization of Intelligence," in *Intelligence and Intelligence Policy in a Democratic Society*, ed. Stephen J. Cimbala (Dobbs Ferry, N.Y.: Transnational, 1987), pp. 25–46; and James J. Wirtz, "Intelligence to Please? The Order of Battle Controversy during the Vietnam War," *Political Science Quarterly* 106 (Summer 1991): 239–263.

22. Michael Herman, *Intelligence Power in Peace and War* (Cambridge: Cambridge University Press, 1996); Arthur S. Hulnick, *Fixing the Spy Machine* (Westport, Conn.: Praeger, 1999).

23. Ray S. Cline, *Secrets, Spies, and Scholars: Blueprint of the Essential CIA* (Washington, D.C.: Acropolis, 1976).

24. Paul Wolfowitz, interviewed by Jack Davis, "The Challenge of Managing 'Uncertainty': Paul Wolfowitz on Intelligence-Policy Relations" (March 1995), unpublished manuscript, p. 8.

25. Report, Joint Committee on Intelligence (Washington, D.C.: U.S. Government Printing Office, 2003); Final Report, National Commission on Terrorist Attacks upon the United States—the 9/11 or Kean Commission, after its chairman, Thomas Kean (Washington, D.C.: U.S. Government Printing Office, 2004).

26. Ronald Kessler, *The Bureau: The Secret History of the FBI* (New York: St. Martin's Press, 2002).

27. Loch K. Johnson, "The Aspin-Brown Intelligence Inquiry: Behind the Closed Doors of a Blue Ribbon Commission," *Studies in Intelligence,* 48 (2004), pp. 1–20.

28. "Appraisal of the Threat Posed by Bin Laden," *New York Times* (April 11, 2004): 13.

29. See Richard K. Betts, "Analysis, War and Decision: Why Intelligence Failures Are Inevitable," *World Politics* 31 (October 1978): 61–89.

30. See Roy S. Godson, *Dirty Tricks or Trump Cards: U.S. Covert Action and Counter-intelligence* (Washington, D.C.: Brassey's, 1996), and Johnson and Wirtz, *Strategic Intelligence,* pp. 289–295.

31. Commission on Government Security, Report (Washington, D.C.: U.S. Government Printing Office, 1957), pp. 48–49.

32. The Church Committee (after its chair, Senator Frank Church, D-Idaho), more formally: Select Committee to Study Governmental Operations with Respect to Intelligence Activities, Final Report, Sen. Rept. No. 94-755, Vol. 1 (Washington, D.C.: U.S. Government Printing Office, 1976), p. 163.

33. Church Committee, Final Report, p. 163.

34. Remarks, Nancy Pelosi, ranking minority member of the House Permanent Select Committee on Intelligence (D-California) to Loch K. Johnson, Athens, Georgia (November 26, 2002).

35. Stan A. Taylor and Daniel Snow, "Cold War Spies and How They Got Caught," *Intelligence and National Security* 12 (April 1997): 101–125.

36. Tom Mangold, *Cold Warrior* (New York: Simon and Schuster, 1991); David Wise, *Spy* (New York: Random House, 2003).

37. Sir John Masterman, *Double Cross System of the War of 1939–45* (New Haven: Yale University Press, 1972).

38. Toby Harden, "CIA 'Pressure' on Al Qaeda Chief," *Washington Post* (March 6, 2003): A1.

39. Loch K. Johnson, *A Season of Inquiry,* and Johnson, *America's Secret Power.*

40. Loch K. Johnson, "Congressional Supervision of America's Secret Agencies: The Experience and Legacy of the Church Committee," *Public Administration Review* 64 (January/February 2004): 3–14.

41. Gregory F. Treverton, *Covert Action: The Limits of Intervention in the Postwar World* (New York: Basic Books, 1989).

42. Stephen F. Knott, *Secret and Sanctioned: Covert Operations and the American Presidency* (New York: Oxford University Press, 1996).

43. Bob Woodward and Dan Balz, "Combating Terrorism," *Washington Post* (February 1, 2002): A1.

44. Johnson, *America's Secret Power* and *Secret Agencies.*

45. Church Committee, Final Report; Treverton, *Covert Action.*

46. David Wise and Thomas Ross, *The Invisible Government* (New York: Random House, 1964).

47. Johnson, *America's Secret Power,* p. 185.

48. Johnson, *A Season of Inquiry,* p. 50.

49. Robert Baer, *See No Evil: The True Story of a Ground Soldier in the CIA's War on Terrorism* (New York: Crown, 2002), p. 21.

50. Tom Wicker et al., "CIA Operations: A Plot Scuttled," *New York Times* (April 25, 1966): 19 ff.

51. Select Committee to Study Governmental Operations with Respect to Intelligence Activities (the Church Committee), *Alleged Assassination Plots Involving Foreign Leaders,* U.S. Senate (November 1975) (Washington, D.C.: U.S. Government Printing Office, 1975), p. 41.

52. Select Committee to Study Governmental Operations, p. 41.

53. Frank Church, "Do We Still Plot Murders? Who Will Believe We Don't?" *Los Angeles Times* (June 14, 1983): part 2, p. 5.

54. Seymour M. Hersh, "Moving Targets," *New Yorker* (December 15, 2003): 48–55.

55. See Frank Church, "Covert Action: Swampland of American Foreign Policy," *Bulletin of the Atomic Scientists* 32 (February 1976): 7–11; and Chambers A. Johnson, *Blowback: The Costs and Consequences of American Empire* (New York: Metropolitan Books, 2004). Chambers Johnson uses the term "blowback" to mean any untoward effects on the United States of America's foreign policy, whether conducted secretly or openly; the CIA uses the term, as explained earlier in this chapter, to mean the hazard of CIA covert propaganda replaying back to the United States.

56. James A. Barry, "Covert Action Can Be Just," *Orbis* 37 (Summer 1993): 375–390.

57. Op-ed commentary, *Boston Globe* (February 1, 1976): 21.

58. See, for example, the argument in Loch K. Johnson and Kiki Caruson, "The Seven Sins of American Foreign Policy," *PS: Political Science* (Spring 2003): 4–10.

59. E. Drexel Godfrey Jr., "Ethics and Intelligence," *Foreign Affairs* 56 (April 1978): 624–642.

PART **FOUR**

Issues of American Foreign Policy

Introduction to Part Four

To this point, *American Foreign Policy: History, Politics and Policy* has focused on the methodology behind, the history of, and the formulation of American foreign policy. In the following four chapters, we examine four general issue areas in American foreign policy: defending the homeland; issues of trade, finance, and currency; military intervention overseas; and the role of human rights and democratization in American foreign policy.

These four general issue areas are not the only ones to which students of American foreign policy, and the broader American and world publics as well, should devote their attention. U.S. international environmental policy, immigration policy, policies toward international law and international institutions, international health policies, and others as well also warrant attention. The four general issue areas examined here, however, are among the most critical in the conduct of American foreign policy. As a general rule, they are also among the most likely to be issues of contention in American political discourse and debate.

The four chapters in Part IV share a similar structure. Each begins with a presentation of the background to American foreign policy in the general issue area under discussion and continues with an examination of specific current problems in that area. This method of analysis inevitably, and intentionally, leads to some repetition of materials presented earlier, especially in Part II of this text.

In Part II, issue areas were examined in their historical context, primarily in relation to other issues that American policymakers faced at a given point in time. In Part IV, each chapter begins with an examination of how the issue area evolved over time. When specific current problems in each issue area are discussed at the conclusion of each chapter, students will thus have the benefit of understanding both the historical context and the contemporary pressures that influence the shaping and conduct of American foreign policy, not only in the broad issue area but also in the specific current problem under discussion.

By the very nature of foreign policy, the specific problems examined in the following four chapters are not exhaustive. Other current problems also exist, but the ones examined here are arguably the most important. After studying the broad issue areas and specific current problems detailed in the following pages, students should be well prepared to join the ongoing American debates about homeland defense; trade, finance, and currency policy; overseas military intervention; and the role of human rights and democratization in American foreign policy.

CHAPTER 12

Defending the Homeland

A Second Day of Infamy: the World Trade Center's Twin Towers shortly after two hijacked planes hit them. Almost 3,000 people were killed in the September 11, 2001, terrorist attacks, which also hit the Pentagon in Washington, D.C.

- What threats to the American homeland has the United States experienced?
- How has the United States over time defended the American homeland?
- What is the nature of the Department of Homeland Security?
- How have American efforts to defend the homeland changed since September 11, 2001?
- How great a threat is posed by weapons of mass destruction?
- Is cyber security a problem for the United States?

The September 11, 2001, terrorist attacks on the United States were a terrible event in American history. Like nothing since Japan's December 7, 1941, attack on Pearl Harbor, the 2001 assault on New York and Washington focused the attention of the public and government on the most fundamental responsibility that a government has, defending the homeland.

One might ask, "What is new about defending the homeland?" The answer is, "Nothing." Since the republic was created, defense of the United States against attacks, either foreign or domestic, has been the most fundamental of all objectives of American foreign policy. In fact, all officers of the federal government must swear to defend the United States against all foes.

Homeland defense has been a constant in American foreign policy, although what made up the homeland and what should be done to defend it have at times been in dispute. Sometimes, homeland defense received lower priority for budget allocations than some believed it should. Nevertheless, the events of September 11, 2001, drove home to Americans once again how important homeland defense is.

EARLY ISSUES OF HOMELAND DEFENSE

Even before the United States was created, defending their homeland concerned the American colonists. Conflicts with the French and with American Indians broke out, and defense was everyone's responsibility, not just the local militia's. However, when the colonies rebelled against Great Britain, the concept of homeland defense took on a different meaning. To most colonists, Great Britain, their erstwhile ally in the fights against the French and the Indians, had become the enemy.

During the American Revolution, it was sometimes difficult to differentiate between friend and foe, and between defense and offense. Thus, one of the first actions the Continental Congress authorized in 1775 was an invasion of Canada. Many American revolutionary leaders envisioned a homeland that included Canada. They were shocked when Canadians met the invasion with stiff resistance at Toronto and defeated it at Quebec. Soon thereafter came American entreaties to France and other European states for loans to prosecute the war.

Post-Independence Dangers and Threats

After it won independence, the United States faced a number of external threats, some real and some imagined, some the result of foreign designs on the American homeland and others generated by the United States itself as it expanded across North America. Spain, France, Great Britain, and the American Indians were the most prominent initial threats to the new nation.

To defend against these threats, the U.S. Congress early on authorized creation of a small army and navy, and building a number of coastal and frontier forts. The army was often supplemented by state militias, and the navy by privateers, that is, by privately owned vessels commissioned to serve as warships, used primarily to capture shipping. The U.S. Navy proved highly effective in the undeclared naval war with France, the Barbary War, and the War of 1812. As for the forts, except during the Civil War, they never fired a shot in anger. American success in the United States' early days in defending the homeland, expanding borders, and gaining more territory was not the result of strength, but of geographical isolation, European geopolitical competition, and occasional international cooperation.

Geographical isolation contributed to early American security because in the eighteenth and most of the nineteenth centuries, transportation and communication technologies had not yet conquered distance. Until the advent of the steamship, transatlantic travel in this era required dangerous and lengthy voyages that sometimes took 70 days. Communications were no better. As you can see from Table 12.1, time and space stood as direct obstacles to communications in the 1700s. Of course, the invention of the telegraph and subsequent electricity-based means of information transmission from the mid-1800s onward revolutionized the transfer of data.

TABLE 12.1
CROSSING THE ATLANTIC

Year	Time Required	Mode of Transportation
1775	42+ days	Sailing ship
1864	10+ days	Screw-driven steamship
1917	5+ days	Steam turbine ship
1941	29 hours	Propeller airplane
2003	8 hours	Jet airplane

The United States was also aided by **European geopolitical competition.** Often, U.S. foreign policy efforts succeeded because France or England used the United States to weaken the other or to complicate the international position of the other. Because of British and French jockeying for global position, the United States, not yet a primary player in the world and a country that existed on the margins of world affairs, sometimes became the beneficiary of European power struggles and secured its objectives with limited interference from the great states of Europe.

Homeland defense also sometimes required cooperation with foreign powers, especially Great Britain. One point of genius in nineteenth-century American foreign policy that contributed substantially to homeland defense was the **demilitarization of the American-Canadian border,** accomplished by several U.S.-British initiatives, such as the 1817 Rush-Bagot Agreement under which neither country could have more than four warships on the Great Lakes and Lake Champlain, the 1818 agreement to extend the 49th parallel as the U.S-Canadian boundary to the Rocky Mountains, the 1842 Webster-Ashburton Treaty that resolved boundary disputes between Maine and Canada, and the 1846 division of the Oregon Territory by extending the 49th-parallel boundary to the Pacific.

These fortunate situations and successful initiatives did not mean that the American homeland was free from threats. Despite the demilitarization of the American-Canadian border, Americans in the late eighteenth and early nineteenth century believed they were threatened by Great Britain. At the same time, France and Spain became involved in North American adventures that included expansion into Mexico.

However, the reality was that foreign powers only rarely attacked the continental United States. The first was Great Britain's attack on various regions of the young republic in the War of 1812. The Great Lakes, New Orleans, and even Washington, D.C., felt British power firsthand.[1] Not counting fighting with Native Americans and the Civil War, no subsequent attacks against the American homeland occurred until 1916, when Mexican revolutionary Poncho Villa crossed the U.S.-Mexican border and attacked Columbus, New Mexico. Seventeen Americans and over a hundred of Villa's men died. In retaliation, the United States sent a military force into Mexico to search for Villa, but never found him.

World Wars I and II

As we saw in Chapter 5, a crisis that involved Mexico helped catapult the United States into World War I when Great Britain intercepted the Zimmermann telegram, in which

Germany offered to help Mexico regain territory it lost to the United States in the Mexican War if Mexico declared war on the United States. London turned the telegram over to Washington, and the United States saw Germany's action as a direct threat to U.S. security. American outrage over the Zimmermann telegram combined with outrage over Germany's sinking of the *Lusitania* and its declaration of unrestricted submarine warfare to precipitate America's 1917 entrance into World War I.

A direct attack against American military bases in territories owned or claimed by the United States also precipitated the United States' entry into World War II. Indeed, until September 11, 2001, the most infamous attack on territory owned or claimed by the United States was Japan's December 7, 1941, attack on U.S. military facilities at **Pearl Harbor**, followed by attacks against American military bases in the Philippines. The deaths of approximately 3,000 Americans at Pearl Harbor left the United States no choice. On December 8, 1941, the United States declared war on Japan. Soon after, Germany declared war on the United States, and America was embroiled in the largest, most violent, and most deadly war in human history.

No meaningful attack occurred against the continental United States during World War II. American cities, especially coastal cities, were blacked out. Japan launched a number of ineffective windborne balloon bombs into the American Northwest, Germany landed an occasional spy on the Atlantic coast, and German submarines wrought havoc with shipping, but the U.S. homeland was never attacked. At the end of World War II, the United States emerged as the only major industrial power whose homeland had not been decimated by war.

The Cold War

After World War II, the world in the late 1940s slipped into the Cold War. After Soviet scientists and engineers developed nuclear weapons in 1949 and the ability to deliver them via long-range bombers in the early 1950s, and then intercontinental ballistic missiles in 1957, the U.S. homeland faced a real threat. Throughout the Cold War, the defense of the American homeland consisted of a combination of conventional and nuclear military preparedness that deterred an enemy attack on the United States and its allies; early warning systems based in Canada, Greenland, Great Britain, and space; air defense and ballistic-missile defense systems; human, signal, and electronic intelligence; careful diplomacy; arms control agreements; military alliances; wisdom; and luck.

Mutual assured destruction (MAD), as we saw in Chapter 6, was at the core of American deterrence and nuclear weapons policy for much of the Cold War. The theory behind MAD, it will be recalled, was that an aggressor state would not strike first if it believed that it would suffer a massive retaliatory strike in response. MAD's effectiveness was strengthened by the fact that from the early 1970s on, neither the United States nor the Soviet Union deployed defenses against a ballistic missile attack. Defense strategist Thomas Schelling suggested that forgoing defensive systems was nothing more than a modern version of the age-old strategy of taking hostages, except that each country's entire population served as hostages without having to leave their homes.[2]

As we will see later in this chapter, both Presidents Ronald Reagan and George W. Bush rejected this logic, with Reagan significantly expanding funding for strategic missile defense and George W. Bush abrogating the 1972 Anti-Ballistic Missile Treaty. Indeed, twenty-first-century proponents of protecting the United States with ballistic missile defenses (BMD) suggest that the United States can no longer rely on deterrence because the logic which held in the bi-polar world of the Cold War does not hold in a world in which there are numerous nuclear powers, each with its own agenda. Furthermore, proponents suggest that a BMD system will enhance stability because the United States would not need to automatically retaliate against missile launches that might be accidental or of a limited nature.

When the Soviet Union collapsed in 1991, Americans breathed a sigh of relief and felt secure. With the Soviet threat substantially curtailed, most Americans had difficulty imagining that other threats to the American homeland still existed. Occasional terrorist attacks against U.S. interests overseas took place, and other challenges to American interests occurred, as when Iraq invaded Kuwait in August 1990, but there seemed to be no substantial threats to America's position. In the early 1990s, an attack against the U.S. homeland seemed more unlikely than any time in recent history.

MODERN TERRORISM AND RESPONSES TO IT

America's sense of safety was short lived. As the 1990s wore on, concern grew that terrorists might acquire **weapons of mass destruction (WMDs)** from a number of sources, but especially from Soviet stockpiles. WMDs include chemical, biological, and nuclear weapons. A subset of nuclear weapons are "radiological weapons," or "dirty bombs," which consist of a conventional explosive encased by radioactive material.

In addition, even though the Cold War was over, Iraqi leader Saddam Hussein remained unpredictable, Iran maintained its anti-U.S. attitude and expanded its nuclear know-how, and North Korea renounced its 1991 agreement to end its nuclear weapons research program. As the American defense community became increasingly concerned about the threats posed by terrorists and by the missile capabilities and nuclear, chemical, and biological research programs of **rogue states** such as Iraq and North Korea, most Americans still considered threats to the homeland distant and unfocused. Indeed, between 1990 and 1994, the FBI reported only 20 domestic acts of terrorism, most of which did not result in casualties. Only the 1993 World Trade Center bombing resulted in substantial casualties during this period.[3]

That may have been the case from a domestic standpoint, but as Figure 12.1 demonstrates, terrorist events were a significant part of the international scene during this time, even if they rarely impacted the American homeland. Figure 12.2 graphically reveals that Americans nevertheless were sometimes the victims of terrorist attacks. Notice especially the years 1993, 1996, and 2001, which correspond to the first attack on the World Trade Center, the bombing of U.S. military quarters in Saudi Arabia, and the second attack on the World Trade Center and the Pentagon on September 11, 2001.

Some Americans also saw the growing numbers of followers of **radical religions,** including radical Islam, as a threat to the United States. Harvard Professor Samuel Huntington proposed that there was a fundamental fault line between the Western and Islamic

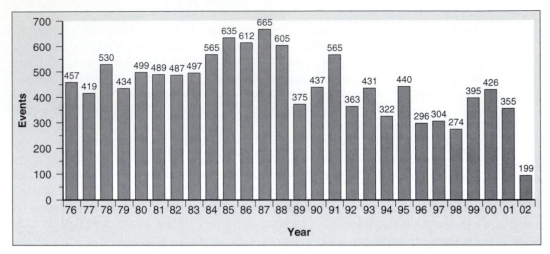

FIGURE 12.1
International Terrorist Events

Source: U.S. State Department, *Patterns of Global Terrorism,* Office of the Coordinator for Counterterrorism, 1995 and 2002 Editions.

worlds, and that these civilizations were likely to be in conflict for quite some time to come. Huntington proposed this thesis in a *Foreign Affairs* article, **"The Clash of Civilizations,"** that broke on the foreign policy community with an impact as loud as its title.[4] Scholars were pitted against scholars and policymakers against policymakers in one of the most profound debates since the Vietnam War. Huntington foresaw a world in which religion and culture would be the major fault lines that divided the world. Religious beliefs and cultural patterns, not political ideologies, would mobilize countries into competing camps, Huntington predicted.

In May 1998, another important development added to the dangers to the American homeland. First India and then Pakistan defied the international nonproliferation regime that had existed since 1968 by testing nuclear weapons. The implications of the **Indian and Pakistani nuclear tests** were unnerving. India and Pakistan had fought several wars against each other since they received independence from Great Britain after World War II, and a real danger existed that if another war broke out, it might become nuclear. In addition, Pakistan had close relations with China, which India saw as its principal threat. Just as foreboding, Pakistan worked closely with several radical Islamic states. Furthermore, with both India and Pakistan having rejected the two-decades-old prohibition on developing nuclear weapons, other countries might now decide to follow suit. While the threat to the U.S. homeland caused by India and Pakistan developing nuclear weapons was not immediate and direct, there were reasons for concern by Washington.

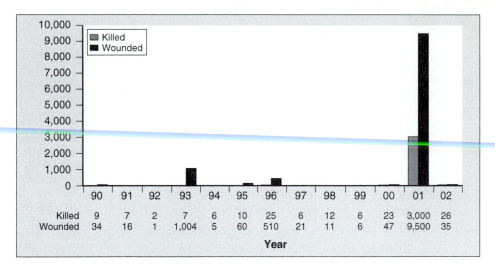

	90	91	92	93	94	95	96	97	98	99	00	01	02
Killed	9	7	2	7	6	10	25	6	12	6	23	3,000	26
Wounded	34	16	1	1,004	5	60	510	21	11	6	47	9,500	35

Year

FIGURE 12.2

U.S. Casualties of International Terrorism

Source: U.S. State Department, *Patterns of Global Terrorism,* Office of the Coordinator for Counterterrorism, 1995, 1999, and 2002 Editions.

The Indian and Pakistani moves to acquire nuclear weapons flew in the face of almost 60 years of international effort to put the nuclear genie back into the bottle. Starting in 1946 with U.S. efforts to internationalize control of nuclear weapons, and proceeding to the 2002 agreement between the United States and Russia, the international community has sought to dampen this march of technology. Much energy has gone into limiting the threat of nuclear, biological, and chemical weapons. Policies to limit the spread of WMD have been common to both Republican and Democratic administrations. Table 12.2 reviews the many agreements that focused on this area of concern.

Beyond the clash of civilizations and nuclear proliferation, there was another reason for growing concern about the defense of the American homeland, namely, the growing reliance of the United States and other developed states on computerized information systems and networks. This gave rise to fears that the United States might become the victim of **information warfare** in which a rogue state or some other unknown enemy might attack American information systems and networks. The dimensions of the dangers that the United States faced from information warfare, detailed in the 1997 report *Critical Foundations: Protecting America's Infrastructures* by the President's Commission on Critical Infrastructure Protection, were so serious that some concluded that the United States might suffer an "electronic Pearl Harbor" that would bring the American economy to a halt.

TABLE 12.2
A HISTORY OF ARMS CONTROL

Year	Name of Agreement	Philosophy/Key Provisions	Status
1946	Baruch Plan	Would have put ownership of all dangerous nuclear technologies under international control	Rejected
1953	Atoms for Peace [Multilateral]	U.S. and USSR would donate fissile material for peaceful uses in other nations	Supplanted by later agreements
1963	Limited Nuclear Test Ban Treaty [Multilateral]	Prohibited atmospheric, underwater, or outer-space testing of nuclear weapons (only underground testing could be performed)	Signed in August 1963 and entered into force in October 1963
1968	Nuclear Non-Proliferation Treaty (NPT) [Multilateral]	Nonnuclear states would forswear obtaining nuclear weapons in exchange for assistance with peaceful nuclear technologies, nuclear powers committed to attempt to disarm	Signed in July 1968 and entered into force March 1970; in 1995 this treaty was indefinitely extended
1972	Biological Weapons Convention (BWC) [Multilateral]	Signatories committed to not develop, produce, stockpile, or acquire biological agents or toxins in quantities beyond those reasonable for protective or peaceful purposes (e.g., vaccine development or research)	Signed in April 1972 and entered into force in March 1975
1972	Strategic Arms Limitation Treaty I (SALT I) [Bilateral: U.S. and USSR]	Froze levels of missile launchers and submarine-launched nuclear weapons pending a more comprehensive agreement	Signed in May 1972 and entered into force October 1972
1972	Anti-Ballistic Missile Treaty (ABM) [Bilateral: U.S. and USSR]	Prohibited the U.S. and USSR from developing antiballistic missile systems, except each side could erect a limited missile shield that would protect their capital and one other area of no larger than approximately 71,000 square kilometers (i.e., roughly the size of Ireland) to protect an offensive missile field	Signed in May 1972 and entered into force October 1972; in 2002 the U.S. withdrew from the treaty by giving 6 months advance notice in accordance with Article XV of the treaty
1974	Threshold Test Ban Treaty [Bilateral: U.S. and USSR]	Restricted the yield of test explosions of nuclear devices to 150 kilotons	Signed in July 1974 and entered into force December 1990
1979	Strategic Arms Limitation Treaty II (SALT II) [Bilateral: U.S. and USSR]	Replaced the SALT I interim agreement; was intended to put limit on the size of nuclear arsenal that could be built	Signed in June 1979 but never ratified; supplanted by START I

A HISTORY OF ARMS CONTROL

Year	Name of Agreement	Philosophy/Key Provisions	Status
1987	Intermediate-Range Nuclear Forces Treaty (INF) [Bilateral: U.S. and USSR]	Bans all ballistic and cruise missiles with ranges between 500 and 5,500 kilometers. The significance of this treaty is that it is the first to eliminate an entire class of weapons	Signed in December 1987 and entered into force June 1988
1987	Missile Technology Control Regime [Multilateral]	This is not a treaty but rather one of several agreements by states to prevent the spread of technologies that could be used for weapons of mass destruction to non–weapons states by creating discriminatory suppliers groups	The U.S. is a member of the MTCR as well as the Nuclear Suppliers Group (NSG), the Australia Group (AG), the Zangger Committee, and the Wassenaar Arrangement
1990	Conventional Forces in Europe (CFE) [Multilateral]	An agreement to limit conventional forces deployed between the Atlantic and the Urals so as to negate the threat of surprise attack or large-scale offensives; one of the few arms agreements limiting conventional weapons	Signed in November 1990 and entered into force in November 1992
1991	Strategic Arms Reduction Treaty I (START I) [Bilateral: U.S. and USSR]	Substantial reduction in the number of intercontinental ballistic missiles (ICBMs), submarine-launched ballistic missiles (SLBMs), and heavy bombers	Signed in July 1991 and entered into force December 1994
1993	Strategic Arms Reduction Treaty II (START II) [Bilateral: U.S. and Russia	Further reduces strategic offensive arms and eliminates Multiple Independent Reentry Vehicle (MIRV) missiles (missiles that can target multiple locations using a single rocket booster)	Signed in January 1993 and ratified January 1996
1993	Chemical Weapons Convention (CWC) [Multilateral]	Prohibits the development, production, stockpiling, and use of chemical weapons, and requires the destruction of stockpiles	Signed in January 1993 and ratified April 1997
1996	Comprehensive Nuclear Test Ban Treaty (CTBT) [Multilateral]	Would eliminate all forms of nuclear test explosions (allowing only tests of the conventional explosives that initiate the chain reaction and "virtual" computer simulation testing)	Signed but not ratified by the U.S.
2002	Moscow Treaty [Bilateral: U.S. and Russia]	Further reduction in strategic offensive weapons down to a level of 1,700–2,200 warheads by December 2012	Signed in May 2002

Sources: Henry D. Sokolski, *Best of Intentions: America's Campaign Against Strategic Weapons Proliferation* (Westport, Conn: Praeger, 2001), pp.8–9 and appendices; NATO, *Key Arms Control Treaties and Agreements (1963–1955), http://www.nato.int/docu/facts/kacta.htm;* Department of State, *Fact Sheet: Start I Aggregate Numbers of Strategic Offensive Arms,* Bureau of Arms Control, 2002, *http://www.state.gov/t/ac/rls/fs/9075.htm;* Department of State, *Moscow Treaty Cuts Top List of U.S. Non-Proliferation Treaty Support,* 2003, *http://www.usinfo.state.gov/topical/pol/terror/texts/03050504.htm.*

Responses to Homeland Vulnerability before September 11, 2001

Even before September 11, 2001, the United States had absorbed several terrorist attacks, some launched by foreign sources and others by American sources. The most infamous were the 1993 bombing of the World Trade Center by foreign Islamic extremists and the 1995 destruction of the Federal Building in Oklahoma City by American radicals. Clearly, the United States was not totally safe, but most Americans did not recognize the extent of the threat.

Some members of Congress, concerned about the implications of terrorist attacks, the proliferation of weapons of mass destruction, the "Clash of Civilizations" thesis, and information warfare, sought to create a government agency that would be responsible for homeland defense. Thus, in 1996, the sponsors of the Nunn-Lugar bill—legislation that addressed the dangers caused by the spread of scientific talent from the collapsed Soviet empire—added language that included a homeland defense czar who would be placed over the many agencies that were involved with protecting the United States from outside threats. Under the proposed legislation, the homeland defense czar

Not all terrorist threats come from overseas. In 1995, American citizen Timothy McVeigh used a truck bomb made of fertilizer to destroy the Alfred P. Murrah Federal Building in Oklahoma City, killing 168 people, the worst terrorist attack on American soil before September 11, 2001.

was to coordinate intelligence about threats, develop countermeasures to respond to threats, and reallocate as much as 10 percent of each agency's budget to address homeland security. However, these aspects of the bill were dropped when the White House, opposed to the idea of a homeland defense czar, threatened to veto it if such provisions were included.[5]

Despite opposing creation of a homeland defense czar, the Clinton Administration recognized that the United States needed to enhance U.S. security in general and homeland security in particular. Thus, in 1998, Clinton formed the United States **Commission on National Security in the 21st Century,** also called the **Hart-Rudman Commission** after its two chairs, to review American security policies. The commission was tasked to "redefine national security in this age and to do so in a more comprehensive fashion than any other similar effort since 1947."[6] The final study recommended significant change in five major areas, the first being "ensuring the security of the American homeland."[7]

The introductory comments of the Hart-Rudman Commission's final report were specific when in came to identifying the need for enhanced homeland security: "The combination of unconventional weapons proliferation with the persistence of international terrorism will end the relative invulnerability of the U.S. homeland to catastrophic attack. A direct attack against American citizens *on American soil* is likely over the next quarter century. The risk is not only death and destruction but also a demoralization that could undermine U.S. global leadership. In the face of this threat, our nation has no coherent or integrated governmental structures." Further, immediately after describing the dangers inherent in the new post–Cold War era, it stated: "We therefore recommend the creation of a new independent National Homeland Security Agency (NHSA) with responsibility for planning, coordinating, and integrating various U.S. government activities involved in homeland security."[8]

Unfortunately, the commission's findings were released during a rancorous period in U.S. political history, the contested presidential election of 2000. Therefore, the study failed to capture the attention of Americans as they focused on the count and recount to determine who would become the president of the United States. Even defense professionals aware of the study were engrossed in other tasks, preparing the final draft of the Quadrennial Defense Review (QDR), the Defense Department's once-every-four-years exercise to sort out defense priorities and responsibilities.

The need for homeland defense received its first attention in the QDR in 1997, although only in passing.[9] It received more detailed attention in the Joint Chiefs of Staff document *Joint Vision 2020*, which called for American forces to be "persuasive in peace, decisive in war, and preeminent in any form of conflict."[10] In calling for effective interagency operations, *Joint Vision 2020* stated: "the future joint force must be proactive in improving communications, planning, interoperability, and liaison with potential interagency participants. These factors are important in all aspects of interagency operations, but particularly *in the context of direct threats to citizens and facilities in the U.S. homeland*"[11] (emphasis added).

The authors further noted: "This Vision is firmly grounded in the view that the U.S. military must be a joint force capable of full spectrum dominance."[12] This "full spectrum" included homeland defense, but homeland defense was not on the tip of everyone's tongue in 2000, nor did it receive widespread attention until September 11, 2001.

The QDR and *Joint Vision 2020* focused on the Department of Defense (DOD) and the capabilities under its control. This was understandable, given the limited amount of attention that was paid both to homeland defense and the need for interagency cooperation before September 2001. Indeed, before the 2001 terrorist attacks on the World Trade Center and the Pentagon, many other agencies were entrusted with homeland security responsibilities, but few recognized either the severity of the threat or the necessity for interagency cooperation to counter the threat. Agencies beyond the DOD that also had a significant responsibility for homeland security included the Immigration and Naturalization Service, the Federal Bureau of Investigation, the Central Intelligence Agency, the Customs Service, the Coast Guard, the Department of Agriculture, the Department of Transportation, the Federal Aviation Administration, various port authorities on U.S. coasts and inland waterways, the Federal Communications Commission, and the Federal Emergency Management Agency. Thus, even before September 11, many people knew that the United States needed to pay more attention to homeland defense, and were responsible for homeland defense, but it was not an urgent issue.

Homeland Defense after September 11, 2001

After the September 11 terrorist attacks, homeland defense became the paramount issue on the government's agenda. Within weeks, under the rubric of defending the United States, the U.S. government developed a plan for a global assault on Osama bin Laden, al Qaeda, and other terrorists. The plan had several components.

First, domestic security was strengthened as the United States created the Office of Homeland Security, which a year later became the Department of Homeland Security. This agency called up reserve forces to protect airports, strengthened laws to deal with terrorists, tightened banking rules to curtail terrorists' flow of funds, and placed combat air patrols above American cities. In addition, on September 24, 2001, President George W. Bush issued Executive Order 13224, which froze terrorist assets and denied access to U.S. markets to foreign banks that refused to cooperate in seizing terrorist assets abroad. Even more importantly, on October 26, 2001, President Bush signed into law the **USA Patriot Act,** which expanded the capabilities of the intelligence and law enforcement communities to investigate terrorist groups by easing restrictions on wiretaps, e-mail monitoring, and "sneak and peak" searches (searches conducted without service of a warrant). The Patriot Act also made information on financial transactions available to intelligence and law enforcement agencies and included many other expansions of government power.

Second, the Bush Administration worked with foreign governments to assemble a coalition of states to combat terrorism. UN resolutions, intelligence sharing, and obtaining promises of military support and overflight rights for American military aircraft were all part of the effort to build an international coalition, as was a conscious American effort to convince the Islamic world that impending military actions were not part of a war against Islam. The United Nations adopted Security Council Resolution 1373 on September 28, 2001, which required all member states to suppress terrorist finances, and UNSCR 1390 on January 16, 2002, which modified and expanded the international sanctions against the Taliban, al Qaeda, and Osama bin Laden.

Third, American military forces were readied for combat against the Taliban government of Afghanistan and al Qaeda forces in that country. The United States also made it clear that the war against terrorism would be carried to other countries if necessary.

Fourth, Congress created a $40 billion Emergency Response Fund to assure that, in the short term, sufficient finances were available for the war against terrorism. For the longer term, Bush requested and received significantly increased spending on homeland defense and the U.S. armed forces in his FY2003 budget.

Fifth, American public opinion ran strongly in favor of exacting retribution for the terrorist attacks, and congressional support was equally strong. Indeed, on September 14, 2001, Congress passed Joint Resolution 23 by a 98–0 vote in the Senate and 420–1 in the House, authorizing the president to use the "United States Armed Forces against those responsible for the recent attacks launched against the United States." According to the resolution: "the President is authorized to use all necessary and appropriate force against those nations, organizations, or persons, he determined planned, authorized, committed or aided the terrorist attacks that occurred on September 11, 2001, or harbored such organizations or persons, in order to prevent any future acts of international terrorism against the United States by such nations, organizations, or persons."

Having received congressional authorization for the use of force, Bush later in September demanded that the Taliban turn Osama bin Laden over to the United States "or face the consequences." When the Taliban refused, the stage was set for the United States to use military force in Afghanistan against the Taliban and al Qaeda.

The Department of Homeland Security

As noted above, shortly after September 11, 2001, President Bush created the Office of Homeland Security, appointing Pennsylvania Governor Thomas Ridge to head the agency. Ridge's authority was not as extensive as that proposed in the 1996 Nunn-Lugar bill, but homeland defense now had an advocate with Cabinet rank, authority to cajole other bureaucratic leaders, and reasonable access to the president. Political bickering over the employee rights of those who would work in the department as well as the hiring and firing authority of the agency head delayed the transition to Cabinet department, but Republican victories in the 2002 congressional elections broke the deadlock, and in late 2002, the largest reorganization of the federal government bureaucracy in half a century led to the creation of the **Department of Homeland Security.**

The new department combined 22 agencies into one and employed 170,000 people. This office must deal with the complex measures needed to identify, prevent, and if necessary respond to an attack on the United States. The challenges are daunting, but failure to meet the challenges might be catastrophic.

Figure 12.3 reveals the size and nature of the Department of Homeland Security, which has five major directorates. The Border and Transportation Security directorate houses the Transportation Security Administration, which most notably provides airport security; the border security elements of the Immigration and Naturalization Service; the Customs Service; the Animal and Plant Health Inspection Service; and the Federal Law Enforcement Training Center. The Emergency Preparedness and Response directorate shares responsibility previously handled by the Federal Emergency Management Agency

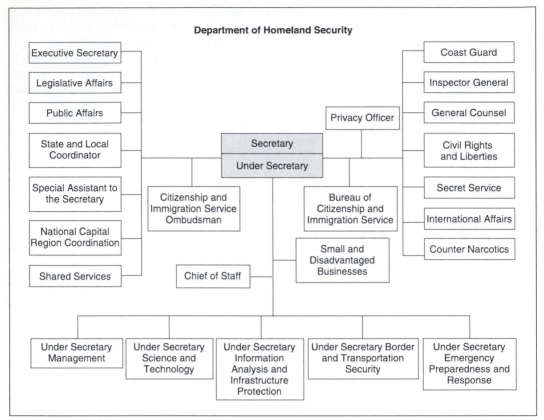

FIGURE 12.3
Organization of the Department of Homeland Security

for response to and recovery from both natural and manmade disasters. The Science and Technology directorate is responsible for research and development of technologies needed for homeland defense, and for responding to terrorist threats involving nuclear, biological, chemical, or radiological weaponry. The Information Analysis and Infrastructure Protection directorate is the intelligence arm of the Department of Homeland Security and is also responsible for coordinating preventive and protective actions to secure critical infrastructure (e.g., the Internet, banking and finance computer networks, and the electrical grid). The Management directorate is responsible for the logistical, budgetary, and human resources tasks that are a critical part of any large organization. The U.S. Coast Guard and the Secret Service were folded into the new department, and Offices of State and Local Government Coordination and a Private Sector Liaison were also created within the agency.

The new department was given a budget of $17 billion, which grew to $44.4 billion for 2003. The "ramp up" or annual increases in funding for the department between 2001 and 2003 are illustrated in Table 12.3. Figure 12.4 shows the allocation of the money by

TABLE 12.3
DIRECT FEDERAL EXPENDITURES ON
HOMELAND SECURITY (WITH SUPPLEMENTS)

FY2001	$17 Billion
FY2002	$29 Billion
FY2003	$44 Billion

Source: Office of Homeland Security, *The National Strategy for Homeland Security,* *http://www.whitehouse.gov/homeland/book,* p. 64. FY2003 budget request for homeland security was $37.7 billion; however, a $6.71 billion supplement was approved in April 2003.

function for Fiscal Year 2003, and Figure 12.5 shows the allocation by recipient. Clearly, homeland defense has become an American priority. (For the 2004 estimated budget outlays for national defense, of which homeland security is a part, see Figure 12.6, which shows the projected budget for the entire U.S. government in billions of dollars.)

Another critical parameter of homeland defense that fell under the aegis of the Department of Homeland Security linked security to economic interdependence and globalization. The reason for this was straightforward, and can best be illustrated by the impact that intrusive control of American borders had in the wake of September 11 in

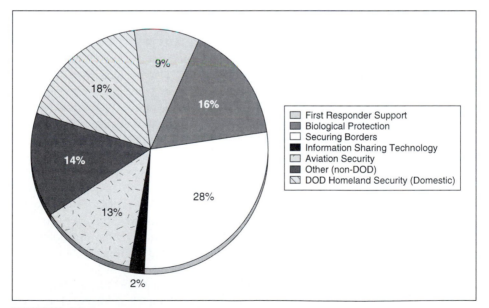

FIGURE 12.4
Homeland Defense Budget Request (FY2003) by Function

Source: Anthony Cordesman, *The Uncertain Costs of Homeland Defense: The Cost and Justification of the FY 2003 Budget Submission.* Washington, D.C.: Center for Strategic and International Studies.

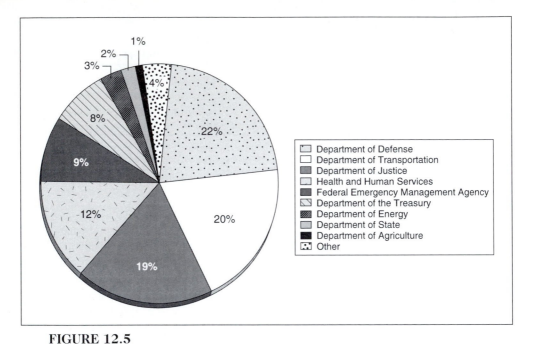

FIGURE 12.5
Homeland Defense Budget Request (FY2003) by Recipient

Source: Steven Kosiak, *FY 2003 Budget Request for Homeland Security.* Washington, D.C.: CBSA. Available at *http://www.cbsaonline.org.*

U.S. manufacturing and retailing sectors. For example, several automobile factories based on just-in-time distribution closed down in the United States and Canada as trucks were unable to deliver across borders and ships were delayed.[13] As one observer pointed out, America's economic infrastructure had become "increasingly more concentrated, more interconnected, and more sophisticated. Almost entirely privately owned and operated, the system has very little redundancy."[14] Thus, as the United States and the world push toward greater globalization and increased international integration of manufacturing and transportation, the disruption of any critical node has the potential to cause significant turmoil in the American economy. The Department of Homeland Security therefore must view American vulnerabilities not just as domestic—restricted to the confines of the territorial United States—but as vulnerabilities that stretch to every country that participates in the global economic system. Globalization implies that homeland defense has come full circle and is deeply and directly related to foreign policy.

Even so, many questions are unanswered about homeland defense. Will the secretary of homeland security be strong enough to implement necessary security measures? Will the secretary's authority be sufficient if a nuclear, chemical, or biological attack occurs and civilian and military authorities must be coordinated? Will the National Guard be able to provide for local defense as it is increasingly used overseas? Will bridges, tunnels, and other transportation, communication, and energy sites need the enhanced secu-

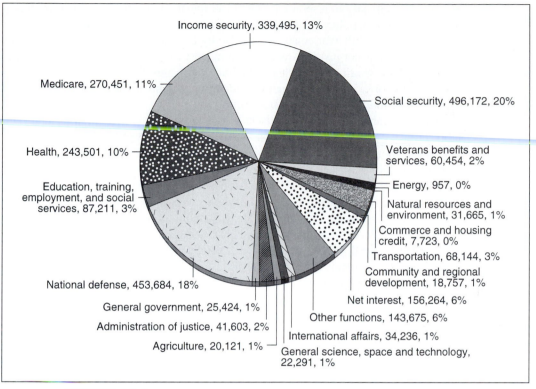

FIGURE 12.6
2004 Estimated Federal Budget Outlays (in billions of dollars)

rity that airports require? Can river and port facilities be made secure, given the massive number of shipping containers brought into the country through these nodes? Can the Immigration and Naturalization Service operate effectively with so few personnel? Can the United States keep track of foreign students and other visitors? Will concerns about visiting foreigners lead to intrusive tracking systems that include automated entry-exit systems, travel documents with "biometric" identifiers for non-U.S. nationals, a consolidated "watch" list to identify suspected terrorists, or a system specifically oriented toward tracking foreign students?[15] And how willing will Americans be to have civil liberties curtailed because of the terrorist threat? The questions are many, and some of the answers may change the very nature of the Republic.

Alliances, Coalitions, and Homeland Defense

Since World War II, in order to preserve and strengthen American security, important considerations in U.S. foreign policy have been the building and maintaining of alliances and coalitions such as NATO and the 1991 coalition that expelled Iraq from Kuwait during the Persian Gulf War. While the post–World War II American alliance system was developed specifically in response to the Soviet threat, alliances have remained important in U.S. security policy even after the Cold War, as shown not only by the expansion of NATO and the Gulf War coalition, but also by George W. Bush's emphasis that the 2003 Iraq War was not just an American war against Iraq but a war of the "coalition of the willing." While critics of Bush and the Iraq War dismiss Bush's claim as politically motivated rhetoric, it was nonetheless evident that the president viewed multilateral action against Iraq as a desirable state of affairs.

The September 2001 terrorist attacks also made it evident that alliances and coalitions played a major role in the defense of the American homeland. Two alliances warrant special attention, NATO and the makeshift coalition that President George W. Bush assembled in the weeks and months after September 11.

As we have seen, after the 1991 break-up of the Soviet Union, NATO evolved into an organization whose purpose was to maintain security in Europe and nearby areas. By 2002, it had 19 members, with 26 other states including Russia associated with it in the Partnership for Peace. Each member of NATO pledged under Article 5 of the North Atlantic Treaty, the document that created NATO, that it considered an "armed attack" against any NATO member "an attack against them all," and that it would help defend any member country that was attacked.

Few people expected that NATO would invoke Article 5 for the first time in defense of the United States, yet that is what happened. On September 12, 2001, NATO invoked Article 5 to help defend the United States. Shortly thereafter, NATO deployed airborne warning and command aircraft to the United States to help defend American airspace. It also accelerated the exchange of counterterrorism intelligence, enhanced the defense of U.S. installations in Europe, and stepped up preparations against biological, chemical, and nuclear attacks. NATO also expanded information exchanges and enhanced anti-terrorist consultations with Partnership for Peace countries. For example, in 2002, NATO and Russian diplomats and military officials met at the NATO Defense College in Rome to discuss civil emergency planning and military cooperation against terrorism.

There was, however, a limit to NATO unity. Some NATO states strongly opposed certain elements of America's post–September 11 security agenda. For example, France and Germany vehemently opposed the U.S. decision to invade Iraq in 2003, instead favoring an approach whereby UN inspectors would continue to carry out inspections to ensure the disarmament of Saddam Hussein's regime. However, other NATO members such as Great Britain, Spain, and Poland supported the U.S. decision to take action against Iraq to enforce UN resolutions demanding Iraqi elimination of weapons of mass destruction and requiring range limitations on Iraqi missiles.

After September 11, George W. Bush also created an **international anti-terrorist coalition** that supported the global offensive against terrorism. Pakistan provided the United States with staging areas at military bases and granted overflight rights that proved invaluable as the United States undertook military operations in Afghanistan. Uzbekistan and Turkmenistan granted base and overflight rights, respectively, that were important as the United States supplied the Northern Alliance against the Taliban forces. The Bush Administration claimed that over 40 countries offered the U.S. war effort military support, base rights, or overflight privileges.[16] Some, such as Great Britain, Canada, France, and Turkey, sent military forces to fight alongside U.S. forces in Afghanistan.

The coalition also cooperated in other ways. Many countries began to share intelligence about suspected terrorists. Interpol and other security agencies stepped up surveillance of known and suspected terrorists. Albania, Belgium, France, Germany, India, Italy, Morocco, Singapore, Spain, the United Kingdom, the United States, and other countries detained suspected al Qaeda members. Over 500 people were detained in the United States and at least 100 were held in Great Britain. Around the world, over a thousand people were detained because of suspected ties to al Qaeda or other terrorist organizations.

Preemptive Defense

Al Qaeda's attack on America had a profound impact on American defense policy. Throughout the Cold War, as we have seen, the United States based much of its defense of the homeland on nuclear deterrence. Thus, the reasoning went, no potential enemy would attack the United States because it knew that the United States would inflict an unacceptable level of damage on it. Deterrence remained a central part of U.S. defense planning after the Cold War, but September 11 led to a fundamental change in U.S. defense thinking.

Concerned that terrorists who were willing to die could not be deterred by massive retaliation, the administration of George W. Bush concluded that new ways that did not rely on deterrence must be found to prevent terrorism. Furthermore, the anonymity of terrorist groups made the threat of retaliation moot because the United States could not credibly threaten a massive response against an enemy whose location was unknown. The need for new ways to prevent terrorists from acting became even more pressing as the Bush Administration concluded that Iraq and other rogue states were acquiring weapons of mass destruction.

Thus, the Bush Administration crafted a new strategic doctrine called **preemptive defense.** First mentioned by Bush in a 2002 speech at West Point, the new doctrine declared when it was unveiled in September 2002, "the United States can no longer solely rely on a reactive posture as we have in the past…. We cannot let our enemies strike first…. As a matter of common sense and self-defense, America will act against emerging threats before they are fully formed." The new strategy also declared that it was essential to identify and destroy security threats before they reached U.S. borders. The new strategy also acknowledged the need to continue the shift from mere nonproliferation to a strategy including counterproliferation that had been emphasized by President Clinton. The difference between nonproliferation and counterproliferation was a recognition that the "genie was out of the bottle" and that military action might be needed to eliminate other countries' programs to develop weapons of mass destruction.[17]

Supporters of the new doctrine praised it as necessary to minimize the threats that terrorism and rogue states posed to the United States. They pointed to the September 2001 attacks, arguing that the United States could not wait to absorb another attack before responding against terrorists and potential terrorists. They also maintained that the threat posed by possible terrorist use of WMDs mandated that the United States act against terrorists and potential terrorists wherever they were, whenever they could be found.

Conversely, critics charged that the United States intended to do whatever it wanted in international affairs, thus becoming an imperial hegemon in the name of homeland security. Critics also claimed that the U.S. position ignored international law and would lead to a more dangerous world.

The consensus view, however, seemed to be that, given the dimension of the new threat, there was nothing inherently wrong with preemptive defense in instances of imminent threat, but that there were dangers in raising preemptive defense to the level of military doctrine. Scholars at the Brookings Institute detailed this perspective, suggesting three dangers with codifying preemption as doctrine. First, it reinforced the perception of the United States as a "loose cannon" that was quick to arms, an image that could lead to the isolation of the United States in the world community. Second, it put rogue actors on warning to hide contraband weapons and change their tactics, thus making them more difficult to combat. Finally, if the United States used preemption, other countries could claim that preemption justified their actions against other states.[18]

Despite the debate, by 2003, preemptive defense was part of America's effort to defend the homeland. Whether it will advance or degrade U.S. security remains to be seen. The invasion of Iraq in 2003 was the first application of the doctrine of preemptive defense after it was formalized in 2002. Proponents of the Iraq War suggest that the world was safer without Saddam Hussein in power and that it was better to fight terrorists overseas than inside America's borders, but critics countered that the war in Iraq created a new cadre of terrorists, distracted the United States from the "real" war against terrorism and al Qaeda, and created the image of the United States as a rogue nation acting without regard for international law or the sentiments of the international community.

THE THREAT OF WEAPONS OF MASS DESTRUCTION

For over 40 years, the United States survived and prospered under the threat of Soviet weapons of mass destruction—nuclear, biological, and chemical. With the demise of the Soviet threat and the rise of global terrorism, however, the danger presented by WMD took on a new dimension. In the post–Cold War world, it is not clear that deterrence will prevent terrorist groups and rogue nations from using weapons of mass destruction if they succeed in developing or attaining them.

The Nuclear Threat

To reiterate, the **nuclear threat** is not new. The world has been living with this form of terror since 1949, and Figure 12.7 shows the estimated stockpiles of nuclear warheads as of 2003. The numbers in Figure 12.7 would be larger if "stored" or "back-up" weapons were included in the case of Russia. Back-up weapons can be used only with some degree of servicing. The numbers for the United States would be lower if only operational weapons—those ready for immediate use—were shown.

To place the current threat in perspective, it is instructive to take a moment to see where the world has been. Figure 12.8 shows the global stockpile of nuclear weapons over time, and Figure 12.9 shows how the number of nuclear warheads held by the five declared nuclear powers varied over the decades.

Clearly, the number of nuclear weapons in the world today has decreased significantly, and the United States and other countries are the safer for it. Whether this is the

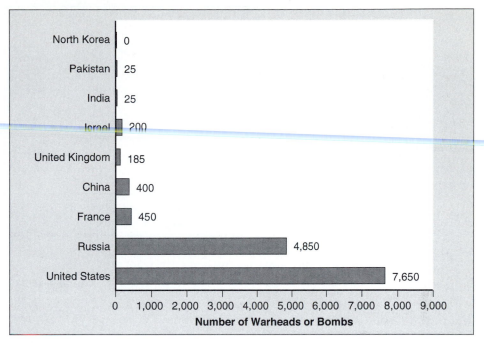

FIGURE 12.7
Nuclear Warheads

Sources: NRDC Nuclear Notebook: U.S. Nuclear Forces, 2003, *Bulletin of the Atomic Scientists* 59(3) (May/June 2003): 74. NRDC Nuclear Notebook: Russian Nuclear Forces, 2003, *Bulletin of the Atomic Scientists* 59(4): 71. Warner Farr, *The Third Temple's Holy of Holies: Israel's Nuclear Weapons. The Counterproliferation Papers: Future Warfare Series No. 2* (Maxwell AFB, Ala.: U.S. AF Air War College, Counterproliferation Center, 1999), p. 13 (Farr cites estimates as high as 400+ nuclear weapons). George Perkovich, *India's Nuclear Bomb* (Berkeley: University of California Press, 1999), p. 2. Zafar Iqbal Cheema, *Pakistan's Nuclear Use Doctrine and Command and Control: Planning the Unthinkable: How New Powers Will Use Nuclear, Biological, and Chemical Weapons* (Ithaca, N.Y.: Cornell University Press, 2000), p. 164. While it is not believed that North Korea has nuclear weapons yet, it may have 7–22 kilograms of separated plutonium and be quite close to becoming a nuclear power. David Alvarez, "North Korea: No Bygones at Yongbyon," *Bulletin of the Atomic Scientists* 59(4) (2003): 44.

result of arms control is a question that will be discussed later this chapter. However, the disintegration of the Soviet Union and the end of communism as an operating ideology in China have been principal vehicles for change. From a high of over 30,000 warheads in the 1980s and as many as 24,000 when the Cold War ended, the United States' total inventory today is below 10,500 weapons.[19] Approximately 13,500 warheads have been removed from the American inventory since the end of the Cold War.[20] This is a remarkable feat that should be celebrated in all countries. And according to the *Bulletin of the Atomic Scientists* 1997 "Nuclear Notebook," the 10,350 nuclear weapons in the United States are located in only 14 states.[21] America's other 150 nuclear weapons are deployed in Germany, Great Britain, Italy, Turkey, Belgium, the Netherlands, and Greece.[22]

The elimination of entire classes of weapons that once had nuclear warheads is also worth noting. For example, there are no more nuclear mines, artillery shells, or

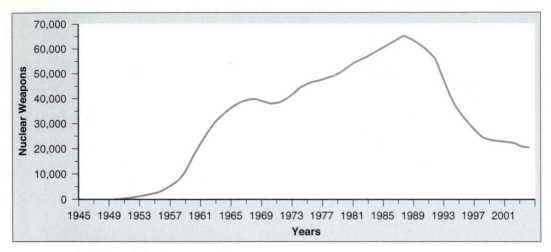

FIGURE 12.8
Worldwide Stockpiles of Nuclear Weapons

Source: Robert Norris, NRDC Nuclear Notebook: Global Nuclear Stockpiles, 1945–2002, *Bulletin of the Atomic Scientists* 58(6) (November/December 2002): 103–104.

medium-range ballistic missiles. This is a stunning reduction. In addition, since 1992, both the United States and Russia have curtailed the deployment of tactical weapons with operational units. These weapons have generally been placed in central storage facilities and are not available to operational forces on a daily basis.

Like the U.S. case, the status of the Russian nuclear stockpile is fluid. Samuel S. Kim of the East Asia Institute at Columbia University stated that the number of Russian

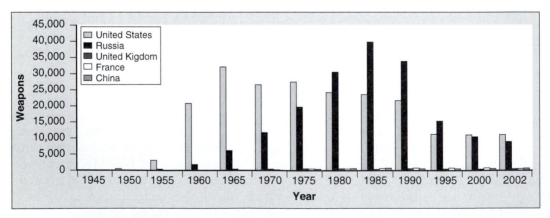

FIGURE 12.9
Nuclear Stockpiles of the Declared Powers

Source: Robert Norris, NRDC Nuclear Notebook: Global Nuclear Stockpiles, 1945–2002, *Bulletin of the Atomic Scientists* 58(6) (November/December 2002): 103–104.

strategic nuclear warheads in 1996 was 6,758, with 8,111 as the corresponding U.S. figure.[23] Totals published in the May/June 2001 *Bulletin of the Atomic Scientists* list Russia as having 6,018 strategic warheads.[24]

Information on Chinese weapons is less precise, but the imprecision is not of as great a concern because of the much smaller Chinese nuclear inventory. The *Bulletin* puts the entire Chinese stockpile at roughly 400 warheads, with 250 strategic and 150 tactical weapons.[25] China's tactical warheads are described as "low yield bombs for tactical bombardment, artillery shells, atomic demolition munitions, and possibly short-range missiles."[26]

Events in 2002 were even more encouraging. The United States and Russia made so much progress on strategic arms discussions that during President George W. Bush's May trip to Moscow, Bush and Soviet President Putin signed a Strategic Offensive Arms Reduction Treaty in which both sides agreed to cut their operational strategic nuclear arsenals to 1,700 and 2,200 warheads, the lowest total in decades.

This, however, is only part of the nuclear picture. Since the end of the Cold War, the nuclear threat to the American homeland is seen as coming less in the near term from Russia or China than from rogue states like Iraq and North Korea and nonstate actors like al Qaeda that have nothing to lose, and perhaps much to gain, by threatening to use or actually using nuclear weapons against the United States. Nuclear threats to the international system involving state actors generally include the tense Pakistan-India border area, the Taiwan Straits area, northeast Asia adjacent to North Korea, and possibly the Middle East.

There is some good news, however. Even though the know-how needed to build a nuclear weapon is available on the Internet and in libraries, a nuclear weapon consists of about 6,000 parts besides the "nuclear package."[27] Thus, in addition to the difficulty of obtaining the required fissile material, the engineering capability needed to build a nuclear weapon may remain beyond the capabilities of nonstate actors. Conversely, if terrorists could obtain already built weapons that do not have disabling devices such as permissive action links, the world would be at risk of nuclear attack by means of civilian aircraft, truck, ship, or some other common form of transportation. To maintain the United States' homeland security, then, it is requisite to maintain, and to help others maintain, tight control over nuclear weapons.

Biological Weapons

Bioweapons, also called the "poor man's nuclear weapons," have been around much longer than nuclear weapons. History abounds with stories of countries using contaminated materials such as blankets to transmit smallpox and measles from one group to another to gain advantage in war, throwing animal carcasses into wells to contaminate drinking water, and in medieval times catapulting dead diseased cows into fortified towns. Indeed, in World War II, every major combatant had a biological weapons program.[28]

The United States began its Biological Research Program in 1942 in its Chemical Warfare Service. The Soviet Union began its program in the 1920s, and the United Kingdom in 1936. Today, the United States believes that Russia, Syria, Iraq, Iran, Libya, North Korea, China, Israel, Egypt, Cuba, Taiwan, Romania, Bulgaria, Pakistan, India, and South Africa have the ability to produce and use biological weapons.[29]

Bioweapons include such diseases as encephalomyelitis, Rocky Mountain spotted fever, psittacosis, Q fever, anthrax, brucellosis, plague, tularemia, smallpox, and other pathogens.[30] These diseases could be distributed by bombs, submunitions, aerial sprays, ballistic missiles, artillery, rockets, cruise missiles, or clandestine delivery systems.[31] They can be extremely effective if conditions are suitable. For example, if 30 kilograms of anthrax spores with a density of 0.1 milligram per cubic meter were used over a ten square kilometer area, 30,000 to 100,000 people could die.[32]

Usually, however, bioweapons are not very effective. The most recent large-scale use of biological weapons occurred in 1985 when Iraq's President Saddam Hussein ordered their use against Shia prisoners at the Salman Pak "pesticide" plant. Saddam possibly also used them in 1987 in conjunction with chemical weapons against rebellious Kurdish villages.[33]

For much of the last three decades, the international community has tried to rid the world of such weapons, but not always with success. As late as 1991, 90,000 people were involved in research on and development of biological weapons in the Soviet Union alone. The Soviet Union built a vast complex, Obolensk, with as many as 3,000 employees dedicated to producing anthrax, smallpox, and plague. Moscow had as many as 100 tons of such bioweapons.[34] In 1992, Russian President Boris Yeltsin terminated Russia's offensive bioweapon programs, 23 years after the United States renounced its bioweapons programs.

When Russia terminated its bioweapons programs, a major concern developed over how to employ the newly unemployed bioweapons scientists. Rogue states and terrorist groups interested in the skills possessed by the now unemployed bioweapons experts could easily offer a grand life to families uncertain of their next month's income. International efforts to employ the unemployed experts were put in place and have ameliorated but not solved the problem. For example, the European Union funds programs to help Russian scientists exchange information with the U.S. Centers for Disease Control. Other collaborative projects on biodefense, funded by the United States, are also underway between U.S. and Russian scientists. Another such enterprise, the International Science and Technology Center, is funded by Western sources that bring Russian and Western scientists together to collaborate on bioweapons research.[35]

Such efforts provided alternatives for some Russian bioweapons experts, but problems associated with verifying the 1972 Biological Weapons Convention (BWC) dulled American enthusiasm for entering additional comprehensive agreements. Verification is difficult because biological weapons labs can be small, and because medical research and military bioweapons research tend to merge, making detection of active programs difficult. As a result of U.S. concerns over these and other issues, negotiations to strengthen the BWC broke down in 2001. They resumed in 2002 with an uncertain future.

The danger of bioweapons stands as one of the most probable threats to the American homeland, well illustrated by the anthrax-contaminated letters sent to media outlets and government officials in Florida, Washington, and New York after the September 2001 attacks. The perpetrator has yet to be found, but the likelihood is that the letters came from domestic sources.

Bioweapons may be used effectively against the United States because of America's open society. Water systems, the postal system, the food distribution system, and other systems all depend on quick, open, and concentrated distribution, making them easy targets for terrorists who seek to inflict significant damage on the United States.

An attack against the United States' agriculture sector would be equally devastating. Because one-sixth of the U.S. gross domestic product involves agriculture, an attack against American agriculture could have a major impact on the American economy. Although few data on such a hypothetical attack have been amassed, at least 21 such incidents occurred during the 1990s. Most had little impact and only a local effect, but a 1989 incident involving a group called the Breeders that released the Mediterranean fruit fly in California to protest the use of pesticides caused considerable damage.

The 1990s incidents were not the first time that biological vulnerabilities were evident. In World War I, horses contaminated with anthrax bacteria were shipped to Europe from the United States, with ineffective consequences.[36] In World War II, several states developed bioweapons. The United States developed a viral agent to use against Japan's rice crop, but never used it. Japan reportedly used bioweapons in World War II in Manchuria, where it employed "anthrax, glanders, 'nose ulcers,' sheep pox, ox plague, and numerous anti-crop agents" against livestock, grains, and vegetables.[37] The United States maintained a robust anti-crop program after World War II, terminating it in 1969.

Biological threats are all the more dangerous because of the many former biological test sites and stores in the world. These could serve as "farms" for terrorists to obtain toxins. For a host of reasons, then, bioweapons are a difficult homeland security challenge for the United States.

Chemical Weapons

Chemical weapons, although not as old as bioweapons, entered the international stage in World War I. Germany first used chemical weapons in 1915, when chlorine-based gases were used. By 1917, Germany had also used other chemical agents such as mustard gas, which was found to stay in the target area longer and was therefore militarily more effective.[38] The United States entered the war in April 1917 and within three months launched a chemical weapons program that eventually involved at least 48 different chemicals.[39]

As a result of the chemical weapons programs of the world's nations since 1917, a new threat has emerged from old munitions either dumped in the sea or buried on land that have begun to leach into the environment. Estimates are that over one million tons of chemical weapons were so disposed between 1945 and 1970.[40] The United States dumped 100,000 tons into the Gulf of Mexico and off New Jersey, California, Florida, South Carolina, Australia, Denmark, India, Italy, Japan, and Norway.[41] Other states also engaged in this practice. The Soviet Union between the end of World War II and 1990 reportedly disposed of 500,000 tons of chemical weapons in the Baltic Sea, Kara Sea, and Sea of Japan. These figures do not include thousands of tons of chemical weapons the Soviet Union buried in unmarked pits.[42]

From the standpoint of defending America's homeland security, the principal threat is that rogue states or terrorists will use chemical weapons against the United States or its interests. As an open society, even with preemptive defense, the United States cannot defend all potential targets against which terrorists might launch chemical attacks. As former President Clinton said, there is a "100 percent likelihood of a biological or chemical terrorist attack on U.S. soil in the next 10 years."[43]

U.S. Policies to Contain Weapons of Mass Destruction

Because of the threats of nuclear, biological, and chemical weapons, the United States has over the years tried to contain the proliferation of these weapons of mass destruction. The ideal way to contain WMD is to attempt to limit proliferation through arms control agreements, disarmament programs, and export and domestic production controls. Such methods limit proliferation without costly use of force, and they can be made beneficial for states that abstain from WMD development. For example, the Non-Proliferation Treaty (NPT) requires nations that have nuclear technology to help those who do not to develop peaceful uses of nuclear energy. Over time, the United States has used a mix of such methods, with uneven success.

The United States has advocated and pursued **arms control** for most of its history. As we have seen, President Woodrow Wilson developed the idea of an international organization whose purpose was to prevent war or, failing that, to lessen the impact of wars upon civilization. Wilson failed to energize Congress to support the League of Nations, but his successor oversaw the beginning of one of the most impressive pre-nuclear arms control processes in history, the Washington Naval Conference, which shook the very foundations of major post–World War I naval establishments.

Indeed, many American presidents embraced the idea that controlling weapons could prevent war, lessen its likelihood, or reduce its impact if it occurred. Even as the United States planned to enter World War II, President Franklin D. Roosevelt, by agreeing to the Atlantic Charter, committed the United States to the idea of a United Nations, an international organization that Roosevelt and other Americans hoped would be created after World War II to maintain peace. And when the UN was created, the United States supported it fully.

Following World War II, the United States, within the context of the UN, proposed the Baruch Plan for the international control of nuclear weapons. Although the Soviet Union refused to accept it, the fact that the United States proposed it indicated once again that America recognized that a supranational body or significant state-to-state agreements must approach the issue of how to control nuclear weapons.

There were no successful nuclear arms control efforts in the late 1940s and 1950s. As we have seen, Cold War fears during this period led to the production of nuclear weapons first by the United States, then the USSR, and then Great Britain, France, and China, as both sides tried to develop a military posture sufficient to deter the other side. Reliance on deterrence seemed to work, at least until the October 1962 Cuban missile crisis, when the United States and the Soviet Union came incredibly close to nuclear war. Frightened, each side understood that steps had to be taken to enhance the security of both sides' homelands, and both sides recognized that it was time to step back from the brink to bring rationality to the process. (For a review of some of the more prominent arms control agreements of the Cold War, see Table 12.2.)

Whether these arrangements actually led to greater security for the American homeland is a matter of debate. However, one would be hard pressed to deny their impact on positive behavioral changes in the international community. At the same time, they slowly built over time a degree of confidence between Washington and Moscow. Indeed, the history of arms control and the process of constant dialogue, even if at times interrupted by increased tension, permitted the United States and Russia in 2002 to agree in the Strategic Offensive Arms Reduction Treaty to reduce nuclear stockpiles to between 1,700 and 2,200 warheads. For those aware of the shadow of imminent destruction under which the United States and the world lived for 40 years, this was a significant accomplishment, even if it did not completely remove the nuclear threat.

However, as previously indicated, during the 1990s American foreign policymakers began to consider whether a more proactive stance toward proliferation was necessary. The early 1990s saw the Clinton Administration considering taking military action to counter proliferation on at least two occasions. In 1993, U.S. intelligence indicated that China was shipping chemical-weapons-related materials to Iran. Clinton considered interdicting the ship, until it was determined that the information was erroneous. Furthermore, in 1994, Clinton believed it might be necessary to preemptively attack the North Korean nuclear reactor at Yongbyong.[44] The Clinton Administration also used counterproliferation actions against Iraq in the late 1990s. Dedication to counterproliferation, not just nonproliferation, has been continued under the administration of George W. Bush, most notably through the invasion of Iraq.

Despite these actions, the threat remains that some international actor, most likely a terrorist group or rogue nation, might use weapons of mass destruction against the American homeland. Countering this threat remains one of the most important tasks and vexing problems that every U.S. administration faces.

OTHER HOMELAND DEFENSE ISSUES

Over the years, good planning, the use of military force, deterrence based on the threat to use military force, skillful diplomacy, military alliances and good luck all played major roles in defending the American homeland. Nevertheless, at the start of the twenty-first century, the international environment is more complex than ever before. Indeed, the threats that the United States faces are as great as ever, or even greater than ever, because of the dangers of weapons of mass destruction and because of the complex ways in which the United States is connected to the rest of the world.

As we have seen, these realities gave rise to the question of whether traditional ways of defending the American homeland remain adequate. The 2002 change in U.S. defense strategy to include preemptive defense and the creation in the same year of the Department of Homeland Security indicate the degree of concern and underline that many Americans believe the answer to the question is "No." What other steps, then, may be required to defend the U.S. homeland as the country and the world move deeper into the twenty-first century? According to many, defense against ballistic missiles, enhanced intelligence, and cyber security lead the list.

Ballistic Missile Defense (BMD)

Defending the American homeland against attack by developing a defensive missile system to protect it from enemy bombers and missiles is an old idea newly discovered. As long ago as the late 1940s, American defense planners conceived of a plan called "Project Thumper" to place a defensive missile shield around the United States to defend it from Soviet bombers. Despite the attractiveness of the idea, the technology was not sufficiently advanced, and Project Thumper faded away.

Throughout the 1950s and 1960s, American scientists and engineers continued to work on defensive missile systems to protect the United States from the Soviet bomber threat. Eventually several defensive systems, such as the Nike-Ajax and Nike-Zeus, were deployed. When the Soviet Union deployed a large number of intercontinental ballistic missiles (ICBMs) in the 1960s, however, it became apparent that the Nike systems were inadequate to meet the ICBM threat.

Throughout these years, as discussed earlier, the United States and the Soviet Union lived with the knowledge that their respective homelands were vulnerable. With no effective defense against ICBMs, both countries relied primarily on nuclear deterrence for a degree of security. One reason both countries relied on deterrence was that the offensive technologies of missiles and bombers always ran ahead of defensive technologies, or anti-ballistic missiles (ABMs).

There was another reason as well. By the early 1970s, strategic thinking had changed to the point that missile defenses were seen as destabilizing. A country that had its cities protected by ABMs might believe that it could escape retaliation if it launched a nuclear first strike. Defensive missiles under this scenario could therefore influence decision makers to launch an attack rather than refrain from an attack. Because of this, the United States and the Soviet Union signed the 1972 ABM Treaty that limited the quantity of ABMs that either side could deploy.

Both sides abided by the ABM Treaty throughout the 1970s, with the Soviet Union deploying a limited ABM system as permitted by the treaty and the United States deciding not to. Both sides also proceeded with ABM research. Then, in 1983, Ronald Reagan turned a low-key debate among defense intellectuals over strategic defense into a major international outcry by calling on U.S. scientists and engineers to develop a defensive system that would render nuclear weapons "impotent and obsolete." Reagan called his program the **Strategic Defense Initiative (SDI).** Critics derided it as **Star Wars.**

SDI proponents defended the program for several reasons. Was it not more moral, they asked, to prevent war by defending populations than by threatening to destroy them? Not only could defenses deter, they argued, but defenses could also protect against accidental launches and rogue states. Critics countered that defense would never be perfect, that it would be prohibitively expensive, that it would set off a new round in the arms race, and that it could be easily confused or degraded by the other side. Opponents also asserted that SDI could cause a nuclear war if the side that had it thought it could launch a nuclear attack, destroy most of the attacked country's nuclear weapons, and then use its defensive shield to protect itself from the few retaliatory weapons that the attacked side still had left. This, of course, was exactly the argument that led the United States and the Soviet Union to conclude the 1972 ABM Treaty.

Despite increased funding for SDI research under Reagan, no system was deployed because of cost, technical difficulties, and improving U.S.-Soviet relations. For most of the late 1980s and early 1990s, the concept of ballistic missile defense was on the back burner as the Cold War ended and the United States grappled with the changes taking place in the world. Late in the Clinton Administration, however, as technology advanced and as fears grew that a rogue state might obtain ballistic missiles, Clinton reconsidered moving forward with a ballistic missile defense (BMD) system.

President George W. Bush, convinced that a BMD system was both possible and desirable, especially as a defense against rogue states that might obtain missiles, declared that he intended to deploy a defensive missile system, hopefully after negotiating revisions with Russia to the 1972 ABM Treaty but, if that proved impossible, unilaterally. The United States issued the necessary notice of abrogation in December 2001 and exited the ABM Treaty in June 2002 to continue development of defensive systems minus the restrictions once imposed.

As of 2004, a BMD system is not deployed, but dates as early as 2006 have been mentioned for deploying existing capabilities. Nuclear deterrence remains a key part of the U.S. strategy to defend the homeland, but so does, at least in concept, ballistic missile defense. With the Patriot 3 point defense system and the Aegis-based mid-course intercept system both maturing, a limited system may be available by mid-decade.

Such a system creates its own problems. It would not be able to protect against a full-scale Russian attack, but it could protect against an attack by China and almost completely negate North Korea's ballistic missile threat. In a worst case scenario, this American capability, combined with a likely Japanese defensive missile system, could signal the beginning of a renewed arms build-up in northeast Asia. Once again, there are no easy answers in formulating national security policy.

Opponents of a national-scale BMD, exemplified by Charles Glaser and Steve Fetter, suggest that it is not worth damaging relations with the only nations that present a current threat, Russia and China, in order to protect against missile threats that are unlikely to materialize for some time.[45] Furthermore, they and other opponents point out that any nation capable of launching nuclear-tipped ballistic missiles would be more than capable of developing decoys that would make the missile defense system ineffective.

Proponents of the system, however, propose that the system will take years to develop and deploy, and that North Korea and Iran will likely have workable missiles by the time the United States can erect a dependable missile shield, even if it starts deployment virtually immediately.[46] Furthermore, proponents argue that a national American BMD is necessary both to prevent death and destruction from another country's accidental launch of a nuclear-tipped ballistic missile and to keep the United States from being deterred from pursuing its national interests by a nuclear blackmailing aggressor. Thus, the debate over the wisdom of ballistic missile defense as a requirement for homeland security continues.

Enhanced Intelligence

As Chapter 11 well illustrated, given both the importance of intelligence in the war on terrorism and other twenty-first-century security issues, one of the prime areas of concern in coming years is improving the quantity, accuracy, and timeliness of U.S. intelligence. Only enhanced intelligence will enable the United States and its allies to identify attacks before they occur and act to prevent them. Improving intelligence is an immensely difficult task.

Enhanced intelligence will require increased emphasis on human intelligence. U.S. decision makers will need to be aware not only of the capabilities but also the intentions of potential enemies. While some of the capabilities of potential enemies may be identified using technology, intentions more often than not can best be discerned by placing intelligence operatives into the field. Highly trained professional men and women with language skills and cultural training who can interact with potential adversaries from within the adversaries' organizations will be needed as never before.

To emphasize the importance of the above, recall the July 2004 report of the Senate Intelligence Committee, which stated: "Most of the major key judgments in an October 2002 National Intelligence Estimate on Iraq's illicit weapons were either overstated, or were not supported by the underlying intelligence reporting." The report was made all the more credible as the committee chair, Senator Pat Roberts of Kansas, was a Republican. Reporting on the committee's findings, the *Atlanta Journal-Constitution* observed that "the most pivotal assessments used to justify the war against Iraq had been unfounded, unreasonable and reflected major missteps on the part of American intelligence agencies."[47]

As we saw in Chapter 11, once intelligence is gathered, it must be transmitted rapidly to analysts so that it can be handled and interpreted expeditiously. Thus, in addition to highly trained field operatives, intelligence agencies must have systems that can access information and transmit it to a centralized fusion center for confirmation. Highly trained analysts are also, of course, requisite. And once intelligence is interpreted and analyzed, conclusions must then be rapidly transmitted to decision makers so that appropriate actions can be planned and taken.

It will require a large amount of money to create such a well-oiled and tightly knit system. After the Cold War, it will be recalled, funding for U.S. intelligence operations decreased significantly, but after the 2001 terrorist attacks, it increased markedly. Almost assuredly, even more funds will be required to improve U.S. intelligence operations.

Enhancing American intelligence operations will also require significant improvements to the interfaces between intelligence agencies and between intelligence agencies and decision makers. In part, the Department of Homeland Security was created to improve these interfaces. Richard Betts has argued that in most of the best known cases of intelligence failure, the most crucial mistakes were attributable to the intelligence consumer, that is, the policymaker, rather than to the collectors or analysts.[48] Most notably, Betts asserts that there are irreconcilable paradoxes involved in getting the intelligence to the consumer. Particularly, the more sensitive one makes the intelligence collection system, the more information and the more false alarms one gets. Inevitably, the more false alarms that are created, the less responsive the policymaker will be when one puts intelligence in front of them.

Finally, the tightly knit intelligence system described above will pose challenges for the oversight of intelligence and of covert operations by responsible elected representatives. Since it will undoubtedly be necessary to move quickly to respond to some intelligence revelations, mechanisms must be developed for quick and secure briefings of elected officials by security decision makers.

In the twenty-first century, American security can only be enhanced if American intelligence is better than it has ever been before. The challenges to achieving this objective are considerable, while the cost of failing to achieve it can be immense.

Cyber Security

The United States' increased reliance on information and communication technologies has opened another avenue of potential American vulnerability to attack, assaults on U.S. information and information systems. Such attacks are called **information warfare** and could take many forms. Computer software and hardware could be destroyed or degraded. Critical information could be acquired or altered. False information could be inserted. Unauthorized access could be obtained and unauthorized directions given. Important services and functions could be denied. Confidence in systems could be undermined.

These dangers led some officials to warn about the possibility of an "electronic Pearl Harbor" in which information warfare could bring the government or corporations to a halt. Other observers dismissed such warnings as overblown. The debate about the extent of the threat continues, but there is no doubt that the threat exists, as shown by the frequent attacks on corporate and government websites. Indeed in late 2002, the Internet came under attack when persons unknown launched a coordinated distributed denial of services attack against eight of the 13 root servers that are the core of the Internet. The servers withstood the attack, but the challenge was the most serious that the Internet had faced.

How serious are the threats? The 1997 U.S. government study *Critical Foundations: Protecting America's Infrastructures* highlighted the weaknesses of critical infrastructures such as communications and telephones, banking, power grids, emergency response systems, water systems, fuel supply networks, and other systems that rely extensively on computers and information systems. Vulnerabilities were further highlighted in a 1997 war game called "Eligible Receiver" in which a team of U.S. Defense Department hackers penetrated military computer networks in Hawaii, Washington, Chicago, St. Louis, and Colorado.

In response to these vulnerabilities and threats, the U.S. government expanded its efforts to improve information and communication security. For example, in 2002, the Bush Administration issued "The National Strategy to Secure Cyberspace," the latest in a series of U.S. government studies that recommended ways to improve information and communications security. It also increased expenditures on creating secure cyber systems.

Inevitably, the competition between those attempting to secure American cyber systems and those attempting to penetrate, degrade, or destroy those systems will continue. Given the ever expanding reliance of American public, private, and personal interests on information and communication technologies, this is as crucial a part of the effort of defending the American homeland as nuclear deterrence or ferreting out terrorists before they can launch an attack.

In the twenty-first century, the challenges of defending the American homeland are perhaps more daunting than ever. Indeed, according to some, the threats that confront the

United States, especially from terrorism and weapons of mass destruction, are so significant that the very nature of American society may be forced to change, a possibility and a danger that we will discuss in detail in Chapter 15. Even so, after over two centuries of American independence, homeland defense remains the central responsibility of, and the central challenge facing, the United States government.

SUMMARY

The September 11th, 2001, terrorist attack on the United States was a terrible event. Like nothing since Japan's 1941 attack on Pearl Harbor, the assault focused attention on defending the homeland.

Even before the United States existed, defending the homeland concerned American colonists. When conflicts with the French and American Indians broke out, defense was everyone's responsibility. After independence, the United States faced several external threats, some the result of foreign designs on the U.S. homeland and others generated as the United States expanded. Spain, France, Great Britain, and American Indians were the most prominent threats. For defense, the United States created a small army and navy, and constructed coastal and frontier forts. Geographical isolation, European geopolitical competition, and the demilitarized American-Canadian border all contributed to early U.S. security.

Before 2001, the most infamous attack against the United States was Japan's December 7, 1941, attack on U.S. military facilities at Pearl Harbor, which led to U.S. entry into World War II. During the war, no meaningful attack occurred against the continental United States. The United States was the only power whose homeland was not decimated by the war.

During the Cold War, Soviet nuclear weapons threatened the United States. Defense of the homeland relied on military preparedness for deterrence; early warning systems in Canada, overseas, and in space; air and ballistic missile defenses; human, signal, and electronic intelligence; diplomacy; military alliances; and arms control. Mutual assured destruction (MAD), which contended that an aggressor state would not strike if it believed that it would suffer a massive retaliatory strike in response, was the core of U.S. defense.

When the Soviet Union collapsed in 1991, Americans believed that, with the Soviet threat gone, no real threat to the homeland existed. However, as the 1990s wore on, the United States absorbed several attacks launched by foreign and American terrorists. The most infamous were the 1993 bombing of the World Trade Center by Islamic extremists and the 1995 destruction of the Federal Building in Oklahoma City by American radicals. Thus, even before 2001, the United States began to pay more attention to homeland defense.

After September 11, 2001, homeland defense became the chief government priority. The United States soon initiated a global war on terrorism that included increasing domestic security, freezing terrorist funds, improving interagency cooperation, launching an assault against the regime in Afghanistan that harbored al Qaeda, devoting $40 billion to fund the war against terrorism, and improving coordination of security. The Office of Homeland Security was created to coordinate homeland defense. In 2002, in the largest reorganization of government in half a century, it became the Department of Homeland Security, combining 22 agencies and employing 170,000 people.

George W. Bush also formed an international anti-terrorist coalition to support the war against terrorism and adopted a new defense strategy, preemptive defense, that declared the United States would "act against emerging threats before they are fully formed." Supporters of the doctrine praised it as necessary to reduce the threat of terrorism. Critics charged the United States intended to do whatever it wanted in international affairs and had become an imperial hegemon in the name of homeland security.

Over the years, good planning, military force, deterrence based on the threat to use force, skillful diplomacy, military alliances, and good luck all played roles in defending the U.S. homeland. At the start of the twenty-first century, the threats that the United States faces are greater than ever because of weapons of mass destruction, international terrorism, and the ways in which the United States is connected to the rest of the world. Thus, the United States has also emphasized ballistic missile defense, for example with the Strategic Defense Initiative. It has also enhanced intelligence, especially since September 2001, and cyber security, that is, protecting computers and the U.S. information and communication infrastructure, as ways to enhance its security.

Defending the homeland is a complex task. The 2001 terrorist attacks made U.S. vulnerability more apparent than it had been and confirmed that homeland defense is a key government task.

KEY TERMS AND CONCEPTS

geographical isolation
European geopolitical competition
demilitarization of the American-
    Canadian border
Pearl Harbor
mutual assured destruction (MAD)
weapons of mass destruction (WMD)
rogue states
radical religions
Clash of Civilizations
Indian and P
ani nuclear tests
information warfare
Commission on National Security in
    the 21st Century (Hart-Rudman
    Commission)

USA Patriot Act
Department of Homeland Security
international anti-terrorist coalition
preemptive defense
nuclear threat
bioweapons
chemical weapons
arms control
Strategic Defense Initiative (SDI), or
    Star Wars
information warfare

THINKING CRITICALLY

1. What major factors contributed to American homeland security during the eighteenth and nineteenth centuries, and how did each help provide security?

2. What were the major threats to American homeland security during the Cold War, and how did the United States defend itself?

3. How can the United States best counter the threat posed by modern terrorism?

4. How can the United States assure that the Department of Homeland Security operates as a well-functioning, mission-oriented agency?

5. How have alliances and coalitions contributed to American homeland security?

6. How serious is the threat posed to homeland security by weapons of mass destruction, and how may the threat best be countered?

7. What are the pros and cons of ballistic missile defense?

8. How vulnerable are the United States computer and communications systems to cyber threats, and how may they best be defended?

9. How may the threat of terrorism and the need to counter the threat change the United States?

10. How can the United States improve its intelligence operations and at the same time assure sufficient oversight of intelligence operations?

NOTES

1. As British forces advanced on Washington, D.C., American troops abandoned the fort at Greenleaf Point, now the site of the National Defense University, hiding powder in a dry well at the end of the point. British soldiers looking for weapons came upon the well and lowered a lantern down to have a look. More British soldiers died in the explosion that followed than in any other battle in defense of the Capital.

2. Thomas Schelling, *The Strategy of Conflict*, 2nd ed. (Cambridge, Mass.: Harvard University Press, 1980), p. 136.

3. FBI, *Terrorism in the United States 1999* (Washington, D.C.: Counterterrorism Threat Assessment and Warning Unit: Counterterrorism Division, 2000).

4. Samuel Huntington, "The Clash of Civilizations," *Foreign Affairs* 72(3) (Summer 1993).

5. Interview with former assistant to Senator Sam Nunn, January 7, 2002, Georgia Tech, Atlanta, Georgia.

6. U.S. Commission on National Security in the 21st Century, *Road Map for National Security: Imperative for Change,* Phase III Report of the Commission, Washington, D.C., January 31, 2001, p. iv.

7. U.S. Commission on National Security in the 21st Century, p. viii.

8. U.S. Commission on National Security in the 21st Century.

9. See especially Michele A. Flournoy, *QDR 2001: Strategy-Driven Choices for America's Security, Defense Strategy Alternatives: Choosing Where to Place Emphasis and Where to Accept Risk* (Washington, D.C.: National Defense University Press), pp. 137–164.

10. "Joint Vision 2020, America's Military—Preparing for Tomorrow," *Joint Force Quarterly* (Summer 2000): 57–76.

11. "Joint Vision 2020," p. 66.

12. "Joint Vision 2020," p. 76.

13. Stephen E. Flynn, "America the Vulnerable," *Foreign Affairs* 81(1) (January/February 2002): 60–74.

14. Flynn, "America the Vulnerable," p. 63

15. Julia Malone, "U.S. Likely to Intensify Tracking of Foreigners," *Atlanta Journal-Constitution* (January 22, 2002): A4.

16. See U.S. Department of State, *Fact Sheet: International Contributions to the War Against Terrorism* (Washington, D.C.: U.S. Department of State, Office of Public Affairs, 2002).

17. White House, *The National Security Strategy of the United States of America* (Washington, D.C.: White House, September 2002).

18. Michael O'Hanlon, Susan Rice, and James Steinberg, *The New National Security Strategy and Preemption* (Washington, D.C.: Brookings Institute, 2002).

19. See *Bulletin of the Atomic Scientists, Nuclear Notebook: Where the Bombs Are, 1997,* September/October 1997.

20. *Bulletin of the Atomic Scientists, Nuclear Notebook.*

21. New Mexico has 2,850; Georgia, 2,000; Washington, 1,600; Nevada, 1,450; North Dakota, 965; Wyoming, 592; Missouri, 550; Texas, 520; Louisiana, 455; Montana, 455; Nebraska, 255; California, 175; Virginia, 175; South Dakota, 138; and Colorado, 138. *Bulletin of the Atomic Scientists, Nuclear Notebook.*

22. *Bulletin of the Atomic Scientists, Nuclear Notebook.*

23. Samuel S. Kim, "China as a Great Power," *Current History* (September 1997): 250.

24. *Bulletin of the Atomic Scientists, Nuclear Notebook*, May/June 2001, pp. 78–79.

25. *Bulletin of the Atomic Scientists, Nuclear Notebook: British, French, and Chinese Nuclear Forces, 1996.*

26. *Nuclear Notebook: British, French, and Chinese Nuclear Forces.*

27. Bret Lortie, "Setting the Scene," *Bulletin of the Atomic Scientists* (March/April 2001): 52.

28. Eileen Choffnes, "Germs on the Loose," *Bulletin of the Atomic Scientists* (March/April 2001): 58.

29. Choffnes, "Germs on the Loose," p. 58.

30. Choffnes, "Germs on the Loose," pp. 59–61.

31. Choffnes, "Germs on the Loose," p. 59.

32. Anthony H. Cordesman, *Global Nuclear Balance* (Washington, D.C.: Center for Strategic and International Studies, 2002), p. 80.

33. Catherine Auer, "A View from Inside," *Bulletin of the Atomic Scientists* (March/April 2001): 69–70.

34. Choffnes, "Germs on the Loose," p. 59.

35. *Japan Times* (January 14, 2002): 17.

36. Gavin Cameron, et al., "Planting Fear," *Bulletin of the Atomic Scientists* (September/October 2001), pp. 40-41.

37. Cameron, "Planting Fear," p. 41.

38. Jonathan B. Tucker, "Chemical Weapons: Buried in the Backyard," *Bulletin of the Atomic Scientists* (September/October 2001): 50.

39. Tucker, "Chemical Weapons," p. 52.

40. Tucker, "Chemical Weapons," p. 56.

41. Tucker, "Chemical Weapons."

42. Tucker, "Chemical Weapons."

43. Frank J. Cilluffo et al., *Combating Chemical, Biological, Radiological and Nuclear Terrorism: A Comprehensive Strategy* (Washington, D.C.: CSIS, December 2000), p. ii.

44. Henry Sokolski, *Best of Intentions: America's Campaign against Strategic Weapons Proliferation* (Westport, Conn.: Praeger Press, 2001), p. 96.

45. Charles Glaser and Steve Fetter, "National Missile Defense and the Future of US Nuclear Weapons Policy," *International Security* 26(1) (Summer 2001): 41.

46. Stephen Hadley, "A Call to Deploy," *Washington Quarterly* 23(3) (Summer 2000): 95–108.

47. *Atlanta Journal-Constitution* (July 10, 2004): 1.

48. Richard Betts, "Analysis, War, and Decision: Why Intelligence Failures Are Inevitable," *World Politics* 31(1) (October 1978): 61.

CHAPTER 13

Economics and Foreign Policy: Trade, Finance, and Currency

Trade has long been a major part of the American economy, and the U.S. economy today is deeply entwined with the global economy. Millions of tons of cargo enter U.S. ports each day, much on container ships, as in the foreground, and tankers, as in the middle background. The Verrazano Narrows Bridge is in the far background.

- What advantages did trade provide for the United States after American independence, and what complications did it cause?
- How did American tariff policy evolve over time?
- What was the Bretton Woods system?
- How did the international trading system evolve following the collapse of the Bretton Woods system?
- How effective are economic sanctions and embargoes as policy tools?

Economic issues play a major role in the foreign policy of every state, and the United States is no exception. In fact, the massive size of the American economy, with a GDP almost as large as the next four biggest economies, allows the United States to have a profound impact on other nations through its economic policies. Ups and downs in the American economy can have ripple effects around the globe. On the other hand, American firms and households rely on foreign countries for imported consumer goods, raw materials, industrial equipment, and labor; therefore, events around the globe can affect the state of the American economy.

The United States' international economic concerns may be grouped under the broad headings of trade, finance, and currency issues. These groupings cover a dizzying array of concerns, including market access, free trade areas, and economic sanctions; interest rates, capitalization, and foreign aid; and exchange rates, speculation, and currency stability.

In each of these areas, foreign policy decision makers have a variety of tools available to them as they pursue their objectives. For example, regarding economic sanctions, decision makers may use embargoes, boycotts, tariff increases, blacklists, unfavorable tariff discrimination, withdrawal of most favored nation status, quotas, license denial, dumping, and preclusive buying as "negative sanctions." Or they may use favorable tariff discrimination, granting most favored nation status, tariff reductions, direct purchases, subsidies to exports or imports, and granting import and export licenses as "positive sanctions."[1]

This chapter will demystify American international economic policy by examining some of the critical international economic issues that the United States faces today. The process will begin with a discussion of how American international economic policy began.

EARLY ISSUES OF INTERNATIONAL ECONOMICS

Even before the American republic was founded, the impact of economics on colonial foreign policy was significant. One of the main reasons the original 13 colonies sought independence from Great Britain was an economic issue. The call "no taxation without representation" that helped drive the American Revolution was both a call for political representation in Parliament and a recognition of the adverse economic impact an unchecked government can have through its power to tax.

International Economics and the War of Independence

After the 1763 Peace of Paris ended the French and Indian War, Great Britain decided it would keep over 10,000 soldiers in its North American colonies. The British government decided that since the troops were posted in North America to protect colonists there, it was only fair that the colonists contribute to the support of these forces by paying a tax. Over the next several years, Great Britain imposed the Stamp Act, the Tea Act, and the Intolerable Acts on the colonies.[2] All of these actions had a detrimental impact on colonists' pocket books.

Seeking to avoid further conflict with France, and to lessen the cost of defending its North American colonies, Great Britain also forbade settlers to move past the Ohio River and placed the Ohio Territory under the control of Canada. This edict was resented because it prevented colonists from taking advantage of the wealth of property and resources to the west, and it led Thomas Paine to write the jingoistic pamphlet *Common Sense,* which asserted that there was not "a single advantage that this continent can reap by being connected with Great Britain."[3] Paine, as many others, believed that the colonies could only benefit from severing ties with Britain.

Recognizing the importance of economics, the Continental Congress sent a commercial agent to France in March 1776, even before the Declaration of Independence was written. The agent's primary objectives were to seek financial and military assistance and to determine the possibility of an alliance.[4] In part because of this, France provided arms to the colonists but disguised the origin of the weapons to prevent Great Britain from having a reason to declare war on France.

The Continental Congress also stressed the role of international economics in its Plan of 1776, known as the **Model Treaty.** Congress believed it was imperative that American diplomats have clear instructions before they left for Europe, because it took a minimum of 84 days for messages to travel back and forth from Europe to America. Drafted in July 1776 by a committee headed by John Adams, the Model Treaty served as basic guidance for American diplomats in Europe. The model declared that commercial connections would always be stressed in treaties, and that political or military ties would largely be absent.[5] For the next quarter century, almost all American treaties were guided by these instructions. An exception was the 1778 Treaty of Alliance with France, which was the first and last American military alliance until NATO in 1949.

Another 1778 treaty with France, the Treaty of Amity and Commerce, reflected the desire of the Continental Congress to have the erstwhile colonies prosper not by sword but through commerce and trade. To the Founding Fathers, trade was a means to insure prosperity for the new country. They favored political isolation, but never commercial isolation. The newly independent colonies were to be free states that traded goods freely the world over.

Trade Conflicts in the Early Years

After independence, the 13 independent states faced several international trade problems. First, they discovered that it was difficult to trade as 13 different entities. Thus, when they asked Great Britain to send a diplomatic mission, London asked if it should send one or 13 representatives. Under the Articles of Confederation, the states issued their own money and often put tariffs and taxes on goods imported from each other. Also, it was difficult to go from being a sheltered member of the British Empire to being in competition with the empire. The creation of the United States under the Constitution rectified some of these problems, especially issues of separate coinage and interstate tariffs and taxes, but trade difficulties with Great Britain, France, and the North African Barbary states remained. **Post-independence trade conflicts** occurred in all three instances.

In the 1790s, the French Revolution led to renewed fighting between Great Britain and France, and Americans traded with both warring countries. Not surprisingly, neither Great Britain nor France appreciated this, and British and French naval vessels therefore often captured American merchant ships bound for the other, sometimes keeping the U.S. ships as prizes of war and forcing sailors from those ships (who were in some cases deserters from the British or French navies) to join their crews. These practices increased tension between the United States and both France and Great Britain, and resulted in the United States fighting an undeclared naval war with France during John Adams's presidency.

Throughout the late eighteenth and early nineteenth centuries, the North African Barbary states—Morocco, Algeria, Tripoli (present day Libya), and Tunis—captured U.S. ships and sailors and demanded tribute for their release or safe passage. Under President Thomas Jefferson, the United States launched naval and marine expeditions against the Barbary states because of these predatory practices.

Trading problems with Great Britain proved even more intractable than the ones with France and the Barbary states, and were one cause of the War of 1812. Great Britain seized American ships, captured American goods, and impressed American sailors as well as Royal Navy deserters who worked on U.S. merchant ships. The United States objected to the British actions, even placing an embargo on shipping, but to no avail. Thus, even though there were other reasons for the War of 1812, such as British support of Indian attacks on American settlers moving west, and the desire of some Americans to annex Canada, trade was a key cause of the war. Indeed, President Madison, in his war message to Congress, listed commercial grievances, "pretended blockades," and Great Britain's efforts to retain its commerce and navigation monopoly as justification for war. Clearly, even in its earliest years, the United States considered free trade an issue worth fighting for.

The Evolution of Tariff Policy

Tariffs played a major role in the United States' early international economic policy. Tariffs, that is, taxes imposed on goods and services being imported into a country, serve two purposes. First, tariffs serve as a source of revenue for the government of the country receiving the goods or services. Second, tariffs make imported goods more expensive, and thus serve to benefit the domestic producers of goods. This is particularly true in cases in which the domestic producer cannot produce the good as cheaply as foreign competitors.

Even though the U.S. Constitution provided Congress the ability to "regulate Commerce with foreign Nations" and to "lay and collect Taxes, Duties, Imposts, and Excises," this did not mean that there was unanimity within the United States about **tariff policy** or other forms of taxes. After the 1789 formation of the United States under the Constitution, Secretary of the Treasury Alexander Hamilton played a major role in establishing the economic policies of the new country. Hamilton's plans included having the new government assume the $25 million debt that the states incurred during the Revolution, honoring the $50 million debt left from the Articles of Confederation period, adding an excise tax on whiskey, and establishing a national bank. Another key element was an effort to make America's infant industrial sector viable by implementing a protective tariff. Hamilton did not succeed. Southerners in particular saw increased tariffs as an impediment to foreign trade and believed tariffs would be counter to their interests. Therefore, it was not until after the War of 1812 that tariff protection was extended to manufacturing interests, largely in the North.

Thus, by the end of the War of 1812, all of the instruments or elements necessary for American international trade, finance, and currency policy were in place. Increasingly, the United States was divided over these issues—generally merchants, financiers, and manufacturers pitted against planters and farmers. By the 1820s, early industrialists such as Matthew Carry argued for tariffs to protect U.S. industries against British dumping of manufactured products.[6] Henry Carry, Matthew's son, further developed the argument for protective tariffs by making the case that a robust domestic economy would remove any reasons for foreign adventures. High tariffs, Carry argued, promoted peace.[7]

Many people, particularly planters and farmers, rejected these arguments. Seeking to export their products and fearing retaliatory tariffs, they advocated free trade, arguing that tariffs were industrial subsidies and an illegitimate use of government power. Some even argued that tariffs were an overt attempt to undermine the true productive class in America, the planters and farmers.

The debate over tariffs and other issues such as slavery continued to divide agricultural and manufacturing interests during most of the early and middle nineteenth century. The Civil War settled the issue of slavery, but during the war, the South had hoped that King Cotton would influence Great Britain to support the Confederacy. This hope was dashed when Great Britain replaced cotton imports from the South with cotton from India and Egypt. Among the South's difficulties was the fact that workers in British cotton mills tended to side with emancipation of the slaves.

As American industrial might grew after the Civil War, U.S. industries generally did not need to be protected. Even so, they were. The 1890 McKinley Tariff Act, with average duties of 49 percent, caused foreign governments to raise their tariffs against American imports. Nevertheless, America enjoyed the benefits of the British-imposed international liberal trading system and was accused of "free riding on free trade."[8]

America Becomes a Global Economic Power

The need for American access to markets, combined with the belief that the U.S. economy needed to export surplus production to prosper, led to demands that American naval power be expanded to protect U.S. trade and interests overseas. Thus, even though exports were a small portion of the overall U.S. economy, Congress funded an increasingly large and powerful navy.

American foreign trade continued to grow, reaching $1.5 billion by 1900 and climbing to $2.5 billion by 1914. The greatest growth in American trade, however, came during and after World War I. By 1915, U.S. trade with England and France alone was $1.3 billion. In 1916, it reached $2.8 billion with those two states. By the end of the war, America had become the world's leading economic power. New York replaced London as the financial center of the world, with foreign interests owing the United States over $13 billion.

The 1920s were called "the Roaring Twenties," and with good reason. The American economy and the economies of many other states recovered, and most societies loosened social values and codes, perhaps to forget the horrors of World War I. But beneath the economic recovery and social frivolity, seeds of economic collapse and renewed world tension were being sown. Many countries shared the blame for this, and the United States was among them. Over the decades since the Great Depression, many causal explanations have been advanced for that tragic economic collapse. Monetarists tend to believe that a cyclical contraction in the money supply was exacerbated by poor decision making on the part of the Federal Reserve Bank and by the ensuing bank failures.[9] Keynesian economists tend to place the blame on decreased investment due to a collapse of investor confidence after the stock market crash of 1929. However, it is generally agreed that high tariffs were a contributing factor. For one thing, the high tariffs created an environment of uncertainty because it was difficult to know how other countries might retaliate, and this made investors fearful. In addition, the restrictive trade environment created a situation in which the reduction in domestic demand could not be offset by purchases by foreign consumers (i.e., increased exports.) American trade and financial policies in conjunction with specific political decisions bore significant responsibility for the economic collapse of 1929, the Great Depression that followed, and ultimately World War II.

Contributing to the grim global economic situation was the hobbling of the German economy in the aftermath of World War I. According to the Treaty of Versailles that ended the war, Germany owed about $33 billion in reparations (or about 750 billion dollars in 2002 dollars). To repay this debt, Germany needed a vibrant international trading system. The United States and other countries, however, created a protective tariff system that gradually slowed trade nearly to a halt. For example, the 1922 Fordney-McCumber Tariff and the 1930 Hawley-Smoot Tariff made is almost impossible for other countries to sell their goods in the United States.

The high tariffs and high war debt had repercussions. In 1922 and 1923, Germany defaulted on its reparation payments for a variety of reasons. France and Belgium in retaliation seized the Ruhr Valley, and states appealed to the United States to forgive some of the debt they had accumulated in World War I. The United States responded with the **Dawes Plan,** which encouraged American investors to loan Germany millions of dollars to pay reparations. This moderated the crisis, and in 1929 German reparations were reduced to $9 billion. In 1931, President Herbert Hoover declared a one-year moratorium on debt payments.

Perhaps if $9 billion had been Germany's initial total reparation, history may have been different, but with increasing tariffs and unceasing demands for reparations, the international trading system imploded. From 1929 to 1933, world trade decreased 40 percent in value and 25 percent in volume.[10] At first, President Roosevelt tried to deal with the economic depression via economic nationalism and reliance on economic unilateralism, but by 1934 Secretary of State Cordell Hull prevailed on Roosevelt to endorse lower tariffs. Under the **Reciprocal Trade Agreements Act,** Congress gave Roosevelt authority to reduce tariffs reciprocally by as much as 50 percent. Congress also created, with Roosevelt's support, the Export-Import Bank to encourage foreign trade with selectively placed loans. These actions helped, but the global economic depression lingered on, eventually helping bring Hitler to power in Germany.

Trade Policy before World War II

Throughout the late 1930s, tensions escalated in Europe, and by 1939 Europe had once again descended into war. As tensions escalated, the United States attempted to remain neutral, with Congress passing a series of Neutrality Acts. However, once war broke out, Roosevelt asked Congress to modify the Neutrality Acts to permit cash-and-carry purchases of war materials by France and England. This was done, paving the way for the March 1941 passage of the Lend-Lease Act, which allowed Roosevelt to "sell, transfer title to, exchange, lease, lend, or otherwise dispose of" weapons for the defense of states he held vital to the defense of the United States.[11] By the end of the war, the United States had spent more than $50 billion on lend-lease.

The United States also used economic levers of statecraft in the Far East. When Japan expanded its war in China in 1937, Roosevelt chose not to implement the Neutrality Act, which would have prevented the United States from selling arms to the Chinese Nationalists. Similarly, in 1940, the United States underlined its opposition to Japan's aggression against China by giving the required six-month notice to abrogate the 1911 U.S.-Japan Commercial Treaty. In the same month, the United States embargoed the sale of aviation fuel and high-quality scrap iron to Japan. In July 1941, the United States added oil to the embargo, and as Japanese forces moved into south Indochina, the United States froze Japanese assets. For all practical purposes, the United States had initiated an economic embargo against Japan.[12]

Japan considered these U.S. actions causes for war. In September 1941, Japan concluded that it must go to war against the United States if embargoed strategic materials were not released by October 15. A clearer picture of the importance of trade policy between two states is hard to find. The United States took restrictive actions, and Japan determined that if the restrictions remained in effect, war would result. This is as clear a cause and effect relationship as possible. Trade policy can be a powerful tool in a country's foreign policy arsenal, but its results are not always those that are intended.

THE RISE AND FALL OF THE BRETTON WOODS SYSTEM

At the end of World War II, most of the prewar powers lay exhausted. The Soviet Union lost 25–30 million killed and suffered colossal economic as well as social losses. China lost 15 million and was soon embroiled in an immensely destructive civil war. Germany and Poland lost 6 million each, Japan 3 million, and Yugoslavia about 1.6 million. The United States lost 405,395 and Great Britain 400,000. All the states mentioned, except the United States, also suffered tremendous physical destruction. The United States benefited from not being ravaged by war on its own soil, emerging from the war with an industrial capacity that produced almost half of the world's output.[13]

The Bretton Woods System and GATT

As World War II neared its conclusion, the global economic system was in shambles. Thus, in 1944, 44 nations met at Bretton Woods, New Hampshire, to approve a plan that included the International Bank for Reconstruction and Development (IBRD), or World Bank; the International Monetary Fund (IMF); and a new global monetary regime. Also in the aftermath of the Second World War, talks began on a General Agreement on Tariffs and Trade (GATT) that would eventually be implemented in 1948. While the GATT agreement was not part of the negotiation or meetings at Bretton Woods, it was an integral part of the international economic system that reigned during the Bretton Woods era.

The primary consideration driving the central bankers and finance ministers who met at Bretton Woods was the desire to create a stable currency exchange system. During the 1930s, a great deal of competitive devaluations and depreciations were made in an attempt to make a country's exports more appealing to foreign buyers. Furthermore, under a floating system of exchange rates, speculators with large monetary resources could influence the value of a currency by flooding a country with currency or by buying up money. These conditions were considered detrimental to the world economy. Therefore, as World War II drew to a close, nations sought an exchange rate regime that would fix the values at which currencies were exchanged, except under conditions in which there was a fundamental disequilibrium. The solution was a system under which currencies would be pegged at a preset rate of exchange to the U.S. dollar, with the value of the dollar being tied to the value of gold held in U.S. coffers. Foreign nations could redeem currency for gold.

However, the new fixed exchange rate regime required the formation of a new organization, since under a system of fixed exchange rates, states that experienced deficits might have to borrow to shore up their foreign currency reserves to pay their debts. The **International Monetary Fund (IMF)** was the body created to cope with the problems of disequilibrium. In cases of temporary deficit, the IMF could make loans to the debtor nation up to a certain value, based on the nation's contribution to the IMF, to replenish the debtor's foreign currency reserves. In cases of a more fundamental disequilibrium, the IMF was the body to whom the debtor nation appealed to receive a revalued exchange rate. The IMF had at its disposal a fund of gold and currencies that it used to credit the accounts of countries that had chronic balance of payments deficits. Most IMF funds came from developed industrial states, determined by a schedule that stated how much each member had to contribute.

Another central issue at Bretton Woods was the need to reconstruct the nations that had suffered severe war damage to their infrastructures, industries, and institutions. Thus, the **World Bank** was formed, originally to provide long-term loans for the post–World War II reconstruction of Europe. Over time, this organization's role shifted to also provide loans to develop impoverished nations.

As the IMF and the World Bank began their operations, and particularly after the global economic conditions that necessitated their creation changed, both the IMF and World Bank became objects of controversy. Detractors accused both agencies of following a "one size fits all" approach that required all borrowers to make the same types of reforms whether they were workable in the particular country or not, and of being too involved in dispensing ideology and not enough in making sound financial decisions. Usually, the World Bank required detailed economic data from countries that requested loans before it granted a loan. This allowed the Bank to assess whether a project made good economic sense. This practice was often criticized by developing states because it was intrusive and because World Bank criteria were demanding. Some critics charged that the conditions the IMF imposed could be counterproductive to making positive changes in a country because the conditions might not be a good fit for the country and could raise animosity.[14]

Formed several years after the Bretton Woods conference was held, the **General Agreement on Tariffs and Trade (GATT)** was nevertheless often considered part of the Bretton Woods era economic institutions. When in 1945–1947 efforts to create an International Trade Organization failed because of U.S. concern that it might infringe on national sovereignty, GATT was created as a temporary organization to reduce tariffs and other nontariff barriers to trade via multilateral negotiations. GATT sought to prevent the resurrection of protectionist trade barriers as occurred between World Wars I and II, to establish rules for trade, and to develop procedures for settling trade disputes.

Proponents of free trade faced opposition both at home and abroad. In the United States, Republicans, who had gained control of the Congress in 1946, tended to favor protectionism to support American industries. This meant that President Truman had considerable opposition to contend with in his attempts to advance a free trade agenda. Furthermore, the delegates who were sent to negotiate the GATT agreement faced difficulties in dealing with other nations who sought to protect their own industries. Most notably, Great Britain was reluctant to eliminate its Ottawa Agreement, which provided for favorable discriminatory trade practices among Commonwealth members. It took about seven months in Geneva to iron out an agreement that would be acceptable to all sides. Of course, from the perspective of the foreign delegates, the major problem was America's unwillingness to make substantial concessions. Ironically, the critical point of contention at the original GATT conference was agricultural, as it was at the most recent WTO conference in Cancun. In the case of the 1947 GATT conference, the issue was wool tariffs and U.S. unwillingness to cut them. The September 2003 WTO meetings came to a halt over the issue of agricultural subsidies in Europe and other developed nations, including the United States.[15]

Known collectively as the **Bretton Woods system,** the organizations and agreements discussed above were designed to help the world's trading economies recover and to prevent a recurrence of the circumstances that led to the Great Depression. These measures, it was hoped, as well as humanitarian aid sent under other programs, would lead to economic recovery throughout the world, but especially in Europe.

The Marshall Plan

The Bretton Woods measures alone were not enough. As detailed in Chapter 6, when in 1947 Great Britain terminated economic aid to Greece and Turkey because of its own financial crisis, President Harry Truman concluded that the United States had to step in to avert communist takeovers in the region.[16] Speaking to Congress, Truman declared his intention to help Greece and Turkey: "I believe that our help should be primarily through economic and financial aid which is essential to economic stability and orderly political process."[17]

Other reports from U.S. diplomats and officials painted a picture of increasing despair across Europe. By June 1947, the picture had become clear enough, as well as depressing. Therefore, Secretary of State George Marshall declared in an address he delivered at Harvard that the United States wanted to provide economic assistance to help revive the world economy to "permit the emergence of political and social conditions in which free institutions can exist." This idea soon evolved into the **Marshall Plan,** under which the United States provided about $13 billion in aid to Europe. American economic aid thus became the key to Europe's economic revival.

Meanwhile, in East Asia, Japan benefited from a different kind of American economic assistance. In 1950, North Korea invaded South Korea, deeply changing both the military and economic situation in Asia. Turning to Japan's war-crippled industrial base as a primary source for material to fight in Korea, the United States radically altered its political and economic course with regard to Japan, and the island country began its rapid return to productivity. In essence, the Korean War became the "Marshall Plan" for Japan.

Also in 1950, American encouragement played a major role in influencing France to take the lead in creating the European Coal and Steel Community, thereby integrating its iron and steel production with Germany's. This was the first step down a path that led, in the 1990s, to the creation of the European Union.

As the Cold War escalated in the 1950s and 1960s and as more and more states threw off the shackles of colonialism, the United States used its economic power to try to help these states develop and to thwart the Soviet Union's efforts to expand its influence in the developing world. The United States and other developed states extended loans that had low interest rates, long payback schedules, and grace periods of up to ten years before first payments were required, stirring hope that the success of the Marshall Plan could be repeated globally. On other occasions, the United States and other states provided outright financial grants. Together, these and other types of economic assistance became know as **foreign aid.**

Debate has arisen over what guides foreign policymakers in their decisions about how to distribute foreign aid. The United States, like many other developed nations, has not typically sent its foreign aid dollars to those countries that are most impoverished. Indeed, a 1998 *World Politics* article examined six different motivating factors in foreign aid disbursement: humanitarian need, strategic importance, economic potential, cultural similarity, ideological stance, and regional identification.[18] It found that the two factors most critical in American foreign aid distribution were strategic interests and ideological stance.[19] Thus, the United States put its money where it believed it would most further its national security interests, also tending to support liberal democracies more often than other types of regime. Lest one believe that the United States is the only country disbursing aid from utilitarian rather than humanitarian motives, the study also found that Japan tended to give aid where it had the greatest economic return for Japan, while France had spreading French culture as one of its top foreign aid objectives.[20]

Official Development Assistance

In certain cases, foreign assistance takes a very specific government-sponsored form. That form is called **official development assistance (ODA).** Specific criteria must be met for aid to be ODA. For one thing, only aid to countries on a list of nations considered to be developing is considered ODA. Furthermore, the aid must be at least partially in the form of grants, that is, transfers that need not be repaid.

Unfortunately, ODA has rarely led to economic development. It took years to appreciate that a difference existed between industrial societies that needed assistance in rebuilding wartorn infrastructures and developing societies that lacked both capital and an educated population. Throughout the Cold War, the United States provided loans and grants to many developing states. Contrary to popular belief, though, except for the Marshall Plan, the United States never provided large quantities of economic assistance, and the United States sent most of the aid to allies such as Israel and Egypt. Indeed, by 2001, the United States devoted only 0.10 percent of its gross national product (GNP) to ODA, the lowest percentage among all industrialized states. Between 1992 and 2001, Japan, which devoted 0.28 percent of its GNP to ODA, provided a larger total of ODA than the United States.[21] In 2001, however, the United States retook the top position in absolute

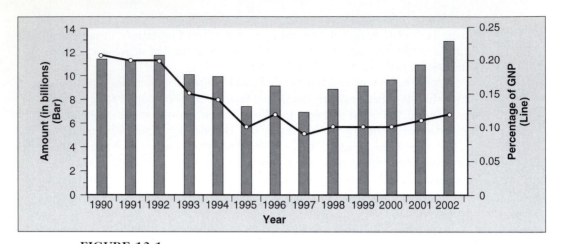

FIGURE 13.1

Official Development Assistance from the United States, 1990–2002

Sources: Lexis/Nexis, *Official Development Assistance from Development Assistance Committee Countries;* OECD, *Official Development Assistance from 1999 to 2002.*

terms, even though America is still not among those who gave the most as a percentage of its national income. Only five northern European nations meet the UN's target of 0.7 percent of GDP devoted to development aid: Denmark, Norway, the Netherlands, Luxembourg, and Sweden.

Perhaps surprisingly, though, the September 2001 terrorist attacks against the United States led to a significant increase in the amount of foreign aid the United States provided. Several senior Bush Administration officials, including the president himself, have observed that poverty breeds terrorism, and Bush in early 2002 called for a "new compact for global development" under which the United States would increase its foreign aid by 50 percent, or $5 billion. Then, in December 2003, Bush announced the largest increase in development assistance since the Kennedy Administration, expanding U.S. ODA transfers by $2 billion.[22] Similarly, while many focused solely on the elements of the new U.S. National Security Strategy that dealt with preemptive defense, Section 7 of the strategy was devoted entirely to poverty-fighting measures. Figure 13.1 provides a summary of U.S. official development assistance.

Currency Intervention

Clearly, trade and aid were significant instruments in the United States' post–World War II international economic arsenal. On occasion, so too was **currency intervention.** One of the most dramatic examples of currency intervention occurred during the 1956 Suez Crisis, when France and Great Britain, attempting to reverse Egyptian President Gamal Abdel Nasser's nationalization of the Suez Canal, and Israel, seeking to acquire territory, invaded Egypt.

The joint British-French-Israeli action caught American leaders completely by surprise. President Dwight Eisenhower declared that the three had made a "complete mess and botch of things,"[23] and Secretary of State John Foster Dulles, in a speech at the United Nations, called the military action "a grave error."[24]

As the situation worsened, the Soviet Union appealed to the United States for joint action. Meanwhile, when Great Britain's dollar reserves fell by 15 percent in three months, London turned to the IMF to shore up the hard-pressed pound.[25] On instructions from Eisenhower, IMF President George Humphrey, an American, refused to release funds unless an immediate cease-fire was implemented and invading forces were withdrawn. Great Britain complied, and French forces, dependent on British logistics, followed suit.

However, withdrawal dragged on for two weeks. Again, the United States used an economic tool of statecraft to goad the British and French into withdrawing. Since the invasion disrupted transcanal shipping, and oil pipelines in Syria had been destroyed, Persian Gulf oil shipments to Europe declined by 36 percent. To replace these losses, America's European allies desperately needed oil from the Western Hemisphere. The United States intervened to prevent such shipments until the invading forces were totally withdrawn. The Anglo-French force was finally withdrawn in late December 1956, and oil shipments began.[26]

The Fall of the Bretton Woods System

The Bretton Woods system was not perfect, but it functioned well enough in the late 1940s, 1950s, and 1960s to provide the Western world with economic stability. During these years, Western economies grew, recovering fully from the ravages of World War II. The American economy was by far the world's largest and strongest.

In the late 1940s, as the system began to operate, a major problem was that, since the U.S. economy was the only one that had not been seriously damaged in World War II and was producing large quantities of consumer goods, too many people wanted U.S. goods, and too few dollars were in foreign hands to pay for them. The question was, "How could more dollars be placed in foreign hands?" The answer was obvious: the United States used transfers such as the Marshall Plan and deficit spending to put dollars overseas. This allowed dollars to flow out so they could be used to purchase American goods. Thus, between 1949 and 1959, U.S. gold assets declined from over $24 billion to slightly under $20 billion, and dollars held abroad climbed from $7 billion to over $19 billion.

Nevertheless, by the 1960s, the system was in trouble, for at least three reasons. First, more dollars were held outside the United States than the United States had gold to cover. Thus, if all countries exercised their option to redeem their dollars in gold, there would have been a run on the U.S. Federal Reserve Bank. Second, as Western economies recovered from World War II, the American share of the world's industrial production declined, and demand for U.S. products declined. Third, during the Vietnam War in the late 1960s, the United States pursued a "guns and butter" economic policy, that is, there was high domestic social spending at the same time the United States was suffering from the burden of war expenditures. As H. Peter Gray put it, the three roles taken on by the United States of military hegemon, financial hegemon, and economic hegemon were irreconcilable. Being a military hegemon required a high level of consumption, and being an economic hegemon required the United States to be a "spender of last resort"—in other words, America buoyed the global economy by maintaining high demand in times of recession. However, the role of safeguarding the value of one's currency, that is, being a financial hegemon, required running a surplus.[27]

By the early 1970s, it was clear that action had to be taken. Facing an uncontrollable outflow of gold and uncontrollable domestic inflation, President Richard Nixon in 1971 unilaterally suspended the dollar's convertibility to gold and levied a 10 percent surcharge on all dutiable imports. Domestically, the U.S. government also instituted a wage and price freeze. For all practical purposes, the United States abandoned the Bretton Woods system, conceding that it could no longer underwrite the system's operations.

By 1972, then, the Bretton Woods system was no more. The exchange value of every major currency now floated with respect to each other based on market action, and orderly changes in the value of international currency no longer took place. While countries with minor currencies had the option of pegging the value of their currency to a major currency like U.S. dollars, British pounds, German marks, or a mixed basket of hard currencies, the major currencies' values were not tied to the value of any commodity, nor were they convertible to a commodity. The great powers had to have strong central banks to control the amount of their money in circulation. Failure to do so could have dire ramifications domestically (e.g., high inflation) or internationally (e.g., deficit spending).

Anarchy and Interdependence: 1974–1995

For the next 20 years, the global community struggled to fashion a viable international economic order. Developed states concentrated on exchange rate management and obtaining currency reserves, and developing states pushed for a new international economic order that would transfer enough capital to them so they could develop and that would create preferential trade arrangements for them so they could sell their products more easily.

For 20 years, little organization existed in the international economic system because of the problems of international trade and finance and because of the end of American financial leadership. For the most part, exchange rates were determined by supply and demand, although an informal agreement existed in which central banks and governments intervened to keep exchange rates within broad imprecise limits.

During these years, several major economic issues buffeted the international community, including the large flow of dollars to oil-producing states, high U.S. interest rates, a growing budget deficit, and the developing world's debt crisis. These concerns were further complicated in the late 1980s as the Soviet Union and its Eastern European communist allies experienced growing economic problems. Little suggested that a new system was over the horizon.

THE GLOBAL ECONOMIC SYSTEM

When the 1990s opened, the international economic system was interdependent and anarchic. American interdependence was demonstrated by the fact that the U.S. economy relied on goods, services, raw materials, labor, and information from other countries. Economic anarchy was also easily documented, with neither the United States nor any other international actor having the will or the ability to provide order to the international economic system.

Why the New System Emerged

As the 1990s progressed, this picture changed, with the United States playing a key role in the emergence of a new global economic system. The United States did this by emphasizing three key factors that the new order required.

First, the United States helped form a consensus among developed states that economic growth could be accelerated and economic power shared through collaborative efforts based on an open economic system. Economic competition would continue, the consensus acknowledged, but a collective system would increase economic prosperity for all. Within the United States, this effort was bipartisan, with most Republicans and Democrats supporting it under the presidencies of George H. W. Bush, Bill Clinton, and George W. Bush.

Second, the United States, in conjunction with other developed states, helped the new noncommunist governments that came to power in Eastern Europe and the former Soviet Union begin integrating their economies with those of the developed states. The United States and other developed states also helped the new governments access development funds from international economic institutions such as the World Bank, and looked on favorably as China and Vietnam increasingly operated their economies on capitalist principles.

Third, the United States, in the late 1980s and throughout the 1990s, encouraged developing nations to seek foreign investment, to cooperate with international lending institutions, and to emphasize privatization and development led by the private sector. Often, the United States provided its own economic aid only to states that followed such programs and policies, a position that began under Ronald Reagan and substantially continued under his successors.

Today's global economic system is very much a by-product of the American vision of an open economic system unencumbered by government-imposed restraints on trade. It is not a completely open system, but it has moved a long way in that direction. It can best be examined in three areas, the first of which we have already explored in some detail: (1) global financial and economic institutions, (2) the increased importance of free trade areas, and (3) annual meetings of the heads of state of the world's leading economic powers.

Global Financial and Economic Institutions

The World Bank and the International Monetary Fund continue to play critical roles in the global economic system. The World Bank, beginning in the 1980s, expanded its role from merely making loans for development projects such as dams, roads, and water systems to lending for more broadly defined structural changes in such areas as financial institutions, labor markets, trade policy, and government spending. The IMF also not only managed to survive the collapse of the Bretton Woods system but expanded its role. While it was intended that the IMF would focus on granting short-term loans for countries in crisis, this institution became involved in reforming the economies of developing nations by placing restrictive conditions on the loans.

It should be noted that the performance of both the IMF and the World Bank have been controversial in their newly revised roles. As James Mittleman points out, the fact that attacks on the IMF and World Bank are coming from all points on the political spectrum, left, right, and center, is an indication that something has definitely gone awry with these two agencies.[28]

The **World Trade Organization (WTO)** also plays a key role in current global economics. The WTO began operating with strong support from the United States and other governments, and often strong opposition from private citizens in America and abroad. Since it replaced GATT in 1995, the WTO has been the world's primary organization for global trade enhancement.[29] The WTO oversees and implements reductions in tariffs and other nontariff barriers that it negotiates, provides procedures for negotiating more tariff reductions, and rules on disputes over trade. In 2004, it had over 150 members.

However, the WTO is not a panacea for all problems of international trade. Indeed, the WTO has been widely criticized as a tool of multinational corporations, an institution that assaults national sovereignty, and an enemy of the environment. These criticisms were the causes behind the demonstrations and riots that greeted the WTO's 1999 Seattle ministerial conference, and most ministerial meeting since then. The WTO may be one of the most influential global economic organizations, but it also has vocal and vehement opponents.

Although the WTO officially must treat all nations equally, developing states sometimes claim that is does not. Indeed, developing states charge that while the United States and other industrialized countries sing the praises of free trade, they often do not practice what they preach. Developing states claim that developed nations are in favor of free trade in principle because it generally benefits these industrially advanced countries, but when it does not benefit them, they are as protectionist as any nation. In no economic sector is this disparity between rhetoric and policy more pronounced than agriculture. Developing nations argue that Western nations must eliminate farm subsidies so that they can compete on a level playing field and take advantage of one of their few advantages, cheap labor. This issue caused India and other nations to walk out on the WTO talks in Cancun, Mexico. Critics point out that the average European cow receives $2.50 per day in agricultural subsidies, more money than 3 billion human beings have to live on.[30] The United States, with a $17 billion a year farm support program, is not far behind.

Free Trade Areas

The United States has been a leading proponent of **free trade areas**.[31] U.S. support of free trade areas is based on the argument that the removal of barriers to free trade accelerates economic growth. As we have seen, the United States during the 1990s played a major role in creating three free trade areas, one of which, the **North American Free Trade Area (NAFTA),** was negotiated during the late 1980s and early 1990s under George H. W. Bush and became operational in the mid-1990s under the Clinton Administration. As we saw in earlier chapters, NAFTA, like other free trade areas, generated controversy. Its supporters claimed that by eliminating tariffs and other economic and noneconomic barriers to trade between the United States, Canada, and Mexico, NAFTA would expand trade and improve living standards in the three countries. NAFTA's critics countered that U.S. capital would move to Mexico to take advantage of lower labor costs and lower environmental standards there.

Undeterred by criticism, the United States under Clinton also worked with 17 Asian and American states, including Canada, China, Japan, and Mexico, to approve in 1994 the **Asian-Pacific Economic Cooperation (APEC) agreement,** which committed all developed signatory states to dismantle barriers to international trade between member states by 2010.[32] Signatory developing states had the same objective set for 2010. By 2000, APEC had grown to 21 members, with a combined gross domestic product equal to half the world's total ($35 trillion) and that included 42 percent of the world's trade.

Later in 1994, the Clinton Administration finalized an agreement for another major free trade area as 34 of the 35 countries in the Western Hemisphere vowed to conclude negotiations for a **Free Trade Area of the Americas (FTAA)** by 2005.[33] Cuba was the only Western Hemisphere country that did not join.

Neither APEC nor FTAA are in force, and many hurdles must be cleared before they are implemented. Nevertheless, free trade areas have gained widespread favor and are important in the global economic community, due in no small part to American support.[34] Table 13.1 provides information on some of the United States' more prominent economic and trade agreements.

G-7 and G-8 Meetings

The United States played a major role in regularizing meetings of the leaders of the world's seven largest Western industrialized countries—Canada, France, Germany, Italy, Japan, the United Kingdom, and the United States. Begun in 1975 and called the G-7 summits, these meetings became the **G-8 summits** in the mid-1990s when Russia became a regular participant. The meetings play a major role in formulating global economic policies, and other policies as well.

For example, at the 1999 G-8 summit in Cologne, Germany, the heads of state agreed to find ways to strengthen Russia's social, structural, and economic reforms and to improve the WTO. They also agreed to support more teacher and student exchanges, develop ways to give globalization a "human face" so that its negative impacts were cushioned, and provide debt relief to heavily indebted poor countries. Similarly, at the 2000 summit in Okinawa, Japan, the heads of state agreed to expand debt relief to developing states and to provide school meals for 9 million children a year in developing states. They also agreed to deposit an additional billion dollars in the World Bank for loans to developing states for education.

Sometimes G-8 summits are criticized for concentrating on discussions and producing few results. They are also sometimes criticized for not following through on previous promises, as when UN Secretary General Kofi Annan, following the 2000 Okinawa G-8 meeting, noted that the leaders did not offer as much debt relief as they had promised in 1999. There is some truth in both criticisms.

Nevertheless, it is important that the leaders of the world's developed states meet to discuss similarities and differences in their perceptions, outlooks, and policies. At a

TABLE 13.1
U.S. ECONOMIC AND TRADE AGREEMENTS

Year	Name	Type	Status	Nature of Agreement
1947	General Agreement on Tariffs and Trade (GATT)	Worldwide multilateral	Superceded by WTO, though the GATT document formed the WTO's umbrella agreement with respect to trade in goods	Post–World War II agreements on international trade in goods; the drive for GATT reflected the desire of the United States to open up trade, and to see an end to discriminatory trade practices between imperial states and their dominions and colonies
1994	World Trade (Organization WTO)	Worldwide multilateral	In effect—over 140 members, with many more in the process of joining	The WTO administers trade agreements, acts as a forum for trade negotiations, settles trade disputes, reviews national trade policies, and assists developing countries with trade difficulties
1989	Asia-Pacific Economic Cooperation (APEC)	Regional multilateral	Not yet in effect, but with regular meetings occurring toward that end. 21 members	Intended to promote economic integration around the Pacific Rim and to sustain economic growth; facilitates discussion among leadership of member states, and encourages financial transparency, reduction of trade barriers, and market-oriented policies
1994	North American Free Trade (Agreement NAFTA)	Regional multilateral	In effect—3 members (U.S., Canada and Mexico)	Phased elimination of import tariffs, elimination of many nontariff barriers, intellectual property rights agreement
2005	Free Trade Area of the Americas (FTAA)	Regional multilateral	Agreement scheduled to take effect in 2005. Currently 34 countries involved in the process	Barriers to trade and investment will be progressively eliminated within the trade area; details of the agreement are still being worked out
1985	U.S.-Israel Free Trade Agreement	Bilateral	In effect—ongoing negotiations are taking place with respect to agricultural product issues	Codifies the nature of acceptable trade barriers, and provides stipulations on trade-relevant issues such as intellectual property rights
1989	U.S.-Canada Free Trade Agreement	Bilateral	In effect—part of this agreement (agricultural agreement) was rolled into NAFTA	Codifies the nature of acceptable trade barriers, and provides stipulations on trade-relevant issues such as intellectual property rights
1999	Agreement on U.S.-China Agricultural Cooperation	Bilateral	In effect	Allows agricultural products (e.g., U.S. wheat, citrus, meat, and poultry) to be directly imported for sale in normal retail stores; reduces tariffs on agricultural products

TABLE 13.1 *(continued)*
U.S. ECONOMIC AND TRADE AGREEMENTS

Year	Name	Type	Status	Nature of Agreement
2001	U.S.- Jordan Free Trade Agreement	Bilateral	In effect	Tariff elimination on industrial and farm products; intellectual property rights agreement
2002	U.S.- Chile Free Trade Agreement	Bilateral	Signed	Reduces barriers on both trade and investment

In addition to the key agreements listed above, the U.S. is engaged in negotiations for free trade agreements with the following countries: Singapore, Morocco, Egypt, and Australia. Furthermore, the U.S. is currently pursuing multilateral free-trade agreement negotiations with many of the nations of Central America to create a regional Central American Free Trade Area (CAFTA).

One should not be led to believe that the term *free trade* means that no tariffs and nontariff barriers exist between the countries. Many more bilateral agreements could be listed here. The subjects of these agreements include trade in specific goods and services, intellectual property rights, investment rights, and mutual recognition of standards of safety and quality. For a more thorough account, visit the United States Trade Representative website at: *http://www.ustr.gov*.

Sources: Thomas Zeiler, *Free Trade Free World: The Advent of GATT* (Chapel Hill: University of North Carolina Press, 1999); U.S. Trade Representative, *http://www.ustr.gov/agreements/index.html;* FTAA website, *http://www.ftaa-alca.org;* WTO website, *http://www.wto.org;* APEC website, *http://www.apec.org;* U.S. Trade Commission website, *http://dataweb.usitc.gov;* Israel-U.S. Free Trade Agreement, available at *http://www.mfa.gov.il*.

Leaders of the world's eight largest industrial economies, with invited leaders from other countries, meet each year at G-8 summits to discuss global issues such as economic and trade policies. Here, G-8 members and guests prepare for a group portrait at the June 2004 Sea Island, Georgia, meeting.

minimum, similarities can be solidified and differences can be prevented from growing. In global economics as elsewhere, this is important. Again, the United States has played a major role in making these meetings occur. Possible topics for future G-8 meetings include terrorism, the AIDS pandemic, the need to advance global free trade, rebuilding Iraq, and "odious debt" relief for Iraq.[35]

The United States, then, has played a major role in shaping today's global economic system. As with the defunct Bretton Wood system, the current system is far from perfect. And questions remain not only about today's global economic system, but also about specific aspects of several U.S. economic policies. We turn to the most important of these now.

CURRENT DEBATES OVER ECONOMIC POLICIES

Despite playing a major role in creating today's global economic system, the United States is not always in complete accord with it. In addition, with so many different viewpoints within the United States about various economic issues, disagreement inevitably exists about American economic policy. Here, we will examine five disagreements and debates over current policies: (1) free trade and globalization, (2) the role of the WTO, (3) revising foreign aid, (4) the role of tariffs and quotas, and (5) the pros and cons of economic sanctions and embargoes.

Free Trade and Globalization

As we saw earlier, the United States has long been committed to free trade and an open international economic system. And the United States is also a major trading nation. In Figure 13.2, we can see the magnitude and direction of American trade. In 2002, for

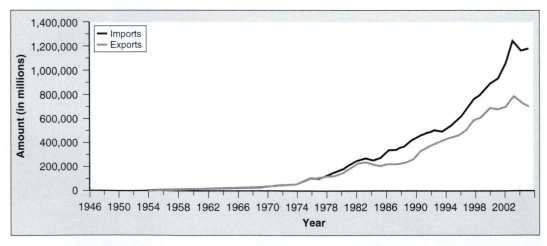

FIGURE 13.2
U.S. Exports and Imports of Goods, 1946–2002

Source: Department of Commerce, Bureau of Economic Analysis.

example, imports to the United States exceeded $450 billion. Access to the U.S. market is critically important to the development of many nations. (America's top ten trading partners are listed in Table 13.2.) South Korea, China, India, Chile, and Poland in particular gain from market access. Trade with these and other states that can receive ODA is almost 40 times larger than ODA and should be followed closely by students of international affairs.[36]

Also, as we have seen, during the last years of the twentieth century and the early twenty-first century, the international economic system moved significantly toward freer trade in goods, services, and financial instruments. This process, known as **globalization,** resulted in the growth and realization of worldwide economic interdependence, that is, the mutual dependence of all but a few of the world's poorest economies on one another.[37] Globalization has been spurred by two factors.

First, during the late twentieth century, many countries, including the United States, began to remove barriers to the movement of people, capital, goods, services, and ideas across national boundaries. The United States was often a leader in this process with NAFTA, APEC, and FTAA, but many other countries and regions of the world were also successfully involved in such efforts, perhaps most notably Europe, where what began as the European Economic Community evolved into the European Community and then the European Union.

Second, technology, especially transportation technology and information and communication technology, spurred the growth of globalization. Technology expanded human ability to move people, capital, goods, services, and ideas reliably and inexpensively over long distances in short periods of time, so the growth of global interdependence was virtually inevitable.

Globalization proceeded as rapidly as it did due in no small part to the policies of several consecutive American administrations, beginning with the Reagan presidency, which committed the United States to pursuing free trade and establishing an open international

TABLE 13.2
AMERICA'S TOP 10 TRADING PARTNERS

	1984	*1994*	*2002*
1	Canada	Canada	Canada
2	Japan	Japan	Mexico
3	Mexico	Mexico	Japan
4	United Kingdom	United Kingdom	China
5	Germany	Germany	Germany
6	Taiwan	China	United Kingdom
7	South Korea	Taiwan	South Korea
8	France	South Korea	Taiwan
9	Italy	France	France
10	Netherlands	Singapore	Italy

Source: International Trade Administration, *Trade Rankings for U.S. Trading Partners, 1984–2002,* *http://www.ita.doc.gov/td/industry/otea/usfth/aggregate/h02t58.html.*

economic regime. George H. W. Bush and Bill Clinton followed suit, as has George W. Bush, who emphasized five points in his administration's international economic policy: (1) establishing global, regional, and bilateral trade agreements; (2) liberalizing trade with the developing world; (3) assisting American citizens adversely affected by globalization; (4) advancing core American values such as the rule of law, freedom and democracy, and strict labor, environmental, and health standards; and (5) encouraging transparent trade negotiations and agreements.[38]

Not all Americans share the U.S. government's enthusiasm for free trade and an open economic system. Domestic U.S. opponents of free trade include trade unions, conservative nationalists, environmentalists, and child welfare and women's health advocates. Trade unions and workers fear that an open trading regime will reduce the number of jobs in the United States as capital goes overseas to find lower labor costs. Conservative nationalists fear that American economic strength will be reduced, U.S. sovereignty compromised, and American strategic capabilities will be diminished. Environmentalists fear that companies will move production overseas where environmental standards are lower. Child welfare and women's health advocates fear that globalization will move production to countries where children and women work for little pay and in miserable working conditions.

On occasion, opponents of free trade and an open economic system succeeded in slowing movement toward globalization. One prime method was to block passage in Congress of bills granting the president and executive branch **trade promotion authority,** or **fast-track authority**—the ability to negotiate and then present Congress with trade pacts that Congress would quickly approve or disapprove as a whole. George W. Bush pushed Congress to pass fast-track legislation almost from his first day in office in 2001, but congressional opponents blocked its passage until mid-2002.

Without such authority, the United States has watched as other countries conclude a host of free trade and special customs agreements. The United States lags far behind many other countries in this regard. For example, the United States has completed only a handful of comprehensive bilateral and multilateral trade agreements. As one might expect, while a president may be very much in favor of free trade, he can expect to run into resistance when it comes to getting the support of legislators, who have a vested interest in protecting industries and economic sectors that feature prominently in their district.

Beyond those that the European Union already participates in, the EU in 2002 had another 15 trade agreements under negotiation.[39] These realities alarm American proponents of free trade, an open economic system, and globalization, causing them to fear that the United States in future years will lose market share, see exports decline, suffer job losses, and go into economic decline. George W. Bush's administration sided with this outlook, asserting that it, like the three administrations that preceded it, remains committed to policies that "will remove trade barriers in foreign markets, while further liberalizing our market at home."[40] Even so, debate over free trade, an open economic system, and globalization are certain to be central elements of the American political landscape for years to come.

The Role of the WTO

Inevitably, the debate over free trade and globalization spills over into questions about the World Trade Organization and the United States' role in it. Successive U.S. administrations have strongly supported the WTO, arguing that it is an institution that will increase American and global economic prosperity. They argue that by reducing tariffs and other barriers to trade and by resolving trade disputes, the WTO will expand global trade. This, they assert, is good because the United States and other countries will be able to concentrate on producing those items that they produce the best and the least expensively. More of everything will therefore be available, they maintain, thereby improving everyone's standard of living. According to World Bank estimates, a new round of reductions of market barriers could raise global output by between $290 billion and $520 billion, and raise 144 million people out of poverty by 2015.

Other Americans see the WTO as a tool of multinational corporations that will eliminate American jobs, assault national sovereignty, permit corporations to destroy the environment, and promote workplace abuse of women and children. The only people who really benefit are those who own, control, or work for multinational corporations, WTO opponents charge. By creating a global economic system where capital and goods can move easily, the WTO encourages American capital and jobs to be exported to countries where labor is cheap, they assert. American workers lose their jobs, they say, even as American sovereignty is jeopardized as the United States depends more and more on imports. What is more, opponents say, free trade and the WTO allow big business to move production to countries where environmental laws and laws protecting workers are lax. This decreases the companies' cost of operation and increases profits, but it also destroys the environment by allowing companies to pollute and to take advantage of workers, especially women and children, critics charge.

This debate is not just intellectual. When the WTO met in Seattle in 1999, many American trade unionists and workers, conservative nationalists, environmentalists, and children's and women's rights advocates attempted to disrupt the meeting. Large-scale demonstrations, violence, and riots broke out in opposition to the WTO, not only in Seattle but in most other city where the WTO has met. Clearly, passions run high over the WTO.

The Role of Tariffs and Quotas

With its commitment to free trade and an open economic system, it is not surprising that the United States, as a rule, opposes tariffs and quotas. Indeed, each year since 1988, the United States has highlighted what it sees as shortcomings in its trading partners' activities in the **National Trade Estimate Report on Foreign Trade Barriers.** Prepared by the Office of the U.S. Trade Representative, the estimate details the U.S. view of trade problems related to tariffs and non-economic barriers to trade.

For example, the 2002 report declared that Japan is "beset with structural rigidity, excessive regulation and market-access barriers," and states that "the Japanese economy continues to under perform." More specifically, the report called for regulatory reforms so that Japan could "more fully realize its economic potential."[41] The report devoted almost 10 percent of its 450 pages to Japan, but it also covered 54 other states, providing harsh commentary on the European Union, China, and South Korea.

The report has also become the tool for beginning debate over trade issues between foreign governments and the U.S. Trade Office. States reviewed particularly harshly usually produce rebuttals. Either the United States or the criticized country often also files a complaint with the WTO following release of the report. At times, the United States may also impose trade sanctions soon after the report is released. The document receives extensive media attention each year, some of which is highly critical of U.S. policy.

Sometimes, despite its preference for free trade and an open economic system, the United States itself resorts to tariffs. For example, both to protect American farmers and steel producers and to gain congressional passage of a trade promotion authority bill that would give him authority to negotiate preferential trade agreements, President George W. Bush in early 2002 approved tariffs and subsidies for farm goods and steel, even though this was contrary to the president's own free market preferences and to prevailing international law and practices favoring reductions in subsidies and tariffs as determined by the WTO.

Japan, the European Union, South Korea, and other states reacted quickly to the U.S. action, filing charges against the United States with the WTO even though Bush claimed he had acted under WTO provisions that tariffs could be imposed if imports caused "serious harm." The WTO ruled against the American agriculture and steel tariffs and subsidies, determining that the EU by itself could impose $4 billion in penalties against the United States because it provided tax breaks to exporters, an action considered an illegal subsidy under international law. The EU announced it would not impose the penalties after the United States modified its tariff position, satisfied that the WTO's ruling had served effectively as a "shot-across-the-bow" of the United States.

The United States has low average tariffs in comparison to most states, and Figure 13.3 shows that average U.S. tariffs for nonagricultual and nonfuel imports have declined

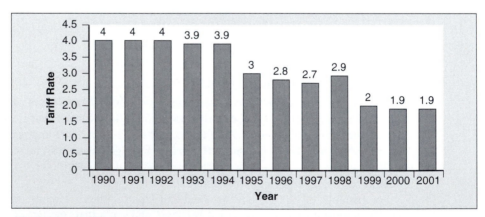

FIGURE 13.3
Average U.S. Import Tariff (nonagricultural and nonfuel)
Sources: UNCTAD (UN Commission on Trade and Development).

over the past decade. Still, many have criticized the structure of U.S. tariffs. For example, according to Edward Gresser, America's tariff system affects the poor the most, both domestically and overseas. Gresser states that, while U.S. tariffs on raw materials and high-tech consumer goods are extremely low, tariffs on low-cost consumer goods are quite high. Thus, domestic buyers of cheap clothing and shoes are disproportionately affected, as are foreign producers that have labor-intensive economies.[42] Low-tech consumer goods have an average tariff of 10.8 percent, while the average tariff on all other items is 0.8 percent.

The Pros and Cons of Sanctions and Embargoes

Economic sanctions and embargoes have been major elements of American economic statecraft dating back to the American Revolution. America's use of sanctions and embargoes was also illustrated earlier in this chapter in the discussion of policies toward Japan before World War II, and in 1956 against Britain, France and Israel for their invasion of Egypt. Often, however, Americans do not realize the extent to which their government uses economic sanctions and embargoes as an instrument of statecraft even today.

Indeed, during the 1990s and into the twenty-first century, the United States used one form or another of economic sanction against 75 states.[43] Some sanctions achieved the desired results, and others did not. Regardless of the success of sanctions in achieving the policy results that the United States desired, they do have an impact. One study concluded that sanctions reduced U.S. exports by almost $20 billion and cost the work force 200,000–250,000 jobs.[44] Critics contend that such activity only results in the antipathy of target states, criticism from allies, and lost market opportunities.

Many policy options fall under the rubric of sanctions. In addition to the economic sanctions addressed in this chapter, there are diplomatic, political, and cultural sanctions as well. Diplomatic and political sanctions include deporting a country's diplomatic mission, refusing to enter negotiations contingent on a desired behavior, and restricting foreign aid. Cultural sanctions include denying a state membership in international organizations or access to international events. However, economic sanctions seem to come to the fore when people think of sanctions.

The most basic type of economic sanction is the trade embargo, which is a prohibition against importing from or exporting to the target country. Other economic sanctions include imposing tariff or nontariff barriers to trade against the target nation, freezing that nation's financial assets, or prohibiting investment in the targeted country. In some cases limited embargoes are put in place to deny the targeted country specific goods or services; such sanctions are called instrumental sanctions. A common form of trade limitation is the arms embargo, in which nonweapon imports are allowed. This method has been put to use in developing nations that are in turmoil (e.g., Liberia, Angola, Rwanda, and Somalia), and in which there is no desire to inflict further economic hardship on the citizens of the targeted country. Other limited embargoes target goods required to build weapons of mass destruction, or focus on strategic resources like petroleum. Table 13.3 gives details of some of the more prominent U.S. and UN uses of sanctions in recent years.

TABLE 13.3
KEY U.S. AND UN IMPOSED SANCTIONS

Nation	Time Period	Action Taken	Desired Effect	Outcome
Cuba	Began 1962, still in effect	Trade embargo, ban on travel from U.S. to Cuba, Cuban assets in U.S. frozen. Recently actions have been taken to ease the embargo	Encourage regime change; end state state sponsorship of terrorism; discourage human rights violations	These long-running sanctions have had little noticeable impact on the Cuban regime
South Africa	U.S. imposed sanctions 1986. Economic sanctions lifted Oct. 1993 and diplomatic lifted April 1994	Export ban imposed by Reagan Administration; UN imposed arms embargo; European Community trade and financial sanctions	End the apartheid system	Objectives were achieved after the imposition of these sanctions, though the effectiveness of the sanctions is in question
Rhodesia	1965–1979	Diplomatic sanctions (nonrecognition of government in power), ending of economic relations by many countries, and an embargo on oil exports	Oust a regime of white minority of elites that had taken control after announcing independence from Great Britain	The role of sanctions appears to be minimal
Iraq	1990–2003	Initially all trade and financial transactions with Iraq were prohibited. As the result of a humanitarian crisis, in 1995 the UN set up an Oil for Food program that allowed Iraq to purchase humanitarian supplies with proceeds from petroleum sales (UN Res. 986)	Initially, to get Iraq to vacate Kuwait, then to force cooperation with the arms inspection process and arms control requirements of peace treaty	The objectives were achieved, though use of force rather than sanctions was the principal factor in success
Guatemala	1993	Diplomatic pressure and threat of economic sanctions	Dissuade the military from supporting a coup	Diplomatic action appeared to be successful

TABLE 13.3 *(continued)*
KEY U.S. AND UN IMPOSED SANCTIONS

Nation	Time Period	Action Taken	Desired Effect	Outcome
Former Yugoslavia	1991–1995	Arms embargo, economic sanctions, and economic assets frozen. Initiated by the European Community	End fighting and force parties to negotiating table; also used to force the government to give up indicted war criminals	Sanctions may have contributed to the decision by Milosevic to come to the bargaining table in Dayton, Ohio; however, NATO bombing and the impact of war were more tangible causes
Libya	UN Security Council imposed March 1992	Embargo on arms and aircraft-related products; tightened in November 1993 to include freezing financial assets abroad and prohibiting oil purchases and foreign direct investment	End Libyan for support terrorism	Libya has made substantial changes with respect to support for terrorism; sanctions may be one element of this success
Haiti	Began in 1990	Trade embargo (except humanitarian goods); later worldwide ban on oil shipments, seizure of financial assets, revoked visas of military leaders	Response to a coup that overturned an election	Sanctions were not effective in changing the military's behavior prior to the military intervention
Liberia	UN began in November 1992	Arms embargo	Create internal order in a wartorn state	Peacekeepers were sent in, and in early 1997 elections took place
Somalia	January 1992 to mid-1994	Arms embargo	Instill order in wartorn state	Arms embargo was not effective because of a previous build-up of weapons

Sources: John Stremlau, *Sharpening International Sanctions: Toward a Stronger Role for the United Nations* (Washington, D.C.: Carnegie Commission on Preventing Deadly Conflicts, 1996); Bruce Bartlett, "What's Wrong with Trade Sanctions?" *Policy Analysis* 64 (December 23, 1985); Arne Tostensen and Beate Bull, "Are Smart Sanctions Feasible?" *World Politics* 54 (3) (2002): 373–403.

The two best known instances of American economic sanctions are those against Cuba and Iraq. Economic sanctions against Cuba began after the 1962 Cuban missile crisis. The United States placed an almost total embargo against the island state, hoping that it would force Castro out, or at least influence him to reduce Cuba's support for revolutionary movements elsewhere in Latin America.

As is often the case with economic sanctions, however, it was difficult to end all trade with Cuba. Cuba had close ties with the Soviet Union and Eastern European states, which bought Cuban products and provided subsidies to lessen the impact of the American embargo. During the Cold War, Cuba received $5–6 billion per year from the Soviet Union.[45] After Eastern Europe's communist states collapsed and the Soviet Union broke up, this money flow ceased, and it was believed that the embargo had a better chance to succeed.

Congress also tightened the embargo in 1992, passing the Cuban Democracy Act, which prohibited foreign subsidiaries of U.S.-owned or -controlled businesses from trading with Cuba. Congress strengthened the embargo again in 1996 with the Cuban Liberty and Democratic Solidarity Act (the Helms-Burton Act), which codified the embargo, strengthened its enforcement, created a base for private lawsuits against Cuba in U.S. courts, and prohibited granting visas to anyone who used "confiscated property claimed by a U.S. national."[46] Many American friends and allies decried the reach of the expanded embargo, with the European Union even taking the issue to the WTO. Nevertheless, despite the embargo, Castro remained firmly in power.

The Iraqi situation is equally instructive. Sanctions were imposed on Iraq after it invaded Kuwait in 1990, first to force Iraq to withdraw and then, after Saddam's forces were expelled from Kuwait, to punish Iraq for noncompliance with a number of UN resolutions. The embargo had a crippling effect on Iraq's economy despite the ability of Iraq to sometimes skirt the embargo and despite the UN's agreement to allow Iraq to sell a small amount of oil to earn hard currency so it could import food.

Nevertheless, Saddam stood defiant against the embargo and the international community, refusing to allow arms inspections and ignoring other UN resolutions as well. In late 2002, Iraq permitted UN inspectors to enter the country once again to search for weapons of mass destruction. This, however, was more the result of a threatened American military assault against Iraq than the embargo. What is more, the question of who was truly hurt by the embargo, Saddam and his government or the Iraqi people, was raised by Human Rights Watch and Amnesty International, among others.

Clearly, evidence is available both to support and to oppose economic sanctions and embargoes as effective elements of statecraft. For either to be effective, it may well be necessary to have specific sets of conditions. What those conditions may be, however, cannot be clearly generalized in all cases. A great deal depends upon the will of the targeted regime to suffer the sanctions, and its ability to transfer the burden of the sanctions onto its citizenry, or a portion of its citizenry, to which it does not feel accountable. For the future, then, it is certain that the United States, and other countries as well, will continue to use economic sanctions and embargoes as tools to try to achieve their foreign policy objectives.

Revising Foreign Aid Policy

One of the most dramatic recent initiatives in American economic statecraft is the revision of foreign aid policy undertaken by George W. Bush's administration. This revision had two historical antecedents. The first was the September 2000 UN Millennium Summit in New York, where world leaders pledged to mount a 15-year campaign against world poverty, illiteracy, and disease. The campaign's ultimate goal is to cut world poverty in half by 2015. The second antecedent was the September 2001 terrorist attack against the United States. Recognizing that poverty and hopelessness were fertile breeding grounds for terrorism, Bush on several occasions in the months after the attack stressed the need to reduce poverty and hopelessness, not only in Afghanistan but in other developing states as well.

These antecedents came together in March 2002 when President Bush announced the creation of a U.S. "Millennium Challenge Account" that would expand official American overseas development assistance by $5 billion between 2002 and 2005.[47] In many people's eyes, this was both a welcome and necessary step, since the United States extended only a small amount of official development assistance, $9.95 billion in 2000—that is only 0.10 percent of its GNP, the lowest percentage in the industrialized world.[48]

As important as the increase was, the manner in which the new aid will be dispersed and the way in which its impact will be monitored may be of even greater significance. Bush stipulated that developing states seeking aid from the United States must have "good governance, attention to health and education, and sound economic policies that fostered the free-market."[49] This was a significant change in the criteria for dispersing foreign aid.

Correspondingly, Bush directed the Department of State to develop "clear and concrete objective conditions" for dispersing aid, with assistance being tied or conditional, depending on the ability of the recipient state to fight corruption and implement supportive political and economic reforms. Aid would also be "results driven" or "results oriented." According to Bush, "For decades, success of development aid was measured only in the resources spent, not the results achieved. Yet pouring money into a failed status quo does little to help the poor, and can actually delay the progress of reform." The president also stressed that developed states should share their wealth, and emphasized that countries that produced wealth, practiced economic freedom, and pursued "political liberty, the rule of law and human rights" should be rewarded. In keeping with his free trade orientation, he also noted that lower tariffs and open markets were critical to development.[50]

Later in 2002, Bush presented his program to more than 50 heads of state who were attending the week-long meeting of the UN International Conference of Financing for Development in Monterrey, Mexico. The heads of state reiterated the need for assistance to the more than one billion people in the world living on less than one dollar per day, and reached what came to be called the "Monterrey Consensus" on the new developmental goals.[51] Even so, domestic and foreign critics assailed the new U.S. effort as too little, too much tied to a conservative economic agenda, and too narrowly focused on America's own interests and ideology.

Free trade, globalization, the role of the WTO, the role of tariffs, the utility of economic sanctions and embargoes, and the revision of foreign aid are not the only critical international economic issues with which twenty-first-century American foreign policy grapples. After defending the homeland, however, they are among the most important. While each of these issues is critical, most analysts would agree that there is no clear-cut answer regarding what policies will result in optimal outcomes for the United States. Inevitably, then, debate will continue. Is free trade and globalization good or bad? How much power should the WTO have? What role should the United States play in the WTO? Are tariffs good or bad? Do sanctions and embargoes work? How much foreign aid should be given, and should it be contingent on reforms? These are a few of the questions that have been central to American economic statecraft for years. Nothing indicates that their importance, or the level of disagreement over them, will diminish.

SUMMARY

After independence, the 13 American states faced a number of international economic problems as each state issued its own money and put tariffs and taxes on goods imported from each other. Also, it was difficult to go from being a member of the British Empire to being in competition with it. The U.S. Constitution solved some of these problems, but trade difficulties soon led to confrontations with Great Britain, France, and the Barbary states.

Tariffs played a key role in early U.S. international economic policy, but agricultural and manufacturing interests disagreed on tariffs for most of the early and middle nineteenth century. After the Civil War, U.S. industries no longer needed to be protected by tariffs, but they were. At the same time, the need for markets and the belief that the United States needed to export surplus production led the United States to build a sizable navy.

U.S. trade grew immensely during and after World War I. By the war's end, the United States had become the world's leading economic power. Its economy grew until 1929, when the Great Depression struck. High tariffs and financial speculation contributed to the grim global economic situation of the time.

Throughout the 1930s, tensions escalated in Europe. In 1939, war again erupted in Europe. After first passing the Neutrality Acts, Congress supported Roosevelt's request to pass the Lend-Lease Act, which allowed him to "sell, transfer title to, exchange, lease, lend, or otherwise dispose of" weapons for the defense of states he held vital to U.S. defense. The United States also used economic levers of statecraft in the Far East. In 1940 and 1941, the United States embargoed oil and metal sales to Japan and froze Japanese assets. Japan considered these actions cause for war and in December 1941 attacked Pearl Harbor.

As World War II drew to a close, the global economy was in shambles. The United States helped create the Bretton Woods system, which included the World Bank, the International Monetary Fund, and the General Agreement on Tariffs and Trade, to help the world's economies recover and prevent another depression. The system functioned well, but by the late 1960s, it was in trouble. In the early 1970s, the United States abandoned the system, conceding it could no longer underwrite it. Every major currency now floated with respect to each other, based on market action.

For the next 20 years, the global community struggled to fashion a viable international economic order. During these years, several major economic issues buffeted the international community, including the large flow of dollars to oil-producing states, high U.S. interest rates and a growing budget deficit, and the developing world's debt crisis. When the 1990s opened, the international economic system was interdependent and anarchic.

As the 1990s progressed, this changed as the United States played a key role in the emergence of a new global economic system. The new system, which remains substantially in place today, includes (1) international financial and economic institutions such as the World Bank, the IMF, and the World Trade Organization; (2) free trade areas such as those under the North American Free Trade Agreement, the Asian-Pacific Economic Cooperation agreement, and the Free Trade Area of the Americas; and (3) regular meetings of the leaders of the world's eight largest Western industrialized countries, called the G-8.

Even though the United States plays a major role in today's global economic system, Americans rarely see eye-to-eye about economic policies. Disagreement over free trade, globalization, the WTO, tariffs, economic sanctions and embargoes, and foreign aid are some of the issues with which Americans grapple. Inevitably, debate will continue.

KEY TERMS AND CONCEPTS

Model Treaty
post-independence trade conflicts
tariff policy
Dawes Plan
Reciprocal Trade Agreements Act
International Monetary Fund (IMF)
World Bank
General Agreement on Tariffs and Trade (GATT)
Bretton Woods system
Marshall Plan
foreign aid
official development assistance (ODA)
currency intervention

World Trade Organization (WTO)
free trade areas
North American Free Trade Agreement (NAFTA)
Asia-Pacific Economic Cooperation (APEC) agreement
Free Trade Area of the Americas (FTAA) agreement
G-8 summits
globalization
trade promotion authority, or fast-track authority
National Trade Estimate Report on Foreign Trade Barriers

THINKING CRITICALLY

1. How and why did the United States become involved in international trading conflicts during the late eighteenth and early nineteenth centuries?

2. What are tariffs, and why did they become controversial in the United States?

3. To what extent did U.S. international trade policy bear responsibility for the Great Depression?

4. How did the United States use economic levers of statescraft in the Far East in the years before World War II, and how effective were they as tools of policy?

5. What was the Bretton Woods system, how did it function, and how successful was it?

6. What was the Marshall Plan, and how successful was it?

7. What is official development assistance (ODA), and what are its pros and cons?

8. A new international trading system began to emerge in the 1990s based on free trade areas, the World Trade Organization, and G-8 meetings. What are these structures, how do they work, and how successful have they been?

9. What is globalization, and to what extent has it helped or hindered the United States?

10. Using specific examples to support your arguments, explain to what extent foreign aid has helped the United States achieve its foreign policy objectives.

11. Provide specific examples to assess the strengths and weaknesses of embargoes and economic sanctions as tools of economic statescraft.

NOTES

1. See David A. Baldwin, *Economic Statecraft* (Princeton: Princeton University Press, 1985), for additional discussion of negative and positive economic sanctions

2. The Intolerable Acts consisted of five distinct acts. The Quartering Act required colonists to house British troops as required. The Quebec Act formed a government for Quebec. The Massachusetts Government Act required the government of Massachusetts Bay to be appointed and not elected. The Administration of Justice Act dictated how justice would be carried out in Massachusetts. Finally, the Boston Port Act was specifically designed to avoid a repeat of the Boston Tea Party by preventing dumping of goods in the harbor.

3. Thomas Paine, *Common Sense,* as quoted in Thomas G. Paterson et al., *American Foreign Relations: A History to 1920,* 5th ed. (Boston: Houghton Mifflin, 2000), pp. 6–8.

4. Thomas A. Bailey, *A Diplomatic History of the American People* (New York: Appleton-Century-Crofts, 1958), pp. 27–29.

5. David McCullough, *John Adams* (New York: Simon and Schuster, 2001), p. 161.

6. Glyndon G. VanDeusen, *The Jacksonian Era: 1818–1848* (New York: Harper and Row, 1959), p. 18.

7. VanDeusen, *The Jacksonian Era,* p. 20.

8. Paterson, *American Foreign Relations,* p. 173.

9. Milton Friedman and Anna J. Schwartz, "Money and Business Cycles," *Review of Economics and Statistics* 45(1) (February 1963): 32–64.

10. Friedman and Schwartz, "Money and Business Cycles," p. 143.

11. Quoted in Paterson, *American Foreign Relations,* p. 213.

12. Hugh Borton, *Japan's Modern Century,* 2nd ed. (New York: Ronald Press, 1970), p. 421.

13. Steven Hook and John Spanier, *American Foreign Policy since World War II* (Washington, D.C.: CQ Press, 2000), p. 54.

14. Joseph Stiglitz, *Globalization and Its Discontents* (New York: Norton, 2002), p. 52.

15. Thomas Zeiler, *Free Trade Free World: The Advent of GATT* (Chapel Hill: University of North Carolina Press, 1999). For a discussion of the wool tariff controversy, see Zeiler, pp. 89–104.

16. Dean Acheson, *Present at the Creation: My Years in the State Department* (New York: Norton, 1969), p. 217.

17. Acheson, *Present at the Creation,* p. 222.
18. Peter Schraeder, Steven Hook, and Bruce Taylor, "Clarifying the Foreign Aid Puzzle: A Comparison of American, Japanese, French, and Swedish Aid Flows," *World Politics* 50(2) (1998): 294–323.
19. Schraeder, Hook, and Taylor, "Clarifying the Foreign Aid Puzzle," p. 299.
20. Schraeder, Hook, and Taylor, "Clarifying the Foreign Aid Puzzle," pp. 301–303.
21. *Atlanta Journal-Constitution* (March 17, 2002): A16.
22. Elizabeth Becker, "$2 Billion Rise in Foreign Aid Is Mostly to Fight AIDS in Africa," *New York Times* (December 7, 2003).
23. Townsend Hoopes, *The Devil and John Foster Dulles* (Boston: Little, Brown, 1973), p. 377.
24. Hoopes, *The Devil and John Foster Dulles,* p. 379.
25. Hoopes, *The Devil and John Foster Dulles,* p. 384.
26. Hoopes, *The Devil and John Foster Dulles,* p. 388.
27. H. Peter Gray, "The Burdens of Global Leadership," in *International Trade in the 21st Century,* ed. Khosrow Fatemi (Tarrytown, N.Y.: Pergamon, 1997), pp. 17–27.
28. James Mittelman, *The Globalization Syndrome: Transformation and Resistance* (Princeton: Princeton University Press, 2000), p. 233.
29. For additional details on the World Trade Organization, see Jeffrey J. Schott, *The WTO after Seattle* (Washington, D.C.: Institute for International Economics, 2000), and Bhagirath L. Das, *World Trade Organization: A Guide to New Frameworks for International Trade* (New York: Saint Martin's Press, 2000).
30. Anne Applebaum, "The New Radical Chic," *Washington Post* (September 10, 2003).
31. See Philip I. Levy, "A Political-Economic Analysis of Free Trade Agreements," *American Economic Review* (September 1997): 506–519; and Edward D. Mansfield and Helen V. Miler, "The New Wave of Regionalism," *International Organization* (Summer 1999): 589–627.
32. For additional discussions of APEC, see Martin Rudner, "APEC: The Challenges of Asia Pacific Economic Cooperation," *Modern Asian Studies* (May 1995): 404–437; and Nicole Gallant et al., "APEC's Dilemmas: Institution Building around the Pacific Rim," *Pacific Affairs* (Summer 1997): 203–218.
33. For additional discussion about the FTAA, see Cesar Gaviria, "The Future of the Hemisphere," *Journal of Inter-American Studies and World Affairs* (Spring 1997): 5–11; and Paulo S. Wrobel, "A Free Trade Area of the America by 2005?" *International Affairs* (July 1998): 547–561.
34. *Atlanta Journal-Constitution* (March 17, 2002): A16.
35. "Odious debt" is money promised by a dictator for projects that did not serve the public in general. Many believe that when a dictatorship is overthrown or collapses, the people should not be held accountable for lavish spending that did not benefit them. The United States has championed relief for Iraq, but other nations, such as France, are reluctant to sign off on this relief and lose money they are owed.
36. *Atlanta Journal-Constitution* (March 17, 2002): A16.
37. See Robert Hunter, "Global Economics," in *The Global Century: Globalization and National Security,* ed. Richard Kugler and Ellen Frost, (Washington, D.C.: National Defense University Press, 2001), p. 111.
38. See Robert B. Zoellick, U.S. Trade Representative, "The United States and the World Trading System," Strasbourg, France, May 15, 2001, *http://www.ustr.gov/speechtest/zoellick/zoellick_4.html.*
39. See Robert B. Zoellick, "Free Trade and the Hemispheric Hope," presented to the Council of the Americas, Washington, D.C., May 7, 2001, *http://www.ustr.gov/speechtest/zoellick/zoellick_2.html.*
40. See Executive Office of the President, "USTR 2001 Trade Policy Agenda and 2000 Annual Report," Washington, D.C., March 6, 2001, *http://www.ustr.gov/releases/2001/03/01-13.html.*
41. *Japan Times* (April 4, 2002): 1.
42. Edward Gresser, "Toughest on the Poor: America's Flawed Tariff System," *Foreign Affairs* 81(6) (November/December 2002): 9–14.
43. Richard E. O'Leary, "Statement to Congress," in *Taking Sides: Clashing Views on Controversial Issues in American Foreign Policy,* 2nd ed., ed. John T. Rourke (Guilford, Conn.: McGraw-Hill/Dushkin, 2002), p. 118.

44. O'Leary, "Statement to Congress," p. 119.

45. Michael Ranneberger, "Statement," in Rourke, *Taking Sides,* p. 125.

46. Michael Ranneberger, "Statement," in Rourke, *Taking Sides,* p. 127.

47. *New York Times* (March 15, 2002).

48. OECD, "A Mixed Picture of Official Development Assistance in 2001: The United States Becomes the World's Largest Donor Again; Most EU Members' Aid Also Rise," *http://www.oecd.org,* May 13, 2002.

49. OECD, "A Mixed Picture of Official Development Assistance."

50. *Atlanta Journal-Constitution* (March 23, 2002).

51. See Kofi A. Annan, "Invest in the World's Future," *Japan Times* (March 22, 2002), p. 18.

CHAPTER 14

Using the American Military Overseas

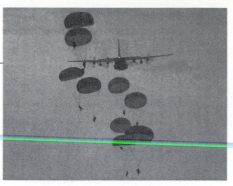

The United States has frequently used its military overseas, and frequently paratroopers, because of the element of surprise they provide, are among the first troops deployed.

- Why should American armed forces be used overseas?
- When should American armed forces be used overseas?
- How should American armed forces be used overseas?"

In one form or another, presidents and other American foreign policy decision makers have faced these three questions since the earliest days of the Republic. George Washington debated these questions regarding U.S. relations with Canada. John Adams pondered them during the undeclared naval war with France. Thomas Jefferson wondered whether to use U.S. military force against the Barbary states of North Africa. Few issues rivet public attention in the United States more than using American armed forces overseas. Few issues have more potential to divide the country than the use of America's armed forces, as the Korean and Vietnam Wars showed—or to unite the country, as in the 1991 Persian Gulf War and the first phases of the war on terrorism.

It continues to be important to ask and answer these questions today: why, when, and how should American armed forces be used overseas? George H. W. Bush had to confront these questions before he determined that it was in the United States' interest to use military force to expel Iraq from Kuwait. Bill Clinton determined that it was in America's interest to use cruise missiles against Sudan and Afghanistan and deploy American armed might to Kosovo to stop ethnic cleansing there. George W. Bush sent American armed forces to Afghanistan and the Philippines to conduct the global war against terrorism, and he sent American armed forces to fight in Iraq to end the reign of a ruler believed bent on developing weapons of mass destruction.

Indeed, between 1798 and 1993 alone, the United States used its military overseas on 234 occasions, sometimes to achieve American objectives via combat and other times to achieve American objectives simply by showing a military presence.[1] Since 1993, American armed force has been deployed to Bosnia, Sudan, Serbia, Kosovo, Afghanistan, the Philippines, Georgia, Yemen, Iraq, and elsewhere. Clearly, armed force continues to be a critical element of American foreign policy. Often, it is the subject of considerable contention as well, as with the U.S.-led invasion of Iraq in 2003, against which numerous U.S. allies, such as France, Germany, and Russia, were vehemently opposed. While polls showed majority domestic support, there was vociferous opposition inside the United States as well, especially after the main combat phase of the war ended and insurgents inflicted a growing casualty count on American forces.

It is vitally important that policymakers determine why, when, and how military force is to be used in advance of its use, and that they develop realistic and precise answers to these questions. Some, most notably Fred Iklé, suggest that it is also critically important to consider how a war will be concluded before one is begun.[2] In this chapter, we explore the dilemmas posed by the reality of American global power and presence, examine several case studies of the use of American armed forces, and speculate on the future of American overseas military interventions.

THE DILEMMAS OF POWER AND PRESENCE

As we saw in Part I of this text, and will see again more concisely in the rest of this chapter, the reality of American power and presence often places American foreign policy decision makers on the horns of multiple dilemmas as they attempt to answer the questions of whether, when, and how to use the U.S. military. The dilemmas they face may be easier to understand if intervention is viewed on a continuum, with one extreme occupied by those who oppose any use of American military force overseas and the other extreme held by those who are willing to intervene anywhere to defend American interests.

Those who oppose using armed force argue that the United States cannot police the world, that no country should impose its will on another, and that national sovereignty is absolute and should not be violated. Some advocates of this perspective are pacifists, arguing that armed force should never be used, while others maintain that armed force should be used only as a last resort, after all other tools of foreign policy have been tried and found wanting.

Proponents of the use of armed force assert that the United States, first as an emerging great power, then as one of two superpowers, and today as the world's only superpower, must actively defend its interests and, if necessary, impose its will via military force on those who threaten American interests, or on those who act aggressively toward the United States or its allies. They argue that the United States should not be reticent about using its military strength to achieve its objectives. Probably no one stated this view more eloquently than President John F. Kennedy in his 1961 inaugural address: "We shall pay any price, bear any burden, meet any hardship, support any friend, oppose any foe, to assure the survival and the success of liberty."[3]

In almost every case, American presidents and other policymakers have held viewpoints between the extremes of "never use armed might" and "use armed force early and often." The times have been rare, as immediately after the Vietnam War in the mid-1970s under Presidents Ford and Carter, when presidents and other policymakers appeared unwilling to take military action. There have been only a few times, during the last years of the nineteenth century and early in the twentieth century, and perhaps today during the war on terrorism, when military force was the preferred tool of presidents and other policymakers. Answering the questions posed earlier thus continues to require careful analysis that balances reasons for restraint with reasons to intervene.

Reasons to Use Military Force

The United States over its history has had several reasons to use military force: enhancing national security and defending the homeland; protecting trade, commerce, and the American economy; acquiring territory in the Western Hemisphere and beyond; defending international law, promoting democracy, and guarding human rights; and undertaking peacekeeping and humanitarian missions.

Enhancing National Security and Defending the Homeland.   Enhancing national security and defending the homeland have been frequent explanations for American use of armed force. Immediately after independence, Americans believed that Great Britain several times incited Indians to attack western outposts during the 1790s and on into the early nineteenth century. Although the term "defending national security" was not used during this era, national defense was one of several reasons that the United States fought the War of 1812 against Great Britain.

The United States entered World War II as a direct result of Japan's attack on the U.S. naval base at Pearl Harbor, in Hawaii, not at the time part of the American homeland, but nevertheless an American possession. Following World War II, almost every American use of armed force between 1947 and 1989, from the Korean and Vietnam Wars through military interventions in Lebanon, the Dominican Republic, Grenada—and elsewhere through a host of covert military operations—was justified on the basis of national security and containing communism.

After the September 11, 2001, terrorist attacks against the United States, the war on terrorism was undertaken for reasons of national security and defending the homeland. Indeed, President George W. Bush declared that the United States would extend homeland defense further than ever before, ferreting out and eliminating terrorists and their supporters no matter where they were. This strategy of homeland defense, as we have seen in previous chapters, was codified as the doctrine of **preemptive defense,** which stated: "The United States can no longer solely rely on a reactive posture as we have in the past…. We cannot let our enemies strike first…. As a matter of common sense and self-defense, America will act against emerging threats before they are fully formed."[4]

Protecting Trade, Commerce, and the American Economy.   Protecting trade, commerce, and the American economy has also been a frequent explanation for

America's use of military force. As we saw earlier, three of the first American uses of armed force—the undeclared naval war with France, the Barbary War, and the War of 1812—were all related to issues of trade and commerce. The same claim can be made about U.S. involvement in the Spanish-American War, the Boxer rebellion in China, numerous interventions in Central America and the Caribbean, and even World War I, when Germany's declaration of unrestricted submarine warfare proved a crucial consideration in influencing the United States to declare war in defense of freedom of the seas. More recently, cynics argue that the real reason the United States went to war against Iraq in 1991 was not to expel Iraq from Kuwait, but to assure American access to oil. That same charge was heard after President George W. Bush used force to remove Saddam Hussein in 2003.

Acquiring Territory.   Although most Americans prefer not to remember, the United States also used its military to acquire territory, especially in land contiguous to the United States, but overseas as well. The United States fought the Mexican War and various wars against and skirmishes with American Indians expressly to acquire territory, usually under the mantle of Manifest Destiny. On several occasions, the United States also undertook military expeditions against Canada, although with less success.

During the late nineteenth and early twentieth centuries, the United States turned to the Pacific, Central America, and the Caribbean as primary regions for expansion. The American military played a major role in helping the United States acquire coaling stations and other island outposts in the Pacific in the 1890s. Shortly thereafter, although the Spanish-American War was fought in part to stop Spanish atrocities in Cuba, acquiring Cuba was a prime war objective in many people's minds. Victory in the war led not only to Spain's expulsion from Cuba, but also to American control of Puerto Rico and the Philippines. When Filipinos rose up in revolt against their new master in the early twentieth century, the United States sent an expeditionary force to the Philippines to defeat the rebellion and maintain American control.

Defending International Law, Promoting Democracy, and Protecting Human Rights.   Several American administrations have used military force to defend international law, promote democracy, and protect human rights. As already noted, one reason the United States went to war against Spain in 1898 was because of Spanish atrocities in Cuba. Similarly, one reason the United States entered World War I was to, in Woodrow Wilson's words, "make the world safe for democracy." World War II has also often been portrayed as a war that pitted the Western democracies against German, Italian, and Japanese dictatorships, even though the Soviet Union, certainly not a democracy, was one of the most important U.S. allies.

In the 1990s and early in the twenty-first century, as we will see later in this chapter, the United States asserted that many of its uses of military force were needed to preserve international law, human rights, and democracy. Operation Desert Storm, the intervention in Bosnia, the war in Kosovo, and to an extent the overthrow of the Taliban regime in Afghanistan all had the defense of international law, human rights, or the promotion of democracy as their rationale. George W. Bush's administration also sought to legitimize the 2003 invasion of Iraq by claiming it was, among other things, pursuing these purposes.

Undertaking Peacekeeping and Humanitarian Missions.   Especially since the end of the Cold War, the U.S. military has been used in peacekeeping and humanitarian missions abroad. American armed forces have been sent to Georgia to help in disaster relief following an earthquake, used in northern Iraq to help distribute food to the Kurds, deployed to Somalia to create conditions so that the UN could provide humanitarian assistance, and served in Bosnia as peacekeepers, to name a few examples. American troops also went to Liberia to rescue U.S. and other foreign nationals who were threatened there during a civil war.

The Complexities of Using Force

Often the United States has used several of these explanations to legitimate its use of military force in a single situation. For example, the United States fought the 1991 Gulf War to expel Iraq from Kuwait, thereby defending international law; to maintain access to oil, thereby protecting the American economy; and to restore a balance of power in the Persian Gulf region, thereby enhancing national security. At the same time, American leaders have recognized that military force does not always have to be used for it to have an impact. Indeed, the threatened use or even mere presence of American military force has sometimes been sufficient for the United States to achieve its desired end.

Clearly, then, the United States has used military force for many reasons, and not always for the most praiseworthy purpose. And to reiterate, the United States often put forward multiple reasons for its use of military force. This does not mean that the United States was searching for a reason to legitimize its use of force. Rather, in most cases, different Americans, including those in senior policymaking positions, saw multiple reasons to use military force.

To Intervene or Not to Intervene

Even during the Cold War, and especially since the Vietnam War, the willingness of American policymakers to use military force overseas has been constrained by several factors. None is more important than the reluctance to send young men and women into battle and risk their death. Many analysts believe that the number of Americans that might be killed has become the litmus test for any intervention.

Some analysts assert that media coverage has led to the **CNN effect,** noting that the bloodiness of war has been brought into American living rooms and influences Americans' responses to the use of force. This phenomenon, some argue, began with Vietnam and accelerated during the 1980s and 1990s as advances in information and communication technologies allowed television to provide real-time coverage of conflicts on the other side of the world. This viewpoint argues that American foreign policy in general and decisions to intervene in particular are often driven by television and the media.[5]

Other analysts hold a different view, arguing simply that many Americans have lost their willingness to sacrifice and their dedication to core American values. This view asserts that "the good life" that many Americans enjoy has softened Americans and undermined their willingness to die for even a just cause.[6]

A third viewpoint holds that, despite advances in military technology that allow the United States to apply force from remote locations, the dangers of intervention have increased. Large numbers of highly sophisticated conventional weapons became available as new centers of arms production developed in the world, and after the Soviet Union collapsed. The **proliferation of weapons,** especially extremely capable automatic weapons, in the hands of militia and paramilitary groups in developing states is astounding. The Pentagon had warned for years about the proliferation of small arms throughout the developing world, but in the 1990s, the warnings became reality.

Military strategist Edward Luttwak takes a different tack to explain why the number of deaths has become the litmus test of overseas military intervention. Luttwak believes that the decline in the size of families over the past century plays a major role. Luttwak asserts that when several sons were born into a family, one or two could be sent to war, with a son remaining at home to carry on. Since this is no longer the case, Luttwak asserts, parents are unwilling to send their only son or daughter on military missions and interventions that are less than a defense of vital American interest.[7]

Figure 14.1 illustrates Vietnam War casualties and public support for the war. The figure shows vividly how public support for an overseas action can decay over time in the face of heavy casualties. Some analysts believe that a similar trend developed in the months immediately following the stated end of major combat operations in the 2003 Iraq War. As casualties and fatalities continued, the political environment in the United States heated up. Critics charged that the Bush Administration had inadequately planned for the after-combat environment in Iraq. Table 14.1 shows U.S. overseas force deployments after World War II and indicates how many U.S. casualties occurred overseas from 1945 to 2003.

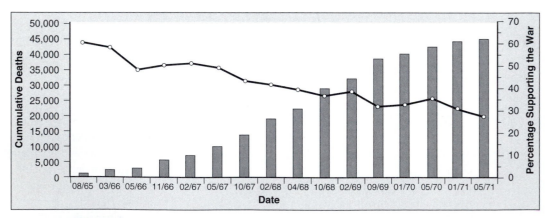

FIGURE 14.1

Vietnam War: Cumulative Casualties and Loss of Public Support

Source: Eric Larson, *Casualties and Consensus: The Historical Role of Casualties in Domestic Support for U.S. Military Operations* (Santa Monica, Calif.: Rand, 1996), p. 111.

TABLE 14.1
DEPLOYMENTS OF U.S. FORCES TO FOREIGN COUNTRIES (POST–WORLD WAR II)

Year	Location	Objective	U.S. Force Deployed	U.S. Casualties
1945–1949	China	Assist in disarming and repatriating the Japanese soldiers still in China; also to help control ports, railroads, and airfields	110,000	40 U.S. marines and seamen killed
1947–1949	Greece	Provide advice and consultation on matters of development (engineers) and the fight against communists; the U.S. provided a large aid package of both financial and military (armaments) assistance designed to keep Greece from falling to communism	Small contingent of officers	3 U.S. dead (2 accidental and 1 aircraft shot down)
1950–1953	Korea	Repel invasion by North Korea into South Korea; containment of communism	178,000 U.S.; with 20,000 allied forces (largely British and Turkish) and 224,000 South Koreans (422,000 total)	36,576 U.S. dead (in-theater dead; another 17,670 nontheater dead; 54,246 total)
1956	Egypt	Evacuate U.S. citizens and others from Alexandria during the Suez crisis	1 marine battalion (approximately 1,000 men)	No known fatalities
1958	Lebanon	Quell an insurrection by a group of leftists	14,300	28 U.S. dead
1958	Panama	Quell an uprising; the uprising began with a dispute over the issue of which flag would be flown in the canal zone	Unknown force strength	No known casualties
1961–1963	Republic of Vietnam	Support the government of the Republic of Vietnam against the National Liberation Front (NLF); containment of communism	10,000 military advisers	Approximately 2,000 U.S. dead
1962	Thailand	Support the government against a threat of communist insurgency	5,000 U.S. marines	177 U.S. dead

(continued on next page)

TABLE 14.1 *(continued)*
DEPLOYMENTS OF U.S. FORCES TO FOREIGN COUNTRIES (POST–WORLD WAR II)

Year	Location	Objective	U.S. Force Deployed	U.S. Casualties
1965	Laos	Support Royal Lao and Hmong forces against the communist Pathet Lao; contain the spread of communism; also interdict and recon the Ho Chi Minh Trail which supplied the Viet Cong and gave Hanoi access to South Vietnam	Varied. These were cross-border operations with no permanent stationing in Laos, because of a 1962 agreement under which U.S., Soviet, and North Vietnamese forces were were all supposed to stay out of Laos. Before the 1962 agreement, the number was 666	733 U.S. dead
1964	Panama	Quell rioting and street warfare; the violence erupted from demonstrations over the fact that the Panamanian flag was not being flown over a school in the canal zone	10,000 garrison force	3 U.S. soldiers dead
1965	Vietnam	Contain the spread of communism; prevent the southern half of Vietnam from falling to a communist regime	530,000 at time of maximum deployment in April 1969	58,198 U.S. dead
1965–1966	Dominican Republic	Quell factional fighting; the justification for the intervention was protecting lives and property, but preventing a communist takeover seems to have been a primary objective	20,463 (22,000 later went to Hispaniola)	47 U.S. dead (27 battle dead and 20 nonhostile deaths)
1966–1967	Guatemala	Advise on counterterrorism after a rash of kidnappings; assist in preventing communists from gaining dominance in the country	A small contingent of military advisers	4 military dead (additionally the U.S. ambassador was assassinated)
1967	Cambodia	Interdict and recon the Ho Chi Minh Trail; prevent the spread of North Vietnamese Army (NVA) influence in Cambodia, and prevent support for communist Khmer Rouge in Cambodia; contain the spread of communism	Varied, cross-border operations	Approximately 500 U.S. dead

TABLE 14.1 *(continued)*
DEPLOYMENTS OF U.S. FORCES TO FOREIGN COUNTRIES (POST–WORLD WAR II)

Year	Location	Objective	U.S. Force Deployed	U.S. Casualties
1975	Cambodia	*Mayaguez* incident; U.S. military forces given the order to retake an American-crewed merchant vessel that had been seized in international waters by Cambodia	1,100	Approximately 41 U.S. dead
1980	Iran	Operation to rescue captured Americans in Tehran; operation was aborted in southern Iran due to mechanical failures in 3 of the 8 RH-53 Sea Stallion helicopters	120 Delta Forces and 200 Rangers, plus the aircrews of 8 RH-53 helicopters, 6 C-130 aircraft, and C-141 transport planes	8 U.S. military members died when a helicopter hit a C-130 ircraft at the desert rendezvous point
1981–1982	El Salvador	Train soldiers for counterinsurgency warfare	3,600 served here (not simultaneously)	20 U.S. dead
1982–1984	Lebanon	Support a peace agreement. Israel agreed to withdraw its invasion force from Lebanon if an international peacekeeping force took up positions in Lebanon	2,000 U.S. military forces (mostly marines); part of a multinational force (MNF) with French, Italian, and British forces	266 U.S. military members killed (241 in an Oct. 1983 terrorist bombing)
1982	Egypt (Sinai)	U.S. participated in multinational force and observers; intended to monitor actions to ensure there were no violations of the 1979 Israeli-Egyptian peace treaty	Approximately 1,000	No known casualties
1983–1989	Honduras	Build military installations near the border with Nicaragua; conduct military exercises; transport Honduran soldiers to the border	1,100	1 helicopter pilot
1983	Grenada (Operation Urgent Fury)	Ensure safe evacuation of the 1,000 American citizens living on the island	8,800	19 U.S. dead
1986	Bolivia	Assist in drug interdiction operations	160	No known casualties

(continued on next page)

TABLE 14.1 *(continued)*
DEPLOYMENTS OF U.S. FORCES TO FOREIGN COUNTRIES (POST–WORLD WAR II)

Year	Location	Objective	U.S. Force Deployed	U.S. Casualties
1989	Philippines	Dispatched from the U.S. naval base in Subic Bay to Manila to protect the embassy	100 marines	No known casualties
1989	Colombia, Bolivia, and Peru	Military forces dispatched to help combat drug producers and traffickers; the Andean Initiative in the War on Drugs	64–184 military advisers	No known casualties
1989–1990	Panama (Operation Just Cause)	Remove Manuel Noriega from power and bring him to the United States to face drug trafficking charges	27,351	23 U.S. dead
1990	Liberia	Provide security for embassy and facilitate evacuation	2,000	No known casualties
1991	Iraq (Operation Desert Storm)	Expel the Iraqi Army from Kuwait; small groups of Special Forces went on "SCUD hunts" in the desert; a small contingent sent into northern Iraq to stop attacks on Kurds	532,000	382 U.S. dead
1992–1994	Somalia (Operation Restore Hope)	At various times between 1992 and 1994 U.S. Marine and U.S. Army units served as part of (or to support) a UN force to assist in a humanitarian mission. October 1983 operation involved abducting two top aides of Somali warlord Farrah Aidid	Varied; up to 25,800, Approximately 160 involved in the October operation	35 U.S. dead (18 died in the October mission)
1994	Rwanda	Provide humanitarian aid	2,300	No known casualties
1994	Haiti	Restore the democratically elected leader to power; instill stability	21,000 with naval blockade force	2 U.S. dead
1995–1996	Bosnia	Enforce Dayton Peace Accords as part of a NATO force	Varied. At peak it reached 22,000, but U.S. forces rotated in and out	12 U.S. dead (1 hostile, 11 nonhostile)

TABLE 14.1 *(continued)*
DEPLOYMENTS OF U.S. FORCES TO FOREIGN COUNTRIES (POST–WORLD WAR II)

Year	Location	Objective	U.S. Force Deployed	U.S. Casualties
1997	Liberia	Evacuate U.S. citizens—noncombatant evacuation operation (NEO)	Unknown force strength (probably 400–2,000)	No known casualties
1997	Albania	Evacuate U.S. citizens—noncombatant evacuation operation (NEO)	Unknown force strength (probably 400–2,000)	No known casualties
1998	Eritrea, Guinea-Bissau, and Congo	Nonnombatant evacuation operations (NEO)	130	No casualties
1999–2000	East Timor	UN force intended to ensure stability	12 U.S. plus rotating multinational force	No known casualties
1999	Kosovo	Uphold UN Security Council Resolution	4,350 U.S. out of a larger multinational force	2 U.S. dead (nonhostile)
2001–2004	Afghanistan	To find and secure key leaders of the al Qaeda terrorist network that was responsible for the September 11 attacks on the Pentagon and World Trade Center; subsequently to remove the Taliban regime harboring al Qaeda and provide stability in the aftermath	9,000	141 dead as of October 8, 2004. However, casualties continue to mount
2003–2004	Iraq (Operation Iraqi Freedom)	To overthrow the regime of Saddam Hussein; to find and secure weapons of mass destruction and any programs to develop weapons of mass destruction	170,000 as of July 2003	1,064 dead as of October 8, 2004, war end. However, casualties continue to mount

Sources: Michael Clodfelter, *Warfare and Armed Conflicts: A Statistical Reference to Casualty and Other Figures, 1500–2000,* 2nd ed. (Jefferson, N.C.: McFarland, 2002), pp. 597–761; Melvin Small and David Singer, *Resort to Arms: International and Civil Wars, 1816–1980,* (Beverly Hills, Calif.: Sage, 1982); CDI, *U.S. Military Deployments/Engagements, 1975–2001* (2001), at *http://www.cdi.org/issues/USForces/deployments.html;* Correlates of War 2, Version 3.0, *http://cow2.la.psu.edu;* NARA, *Statistical Information About Casualties of the Vietnam Conflict* (1998), at *http://www.archives.gov/research_room;* DOD, *Casualty Summary,* Washington Headquarters Services, Directorate for Information Operations and Reports (2003); Ellen Collier, *Instances of Use of United States Forces Abroad, 1798–1993* (Washington, D.C.: Congressional Research Service, at http://www.history.navy.mil/wars/foabroad.htm; US Navy, *Casualties: U.S. Navy and Marine Corps Personnel Killed and Wounded in Wars, Conflicts, Terrorist Acts, and Other Hostile Incidents* (2002), at *http://www.history.navy.mil/faqs/faq56-2;* Steven Metz, *Stay the Course in the Balkans* (Carlisle Barracks, Pa.: Strategic Studies Institute, 2000); Clyde Mark, *Lebanon,* Issue Brief for Congress, Congressional Research Service, Library of Congress, 2003.

Lee Hamilton, a former chair of the House Foreign Relations Committee and currently chair of the U.S. Institute of Peace, contends that the United States cannot intervene in every situation that may develop, since it does not have enough resources to do so. However, he stated, "we must intervene sometimes. If we never intervene, our international standing is diminished, our moral leadership is questioned, our commitment to peace, justice, and prosperity appears thin, and people suffer." He further suggested that "we must adopt a middle course between intervention everywhere and intervention nowhere."[8] This is a far cry from John Kennedy's 1961 "Go any place, pay any price" rhetoric.

As we have seen, the justification for the use of military force overseas has taken many forms. And Americans have not always agreed on or supported the overseas use of armed force. Opposition to the Vietnam War is a classic example of opposition, but there are others as well. As Major General Smedley Butler, who retired from the U.S. Marine Corps in 1933 after 33 years of service, commented: "I wouldn't go to war again as I have done to protect some lousy investment bankers. There are only two things we should fight for. One is the defense of our homes and the other is the Bill of Rights. War for any other reason is simply a racket."[9]

Teddy Roosevelt stood at the other end of this spectrum. Roosevelt approached war and the use of military force as an almost mystical experience. According to historian Edward J. Renehan Jr., when war was inevitable, Roosevelt insisted that war "should be seized upon as a purifying, unifying moment in the life of a country and a people. Out of the deadly fire of battle, the metal of nationhood would emerge stronger and more resilient than before. Without the occasional trial and trauma of war, a country would grow too fat, too smug, and too complacent for its own good, its citizens totally caught up in the self-centered concerns of commercialism and pampered modern living."[10]

The Ongoing Debate

Teddy Roosevelt's view has little legitimacy today. Indeed, especially after the Vietnam War, Americans were unwilling to commit armed forces to use overseas. Many Americans believed that the United States lost its moral compass during Vietnam and became simply another classic imperialist power. After the United States withdrew from Vietnam, Americans thought long and hard about the conditions under which American armed forces would once again be committed overseas. Under Presidents Ford and Carter, the United States was particularly hesitant to use its military as a policy instrument. This began to change in 1979 after the U.S. embassy in Teheran, Iran, was overrun by radicals and the embassy staff was taken hostage, and after the Soviet Union invaded Afghanistan.

When Ronald Reagan became president in 1981, the time was ripe for a review of conditions under which American forces would be used overseas. It was with the memory of Vietnam in mind that Secretary of Defense Casper Weinberger, assisted by Brigadier General Colin Powell, developed criteria for using American armed forces overseas. Called the **Weinberger Doctrine,** it declared that American forces should not be used in conflict overseas unless: (1) long-term public and congressional support was available, (2) "clearly defined political and military objectives" were present, and (3) the United States had a "clear intention of winning."[11] Clearly, intervention and the use of military force would be possible, but Weinberger sent a clear signal that if the United States were to intervene, it would do so to win.

Secretary of State George Shultz, however, considered the Weinberger criteria too restrictive, arguing that the United States would become "the Hamlet of Nations," continually pondering whether enough support were present under the terms of the Weinberger Doctrine to use armed force. Schulz wanted a freer hand to use the military than the Weinberger Doctrine provided.

Weinberger and Schulz left office disagreeing over when American armed forces should be used. As complicated as the picture was, it became even more confusing in the late 1980s and early 1990s, as more and more Americans, Representative Hamilton included, adopted the view that the United States had the right, perhaps even the duty, to stop extreme violations of human rights by intervening with whatever instrument of foreign policy is needed, including the military. This was far from the extreme on the continuum that asserted that state sovereignty is inviolate and total. Indeed, as we will shortly see, American forces during the post–Cold War era were deployed to Bosnia in the 1990s and fought a war in Kosovo in 1999 to stop Serbian ethnic cleansing, a euphemism for slaughtering Bosnian Muslims and Albanian Kosovars.

Clearly, then, the why, when, and how of military intervention have changed over time, with even senior policymakers in the same administration disagreeing over the criteria for the use of U.S. armed force. It will be instructive, then, in order to understand past decisions and inform present and future policies, to examine this evolution in some detail.

EARLY ISSUES OF AMERICAN USE OF ARMED FORCE

Early in U.S. history, the United States rarely used military force abroad, primarily because the American military was small, U.S. overseas interests except for trade were limited, the United States was isolated, and technology was primitive. Over time, this changed as the U.S. military became more capable, American interests expanded, the United States became an active participant in world affairs, and technology advanced.

The Early Years: Defense and Expansion

Under Washington and Adams, the United States had only a small army and navy. The navy acquitted itself well in an undeclared naval war with France in the 1790s, but it was not until the Jefferson Administration that the United States for the first time used its military power beyond North America or the high seas, sending naval forces, marines, and mercenaries against the Barbary pirates in Morocco, Algiers, Tunis, and Tripoli to try to stop them from seizing American ships. This expedition had some successes, but it also experienced several setbacks.

After the **Barbary War,** the United States, with only one major exception, used its military primarily for occasional forays against Canada and Mexico, and during the Civil War. The single major exception was, of course, warfare against American Indians. Concentrating on continental expansion, the United States during most of the nineteenth century had little time for foreign adventures. At the end of the nineteenth century, as we saw especially in Chapter 4, this changed.

Imperial America

Combining Manifest Destiny, militarism, claims of Christian duty, commercial opportunity, and modern communication with self-proclaimed moral and racial superiority, the United States leaped full force into the international arena as an imperial power as it acquired interests and territories in the Pacific. After acquiring a few isolated islands in the Pacific, the United States went to war for the first time with a European power other than Great Britain—Spain.

The United States justified the 1898 **Spanish-American War** in part on humanitarian grounds, accurately charging the Spanish with committing atrocities against the Cuban people when Spain attempted to quell an independence movement on the island. But there were other reasons for war as well, including commerce, territory, and empire, several of which were addressed by President William McKinley as he explained why the United States kept the Philippines:

> The truth is I didn't want the Philippines and when they came to us as a gift from the gods, I did not know what to do about them…. I sought counsel from all sides—Democrats as well as Republicans—but got little help. I thought first we would take only Manila; then Luzon; then other islands, perhaps, also. I walked the floor of the White House night after night until midnight; and I am not ashamed to tell you, gentlemen, that I went down on my knees and prayed to Almighty God for light and guidance more than one night.
>
> And one night late it came to me this way—I don't know how it was, but it came: (1) that we could not give them back to Spain—that would be cowardly and dishonorable; (2) that we could not turn them over to France or Germany—our commercial rivals in the Orient—that would be bad business and discreditable; (3) that we could not leave them to themselves—they were unfit for self-government—and they would soon have anarchy and misrule over there worse than Spain's was; and (4) that there was nothing left for us to do but to take them all, and to educate the Filipinos, and uplift and civilize and Christianize them, and by God's grace do the very best we could by them, as our fellow-men for whom Christ also died. And then I went to bed, and went to sleep and slept soundly."[12]

The treaty ending the Spanish-American War was inked in late 1898 and gave Cuba, the Philippines, Puerto Rico, and Guam to the United States. However, a revolt broke out in the Philippines against American rule. The United States intervened to end the revolt, but by the time order was restored in 1902, 5,000 Americans and some 200,000 Filipinos had died.[13]

Despite this foray into imperialism and the cost in American and Filipino lives, Americans as a general rule supported overseas military intervention and adventures abroad. Indeed, in the late nineteenth and early twentieth century, such activities were the mark of a great power, and it bordered on treason not to support them. Thus, when Theodore Roosevelt was assistant secretary of the U.S. Navy a year before the Spanish-American War, he captivated an audience at the Naval War College, declaring that "no triumph of peace is quite so great as the supreme triumphs of war." Roosevelt was not the only enthusiastic supporter of warfare. Others included Oliver Wendell Holmes Jr., who called war "Divine," and naval strategist Alfred Thayer Mahan, who believed war "a remedy for greater evils, especially moral evils."[14]

Not everyone believed in the cleansing power of war and the majesty of military force, and Roosevelt and his views were not universally admired. Mark Twain considered Roosevelt "insane … and insanest upon [the subject of] war and its supreme glories."[15] An anti-imperialist movement called the **Anti-Imperialist League** also developed but never gained much influence.

Even so, for the most part, the end of the nineteenth and beginning of the twentieth century was a period during which chest thumpers and saber rattlers reigned supreme in the United States and elsewhere. Many had access to corridors of power, and in some cases they held power. This was a period in the United States when moral superiority, racial superiority, militarism, Manifest Destiny, Christian duty, commercial opportunity, and modern communication came together in a way never before or since seen.

Into the 1920s, the United States frequently used military power overseas, for the most part for **interventions in the Caribbean, Central America, and Mexico.** From 1900 to 1925, the United States intervened militarily in the Caribbean and other Latin American countries for a host of political, economic, and security reasons. American armed forces were deployed in 1901 and 1902 in Colombia; in 1903, 1907, 1911, 1912, 1919, 1924, and 1925 in Honduras; in 1903, 1904, 1914, and from 1916 to 1924 in the Dominican Republic; from 1903 to 1914 and again in 1918–1920, 1921, and 1925 in Panama; from 1906 to 1909, in 1912, and between 1917 and 1922 in Cuba; in 1910 in Nicaragua; in 1914 and from 1915 to 1934 in Haiti; in 1920 in Guatemala; and in 1921 in Costa Rica. The United States also sent troops into Mexico in 1913 and from 1914 to 1917.

Interventions were usually undertaken for political or economic reasons, specifically to restore order and to insure that debts were paid to American firms or European creditors. U.S. decision makers often reasoned that it was better to send in the U.S. Marines to collect tariffs and taxes so that Caribbean and Central American states could pay their debts than to allow British or German forces to intervene for the same purpose. American leaders "knew" that U.S. forces did not intervene to establish a colony or take over a country permanently. They were not sure that the same would be true if Great Britain, Germany, or some other European country sent troops in to restore order and collect taxes.

Most American interventions were carried out under the auspices of the **Roosevelt Corollary** to the Monroe Doctrine, which, as we have seen, asserted that "civilized" countries, particularly the United States, had responsibilities as the world's "policemen" to intervene to establish order. As Roosevelt told Congress in 1902: "If a nation shows that it knows how to act with decency in industrial and political matters, if it keeps order and pays its obligations, then it need fear no interference from the United States. Brutal wrong-doing, or an impotence which results in a general loosening of the ties of civilized society, may finally require intervention by some civilized nation, and in the Western Hemisphere the United States might act as a policeman, at least in the Caribbean region."[16]

American reasons to intervene were not limited to maintaining order and collecting bad debts. The United States acquired the Panama Canal Zone in 1903 by using military power to obtain a geostrategic objective: constructing the Panama Canal. When Colombia refused to allow the United States to build a canal across Panama, events unfolded in which local advocates of independence who favored building a canal declared and gained independence from Colombia, backed by a nearby American naval force. While the United States did not actually use force against Colombia, the presence of the U.S. Navy was a major factor in achieving Panamanian independence. Years later, the United States paid Colombia $25 million in "canalimony," but never apologized.[17]

During this era, the United States twice deployed sizeable contingents of American troops beyond the Western Hemisphere. In 1900, the United States sent 2,500 troops to join 15,500 soldiers from Britain, France, Germany, Russia, and Japan to rescue besieged international legations in Beijing, China. The other occasion was the already mentioned U.S. intervention in the Philippines to quell a rebellion.

Roosevelt's use of the U.S. Navy as a tool of diplomacy was striking. For example, relations between the United States and Japan had advanced positively after the Perry Mission opened Japan to the United States and the world in the 1850s. The United States also helped settle the 1905 Russo-Japanese War. Even so, racial tension developed on the U.S. west coast, and in 1906 the San Francisco School Board separated students of "Oriental" descent from "Americans." Japan lodged an official protest, and Japanese newspapers printed strongly worded anti-American articles. The matter was settled with the 1907 "gentlemen's agreement" in which Japan restricted emigration to the United States. But racial tensions and incidents continued.

At this point, Roosevelt sent 16 American battleships, known as the **Great White Fleet**, on a world cruise, with Tokyo as a principal stop. The fleet enjoyed a successful visit to Tokyo that led to the Root-Takahira Agreement, which normalized U.S.-Japanese relations and affirmed the integrity of Japanese and American possessions and interests in the Pacific. It was a clear case of the diplomatic use of the military, but not a shot was fired.

Before World War I, then, it is indisputable that the United States intervened militarily overseas on numerous occasions. Generally speaking, these interventions took place in situations in which there were no threats to American vital strategic interests, to U.S. sovereignty, or to American territorial integrity. Between the War of 1812 and the American entry into World War I, the only instance in which the United States itself was threatened occurred in 1916 when rebel Mexican General Poncho Villa attacked Columbus, New Mexico. Seventeen Americans and over 100 of Villa's men died in the fighting. In response, the United States sent an expeditionary force into Mexico, but it never found Villa.

From World War I to World War II

Before World War I, the United States' use of military force overseas occurred in instances in which the United States had overwhelming advantage, and in which America was impelled by commerce, territory, prestige, and empire. The U.S. entry into World

War I changed this pattern. The American rationale for using force shifted toward higher moral and political plains as defense of democracy, freedom of the seas, freedom for oppressed peoples, and national self-determination became the elements upon which the United States justified its use of military force.

As we saw in Chapter 5, several specific events and general trends led to **American entry into World War I,** but it was the combination of Germany's declaration of unrestricted submarine warfare and the Zimmermann telegram that made an American declaration of war against Germany inevitable. As submarines sank ship after ship in early 1917, Woodrow Wilson opted for war. Addressing a joint session of Congress on April 2, 1917, Wilson declared that Germany had unleashed "warfare against mankind" with its submarines and that Germany endangered the "very roots of human life." Declaring that "the world must be made safe for democracy," Wilson asked Congress for a declaration of war against Germany. Congress supported the request, and the United States went to war with Germany, with Wilson's rhetoric making it clear that the United States intended to win the war, overthrow autocracy, and impose its view of human rights, self-determination, and democracy on Europe once Germany and its allies were defeated.

As the war wound down, the United States intervened in Russia.[18] Wilson dispatched 10,000 U.S. troops to Siberia to participate with French, British, and Japanese forces to help thousands of Czech troops, who had been fighting in Russia against Germany, to return home. Cut off by the Russian revolution, the Czechs were isolated. Wilson, firm in his desire to help the Czech legion return home, also had an ulterior reason for sending troops to Siberia. By the end of World War I, Japan had 70,000 troops in Russia's Far East,[19] and Wilson was concerned that Japan's real intent for having so many troops in Russia was to acquire the region. Thus, U.S. troops were in Siberia as much to watch the Japanese as to help the Czechs. In any event, U.S. troops departed Russia in 1920, while the Japanese stayed until 1922. The U.S. **intervention in Russia** accomplished little, but it soured Russian attitudes toward the United States for years. Even as late as 1959, Soviet leader Nikita Khrushchev complained, "Your soldiers were on Russian soil."[20]

For a time, World War I destroyed the myth of the glory of war. U.S. losses were comparatively few, "only" 116,000, but the rest of the world lost some 14,700,000 people. As a result, concepts like the League of Nations, collective security, naval arms control treaties, and outlawing war were advanced to make the world a safer place. In the United States, demobilization rendered the U.S. Army one of the smallest in the world for a major power. The United States still had an occupying force in the Philippines, a few naval vessels patrolling Chinese rivers, and a token troop presence in Germany near Koblenz.[21]

On several occasions, the United States also intervened after World War I in the Caribbean and Central America, but this changed when Franklin D. Roosevelt became president in 1933 and instituted the **Good Neighbor Policy** toward America's southern neighbors. Believing that dollars and trade were better instruments of diplomacy than guns and bayonets, Roosevelt said that the era of U.S. military intervention was over.

As the world sank into the Great Depression in the 1930s and the United States declared its intention not to intervene in Latin America and the Caribbean, Asia and Europe slid toward war. Japan in 1931 seized Manchuria, a Chinese province, and converted it into the "sovereign" state of Manchukuo. Meanwhile, after Hitler became German chancellor in 1933, Germany withdrew from the League of Nations and two years later announced it was rearming. Thereafter, throughout the 1930s, Europe careened from crisis to crisis. Finally, in September 1939, Germany invaded Poland. Two days later, France and Great Britain declared war on Germany. World War II had begun.

The United States, like the rest of the world, did little to oppose German, Japanese, and Italian aggression throughout the 1930s. Congress expressed its isolationism by passing a series of Neutrality Acts from 1935 to 1937 to keep the United States out of foreign conflicts, and until late in 1938, Roosevelt was as much of an isolationist as anyone. As we saw in Chapter 5, there were several reasons for **American isolationism and neutrality.**

First, the United States was in the midst of the Great Depression, and most Americans saw economic recovery as the primary national objective. Second, most Americans were convinced that Europe and Asia were far away and should handle their own problems. Third, some Americans believed that Germany was justified in regaining land taken from it by the 1919 Treaty of Paris. Some also argued that Great Britain and France were as much to blame for World War I as Germany, and that U.S. involvement in World War I was a mistake not to be repeated. Fourth, some remembered how, during World War I, the Wilson Administration curtailed civil liberties to quell opposition to the war. They did not want that to happen again. Fifth, having substantially disarmed following World War I, the United States was unprepared to respond to overseas aggression even had it so desired.

Despite these reasons for isolationism and neutrality, German and Japanese aggression troubled Roosevelt. Even after Germany invaded Poland, however, the United States did not go to war. As in World War I, the United States remained aloof from the conflict, this time for 26 months. Throughout this time, again as detailed in Chapter 5, Roosevelt moved the United States closer to an alliance with Great Britain, providing as much aid as possible without going to war.

Meanwhile, U.S.-Japanese tensions mounted as Japanese aggression in China continued. Roosevelt in 1940 embargoed shipments of aviation fuel and scrap iron to Japan, although U.S. oil shipments to Japan continued. Nevertheless, Japan's assault on China continued. After Germany defeated France in 1940, Japan occupied France's colonies in northern Indochina. When in July 1941 the United States discovered Japanese troop ships heading toward southern Indochina, Roosevelt froze Japanese funds in the United States and stopped all trade with Japan, including oil. With a U.S. embargo in place, and having depended on the now-embargoed U.S. oil shipments, Japan had two options. It could end its effort to take over China or it could invade the oil-rich Dutch and British East Indies. The latter action would require Japanese military action against the Philippines, and that would mean war with the United States. Japan chose the second option.

On December 7, 1941, Japan attacked the U.S. naval base at **Pearl Harbor,** killing 2,400 Americans and sinking seven battleships. The next day, Roosevelt asked Congress to declare war. The Senate supported the request unanimously, and there was only a single negative vote in the House. The United States was at war with Japan. Three days later, Hitler declared war on the United States, and the United States was in a two-front war.

World War II from the American perspective began with a series of disasters in the Pacific. An introspective America awoke to news reports from Pearl Harbor, Bataan, Midway, Guadalcanal, Tulagi, Gavutu, and Tanambogo.[22] The glory of war, so often referred to by Teddy Roosevelt, was nowhere to be found. With only rare exceptions, such as the early 1942 Doolittle air raid on Tokyo, the United States experienced disaster after disaster, not glorious victory. However, by early 1943, the U.S. Marines had won the battle for Guadalcanal, and in mid-1943 the United States won a resounding naval victory at the Battle of Midway. The process of island hopping to evict Japan from its holdings in the Pacific soon began.

The war's grand strategy put victory in Europe ahead of victory in the Pacific even though the war had begun for the United States in the Pacific. Thus, American forces concentrated on defeating the Axis Powers in North Africa first, then moved into Italy, next launched the D-Day invasion of France in June 1944, and finally defeated Germany, meeting Soviet forces along the Elbe River in Germany in April 1945. The Pacific war ended with the U.S. use of atomic bombs against Hiroshima and Nagasaki in August 1945.

World War II cost the United States dearly, but its losses were nowhere near as much as those of other nations. The United States suffered approximately 400,000 deaths, but the rest of the world lost approximately 55 million people. The Soviet Union suffered the most, with 25–30 million killed. China lost 10 million, Germany and Poland 6 million each, Indonesia 4 million, Japan 3 million, Vietnam 1 million, and Great Britain 400,000.[23]

The Cold War and Containment

When World War II ended, most Americans hoped that an era of global peace had arrived that would not require the overseas use of America's armed forces. This hope was in vain. Gradually at first, but then more rapidly, Americans realized that their country had become the leader of the Western world. This reality led to widespread overseas deployment of American forces, and frequently to the use of armed force.

Details of the American role in the Cold War were provided earlier and will not be repeated here. Suffice it to say that the Cold War forced a general reversal of American attitudes about intervention overseas during times of peace, especially intervention and involvement in Europe. Throughout the Cold War, the United States found it imperative to intervene almost anywhere that it perceived the possibility of a communist takeover. The use of military force, sometimes in combat and sometimes for display purposes to back up other aspects of American diplomacy, was a crucial element of **containment.**[24] A partial list of the occasions when American armed force was used during the Cold War can be seen in Table 14.1.

American interventions were not without controversy. Hundreds of thousands of Americans went to the streets to protest America's involvement in the Vietnam War. Nevertheless, for most of the Cold War, the American public remained committed to the idea that it was the United States' global responsibility to prevent the expansion of communism.

With the collapse of communist regimes in Eastern Europe in 1989 and the break-up of the Soviet Union in 1991, containment disappeared as a motivating factor for the use of U.S. military force overseas. Nevertheless, the U.S. government still had ample opportunity to deploy and use American armed forces overseas, and in the eyes of many, ample justification to do so. It should come as no surprise, then, that with the world being significantly different after the demise of communism in Eastern Europe and the collapse of the Soviet Union, the pattern of American use of armed force overseas changed once again.

AMERICAN USE OF ARMED FORCE AFTER THE COLD WAR

Since the end of the Cold War, the United States has continued to use military force overseas, justifying its actions as being needed to defend international law, promote democracy, protect human rights, provide peacekeeping operations, perform humanitarian missions, and defend the American homeland. Almost all of these justifications for the overseas use of armed force are similar if not identical to those we have seen in our survey of history. Perhaps surprisingly, however, the years since the end of the Cold War have seen a greater number of American uses of military force than any other corresponding period since World War II. There are several reasons for this, not the least of which is the end of the Cold War.

The Emerging Global Setting

During the Cold War, there was a clear distribution of global power, and the international system was unambiguously bi-polar. The United States and the Soviet Union were for the most part deterred from infringing on each other's sphere of influence by the threat of either a nuclear holocaust or a massive conventional conflict. The American decision to avoid any but the most covert proxy support for anti-communist action in Eastern Europe despite its rhetoric about "rolling back" communism is one example of this.[25] On the Soviet side, the stability that the bi-polar system imparted was seen in the Soviet withdrawal of missiles from Cuba during the 1962 Cuban Missile Crisis.[26]

Indeed, even though during the Cold War it may have seemed that the world was on the brink of annihilation, in retrospect, bi-polarity helped stabilize the international system. The analogy has been made that events in the bi-polar world were like a game of "chicken" in which two drivers head their cars toward each other at high speed. Possible outcomes are that one swerves, both swerve, or there is a devastating and deadly crash. During the Cold War, both sides regularly swerved to avoid a crash.

With the end of the Cold War, a more ambiguous international structure developed. As we saw earlier, some saw this as a "uni-polar moment," that is, an opportunity for the United States to assert its hegemony, but others, recognizing the growing importance of a consolidating Europe and a vibrant China, believed that a multi-polar world was developing, albeit one heavily skewed toward the United States because of the preponderance of American military might, economic strength, and cultural influence. This view recognized that the United States was the only power with global reach but accepted that regional powers such as China, the EU, and perhaps even Iran had sizeable influence in their own regions of the world.

Regardless of whether the world is now uni-polar or multi-polar, the United States, even with its preponderance of military might, cannot assume that it will succeed when it uses its armed forces. First, conflicts like the Vietnam War and the Soviet-Afghan War demonstrated that having even immensely superior firepower does not ensure victory. Realizing that defeating a country with a superior military force in a conventional war is not possible, potential enemies may employ **asymmetric strategies,** that is, strategies that do not directly engage the full armed forces of a military power, instead taking advantage of anonymity, patience, and willingness to suffer casualties to counter an adversary's advantage in firepower. Guerrilla warfare as employed by the Vietcong in Vietnam against the United States and the *mujahadeen* against the Soviet Union in Afghanistan are examples of asymmetric strategies. Similarly, terrorism is an asymmetric strategy, employed by international actors such as Osama bin Laden and by anti-U.S. insurgents in Iraq following the 2003 American military victory in that country. Both bin Laden and Iraqi insurgents believe that the United States can be defeated because it has a limited willingness to suffer casualties.[27]

Second, in recent years, there has been a growing expectation that all military actions except those conducted in self-defense will be carried out multilaterally, or at least with multilateral approval. A prime example can be seen in George H. W. Bush's 1991 decision to go to war in the Persian Gulf to expel Iraq from Kuwait. This action was carried out with the support of a sizeable coalition of states both in the region and around the world. Indeed, most U.S. military actions in the post–Cold War era have been carried out with the support of the United Nations, or at least with substantial regional support, as in the U.S. role in NATO's actions in the Balkans.

Even George W. Bush, often accused of being prone to unilateral action, recognized the value of multilateralism. While many cite the 2003 Iraq War as an example of Bush's unilateralism, both he and Secretary of State Colin Powell went before the UN in an attempt to gain support for U.S. actions. Bush also developed a coalition of like-minded countries, the "coalition of the willing," including Great Britain, Poland, and Spain, which supported the war against Iraq. Thus, while one may argue that Bush should have done more to gain wider support, it cannot be argued that the desire for multilateral approval was not a consideration in Bush's decision making.

Finally, the United States is keenly aware of the fate that previous hegemons have suffered: eventual decline.[28] The cost of the war in Iraq has been on the minds of policymakers and taxpayers alike, as Bush in 2003 requested $87 billion to maintain U.S. military forces overseas and aid in reconstruction of a battered Iraq. While there was speculation that Iraq might be only the first in a chain of U.S.-imposed regime changes that would include Syria, Iran, and North Korea, it seems unfathomable that the United States could take on any additional such dauntingly expensive projects any time in the near future.

With these considerations in mind, and with the easy guideline of containing communism gone, it has become more difficult than ever for American policymakers to determine whether, when, and how the United States should use its military forces overseas. Now more than ever, before committing American troops overseas, foreign policy decision makers must ask and answer the three questions posed earlier: "Why should American armed forces be used overseas?" "When should American armed forces be used overseas?" "How should American armed forces be used overseas?"

The record of America's use of armed force in the 1990s well illustrates how difficult a task answering these questions is. Leaving an examination of the use of the American armed forces against terrorism until later, we will turn to a review of nine situations in which the United States used or may have been expected to use military force during the 1990s and early twenty-first century. It is worth noting, however, as Figure 14.2 shows, that most American forces are based in the United States. Nevertheless, U.S. armed forces are deployed around the world. Figure 14.3 shows the total distribution of U.S. forces overseas; Figure 14.4 shows distribution within Europe; Figure 14.5 shows distribution in East Asia. Clearly the United States in the post–Cold War world retains global reach and global interests.

The Persian Gulf War

In August 1990, Iraq invaded and occupied Kuwait.[29] President George H. W. Bush saw the Iraqi action as a threat of immense political, economic, and military significance. Bush likened it to Hitler's 1939 invasion of Poland and considered it an extreme and blatant violation of international law. The United States also feared that the Iraqi action was a precursor to an invasion of Saudi Arabia that would place Iraq's ruler, Saddam Hussein, in a position to dictate world oil production and prices.

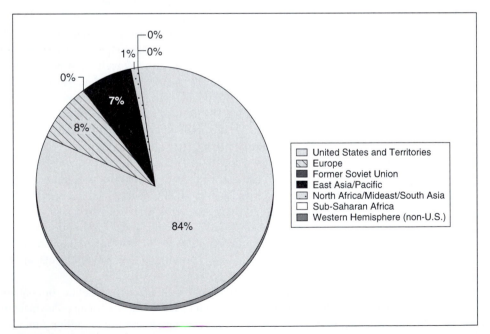

FIGURE 14.2
Distribution of U.S. Forces Worldwide

Source: Department of Defense, Worldwide Manpower Distribution by Geographical Area (Washington, D.C.: Directorate for Information, December 31, 2002), pp. 1–5.

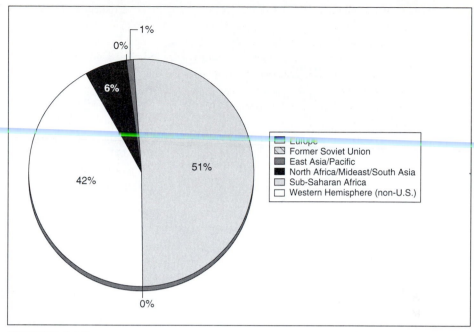

FIGURE 14.3
Overseas Distribution of U.S. Forces

Source: Department of Defense, Worldwide Manpower Distribution by Geographical Area (Washington, D.C.: Directorate for Information, December 31, 2002), pp. 1–5.

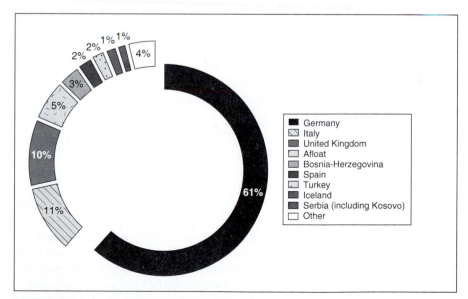

FIGURE 14.4
U.S. Forces in Europe

Source: Department of Defense, Worldwide Manpower Distribution by Geographical Area (Washington, D.C.: Directorate for Information, December 31, 2002), pp. 1–2.

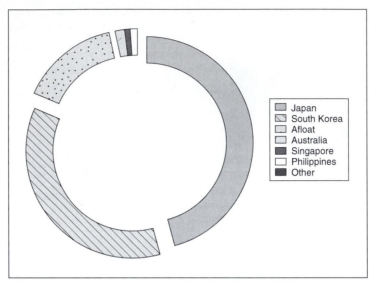

FIGURE 14.5
U.S. Forces in East Asia

Source: Department of Defense, Worldwide Manpower Distribution by Geographical Area (Washington, D.C.: Directorate for Information, December 31, 2002), p. 2.

After several months of a massive military build-up called "Operation Desert Shield," passage of a UN resolution authorizing the use of force to expel Iraq from Kuwait, and the U.S. Senate's vote to allow American use of its military against Iraq, the Persian Gulf War began. For a month, U.S. and other allied aircraft attacked Iraqi military and strategic targets. Then, the U.S. Army and Marines as well as the armed forces of other states launched a massive tank attack into Iraq and Kuwait. Within 100 hours, Iraq was defeated. **Operation Desert Storm,** the U.S. name for its military action against Iraq, had been an immense success, and the United States and its allies had suffered relatively few casualties.

Somalia

As civil war ravaged the poverty-stricken country of Somalia on the Horn of Africa, the United States inserted troops in 1992 to help create conditions favorable for the United Nations and international relief agencies to distribute food.[30] The **U.S. intervention in Somalia** soon became more than a humanitarian mission.

In 1993, President Clinton, with considerable urging by and support from the United Nations, expanded the U.S. mission to include capturing a Somali warlord, General Mohammed Aidid. In pursuit of this new objective, U.S. Army Rangers and Delta Force members in October 1993 attempted to take two of Aidid's lieutenants into custody. However, when an American Blackhawk helicopter was shot down, more troops were inserted to rescue the downed soldiers. During the ensuing battle, depicted in the movie

Blackhawk Down, U.S. forces suffered 18 fatalities in what was at the time the longest sustained firefight involving American forces since the Vietnam War.[31]

The images broadcast by CNN and other news outlets of the lifeless Blackhawk crew chief being dragged through the streets of Mogadishu had an immense impact on the American public. Whereas before the raid on Aidid three out of four Americans supported the mission in Somalia, a *Time*/CNN poll conducted just after the ill-fated raid showed that 60 percent of the American public agreed with the statement: "Nothing the United States could accomplish in Somalia is worth the death of even one more soldier."[32] This indicated how sensitive the American public was to the loss of American lives in instances where the nation's strategic interests were not clearly at stake. The United States withdrew it troops in 1994, having accomplished little, and UN forces departed Somalia in 1995 as the fighting continued.

Bosnia

Bosnia-Herzegovina (hereafter Bosnia) was one of the provinces of multi-ethnic, multi-religion Yugoslavia.[33] Orthodox Serbs, Orthodox Macedonians, Orthodox Montenegrins, Catholic Croats, Catholic Slovenes, Catholic Hungarians, Muslim Slavs, and Muslim Albanians all lived in Yugoslavia's six provinces—Bosnia-Herzegovina, Croatia, Macedonia, Montenegro, Serbia, and Slovenia—and its two autonomous regions, Vojvodina and Kosovo. Many nationalities lived peacefully together, worked with each other, and intermarried. Even so, some disliked and hated each other.

Then, in 1980, Yugoslavia's longtime leader Josef Tito died, and Yugoslavia began to drift apart. In 1987, Slobodan Milosevic, a Serb nationalist, became Yugoslavia's leader. Non-Serbian Yugoslavs saw Milosevic as a threat, and the trend toward break-up accelerated. By the early 1990s, Slovenia, Croatia, Bosnia, and Macedonia had declared independence, but Milosevic did not intend to allow Yugoslavia to dissolve. After failing to prevent Slovenia's and Macedonia's secession, he tried to keep Croatia and Bosnia, where many Serbs lived, within Yugoslavia.

During World War II, the government that ruled Croatia for the Nazis killed 400,000 Serbs. Serbs in Croatia therefore were terrified by Croatian independence and wanted to remain with Yugoslavia. This led to fighting during 1991 and 1992. Both sides were brutal, and both sides massacred civilians. The fighting ended in 1992 when Croatian forces gained the upper hand and UN peacekeepers moved in.

Bosnia was less fortunate. Although almost half of Bosnia's population was Muslim Slav, Milosevic's government and Bosnian Serbs tried to expel them, using ethnic cleansing and rape as policy tools. As fighting escalated and deaths mounted, UN peacekeepers deployed to Bosnia in 1992. Although UN forces were deployed until 1995, over half a million people were killed in Bosnia as Serb forces ignored and often overran UN safe areas, even taking UN peacekeepers as hostages. Ethnic cleansing, rape, and mass executions of civilians continued. Throughout these years, the United States refused to intervene militarily.

Then, in 1995, the United States brokered a peace agreement, the Dayton Accord, between Croats, Bosnian Muslims, and Serbs. The agreement arranged a division of land along ethnic lines to be enforced by NATO. In late 1995, peacekeeping in Bosnia passed from the UN to NATO. NATO deployed an Implementation Force (IFOR) of 20,000 U.S. troops, 43,000 French and British soldiers, and several thousand troops from other countries, including 2,500 Russians. IFOR in 1997 transitioned into a smaller 30,000 person NATO Stabilization Force (SFOR) whose mission was to keep the warring parties apart, map minefields, and destroy weapons. Warfare stopped, but the situation in Bosnia remained unsettled. SFOR is still deployed there today.

North Korea

When **North Korea** accelerated its effort to acquire nuclear weapons, some Americans urged President Clinton to attack North Korea's nuclear facilities, but he chose diplomacy instead.[34] After protracted negotiations, an agreement was reached in 1994 under which North Korea agreed to shut down a reactor that could make nuclear weapons in return for obtaining two reactors from South Korea that made inspections easier and producing weapons-grade nuclear materials more difficult.

The agreement ran into snags on the North Korean side and was not implemented for several years. Nevertheless, even after it was implemented, the United States remained convinced that North Korea was a rogue state, with President George W. Bush in 2002 denouncing it as part of an "axis of evil." Then, when U.S. negotiators accused North Korea of engaging in a surreptitious uranium enrichment program, North Korea left the nuclear nonproliferation treaty and recommissioned its weapons-capable reactor. In 2003, it started to reprocess spent fuel, the first step toward developing nuclear weapons.

Even so, throughout these years, the United States never came close to using military force against North Korea, despite the threat it presented to global stability. Indeed, in August 2003, regional talks involving China, Japan, North and South Korea, Russia, and the United States began, seeking to develop a compromise solution that would end North Korea's nuclear threat and provide security for the country.

Rwanda

Rwanda presents a case study of a crisis where human rights were blatantly violated, but the United States chose not to act.[35] In Rwanda, a violent civil war broke out in 1994 between the Tutsi and Hutu tribes. Over half a million people, mainly Tutsi, were killed. The United States, along with the rest of the world, chose not to intervene to stop the slaughter.

Some believed that the U.S. decision to stand apart from the fighting was based on geopolitics, since Central Africa was strategically not very important to the United States. Others asserted that the lack of U.S. intervention was based on racial motives, that the United States chose not to intervene because Rwanda was a "black" nation. However, the United States stayed apart from the fighting in Yugoslavia, a "white" nation, for over three years before it deployed its forces, and even then only as part of a NATO mission.

Other evidence indicates the decision not to intervene was based on criteria such as the sheer magnitude of the force that would have been required, the existence of more pressing needs for U.S. military capabilities, the failure of efforts in Somalia, and perhaps most importantly, the decision of the United Nations to stay aloof from Rwanda.

Even so, U.S. troops, and forces from Belgium, France, and elsewhere, provided humanitarian assistance to refugees in Rwanda.

Haiti

In **Haiti** in 1992, a coup led by General Raoul Cedras removed democratically elected President Jean-Bertrand Aristide from power.[36] Cedras instituted a brutal regime that arrested many and killed hundreds. The combination of Cedras's brutality and Haiti's appalling economic conditions led thousands of Haitians to flee, most going to the United States. By 1994, the Haitian refugee tide reaching southern Florida was overwhelming.

Meanwhile, the international community pressured Cedras to resign, but to no avail. Then, in 1994, the UN Security Council approved the use of "all means necessary" to overthrow Cedras, and the United States began to assemble an invasion force to overthrow him. Lead elements of the invasion force were already on the way to Haiti when former U.S. President Jimmy Carter, in Haiti as part of a last-ditch American effort to resolve the crisis peacefully, negotiated an agreement for Cedras and his military government to resign and leave Haiti.

U.S. forces nevertheless went to Haiti, staying there for some time to provide law and order as Aristide returned to the presidency. Haiti's grinding poverty remained, but American military power had helped restore democracy to Haiti.

Iraq

In **Iraq,** Saddam Hussein in October 1994 again sent troops toward Kuwait. The United States responded quickly, sending army, air force, and naval units to deter Iraq. Saddam quickly backed down. In August 1995, following the defection of his daughters and sons-in-law to Jordan, Saddam moved forces toward that country. The United States once again responded, sending an aircraft carrier to the eastern Mediterranean and U.S. troops to Jordan for joint maneuvers with the Jordanian military. The Iraqi leader was again deterred. Twice in less than a year, then, the United States used its armed forces to deter the Iraqi dictator.

Kosovo

Kosovo, a region of Yugoslavia whose population is over 90 percent Albanian Muslim, presented the next challenge for the use of American military power.[37] In 1997, the region's Muslim population began to push for autonomy for Kosovo. Radical elements agitated for independence, forming the Kosovo Liberation Army and taking up arms against Serb troops and police in Kosovo.

Slobodan Milosevic, still in power, directed Yugoslav forces to fight in Kosovo as they had in Bosnia, with repression, brutality, and ethnic cleansing. The United States and most Western European states ignored the fighting, but as it escalated in 1998 and early 1999, they attempted to change Milosevic's policies with diplomacy and negotiations. The United States and Western European states also warned that they might resort to armed force.

In March 1999, NATO initiated a massive bombing campaign against Yugoslavia to force Milosevic to change his policies. This was the first time NATO forces were ever engaged in full-fledged fighting. U.S. planes flew most of the missions. According to the NATO commander, General Wesley Clark, the air strikes were conducted using several "measures of merit" meant to "minimize the loss of aircraft," with the objective of not losing any; to "impact the Yugoslavian military and policy activities on the ground as rapidly and effectively as possible"; to "protect our ground forces" and those of our allies; and to "retain Alliance solidarity and the full support of our regional partners."[38]

Milosevic responded by increasing Serbian brutality and repression. Meanwhile, hundreds of thousands of Kosovar refugees flooded into Albania, Macedonia, and Montenegro, destabilizing all three. Finally, in June 1999, after three months of air attacks, Milosevic conceded. Negotiations led to the June 1999 deployment into Kosovo of a NATO-led peacekeeping force. This force remains on the ground today, but the situation remains tense and dangerous.

From the U.S. perspective, Western restraint in Kosovo during 1997, 1998, and early 1999 had not succeeded and may have worsened the situation. From Washington's viewpoint, diplomacy and negotiations had been tried time and again, never working except when Milosevic was confronted by superior military force. Yugoslavia's repression and brutality legitimized NATO air strikes, many Americans agreed, despite the unintended suffering and death the military intervention caused among Yugoslavians. Support for the intervention was not unanimous in the United States, but opposition was muted and unfocused.

The Iraq War

The United States had contained Saddam Hussein's expansionist dreams with the 1991 Persian Gulf War and its expulsion of Iraqi forces from Kuwait, but by 2002, the United States had become increasingly concerned about Saddam's programs to develop weapons of mass destruction, especially the potential for Iraq to provide WMD to nonstate terrorist actors. Under pressure from the United States, the UN passed a series of resolutions regarding Iraqi WMD programs. As a result, Iraq allowed international weapons inspections to resume but refused to provide clear and sufficient information to the inspectors. Nevertheless, the UN refused to take action, arguing instead that Iraq should receive more time to comply with the UN resolutions. U.S. Secretary of State Colin Powell warned the UN in early 2003 that it risked "irrelevance" if Iraq were to "continue to defy its will."[39] It soon became clear that the United States intended to launch a military strike against Iraq, unilaterally if necessary, if the UN failed to act.

In March 2003, American and British armed forces invaded Iraq. Advancing rapidly, U.S. troops entered Baghdad, the Iraqi capital, within weeks of initiating the action, and on May 1, 2003, President Bush declared that major combat operations in the **Iraq War** were over. Despite this, anti-U.S. insurgents continued to attack U.S. troops, inflicting a mounting toll on American forces and innocent Iraqi citizens, especially those who cooperated with the Americans. Insurgents also kept up a campaign to sabotage Iraq's weak economic infrastructure. The United States had won the war, but peace remained elusive.

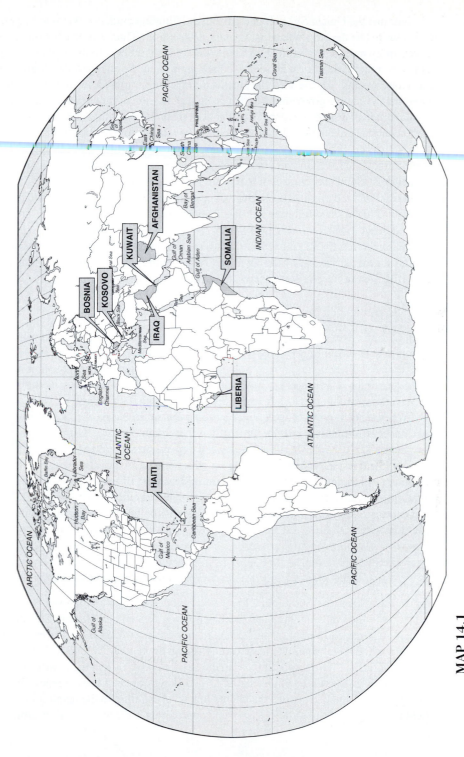

MAP 14.1
Major Post–Cold War American Military Interventions: 1990–Today

Nor had the United States found any but the flimsiest evidence that Iraq had renewed its programs to develop weapons of mass destruction. Thus, the Bush Administration increasingly moved its justification for having initiated the war to the argument that Saddam was a brutal dictator who repressed and murdered his own people. Regime change was cause enough for the war, the Bush Administration argued, even as it continued to assert that Saddam's government had presented an imminent threat to the United States.[40]

Long after Bush declared the Iraq War over, then, debate within and beyond the United States continued about the wisdom of the war, the reasons for the war, and what to do next. As organized resistance continued against American and other foreign forces that had entered Iraq to help reconstruct the country, efforts to develop an effective new Iraqi government that could take control of the country intensified. But the old saying, "It is easy to start a war, but hard to end one," seemed to be increasingly appropriate to describe the Iraqi situation. Indeed, the United States faced a genuine dilemma. On one hand, the United States desired to hand the reigns of power back to Iraqis so it would not be viewed as an occupying power. On the other hand, the United States was also concerned that turning over power too rapidly, and vacating too quickly, would result in the formation of a chaotic state with a weak government that might fall prey to or harbor terrorists.

Interim Conclusions

In these nine crises of the post–Cold War era, is any pattern evident concerning the use or non-use of U.S. military force overseas? It appears not. In each case, different situations dictated different responses. Sometimes military force was used; sometimes it was not. Sometimes it was successfully employed; sometimes it was not. Additional cases are available, and they add more evidence for the absence of a pattern.

Whether U.S. armed forces will be used overseas in the post–Cold War world, and how successful that use will be, probably will continue to be determined on a case by case basis. The use of U.S. armed force will depend on the type of interest at stake, the size of the interest at stake, the type and severity of threat to the interest, the cost of potential intervention, and the political and strategic context of each situation. This is not a satisfying conclusion for anyone who desires perfect policy clarity, but in the twenty-first century, aside from the issue of terrorism, this is the most concise conclusion that can be reached.

USING MILITARY FORCE IN THE WAR ON TERRORISM

As we have seen, the September 11, 2001, terrorist attacks against the United States focused attention on homeland defense like no event since Pearl Harbor. The attacks also created an American resolve to use armed force overseas to eliminate terrorists and those who supported them, wherever they were. Thus, on September 14, 2001, Congress passed Joint Resolution 23 by a vote of 98–0 in the Senate and 420–1 in the House, authorizing the president to use the "United States Armed Forces against those responsible for the recent attacks launched against the United States." According to the resolution: "the President is authorized to use all necessary and appropriate force against those nations, organizations, or persons, he determined planned, authorized, committed or aided the terrorist attacks that occurred on September 11, 2001, or harbored such organizations or persons, in order to prevent any future acts of international terrorism against the United States by such nations, organizations, or persons."[41]

Using American armed forces against terrorists and those who support them is a central part of the **war on terrorism.**[42] Within a month of the passage of the resolution, U.S. forces were deployed to Afghanistan and elsewhere to find, fight, and eliminate terrorists and their supporters.

Historical Precedents

This was not the first time that American armed force had been used overseas against terrorism. During the 1980s, in response to **state-supported terrorism** (terrorism undertaken by individuals and groups who act independently but are supported by states), the United States used armed force on several occasions. For example, in 1985, U.S. jets intercepted and forced down an Egyptian airliner carrying the terrorists who hijacked an ocean liner and killed an American passenger. Similarly, in 1986, the United States twice struck against Libyan military targets and terrorist training camps in response to Libyan-supported terrorist actions against American forces in Germany and the destruction of a U.S. airliner over Scotland.

American military action against terrorism continued during the 1990s as the terrorist network **al Qaeda,** masterminded by one-time Saudi Arabian businessman **Osama bin Laden,** became more and more active. Attacks linked to al Qaeda included the 1993 bombing of the World Trade Center, the 1995 and 1996 bombings of U.S. military facilities in Saudi Arabia, the 1998 bombings of U.S. embassies in Kenya and Tanzania, and the 2000 attack against the U.S. Navy frigate U.S.S. *Cole.* The United States responded by launching cruise missiles against al Qaeda training sites in Afghanistan, and against a pharmaceuticals plant in Sudan that was believed to be a biological weapons production facility.[43] The United States also foiled several terrorist plots in the 1990s, including plans to destroy 11 American airliners over the Pacific and attack Los Angeles during the 2000 New Year's Eve celebrations.

Armed Force in Afghanistan

After September 2001, the scale and ferocity of American use of force against terrorism increased immeasurably.[44] Having received congressional authorization to use armed force, President Bush first demanded that the Taliban government of Afghanistan, which sheltered al Qaeda and bin Laden, turn the terrorist leader over to the United States "or face the consequences." When the Taliban refused, the stage was set for the United States to use military force.

On October 7, 2001, the United States initiated an aerial and ground **war in Afghanistan** against the Taliban and al Qaeda bases and fighters. By year's end, American aircraft had flown over 17,000 sorties. Almost every type of plane in the American arsenal was used. British aircraft joined in the attacks as well. At sea, U.S. and British naval vessels launched cruise missiles against Taliban and al Qaeda targets, especially during the first few weeks of the war.

The United States also used a significant number of new and upgraded weapons. Kits called Joint Direct Attack Munitions that consisted of a global positioning system and an inertial navigation system were attached to the tails of conventional bombs, turning dumb bombs into deadly accurate smart bombs, which were used to great effect. Fuel air explosive weapons called Daisy Cutters incinerated everything within a kilometer radius. Thermobaric bombs that penetrated deep underground before exploding destroyed many caves, caverns, and tunnels that hid al Qaeda forces.

New reconnaissance capabilities were also unveiled, especially two unmanned aerial vehicles (UAVs). One, the Global Hawk, flew as high as 65,000 feet, loitering for as long as 20 hours, sending intelligence via satellite back to its on-the-ground operator several hundred miles away. Another UAV first used in the 1999 Kosovo war, the Predator, flew at about 30,000 feet and could remain on station for 16 hours. One version of the Predator was modified to carry a Hellfire air-to-surface missile, one of which was credited with killing a member of bin Laden's inner circle.

Psychological operations also played a key role in the war. American aircraft dropped millions of leaflets on Afghanistan's population, urging them to support anti-Taliban forces and assuring them of a better future once the Taliban was ousted. On February 3, 2002, alone, the United States dropped over 300,000 leaflets. Specially modified C-130s also flew over Afghanistan, blanketing the country with anti-Taliban, pro-alliance radio messages.

Obtaining base rights and overflight rights was important. After initial hesitation because of internal elements sympathetic to the Taliban and al Qaeda, Pakistan supported the war effort, buoyed by the cancellation of much of its foreign debt. Pakistan provided the United States with staging areas at several military bases, granted the United States overflight rights, and deployed ground forces along the Afghan-Pakistani border to attempt to prevent Taliban and al Qaeda fighters from disappearing into Pakistan. To the north, Uzbekistan granted the United States base rights and overflight rights, and Turkmenistan granted a land transportation corridor, as well as humanitarian overflight rights.[45] The United States claimed that over 40 countries offered military support, base rights, or overflight privileges.

Within two weeks of the beginning of the air campaign, the United States also acknowledged that Special Operations forces, Army Rangers, and Central Intelligence Agency operatives were on the ground in Afghanistan, supporting the Northern Alliance and providing intelligence, as well as serving as spotters and illuminators for American air strikes. U.S. forces during the early phases of the war never numbered more than a few hundred, but they were extremely effective in all their capacities.

By late November, Taliban forces were in retreat in the north, and by December throughout most of Afghanistan. By this time, several thousand American soldiers and marines were in Afghanistan, sometimes engaged in main force fighting. By mid-December, the Taliban no longer ruled, and an interim government under Hamid Karzai had taken power, attempting to establish its authority and extend its influence in Afghanistan.

The task was not easy, since fighting continued. In December, Afghan and American forces engaged Taliban and al Qaeda fighters in the Tora Bora region near the

When the United States deploys its armed forces overseas, it must also supply them. Thus, the United States has immense aircraft like the C-5, shown here, capable of delivering oversize cargo such as tractor trailers and tanks to large airfields anywhere in the world, and high-speed cargo vessels that are slower than aircraft but carry much more.

Pakistani border. The fighting raged for several days. Hundreds of Taliban and al Qaeda troops were killed. Afghan and U.S. forces found more Taliban and al Qaeda fighters near Gardez in early 2002, again close to the Pakistani border, and initiated Operation Anaconda, the largest operation of the war. Several hundred more Taliban and al Qaeda troops died.

Since the Taliban and al Qaeda had cave and tunnel complexes scattered throughout Afghanistan's rugged countryside, and since some elements in Afghanistan continued to support the Taliban and al Qaeda, sporadic fighting continued throughout 2002 and on into 2004, even though the Taliban and al Qaeda had been decimated as a fighting force. More foreboding, al Qaeda cells continued to operate outside Afghanistan.

The Global War on Terrorism outside Afghanistan

The war against terrorism began only days after the 9/11 attacks as many countries began to share intelligence about known and suspected terrorists. Interpol and other security agencies stepped up their surveillance of and attention to known and suspected terrorists. Albania, Belgium, France, Germany, India, Italy, Morocco, Singapore, Spain, the

United Kingdom, the United States, and other countries detained suspected al Qaeda members. Over 500 people were detained in the United States alone, and at least 100 were held in the United Kingdom. Around the world, over a thousand people were detained because of suspected ties to al Qaeda or other terrorist organizations. However, many were soon released.

The U.S. military provided anti-terrorist training in Georgia, the Philippines, and Yemen. Over 200 American military personnel arrived in Georgia in early 2002 to train Georgian anti-terrorist squads. Georgia, which borders Russia's breakaway province of Chechnya, was believed to be a main transit route for Chechen fighters to Afghanistan. Also in early 2002, almost 700 U.S. military personnel took up stations in the southern Philippines to help the Philippine military combat terrorist groups. Another 100 U.S. troops arrived in Yemen about the same time to help Yemeni internal security forces find, track, and counter al Qaeda elements in that country.

President Bush declared that the United States would pursue terrorists in other countries and take the war against terrorism to countries that aided or sheltered terrorists. In 2002, this became the doctrine of preemptive defense, discussed earlier in this chapter. Iraq, Iran, and North Korea dominated American attention, with Bush referring to these states as the "axis of evil" in his 2002 State of the Union message. Other officials pointed to Cuba, Libya, Somalia, Syria, and Sudan as other states that assisted or shielded terrorists. And as we have already seen, the concern that Iraq under Saddam Hussein was developing weapons of mass destruction and supporting terrorism melded nicely with the new U.S. doctrine of preemptive defense, providing the Bush Administration with what it claimed were legitimate reasons for going to war against Iraq in 2003.

Advanced information and communication technologies played key roles in helping U.S. and allied forces identify, track, and occasionally attack terrorist operatives. On at least one occasion outside Afghanistan (as well as several within it), Predator UAVs armed with Hellfire missiles not only identified terrorists but also killed them.

Despite successes, the war on terrorism by 2004 was not won. It is therefore assured that American armed forces will continue to be used overseas against terrorists and those who support them for years into the future.

Enhancing national security and defending the homeland is clearly the most important single reason in the early twenty-first century to use American armed force overseas. Nevertheless, at some point, it may be necessary again to use armed force to protect trade, commerce, and the economy; defend international law, promote democracy, and guard human rights; and perform peacekeeping and humanitarian missions, even as in the recent past. Among the historic reasons the United States has used armed force overseas, only acquiring territory is beyond the pale in the current era.

Even so, despite the importance of the war on terrorism and the possibility of using U.S. armed force overseas for other reasons, American presidents and other policymakers would do well to heed the advice of Ronald Reagan's Secretary of Defense Caspar Weinberger before committing U.S. forces to missions overseas. Weinberger's criteria included long-term public and congressional support, clearly defined political and military objectives, and a clear American intention to win.

Much has changed since the early days of the Republic when it comes to the use of the American military overseas. But the importance of American presidents asking why, when, and how to use American armed forces overseas remains as great as ever.

SUMMARY

Few issues unite the United States, or divide it, any more than the use of armed force overseas. Those who oppose using armed force overseas often argue that the United States cannot police the world, that no country should impose its will on another, and that sovereignty should not be violated. Those willing to use armed force overseas assert that the United States must defend its interests and, if necessary, impose its will on those who threaten American interests.

The United States has used armed force overseas for several reasons, including enhancing national security, defending the homeland, protecting trade, acquiring territory, defending international law, promoting democracy, guarding human rights, and undertaking peacekeeping and humanitarian missions. Early on, the United States rarely used military force abroad because its military was small, its overseas interests except for trade were limited, it was isolated, and technology was primitive.

The United States used its military power beyond North America or the high seas for the first time during Jefferson's presidency, sending naval forces, marines, and mercenaries against the Barbary pirates to stop them from seizing American ships. After the Barbary War, the United States used its military primarily for forays against Canada and Mexico, and during the Civil War, but also in warfare against American Indians.

In the late 1800s, combining Manifest Destiny, militarism, claims of Christian duty, commercial opportunity, and modern communication with self-proclaimed moral and racial superiority, the United States became an imperial power, acquiring a few isolated islands in the Pacific, and in 1898 going to war with Spain, acquiring Cuba, the Philippines, Puerto Rico, and Guam.

From the Spanish American War into the 1920s, the U.S frequently intervened militarily in the Caribbean, Central America, and Mexico. Many interventions were carried out under the Roosevelt Corollary to the Monroe Doctrine, which asserted that the United States had a responsibility to establish order. The United States acquired the Panama Canal Zone in 1903 and deployed troops in 1900 to China and, for a number of years, to the Philippines to quell a rebellion.

With World War I, the U.S. rationale for using force included defense of democracy, freedom of the seas, freedom for oppressed peoples, and national self-determination. Even so, the United States on occasion intervened in the Caribbean and Central America. This changed in 1933 when Franklin Roosevelt initiated his Good Neighbor policy, saying the United States would no longer send troops into its southern neighbors. Meanwhile, throughout the 1930s, the United States did little to oppose German, Japanese, and Italian aggression.

When World War II broke out in Europe in 1939, the United States avoided the conflict for 26 months, not entering the war until December 1941, when Japan attacked Pearl

Harbor. When the war ended in 1945, most Americans hoped that global peace had arrived and the United States would not have to use armed force overseas again. This hope was in vain as Americans realized their country was the leader of the Western world. This led to many overseas deployments of U.S. armed forces and frequent use of armed force.

The Cold War changed many U.S. attitudes about intervening overseas. Throughout the Cold War, the United States intervened where it perceived the possibility of a communist takeover. The use of military force, sometimes in combat and sometimes for display to back up diplomacy, was a key element of containment. Some interventions were controversial; hundreds of thousands of Americans protested U.S. involvement in the Vietnam War.

After the Cold War ended, the United States justified its use of armed force overseas as needed to defend law, promote democracy, protect human rights, support peace-keeping operations, perform humanitarian missions, and defend the American homeland. No pattern was evident in these interventions.

The September 11, 2001, terrorist attacks against the United States led George W. Bush to declare war on terrorism, a central part of which is the use of force against terrorists and those supporting them. Thus, the United States sent troops to Afghanistan to overthrow the Taliban government that supported al Qaeda; provided anti-terrorist training in Georgia, the Philippines, and Yemen; used high-tech weapons to kill terrorists in several countries; and, under the doctrine of preemptive defense, invaded Iraq to overthrow Saddam Hussein.

Much has changed since the early days of the Republic when it comes to the use of the U.S. military overseas. But the importance of American presidents asking why, when, and how American armed forces should be used overseas remains as great as ever.

KEY TERMS AND CONCEPTS

preemptive defense

CNN effect

proliferation of weapons

Weinberger Doctrine

Barbary War

Spanish-American War

Anti-Imperialist League

interventions in the Caribbean, Central America, and Mexico

Roosevelt Corollary

Great White Fleet

American entry into World War I

interventions in Russia

Good Neighbor Policy

American isolationism and neutrality

Pearl Harbor

containment

asymmetric strategies

Operation Desert Storm

U.S. intervention in Somalia

Bosnia

North Korea

Rwanda

Haiti

Iraq

Kosovo

Iraq War

war on terrorism

state-supported terrorism

al Qaeda

Osama bin Laden

war in Afghanistan

THINKING CRITICALLY

1. Why is it important for American presidents and policymakers to carefully address why, when, and how American armed forces should be used overseas?

2. What reasons have been advanced for using American armed forces overseas? To what extent do you believe these reasons are legitimate in the post–Cold War world?

3. What factors constrain the use of American armed forces overseas, and how does each factor act as a constraint?

4. Describe the debate that took place between President Ronald Reagan's Secretary of Defense Casper Weinberger and Secretary of State George Shultz over the use of American armed forces overseas, and assess the extent to which their viewpoints are valid or invalid in the post–Cold War world.

5. In what locations and for what reasons did the United States use military force overseas before World War I?

6. In what locations and for what reasons did the United States use military force overseas during the Cold War?

7. In what locations and for what reasons has the United States used military force overseas since the end of the Cold War?

8. How has the American willingness to use armed force overseas changed as a result of the terrorist attacks of September 11, 2001?

9. Why, when, and how should American armed forces be used overseas?

NOTES

1. Ellen C. Collier, "Instances of Use of United States Forces Abroad, 1798–1993," CRS Issue Brief, Foreign Affairs and National Defense Division, Washington, D.C.: Library of Congress, October 7, 1993, p. 1.

2. Fred Iklé, *Every War Must End* (New York: Columbia University Press, 1991). This seminal work argues that countries usually enter wars without any thought about how they will end, and that this creates hardship down the line.

3. John F. Kennedy, *Public Papers, Kennedy, 1961* (Washington, D.C.: U.S. Government Printing Office, 1962), p. 3.

4. White House, *The National Security Strategy of the United States of America* (Washington, D.C.: U.S. Department of Defense, September 2002).

5. For a detailed discussion of the CNN effect, see Steven Livingston and Todd Eachus, "Humanitarian Crises and U.S. Foreign Policy: Somalia and the CNN Effect Reconsidered," *Political Communication* 12, (1995): 413–429; and Steven Livingston, "Clarifying the CNN Effect: An Examination of Media Effects According to Type of Military Intervention," Research Paper R-18, June 1997, Harvard University, John F. Kennedy School of Government, Joan Shorenstein Center for Press, Politics and Public Policy.

6. For an in-depth look at the role military casualties play in the people's support for war, see Eric Larsen, *Casualties and Consensus: The Historical Role of Casualties in Domestic Support for U.S. Military Operations* (Santa Monica, Calif.: Rand Corporation, 1996).

7. Edward Luttwak, "Where Are the Great Powers? At Home with the Kids," *Foreign Affairs* 73(4) (July/August 1994).

8. Lee H. Hamilton, Remarks, Woodrow Wilson International Center for Scholars, Washington, D.C., May 2, 2001, accessed at *http://wwies.si.edu/director/speeches/intervene.*

9. Major General Smedley Butler, speech delivered in 1933, accessed at *http://www.fas.org/man/smedley.htm.*

10. Edward J. Renehan Jr., *The Lions' Pride: Theodore Roosevelt and His Family in Peace and War* (New York: Oxford University Press, 1998), p. 26.

11. Thomas G. Paterson et al., *American Foreign Relations: A History since 1895,* Vol. 2 (Lexington, Mass.: D. C. Heath, 1995) p. 511.

12. Thomas A. Bailey, *A Diplomatic History of the American People* (New York: Appleton Century-Crofts, 1958), pp. 473–474.

13. Paterson, *American Foreign Relations,* p. 26.

14. Renehan, *The Lions' Pride,* pp. 24–25.

15. Renehan, *The Lions' Pride,* pp. 24–25.

16. For details on how the United States interpreted the Monroe Doctrine and used the Roosevelt Corollary during this era, see Dexter Perkins, *The Monroe Doctrine: 1867–1907* (Baltimore: Johns Hopkins University Press, 1966).

17. Renehan, *The Lions' Pride,* p. 43.

18. See Richard Pipes, *The Russian Revolution* (New York: Vintage Books, 1990), pp. 606–670.

19. Hugh Borton, *Japan's Modern Century*, 2nd ed. (New York: Ronald Press, 1970), p. 327.

20. Paterson, *American Foreign Relations,* p. 119.

21. Paterson, *American Foreign Relations,* p. 134.

22. These last three islands surrounded the Guadalcanal beach approaches and became known as "the Slot." See Michael Coffey, *Military Blunders* (New York: Hyperion, 1999), p.135.

23. See Paterson, *American Foreign Relations,* p. 255, for a summary of the worldwide human costs of World War II.

24. As discussed in Chapter 6, George F. Kennan was the architect of the policy of containment. He wrote a telegram, often called the "long telegram," laying out his rational for believing that containment would lead to an eventual Soviet collapse. The essence of this piece was later published as the famous "X" article. See George F. Kennan ("X"), "The Sources of Soviet Conduct," *Foreign Affairs* (July 1947): 566–582.

25. See Peter Grose, *Operation Rollback: America's Secret War behind the Iron Curtain* (Boston: Houghton Mifflin, 2000).

26. For a detailed look at decision making during the Cuban missile crisis, primarily on the American side, see Graham Allison, *Essence of Decision: Explaining the Cuban Missile Crisis* (New York: Harper Collins, 1971).

27. Bin Laden's comments can be found in his 1996 Declaration of War. See Barry Rubin and Judith Colp Rubin, eds., *Anti-American Terrorism in the Middle East: A Documentary Reader* (New York: Oxford University Press, 2002), pp. 137–142.

28. There are many explanations for the rise and fall of hegemonic powers. Paul Kennedy used the term "imperial overreach" to describe the phenomenon of a nation's tendency to expand beyond its capability to support such actions. Some propose that hegemonies are cyclical. For this view, see George Modelski, "The Long Cycle of Global Politics and the Nation-State," *Comparative Studies in Society and History* 20 (April 1978): 214–235.

29. For details on the Persian Gulf War, see Janice Gross Stein, "Deterrence and Compellence in the Gulf, 1990–1991," *International Security* 17(2) (1992): 147–179; Robin Wright, "America's Iraq Policy: How Did It Come to This?" *Washington Quarterly* 21(3) (Summer 1998): 53–70; Marc Weller, "The U.S., Iraq, and the Use of Force in a Unipolar World," *Survival* 41(4) (Winter 1999–2000): 81–100; and

Lawrence Freedman and Efraim Karsh, *The Gulf Conflict, 1990–1991* (Princeton,: Princeton University Press, 1993).

30. For more information on events in Somalia, see Mark Bowden, *Black Hawk Down: A Story of Modern War* (New York: Signet Books, 1999); Daniel Bolger, *Savage Peace: Americans at War in the 1990's* (Novato, Calif.: Presido, 1995), chapter 7; Michael Maren, *The Road to Hell* (New York: Free Press 1997); Robert Oakley, *Somalia and Operation Restore Hope* (Washington, D.C.: U.S. Institute for Peace Press, 1995).

31. See Bowden, *Black Hawk Down*.

32. Eric Larson, *Casualties and Consensus: The Historical Role of Casualties in Domestic Support for U.S. Military Operations* (Santa Monica, Calif.: Rand, 1996), pp. 12–17.

33. For more details, see Noel Malcolm, *Bosnia: A Short History* (New York: New York University Press, 1994); Wesley K. Clark, *Waging Modern War: Bosnia, Kosovo, and the Future of Combat* (New York: Public Affairs, 2001), pp. 183–184; Steven Burg and Paul Shoup, *The War in Bosnia-Herzegovina: Ethnic Conflict and International Intervention* (Armonk, N.Y.: M. E. Sharpe, 1999); and Ronald Wixman, "Ethnic and Territorial Conflicts in Eastern Europe," *The Challenge of Ethnic Conflict to National and International Order in the 1990's: Geographic Perspectives,* A Conference Report, Central Intelligence Agency, October 1995.

34. For more information, see Rosemary Foot, *The Wrong War: American Policy and the Dimensions of the Korean Conflict, 1950–1953* (Ithaca, N.Y.: Cornell University Press, 1985); and Joseph Bermudez, "The Democratic People's Republic of Korea and Unconventional Weapons," in *Planning the Unthinkable: How New Powers Will Use Nuclear, Biological, and Chemical Weapons,* ed. Peter Lavoy, Scott Sagan, and James Wirtz (Ithaca, N.Y.: Cornell University Press, 2000), pp. 182–201.

35. For more information, see Gerard Prunier, *Rwanda Crisis: History of Genocide* (New York: Columbia University Press, 1995), and Philip Gourevitch, *We Wish to Inform You That Tomorrow We Will Be Killed with Our Families: Stories from Rwanda* (New York: Farrar, Straus, and Giroux, 1998).

36. For more information and background, see John Ballard, *Upholding Democracy: The United States Military Campaign in Haiti, 1994–1997* (Westport, Conn.: Praeger, 1998); Georges Fauriol, ed., *Haitian Frustrations: Dilemmas for U.S. Policy* (Washington, D.C.: Center for Strategic and International Studies, 1995); and Roland Perusse, *Haitian Democracy Restored, 1991–1995* (New York: University Press of America, 1995).

37. For details on Kosovo, see Misha Glenny, *The Rebirth of History: Eastern Europe in the Age of Democracy* (New York: Penguin Books, 1990), pp. 120–136; Daniel Byman and Matthew Waxman, "Kosovo and the Great Airpower Debate," *International Security* 24(4) (Spring 2000): 5–38; and Chris Hedges, "Kosovo's Next Masters?" *Foreign Affairs* 79(3) (May/June 1999): 24–42.

38. Clark, *Waging Modern War,* pp. 183–184.

39. Mats Berdal, "The UN Security Council: Ineffective but Indispensable," *Survival* 45(2) (Summer 2003): 7.

40. Adam Roberts, "Law and the Use of Force After Iraq," *Survival* 45(2) (Summer 2003): 39.

41. U.S. Congress, Joint Resolution 32, September 14, 2001.

42. Other dimensions of the war on terrorism included strengthening domestic security by creating the Department of Homeland Security, calling up reserve forces, strengthening laws dealing with terrorists, tightening banking rules to curtail the terrorists' flow of funds, placing combat air patrols above American cities, working with foreign governments to assemble a coalition of states to combat terrorism, creating a $40 billion Emergency Response Fund to assure that in the short term sufficient finances would be available for the war against terrorism, and requesting significantly increased funds for homeland defense and the armed forces in the FY2003 budget.

43. For details of the effort that have become public, see Barton Gellman, "Clinton's Covert War," *Washington Post Weekly Edition* (January 7–13, 2002): 6–8.

44. For more information and background on the war in Afghanistan, see Stephen Bidle, "Afghanistan and the Future of Warfare," *Foreign Affairs* 82(2) (March/April, 2003): 31–46; and "A Puzzling Kind of War," *Economist* (October 27–November 2, 2001).

45. U.S. Department of State, *Fact Sheet: International Contributions to the War against Terrorism* (Washington, D.C.: U.S. Department of State, Office of Public Affairs, 2002).

CHAPTER 15

Human Rights and Democratization

Expanding the reach of human rights and democracy is a key part of U.S. foreign policy. Despite American occupation in the early twentieth century, a dictatorship for a half-century thereafter, a pro-Soviet government in the 1980s, and the decade-long Contra War in the 1980s, democracy came to Nicaragua in a 1990 election supervised by international observers, including former U.S. President Jimmy Carter, seen here watching the voting at a Nicaraguan polling station in 2001.

- What do "human rights" and "democratization" mean?
- How have human rights and democratization as concepts evolved over time?
- What roles have human rights and democratization played in U.S. foreign policy?
- What are today's major international debates over human rights and democratization?
- What impact is the war on terrorism having on U.S. policies toward human rights and democratization?

Human rights and democratization have been key considerations in American foreign policy almost since the United States was founded. Sometimes they played central roles in American foreign policy, as during the 1990s following the collapse of communist governments in Central and Eastern Europe and during the 1970s during the presidency of Jimmy Carter. Earlier, following World War II, the United States was the strongest proponent not only of the United Nations but also of the Universal Declaration of Human Rights. Similarly, American involvement in World War I was driven by elements of human rights and democratization, which Woodrow Wilson made clear as he argued for independent governments based on national self-determination. Earlier still, one reason that the United States invaded Cuba during the Spanish-American War was Spain's denial of human rights to Cuba's population.

On other occasions, human rights and democratization took a back seat in U.S. foreign policy to trade and commerce, containing communism, and fighting the war on terrorism. During the Napoleonic Wars, Americans paid lip-service to human rights and democracy but traded with whomever they could. During the Cold War, the United States praised human rights and democracy but often found it necessary to side with African, Asian, and Latin American dictators. Some see the same trend occurring today as the United States pursues the war on terrorism.

Other times, as during America's westward expansion across continental North America, the acquisition of Hawaii, the Philippines insurrection in the late nineteenth and early twentieth centuries, the internment of Japanese Americans during World War II, the widespread use of free-fire zones during the Vietnam War, and some would say during the Nixon-Kissinger era of Cold War realpolitik, it was difficult to argue that human rights and democratization were important American foreign policy objectives.

Unarguably, the role that human rights and democratization play in American foreign policy is complex. In this chapter, we attempt to decipher some of that complexity. Do not be surprised, however, if as a greater understanding of the issues is developed, even more questions are raised.

EARLY ISSUES OF HUMAN RIGHTS AND DEMOCRATIZATION

For most of history, kings, queens, emperors, and other rulers did what they wished to their subjects, limited only by personal whims, religious or philosophical beliefs, or the intervention of others who were more powerful. When political, economic, or social conditions became too burdensome, subjects on occasion rebelled against their rulers, but individual freedom and the natural rights of human beings—the core of what is today widely recognized as human rights—rarely caused rebellions. Except for a few religious leaders and philosophers, human rights and democracy were not parts of human consciousness. For example, Niccoló Machiavelli in *The Prince* presented a practical formula for how and when to treat one's subjects poorly and when to treat them well, not based on morality or rights, but on maximizing the length of one's reign.[1] For centuries, rulers ruled, and the ruled were ruled. That was the way it always had been and always would be, or so it seemed.

This began to change in the seventeenth and eighteenth centuries as British philosophers such as John Locke and John Stuart Mill wrote about political democracy, equal opportunity, individual rights, and limited government, while Adam Smith and other economists developed ideas about free-market economics. Gradually, the ideas of these **classical liberal philosophers and economists** found a wider audience in Europe, especially within a small middle class that resented the inherited control and authority of the aristocracy and was appalled by the living conditions of peasants. By the nineteenth century, these ideas reached the growing industrial worker class.

It was in Great Britain's colonies in North America that, in the late eighteenth century, the ideas of the classical liberals first found their way into widespread national policy. Although it is perhaps an overstatement, the words of twentieth-century President Jimmy Carter come to mind: "America did not invent human rights … human rights invented America."

The American Role

The American Declaration of Independence in 1776 and the U.S. Constitution in 1789 put forward as the new nation's founding concepts the ideas of political democracy, equal opportunity, individual rights, limited government, and free-market economics. By the end of the eighteenth and beginning of the nineteenth century, the ideas of human rights and democracy were well established in North America and beginning to make inroads in Europe as more and more people became persuaded about the legitimacy of classical liberal thought. Few governments other than that of the United States translated those thoughts into policy, however, and the expansion of political democracy, equal opportunity, individual rights, limited government, and free-market economics was slow.

This led Americans to view the United States as different from other countries. This sense of **American exceptionalism,** as we saw in Chapter 2, dated back to the founding of the nation, with Thomas Jefferson opining that the United States was "a sanctuary for those whom the misrule of Europe may compel to seek happiness in other climes. This refuge once known will produce reaction on the happiness even of those who remain there." Jefferson saw the United States as "the last best hope of mankind" and a "barrier against the returns of ignorance and barbarism," while Benjamin Franklin declared that the United States would "have some effect in diminishing the misery of those, who in other parts of the world groan under despotism, by rendering it more circumspect, and inducing it to govern with a lighter hand."

Conversely, throughout the nineteenth century, critics of the American experiment pointed out that the United States regularly flouted its expressed ideals, especially in the way it treated American Indians, African Americans, and immigrants from Asia and some parts of Europe. U.S. claims that it initiated the Spanish-American War because of Spain's abuses of Cuba's population were also viewed in some quarters as little more than a cover for American territorial expansion in the age of imperialism.

The role of human rights and democratization in American foreign policy received a boost during World War I as President Woodrow Wilson announced that the United States was entering the war to "make the world safe for democracy." After the war, the Versailles Peace Treaty gave human rights and democratization another boost, promoting national self-determination for those who lived in defeated countries. Even so, many European leaders considered Wilson's ideas hopelessly naive.

World War II and Its Aftermath

Human rights and democratization were firmly on the American foreign policy agenda during World War II. As early as 1941, President Franklin Roosevelt and British Prime Minister Winston Churchill signed the **Atlantic Charter,** pledging support for national self-determination, collective security, economic collaboration leading to "social security," and a future in which "all the men in all the lands may live out their lives in freedom from fear and want."[2] A year later, 26 states signed the Declaration of the United Nations, which pledged cooperation in achieving the aims of the Atlantic Charter. Also in 1942, the United States and Great Britain issued the St. James's Palace Declaration, which stated, regarding the issue of war crimes: "There will be punishment of those guilty or responsible for the crimes, whether they have ordered them, perpetrated them, or participated in them."

After the war, the Allies were as good as their word. The United States and other victorious states, under UN auspices, held the 1946 **Nuremberg and Tokyo tribunals** as forums to try German and Japanese officials charged with war crimes and other crimes against humanity. Condemned by some as "victor's justice," the Nuremberg and Tokyo tribunals sentenced some defendants to death, gave others life in prison, levied extended sentences against others, and acquitted only a few.[3] The Nuremberg trials were particularly noteworthy, with 21 senior Nazi leaders being convicted and sentenced to death for their role in World War II, and 98 lower-level officials also being convicted. At the same time, the Nuremberg trials added two principles to international law that remain central elements of the defense of human rights today: following orders given by superiors does not legitimize the violation of human rights, and individuals as well as governments may be held accountable for war crimes.

After the trials, the United States continued to play a major role in keeping human rights on the agenda of the international community, and over time in expanding inclusion of principles of human rights into international law. For example, the United States strongly supported the United Nations' adoption of the **Universal Declaration of Human Rights** as a "common standard" of human rights "for all peoples and all nations."[4] Adopted by the UN in 1948, the Universal Declaration nevertheless faced two major difficulties.

First, the Soviet Union and the United States differed over how to track the status of human rights. The United States favored having the United Nations issue a county-by-country report on human rights, but the Soviet Union wanted individual countries to submit reports on their own internal human rights. In the UN's early years, this deadlock frustrated progress on human rights. Indeed, despite U.S. and Western protestations that human rights remained critically important foreign policy issues, the Cold War confrontation between the United States and the Soviet Union, and between East and West, led the United States and most other Western states to deemphasize human rights as foreign policy issues throughout much of the Cold War. As for the Soviet Union and its allies, human rights and democratization were never primary concerns.

Second, when the Universal Declaration was adopted, it was not a binding legal document, but simply a plan to advance human rights.[5] Over time, with American support and the support of other particularly Western states, this changed as the UN created agreements such as *The International Covenant on Economic, Social and Cultural Rights* (1966) and the *International Covenant on Civil and Political Rights* (1966) that included many of the Universal Declaration's provisions. These and other conventions that include human rights guarantees, listed in Table 15.1, converted the Universal Declaration into a document that was legally binding.

The Cold War

Throughout the Cold War, the United States continued to claim to support human rights, and frequently it in fact did. On other occasions, however, the U.S. government concluded that strategic considerations arising from the struggle to contain communism were more important than human rights. Thus, the United States often allied itself with autocratic and dictatorial governments that violated the human rights of their citizens as it constructed its global alliance system during the 1950s and attempted to keep Soviet influence out of Africa, Asia, and Latin America. For strategic reasons of national

TABLE 15.1
MAJOR HUMAN RIGHTS CONVENTIONS

Year in Effect	*Name*	*Intent*	*Status*
1927	Slavery Convention	To prevent or suppress slave trade; to bring about abolition of slavery in all its forms	Signed, Ratified: 3/29, U.S. reservation: labor as criminal punishment
1950	Geneva Convention for the Amelioration of the Condition of the Wounded and Sick in Armed Forces in the Field (Geneva Convention)	Requires that noncombatants and surrendering soldiers be treated humanely; prohibits torture, mutilation, hostage taking, and degrading treatment; wounded and sick must be given adequate medical attention; all captured persons shall be documented and accounted for; medical facilities and personnel shall not be attacked or subjected to violence; provides for red cross insignia to designated medical noncombatant personnel and facilities	Signed: 12/49, Ratified: 2/55
1950	Geneva Convention for the Amelioration of the Condition of Wounded, Sick, and Shipwrecked Members of the Armed Forces at Sea	Similar provisions to the first protocol, but applies to sailors and noncombatants at sea	Signed: 12/49, Ratified: 2/55
1950	Geneva Convention relative to the Treatment of Prisoners of War	Provides guidelines for the humane treatment of prisoners of war, including prohibition of torture of both physical and mental natures; requires adequate food, clothing, and medical attention for prisoners; requires that chaplains and medical personnel not be considered POWs (though they are still detained); stipulates the type of work that prisoners may be required to conduct	Signed: 12/49, Ratified: 2/55
1969	Convention on the Elimination of All Forms of Racial Discrimination (CERD)	Prohibits states from making distinctions, exclusions, or restrictions on the basis of race; states agree to not sponsor or defend groups, organizations, or individuals that do engage in such discrimination; states agree to take whatever action allowable by law to discourage such discrimination; establishes a UN Committee on Elimination of Racial Discrimination	Signed: 9/66, Ratified: 10/94

(continued on next page)

TABLE 15.1 *(continued)*

Year in Effect	*Name*	*Intent*	*Status*
1976	Covenant on Economic, Social, and Cultural Rights (CESCR)	Includes the following rights: to self-determination, to wages sufficient to support a minimum standard of living, to equal pay for equal work, to form trade unions, to strike, to maternity leave, to free primary education, to protection of intellectual property (e.g., copyright, patents, and trademarks)	Signed in 1971, Unratified
1976	Covenant on Civil and Political Rights (CCPR)	Includes the following rights: for countries: to own property and exercise control over as they see fit; for individuals: to recourse when one's rights are violated, to life, to freedom of movement, to equality before the law, to the presumption of innocence in criminal matters, to appeals upon conviction, to expression, and to peaceful assembly	Signed: 10/77, Ratified: 6/92
1976	Optional Protocol on the Covenant on Civil and Political Rights (CCPR-OP)	Allows the Human Rights Commission to investigate and adjudicate complaints of human rights violations of individuals from signatory countries who have exhausted the legal remedies of their own country	Unsigned and Unratified
1976	Second Optional Protocol on the CCPR (CCPR-OP2-DP)	Prohibits the death penalty in signatory countries, except for grave crimes against the state in times of war	Unsigned and Unratified; the U.S. looks unfavorably on covenants and conventions that ban capital punishment
1980	Convention on Prohibitions or Restrictions on the Use of Certain Conventional Weapons Which may be Deemed to be Excessively Injurious or to have Indiscriminate Effects and Protocols	This convention consists of four protocols that stipulate limitations on the use of certain classes of conventional weapons, which are deemed to be particularly indiscriminate in their effects; the intent is to prevent excessive civilian injuries	Signed, Ratified: 3/95; the U.S. has ratified 2 of the 4 protocols (those that deal with undetectable projectile weapons, and mines and booby-traps)
1980	Protocol I: Prohibition on nondetectable weapons	Prohibits the use of any weapon whose projectiles or fragments are not detectable by X-ray	Signed, Ratified: 3/95

TABLE 15.1 *(continued)*

Year in Effect	Name	Intent	Status
1996	Protocol II: Protocol on Prohibitions or Restrictions on the Use of Mines, Booby-traps, and other devices	(Does not apply to anti-ship mines or command-detonated mines); nonremotely placed mines are prohibited in built-up areas except when deployed around military targets and actions have been taken to protect the civilian populace, remotely delivered mines are prohibited unless their positions can be accurately mapped and they have a neutralizing mechanism in place; booby-traps cannot be hidden under or disguised with: wounded persons, corpses, burial sites, apparently harmless portable objects, children's toys, or food or drink; minefields must be recorded and published and upon the cessation of hostilities actions must be taken to neutralize the threat produced by the minefields	Signed, Ratified: 3/95 (This protocol was amended in 1996, and the U.S. ratified the amended protocol in 5/99)
1980	Protocol III: Prohibition on Incendiary Weapons	Does not apply to tracer rounds or other projectiles that have an incidental incendiary effect; prohibits the use of such weapons against concentrations of civilians	The U.S. has not ratified this protocol
1995	Protocol IV: Prohibition on Blinding Laser Weapons	Prohibits laser weapons that cause permanent blindness	The US has not ratified this protocol
1981	Convention on the Elimination of All Forms of Discrimination Against Women (CEDAW)	Prohibits distinctions, exclusions, or restrictions made on the basis of sex; states agree to take appropriate action to prevent discrimination against women; prohibits all practices which are based on the idea of inferiority of women; requires equality in educational and vocational guidance; right to the same employment opportunities; right to maternity leave; right to freely choose a spouse	Signed: 7/80, Unratified
2000	Optional Protocol for the CEDAW (CEDAW-OP)	Allows for a UN committee to hear complaints of violation of the CEDAW provisions in signatory states when remedies within the country have been exhausted	Unsigned and Unratified

(continued on next page)

TABLE 15.1 *(continued)*

Year in Effect	Name	Intent	Status
1987	Convention against Torture and Other Forms of Inhuman or Degrading Treatment or Punishment (CAT)	Bans torture under all circumstances; establishes a UN Committee against Torture; requires nations to provide appropriate punishment for those who engage in torture; requires nations provide training to military and law enforcement on torture prevention	Signed: 4/88, Ratified: 10/94
1990	Convention on the Rights of the Children (CRC)	Prohibits discrimination based on parents' race or nationality; requires children be cared for and provided a proper environment for their growth and development; right of the child to know and be cared for by their parents (except in cases where a competent legal authority determines the care of the parents is not in the child's best interest); children are given the right to express their views if they are capable of doing so, and these views must be given due weight considering the age and maturity of the child; no child shall be subjected to arbitrary or unlawful interference with his or her privacy	Signed: 2/95, Unratified
2002	Optional Protocol to the CRC (CRC-OP-AC)	To the degree possible children under 18 should not participate in hostilities and should not be drafted into military service	Signed: 7/00, ratified: 12/02
2002	Optional Protocol to the CRC on the Sale of Children, Child Prostitution, and Child Pornography (CRC-OP-SC)	Prohibits the sale of children, child prostitution, and child pornography (child is any person under the age of 18)	Signed: 7/00, ratified: 12/02
2002	Rome Statute of the International Criminal Court (ICC)	Creates a permanent legal body to adjudicate cases of genocide, war crimes, and other violations of international law of similar gravity; prior to the ICC such crimes were tried by ad hoc tribunals, and some propose this led to selective enforcement of the law	The U.S. opposes the ICC out of a concern that U.S. peacekeeping forces or military and political leaders could be indicted and tried by the court; proponents counter that it is a "court of last resort" and therefore

TABLE 15.1 *(continued)*

Year in Effect	Name	Intent	Status
			countries would retain the first opportunity to try their own citizens; currently the U.S. is seeking bilateral agreements with other countries to ensure these countries will not turn over U.S. citizens to the ICC
2003	Convention on the Protection of the Rights of All Migrant Workers and Members of their Families (MWC)	Prohibits discrimination against those that work in one country but are citizens of another; protects migrant workers' rights to life, freedom from torture, from slavery, to thought, to conscience, to religion, and to basic legal rights; requires freedom of movement (except where laws intended to provide for national security, public order, or public health take precedence)	Currently Unsigned and Unratified
Not yet in effect	Convention against Transnational Organized Crime	States agree to criminalize money laundering and corruption; codifies cooperation on: extradition of criminals, confiscation of the proceeds of criminal activities, criminal investigations and law enforcement activities, and information sharing	Signed: 12/00
Not yet in effect	Protocol to Prevent, Suppress, and Punish Trafficking in Persons, Especially Women and Children (Supplements the Convention against Transnational Organized Crime)	Prohibits recruitment, transport, transfer, harboring, or receipt of a human being by force or fraud; each state agrees to criminalize such activities; codifies requirements for protecting the victims of trafficking, including: protecting life, safety, and identity; provides for repatriation of the trafficked individual	Signed: 12/00

Sources: University of Minnesota Human Rights Library, available at *http://www1.umn.edu/humanrts/instree/ainstls1.htm;* Office of the United Nations High Commissioner for Human Rights, *Status of Ratifications of the Principal International Human Rights Treaties,* updated May 2, 2003; UN, *A Summary of United Nations Agreements on Human Rights,* available at *http://www.hrweb.org/legal/undocs.html,* last edited January 1997; UN, *Rome Statute of the International Criminal Court: Overview,* available at *http://www.un.org/law/icc/general/overview.htm;* UN, *Multilateral Treaties Deposited with the Secretary-General, http://www.untreaty.un.org;* International Red Cross, *States Party to the 1980 Convention on Certain Conventional Weapons,* available at *http://www.icrc.org/eng/party_ccw.*

security, the United States during the Cold War thus supported governments in Chile, the Dominican Republic, Greece, Guatemala, Honduras, Iran, Nicaragua, Panama, the Philippines, South Africa, South Korea, South Vietnam, and elsewhere that regularly and sometimes egregiously violated their citizens' human rights.

At the same time, the United States often criticized the Soviet Union and other communist states for violating the human rights of their citizens. The UN became a favorite American forum for this, especially during the 1950s. Later, during the 1970s, the United States used the Conference on Security and Cooperation in Europe to keep human rights violations in the communist bloc on the agenda of the international community. During the 1980s, the Reagan Administration was particularly vocal in its criticism of human rights violations in the Soviet Union and other communist countries.

The contradiction between claiming to support human rights and allying their country with autocratic and dictatorial regimes often placed American policymakers squarely on the horns of a dilemma. In his confirmation hearings before the U.S. Senate to become secretary of state, Henry Kissinger in 1973 well outlined both the dilemma that numerous American foreign policymakers faced, and his thinking about how it could be resolved. When it came to a potential conflict between human rights and security, Kissinger declared that policy "would have to be decided from case to case. If it is a borderline case, human liberty should weigh very heavily, maybe a little more heavily. But there are situations in which national security considerations will have to predominate, and in that case the executive branch owes it to the public and to the legislative branch to be able to make a convincing demonstration that the necessity [to overlook violations of human rights] in fact existed."[6]

Kissinger also had strong convictions about the thinking that American policymakers needed to employ as they made decisions about whether the United States should intervene in other countries to respond to human rights violations that may be taking place there. According to Kissinger, the United States "stands always for human liberty, for individual rights, for freedom of movement, and for freedom of the person," but before acting against those who infringed human rights, American policymakers had to ask themselves: "First, what is our capability for changing the domestic structure of other countries; second, what price are we going to pay for it; and third, what are the consequences of getting ourselves so directly engaged [and what are] the sort of obligations we might assume toward other countries if we succeed?"[7]

Both Kissinger and the president that he served, Richard Nixon, were extensively criticized for downplaying and even ignoring human rights in their foreign policy. In keeping with their emphasis on strategic considerations in foreign policy, the Nixon-Kissinger team maintained close relations with the military juntas that ruled Greece and Chile, tacitly supported South Africa despite its policies of apartheid, and argued that the United States should overlook Soviet human rights violations, all because of U.S. strategic interests.

Despite Nixon and Kissinger's emphasis on strategic interests at the expense of human rights, negotiations began during the Nixon Administration on what became the **Helsinki Accords,** finally signed for the United States by President Ford in 1975. The Helsinki Accords, (Table 15.2), contained three parts, called "baskets," that many people later said played a major role in the fall of communist governments in Eastern Europe

TABLE 15.2
A DESCRIPTION OF THE HELSINKI ACCORDS' THREE BASKETS
AUGUST 1973

Basket 1

The Declaration of Principles on Political Relations among the States

This basket consists of ten principles to guide relations among the 35 states that signed the accords. The principles include respect for "sovereign equality," the "inviolability of frontiers," "respect for human rights and fundamental freedoms," "cooperation among states," "peaceful settlement of disputes," and "non-intervention in the affairs of states."

Basket 2

A Call for Economic, Scientific, Technical, and Environmental Cooperation among the States

This basket contains recommendations to enhance East-West cooperation in the above areas.

Basket 3

A Call for Humanitarian Cooperation between East and West

This basket calls for the "freer movement of people, ideas, and information" between the East and the West. The reunification of families, binational marriages, and freer travel should be encouraged; greater exchange of information should be allowed; and cultural and educational cooperation should be supported.

Source: Modified from "Conference on Security and Cooperation in Europe," Department of State Bulletin, September 26, 1977, pp. 404–410.

in the late 1980s. Although the Helsinki Accords remained matters of East-West debate for years, many observers claimed that they provided hope to many in Eastern Europe that the United States and the West still had the restoration of human rights in Eastern Europe high on its list of international priorities.

When Jimmy Carter assumed the presidency in 1997, he resolved to base much of his administration's foreign policy on human rights. Rejecting Nixon and Kissinger's "realpolitik," Carter believed that human rights should be a central feature of American foreign policy. Declaring that the United States had abandoned its "inordinate fear of communism" that had led it to support autocrats and dictators around the world during the height of the Cold War, Carter also decided that the United States should focus more of its foreign policy on developing states. Once more, Carter claimed, the United States' foreign policy would stand for something.

Coming in the midst of détente and in the wake of Vietnam, Carter's view of what American foreign policy should have gained the support of many Americans, at least at first. Soon, however, as we saw in Chapter 6, Carter's idealism ran into the roadblocks of Soviet expansionism in the Third World, runaway inflation fueled by large increases in the price of imported oil, and eventually the capture of American hostages at the U.S. embassy in Teheran, Iran, and the Soviet invasion of Afghanistan. By the end of Carter's term in office, détente was dead, the memory of Vietnam was fading, and the idea of basing foreign policy primarily on human rights had been substantially discredited.

As we saw in Chapter 6, Ronald Reagan took office in 1981 with a clear anti-communist agenda that emphasized military strength and containing Soviet expansionism. Reagan also claimed that human rights remained a central part of his foreign policy agenda, although he intended to pursue human rights differently than Carter had. Reagan maintained, for example, that the U.S. supported human rights by meeting with the South African government to discuss why apartheid should be abolished rather than by breaking relations with South Africa. Calling this "constructive engagement," Reagan argued that diplomatic pressure applied by discussions and warnings had a greater chance of dismantling apartheid and instituting human rights in South Africa than diplomatic pressure applied by breaking relations.

Reagan also asserted that open and free elections, freedom of the press and speech, and support for private enterprise were fundamental human rights denied by the Soviet Union and pro-Soviet Third World governments. Thus, Reagan argued, it was appropriate for the United States to criticize Soviet human rights violations and to support the *contras* against the Sandinistas in Nicaragua. As for the criticism that the United States ignored human rights violations in countries that were friendly with the United States, the Reagan Administration replied that a fundamental difference existed between authoritarian dictatorships of the right, that is, those with which the United States was more likely to be friends, and totalitarian dictatorships of the left, that is, those that were pro-Soviet. Authoritarian dictatorships could change over time of their own volition if the United States applied subtle pressure to them, the Reagan Administration argued, and totalitarian dictatorships could not.

These arguments divided the American body politic. Some people accepted them, but others saw them as conservative ideology, not as proof of support for human rights. Few disputed that human rights should be central tenets of U.S. foreign policy, but disagreement existed over what human rights meant and which policies should be implemented to achieve them.

HUMAN RIGHTS AND DEMOCRATIZATION AFTER THE COLD WAR

When communist governments collapsed in Eastern Europe in 1989 and the Soviet Union dissolved soon thereafter, the United States and other Western governments were faced with the challenge of how to help construct not just new governments but complete societies. During the 1990s, human rights and democratization therefore moved to the forefront of American foreign policy in a way rarely before seen. The administrations of George H. W. Bush, Bill Clinton, and George W. Bush all cast spotlights on human rights and democratization. Even with the renewed emphasis on human rights and democratization, however, all three presidents faced an issue that confronted many of their predecessors: when should the United States emphasize human rights and democratization in its foreign policy perhaps above all else, and when should strategic issues, trade, national security, and other concerns play greater roles in U.S. foreign policy than human rights and democratization?

The Presidency of George H. W. Bush

As communist governments crumbled in Eastern Europe in 1989, George H. W. Bush faced the daunting yet welcome task of helping the peoples of Eastern Europe reconstruct their societies politically, economically, and socially. Human rights and democratization were central elements in this task. By 1991, he faced the same challenge in the former Soviet Union.

Following the collapse of communist governments, the United States and other democratic states provided economic aid, technical assistance, and political advice to the new noncommunist Eastern European governments, most of which tried to guarantee human rights, establish democratic political systems, and institute free-market economies. U.S. and Western aid and assistance was provided via three major avenues: through direct government-to-government programs, through government-to-NGO efforts such as trade unions and professional societies, and through private businesses and interest groups. The task was difficult, and all former communist states struggled, finding old ways difficult to abandon and new ways difficult to embrace. In Eastern Europe, the Czech Republic, Hungary, and Poland made the most progress toward remaking societies where human rights and democracy were widely accepted. In the former Soviet Union, the Baltic states of Latvia, Lithuania, and Estonia progressed most rapidly. And in East Germany, elections were held that led to reunification with West Germany. In many Eastern European states and several of the republics of the former Soviet Union, then, human rights, democracy, and a free-market economy slowly took hold, with George H. W. Bush's administration strongly supporting the process.

Bush's human rights and democratization challenges were not confined to Eastern Europe and the former Soviet Union. China's human rights practices also created problems for Bush, both in regards to the Tiananmen Square massacre and trade. In the wake of the 1989 Tiananmen Square massacre, discussed in Chapter 7, the United States condemned China and suspended diplomatic, military, trade, and other contacts. Americans of all political persuasions were repulsed by the massacre. Many advocated breaking diplomatic relations with Beijing. On the whole, however, the American response was restrained, with relations edging back to where they were before the massacre as pragmatic strategic interests took precedence over human rights. Similarly, the Bush Administration annually approved the extension of most favored nation status to China despite its human rights violations, arguing that this was necessary for economic and strategic reasons. Others charged that the Bush Administration ignored China's human rights violations.

The Tiananmen massacre had barely left the headlines when a crisis unfolded in the Philippines. In 1986, the Filipino people had overthrown the dictatorial Marcos regime, bringing Corazon Aquino to power. Well-liked but politically untested, Aquino survived five coup attempts in her first three years in power. In late 1989, units of the Philippine military tried again to overthrow Aquino. This time, the United States provided air cover to military units loyal to Aquino. Thus, in the Philippines, the United States stood squarely behind the rule of a democratically elected government.

Closer to home, Central America offered Bush other human rights and democratization challenges. In Panama in the late 1980s, the U.S. stalemate with Panamanian dictator Manuel Noriega, whom the United States had earlier supported because he was anti-communist and because he provided the U.S. information about drug smuggling, continued. For several years, the United States had been displeased with Noriega's growing anti-Americanism and had attempted to force him out of power using diplomatic pressure and economic sanctions. Despite this pressure, Noriega retained power.

At first, the United States was unwilling to use military force, not acting even in mid-1989 when dissidents in the Panamanian Defense Force revolted against Noriega. When U.S.-Panamanian relations deteriorated further, however, Bush concluded that it was time to act. Thus, in December 1989, the United States invaded Panama and overthrew Noriega, bringing him to the United States for trial. At least in a theoretical sense, with U.S. assistance, human rights and democracy became possible in Panama.

Meanwhile, Cuba continued to supply arms to Nicaragua's Sandinista regime. The Bush Administration believed that the Soviet Union remained involved in the arms traffic as well, although at a lower level. Concerned about future Soviet support, wanting to confirm its legitimacy, and confident of its popularity, the Sandinista regime, under pressure from other Central American states, the Organization of American States, and the UN, with the United States lurking in the background, agreed to hold elections under international supervision in early 1990. To most peoples' surprise, when the Sandinistas lost, they stepped down peacefully, with Violeta Chamorro becoming president. Thus, with U.S. support, human rights and democracy became part of Nicaragua's political scene.

George H. W. Bush left office in 1993 having presided over American foreign policy during an era of immense international change. His legacy in the areas of human rights and democratization remains a subject of controversy. Bush's supporters point to his support for human rights and democratization in Eastern Europe and the former Soviet Union, to his condemnation of China's human rights violations, to his support of a democratically elected government in the Phillipines, to the American overthrow of Noriega, and to the U.S. support of elections in Nicaragua. Bush's critics assert that the United States should have done more to further human rights and democratization in Eastern Europe and the former Soviet Union, that Bush ignored China's human rights violations in the interests of trade and global strategy, and that the United States provided funds to Noriega and then failed to act against him for too long before overthrowing him. Controversy over human rights and democratization also plagued Bush's successor, Bill Clinton.

The Clinton Legacy

As a presidential candidate, Bill Clinton had pledged to keep human rights and democratization at the forefront of American foreign policy. Speaking in Milwaukee in October 1992, Clinton discussed his view of democratic realism, stating that the United States had a practical and moral responsibility to support oppressed peoples and the process of democratization overseas. On other occasions, he declared that trade and aid had to be linked to improvements in human rights and that the United States needed to act when necessary to stop egregious violations of human rights. Like George H. W. Bush, however, Clinton discovered that promoting and defending human rights and democratization in the post–Cold War world was a task that included many shades of gray.

During the early years of the Clinton Administration, the United States adopted a strong declaratory policy against the ethnic cleansing that took place in Bosnia and elsewhere in the former Yugoslavia but did little except issue press statements and diplomatic notes, asserting that Bosnia was a problem that Europeans had to resolve. Eventually, the United States played a major role in ending the Bosnian conflict, including deploying American troops. Similarly, in Haiti and Kosovo, the United States under Clinton at first sought to resolve affronts to human rights and democratization diplomatically but eventually concluded that military force had to be used. In all three cases, Clinton's supporters praised him both for emphasizing human rights and democratizations and for pursuing diplomatic paths to defend human rights and democratization before resorting to military force.

Conversely, human rights and democratization advocates charged that Clinton had relied on diplomacy too long and had not been resolute enough in using armed force once it was employed, and that thousands had died because of Clinton's restraint. Other critics chastised Clinton for being too much of an idealist and not enough of a realist, using armed force too often to pursue goals that were not related to global strategy, economic benefit, or national security. Still others complained that Clinton used the military too frequently for jobs for which it was not trained, thereby undermining American military strength.

Clinton also was sometimes criticized for ignoring human rights when he did not intervene militarily. For example, in Rwanda the United States never used armed force to end the slaughter taking place there. Clinton's critics charged that he was ignoring genocide. Others argued, however, that the United States had no strategic, economic, or security interests in Rwanda, and that the United States neither could nor should act against violations of human rights everywhere.

Human rights proponents also reviled Clinton for deemphasizing the linkage between human rights and trade in his policies toward China and Vietnam, for providing military aid to Colombia for anti-drug programs, and for not being vocal enough in his condemnation of Russian policies toward its breakaway province of Chechnya. In the case of trade with China, despite his campaign rhetoric, Clinton regularly reported to Congress that the human rights situation within China was improving, thereby legitimizing extending favorable trading status to China. Similarly, when the United States opened diplomatic and trade relations with Vietnam, critics charged that the United States was ignoring Vietnam's human rights violations and rewarding the Vietnamese government's dictatorial rule. Clinton defended his actions, claiming that they supported the struggle for human rights and democratization within China and Vietnam as well as helped American strategic interests, served American economic needs, and promoted American security.

As for Colombia, Clinton in 2000 provided the country a $1.3 billion aid package to aid its fight against drug production and the drug trade even though it had not met human rights conditions established by the U.S. Congress for the provision of aid and was identified by the U.S. Department of State as a country whose government violated human rights. Once again, detractors charged that Clinton was ignoring human rights violations. Clinton countered that the war against drugs and the struggle to stabilize Colombia required the United States to provide aid.

Meanwhile, even though the Clinton Administration often lambasted Russia for its brutal military operations in Chechnya in its effort to reassert control there, critics on the political left and the political right assailed the president for not implementing economic or other sanctions against Russia. Clinton countered that he was properly balancing strategic, economic, national security, and human rights concerns in American policy toward Russia not only in regard to Chechnya, but also in regard to overall American policy toward the former "other superpower."

Meanwhile, the Clinton Administration pursued or supported numerous other human rights and democratization initiatives, for example, establishing an interagency working group within the U.S. government to help implement human rights treaties that the United States had signed and to make recommendations about which new human rights agreements the United States should support; signing the International Labor Organization's "Convention on the Elimination of the Worst Forms of Child Labor"; supporting the creation of the International Criminal Tribunal for the former Yugoslavia in 1993 and the International Criminal Tribunal for Rwanda in 1995; and despite congressional opposition, committing the United States to the International Criminal Court (ICC), which would have jurisdiction over crimes against humanity, war crimes, and genocide. The tribunals and ICC will be discussed in more detail later in this chapter.

Like Bush before him, Clinton was praised by supporters and chastised by critics, often for the same action. Indeed, the foreign policies of George H. W. Bush and Bill Clinton in the area of human rights and democratization had many similarities. Both emphasized internationalized and multilateral approaches to human rights and democratization, and both attempted to strike a balance between human rights and democratization on the one hand, and strategic, economic, and security considerations on the other. This approach left them open to criticism from human rights and democratization advocates that they ignored human rights and democratization, and to advocates of realpolitik, unilateralism, and isolationism that they were too idealistic, too multilateral, and too internationalist. America's first two post–Cold War presidents thus left a legacy of controversy on human rights and democratization.

George W. Bush, Human Rights, and Democratization

By the time George W. Bush took office in 2001, the United States and the rest of the world were embroiled in four major debates about human rights: (1) Should human rights be broadly or narrowly defined? (2) Were human rights universal or relativist? (3) Did human rights take precedence over sovereignty? (4) How should human rights norms and agreements be enforced?

Disagreement also existed both within the United States and around the world about the extent to which democratic states, and particularly the United States with its immense economic clout and massive military power, should promote the establishment of democratic governments and undermine nondemocratic regimes. Proponents of active American support for democratization argued that the United States should use its strength to enlarge the number of countries under democratic rule. Opponents of this perspective asserted that such actions were simply a thin cover for American hegemony.

The policies and positions of George W. Bush's administration on these and related human rights and democratization issues were just beginning to emerge when the terrorist attacks on the World Trade Center and the Pentagon forced the most significant reordering of American foreign policy priorities since the end of World War II. To be sure, human rights and democratization remained important American foreign policy priorities after the attacks, but the way that the Bush Administration and many other Americans looked at the role of human rights and democratization in U.S. foreign policy changed significantly on September 11, 2001.

Even so, Bush stressed that human rights and democratization remained central elements in U.S. foreign policy despite the preeminence of the war on terrorism. Indeed, the United States in 2003 began to publish *Supporting Human Rights and Democracy: The U.S. Record,* an annual compilation of the United States' international support for human rights and democracy, to accompany **The Country Reports on Human Rights Practices,** in which the State Department's Bureau of Democratization, Human Rights, and Labor provides to Congress a detailed report, sometimes as long as 5,000 pages, on human rights conditions in 196 countries. *The Country Reports* cover institutional and structural changes regarding human rights and democratization; political rights; internal conflicts; arbitrary detention, torture, and extrajudicial killings; press freedom; religious freedom; the status of women; efforts to protect children; worker rights; trafficking in persons; and corporate social responsibility. In contrast, *Supporting Human Rights and Democracy* details the policies that the United States implemented in the 92 countries around the world that have the most egregious violations of human rights and democracy. This, the Bush Administration maintained, provided proof positive that the United States remained committed to human rights and democracy.

Before we examine the impact of the war on terrorism on the role of human rights and democratization in U.S. foreign policy, however, we will first explore the twenty-first-century debates over human rights and democratization that emerged before the events of September 11, 2001. Such an exploration will considerably aid our ability to understand the human rights and democratization issues that the war on terrorism raises.

TWENTY-FIRST-CENTURY HUMAN RIGHTS DEBATES

As noted above, as the twenty-first century began, the United States and the rest of the world were embroiled in four major debates about human rights: broad versus narrow definitions; the universal versus relativist nature of human rights; the conflict between human rights and sovereignty; and the problem of enforcing human rights norms and agreements. Although the war on terrorism overshadowed many of these debates, they remain important, and the United States has strongly held positions on each. Each requires detailed discussion.

Broad versus Narrow Definitions of Human Rights

First, there is a struggle over whether human rights should be broadly or narrowly defined. The preamble to the Universal Declaration of Human Rights states that "recognition of the inherent dignity and of the equal and inalienable rights of all members of the human family is the foundation of freedom, justice, and peace in the world," but what this means in practice is a matter of considerable debate.

For the most part, the United States prefers a **narrow definition of human rights** identified in the Universal Declaration and elsewhere, restricting the concept of human rights to political and legal rights such as freedom of religion and speech, maintenance of democratic political systems and practices, equality of opportunity, opposition to racial and ethnic discrimination and violence, prevention of imprisonment without fair trial, and opposition to other abuses of individual freedom associated with classical liberal political thought.

Conversely, other countries, especially developing states, believe that definitions of human rights that concentrate on political and legal issues are inadequate. They prefer a broader definition that includes economic and social quality of life concerns. Sometimes called the **basic human needs approach** to human rights, this interpretation includes availability of food, health services, education, and a clean environment as human rights.[8]

During the Cold War, most communist regimes argued for a broad definition of human rights and democracy, asserting that in the absence of "economic democracy," that is, the evenly shared distribution of wealth allegedly favored by communist governments, the United States and the Western world's preferred narrow definition of political and legal democracy meant nothing. No communist regime achieved its claimed objective of economic democracy, but this did not stop the Soviet Union, Eastern European states, China, Cuba, and other communist states from claiming that the American and Western emphasis on political and legal human rights and democratization were irrelevant. Indeed, disagreements between communist governments and the United States over human rights and democratization continue today, as will be seen later in this chapter in regards to Cuba.

Clearly, the debate over narrow versus broad definitions of human rights has policy implications. For example, although it historically accepted narrow political and legal definitions of human rights, the United States at the 1993 Vienna Conference on Human Rights expanded its view to include economic and social rights as human rights "goals." It did this to gain the support of developing countries for its view of universal as opposed to relativist human rights.

Since then, the United States on occasion has accepted broader definitions of human rights, acknowledging that economic issues have an impact on both human rights and democracy. Since the end of the Cold War, this has even been reflected in U.S. economic assistance policy, as we have seen. Nevertheless, in comparison to most nations, the United States' viewpoint on human rights and democratization is narrowly defined, concentrating on political and legal parameters of both.

Universal versus Relativist Human Rights

The second debate is over whether human rights are universal or relativist. The United States and Western states argue that human rights are universal, but many developing states such as Burma, China, Cuba, Iran, Libya, North Korea, Singapore, and the Sudan argue that universal human rights are a creation of the developed world in which the West attempts to impose its values on developing states. **Universal human rights** rarely if ever exist, they argue, because in their eyes human values are culturally determined. They also point out that Western states were the authors of the Universal Declaration of Human Rights, with developing states having no input because almost all at the time were European colonies. They also argue that culture determines human values. The viewpoint that human rights are culturally determined and not universal is sometimes called **cultural exceptionalism.**

Two examples help illustrate the point. In 1994, Singapore caned an American teenager for vandalism. This was a typical sentence for the crime in Singapore, but it caused an uproar in the United States, where caning is considered cruel. The uproar over the caning incident for a time caused a serious deterioration in U.S. relations with Singapore.

Second, lest one think that disagreement over universalist versus relativist human rights divides only the developed and developing worlds, many Americans support capital punishment, which is legal in many U.S. states. Most Europeans consider capital punishment a clear violation of human rights.[9] The issue of capital punishment has also created difficulties for Turkey in its effort to join the European Union. Turkey believes that there is value in having death sentences for capital crimes, whereas EU states forbid capital punishment.

The debate over whether human rights are universal or relativist has unleashed some deeply held feelings. For example, in preparation for the 1993 Vienna Conference on Human Rights, developing countries held three regional meetings to formulate their positions for Vienna. The Asian meeting, held in Thailand, issued a statement called the Bangkok Declaration, signed by 40 Asian states, which declared that the definitions of core human rights concepts such as freedom and democracy flowed from "regional particularities and various historical, cultural, and religious backgrounds." To them, human rights were clearly relativist.[10]

Singapore, Malaysia, Indonesia, and other Southeast Asian states and their leaders have long been associated with the notion of cultural exceptionalism, espousing a concept they call "Asian values." For example, former Malaysian Prime Minister Mahathir bin Mohamad objected to the Universal Declaration on Human Rights so much that he recommended it be revised or repealed, claiming that its emphasis on individual rights ignored the rights of the society or "the common good."[11] Others have also argued for greater emphasis on collective rights as opposed to individual rights.

On occasion, cultural exceptionalism is used as an argument to justify extreme policies. Such was the case with the Taliban government of Afghanistan when it reintroduced Islamic law punishments such as stoning women to death for adultery, claiming that Islamic law was socially stabilizing. Arguing that Western influences such as movies, television, and women's rights weaken the bonds that keep families and societies together, the Taliban and other advocates of extremist views of Islamic law maintain that their strict laws "reintroduce social cohesion, decency, and family values into societies corrupted by colonialism and globalization."[12] Other Islamic states such as Iran, Pakistan, the Sudan, and Malaysia are seriously considering or have already reintroduced strict adherence to very specific requirements of personal and interpersonal behavior.

The international community, with strong support from the United States, has increasingly rejected extreme behavior justified by cultural exceptionalism. Just as the global community no longer accepts colonialism, states that subject their citizens to "cruel, inhuman, or degrading treatment or punishment" find themselves outside Article 7 of the International Covenant on Civil and Political Rights. Other international agreements such as the 1980 Convention on the Elimination of All Forms of Discrimination against Women clearly prohibit actions that egregiously violate human rights. In the case of the Taliban, its failure to gain acceptance at the UN as the legitimate government of Afghanistan and its unanimous censure by the UN Security Council in 1999 were visible demonstrations that such actions are outside accepted bounds of state behavior.

The United States and other Western states are not the only critics of cultural exceptionalism. Former UN General Secretary Boutros Boutros-Ghali observed that most states that argue for relativist human rights are authoritarian states that "cloak their wrong-doing in terms of exception," and further declared that there "is no one set of European rights, and another of African rights.... They belong inherently to each person, each individual."[13]

Even so, many states still assert that national cultural practices determine human rights, and that human rights are relative, not universal. Thus, the debate continues, with the United States at the forefront of the argument that human rights are universal.

Sovereignty and Human Rights

The debate over universal versus relativist human rights is closely associated with the relationship between **sovereignty and human rights.** Clearly, if human rights are relative, then states have as part of their sovereign power the ability to define and protect human rights as they see fit within their own borders. Conversely, if human rights are universal, how human rights are defined and protected is the concern not only of individual states but also of the broader international community.

The world's major states have been particularly sensitive to the relationship between human rights and sovereignty. Until recently, China, Russia, and the United States all opposed the creation of transnational legal institutions that had the ability to try cases involving human rights. China and Russia often claimed that international criticism of their domestic human rights practices and records was tantamount to meddling in their domestic affairs. The United States took a different line, claiming as we will see later that its opposition was not based on concern about sovereignty but over the possibility that human rights courts might be used for political purposes against Americans and American interests overseas.

Despite this concern, the United States for the most part supported international action against those who egregiously violated human rights, as shown by U.S. support for UN action in Bosnia, U.S. leadership in the Kosovo War, and U.S. efforts in Afghanistan. U.S. actions are thus closely in line with the UN. Thus, for example, UN Secretary General Kofi Annan, in a meeting of the General Assembly in 2000, stated that the UN should "forge unity behind the principle that massive and systematic violations of human rights—wherever they may take place—should not be allowed to stand.... If states bent on criminal behavior know that frontiers are not the absolute defense; if they know that the Security Council will take action to halt crimes against humanity, then they will not embark on such a course of action in expectation of sovereign immunity."[14]

The existence of the United Nations and the Universal Declaration of Human Rights thus help to create a context in which the United States can advocate and pursue universal human rights, blunting criticism that the United States meddles in the internal affairs of other states. George W. Bush directly confronted this claim, declaring: "We have no intention of imposing our culture. But America will always stand firm for the non-negotiable demands of human dignity: the rule of law, limits on the power of the state, respect for women, private property, free speech, equal justice and religious tolerance."[15]

Admittedly, this statement ignored the shades of gray that form the basis for much of the discord experienced in the world over the potential for conflict between human rights and sovereignty. As the *U.S. Country Reports on Human Rights Practices for 2001* declared, "the battle of ideas between those who suppress democracy and human rights and those who would see them flourish remains far from over."[16]

Enforcing Standards and Agreements

Despite the precedent of the Nuremberg and Tokyo war trials, the international community did little during the Cold War about human rights violations even when there was agreement that human rights had been violated. Sovereignty was a primary issue, but so were questions of definition, power, and intent. Enforcing human rights standards and agreements requires not only standards and agreements, but also mechanisms and institutions to carry out punishment, and the will to use them.

By the 1990s, with the Cold War over and tensions between East and West almost gone, a new international regime for human rights began to emerge, generally with strong support from the United States. Atrocities in Rwanda and Bosnia, earlier egregious assaults on human rights such as the Khmer Rouge's genocide against fellow Cambodians in the late 1970s, Iraq's use of gas in the 1980–1988 Iran-Iraq War, the 1991–1994 attacks by Somali factions against civilians and international relief efforts, and indiscriminate use of landmines in many conflicts combined to galvanize the international community into action to improve the protection of human rights.

Thus, the UN established in 1993 the **International Criminal Tribunal for the former Yugoslavia (ICTY)** and in 1995 the **International Criminal Tribunal for Rwanda (ICTR).** At first, the Yugoslavia tribunal was not too effective, but between 1996 and 2000, NATO-led peacekeeping forces in Bosnia began to arrest more people accused of crimes and bring them before the ICTY. The ICTY adjudicated the cases, in 1999 indicting Yugoslav President Slobodan Milosevic for Serb actions in Kosovo. Meanwhile, the ICTR also became more effective as it adjudicated more and more cases, even convicting a Rwandan of genocide. This was the first time that an international court had handed down a genocide conviction.[17]

The UN soon went further than the tribunals. In 1998, a United Nations conference finalized a treaty establishing an **International Criminal Court (ICC)** that would have jurisdiction over crimes against humanity, war crimes, and genocide once 60 states ratified it. By 2001, 139 states had signed the treaty, and by 2002, 78 had ratified it, enough so that the ICC became operational. However, the United States was not among the ratifiers.

Why not? As we have seen, the United States opposes crimes against humanity, war crimes, and genocide. In the mid-1990s, it deployed thousands of troops to Bosnia to help prevent genocide. In the late 1990s, it supported the creation of a UN tribunal that indicted Yugoslav President Milosevic of war crimes and convicted other Serbs of crimes against humanity for their ethnic cleansing campaign against Bosnian Muslims. In 1999, the United States contributed most of the armed forces for NATO's military operation against ethnic cleansing in Kosovo.

Many Americans believed, however, that the ICC statutes gave the court power that might lead to politically motivated prosecution of U.S. personnel involved in peace-keeping missions. Fearing that frivolous charges might be made against Americans engaged in legitimate activities, Senator Jesse Helms argued that a government that committed human rights abuses against its citizens might charge that a member of the U.S. armed forces trying to prevent such abuses was violating the rights of its citizens and bring charges against him or her in the ICC. ICC defenders asserted that this could not occur, since the statutes allowed peacekeeping states to preempt the ICC by first trying anyone so accused in their own national courts.

In late 2000, the United States under Bill Clinton signed the treaty. However, the Senate never ratified it, and when George W. Bush took office in 2001, he renounced it. As the court neared operational status in 2002, Bush threatened to oppose all UN peace-keeping missions if the ICC began operations, to refuse to provide U.S. funding for such operations if they were approved, and to refuse to have U.S. forces participate in any peacekeeping efforts.

Bush also initiated an extensive diplomatic offensive to conclude one-on-one agreements with other countries so that they would not prosecute or bring charges against U.S. peacekeepers. By late 2002, a number of countries had signed such agreements, mostly close U.S. allies such as Israel, small countries like Micronesia, and countries strongly influenced by U.S. preferences, such as Tajikistan and Honduras. The U.S. diplomatic effort was widely criticized outside the United States as an attempt to circumvent the ICC. For example, the European Union and most of its members chastised the United States, and Amnesty International considered the effort an attempt to undermine the ICC.

By the early twenty-first century, then, the international community had begun to create enforcement mechanisms and institutions for laws of war and human rights. Issues over sovereignty, definitions, politically motivated prosecutions, and the extent to which human rights were universal still remained, but the new century dawned with new possibilities for the protection of human rights and the expansion of democracy.

DEBATING DEMOCRATIZATION

Democratization has been almost as controversial as human rights. Although the United States became a democracy in the eighteenth century, only a few other states, most in Europe, followed suit in the nineteenth century. After World War I, more states became democracies, some because of Woodrow Wilson's concept of national self-determination that was included in the Treaty of Versailles.

Even so, questions continued about what democracy meant.[18] If a country held a free election, did that mean it was a democracy? What if voting was restricted to one economic class, gender, or race? Did democracy exist then? What if an election was controlled or inordinately influenced by those with money? Was a country democratic if the electoral process favored one party or candidate, or if all parties or candidates came from one economic class? If a freely elected government became repressive, violated human rights, favored the economic interests of a few, or canceled elections, was it still democratic? V. I. Lenin and the Bolshevik Party, which came to power in Russia at the end of World War I, raised some of these questions, but many were asked by people in Western states who looked at the United States and other allegedly democratic countries in Europe and found their political practices wanting.

As the world sank into the Great Depression in the 1930s, economic concerns replaced political concerns as the leading issues in most countries. Autocratic and dictatorial governments came to power in several states, legitimizing their monopoly of authority by saying that it was necessary to cope with the economic problems and security issues of the time. When World War II erupted, it for the most part arrayed autocratic and dictatorial governments against democracies. Thus, it was inevitable that the type of government that a country had became a key war issue.

Democratization was also on the minds of American and British leaders during and after World War II, as shown by the Atlantic Charter, the Declaration of the United Nations, and the Universal Declaration of Human Rights. Nevertheless, despite hope that the postwar world would become democratic, disagreements over democracy, national security, and economics that existed before the war between the Western powers on the one hand and the Soviet Union on the other divided the victors. The world thus became mired in the Cold War.

Throughout the Cold War, democratization remained a long-term objective of the United States, but it often took a back seat to more pressing strategic and national security concerns. Often, as we have seen, the United States allied itself with autocratic and dictatorial leaders in Africa, Asia, Latin America, and the Middle East despite its professed allegiance to democracy.

During the 1980s, a trend toward democratization began in Latin America as country after country rejected authoritarianism and dictatorship and moved toward democracy. The United States favored and supported this trend, which spread to Africa and Asia in the late 1980s and early 1990s. (Figure 15.1 shows this increasing trend toward democratization in the twentieth century.) But the most surprising and important advances

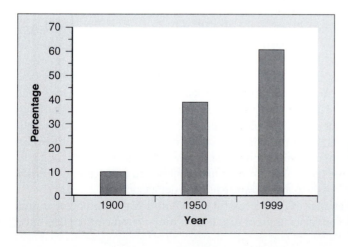

FIGURE 15.1
The Increasing Proportion of Democratic States

Source: Julian Simon and Stephen Moore, *It's Getting Better All the Time: 100 Greatest Trends of the Last 100 Years* (Washington, D.C.: Cato Institute, 2000), p. 257.

occurred in Eastern Europe in 1989 when one communist government after another was overthrown and in most instances eventually replaced by freely elected governments. The same thing happened in the Soviet Union in 1991, where one state became 15 states, several of which instituted free elections.[19]

The trend toward democratization should not be overstated. Many countries still do not have democratic governments. In some, such as China in 1989, democracy was brutally repressed. In some states where free elections have been held, democracy's hold is tenuous as economic problems, ethnic unrest, civil strife, extremist movements on the left and right, and continuing disagreements over what democracy means threaten to undermine freely elected governments. Thus, even though the United States placed democratization at the center of its foreign policy agenda after the Cold War, much remained undecided.

Two undecided issues regarding American support for democratization were the extent to which the United States should support struggling democracies overseas, and the extent to which the United States should seek to impose democracy on nondemocratic countries. These issues began to be debated seriously by the scholarly and policy communities during the 1990s as the Clinton Administration postulated that enlargement of the democratic community of nations was an important American foreign policy objective. The debate became louder and more confrontational during George W. Bush's administration as the United States, having failed to find weapons of mass destruction in Iraq, increasingly legitimized its overthrow of Saddam Hussein's regime on the basis of the brutality of Saddam and the need to establish a democratic government in Iraq. Bush's supporters argued that it was just and proper for the United States to overthrow a brutal government and to try to build a democratic government in its place. Bush's critics charged that the United States had adopted a policy of twenty-first-century imperialism.

In addition to the intrinsic value of democracy, some international relations scholars argue that there is a relationship between democracy and peace, noting that there are few examples of democracies going to war with other democracies. This phenomenon has been labeled the **democratic peace theory,** and it has raised some interesting questions. For example, if democracies do not fight each other, then wouldn't a world with more democracies be more peaceful? Should not U.S. policymakers therefore seek to convert non-democratic regimes to democracy in the interest of world peace?

While the democratic peace thesis argues that the answer to these questions is yes, other studies make the answers less clear. For example, scholars have identified seven other tendencies of democratic states.[20] First, just because democracies do not fight other democracies does not mean that they are less likely to fight wars in general. Second, when democracies go to war, they are more likely to win than nondemocracies. Third, when two states have a conflict, they are more likely to opt for peaceful means of dispute resolution if they are democracies. Fourth, a democracy is more likely to initiate a war with an autocratic government than an autocratic government is to begin one with a democracy. Fifth, democracies tend to fight shorter wars and suffer lower casualty rates than nondemocracies. Sixth, transitional democracies are more likely to fight than established democracies. Finally, small democracies are less likely to avoid wars than large democracies.

Some point to the examples of the successful post–World War II democratizations that occurred in Germany and Japan as proof that democratic governments are less likely to go to war than nondemocratic governments. As Bruce Russett points out, however, three points must be kept in mind when making this argument.[21] First, Germany and Japan had a base to build on in terms of individuals and institutions with democratic experience. Second, the allies had completely defeated these countries, and therefore had a great deal of leverage in creating new governments. Finally, the process was extremely expensive.

HUMAN RIGHTS, DEMOCRACY, AND THE WAR ON TERRORISM

Since September 11, 2001, the war on terrorism has taken precedence over human rights, democratization, and almost every other element of American foreign policy. As the United States made alliances of convenience with governments that have less than stellar records on human rights and democratization, concerns grew in some quarters that the United States would no longer push for human rights and democracy. American accommodations with governments with poor records on human rights and democracy also opened the United States to charges that it had a double standard on human rights and democratization. Conversely, the war on terrorism helped influence the Bush Administration to alter long-standing U.S. policies on foreign aid and to reemphasize the American and Western view that human rights are universal. Each issue will be examined individually.

Is the United States Ignoring Human Rights and Democracy?

As the United States began and then accelerated the global war against terrorism after the 9/11 terrorist attacks, it found it necessary to collaborate with regimes in Pakistan, Kazakhstan, Uzbekistan, Turkmenistan, Kyrgyzstan, Tajikistan, and elsewhere that sometimes violated the human rights of their citizens and ignored democratic governing practices. This understandably led critics of American policy to charge that the United States was ignoring human rights.

The Bush Administration defended its policies in two ways. First, it maintained that it was necessary to cooperate with some governments that had less than perfect records on human rights and democracy because of the threat posed by terrorism and because they were critical to the American conduct of the war on terrorism. Second, it asserted that the United States had a better opportunity to influence these governments if it was closely engaged with them.

The Bush Administration's policies and defenses of its policies were closely akin to those of most American administrations during the Cold War, when the United States argued that, out of strategic necessity and military and political convenience, it had to ally itself with autocratic and dictatorial regimes that had little use for human rights or democracy. Several examples help illustrate the point.

According to the NGO Human Rights Watch, U.S. military assistance provided to several regimes to enable them to wage war against terrorism had a serious negative impact on human rights. Human Rights Watch asserted that much of the American aid to Pakistan and several central Asian states were being used by those states for "torture, political killings, illegal detention, religious persecution, and attacks on civilians."[22] For example, the eight-year-old ban on arms sales to Tajikistan was lifted after the 9/11 terrorist attacks despite that state's history of "torture, suppression of political opposition and the media, and arrests based on religion."[23]

Similarly, before September 2001, the United States harshly criticized Russia's policies in Chechnya, where Moscow employed brutal tactics against civilians to try to end Chechnya's drive for independence. However, Russia strongly supported the initiation of the war on terrorism, helping the United States gain access to military bases in central Asian states. In recognition of Russian assistance, U.S. criticism of Russia's Chechnya policy moderated. For example, during a May 2002 meeting with Russian President Vladimir Putin, George W. Bush asked Russian troops not to harm unarmed civilians, even suggesting that the example of American operations in Afghanistan be taken seriously by Russian troops. The war "can only be won by simultaneously protecting the rights of the population, particularly ethnic minorities," Bush declared, without criticizing Russian excesses.[24]

Obviously, the United States dampened its concerns over Russian human rights abuses in Chechnya in light of Putin's support for the U.S. war on terrorism. Russian human rights abuses, for the near future, will undoubtedly be placed in the annual State Department review of human rights practices, but probably not on the agenda for meetings between Russian and American leaders.

U.S. commentary on Chinese abuses of human rights followed a similar path after September 2001. Although the Department of State's annual report singled out religious freedom and workers rights as areas where China had significant shortfalls,[25] the February 2002 meeting between President Bush and China's President Jiang Zemin in Beijing had few human rights issues on the agenda. Only the issue of religious freedom surfaced during the visit, focusing on China's handling of the Fulun Gong movement, and U.S.-Chinese relations were described as "on the mend since China declared its support for the war on terrorism."[26]

Human rights abuses and problems and democratization in Latin America also received less emphasis from the United States after September 2001. This has not helped the cause of human rights in an area one source sees as "plagued by weak institutions, constrained civilian authority, endemic violence, unreformed or resistant security forces and enduring poverty."[27]

One case in point is Colombia, where the Colombian military and paramilitary supporters are engaged in a struggle with two guerrilla organizations, the Revolutionary Armed Forces of Colombia and the National Liberation Army. The Colombian military and its paramilitary allies have often been accused of human rights abuses in the conflict, such as abductions, recruitment of minors, and indiscriminate and selective killings. In turn, the U.S. government pressured the Colombian government to abandon such actions and find and prosecute those who undertook them.

As required by Congress, the Department of State must certify that aid recipients meet minimum human rights conditions before military aid can be dispersed. As we have already seen, Bill Clinton in 2000 provided $1.3 billion in aid to Colombia even in the absence of State Department certification. Then, in 2002, the State Department certified

Columbia, and military aid was released. However, Human Rights Watch, the Washington Office on Latin America, and Amnesty International contested this certification. While they did not criticize the United States, they accused the Colombian government of circumventing American efforts to verify human rights.[28] Most people, however, speculated that the United States simply was seeking another ally in the global war on terrorism.

Does the United States Have a Double Standard?

The actions described above have led some NGOs such as Amnesty International, Human Rights Watch, and the International Federation of Human Rights Leagues, a few governments, and concerned individuals to question whether the United States has a double standard when it comes to human rights and democratization. The United States rejects such accusations, asserting that these are short-term actions undertaken both to further other critical American objectives and to position the United States to better influence the policies and practices of human rights violators.

Nevertheless, concerns persist. Critics of American policy argue that the United States has allied itself in the war on terrorism with some governments whose abuses of human rights and denial of democracy to their citizens far exceed the excesses of Castro and Cuba, yet with Castro and Cuba the United States insists on maintaining an embargo, whereas with the other states, it provides weapons. This, critics charge, is clear proof of an American double standard.

Critics of the United States also point to U.S. actions at Camp X-Ray at Guantanamo Bay, Cuba, where the United States transferred Taliban and al Qaeda prisoners following the fall of the Taliban government in Afghanistan. Since the installation had been used on several occasions as a processing point for refugees, the United States decided that it would be a good location at which to hold detainees indefinitely while they were questioned regarding al Qaeda. The detainees' legal status remains unclear. They are not considered Prisoners of War, whose rights are outlined in the Geneva Convention, but they are also certainly not being treated in accordance with U.S. criminal law.[29] They are in a netherworld, classified only as unlawful combatants. Human Rights Watch and other NGOs charge that the United States is holding the Camp X-Ray prisoners in poor conditions without filing charges against them. This, they maintain, is a violation of human rights. The United States is under close scrutiny by the international human rights community to see how the situation at Camp X-Ray evolves.

The United States received even more criticism about alleged double standards on human rights as a result of the way some American soldiers treated Iraqi prisoners at the Abu Ghraib prison near Baghdad. Video footage of U.S. troops physically abusing and sexually degrading prisoners provided incontrovertible proof that the human rights of prisoners were being abused. While the Bush administration attempted to dismiss the abuses as the extreme actions of a few undisciplined soldiers, critics of the United States and the Bush administration asserted that the excesses could be traced to a directive that Secretary of Defense Donald Rumsfeld had issued permitting extreme measures to extract intelligence from prisoners.

The U.S. government has also come under fire for actions taken within America's borders that are seen as attacks on civil liberties. In the aftermath of the September 11

Camp X-Ray, Guantanamo Bay Naval Base, Cuba. Critics of the United States maintain that it is violating international standards of human rights and treatment of prisoners here, treating prisoners captured in Afghanistan and elsewhere in the war on terrorism poorly and holding them without charges. The United States denies the first charge, and says it can hold them without charges because of their involvement with terrorism.

attacks, the U.S. Congress enacted the Uniting and Strengthening America by Providing Appropriate Tools Required to Intercept and Obstruct Terrorism legislation—more commonly known by its acronym as the **USA PATRIOT Act,** or Patriot Act—which some believe has severely curtailed legal rights within the United States. Included in the Patriot Act are provisions easing requirements for wiretaps, financial information disclosure, and "sneak and peak" searches (searches conducted without advance service of a warrant). Furthermore, the September 11 attacks led to numerous arrests that many believe were no more than "fishing expeditions" in the hopes of stumbling into useful information. By the end of October 2001, more than 1,100 persons had been arrested and were being held without bail.[30] Legal aliens can be held up to seven days without being charged, under provisions of the Patriot Act.

Ironically, the United States in 2002 sided with Islamic states to oppose a proposal by Mexico and several NGOs that sought to establish a mechanism to ensure that the war on terrorism would be conducted within the bounds of international human rights laws. The Mexican resolution to give the UN Human Rights Commissioner special review capabilities to analyze the impact of anti-terrorist policies was withdrawn at the annual

UN human rights meeting in Geneva. Thus, many people are convinced that despite American assurances to the contrary, the war on terrorism will be used in some states as a pretext for repression, with human rights and democracy suffering in the end.[31]

Changes in Aid Policies

The war on terrorism also provided impetus for the United States to alter its policies on foreign aid. Recognizing that poverty contributes to terrorism, the United States in 2002 declared that a country's performance on human rights and democratization would be considered before the United States provided economic assistance. President George W. Bush made this new linkage public at a March 2002 UN conference on Financing for Development held in Monterrey, Mexico, where he declared that countries seeking U.S. economic assistance in the future would have to "govern justly, invest in their people, and encourage economic freedom."[32]

Thereafter, Bush directed Secretary of State Colin Powell to develop concrete requirements for the Millennium Challenge Account. These requirements will encourage the production of "wealth, economic freedom, political liberty, the rule of law and human rights." By 2006, Bush promised, $15 billion a year would be available under these terms. This is a clear indication that the United States remains deeply committed to human rights and democratization despite the compromises that have just as clearly been made to initiate and fight the war on terrorism.

Reemphasizing Universal Human Rights

The United States also under the auspices of the war on terrorism reemphasized its commitment to universal human rights. As if previous American rhetoric and the history of American actions in Bosnia, Kosovo, and Afghanistan were not enough evidence that the United States was committed to universal human rights, President Bush in a speech to graduates of the U.S. Military Academy at West Point in June 2002 declared, "Our nation's cause has always been larger than our nation's defense."[33]

Continuing, Bush outlined three foreign policy objectives: (1) to "defend the peace against threats from terrorists and tyrants," (2) to "preserve the peace by building good relations among the great powers," and (3) to "extend the peace by encouraging free and open societies on every continent." Bush also laid out a roadmap for the role that human rights and democratization would play in future American foreign policy: "In our development aid, in our diplomatic efforts, in our international broadcasting and in our educational assistance, the United States will promote moderation and tolerance and human rights…. The requirements of freedom apply fully to Africa and Latin America and the entire Islamic world."[34]

On the surface, these views were laudable and well within the American tradition of supporting human rights and democratization. But under the auspices of the war on terrorism, they raised serious questions about the future direction of American foreign policy. Would the United States use its support for human rights and democracy and the necessity to prosecute an effective global war on terrorism to legitimize armed intervention wherever it saw fit? And if the United States chose such a policy course, would the rest of the international community react by supporting or opposing the United

States? The 2003 Iraq War and its aftermath provided no clear answer to either of these questions. Both the war and its aftermath guaranteed, however, that human rights, democratization, and the war on terrorism would continue to be central elements of American foreign policy debated far into the future.

As we have seen throughout this chapter, human rights and democratization have been core foreign policy values that the United States has espoused since its creation.[35] Even so, the definition of human rights and democratization, and how best to achieve them, remain among the most controversial issues in American foreign policy. The United States over its history has had a profound impact on these concepts as they became increasingly accepted in the international community, playing a major role in helping expand the reach and meaning of the ideals of both human rights and democratization over time. It is to the United States' credit that it has continued to espouse these ideals, to expand the meaning of the terms, and to work to improve its own performance and the performance of others in achieving them.

In its foreign and domestic policies, the United States on occasion has admittedly ignored or abandoned the principles of human rights and democratization. This was true during the nineteenth century as the United States expanded westward at the expense of Native Americans and Mexico, in the late nineteenth and early twentieth centuries as its influence grew in the Caribbean and Central America, and during the same period as it gained control of territories in the Pacific. On other occasions, the United States made short-term pragmatic compromises that placed other priorities above human rights and democratization. For example, the nation's founders agreed to the existence of slavery as they developed the U.S. Constitution in 1789. Similarly, American leaders during the Cold War found it necessary to overlook human rights violations and dictatorial policies on the parts of numerous countries that the United States enlisted in its efforts to contain communism. Similar steps backward may be taken as part of the war on terrorism.

This, then, is the special nature of the American quandary over human rights and democratization: when should the pursuit of short-term objectives supercede long-term ideals, given that defense of human rights and democratization are key elements of American foreign policy, of being American, and of American exceptionalism? This has never been an easy question to answer.

SUMMARY

Human rights and democratization have been key elements in U.S. foreign policy almost since the United States was founded. Sometimes they played central roles in U.S. foreign policy; other times they took a back seat to trade and containing communism.

For most of history, rulers did what they wished. In the seventeenth century, British philosophers challenged this practice as they wrote about political democracy, equal opportunity, individual rights, and limited government. These ideas found their way into policy in the United States in the late eighteenth century as the Declaration of Independence and the U.S. Constitution put forward political democracy, equal opportunity, individual rights, limited government, and free-market economics as the new nation's founding concepts.

In the nineteenth century, critics claimed the United States flouted its ideals, given the way it treated American Indians, African Americans, and many immigrants. Human rights and democratization were praised in World War I as Woodrow Wilson said the United States entered the war to make the world safe for democracy. After the war, the Versailles Peace Treaty gave human rights and democratization a boost, promoting national self-determination.

Human rights and democratization were on the U.S. agenda in World War II. After the war, the United States kept human rights on the agenda of the international community, supporting the UN's Universal Declaration of Human Rights. During the Cold War, the United States frequently supported human rights. On other occasions, the United States concluded that strategic considerations were more important as it allied itself with dictatorial governments.

The contradiction between claiming to support human rights and allying their country with dictatorial regimes often placed American policymakers in a dilemma. Thus, the United States under Richard Nixon was criticized for ignoring human rights as Nixon emphasized strategic considerations. When Jimmy Carter became president in 1997, he based much of his foreign policy on human rights. Many Americans supported Carter, but soon Soviet expansionism, the capture of American hostages at the U.S. embassy in Iran, and the Soviet invasion of Afghanistan ended Carter's emphasis on human rights. Ronald Reagan took office in 1981 with an anti-communist agenda emphasizing military strength and containing the Soviet Union.

When communist governments collapsed in Eastern Europe in 1989, human rights and democratization moved to the forefront of U.S. foreign policy. George H. W. Bush, president from 1989 to 1993, left a controversial legacy. His supporters praised his support of human rights and democratization in Eastern Europe and the former Soviet Union, while his critics charged he should have done more. Under Bill Clinton, the United States played a major role in ending conflicts in Bosnia, Haiti, and Kosovo, first seeking to resolve affronts to human rights and democratization diplomatically, but eventually using military force. Human rights advocates charged that Clinton ignored genocide in Rwanda.

When George W. Bush took office in 2001, the world was embroiled in four human rights debates: (1) Should human rights be broadly or narrowly defined? (2) Were human rights universal or relativist? (3) Did human rights take precedence over sovereignty? (4) How should human rights norms and agreements be enforced?

Another issue regarding democratization was the extent to which the United States should impose democracy on nondemocratic countries. The debate became pointed during George W. Bush's administration when the United States, having failed to find weapons of mass destruction in Iraq, claimed it overthrew Saddam Hussein to establish a democracy. Bush argued it was proper for the United States to overthrow a brutal government and put a democratic government in its place. Critics charged the United States had adopted imperialism.

After September 2001, the war on terrorism took precedence over human rights and democratization. As the United States made alliances with governments with weak human rights and democratization records, concern grew that the United States no longer pushed for either. Conversely, the war on terrorism influenced Bush to alter long-standing U.S. policies on foreign aid and reemphasize the American view that human rights are universal.

This, then, is the U.S. quandary over human rights and democratization: when should short-term goals replace long-term ideals, given that human rights and democratization are key elements of American foreign policy and of being American?

KEY TERMS AND CONCEPTS

classical liberal philosophers and economists

American exceptionalism

Atlantic Charter

Nuremberg and Tokyo tribunals

Universal Declaration of Human Rights

Helsinski Accords

The Country Reports on Human Rights Practices

narrow definition of human rights

basic human needs approach

universal human rights

cultural exceptionalism

sovereignty and human rights

International Criminal Tribunal for the Former Yugoslavia (ICTY)

International Criminal Tribunal for Rwanda (ICTR)

International Criminal Court (ICC)

democratic peace

USA PATRIOT Act

THINKING CRITICALLY

1. What are the historical and philosophical precedents for the modern concepts of human rights and democratization?

2. What effect did the Cold War have on American policies regarding human rights and democratization?

3. Contrast American foreign policy regarding human rights and democratization under the Nixon and Carter administrations.

4. Contrast American foreign policy regarding human rights and democratization under the Carter and Reagan administrations.

5. What similarities and differences regarding human rights were apparent in the foreign policies of George H. W. Bush and Bill Clinton?

6. What impact has terrorism had on American policies regarding human rights and democratization?

7. Compare and contrast the differing viewpoints regarding broad versus narrow definitions of human rights, the universal versus the relativist nature of human rights, the conflict between human rights and sovereignty, and the problems of enforcing human rights norms and agreements.

8. Detail the generally accepted American foreign policy perspective regarding broad versus narrow definitions of human rights, the universal versus the relativist nature of human rights, the conflict between human rights and sovereignty, and the problems of enforcing human rights norms and agreements.

NOTES

1. See Niccoló Machiavelli, *The Prince* (New York: Dover Publications, 1992).

2. For the Atlantic Charter, see David R. Facey-Crouther, *The Atlantic Charter* (New York: Saint Martin's, 1994).

3. The stories of the Nuremberg and Tokyo trials may be found in Robert E. Conot, *Justice at Nuremberg* (New York: Carroll and Graf, 1984), and Antonio Cassese and B. V. Roling, eds., *The Tokyo Trial and Beyond* (Malden, Mass.: Blackwell, 1994).

4. The Universal Declaration of Human Rights may be found in Johannes Morsink, *Universal Declaration of Human Rights: Origins, Drafting, and Intent* (Philadelphia: University of Pennsylvania Press, 2000).

5. See *http://www.un.org/rights/dpi1774e.htm* for discussions of the UN and human rights.

6. See Henry A Kissinger, *American Foreign Policy* (New York: Norton, 1974), p. 208.

7. Kissinger, *American Foreign Policy*, p. 206.

8. For fuller discussions of basic human needs, see Bruce E. Moon, *The Political Economy of Basic Human Needs* (Ithaca, N.Y.: Cornell University Press, 1991), and Len Doval and Ian Gough, *A Theory of Human Need* (New York: Guilford Publishers, 1991).

9. For a European perspective on capital punishment, see "The Cruel and Even More Unusual Punishment: Capital Punishment in the U.S. and the World," *Economist* (May 15, 1999): 95–97.

10. China's view of the Declaration can be found in "Bangkok Declaration," *Beijing Review* (May 31, 1993): 9–11.

11. See Thomas M. Franck, "Are Human Rights Universal?" *Foreign Affairs* (January/February 2001): 191–204.

12. Franck, "Are Human Rights Universal?"

13. Franck, "Are Human Rights Universal?" p. 197.

14. Franck, "Are Human Rights Universal?" p. 194.

15. As quoted by Lorne W. Craner, Assistant Secretary of State, Bureau of DRL, at the State Department website, *http://www.state.gov/g/drl/rls/hrrpt/2001/8147.htm.*

16. Craner, State Department website.

17. Even so, by 2000, more suspects had been detained by the Rwandan national courts for the crime than by the ICTR.

18. See Alain Touraine, "What Does Democracy Mean?" *International Social Science Journal* (1991): 259–268.

19. Democratization is discussed in detail in Larry Diamond and Mark F. Plattner, eds., *The Global Resurgence of Democracy* (Baltimore: Johns Hopkins University Press, 1993); Laurence Whitehead, ed., *The International Dimension of Democratization: Europe and the Americas* (New York: Oxford University Press, 1996); Lisa Anderson, ed., *Transitions to Democracy* (New York: Columbia University Press, 1999); and Mark Robinson and Gordon White, eds., *The Democratic Developmental State: Political and Institutional Design* (New York: Oxford University Press, 1999).

20. Bruce Bueno De Mesquita, James Morrow, Randolph Siverson, and Alastair Smith, "An Institutional Explanation of the Democratic Peace," *American Political Science Review* 93(4) (December 1999): 791.

21. Bruce Russett, "Why Democratic Peace?" in *Debating the Democratic Peace*, ed. Michael Brown, Sean Lynn-Jones, and Steven Miller (Cambridge, Mass.: MIT Press, 1996), pp. 111–112.

22. Human Rights Watch, "Dangerous Dealings: Changes to U.S. Military Assistance after September 11," February 15, 2002, at *http://www.hrw.org/us/us.php.*

23. Human Rights Watch, "Dangerous Dealings."

24. Radio Free Europe, "Russia: Bush Urges Respect for Human Rights in Chechnya," May 24, 2002, at *http://www.rferl.org/nca/features/2002/05/24052002104227.asp.*

25. See the Department of State's Annual Review at *http://www.state.gov/g/drl/rls/hrrpt/2001/8147.htm.*

26. "Bush Pushes Jiang on Missiles," *Japan Times* (February 22, 2002): 1, 4.

27. "Facing the 21st Century: Challenges and Strategies of the Latin American Human Rights Community," at *http://www.wola.org/hrworkshopintro.html.*

28. See Human Rights Watch Documents on Colombia, "HRW Disputes State Department Certification," May 16, 2002, Washington, D.C., at *http://www.hrw.orp/press/2002/05/colombia0516.htm.*

29. "Decision Not to Regard Persons Detained in Afghanistan as POWs," *American Journal of International Law* 96(2) (April 2002): 475–480.

30. "U.S. Detention of Aliens in Aftermath of September 11th Attacks," *American Journal of International Law* 96(2) (April 2002): 470–475.

31. VOA News, "UN Drops Plans for Human Rights Scrutiny of Anti-Terrorism Measures," April 26, 2002, at *VOANews.com.*

32. "Bush Puts Price on Aid," *Atlanta Journal-Constitution* (March 23, 2002): A1.

33. "Bush Puts Price on Aid," p. A7.

34. "Bush Puts Price on Aid."

35. For additional views on approaches to human rights, see Jack Donnelly, *International Human Rights*, 2nd ed. (Boulder, Colo.: Westview Press, 1997); Seyom Brown, *Human Rights in World Politics* (New York: Addison Wesley, 2000); and Wm. Theodore de Bary, *Asian Values and Human Rights: A Confucian Communitarian Perspective* (Cambridge, Mass.: Harvard University Press, 2000).

Concluding Thoughts

President George W. Bush: In charge of U.S. foreign policy from 2005 to 2009, but not solely responsible for it. You, too, have the knowledge, the opportunity, and the responsibility to help guide U.S. foreign policy.

In the years after the September 11, 2001, terrorist attacks on the World Trade Center and the Pentagon, a great debate unfolded in the United States—and around the world—about the future of American foreign policy, and more particularly, about its goals and purposes. The debate revolved around three related questions: What is the best strategy to preserve American security against terrorism? to protect American interests and principles? to promote the American mission?

On the surface, the debate was a matter of disagreement specifically over the way that President George W. Bush and his administration conducted the global war on terrorism. Few Americans—or for that matter, citizens of the civilized world—objected to the first phase of the war, the 2001 American intervention in Afghanistan to help Afghan insurgents overthrow that country's Taliban regime, the protector of Osama bin Laden and al Qaeda terrorists. The same was not true of later phases of the Bush administration's war on terrorism.

Bush's 2002 announcement of a new American defense strategy of preemptively attacking those who threatened American security was praised by many as necessary in a new era in which both state and nonstate actors, including terrorists, could obtain weapons of mass destruction. However, many others called the policy a cover under which the United States could impose its will on other nations, and an unworkable strategy in a world of imperfect intelligence.

Similarly, the 2003 war in Iraq was praised by Bush and his supporters first as a "coalition of the willing" necessary to eliminate the threat posed by possible Iraqi weapons of mass destruction and then, after no weapons of mass destruction were found, as necessary to free the Iraqi people from Saddam Hussein's tyranny and bring democracy to Iraq. Critics claimed the war was being conducted by a "coalition of the billing," whose actions were based on some combination of poor intelligence, faulty strategy, and/or American imperial design.

As the struggle in Iraq continued into 2004, the Bush Administration insisted that the United States had to stay the course, even though anti-American forces inflicted mounting casualties on U.S. troops, international aid providers, and Iraqi civilians. Critics of the war chastised Bush and his administration for planning inadequately for the aftermath of main force fighting, providing too few troops to ensure stability, and distracting world attention from more important facets of the war on terrorism.

The debate over how to conduct the war on terrorism, and over the war in Iraq and its aftermath, was perhaps inevitable. As we saw particularly in Chapter 7, the 1991 collapse of the Soviet Union rendered irrelevant the long-standing American strategy of containment, which the United States had followed essentially without interruption since 1947. Since the Soviet collapse, the United States had been searching for a new strategy on which to base its foreign policy. Neither George H. W. Bush's conception of a "new international order" nor Bill Clinton's arguments for "enlargement" and "engagement" captured the imagination of the American public or the international community.

As we have previously seen, the current debate is not the first time that Americans and others have disagreed about the strategy behind and the conduct of American foreign policy. Indeed, dating back to the days of Washington, Adams, and Jefferson, disagreement has often been a hallmark of American foreign policy. As the United States and the world move deeper into the twenty-first century, then, Americans and others are understandably debating and discussing what America's foreign policy strategy should be, both in the war on terrorism and more broadly, and arguing over how the United States should conduct itself in foreign policy as it pursues the war on terrorism and its other national interests.

On the surface, these debates, discussions, and arguments involve disagreements over American policy, specifically the way that President George W. Bush and his administration have conducted the global war on terrorism. But underlying these disagreements over policy are widely divergent viewpoints about the American mission, and about two of the three sets of competing themes that we have explored throughout this text, namely, the extent to which the United States should be realistic or idealistic in its foreign policy, and the extent to which the United States should act unilaterally or multilaterally.

The debate over mission concerns the extent to which, and the ways in which, the United States should attempt to spread its values and principles to other countries. As we saw in Chapter 2, during Jefferson's time and throughout the first century and a half of its existence, the United States believed that its mission was primarily to serve as an example for those who sought and fought for political freedoms. Following World War II, the United States adopted a more activist way to pursue its mission as it supported and aided foreign nations and individuals who desired political freedom as defined by the United States. By 2003, the United States had both the capability and the will to overthrow Saddam Hussein in Iraq and to try to bring American-style democracy and freedom to the Iraqi people.

But should an American foreign policy mission be to overthrow dictatorships and bring American-style democracy and freedom to other countries and peoples? This is the core of the twenty-first-century debate over the American mission: should the United States use its unrivaled position in foreign affairs, its immense power and strength, to bring its values and principles to—some would say to attempt to impose its values and principles on—other countries and peoples?

The controversy over realism versus idealism is similarly divisive, and can best be framed as a debate over where on a spectrum (see again Chapter 2) American foreign policy should be, with realism being at one extreme of the spectrum and idealism at the other. Proponents of foreign policy approaches that stress realism point to the threat posed by terrorists who are willing to die for their cause and who might gain access to weapons of mass destruction. They argue that the United States has to act preemptively against potential terrorists whenever and wherever it can identify them, even if such actions might compromise the sovereignty of other states, ignore tenets of international law, or abrogate individual human rights. Proponents of a more idealistic approach to foreign policy often concede that given the nature of the threat, more extreme steps are needed to provide for American security than were required in earlier eras, but they reject the arguments that sovereignty should be compromised, international law ignored, or human rights abrogated.

Similarly, the controversy over unilateralism versus multilateralism could best be framed as a debate over where on another spectrum American foreign policy should be, with unilateralism being at one extreme and multilateralism at the other. Proponents of a unilateralist American approach to foreign policy assert that the United States should do whatever it needs to do, by itself if necessary, to counter international terrorism. Proponents of multilateralism counter that success in the war on terrorism requires multilateral action, and that a unilateralist approach will ultimately lead to an anti-American backlash from the international community that will complicate and undermine the war on terrorism.

Having read this text and studied American foreign policy, you are now in a position to join intelligently this great national and global debate over American foreign policy. You now have an excellent grounding in the history, politics and process, and issues of American foreign policy on which to base your viewpoints and opinions. But keep in mind that what you have read in this book is only one set of views concerning issues of American foreign policy.

Indeed, the three authors who wrote this text collectively have over a century of experience in the formulation, implementation, and analysis of American foreign policy, but they frequently debated and argued over the content and interpretation of what you just finished reading. The fact that three experts on American foreign policy can debate and argue over the history, politics and process, and issues of U.S. foreign policy is critically important for several reasons.

First, it makes it clear that American foreign policy can be viewed from many perspectives. There is not necessarily a single "right" answer about what the United States has done, is doing, or will do in its foreign policy, despite what some policymakers, policy implementers, policy analysts, and yes, sometimes even professors, would have us believe. There is room for debate over the history, politics and process, and issues of American foreign policy. Indeed, if the authors of this text agree about one thing, it is that nothing is more likely to improve understanding about the United States' conduct in foreign affairs, and to lead to more effective and successful policies, than informed, respectful, and open debate and discussion about American foreign policy. Put more simply, American foreign policy is too important to be left to the ideologues.

Second, the authors' discussions and debates as they wrote this text confirm that the history, politics and process, and issues of U.S. foreign policy are dynamic, ever changing, and laden with controversy. Rarely is there a final word on any of the three major components of American foreign policy presented here. History can be—and often is—rewritten and reinterpreted as new facts come to light and as outlooks and values change. Similarly, the politics and process of foreign policy change on a year-to-year and sometimes month-to-month basis as prevailing political winds emphasize one facet of or input to policy and deemphasize another. What is seen as good policy today may be considered bad policy next year, or the year after, as long-term impacts of past policy become more apparent, and as short-term impacts of policy become less relevant.

Third, as the world's most powerful country, the United States has immense power and influence, and immense responsibilities. No other country or international actor rivals the United States in military power, economic strength, political clout, or cultural influence. The American economy is almost twice as large as that of Japan, the state with the second largest economy. The United States' armed forces are unparalleled, projecting American power to every corner of the globe. Washington's position on every important international political issue is a matter of utmost concern to all involved. And American culture for better or worse penetrates many non-U.S. cultures and extends American influence throughout the world. To reiterate, with its immense power and influence, the United States has immense responsibilities.

With your new understanding of American foreign policy, you can now join intelligently and responsibly the ongoing discussions and debates. You have the knowledge, you have the opportunity, and indeed, you have the responsibility, to help the United States find its proper direction and follow its proper course. Use these gifts wisely and well.

Index